► *Theory and Methods of Scaling*

► *Theory and*

JOHN WILEY & SONS, INC.

New York · London · Sydney

Methods of Scaling

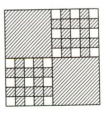

WARREN S. TORGERSON

Staff Member, Lincoln Laboratory
Massachusetts Institute of Technology

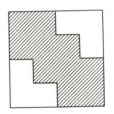

► *Foreword*

Psychophysics was defined by Gustav Theodor Fechner (1801–1887) as "an exact science of the functional relations of dependency between body and mind." As developed by Fechner, psychophysics included both the measurement of sensory attributes and the quantification of perception, in order to correlate these psychological scales with physical measurements of the stimuli. Louis Leon Thurstone (1887–1955) pointed out that many of these "psychophysical" scaling methods could be used for accurate measurement of psychological attributes of stimuli which had no relevant measurable physical correlate. Thurstone developed the law of comparative judgment for data collected by Fechner's method of paired comparisons and showed that it was possible to obtain internally consistent measurements for various psychological attributes such as, for example, the intensity of feeling toward various "nationalities," the judgment of the relative merits of compositions, or preferences for various foods or gifts.

Since Thurstone's first paper on the law of comparative judgment in 1927, a tremendous amount of work has appeared on the psychological scaling methods. Many linear scaling procedures have been developed; the theory for multidimensional methods has been formulated and applied successfully in various areas; appropriate statistical procedures have been formulated.

A Committee on Scaling Theory and Methods, comprised of Harold Gulliksen, chairman, Paul Horst (1950–54), John E. Karlin, Paul F. Lazarsfeld, Henry Margenau, Frederick Mosteller, and John Volkmann, was appointed by the Social Science Research Council late in 1950 to

v

review the status of scaling procedures and their relation to basic research in the social sciences. The conclusion was reached that the theoretical and experimental work on psychological scaling methods should be significant in other social science fields since social scientists frequently deal with psychological attributes that have no apparent relevant physical correlates—such as esthetic merit, preference, utility, prestige, friendship, or value.

The potential usefulness and wide applicability of these scaling methods is indicated by past studies of sensory problems, such as scaling of preferences for, or other characteristics of, tastes, colors, sounds, or odors. Scaling methods have also been used to study the meaning of words, esthetic merit of pictures, and the appropriateness of various filters for color photography, as well as preferences for various sets of objects such as foods, gifts, and goals of life. Scaling procedures have been found useful in studies of discrimination learning, generalization, and personality.

A survey of the literature showed that several hundred pertinent articles were available in journals in a variety of fields such as psychology, biometrics, agriculture, and optics. The student had no single readily available source for studying the various methods and becoming acquainted with their relative merits. Furthermore, no general survey of scaling methods had appeared since Guilford's *Psychometric Methods* (1936),* whereas much important work had appeared, particularly on the law of categorical judgment and on multidimensional scaling. The committee thought that a monograph making these developments readily available to the student would be desirable.

Warren S. Torgerson was engaged to review and summarize the material on psychological scaling. He was selected for this assignment because of his intensive work on psychological scaling. His doctoral dissertation presented original theoretical developments in multidimensional scaling, gave experimental applications of these theoretical formulations, and included a thorough review of the literature in the field. During its early meetings the Committee hoped that a monograph might be issued in 1954. However, from 1952 to 1954 Torgerson was recalled to active service with the Navy; this service and subsequent new obligations made it necessary to abandon the schedule originally set.

The Committee assisted and advised in outlining the monograph and compiling the bibliography, as well as offering suggestions during the

---

* Since the project was started, Guilford's *Psychometric Methods* (1954) has appeared. It gives an up-to-date account of scaling methods but devotes far less emphasis to derivations and to the method of successive intervals and the multidimensional methods than the present monograph.

preparation of the manuscript. It is hoped that the survey of psychological scaling methods presented here will not only encourage their use by research workers in various social sciences, but will also lead mathematicians and statisticians to continue with the needed theoretical and analytical developments.

HAROLD GULLIKSEN

July 1958

► *Preface*

Psychological scaling methods are procedures for constructing scales for the measurement of psychological attributes. Many methods have been developed, with contributions coming from a variety of different fields. This monograph represents an attempt to bring together the major developments in both the theory and the method of psychological scaling. It was prepared for the Committee on Scaling Theory and Methods of the Social Science Research Council. The considerations that led the Committee to sponsor this monograph are discussed by Professor Gulliksen in his foreword.

A word about the scope of the monograph is in order, since scaling methods overlap other quantitative techniques to a considerable extent. Mathematical learning theories, for example, often contain one or more free parameters to provide for individual differences. Since the process of fitting curves to individual data involves estimating these individual parameters, the learning theory can also be considered to be a theory for scaling individuals. Factor analysis, though primarily a technique for studying interrelationships among quantitative variables, can also be used, with certain assumptions, to scale items. Much the same can be said for other quantitative techniques. Procedures such as these, which are primarily concerned with other problems, are not covered in this monograph. It was necessary to limit the coverage to those methods that are primarily concerned with scaling. For the most part, the methods considered here meet the following three criteria: First, they are *general* methods; i.e., methods that might be applied to a number of different psychological attributes. Procedures specific to a particular attribute are not discussed. Second, they yield at least an ordering of the stimuli along the one or more dimensions of the attribute of interest. The broader, and perhaps more complex, problems concerned with classification of stimuli into unordered or partially ordered groups or types are not treated. Third, when successfully applied, the methods considered result in scales that reflect the operation of empirical laws, at least to some extent. The notion of goodness of fit is relevant. Procedures that rely solely on definition are not covered in any detail.

The first two chapters are concerned with measurement in general. In the third chapter, a classification of psychological scaling methods is presented, based primarily on theoretical approach to the scaling problem. After this, each class of methods is discussed in terms of theory, experimental procedures for obtaining the observations, analytical procedures for estimating the quantities of interest, and ways of evaluating goodness of fit. Throughout, I have attempted to keep the mathematical development of the model itself separate from the mathematics involved in statistical problems of estimation. Detailed derivations are given in each case.

It is assumed that the reader's mathematical background includes a course in elementary differential and integral calculus and a course in statistics. In addition, some of the derivations of least-squares procedures require knowledge of the elements of matrix algebra, including familiarity with latent roots and vectors. The multidimensional models of Chapter 11 also assume a knowledge of the mechanics of factor analysis.

It is a pleasure to acknowledge the great debt the book owes to Professor Gulliksen and the members of the Committee on Scaling Theory and Methods of the Social Science Research Council. Discussions of scaling problems, both in Committee meetings and with the individual members, did much to set the course of the book. The comments of the members on the manuscript contributed greatly to its improvement. Thanks are also due to Paul Webbink, of the Social Science Research Council, who aided the development of the project in many ways.

Dr. Bert F. Green read the entire manuscript in most of its versions and saved it from many inaccuracies and ambiguities. Others whose careful reading of chapters has aided and improved the work include Drs. R. Bahadur, J. F. Bennett, C. H. Coombs, J. Keats, F. M. Lord, S. J. Messick, J. E. K. Smith, and L. R. Tucker. Their help is greatly appreciated. Lorraine M. Torgerson typed much of the manuscript, mimeographed chapters, helped with the proof, and, above all, provided the encouragement necessary to get the job done.

Most of the manuscript was written while I was a research associate for the Committee on Scaling Theory and Methods. During this period, office space and library facilities were kindly made available by Princeton University. I also wish to thank the Educational Testing Service and the Massachusetts Institute of Technology for their interest and support during the final phase of the project.

WARREN S. TORGERSON

Lexington, Massachusetts
July 1958

► Contents

1 ◄

► *The Importance*

of Measurement in Science

1. INTRODUCTION

The principal objective of a science, other than the description of empirical phenomena, is to establish, through laws and theories, general principles by means of which the empirical phenomena can be explained, accounted for, and predicted. In carrying out this objective, sciences concern themselves with gathering and comparing data in order to establish the correlations, mathematical equations, and theories that are the goal of inquiry. As we shall see, measurement is one of the things that enables these processes to be carried out. In large part, measurement enables the tool of mathematics to be applied to science.

Before the place of measurement in science can be discussed, it is first necessary to consider briefly something of the nature of science itself. The various scientific disciplines differ from one another in a variety of ways. These ways have been used in various classifications of the disciplines. One such classification, suggested by Margenau, is according to the degree to which *theoretical* procedures or explanations are used as contrasted with *correlational* procedures or explanations (Margenau, 1950, pp. 27–30). The distinction here is between a science that consists largely of statements describing the degree of relationship among more or less directly observable variables and a science that attempts (successfully) to derive, account for, or explain these relationships from principles that are not immediately given, but lie beyond straight empirical knowledge.

Although no science is all correlational or entirely theoretical in this sense, yet it is clear that sciences do differ in the degree to which they rely on one or the other level of explanation. It may be also noted that all sciences begin as largely correlational, and progress toward the theoretical. In this sense, we might say that the social sciences are largely correlational, as are most of biology and psychology, though possibly less so. Physics and chemistry would be examples standing at the other extreme.

It is more than a mere coincidence that the sciences would order themselves in largely the same way if they were classified on the basis of the degree to which satisfactory measurement of their important variables has been achieved. The development of a theoretical science, in Margenau's sense, would seem to be virtually impossible unless its variables can be measured adequately. And one of the primary differences between the social and behavioral sciences on the one hand and the physical sciences on the other lies in the procedures used for measuring their important concepts.

Let us consider briefly, and in an oversimplified way, the structure of a well-developed science such as physics, and then compare this structure with that which seems typical of some of the less well-developed social and behavioral sciences. We shall see that certain differences involve to a considerable extent the measurement problem.

2. THE STRUCTURE OF A WELL-DEVELOPED SCIENCE

Overview

Science can be thought of as consisting of theory on the one hand and data (empirical evidence) on the other. The interplay between the two makes science a going concern. The theoretical side consists of constructs and their relations to one another. The empirical side consists of the basic observable data. Connecting the two are rules of correspondence which serve the purpose of defining or partially defining certain theoretical constructs in terms of observable data. In part, these rules have to do with the process of measurement. Margenau has diagrammed the situation in the manner shown in Figure 1.

In this diagram, the vertical line stands for the observable data (Nature with a capital N). The area to the left of the vertical line corresponds to what we shall call the theoretical space. The circles within this space stand for the theoretical constructs. Double lines indicate rules of correspondence (also called operational definitions or rules of interpretation) between theoretical constructs and observable data, and single lines connecting two constructs indicate a theoretical connection between the two. Single lines thus stand for the formal, logical relationships between constructs, whereas the double lines give the empirical, experimental procedures relating a construct to the data.

A single line might, for example, indicate that the volume of a sphere is proportional to the cube of the radius, whereas the double line would give the rules for determining experimentally the length of the radius or the volume of the sphere.

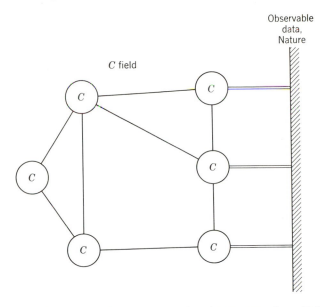

Figure 1. A schematic diagram illustrating the structure of a well-developed science. The circles stand for constructs, single lines for formal connections, and double lines for rules of correspondence linking certain constructs with data. (For more detailed consideration of the notions presented here, see Margenau, 1950, Chapters 5 and 12.)

In terms of Figure 1, we could characterize physics as having many constructs, many rules of correspondence, and a great many connections between the constructs. The rules of correspondence are often operational definitions of quantities—rules that enable assignment of numbers to represent quantities, which in turn enables substitution of formal mathematical symbols for empirical events. Hence the connections between the quantitative constructs can be in the form of mathematical equations.

The multiplicity of connections between quantitative constructs expressed as mathematical equations enables us to progress from one set of observables through a rule of correspondence into the theoretical space. Within this space, progress can be made from one construct to another via mathematical transformations, finally returning again to a different set of observables via different rules of correspondence. Comparison can then be made between the "predicted" result and the observations.

With an established theory, this procedure can be used in place of actually carrying out the second set of experiments. Given certain data, we can *compute* those remaining. With an untested theory, the procedure can be used in its verification, by actually carrying out the second set of experiments and comparing the experimentally obtained values with those predicted by the theory.

Constructs and Connections

In a sense, we can say that the set of constructs with their formal connections forms a model. When certain of the constructs are connected to the empirical world by rules of correspondence, the model becomes a *theory*, and, as such, is subject to empirical test. A model with no terms subject to empirical interpretation can be evaluated only on logical grounds and is not subject to empirical test. Until empirical interpretation can be given to a sufficient number of its terms, the model, along with all of its terms, lacks empirical import, and does not constitute a scientific theory. (See Margenau, 1950; Hempel, 1952, p. 39; also Coombs, Raiffa, and Thrall, 1954, pp. 132–144.)

In a satisfactory theory, the set of constructs is characterized by two different types of definitions. A given construct may be defined in terms of other constructs in the set. Thus, for example, *time* might be defined as the independent variable in the equations of mechanics. In Figure 1, formal connections represented by single lines can be considered to be equivalent to definitions of this type. A formal equation expressing the interrelation of two or more constructs can be thought of as defining any one of the constructs in terms of the others. Thus force can be defined constitutively as the product of mass and acceleration. Equivalently, mass can be defined as the ratio of force to acceleration, and acceleration defined as the ratio of mass to force. We shall call this kind of definition a *constitutive* definition (Margenau, 1950, p. 236). Constructs that have one or preferably more constitutive definitions possess theoretical or systematic import in Hempel's sense (1952, p. 39).

As against the constitutive definition of constructs, which must, of and by itself, be circular, a satisfactory theory contains constructs that are also defined, not in terms of other constructs in the set, but rather, directly in terms of observable data. Thus, periods of time might be defined in terms of one or another periodic system, such as the rotation of the earth or the initial and final states of an hourglass. Indeed, as was mentioned above, a model does not become a scientific theory *until* a sufficient number of its terms possess such *operational* or *epistemic* definitions. In Figure 1, the rules of correspondence represented by double lines can also be considered as operational or epistemic definitions. A given construct may possess several constitutive and several epistemic definitions.

It should be immediately noted that, in order to be useful, *all constructs must possess constitutive meaning* (Margenau, 1950, p. 236). They must permit themselves to take part in the formation of laws and theories. However, it is *not* necessary that *all* constructs possess a direct operational definition, as the earlier forms of operationalism and empiricism would require. It is rather necessary only that a sufficient number in any system be operationally defined. It is true, on the other hand, that, although constructs need not themselves possess operational definitions directly, they must at least be connected with observable data indirectly through other constructs that do. Constructs with neither direct nor indirect empirical meaning can serve no explanatory purpose at all.

3. SOCIAL AND BEHAVIORAL SCIENCES

The situation in these less well-developed sciences is not nearly as neat, even though here, too, we have a wealth of observables and certainly no lack of constructs. There is, however, a rather serious shortage of important connections. Without stretching the point too far, a typical situation might be diagramed something like that in Figure 2. In this

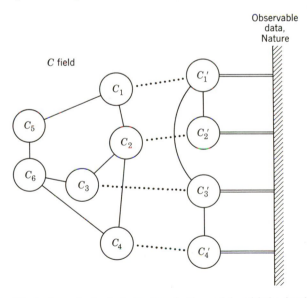

Figure 2. Illustration of a typical structure in the social and behavioral sciences.

diagram we have two sets of constructs: those on the right, lying very close to Nature, interconnected with one another, and each with a rule of correspondence connecting it to the observable data; and those on the left, also interconnected with one another but with no operational definitions. Further, we have some dotted lines connecting the two groups of constructs. These dotted lines are something new.

In this schematic diagram, the set of constructs on the left might represent the "socially or behaviorally important" concepts that a theoretically minded person might have in mind when he begins to work on constructing a theory of personality, of social behavior, of intelligence, and the like. Such concepts, for example, as socioeconomic status, tension, intelligence, learning ability, satisfaction, motivation, attitude, etc. The connections between concepts indicate theoretical relationships between these concepts. Perhaps most often, these connections are expressed verbally rather than mathematically, and with a good deal less rigor. For example, we might have statements such as "The intelligence of an individual is a product of his heredity and his environment"; "An individual's achievement in a given area is a function of his aptitude and his motivation"; "Intelligence is the ability to learn." However, occasionally more precise statements are made. In one theory of personality, it is stated that "Other factors being equal, the degree of satisfaction is roughly proportional to the amount of tension that is reduced per unit of time" (Kluckhohn and Murray, 1948, p. 15). This latter statement could be expressed mathematically as:

$$s = -k\frac{dT}{dt}$$

This equation could thus be considered as expressing a set of formal connections among the three constructs of satisfaction, tension, and period of time.

Let us now consider the set of constructs on the right side of Figure 2. These constructs all possess operational definitions—rules of correspondence relating them to observable data. Very often they have the same names attached to them as those previously discussed. For example, we might have

Intelligence as defined by a score on a particular intelligence test.

Socioeconomic status as defined by some particular weighted sum of income and job prestige as determined by ratings.

Motivation as defined by period of time of food deprivation.

Learning ability as defined by the difference in total score between a particular pre- and post-test with a specified amount and kind of interpolated practice.

These latter constructs have rules of correspondence which enable numbers to be attached to objects possessing them. The degree of relationship between the constructs, as expressed by correlation coefficients or other mathematical terms, is then determined. This is indicated in the diagram by the single lines connecting the constructs on the right. We can thus determine the relationship between intelligence and socioeconomic status, between motivation and rate of learning in a maze, between aptitude and achievement.

But it is important to note that this operationally defined intelligence, socioeconomic status, etc., is not universally agreed to be the same thing as the theoretically defined term having the same name. Hence, the dotted lines. In these sciences we often have the concept as one thing *and* a measure of it as another. The operationally defined construct on the right is an *indicant* (Stevens, 1951*b*) or an index of the equivalent on the left. At best, the two are *presumed* to be monotonically related to each other. At worst, merely a positive correlation of unknown magnitude is *presumed* to exist. A dotted line then stands for a presumed relationship between the construct with operational meaning and the equivalent concept which possesses a wealth of constitutive meaning.

It will be instructive to see what happens to the process of verification or rejection of a theory in this situation. It will be recalled that in physics we may pass from one set of observable data through operational definitions into the theoretical space, travel across the theoretical space from one construct to another via constitutive connections, return to the plane of observation via other operational definitions, and finally predict the results of a different set of observations. The theory can then be *accepted* or *rejected*, depending upon the agreement between the predicted and the observed data. Here we may carry out essentially the same procedure except that part of the journey in the theoretical space is over the dotted lines. If the predictions made using the constitutive connections agree with the observed data, the theorist is happy. He has added evidence in support of his theory. If disagreement is found, however, things are not as neat. He may conclude that the theory is incorrect, or he may equally well conclude that the operationally defined variables are, after all, not really measures of the corresponding constitutively defined variables, but are only presumed to be related to them, and hence, that the theory may still be correct and the experiments simply inappropriate. Thus, in this kind of situation, statements expressing the relationship between the more theoretical concepts are immune, to a fairly large extent, to adverse results obtained in determining experimentally the relationship between their operationally defined mates. Intelligence can thus remain the ability to learn, even though most experiments show that intelligence, as operationally defined, is virtually unrelated to learning ability as independently defined operationally (Woodrow, 1946).

This, of course, is not a particularly happy state of affairs. The concepts of theoretical interest tend to lack empirical meaning, whereas the corresponding concepts with precise empirical meaning often lack theoretical import. One of the great problems in the development of a science is the discovery or invention of constructs that have, or are likely to have, both.

The more "theoretical" constructs are often not far removed from simple common-sense or prescientific conceptions. Though they have a great deal of common-sense meaning attached to them, the meaning is not specified precisely. The terms are thus somewhat vague, and more often than not are complex. Before a satisfactory state of affairs is reached, it is necessary somehow to transform these inexact, complex concepts into exact ones which can be specified precisely. This is what Carnap (1950) calls the task of *explication*. Though this task seems common to all sciences, it is particularly acute in those disciplines that are in their initial stages of development. It is especially true at the present time in the social and behavioral sciences, where an immense amount of time has been devoted to construction of complex and elaborate theoretical super-structures based on unexplicated, inexact constructs.

When we devise a rule of correspondence for relating one of these pre-scientific concepts to observable data, we are in fact carrying out an explication of the original concept. Our purpose is to replace the original concept with one that is defined more precisely. It is only after such a substitution has been made that the empirical investigation of hypotheses concerning theoretical connections can proceed. Unfortunately, there seems to be virtually an unlimited number of ways in which such rules of correspondence can be devised. Since each way *is* an operational definition of the explicated concept, and since different ways ordinarily lead to different results, it is clear that the problem of determining which way if any is likely to prove fruitful is a serious one. The best of theoretical models is of no use if rules of correspondence are chosen unwisely or unfortunately. Yet chosen they must be, since models without constructs which are anchored firmly to observable data have no scientific import whatsoever.

Often, the problem of establishing a rule of correspondence for relating a construct to observable data reduces to the problem of devising rules for the *measurement* of the construct. This is not always so, however, since many of the constructs useful in science are intrinsically immeasurable. In the next section we consider the relation of measurement to two of the important kinds of scientific constructs.

4. SYSTEMS, PROPERTIES, AND MEASUREMENT

The constructs used in science can be classified into several different types. For our purposes at the present time, it will only be necessary to distinguish between two—systems and properties.

The relation of system to property is an intimate one. Properties are essentially the observable aspects or characteristics of the empirical world. Whenever we define or denote a property, it always seems to be a property *of* something. For this something, we use the term *system*. Thus, properties, where they occur, occur as aspects or characteristics of systems. To make the circle complete, we might define a particular system as roughly that which possesses such and so properties.

Systems thus include the objects and things of ordinary experience, such as flowers, houses, sheets of paper, persons, and shot-filled bottles. Systems also include, however, such "things" as spots of light, tones, electrons, genes, and waves. Properties, on the other hand, are the observables. Here, we might mention weight, length, width, color, and thickness as examples of properties of a sheet of paper; pitch and loudness as properties of a tone; and mass and charge as properties of an electron.

While this distinction between systems and their properties is perhaps obvious, it is nevertheless an important distinction. It is of special importance here because of the fact that it is always the properties that are *measured* and not the systems themselves. Measurement is always measurement of a property and never measurement of a system.

This, too, would seem obvious. Consider the system-construct "book" and the property-constructs "weight" and "thickness." The book itself can never be measured. The weight of the book, or its thickness, can. Similarly, electrons, mass points, individuals, cultures, and chromosomes are immeasurable by their very nature. Each, however, possesses properties that perhaps can be measured.

Now we should note immediately that books (and other systems) can be *classified.* They can be sorted into various categories of very complex classificatory structures. Furthermore, numerals can be used to name the classes. Actually, of course, this is commonly done. However, the fact that Russell's *Principles of Mathematics* is assigned the numerals 8105.793.11 in the Princeton University library does not mean that the librarian has *measured* the book, but only that it falls into a particular class of a complex classificatory structure which has been given this numerical name.

Measurement, then, where it occurs, is concerned with the definition of properties of systems, and not with the systems themselves. However, it should not be assumed from this that a property is always defined or denoted in terms of measurement. Many property concepts are essentially classificatory, particularly in the early stages of inquiry. For example, in the following:

X is close to Y,
X is red,
X is triangular,
X is warm,

the words close, red, triangular, and warm represent property concepts that are classificatory in nature. X is either close to Y or it is not. X is either red, or triangular, or warm, or it is not.

As a science progresses, however, many of the classificatory concepts dealing with properties tend to be replaced by quantitative concepts. Measurement of properties has a number of advantages over mere classification from a standpoint both of scientific description and of explanation. Hempel lists the following four advantages which seem to summarize the subject well (1952, pp. 56–57):

   a. By means of ordering or metrical concepts, it is often possible to differentiate among instances which are lumped together in a given classification; in this sense a system of quantitative terms provides a greater descriptive flexibility and subtlety. [Thus, among objects which might all be classified as warm, some are warmer than others. The quantitative construct of *temperature* gives a much finer distinction.]
   b. A characterization of several items by means of a quantitative concept shows their relative position in the order represented by that concept. [Thus, an object with a temperature of seventy degrees is *warmer than* one of sixty degrees. Classificatory concepts only indicate that they are different.]
   c. Greater descriptive flexibility also makes for greater flexibility in the formulation of general laws. [The law that an increase in the temperature of a column of mercury is accompanied by an increase in the height of the column would be virtually impossible to state in terms of classificatory concepts.]
   d. The introduction of metrical terms makes possible an extensive application of the concepts and theories of higher mathematics: General laws can be expressed in the form of functional relationships between different quantities. [We may thus state precisely in mathematical terms the relation between the height of the column of mercury and its temperature.]

These four advantages serve to define in a concise manner the purposes of measurement in science. They deal with the "why" of measurement. The remainder of the monograph is more concerned with the "what" and the "how" of measurement, particularly as applicable to the social and behavioral sciences.

In Chapter 2, we discuss the general logical nature of measurement. Chapter 3 offers a classification of procedures used in the social and behavioral sciences for developing scales of measurement. In Chapters 4 through 14, the different classes of scaling procedures are each discussed in detail with respect to underlying rationale, experimental procedures, and methods of analysis. Finally, in Chapter 15, we consider something of the progress to date in the application of these methods to measurement problems.

5. SUMMARY

Before we embark on a discussion of the nature of measurement itself, it may be well to summarize the ground we have covered thus far.

The structure of a science was pictured as a complex interplay between theory and data, the theory side consisting of a network of constructs and their interconnections, and the data consisting of observable phenomena of the world. Linking the theory with data are the rules of correspondence. The formal connections between constructs on the one hand and the rules of correspondence on the other establish two different kinds of definitions which are used in science. The former were called constitutive definitions and the latter operational or epistemic definitions.

Constructs, to be useful in a science, must possess both systematic and empirical import. By systematic import is meant simply that the construct must be such as to lend itself to the formation of multiple connections with other constructs in the structure. By empirical import is meant that the construct must be connected, either directly or through other constructs, to the observable data. One of the important concerns in science is the search for or the invention of constructs with both empirical and systematic import. In this concern the processes of concept formation and theory formation go hand in hand. In the discussion of the social and behavioral sciences, a tendency was noted for concepts to have either operational or systematic import, but not both. This was illustrative of an unsatisfactory state of affairs in these disciplines.

The scientific constructs are of several different kinds. Of these, systems and properties were singled out for special consideration. Systems include the objects and things of ordinary experience. Properties refer to their observable aspects. Measurement refers to the properties of systems and not to the systems themselves. Measurement was seen as one way of defining a property.

Given that a property is measurable (this is not necessarily true of all properties), the advantages of defining it in terms of measurement, as contrasted with a purely classificatory definition, accrue both in the descriptive and in the explanatory functions of science. In terms of description, it makes for greater descriptive flexibility, since the number of classes is theoretically unlimited. It also gives information about the relations between various quantities of the property. In terms of explanation, it allows for more precise formulation of general laws relating different constructs, and it enables the paraphernalia of mathematics to be extensively applied to science. Functional relations between constructs can be expressed in terms of mathematical functions. Theories and laws can be formulated in terms of mathematical equations.

It is most important to keep these latter advantages of measurement in mind as we embark on a consideration of the logic of measurement. We might almost say that the primary purpose of measurement in science is to enable us to express the functional relations between constructs in terms of mathematical equations. As Nagel says, "If we inquire why we measure in physics, the answer will be that, if we do measure, and measure in certain ways, then it will be possible to establish the equations and theories which are the goal of inquiry" (Nagel, 1931, p. 314). Yet it seems that, when one gets into a discussion of the logic of measurement, there is a tendency to lose sight of these considerations. There seems to be a tendency to become so involved with one or another preferred method of developing a scale of measurement that the means itself becomes the end.

While we shall see that there are certain criteria that any measuring procedure must meet, there are often several ways in which these criteria can be met. It is only with reference to a larger theoretical system that scales differing with respect to *ways* of meeting the criteria can be evaluated.

2 ◄

► *The Nature*
of Measurement

1. INTRODUCTION

There seems to be little difficulty in defining the term "measurement."
Various definitions put forth by different writers on the subject seem, at
first glance at least, to be merely alternative ways of saying the same thing.
Thus, to Russell, "Measurement of magnitudes is, in its most general
sense, any method by which a unique and reciprocal correspondence is
established between all or some of the magnitudes of a kind and all or some
of the numbers, integral, rational, or real as the case may be" (1938,
p. 176). To Campbell, measurement is "the assignment of numerals to
represent properties of material systems other than number, in virtue of
the laws governing these properties" (1938, p. 126). To Stevens, "Measurement is the assignment of numerals to objects or events according to
rules" (1951*b*, p. 22).

In spite of the apparent similarity in definition, subsequent treatment of
the subject differs considerably among the three authors. Other writers,
when dealing with the same topic, generally take viewpoints similar to one
of the three, though occasionally with modifications and additions. In
spite of the difference in treatment, it is clear, however, that they are
dealing with the same general problem. This problem concerns the
process and rationale involved in the construction of a scale or measuring
device and the properties that can be ascribed to it.

There are other uses of the term "measurement" which are not particularly relevant to this problem. Indeed, in the popular usage, "measure"

13

is applied to a great number of different situations.   Lorge mentions that "in a count of its occurrence in a sample of two and a half million words, 'measure' occurred more than four hundred times and was used in forty different ways" (1951, p. 533).   In this monograph, we are, of course, interested in but one of the ways.   The logic of measurement deals with the conditions necessary for the construction of a scale or measuring device.   Measurement as used here refers to the process by which the yardstick is developed, and not to its use once it has been established, in, say, determining the length of a desk.   It is essential that we keep this distinction in mind.   The use of the established yardstick in "making a measurement" is a rather simple procedure involving merely the comparison of the quantity to be measured with the standard series, or perhaps only reading the pointer or counter of an instrument designed for the purpose.   We are here concerned with the more basic problem of establishing a suitable scale of measurement.

On closer inspection of the three definitions quoted above, certain differences become apparent.   To Russell, numbers correspond to *magnitudes*; to Campbell, they represent *properties of material systems*; but to Stevens, they are assigned to *objects* or *events*.   Now, Russell's *magnitude* is roughly an amount of a property of a system;   hence, Russell is in agreement with Campbell on this point.   Stevens' definition, however, does not mention property.   For him, if numerals are assigned to objects according to rules (presumably any rules), we have measurement.   And apparently it is the object that is measured, and not (at least not necessarily) a property of the object.   At least, he does not object to the use of the term measurement to denote, say, the sorting of sticks into piles according to whether they grew on oak, elm, or pine trees—as long as numerals are used for naming the piles rather than words.   According to this view, we have measured or scaled a stick, though only at a primitive, nominal level, when we determine that that particular stick is a "two."   Thus, for this approach, classification, and even naming of individual instances, becomes a kind of measurement.

We shall not use the term measurement in this way.   We shall rather retain the more traditional view, that measurement pertains to properties of objects, and not to the objects themselves.   Thus, a stick is not measurable in our use of the term, although its *length, weight, diameter, and hardness* might well be.

2. ISOMORPHIC CHARACTERISTICS

Measurement of a property then involves the assignment of numbers to systems to represent that property.   In order to represent the property, an isomorphism, i.e., a one-to-one relationship, must obtain between certain characteristics of the number system involved and the relations between various quantities (instances) of the property to be measured.

The essence of the procedure is the assignment of numbers in such a way as to reflect this one-to-one correspondence between these characteristics of the numbers and the corresponding relations between the quantities.

Without here going into a logical or axiomatic discussion of number, we can list the important features of the real number series itself (as distinguished from various operations we can perform on the numbers) as follows:

1. Numbers are ordered.

2. Differences between numbers are ordered. That is, the difference between any pair of numbers is greater than, equal to, or less than the difference between any other pair of numbers.

3. The series has a unique origin indicated by the number "zero." An important feature of this origin is that the difference between any pair of numbers containing zero as one member is the number of the other member.

For brevity we shall call these, respectively, the characteristics of *order, distance, and origin*.

For some, but not necessarily all properties, it is possible to give empirical meaning to one or more characteristics which are analogous to the characteristics of numbers listed above. It is then possible to establish a one-to-one relationship between objects possessing this property and those characteristics of numbers. Numbers are then assigned to the objects so that the relations between the numbers reflect the relations between the objects themselves with respect to the property. Having done so, we have measured the property; i.e., established a scale of measurement.

These three characteristics form the basis for two different methods of distinguishing among different kinds of measurement.

A first distinction can be made according to whether the numbers reflect one, two, or all three of the characteristics. This leads to a classification of *types of scales*.

A second distinction can be made according to the meaning of the characteristics themselves. This distinction leads to a classification of different *kinds of measurement*. We shall first discuss the different types of scales, and then go on to a discussion of the different kinds of measurement.

3. TYPES OF SCALES

Of the three characteristics listed in the preceding section, order is the only one that is invariably involved in measurement as it is usually conceived. (We shall make no exception to this until the latter part of this chapter, when we discuss multidimensional scaling.) Campbell states: "The conception of a magnitude is inseparable from that of the order characteristic of it" (1928, p. 8). His first law of measurement is a statement that the property to be measured has a definite order (1928, p. 2).

In addition to order, a scale may possess either or both of the remaining two characteristics of distance and origin. We thus distinguish between four types of scales which can be arranged in a fourfold table as shown in Figure 1. Any unidimensional scale falls into one or another of the four

	No natural origin	Natural origin
No distance	Ordinal scale	Ordinal scale with natural origin
Distance	Interval scale	Ratio scale

Figure 1.   The four types of scales.

scale types: ordinal, ordinal with natural origin, interval, and interval with natural origin. In the ordinal scale the numbers are assigned to the various instances of the property, so that the order of the numbers corresponds to the order of magnitude of the instances. Examples of ordinal scales are the replacement series of chemistry, the Mohs hardness scale of physics, and the peck order of chickens in psychology. The ordinal scale with natural origin has the additional restriction that the number "zero" is assigned to the zero amount of the property. Many of the scales of experimental esthetics are of this type. In these scales, the order of the numbers corresponds to the order of pleasantness of a set of stimuli, while the origin divides the series at the point of transition from pleasant to unpleasant. With the interval scale, in addition to the order of the numbers corresponding to the order of magnitude of the various amounts of the property, the size of the difference between pairs of numbers has meaning, and corresponds to the distance (in some generalized sense) between the corresponding pairs of amounts of the property. The physical scales of time and energy are well-known examples of interval scales. With the interval scale having a natural origin, we have the additional restriction that the numbers assigned to the instances correspond to the distances of these instances from the natural origin of the property.

Since in this scale the ratios of the numbers assigned have meaning, we shall henceforth call this type of scale a ratio scale.

Comparison with Other Classifications

It might be well to compare this classification of scales with those given by other writers on the subject. Our classification is similar to that given by Stevens (1951*b*, p. 25). Stevens distinguishes among nominal, ordinal, interval, and ratio scales. The present classification differs from Stevens, first, in that we distinguish between ordinal scales with and without natural origins, and, second, in that Stevens includes what he calls a nominal scale. His nominal scale refers to the processes of reification and classification, with the trivial restriction that numbers be used to name the objects or name the classes of objects. One example of a nominal scale would be as follows: Given a number of discrete objects, we simply assign a different numeral to each of them. The numerals can then serve as names for the different objects. This set of numerals corresponds to one kind of nominal scale. A second kind of nominal scale would be obtained if we sorted the objects into a number of piles or classes, according to some more or less well-defined complex of properties. In this task, for example, two stones may be sorted into the same class, whereas a stone and a tree would be sorted into two different classes. We would then assign one and the same numeral to the stones, and a different numeral to the tree. Here, the numerals serve to identify classes of objects. In the immediately preceding method it was the objects themselves. It should be noted that the use of numerals here is unnecessary. Other sets of distinguishable marks would serve as well. As a matter of fact, words are ordinarily used for this purpose. In measurement as we use the term, the number assigned refers to the relative amount or degree of a property possessed by the object, and not to the object itself, whereas, in the different nominal scales, the numbers refer to the objects or classes of objects: it is the object that is named or classified. In terms of the previous discussion of constructs, we may say that, in classification, the construct of primary interest is the object or class of objects; in measurement, it is the property. Now, it is true that, when objects are classified, it is always with respect to some particular property or complex of properties, and therefore, the notion of property is also important in classification. However, the role played by the concept of property is somewhat different in the two processes. In the one case, objects are classified according to presence or absence of one or more properties; in the other, the degree or amount of the property itself is determined.

A second, and more complex, classification of scales has been given by Coombs (1952, p. 4). Coombs first of all adds to Stevens' four types of

scales a fifth, which he calls a partially ordered scale.   In Stevens' hierarchy, this scale falls between the nominal scale and the ordinal scale.
He then notes that we can think of a scale in terms, first, of the objects
themselves and, second, of the distances between the objects.   The
objects may be simply classified, may be partially ordered, or may be
completely ordered.   The distances between objects, he holds, may also
be classified, ordered, or partially ordered.   This leads to a distinction
between eleven different kinds of scales, with nine of the eleven falling
below the interval scale in Stevens' hierarchy.   Each of his scales is
named by a pair of terms, where the first term refers to the object, and the
second term refers to the distance.   For example, we have such things as
ordered–nominal scale, nominal–partially ordered scale, and partially
ordered–ordered scale.   A somewhat different classification, but in the
same general spirit, has subsequently appeared in Coombs, Raiffa, and
Thrall (1954).

Here again the discussion seems to be in terms of objects and distances
between objects, rather than in terms of a property and amount of difference between various instances of the property.   Coombs thus seems to be
dealing primarily with what might better be called different methods for
the systematic classification of various limited sets of objects, rather than
methods for measurement of a property.   It would seem to be closely
analogous to such things as the development of the periodic table for the
classification of elements in chemistry and the development of the phylo-
genetic system of classification in biology.   The classificatory system given
in Figure 1 seems adequate for classifying the various types of *measurement
of a property*.   The additional categories in the classificatory systems
presented by Stevens and Coombs are relevant more to classification of
sets of objects than measurement of a property.

Our primary distinction between ordinal and interval scales corresponds
closely to Carnap's distinction between comparative and quantitative
concepts (Carnap, 1950, p. 8).   Our ordinal and interval classification also
corresponds to the economists' distinction between ordinal and cardinal
in their discussions on measurement of utility.   (See for example Edwards,
1948, p. 384.)

Campbell's (1928) primary dichotomy of scales corresponds to the
principal diagonal of our Figure 1.   He distinguishes between the ordinal
scale on the one hand and a ratio scale on the other.   Indeed, this distinction seems to be the rule among those interested in measurement in the
physical sciences, where, however, the distinction is of little importance
since ordinal scales are not often used.   Though interval scales also occur
in the physical sciences, as, for example, in the measurement of time, of
energy, and of spatial position, since these properties can all be defined in

terms of other properties measurable on ratio scales, they have not been emphasized.

Invariance Characteristics of the Four Types of Scales

Measurement, we have seen, concerns the assignment of numbers to objects to represent amounts or degrees of a property possessed by all of the objects. An important characteristic of measurement is its power to enable us to decide, within limits, which of the inexhaustible number of sets of numbers that might be assigned to the set of objects is appropriate. Each of the four types of scales accomplishes this basic feature of reducing the completely arbitrary element in the assignment of numbers to represent the property to a different degree. We shall discuss each in turn. In our discussion we shall make use of the excellent notion of relating scales of measurement to transformation groups, as developed by Stevens (1951*b*).

ORDINAL SCALE. Given only that the objects can be arranged in serial order with respect to the property, and the rule that numbers are to be assigned in such a manner that the order of the numbers assigned agrees with that of the property, we see immediately that a great deal of the freedom has disappeared. It is equally true, however, that a great deal remains. The freedom remaining amounts to this: Given any set of numbers assigned in such a way as to fulfill the prescribed requirements, any order-preserving (i.e., monotonic) transformation of these numbers will also fulfill the requirements, and hence will serve as well. We thus say that, in an ordinal scale, the numbers are determined to within a monotonic-increasing transformation. Such transformations are illustrated in Figure 2*a*.

ORDINAL WITH NATURAL ORIGIN. Given, in addition to the above, that a unique natural origin can be established with respect to the property, we are further limited. Now, instead of any monotonic-increasing transform of the numbers, we are limited to those that leave the origin unchanged. Figure 2*b* gives an illustration of two varieties of such transformations. Curve *U* refers to a situation where the origin occurs at one end of the series, whereas for curve *V* the origin occurs within the series.

EQUAL INTERVAL. Given, in addition to the requirements of an ordinal scale, that we can also determine differences between different amounts of the property (distances), and the further rule that numbers are to be assigned so that their *differences* reflect the sizes of the corresponding *distances*, the freedom remaining is reduced to the assignment of two numbers arbitrarily: e.g., the selection of a unit and an origin. To put it another way: a set of numbers satisfying the requirements of an interval scale is insensitive to a linear transformation of the numbers. In an interval scale, then the numbers are determined to within a linear transformation of the form $y = ax + b$, where a is any positive number, and b is any finite number whatsoever.   Figure 2c gives examples of two such transformations.

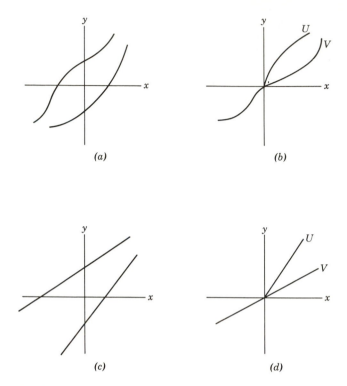

(a)   (b)

(c)   (d)

Figure 2.   Examples of permissible transformations for each of the four types of scales.   Let the abscissa x give the numbers originally assigned to the quantities.   The values of the quantities on the ordinate y then also fulfill the requirements of the scale type.

(a) Ordinal scale: monotonic transform
(b) Ordinal scale with natural origin: monotonic transform through origin
(c) Interval scale: linear transform of form $y = ax + b$
(d) Ratio scale: linear transform of form $y = ax$

RATIO.   If we add the determination in some sense of a unique natural origin to the requirements of the interval scale, we find that only one number may be assigned arbitrarily.   After one number has been assigned to one object, the numbers to be assigned to those objects remaining are completely determined.   The set of linear transformations available in the interval scale is now reduced to those that leave the natural origin (zero point) unchanged. In a ratio scale, then, the numbers are determined to within a linear transformation of the form $y = ax$, where a is any positive number as is illustrated in Figure 2d. As in Figure 2b, curve U refers to a situation where the origin occurs at one end of the scale, and curve V to one where the origin occurs within the scale.

Thus, the four different types of scales restrict the arbitrary element in assignment of numbers to different degrees. As a result, when using the numbers to stand for the property, we are in like manner restricted in the characteristics of the numbers that are available for meaningful use. For example, if we wish to express the relation between one property and another, say, the areas and the radii of circles, we are limited as follows by the use of the four different scales:

1. *Ordinal.* Area is a monotonic function of radius. That is, if either area or radius, or both are measured only on an ordinal scale, we could only determine that the relation between the two is monotonic.

2. *Ordinal and Natural Origin.* Area is a monotonic function of radius through the origin: that is, whenever the radius is equal to zero, the area is equal to zero.

3. *Equal Interval.* Area is a quadratic function of the radius.

4. *Ratio.* Area is proportional to the square of the radius. When the units of area and length are chosen in a particular way, and both are measured on ratio scales, the constant of proportionality turns out to be pi.

4. KINDS OF MEASUREMENT

The classification of scales into scale types was, in a sense, based on how *much* information about the property the numbers represented (which may depend on the nature of the property). It is also necessary to distinguish among what might be called the *kinds* of information the numbers represent. This amounts to a consideration of the sorts of meaning attributed in a particular scale to those characteristics of order, distance, and origin that are represented. Here we distinguish three different ways in which these characteristics might obtain meaning. First of all, they might obtain meaning through *laws relating the property to other properties.* Density is an example of this kind of measurement. The law refers to the fact that the ratio of mass to volume for any amount of a given substance is a constant. Further, the ratio turns out to be different for different substances. Hence, the value of the ratio can be taken as the *density* of the substance. Campbell has called this kind of measurement, *derived measurement*, or measurement of *B magnitudes.*

A second way in which these characteristics might obtain meaning, after a fashion, is simply by arbitrary definition. We might call this *measurement by fiat*. Ordinarily, it depends on *presumed* relationships between observations and the concept of interest. Included in this category are the indices and indicants so often used in the social and behavioral sciences. This sort of measurement is likely to occur whenever we have a prescientific or common-sense concept that on a priori grounds seems to be important but which we do not know how to measure directly. Hence, we measure some other variable or weighted average of other variables presumed to be related to it. As examples, we might mention the measurement of *socioeconomic status*, of *emotion* through use of GSR, or of *learning ability* through the number of trials or the number of errors it takes the subject to reach a particular criterion of learning. Whereas, with derived measurement, the characteristics possess constitutive meaning directly, and operational meaning only indirectly through the measurement of other variables, the indices and indicants possess operational meaning alone, at least initially.

A third kind of measurement depends upon laws relating various quantities of the construct to each other. Campbell calls this kind of measurement *fundamental* measurement or measurement of *A magnitudes*. Fundamental measurement is a means by which numbers can be assigned according to natural laws to represent the property and yet which does not presuppose measurement of any other variables. *A construct measured fundamentally possesses both operational and constitutive meaning of and by itself.* The former, since definite rules are available for assigning numbers to represent particular quantities, and the latter, since the numbers reflect natural laws relating different quantities of the property.

The extensive properties of physics, e.g., length, resistance, number, and volume, are examples of properties measurable by a fundamental procedure. A ratio scale can be constructed for each of these properties which is based on laws relating different quantities of the particular property itself. The characteristics of order, distance, and origin have constitutive meaning in terms of these relations, and independent of any consideration of laws and theories relating the property to other, different variables. Each of these properties, of course, also enters into a great many relations with other variables. Indeed, the properties would not be particularly important if they did not. Further, it should be noted that, once relations with other variables have been established, these can be used in place of the fundamental process to measure the property itself.

It should be noted that any particular *scale* may be a mixture of different *kinds of measurement*. For example, the ordinal characteristic may be determined fundamentally, and the interval characteristic derived from laws relating the construct to other variables. Or both may be derived, or both fundamental. A common occurrence in the social and behavioral sciences is for the order to be determined fundamentally, and the intervals to be defined by fiat. The usual speed test scores would be an example of this situation.

It might also be noted that the kind of measurement for a particular scale might change as we go from the very small to the very large. As a matter of fact, in physics, properties that are measurable fundamentally are usually so measurable only in the middle range. Measurement of the very small and the very large is accomplished through the derived process, using laws or extrapolations of laws discovered through experimentation on the quantities lying in the middle range that are fundamentally measurable. It might further be noted that, as a science progresses, fruitful quantitative concepts obtain what amounts to more and more definitions of the derived sort. In addition, new quantitative constructs tend to be introduced more and more by a derived process, in terms of other already established variables. Thus, out of all the measurable quantities of physics, only a very few are measurable fundamentally. In nearly all instances, the equality of intervals or ratios derives its meaning entirely through laws, theories, or simply definitions relating the property to other variables.

If we could measure amount of tension on an interval scale, we could then define degree of satisfaction in terms of Kluckhohn and Murray's equation as given in Chapter 1:

$$S = -k \frac{dT}{dt}$$

where S is the degree of satisfaction, T is the amount of tension, and t is time. We would not have *discovered* or *proved* anything about the relationship among these three variables, of course. We would have simply introduced the concept of degree of satisfaction into the system by specifying its relationship to two other measurable variables. The usefulness of the concept as so defined would hinge on its entering into lawful relationships with other important variables of the theoretical system.

Since, in the social and behavioral sciences, we do not yet have a previously established theoretical system which would enable us to introduce new concepts by way of the derived process, we are reduced largely to measurement either by fiat or by a fundamental process, or by some combination of the two.

There is little we can say about measurement by fiat, since it depends so heavily on the intuitions of the particular experimenter. One thing should be emphasized, however: there is certainly nothing *wrong* or *logically incorrect* with the procedure. (For different views on this matter, see, for example, Stevens, 1951*b*; Weitzenhoffer, 1951; Johnson, 1936; and Reese, 1943.) It has led to a great many results of both practical and theoretical importance. For example, a major share of the results of the field of mental testing and of the quantitative assessment of personality traits has depended upon measurement by fiat. Measurement of morale, efficiency, drives, and emotion, as well as most sociological and economic indices, is largely measurement of this type.

In all these cases, one or more observable properties are selected which on a priori grounds are judged to be related to the concept of interest. A measure of the observable property itself or of a simple or weighted sum of several such observable properties is taken as the measure of the concept of interest. Ordinarily, the values so obtained are treated as though they were measures on an interval or ratio scale. This is clear, for example, when curves are fitted by the process of least squares or when product–moment correlations, means, or standard deviations are computed. All of these presuppose that distance has meaning. Hence, either explicitly or implicitly, the experimenter is measuring the attribute on an interval scale whose order and distance characteristics have obtained meaning initially through definition alone.

The discovery of stable relationships among variables so measured can be as important as among variables measured in other ways. Indeed, it really makes little difference whether the present scale of length, for example, had been obtained originally through arbitrary definition, through a relation with other, established variables, or through a fundamental process. The concept is a good one. It has entered into an immense number of simple relations with other variables. And this is, after all, the major criterion of the value of a concept. If the result is the same, the way in which a concept is originally introduced is of little importance.

The major difficulty with measurement by fiat is the tremendous number of ways in which such defined scales can be constructed. We might measure strength of food drive by the number of hours of food deprivation, by the amount of shock an animal is willing to take in order to reach food, by the amount of weight lost during a particular period of deprivation, and so on.

In the field of mental testing, the possibilities are enormous. We have only to consider that, since any single arithmetic problem can be considered to be an indicant of arithmetic ability, any combination of any number of arithmetic items, presented orally or written, under speed or power conditions, or anywhere in between, can be taken as the defined measure of this ability. Each is a separate explication of an initial concept of arithmetic ability. Although subsequent investigations may establish that many lead to virtually the same result and hence may be considered to be equivalent operational definitions of the same concept, many will also lead to quite different results, in which case they are operational definitions of different concepts. The same state of affairs occurs as well in measurement of attitudes and personality traits, sociological and economic indices, and the like.

Since there are so many possibilities, since such scales come so cheap, the confidence in any particular explication of this type can be expected to be low. As a result, we cannot always blame the theoretician for rejecting the explication rather than his model when the experimental results do not go in the direction indicated.

It is at this stage of scientific inquiry that the development of procedures for the fundamental measurement of important constructs would seem to be most crucial. A great deal of arbitrariness is removed by this process. Concepts explicated in this way *begin* with a certain amount of theoretical significance, since numbers assigned to particular quantities reflect the operation of empirical laws. Actually, as we shall see in the next sections, fundamental measurement itself is an example of the construction and verification of theories. Any particular scale type can be considered to be a formal model. If rules of interpretation are laid down which connect the model to observable data, the model becomes a theory, and as such can become subject to empirical test.

Perhaps the primary justification for the great amount of effort devoted to fundamental measurement in the social and behavioral sciences lies in the expectation that scales so constructed, based initially as they are on empirical law rather than on arbitrary definition alone, will ultimately prove to be a more fruitful basis for a science of behavior than the more arbitrary procedures now in common use.

5. ORDINAL SCALES

Definitions of Terms

In the preceding sections we have been using a number of terms rather loosely. Henceforth, we shall have need to distinguish rather carefully among a number of rather closely related concepts. More particularly, we shall have need for the following distinctions: between measurable and nonmeasurable properties, between property and system, between the property and a particular amount of the property, and, finally, between two instances of the same amount of the property. We shall use the following definitions:

1. *Object* will refer to a system: that is, to the "thing" which carries or possesses properties.

2. *Attribute* will refer to a measurable property: that is, to a property capable of gradations. Length, pitch, wavelength, mass, and weight are examples of attributes.

3. *Magnitude* (we shall use Russell's meaning of the term) is, essentially, anything capable of being greater than or less than something else. A magnitude is a particular amount of an attribute. In like manner, the class of all magnitudes of a kind (such that, of any pair, one is either greater than or less than the other) corresponds to the attribute. The attribute then is analogous to a *continuum* of points, and the magnitude to a *point* in the continuum. A length of seven inches, a pitch of one hundred mels, and a weight of ten pounds are examples of magnitudes.

4. *Quantity* is a particular instance of a particular magnitude. Russell defines it as follows: "When a magnitude can be particularized by temporal, spatial, or spatial–temporal position, or when, being a relation, it can be particularized by taking into a consideration a pair of terms between which it holds, then the magnitude so particularized is called a *quantity*. Two magnitudes of the same kind can never be particularized by exactly the same specifications. Two quantities which result from particularizing the same magnitude are said to be *equal*." (1938, p. 167.)

Thus, for example, in terms of length, the four expressions would have the following meaning: *Object* might refer to a particular stick which has many other properties besides length. *Attribute* would refer to the continuum of length. *Magnitude* would be the point in the continuum corresponding to the length of the stick. *Quantity* would refer to the length of the stick itself. The distinction between quantity and magnitude here would be as follows: If we have two sticks, both eleven inches long, the quantity of length associated with one is *equal* to that of the other. The two quantities are equal because the sticks both possess the *same* magnitude of length.

This distinction between quantity and magnitude is of some importance because the model or theory underlying an ordinal scale may be stated in terms of either quantities or magnitudes. The postulates are slightly different in the two cases. If the distinction is not kept clearly in mind, a certain amount of confusion could result. For example, if the model is stated in terms appropriate for magnitudes, and the rules of correspondence are appropriate for quantities, we might find ourselves concluding that an ordinal scale of a particular attribute does not exist, when in fact it does—as will be illustrated in the following section.

Postulates of Order

We shall first present a set of postulates which are appropriate for constructing an ordinal scale if we are thinking in terms of magnitudes.

These are Huntington's three postulates of order and are taken from Stevens (1951b, p. 14).

All of the magnitudes of a kind form the class of elements. Let a, b, and c be any three magnitudes of a kind. We then introduce the symbols for two relations: $<$ (less than) and $\neq$ (is different from). The latter relation is symmetrical.

The three postulates then are as follows:

1. If $a \neq b$, then either $a < b$ or $b < a$.
2. If $a < b$, then $a \neq b$.
3. If $a < b$, and $b < c$, then $a < c$.

This model is simpler than the next to be discussed. However, this simplicity is illusory. When we seek a rule of correspondence to connect the relation $\neq$ and the elements a, b, and c with observable data, we are likely to run into some difficulties. For example, considering length again, if we let the elements a, b, and c correspond to the lengths of three sticks, then we do not want the relation $a \neq b$ to mean that stick a is different from stick b since stick a and stick b might be quite different from each other and yet both possess the *same magnitude* of length. If these rules of correspondence are used, we would have to conclude that such attributes as length, mass, and volume, for example, are not measurable on an ordinal scale. On the other hand, if the terms a, b, and c, refer to magnitudes rather than objects or quantities, then the set of postulates can determine an ordinal scale as we usually think of it.

Since magnitudes are themselves fairly abstract concepts, it would seem that a more satisfactory set of postulates would be one that allowed its terms to be related directly to quantities of observable data. Such a set of postulates in terms of quantities rather than magnitudes has been given by Hempel (1952, p. 59). The postulates given below determine what Hempel calls a quasiseries to distinguish it from a series as determined by the postulates given above. A quasiseries differs from a series only in the fact that several elements may occupy the same place.

We first specify the class of elements as all those objects possessing the attribute. We then introduce two relations: P for *precedence*, and C for *coincidence*. Then, if we again designate any three elements as a, b, and c, the relations must meet the following conditions: First, C must be transitive, symmetric, and reflexive. One easy and conventional interpretation of C is the arithmetical relation $=$. Second, P must be transitive, C-irreflexive, and C-connected. An easy and conventional interpretation of P is the arithmetic relation $>$. The meaning of each of these requirements is spelled out in more detail below.

1. C is transitive. That is, whenever a coincides with b and b coincides with c, then a coincides with c.

2. *C* is symmetric.   That is, whenever *a* coincides with *b*, then *b* coincides with *a*.

3. *C* is reflexive: Any element coincides with itself.

4. *P* is transitive: Whenever *a* precedes *b*, and *b* precedes *c*, then *a* precedes *c*.

5. *P* is *C*-irreflexive: If *a* coincides with *b*, then *a* does not precede *b*.

6. *P* is *C*-connected: If *a* does not coincide with *b*, then *a* precedes *b* or *b* precedes *a*.

If the requirements hold, we may then assign numbers to the elements so that for any two elements, if *a C b*, then *a* and *b* are given the same number, and, if *a P b*, then *a* is given a smaller number than *b*.

This, then, is a basic model for an ordinal scale.   All that remains is to develop rules of correspondence relating the model to observable data and then to test the theory to see if it fits the data.   Two examples of this procedure are given below, a very elementary one from physics and one from psychology:

1. Let the class of elements refer to the length of medium-sized objects where the objects are rigid bodies having ends.

Let the relation, *a P b*, correspond to "*a* is shorter than *b*," which is determined by superimposing the objects *a* and *b* so that one end coincides, and then determining for which object the other end extends farther. Furthermore, let the relation, *a C b* mean that whenever *a* and *b* are placed side by side so that one end coincides, the other does also.

These two relations will then satisfy the requirements for an ordinal scale.   The relation *C* is symmetric and reflexive by *definition* or *stipulation* since, whenever the ends of *a* coincide with *b*, then *b* must coincide with *a*, and since the length of *a* must coincide with itself.   Further, *P* is *C*-irreflexive and *C*-connected also by stipulation since our operation of comparing *a* and *b* must result in either *a C b* or *a P b* or *b P a*.   Any element for which this is not true is simply not a member of the class.

It is very important to note, however, that the *transitivity requirements* on the relations *C* and *P* are not merely a matter of definition or stipulation but rather take the form of *testable hypotheses*.   It is this latter fact that sets fundamental measurement apart.   The transitivity requirements enable us to test whether the theory (that is, the model, along with the rules of interpretation) actually fits the observable data.   Whether or not it does depends on the existence of natural laws.   The transitivity requirements on both the relations *P* and *C* are subject to experimental test.   If they hold, the attribute is measurable fundamentally on an ordinal scale.   If not, it is not.   In interpreting whether or not the requirements hold, we must keep in mind, of course, the limitations of our procedure. Thus, for example, it would probably be possible to find a set of elements such that $a \, C \, b$, $b \, C \, c$, $c \, C \, d$, and yet $a \, P \, d$, which would be due to the fact that the procedure corresponding to the relation C is not infinitely sensitive. This type of difficulty is always present in all physical as well as psychological measurement. One way around the difficulty is to obtain a large number of repeated observations of each pair and then stipulate that $a \, P \, b$ only if b is observed to exceed a more often than a is observed to exceed b; and that $a \, C \, b$ only if the observation b exceeds a and the observation a exceeds b occur equally often. Some such modification would actually be used if the differences among quantities approached the sensitivity of the procedure. A forced choice version is given below in the example from psychology, where this is often the case.

2. An example from psychology: Let the class of elements refer to the pitch of tones.

We shall take the method of paired comparisons as our experimental method. We have a set of stimuli, which in this case are pitches. Each pair of stimuli is presented to the subject a large number of times. We shall say that $a \, P \, b$ whenever the percentage of times a is judged lower in pitch than b exceeds 50%. And we shall say that $a \, C \, b$ whenever the percentage of times a is judged lower in pitch than b is exactly equal to 50 per cent. This, then, sets up our rules of correspondence. Again the relation C is symmetric and reflexive by definition or stipulation, and P is C-irreflexive and C-connected by definition or stipulation. Once more, however, the transitivity requirements on C and on P are a matter of experimental test. As a matter of fact, again within limits, both are found to hold. We can thus conclude that pitch is measurable on an ordinal scale fundamentally.

Derivative Procedures

The development given above refers to the most simple case, where the attribute and the defining operations are such that each object can be compared directly with each other object. Suppose now that for some reason or other some of the quantities cannot be directly compared with some of those remaining. In particular, suppose we have two subsets of elements such that any element from one subset can be directly compared with any element from the other subset, but no two elements from the same subset can be compared directly with each other. This would occur, for example, in establishing an ordinal scale of density of liquids through use of the ordering relation "floats on," if all of the liquids could be divided into two subsets such that all pairs of liquids within a subset mixed with one another (i.e., formed solutions) and no pair of liquids from different subsets mixed.   The observational relation "floats on," which is interpreted as "is less dense than" could then be determined *directly* only for those pairs of elements consisting of one member from each subset.   Given n elements in one subset, and N elements in the other, we could observe directly only nN of the $(n+N)(n+N-1)$ possible relations.   However, *if* the attribute behaves in the manner specified by the ordinal scale, we can then *deduce* the remaining relations (those between members of a single subset).   Further, we can test whether the attribute does in fact behave in the prescribed manner.   From the postulates underlying the ordinal scale, the following relation between any two elements a and b of the same subset occurs: If $a\,P\,b$, then a precedes every element that b precedes plus at least one more.   Further, if $a\,C\,b$, then a and b precede exactly the same elements.   These two theorems suffice to scale the entire set of nN elements (within the sensitivity of the procedure), provided that the observable relations do in fact behave in the manner prescribed by the postulates of the ordinal scale.   The experimental test of the procedure consists simply of determining if an order exists for which neither of the two deductions given above is violated.   That is, in a derivative procedure such as this, certain deductions from the formal model are put to experimental test rather than certain of the postulates themselves.   We shall have more to say about this in a subsequent section. Suffice it to say here that such derivative procedures are also examples of fundamental measurement, since they depend on the existence of empirical laws.   The particular procedure illustrated is actually a prototype of one of the more important procedures developed in the field of attitude measurement.   It is discussed more fully in Chapter 12.

6. THE NATURAL ORIGIN

There has been nothing in the procedures thus far that serves to establish a natural origin for the ordinal scale.   Yet it seems clear that for some attributes, at least, that are measurable on ordinal scales, natural origins do exist.   Whether or not a natural origin can ever be determined *fundamentally* for an ordinal scale, in the sense that "fundamental" has been used, is a matter of question.   Nonetheless, procedures have been devised in several different disciplines for determining some type of natural origin. In psychophysics the absolute limen ordinarily serves as the natural origin. In the measurement of such attributes as attitudes, esthetics, preferences, and value, the natural origin occurs within the series and can be described as a neutral point such that all stimuli or individuals in one direction are favorable, pleasant, liked, or wanted as the case may be, whereas all those on the other side are unfavorable, unpleasant, disliked, or not wanted.

There is little more to say at this time about the natural origin in connection with ordinal scales other than that, when it is determined by some additional operations, the numeral zero is assigned to the element at the natural origin. Furthermore, for those attributes such as attitudes, esthetics, and the like, the numbers assigned to the elements on one side of the natural origin have negative signs, and those on the other side have positive signs.

7. INTERVAL AND RATIO SCALES

The interval and ratio scales are by far the most useful measurement scales employed in science. As a matter of fact, the term measurement is often restricted to these kinds of scales, both in the ordinary use of the term and in the more advanced discussions of the topic. (See, for example, Carnap, 1950, p. 9; Hempel, 1952, p. 58; and Campbell in Ferguson et al., 1940, p. 347.) It might further be noted, that, in discussion of the nature of measurement, the distinction between fundamental and derived measurement is also commonly made only in terms of interval and ratio scales. (Measurement by indices is usually not considered.)

As was done with ordinal scales constructed by the fundamental process, we shall consider the fundamental process of establishing interval and ratio scales in terms of a scientific structure, i.e., in terms of a model, a model interpreted through rules of correspondence or theory, and the empirical testing of the theory in terms of observable data.

The model underlying both these scales would seem to be that of the real-number system. The construction of an interval or ratio scale is accomplished when we have assigned one real number to each of the quantities to be measured.

The statement that the model underlying the interval and ratio scales is that of the system of real numbers rather than that, say, of the rational numbers or of the integers requires further comment. Actually, certain procedures for fundamental measurement result directly only in the assignment of integers (or integers multiplied by a fractional constant) to the quantities. Other procedures result in the assignment only of rational positive numbers. Thus, there are two alternative ways of looking at the process of fundamental measurement. We could speak in terms of a separate model for each of the different procedures, such as those mentioned above, or we could speak in terms of one single over-all formal model, where the procedures differ with respect to the number and kinds of terms in the formal model which are given rules of correspondence, and which thus, then, enable us to test the theory and to assign numbers to the quantities. Of the two, the latter seems to be the more fruitful. A conception of length which implies that the Pythagorean theorem is exact only for those right triangles for which the sum of squares of the lengths of the two shorter sides is a perfect square does not seem desirable.

Two broad approaches to the construction of interval and ratio scales by the fundamental processes can be distinguished. The distinction corresponds to the difference between fundamental measurement as used in physics (i.e., fundamental measurement of extensive attributes) and that used in other disciplines such as, for example, psychology. The difference between the two does not seem to be as earthshaking as we would be led to believe from reading various discussions of the subject. The distinction would seem to involve little more than noting which terms of the formal model are interpreted through rules of correspondence relating them to observable events. The distinction here is similar to that made in the preceding discussion of ordinal scales, where we considered both the simple, direct test of the ordinal scale model and the more complex tests based on derivations from the postulates of the model. In fundamental measurement in physics, the primitive terms of the model, or at least certain of them, receive rules of interpretation. The elements, the class of elements, the relations of precedence and coincidence, and the operation of addition all are interpreted directly in terms of physical events. For example, in the construction of a scale of length, the element is a rigid body possessing ends. The class of elements is the class of all rigid bodies possessing ends. The relation of precedence is determined by placing two elements side by side, so that one end of one is coexistent with one end of the other, and then checking to see whether the other end of one extends farther. The relation of coincidence can be defined in much the same way or alternatively can be defined in terms of the relation P and its converse. And finally the operation of addition is defined by the placing of two elements end to end in a straight line so that one end of one coincides with one end of the other.

In the second kind of approach various deductions from the formal model are given interpretation. For example, in the formal model the *difference* between any two elements is equal to, greater than, or less than the difference between any other two elements. That is, for any four real numbers a, b, c, and d, $(b - a)$ is greater than, equal to, or less than $(d - c)$. In like manner, in the formal model, given any three elements in serial order a, b, and c, then $(b - a) + (c - b) = (c - a)$. In several forms of fundamental measurement in psychology, the difference between two elements is interpreted as a distance, and this distance is defined in terms of observations through a rule of correspondence.

In these forms of psychological measurement, the relation *distance* is of central importance, whereas in physical measurement the operation of *addition* is of central importance. This distinction, incidentally, corresponds closely to Russell's distinction between attributes whose quantities are divisible and attributes whose quantities possess the relation *distance*. (Russell, 1938, Ch. 10.)

Now, the distinction between a theory whose primitive terms are interpreted and one whose derivative or defined terms are interpreted is not a particularly crucial one. Very respectable theories of both kinds occur in science. Indeed, in many instances it is difficult to tell which terms are primitive and which terms are defined in terms of primitives. The relation of equality or coincidence may be defined in terms of the primitive relations greater than and less than, these relations then being sufficient to generate a quasiseries. But the quasiseries may be generated also by considering the relations of equality and less than as primitives. Very often the choice of which terms are to be considered as primitive terms and which as derivative is a matter of convention. In any event, empirical confirmation of a theory, whether interpreted in terms of primitives or of derivatives, confers some empirical meaning on the entire theory. In the one case, meaning is conferred on the primitive terms directly, in the other case, mediately. (See Hempel, 1952, p. 35.)

Fundamental Measurement in Physics

Let us return now to a closer look at the specific conditions imposed in physics in the construction of a scale of an extensive attribute by a fundamental procedure. The actual specification of these conditions can be made in a number of different ways. The following presentation follows Hempel:

We first define a quasiserial order for the domain in terms of the relations P and C as presented in the preceding section on ordinal scales. We then must specify some way of combining two quantities a and b such that the combination is a new quantity of the same kind. Thus, for example, in the fundamental measurement of length, the combination would be obtained simply by placing the two quantities end to end; with resistance, by connecting the two quantities in series; with conductivity, by connecting the two quantities in parallel. Following Hempel, we will denote the operation of combination by a small circle. Thus $a \circ b$ will mean the quantity formed by the combination of a and b. We may now state the additional conditions which $\circ$ together with C and P must obey:

1. $a \circ b \, C \, b \circ a$.
2. $a \circ (b \circ c) \, C \, (a \circ b) \circ c$.
3. If $a \, C \, b$ and $c \, C \, d$, then $a \circ c \, C \, b \circ d$.
4. If $a \, C \, b$ and $c \, P \, d$, then $a \circ c \, P \, b \circ d$.

5. If $a\,P\,b$ and $c\,P\,d$, then $a \circ c\,P\,b \circ d$.
6. If $a\,C\,b$, then $a\,P\,b \circ c$.
7. If $a\,P\,b$, then there exists a c such that $b\,C\,a \circ c$.

These conditions are much easier to read if the $\circ$, C, and P are replaced by the usual arithmetic signs of $+$, $=$, and $<$, respectively. It is readily seen that the class of all positive real numbers meets these conditions.

Though in a particular situation some of these conditions may be true by definition, others will be in the nature of testable hypotheses. Thus, for example, in the fundamental measurement of length, the first might possibly be considered to be true by definition, whereas all the rest are testable hypotheses which prior to experimental investigation may or may not be true.

Assuming that the hypotheses are all verified, it is then a simple matter to assign numbers to the quantities considered in such a way that for any two quantities the following are true:

1. If $a\,P\,b$, then the number assigned to a is less than that assigned to b.
2. If $a\,C\,b$, then the number assigned to a is the same as that assigned to b.
3. The number assigned to the combination of a and b ($a \circ b$) is equal to the number assigned to a plus the number assigned to b.

In carrying out this task, we find that we can assign one number to one of the objects arbitrarily. Once we have done so, the numbers to be assigned to the remaining quantities are determined. Hence, fundamental measurement in physics, or, for that matter, any fundamental measurement based in this manner on the empirical addition or combination of quantities, results in a ratio scale. All fundamental measurement used in physics seems to be of this type. Indeed, it is commonly held that this is the only fundamental procedure that will yield scales having more than ordinal characteristics. However, as we stated earlier, other types of approaches are possible and are being used. Let us turn now to consider these in somewhat more detail.

Fundamental Measurement Based on Distance

There seems to be no general set of conditions stated in the literature which must be obeyed by quantities before a scale based on the distance relation can be constructed. Nevertheless, the following seems to be true.

We first establish a quasiserial order for the quantities under consideration by the same procedures as discussed previously under the section on ordinal scales. We then deduce from the formal model (the real-number system) certain propositions concerning the properties of differences between real numbers. In addition, we may deduce certain propositions concerning the behavior of ratios of real numbers. The differences and/or ratios are then given empirical interpretation in terms of distances between quantities and/or ratios of quantities.

Finally, an experimental test is made to determine whether the distances between quantities behave in the same manner as the differences between real numbers and/or whether the ratios between quantities behave in the same manner as ratios between numbers. If so, numbers can be assigned to the quantities so that the order of the numbers corresponds as before to the order of the quantities, and, furthermore, the relative size of the distances between quantities corresponds to the relative size of the differences between numbers assigned to the quantities. Finally, if ratios have been interpreted, numbers can be assigned with the additional restriction that the ratio of one quantity to another corresponds to the ratio of the numbers assigned to the quantities.

If distances only are interpreted, then, when numbers are assigned to the quantities, we find that we may assign numbers to two different quantities arbitrarily. Once we have done so, the rest of the numbers are determined. Hence, fundamental scales based on distance and order are interval scales. If, in addition, testable hypotheses concerning ratios are verified, or if distances from a natural origin are interpreted in some other manner, we find that we may arbitrarily assign a number to one quantity only. Hence, the resulting scale in this case is a ratio scale.

The different procedures for the construction by fundamental process of interval and ratio scales based on the distance relation are discussed in detail in subsequent chapters. However, we shall give here an example of how one such procedure might be applied to the fundamental measurement of a physical variable which is ordinarily considered to be measurable only in terms of its relation to other variables; e.g., volume or pressure. The attribute to be considered, namely, that of temperature, has long been a favorite of measurement theorists.

The procedure will be, first, to define a temperature distance as simply the amount of difference in warmth between any pair of quantities, and, second, to postulate that a particular set of operations bisects, trisects, or, in general, n-sects this distance. Through a number of successive sections we shall be able to test our theory empirically.

We first establish an ordinal scale of temperature, using any of the customary procedures: e.g., by correlating warmth of some substance, say water, with, say, the height of a column of mercury. This will enable us to *identify* various specimens of water having particular temperatures, even though we do not know what number should be assigned to the temperatures. We shall use the column of mercury to reproduce specimens of water at a given unknown temperature. The next step is to take a beaker, fill it to a particular mark with water at temperature a, and pour it into some larger container. We then fill the beaker to the same mark with water at temperature a, and heat the water to temperature e, after which we pour the water at temperature e into the same larger container. We then mix the two quantities, obtaining a quantity of water at the new temperature c. We hypothesize that the temperature c is halfway between temperatures a and b. In other words, it is hypothesized that the procedure followed thus far bisects the temperature distance $(a - e)$, giving a new temperature c halfway between the two. In order to test the hypothesis, we use the procedures employed by Gage (1934) and by Newman, Volkmann, and Stevens (1937) in their experiments on loudness. We repeat the experiment, using temperatures a and c to get a new temperature b halfway between a and c. We also repeat the procedure, using temperatures c and e to get a new temperature d halfway between temperature c and e. Finally, the crucial phase is to repeat the experiment, using temperatures b and d. If our hypothesis is correct, the result will be temperature c, which is the same temperature as that resulting from the initial bisection. Assuming that the procedure works, and it does work fairly well, we may then assign numbers to our five temperatures so that the number assigned to a is less than that assigned to b, which is less than that assigned to c, and so forth, and so that the differences between the numbers correspond to equal temperature distances. The scale developed would be an interval scale of temperature of water. The scale is based on distance and not on additivity. And it is not a derived or defined scale in Campbell's terminology, since it does not depend on the previous fundamental measurement of any other attribute. Fundamental measurement in this sense is analogous to several types of measurement in psychology.

More Complex Measurement Models

The illustration given above is an example of one of the simplest and most straightforward of the scaling models. Others become considerably more complex and elaborate.

The more complex models involve a certain amount of theoretical superstructure above and beyond that of the interval or ratio scale itself. In general, these additional postulates enable us to make use of notions of probability in establishing a scale with interval or ratio properties. For example, in Thurstone's judgment model, discussed in Chapters 8 through 10, the additional postulates enable us to derive a relationship between the probability that an element a will be judged greater than an element b and the distance between the two elements. An empirical estimate of this probability can then be used to estimate the distance. The additivity of independent estimates of distances between sets of three ordered stimuli can then be used to evaluate the goodness of fit of the theory to the data.

The more elaborate models, such as are discussed in Chapter 13, involve postulates relating the probability that an individual will agree with or pass an item, to certain scale parameters of both the item and the person. When enough restrictions are made, the number of independent observations is sufficient not only to estimate the relevant parameters but also to test the goodness of fit of the theory to the data.

In all these approaches we are dealing with fundamental measurement in our sense of the term, since the procedures used for establishing the scale depend on the existence of empirical laws relating the different quantities of the attribute scaled.

8. MULTIDIMENSIONAL SCALING

Heretofore, we have limited ourselves to a consideration of unidimensional attributes. The measurement problem consisted of developing procedures which would enable us to assign a number to each quantity of the attribute in such a way that certain relations between the numbers reflect analogous relations between the quantities. This procedure is possible for those attributes whose quantities form a one-dimensional quasiseries. In this case, we can conceive of the attribute as a one-dimensional continuum, analogous to the straight line in geometry. Assigning numbers to quantities is analogous to specification of the position of points on the straight line.

For those attributes whose quantities form a multidimensional series, such as the attributes of *spatial position* and *color*, for example, the measurement problem is somewhat more complex. Here the problem is to develop procedures to assign a *set* of numbers to each quantity so that the numbers, when considered in terms of a specified geometrical system, reflect relations among the various quantities. The number of numbers to be assigned to each quantity corresponds to the dimensionality of the attribute. Thus, the analogy now is with a multidimensional geometrical space. Whereas in unidimensional measurement, the attribute corresponds to the straight line (a unidimensional space), and the quantity to a point on the line, in multidimensional measurement, or scaling as it is usually called, the attribute corresponds to an *n*-dimensional space, and the quantity to a point in that space. Where the process of assigning numbers in unidimensional measurement corresponds to the location of points on a line, in terms of the order of the points, their distances from one another, and/or their distances from an origin; so, in multidimensional scaling, the process of assigning sets of numbers corresponds to locating the points in a multidimensional space, in terms of a set of relations between the points as specified by the particular geometrical model. Hence, multidimensional scaling can be considered to be a generalization of measurement as ordinarily considered.

The geometrical models that might be employed are, of course, of many different varieties. Besides the metric spaces, such as the familiar Euclidean model, other non-Euclidean models, and more peculiar spaces like the "city-block" space proposed by Attneave (1950), various non-metric models, such as have been proposed by Coombs and his students (e.g., Coombs and Kao, 1954, 1955; Bennett, 1951, 1956; Milholland, 1953; Hays, 1954) might be used.

Regardless of the particular model, the nature of the problem remains essentially the same.   The meaning of the numbers assigned to the elements of the model is specified by the model.   Rules of correspondence are established, relating elements and properties of the model to observable data, thus converting the model into a testable theory.   If the theory is verified, numbers are assigned to the quantities of the multidimensional attribute as specified by the theory.   Once this is done, we have scaled or "measured" the multidimensional attribute in question.

In an n-dimensional real Euclidean space, for example, each number associated with a given element gives the projection of the element on one of the coordinate axes of the space; i.e., gives the distance in terms of real numbers, of the projection on the axis from the origin.   Each element is, therefore, assigned n numbers, one for each dimension of the space.

An important feature of a Euclidean space is that the distance between any two points is equal to the square root of the sum, over all n orthogonal axes, of the squares of the differences of the projections of the points on the axes.   That is,

$$d_{jk} = \left[\sum_{r=1}^{n} (p_{rj} - p_{rk})^2 \right]^{1/2}$$

where j, k are indices for any two points.

r is an index for axes.

n is the number of orthogonal axes.

p_{rj} refers to the projection of point j on axis r.

Hence, given the projections, we may determine distances between points.   Furthermore under some circumstances, we can also proceed the other way around.   Given the distances between all pairs of points, we can solve for the projections of the points on an arbitrary set of orthogonal axes of the space.   This latter fact gives us a lever whereby we can convert the formal model into a testable multidimensional-scaling theory.   If we can develop a rule of correspondence relating the formal construct "distance" to empirical observations (i.e., if we can devise a procedure for determining distances between quantities of a multidimensional attribute), we then have a testable theory, which, if not in conflict with the data, enables us to assign numbers to each quantity to represent the projections of that quantity on each of the dimensions of the attribute.

The numbers assigned will be determined to within, first, the unit of measurement, and, second, a rotation and translation of the set of axes. The second limitation holds since, in a real Euclidean space, the interpoint distances are invariant over all orthogonal rotations and translations of the reference axes.

In this example, the problem can be considered as twofold:

1. To develop a unidimensional-scaling procedure for determining values of distances between pairs of quantities.
2. To determine whether these distances can be considered as distances between points lying in a real Euclidean space of some minimal dimension n, and, if so, to obtain the projections of quantities on dimensions of the attribute.

The general procedure is discussed in greater detail in Chapter 11.

Another approach, which depends on establishing some rule of correspondence for the interpretation of the distance between two quantities, has been developed by Attneave (1950). He uses a spatial model where the distance between two points is simply equal to the sum of the absolute values of the differences of their projections on the axes. That is

$$d_{jk} = \sum_{r=1}^{n} |p_{rj} - p_{rk}|$$

The model here implies a unique set of directions for the reference axes. It will also be discussed in greater detail in Chapter 11.

Bennett (1956) has discussed a model where the rule of correspondence is sufficient only to determine the rank order of distances of some of the quantities from certain other of the quantities. The problem here is at a more primitive level—to determine the dimensionality of the space and the order of the projections of quantities on each of the dimensions. At the present time, however, this is largely a program for the future.

A somewhat different set of models, in which the relation that receives interpretation via a rule of correspondence is not one of distance but rather one of "dominance" has been developed by Coombs and Kao (1955). The dominance relation is essentially a generalization of the relation "greater than" discussed in the section on ordinal scales, although the precise formal meaning of the term differs somewhat for the different models. These procedures too might at the present time be considered as representing mainly problems for future research. Bennett's model and Coombs' various models are considered in somewhat greater detail in Chapters 12 and 14.

The important thing to note at the present time is that the process of assigning numbers to represent quantities of the attribute is much the same, whether we are dealing with unidimensional or with multidimensional attributes.

3 ◄

► *Classification*
of Scaling Methods

1. INTRODUCTION

A considerable number of procedures have been devised to enable social scientists, psychometricians, and psychophysicists to determine scale values of a series of objects, events, or individuals with respect to some attribute. In all too many cases there has been too little communication between and within the various disciplines in developing, naming, and using the various techniques. In some cases, the same techniques are used in different areas under different names. In others, similar names have been applied in different fields to techniques that differ considerably. For example, the method of graded dichotomies, the method of successive intervals, and the equidiscriminability method all refer to a single general procedure. Equal appearing intervals and the method of equisection are two basically different techniques that have often been considered in terms of a single method.

In order to discuss these many methods intelligibly, we find it first necessary to devise some kind of an inclusive framework within which the different methods can be classified. The development of such a framework or classificatory system is the topic of the present chapter. We shall first consider briefly a number of classificatory principles which might be used as the basis for such a framework. We shall then indicate which of these seemed most appropriate for the purposes of the present monograph.

Finally, using these principles, we shall develop the system of classification which serves to organize the presentation in the remainder of the monograph.

2. PRINCIPAL WAYS IN WHICH THE PROCEDURES DIFFER

The various methods differ from one another in several different aspects. Any number of these aspects might be used in an attempt to classify the methods.   Some are listed below.

Properties of the Final Scale

The methods differ from one another with respect to the properties ascribed to the final scale.   In the previous chapter, the problem was considered in terms of three characteristics of number important in measurement: namely, the characteristics of order, origin, and distance. Scales were first classified into the four *types* (ordinal, ordinal with natural origin, interval, and ratio) on the basis of whether one, two, or all three of these characteristics were present in the scale.   A second classification dealt with the meaning of each of those characteristics present in a given scale.   Here we considered three ways in which each of the three characteristics might be introduced: by definition or stipulation, through relations to some larger theory, or through application of an independent scaling theory.   These three *kinds of measurement* were called measurement by fiat, derived measurement, and fundamental measurement, respectively.

Either *type of scale* or *kind of measurement* might serve as a basis for classifying measurement procedures in the social and behavioral sciences. Stevens (1951b), for example, discusses procedures largely in terms of his own set of scale *types*.   For Campbell (1928), on the other hand, a distinction similar to the three *kinds* of measurement given above serves as a basic classificatory principle.

Discriminability among Stimuli

The methods differ with respect to the discriminability among the stimuli to which they are ordinarily applied.   The dichotomy of *subliminal* methods versus *supraliminal* methods is a traditional one of psychophysics.

Use of a Related Physical Continuum

The procedures differ in whether or not a related physical continuum is either necessarily or ordinarily available.   Guilford's *Psychometric Methods*, for example, had as two of its basic subdivisions the *psychophysical methods*, in which a physical continuum is ordinarily available, and the *psychological methods*, in which it is not.

Nature of the Response

The procedures differ in the nature of the response obtained from the subject. We have first of all the distinction between those methods where the response is concerned with the relation between characteristics of the stimulus and the subject (the subject agrees with, passes, or endorses a stimulus, for example) and those methods where the response concerns the relation between the stimulus and a specified attribute (the subject orders the stimuli with respect to brightness, loudness, or sweetness, for example).

A further distinction can be made, depending on whether the form of the response is *comparative* or *categorical*. A *comparative* response explicitly states a relation between two or more stimuli: e.g., stimulus A is brighter than stimulus B, or subject X prefers stimulus A to stimulus B. In the *categorical* response, on the other hand, the stimulus is classified into one of two or more classes (which may or may not have an a priori order): e.g., the subject sorts the stimuli into seven classes according to heaviness, or the subject indicates whether he agrees or disagrees with each of the stimuli.

These two distinctions form the basic two-way classification in Coombs's theory of data (1952), and in his discussions of scaling methods. Coombs's *task A* and *task B* refer to whether or not the response concerns the relation between the stimulus and the subject or the relation between the stimulus and a designated attribute, whereas his *relative–irrelative* dichotomy corresponds to our distinction between comparative and categorical responses.

Field of Specialization

The procedures differ with respect to the particular field of specialization in which the continuum being scaled lies. Thus we have, for example, attitude scaling procedures, psychophysical scaling methods, psychometric or mental test methods, merit rating methods, and esthetic preference scaling methods.

Latent Continuum versus Manifest Data

They differ with respect to whether or not the originator was interested in the manifest data themselves or in a hypothesized latent continuum which acts as a causal agent in determining the manifest data. Stouffer, Guttman, and Lazarsfeld (in Stouffer et al., 1950) and Coombs (1952) all emphasize this factor as a basic variable.

Experimental Procedures

They differ with respect to the particular experimental procedures involved. We thus have rating methods, sorting methods, method of paired comparisons, method of rank order, method of choice, and the like.

Any of these principles (undoubtedly there are others as well) might serve as a basis for organizing a monograph on scaling methods. In one sense, the notion of the three kinds of measurement, i.e., by definition, by derivation from a larger theoretical framework, or by a fundamental process, has played a central part in the development of the present work. The methods with which we shall be concerned fall in general into the fundamental measurement class.

We do not consider measurement by derivation from a larger theoretical system because few if any such systems exist at the present time in the social and behavioral sciences. As these disciplines advance, this form of measurement will undoubtedly become more important. But this is largely a matter for the future. Actually, when these disciplines reach the point where a good share of their quantitative concepts are introduced in this way, much of the present practical concern with measurement procedures will likely have disappeared, and there will be little need for a work of this kind.

We do not consider measurement by definition primarily because the major problems in such procedures, e.g., selection and weighting of indicants, are largely dealt with intuitively and are tied very close to the particular subject-matter area. Few rigorous statements can be made with regard to these problems. In addition, the mathematical procedures for carrying out the weighting procedures decided upon, along with quantitative procedures for evaluating, improving, and using such scales, are discussed adequately in detail in books dealing with the subject matter of the area involved.

The more important among the remaining classificatory principles discussed above can be summarized as dealing with differences in *theoretical approach* to the scaling problem, in *experimental procedures* used for obtaining the data, or in *analytical procedures* that are applied to the data. It is essential that these three classes of variables be clearly distinguished. Among the scaling methods which appear in the literature, some refer only to a single one of the variables; others refer to various combinations of the three.

A given underlying theory may be applicable to data obtained from several different experimental procedures, each of which might be analyzed in somewhat different ways. For example, Thurstone's basic judgment model (discussed in Chapter 8) can be applied to data gathered by, among others, the *experimental* methods of paired comparisons, rank order, successive intervals, and single stimuli. With each kind of data, several *analytical* solutions are available—graphic procedures, procedures based on medians or means, or, in some cases, least-squares solutions. Scaling methods of fractionation may utilize any of a number of experimental methods in gathering data. Again, given the data, several alternative analytical procedures are often available. In each case, however, the basic theoretical approach remains the same.

In like manner, a given experimental procedure may be utilized by several different theoretical approaches. For that matter, the experimental procedure may be used in experiments that do not involve problems of scaling at all. The experimental method of average error might be used to determine scale values in conjunction with the scaling methods of equisection or fractionation, to determine absolute or difference limens, or simply to determine the physical extent of an illusion or the physical weight of an object. The experimental method of paired comparisons might be used to determine scale values in conjunction with the law of comparative judgment, or simply to determine whether or not one object is preferred to another.

Of the three basic aspects of scaling, use of either theoretical approach to the problem or experimental method might be justified as the primary basis for classifying and organizing the scaling methods. Perhaps the most usual procedure is to organize in terms of experimental procedures. In this case we would have as major divisions the method of average error, method of paired comparisons, method of single stimuli, and the like. Within each division would then be a section describing the experimental procedure, followed by a series of sections devoted to various methods of analyzing the data obtained. There are certain arguments in favor of such an arrangement. Perhaps the principal one is that it conveniently allows a person with a set of data to compare the various methods that might be used to analyze it.

However, from the standpoint of a system to enable better understanding of the different approaches and of their relationships to one another, a system based upon underlying theoretical approach to the scaling problem would seem superior. Indeed, even in the case of the practical question of deciding which procedure to use for a particular problem, it would seem more reasonable to consider theoretical approach first and experimental procedure only after the theory is decided upon.

In the remainder of this chapter will be presented a system of classification based largely on underlying theoretical approach, which will permit a consideration of the scaling methods themselves in terms of their logical relationships.

3. THREE BROAD APPROACHES TO SCALING

In most measurement situations in the social and behavioral sciences, the raw data consist of a number of responses to each of a number of stimuli or stimulus combinations. This may take the form of many subjects each responding once, one subject responding many times, or several subjects responding several times, to each of a number of stimuli or stimulus combinations. For simplicity in the present discussion, it will be assumed that n subjects have each responded once to each of m objects. The same reasoning is applicable to the other cases as well.

We shall consider three different approaches to the measurement problem. The distinction is based primarily on differences in the allocation of the variability of the responses to the stimuli. This point of view parallels certain models used in analysis of variance designs if the notion of interaction is ignored.

The Subject-Centered Approach.   The systematic variation in the reactions of the subjects to the stimuli is attributed to individual differences in the subjects.

The immediate purpose of the experiment is to scale the subjects, who alone are assigned values. The stimuli are considered as replications. Adding or deleting stimuli from the same stimulus-population at random would have no effect on procedure or results other than those due to the usual sampling fluctuations. Insofar as the stimuli are replications, this approach is analogous to a one-way classification in the analysis of variance table with several observations per column, the subjects corresponding to the columns.

The Stimulus-Centered or Judgment Approach.   The systematic variation in the reactions of the subjects to the stimuli is attributed to differences in the stimuli with respect to a designated attribute.

The immediate purpose of the experiment is to scale the stimuli, which alone are assigned scale values. In this approach, the subjects are considered as replications. Adding subjects chosen at random from the same population, or deleting subjects at random, would have no effect on either the procedure or the results other than the usual sampling fluctuations. The analogy here is also with a one-way classification in analysis of variance. In this case, however, it is the subjects that are considered as replications.

The Response Approach.   Variability of reactions to stimuli is ascribed to both variation in the subjects and in the stimuli.

Both subjects and stimuli might be assigned scale values. The immediate purpose of the experiment might be to scale either the stimuli or the subjects or both. The analogy now is with a two-way analysis of variance with (ordinarily) one observation per cell.

It should be noted immediately that, with both the subject- and the stimulus-centered approaches, precautions are taken to eliminate, balance out, or otherwise control the effects of the secondary source of variation. Thus, in the stimulus-centered or judgment procedures, for example, the task set for the subject is usually such as to minimize inter-individual differences. In addition the experimenter may select a homogeneous group of subjects or may use a single subject over many trials, either of which procedures will tend to minimize variability due to factors other than the differences between the stimuli with respect to the attribute under consideration. Similarly, in the subject-centered procedures, the experimenter selects those stimuli and responses that tend to emphasize the individual differences between the subjects.

The three approaches can perhaps be illustrated most clearly by examples from the area of attitude measurement where all three have been popular. Typical of the judgment approach is the method of equal-appearing intervals (discussed in Chapter 4) for the *construction* of an attitude scale. The task set for the subjects (judges) is such as to minimize any variation due to their own position with respect to the attitude. Typically, it consists of sorting, according to degree of the attitude reflected by each statement, a number of attitude statements into eleven piles so that the piles are ordered and equally spaced with respect to the attitude continuum. Judges are treated as replications, and the stimuli alone receive scale values. The Likert technique provides an example of the testing approach. Here, the task set for the subjects is such as to allow individual differences with respect to the attitude continuum to be expressed. Subjects respond to each item on the basis of the extent to which they are willing to endorse the item. Subjects alone receive scores. Stimuli are selected so as to increase the individual differences with respect to the attitude continuum. Different weights might be given to the stimuli, but, if so, it is on *the basis of their power to discriminate between subjects, and not on the basis of their relative positions on the attitude continuum.* The response approach can be illustrated with the Guttman technique of scale analysis (discussed in Chapter 12). The task set for the subject is essentially the same as in the Likert technique. But here an attempt is made to order both subjects and stimuli with respect to the attitude continuum. Both subjects and stimuli can thus be assigned scale values.

The subject-centered approach has not yet led, to any great extent, to the development of scaling models. The applications in general are examples of measurement by definition. By far the major part of the field of mental testing is based on measurement of this kind. Most aptitude, achievement, and intelligence tests, where the individual's score is a simple or adjusted sum of the number of items answered correctly, are essentially examples of measurement by definition. It is interesting to note that, in those areas where the primary interest is in scaling subjects, the change from measurement by definition to measurement by a fundamental process has ordinarily involved a shift from the subject-centered approach to the response approach.

Since we are not concerned in this monograph with measurement by definition, we shall have little more to say about the subject-centered approach. Since it falls within the province of mental testing, readers interested in this approach are referred to any of the standard works in the mental testing field (for example, Gulliksen, 1950; Lindquist, 1951; Cronbach, 1949).

We thus have remaining, as the basic dichotomy of scaling methods to be considered, the *stimulus-centered* or *judgment* methods, in which the differences in reactions of subjects to stimuli are attributed to differences in the stimuli with respect to some attribute, and the *response* methods, in which the differences in reactions are attributed to differences both in the stimuli and in the subjects.

4. JUDGMENTS VERSUS RESPONSES

Associated with the two approaches to scaling is a basic difference in the task set for the subject. In the stimulus-centered or judgment approach, the task set for the subject is to evaluate the stimuli with respect to some designated attribute. The subject responds to a stimulus with respect to its relation among other stimuli in the defined continuum. (Other stimuli here may refer either to stimuli that are present at the time of the judgment or to stimuli experienced at some time previous to the particular judgment.) Since the subject responds to the stimulus on the basis of its relative position among other stimuli, the effect of his own bias is minimized.

In the response approach, the task set for the subject is to respond to a stimulus on the basis of the position of the stimulus in relation to the subject's own position with respect to the attribute. The subject's own attitude, feeling, or ability is an important factor in his response. It should be remarked that this distinction is essentially the same as that used by Coombs (1952). Our "judgments" are his "task *A*," and our "responses" his "task *B*."

As an illustration to distinguish between the two kinds of tasks, consider two attitude statements taken from Thurstone and Chave's monograph (1929, p. 61).

1. I find the services of the church both restful and inspiring.
2. I think the church is a parasite on society.

In the judgment approach, the task set for the subject might be to judge which statement is more favorable to the church. A subject would be expected to pick statement 1 regardless of his own attitude toward the church. In the response approach, the task set for the subject might be to pick the statement with which he is in closest agreement. In this case, of course, both his own attitude and the attitude reflected by the stimuli act to determine his response.

There is at least one area, however, in which the ability to distinguish between the two approaches on the basis of the task set for the subject breaks down. This area includes preferences, esthetic judgments, judgments of pleasantness, and the like. Here either approach might possibly be used on a given set of data. Whether or not to consider the responses as reflecting variation in the position of the stimuli on a given continuum that is common to or typical of a given population of subjects, or as also reflecting opinions that may differ with each subject, would depend on the purposes and preferences of the experimenter.

5. THE DETERMINATION OF ORDER

The two approaches to scaling can also be differentiated in terms of the way in which the problem of order is treated. Indeed, from a more formal standpoint, this probably provides the clearest differentiation between the two types of approaches.

In Chapter 2, we saw that an ordinal scale can be characterized by two relations, C and P, where C is transitive, symmetric, and reflexive and P is transitive, C-irreflexive, and C-connected. In the judgment methods, the two relations are *interpreted directly* in terms of the proportion of times one stimulus is judged *more x than* another, where x refers to a designated attribute. Since for each pair of stimuli we have a single proportion, the relation C is symmetric and reflexive by definition. In like manner the relation P is C-irreflexive and C-connected by definition. The transitivity of C and P, which can be examined experimentally, is used to determine whether or not the attribute under consideration can be represented by an ordinal scale.

Now, for *any* two stimuli possessing the attribute, either one precedes the other, or they coincide with respect to the attribute. This gives a way of specifying the class of stimuli under consideration: the class of all stimuli that possesses the attribute is made up of all those stimuli such that, for any pair, either one precedes the other, or they coincide with respect to the attribute. Any stimulus for which this is not true is simply not a member of the class.

With the judgment methods, *the rule of interpretation allows for direct empirical determination of the relation between any two stimuli in the class.* It also involves *specification of the attribute under consideration.* The proportion refers to the proportion of times, for example, that one stimulus is judged *brighter than, more favorable to the church than, more pleasing than,* or *louder than* another stimulus. In each case, the attribute is clearly specified: judged *brightness, favorableness to the church, pleasantness, loudness.*

In the judgment methods, if the transitivity requirements are satisfied, we conclude that the attribute can be represented by an ordinal scale. If these requirements are not satisfied, we conclude that the attribute cannot be represented by an ordinal scale. The point to be emphasized here is that it is an hypothesis about the nature of the *attribute* that we are evaluating.

When we turn to the response methods, we are confronted with a somewhat different approach. We note first of all that we have two subclasses of elements—stimuli and subjects—rather than one single class. Further, the data obtained pertain in general to relations between elements of one subclass and elements of the other subclass. In one response situation we have data of the form "subject *i agrees with, passes,* or *is characterized by* stimulus *g*," in which case no corresponding comparisons of subject *i* with subject *j* or stimulus *g* with stimulus *h* are obtained. In another situation, the order of preference of the stimuli is obtained for each subject, but the subjects themselves are not directly compared.

In general we thus do not have a direct interpretation of the relations *P* and *C* with respect to the attribute for *all* pairs of elements in the class. Hence, a *direct* and *complete* test of the primitive postulates for order as given in Chapter 2 cannot be made. Rather, the different response methods handle the problem of order by various *derivative* procedures. That is, from the properties of an ordinal scale (or, as we shall see, even an interval or ratio scale) are deduced various propositions, which are then related to observable data. An example of one such procedure was given in Chapter 2.

The nature of the response, along with the two subclasses of elements, leads to several interesting differences between the two approaches. First, where in the judgment procedures a clear-cut way of defining the class of elements is available which is independent of whether or not the attribute forms a scale, the response methods lack this convenience. The response of "agree–disagree" or "pass–fail" can be made to each of two items with respect to entirely different attributes. *Hence, additional procedures are needed to specify the class of elements.*

Second, in the judgment methods, the attribute under consideration was specified clearly: Stimulus *A* was *judged brighter* than stimulus *B*. The relations C and P were different for each attribute. In the response methods, this is not so. The response "agree–disagree" or "pass–fail" does not itself distinguish between attributes. Hence, additional factors must determine the nature of the attribute.

Third, in the judgment methods, when the requirements are not satisfied, we would conclude that the attribute (e.g., judged brightness) does not form an ordinal scale. With the response methods, the conclusion is somewhat more complex.

We might, first of all, conclude that, though the responses are all generated by a single property, this property cannot be represented by an ordinal scale; e.g., we might conclude that the concept "attitude toward the church" represents a single property, but that the property cannot be characterized by a linear order.

We might also conclude that the property *could* be represented by an ordinal scale if we only had a better rule of correspondence; i.e., we might conclude that other factors besides "attitude toward the church" enter into the determination of whether a response to any given item will be positive or negative.

We might instead conclude that the property could be represented by an ordinal scale if we only had a better way of specifying the class of stimuli; for example, considering all the stimuli that look as though they reflect "attitude toward the church," the responses to some of the stimuli may be entirely dependent on this property, whereas the responses to others may be dependent on one or more other properties as well.

Much the same could be true of the *subjects*. Some might respond entirely in terms of the "attitude toward the church." Others might respond on the basis of a number of other attributes of the stimuli.

Different interpretations of the reason for failure to obtain an ordinal scale can lead to different subsequent steps. One experimenter might proceed to see if, by removing certain subjects, a scale would be obtained. If successful, this would lead to a class of "scalable" subjects and a class of "nonscalable" subjects. Another might attempt to eliminate or revise stimuli in order to obtain a scale. A third might develop a more elaborate model which attempts to take into account the idea that a response of subject i to stimulus g is mediated not only by ordinal position on the attribute of interest but also by various irrelevant factors. All three, it should be noted, would be attempting to carry out some modification which would result in a procedure for establishment of an ordinal scale of subjects, of stimuli, or both.

A different approach would be to accept the responses of the set of subjects to the set of stimuli at face value and ask: If these responses do not form the pattern required by the ordinal scale model, then what sort

Framingham State College
Framingham, Massachusetts

of a pattern *do* they form? It is here that a gradual shift can occur from the problems relating to measurement of an attribute to the equally important, but much broader, set of problems concerning the systematic classification of a set of events.

In measurement, the primary concern is in constructing a scale of an attribute. In classification, the primary interest is in the pattern of responses of a particular set of subjects to a particular set of stimuli (or *population* of subjects of which this set of subjects is a sample and/or *universe* of stimuli defined in some fashion of which this set of stimuli is a sample). If the response patterns can be considered as being generated by a linear order, well and good. The ordinal scale is one of the neatest of classificatory systems. If not, perhaps another less restrictive system will be satisfied. Even if no systematic relationships among the various response patterns can be seen, we can at least obtain what Stevens calls his "nominal scale." That is, we can at least classify the subjects according to whether their response patterns are the same or different.

Coombs, Raiffa, and Thrall (1954) have given a considerable number of classificatory systems of this type, which in a sense lie between the nominal "scale" (which, to be sure, is hardly even a classificatory *system*, since the only systematic relation among different classes is one of difference itself) and the ordinal scale (which in our view represents the most primitive level of measurement of an attribute). Perhaps the best known of these is the partially ordered "scale," a classificatory system that orders some but not all of the elements.

In the present monograph we shall keep substantially within the framework of methods for measurement of an attribute. Hence we shall have little more to say about various alternative systems for classifying data. Readers interested in the latter problem are referred to Coombs, Raiffa, and Thrall (1954).

From the standpoint of measurement, the more important consideration dealt with in this section is the differentiation between the judgment and response methods, in terms of a *direct* test of the postulates of order on the one hand, and an indirect test of derivative propositions on the other, along with the consequences of the latter procedure with respect to delineation of the class of elements and the specification of the nature of the attribute.

6. JUDGMENT METHODS

General Characteristics

We have seen that the ordering of a stimulus series with respect to a designated attribute presents, at least theoretically, few problems for the methods of the judgment approach. It is true that, for stimuli that are very close together on the attribute continuum, or for attributes that have not been clearly defined, practical problems often arise which may make the ordering of the stimuli difficult, or which may render the final result somewhat questionable. This is particularly true if, for one reason or another, repeated independent judgments of each stimulus or stimulus combination cannot be made. For most situations, however, the problem of ordering the stimuli is not pressing. Indeed, in many situations, such as those wherein a related physical magnitude is available, the ordinal characteristics of the stimuli are known to a high degree of certainty before any experiment is performed. For those stimulus series in which the order along the given attribute is not obvious, and thus must be determined experimentally, the criterion for order is based on the proportion of times any stimulus is designated as possessing more of the attribute than any other stimulus. More specifically, if stimulus A is designated as greater than stimulus B over 50 per cent of the time, it is concluded that stimulus A is greater than stimulus B with respect to that particular attribute. There is considerable evidence that the rank order obtained is substantially invariant with respect to the different experimental methods that might be used. For example, we would expect substantially the same rank order to obtain for a given set of stimuli with respect to a designated attribute, whether we used judgments involving paired comparisons, ranking, single-stimulus rating, or sorting into successive intervals to obtain the data.

It should be noted, however, that paired comparisons is the only method of those mentioned in the preceding paragraph that does not force transitivity on the data. That is, in ranking, rating, or sorting procedures, if stimulus A is placed above B over 50 per cent of the time, and B is placed above C over 50 per cent of the time, then stimulus A must have been placed above stimulus C over 50 per cent of the time, simply as a result of the experimental procedure used. The procedures do not allow for the possibility of C being greater than A under these circumstances. Paired comparisons, on the other hand, is permissive rather than coercive with respect to transitivity. It is experimentally possible to obtain 100 per cent judgments of A greater than B, B than C, and C than A. Thus, if the attribute is such that the property of transitivity is questionable, then paired comparisons (or variants, such as the method of triads) is the best method to use for answering the question. The other procedures mentioned above force transitivity on the data and are thus not suitable for testing the property itself. Ordinarily, however, the attribute of interest is such that transitivity may safely be assumed. In such cases, each of the different kinds of tasks usually set for the subject may be expected to result in substantially the same rank order of the stimuli.

It is in the rationale used in obtaining a *unit of measurement*, i.e., in constructing a scale with interval or ratio properties, that the unidimensional judgment methods can perhaps be differentiated most profitably. When considered in this light, it is seen that these methods fall into two distinct groups: the *quantitative judgment* approach and the *variability* approach.

In the quantitative-judgment methods, the unit is obtained directly from quantitative judgments of the stimuli with respect to the attribute. The task set for the subject always requires more than the mere ability to differentiate stimuli on the basis of their order. That is, the subject must be able not only to give judgments of the general form "*A* is greater than *B*," "*B* is greater than *C*," etc., but also, in some form or other, to indicate relationships among the psychological distances or ratios between the stimuli. Examples of such tasks, all given with respect to some designated attribute, are:

(*a*) Adjust stimulus *B* so that it is subjectively halfway between stimuli *A* and *C*.

(*b*) Adjust stimulus *B* so that it is 1/3 as great as stimulus *A*.

(*c*) Rate each stimulus on a scale of 10 equal steps.

(*d*) Sort the stimuli into 11 piles so that the intervals between the piles are subjectively equal.

(*e*) Given that stimulus *A* is 100 units, report the value of stimulus *B*.

(*f*) Report whether *B* is closer to stimulus *A* or to stimulus *C*.

Contrasted with the quantitative-judgment approach are those judgment methods wherein the variability of judgments with respect to each stimulus or stimulus combination is used to derive a unit of measurement. The task set for the subject requires only the ability to differentiate stimuli on the basis of the order, such as

(*a*) Which is greater, stimulus *A* or stimulus *B*?

(*b*) Place the stimuli in rank order.

(*c*) Place the stimuli into 11 piles, which are ordered with respect to the attribute.

It will be noted that task *c* here is very similar to task *d* in the quantitative-judgment methods. The present case, however, requires that the piles simply be ordered, whereas the quantitative-judgment case requires that they also be separated by equal intervals. Actually, of course, the variability methods that can use data gathered by task *c* can also use data gathered by the corresponding quantitative-judgment methods. When they do so, they simply assume that the piles are merely ordered and treat the data accordingly.

In the quantitative-judgment methods, variability of judgment with respect to a particular stimulus or stimulus combination is troublesome. By troublesome we do not mean that it is necessarily difficult to deal with, but only that it is a factor which presents problems additional to the basic theory. Experimenters using a quantitative-judgment approach would not, to say the least, be handicapped if the subjects always gave the same response to a given stimulus situation. For example, with the method of bisection, if the world were such that all subjects always selected the same stimulus as lying halfway between two given standard stimuli, it would be all to the good. With the variability methods, however, this is not true. These models can obtain an interval scale from ordinal-type judgments only because hypotheses relating the variability of judgments with respect to each stimulus situation to the relative positions of the stimuli on a psychological continuum can be accepted. Without variability of judgment, the variability models can obtain only a scale with ordinal properties.

Quantitative-Judgment Methods

Quantitative-judgment methods can be further subdivided according to how much more they require of the subject than mere knowledge of the ordinal characteristics of the stimuli. Three general classes will be distinguished:

THE SUBJECTIVE-ESTIMATE METHODS. These methods would seem to require the most of the subject. It is assumed that he can rate, sort, or arrange members of the stimulus series in such a manner that the ratios of differences between the numbers assigned to the stimuli are equal to the ratios of the distances separating the stimuli on the psychological continuum. Under some circumstances, it might be further assumed that the ratios of the numbers themselves are equal to the ratios of the distances of the corresponding stimuli from a natural origin. Typical tasks set for the subject are the rating and sorting tasks (tasks c and d given above). Note that a unit and an origin are implied. For example, a rating of 7 implies that the stimulus is seven equal units from an origin. If we conceive of a subjective continuum along which the stimuli are located, we may consider the subjective-estimate methods as making the following requirements of the subject:

(a) He must be able to perceive directly the position of each stimulus on the psychological continuum.

(b) Although origin and unit in which the judgments are expressed may be arbitrary for any given experiment, they must remain constant throughout that experiment. That is, in any single experiment, a rating of 7 must, within error, always refer to the same distance from the same origin for a given subject.

The subjective-estimate methods will be discussed in Chapter 4.

FRACTIONATION METHODS. Fractionation methods require in one sense somewhat less of the subject than the subjective estimate methods. It is assumed either that the subject is capable of directly reporting the ratio of the amounts of the attribute of interest associated with two stimuli, or that he can adjust or select a stimulus which bears a given ratio to a second stimulus. Typical fractionation tasks are tasks *b* and *e* given above. The judged ratios are treated as though, within error variation, they are equal to the ratio of the distances between an absolute zero and the two stimuli on the attribute of interest. If we again conceive of a subjective continuum along which the stimuli are located, we may consider the fractionation methods as making the following requirement of the subject:

He must be able to perceive and report directly the ratio of two sense magnitudes. Note that this requires an absolute zero which remains fixed. The problem of unit does not enter since a ratio is the same, regardless of unit. It is in this sense that the fractionation methods require less of the subject than the subjective-estimate methods.

Fractionation methods are discussed in Chapter 5.

EQUISECTION METHODS. These methods require much less of the subject than either the subjective-estimate or the fractionation methods. In the equisection methods, it is assumed that the subject is capable of equating sense distances. To put it another way, it is assumed that he can make *ordinal* judgments of sense *distances*, that he can report whether the subjective distance between stimuli *A* and *B* is greater than or less than that between, say, *B* and *C*. It is apparent that, in the special case of half or double judgments in the fractionation methods, the task is formally identical with that in the method of bisection when one of the standards has associated with it a zero amount of the attribute of interest.

Equisection methods are discussed in Chapter 6.

Variability Judgment Methods

The variability methods may also be further differentiated into three groups. One procedure, based on variability, for "achieving" equality of units relies on the assumption that the distribution of scale values of the stimulus series is normal on the psychological continuum. This assumption has been used to a considerable extent in test theory. With respect to scaling procedures, it has been most popular in those situations where the *stimuli* are individuals or products of individuals. For example, when a group of individuals are rated with respect to a trait of personality or character, or when essays are rated with respect to excellence, the assumption of a normal distribution of stimuli is commonly made. Given this assumption, the only necessary experimental operations to determine scale values with equal-interval properties are those sufficient to determine the order of the stimuli. Once the stimuli have been ordered, it is a simple matter to assign values so that the stimuli project a normal distribution on the attribute of interest. It is obvious, of course, that any other distribution function could be assumed instead as representing the "true" distribution of the stimuli on the attribute. Since this procedure involves simply an arbitrary transformation of ranked data, it will not be discussed further.

A second approach "achieves" equality of intervals through use of the definition of equality of just noticeable differences. Examples of this approach are Fechner's law and the differential sensitivity scales of traditional psychophysics, as well as the pioneering work of Cattell and his students on the construction of scales of such strictly psychological magnitudes as eminence of scientists, quality of handwriting, and degree of humor. If we are willing to grant this definition of equality of intervals, we can then proceed to obtain scales with equal-interval properties for just about any attribute with respect to which subjects can differentiate stimuli. The difficulty, of course, lies in the fact that no criteria are given for determining when to accept and when to reject the definition. It implies, for example, that the proportion of times a difference between two stimuli is noticed depends only on the magnitude of the psychological distance between them, and thus is invariant with respect to the psychological order of magnitude of the stimuli themselves. It could equally well be assumed, however, that the proportion is also a function of the portion of the psychological continuum in which the stimulus difference occurs. Definitions of equality of intervals could thus be made which again would attribute the equal-interval property to any given monotonic transform of the original differential sensitivity scale. In each case, a scale could be constructed. In the absence of a more complete theory, there would be no really sound means of choosing among them. However, the notion of equality of just noticeable differences has a certain amount of reasonableness to it. It does determine scale values uniquely and has proved to be of use in many situations. These differential sensitivity scales are discussed in more detail in Chapter 7.

We are largely indebted to Thurstone for the third class of methods using variability of judgments to obtain a unit of measurement. These variability methods differ from those discussed above in the very important sense that the validity of the theoretical model is subject to statistical test. Where, with the former methods, the interval property is obtained solely through definition, in Thurstone's procedures, the interval property becomes a matter for empirical test. The fundamental nature of this distinction between this method of using variability to derive units and those discussed above is often overlooked.   Perhaps this results from the fact that the most popular variability model—Thurstone's case V of the law of comparative judgment—includes the requirement that equally often noticed differences are equal.   Even in this most simple case of the model, however, the contrast between merely defining a unit, on the one hand, and fitting a mathematical model, on the other, should be apparent. If the subjects do not behave in the manner required by the model, then the theory will not fit the experimental data, and the model will be rejected. An equal-interval scale will be obtained only in those situations where the behavior of the subject can in fact be accounted for by equations derived mathematically from the theoretical model.

Thurstone's variability model, with its various special cases, is discussed in Chapters 8, 9, and 10.

7. RESPONSE METHODS

General Characteristics

It will be recalled that the general category of response methods includes all those scaling methods in which the systematic variation in responses of the subjects to the stimuli is attributed to variation in amounts of the attribute with respect to both subjects and stimuli.   The endorsement or rejection of the particular stimulus by a particular subject is considered to depend both on his own attitude, belief, ideas or characteristics, and also on those reflected by the stimulus.   In like manner, a choice by a subject of one stimulus over another is considered to depend not only on the nature of the two stimuli, but also on the nature of the particular subject.   We saw earlier that one salient feature of all response methods is the use of indirect derivative procedures in establishing (or rejecting) the ordinal characteristics of the scale.   The nature of the problem here considered is such that direct test of the postulates of order is not feasible.   While a subject may respond to one or more stimuli, one stimulus does not in general respond to another.   Hence, indirect, derivative procedures are indicated.

The various methods that have been proposed differ from one another in a variety of ways.   Of these, two would seem to be of particular importance in forming a basis for grouping the methods into different classes. The first concerns the provision for (or treatment of) *error* or *unsystematic variance*.   This leads to a differentiation between the *deterministic models* as against the *probabilistic models*.   The second concerns the kind of data to which the models are applicable, or, to put it another way, the nature of the task set for the subject.   This leads to a classification into methods based on *categorical responses* as against those based on *comparative responses*.   Both dichotomies are discussed more fully below.   A third dichotomy, that differentiating the *unidimensional* from the *multidimensional* models, is also of importance. However, the present multidimensional models are more or less direct extensions of corresponding unidimensional models. Hence, we shall base our grouping solely on the differences amongst the latter. Multidimensional extensions of a particular unidimensional model will be considered along with the unidimensional model itself.

Deterministic versus Probabilistic Models

A basic distinction among the various response methods concerns the way in which they treat the problem of error. In the deterministic models, the formal model is stated in terms of the ideal case which is not expected to hold true exactly with real data. The model itself makes no provision for any error or unsystematic variance. All the variations in the responses of subjects to stimuli are accounted for in the model by the positions of the subjects and the positions of the stimuli. Since these models are thus completely deterministic, presumably one aberrant response could serve as sufficient evidence for rejection of the model. Since, in virtually any experiment with real data, such aberrant responses will occur, testing such a model against the data would virtually always yield a negative conclusion. However, even though the formal model itself does not fit the data exactly, it may serve as a very close approximation to the real data. Furthermore, various useful though arbitrary indices can be developed which will serve to indicate how good an approximation it is. The situation here is somewhat analogous to that of the ideal-gas laws or of the notion of a black-body radiator in physics. No real gas behaves exactly like an ideal gas and no real body is a perfect black-body radiator. Nonetheless, the approximation is very close and can be evaluated. Hence the ideal models can serve to represent the data to within a rather small degree of error. It can perhaps be argued that a theory of error is involved whenever the deterministic model is used along with an index for indicating degree of approximation to the ideal. However, such a theory of error is ordinarily implicit. It is not intrinsic to the model itself but is rather something that is added, subtracted, or changed as the circumstances warrant.

In contrast to this general approach, the probabilistic models do incorporate within themselves the notion of error or unsystematic variation. Variation above that provided for by the parameters of the stimuli and subjects can be accounted for in the formal model itself. This latter approach lends itself, theoretically, to the setting up of statistical criteria on goodness of fit of the model to the data, and thus gives a somewhat less arbitrary procedure for acceptance or rejection of the scaling method.

Categorical versus Comparative Responses

The second principle of classification deals with the nature of the task set for the subject. In the one case the subject responds to each stimulus with some sort of a *categorical response*. He *agrees* or *disagrees* with it, he *passes* or *fails* it. In the other, the subject *compares* two or more stimuli, and then orders them in some sense. The subject may indicate that he *prefers* one to the other, or he may indicate which of a set he agrees with most, which next most, etc. The kind of information given by the subject is different in the two examples. In general, a particular model will require information of one or the other kind, but not both. In the present monograph we shall call the two kinds of responses *categorical* responses and *comparative* responses. Other terms used in the literature are *single stimulus* and *irrelative* for categorical responses, and *relative* or *choice* for the comparative responses. Although most of the models that require categorical information need only two categories of response for each item, such as pass–fail or agree–disagree, use of additional categories in actual collection of the data is not uncommon. For example, the subject might not only indicate whether or not he agrees or disagrees with the stimulus, but also in some form or another indicate the strength of his agreement or disagreement. In like manner, for the methods that require comparative information, the subject might indicate directly for each pair of stimuli which one he prefers, as is done in the method of paired comparisons, or, alternatively, he might rank the stimuli in order of his preference, or might simply choose that stimulus out of a larger number of stimuli which he prefers most.

In Chapter 12, we discuss deterministic models for categorical data along with their multidimensional extensions. This chapter is largely concerned with the approaches of Guttman and Coombs. Chapter 13 deals with the equivalent probabilistic approaches to categorical data. Here we are concerned primarily with the approaches of Lazarsfeld, Thurstone, Tucker, and Lord. In Chapter 14, we discuss Coombs's deterministic response model for comparative data, along with its multidimensional extensions.

4◄

► *The Subjective*

Estimate Methods

1. THEORY

The Basic Rationale

Methods have been devised in many subject-matter areas in which an attempt is made to construct a subjective scale directly from the subject's own quantitative estimates of the scale values of a series of stimuli. They all have in common the fact that the subject is required to give, in one form or another, a direct report of the subjective scale value of each member of the stimulus series. The subject is instructed, either explicitly or implicitly, to base his reports on an equal-interval scale of the attribute of interest. The zero point of this scale may be arbitrary or absolute, depending on the particular experimental situation. In psychophysics, the methods are generally referred to as methods of absolute judgment (McGarvey, 1943). Corresponding methods developed in the field of esthetics are known as rating methods (Woodworth, 1938), as are equivalent procedures in the field of personnel evaluation (Tiffin, 1947; Ghiselli and Brown, 1955), and in the study of personality and character traits (Stagner, 1948). In education, much the same procedures are often applied to the scoring of essay tests (Ross and Stanley, 1954). In the construction of attitude scales, an equivalent procedure is known as the method of equal appearing intervals (Thurstone and Chave, 1929). Undoubtedly a great number of other uses could be cited.

The rationale is basically the same, regardless of the subject-matter area in which the methods are used. The procedures are as follows: a series of stimuli is presented to a subject (judge, observer), who is instructed to render a direct, quantitative judgment of the amount of a specified attribute that is possessed by each of the stimuli. For example, the task set for the subject might be to rate each of a group of essays on a ten-point equal-interval scale with respect to excellence. It is assumed that the subject is capable of carrying out this task. That is, if he rates three essays as 4, 5, and 6, respectively, it is assumed that, except for a certain amount of error, the difference in the degree of excellence between the first and second essay is equal to the difference between the second and third. He is thus required to make his reports so that they may be treated as scale values on a linear scale of the attribute of interest. Since variability in judgment with respect to a given stimulus occurs, it is necessary to obtain repeated judgments (either over judges or over trials with a single judge) in order to arrive at more stable estimates of the scale values of the stimuli.

It is apparent that the requirements set by the instructions solve the problem of obtaining an equal-interval scale for us—provided, of course, that the subject can fulfill these requirements. If we assume that the subject actually has been able to carry out the task, then the scale values of the stimuli on an equal-interval scale are directly given by his reports, and the scaling problem becomes merely a problem of averaging.

There are, of course, a number of variations of the basic experimental procedures. These will be discussed in the next section. There is also some variation in the analysis of the data, due to different approaches to the treatment of the variability of judgment with respect to a single stimulus. The basic rationale, however, underlying all the variations of the subjective-estimate methods is the same. If we wish to think in terms of a theoretical model underlying the subjective-estimate methods to be discussed in this chapter, it could be summarized as follows:

1. We take as given a series of stimuli that vary along some discriminable attribute. We assume that the subject is capable of making direct quantitative judgments of the amount of the attribute associated with each stimulus.

2. The subject's judgment is considered to be a direct report of the value of the stimulus on a linear subjective continuum of the attribute of interest. The reports may be referred to an arbitrary point or to an absolute reference point, depending on the instructions and the particular experimental situation.

3. Some variability of judgment with respect to any given stimulus may occur as is true of any measurement procedure. If so, the variability is

treated as error, and some averaging procedure is used to give an estimate of the scale value of each stimulus.

4. Except for this error, the subject's report gives the scale value of the stimulus directly on a linear continuum of the attribute of interest.

It is recognized that other approaches are available for treating the problem which can and do make use of the *experimental* procedures.   We could, of course, simply deny the possibility of obtaining equal units from judgments of this sort and treat the results as an ordinal scale.   Alternatively, we could assume that the attribute is distributed normally, and then either require the subjects to rate in such a manner that the ratings of the stimuli are normally distributed initially, or transform the scale values obtained by the methods to be described in this chapter so that they are normally distributed.   A third approach, to be covered in Chapter 10, which can make use of the same experimental procedures, represents an attempt to account for the data through use of a mathematical model.

The Origin and Unit

ERROR-FREE CASE.   It might be well to examine the nature of the task set for the subject in some detail.   Consider, for example, the following experiment: The subjects are presented with a series of objects differing only in weight.   They are instructed to rate these objects on a ten-point, equal-interval, subjective scale of weight, with the higher digits corresponding to the heavy end of the continuum, and the lower digits to the lighter end.   Assume for the moment that the subjective weight continuum is the same for all subjects, and that the locations of four of the stimuli on this subjective continuum are as marked off below:

Light s_1 s_2 s_3 s_4 Heavy
_____

If we further assume that the subjects do not make any errors in perceiving the weights of the stimuli, does this then guarantee that all subjects will give the same rating to any given stimulus?   It does not.   Four subjects may rate the four stimuli as follows:

		Subjects			
		A	B	C	D
	(1)	1	2	2	1
	(2)	2	3	4	3
Stimuli	(3)	3	4	6	5
	(4)	5	6	10	9

The four subjects each report a different set of scale values, even though they are basing their reports on the same subjective continuum. The reason, of course, is obvious. The instructions to the subject leave him free (indeed, require him) to select his own unit and origin in terms of which the scale values of the stimuli are to be reported. In the example, subjects A and B gave their reports in the same unit but referred to different origins. The unit used by subjects C and D is half that used by subjects A and B. The scale values assigned by the different subjects are, however, invariant within a linear transformation of the form $y = ax + b$, where a is a proportionality factor that allows for the difference in unit, and b is an additive constant to allow for differences in origin. The subjective-estimate methods are unique among the different scaling approaches in that they are the only ones in which both a fixed (though perhaps arbitrary) origin and unit are necessarily implied in the judgment.

Suppose we had made the additional restriction that each subject rate on a ten-point (0 to 9) equal-interval scale, where zero is to denote an object that has "just no perceptible weight." We would then, through our instructions, have fixed the origin from which the reports are to be made. The subjects would now be free to choose only a unit in which to express the scale values of the stimuli. Again, assuming no error, the scale values reported by the different subjects must now agree to within a linear transformation of the form $y = ax$ if the requirements are to be met. If, in addition, we had also specified that the heaviest stimulus in the series was to define a rating of 9, then we would also have specified the unit of measurement, and the scale values reported by the subjects must then agree to within the identity transformation, $y = x$: that is, must agree perfectly. The instructions would then have specified the scale completely. If the subjective continuum were the same for all subjects, they must all give identical reports for any given stimulus.

In the preceding paragraph one of the points specified was an absolute zero, but this is not necessary if merely an equal-interval scale is desired. It is apparent that specifying the values of *any* two different stimuli would serve to fix the unit and origin as well, although, in this case, the origin is arbitrary. This is much the same situation as is found in the early measurement of temperature. The Fahrenheit and centigrade scales are equal-interval measures of the same continuum, but have different arbitrary origins and units. In the centigrade scale, zero and one hundred degrees are specified as the freezing and boiling points of water, respectively. These two points determine the origin and unit of the centigrade scale. In the Fahrenheit scale, 32 and 212 degrees are specified as the freezing and boiling points of water, and these values determine the Fahrenheit unit and origin. Since the two scales are linear measures of the same continuum, however, they are related by a linear equation of the form $y = ax + b$, namely,

$$F = (9/5)C + 32$$

Occasionally, an attempt is made to specify *three* points on the subjective continuum. Consider, for example, the following instructions: "Rate the stimuli on a seven-point equal-interval scale, extending from -3 through 0 to $+3$ with respect to pleasantness. Let -3 stand for the most unpleasant stimulus in the series, $+3$ for the most pleasant stimulus in the series, and zero for any stimuli that are neither pleasant nor unpleasant." Though this may seem like a reasonable task, it actually may be impossible to perform. It is only possible to fulfill the conditions when the distance between the most unpleasant stimulus and zero is exactly the same as that between the most pleasant stimulus and zero. In general, when we attempt to *construct* a scale for a set of stimuli using one of the subjective estimate methods, we are free to specify two and only two points on the continuum. If the scale is to possess ratio properties, we are free to specify only one point, other than the rational zero point itself.

TREATMENT OF ERROR. In the discussion thus far, we have assumed that the subject behaved perfectly consistently. Actually, of course, he does not do so. If subject A in the illustration were given repeated trials, something like the following might be obtained.

		Trial				
		a	b	c	d	e
Stimuli	(1)	1	2	1	1	2
	(2)	2	3	3	1	2
	(3)	3	3	4	2	3
	(4)	5	4	5	4	5

This variation might be accounted for in two different ways. Consider again the subjective continuum on which the reports are based. In the illustration below the arrows indicate the locations of the four stimuli and the vertical lines the boundaries separating the ten intervals of judgment for subject A.

Stimuli	(1)	(2)	(3)		(4)					
Categories	1	2	3	4	5	6	7	8	9	10

The minor variation in the response to any given stimulus can be attributed to either variation in the perception of the *stimulus* along the continuum or variation in the location of the *category boundaries* along the continuum. In the first case, we may think of the stimulus as projecting a distribution on the continuum, and the categories as fixed; in the latter, the stimuli are fixed, and the category boundary projects a distribution on the continuum. In general, experimenters working in areas where no correlated physical attribute is available have preferred the former notion, while those working with stimuli that have a known related physical attribute have preferred the latter.

In the sections to follow, we shall first discuss various experimental procedures which might be used to obtain data for the subjective-estimate approach. Following this will be sections on analytical procedures, behavior of the scales constructed by this approach, and problems connected with the use of such scales.

2. EXPERIMENTAL PROCEDURES

A Two-Way Classification

A two-way classification of the different experimental procedures used in obtaining data in the subjective-estimate approach is given below, along with the name of a typical method associated with each category.

	Single Stimulus	Multiple Stimuli
Limited Categories	Usual method of single stimuli	Equal-appearing intervals
Unlimited Categories	Graphic rating scales	Arrangement methods

In this table, *single stimulus* refers to those methods in which the judgment follows the presentation of a single stimulus. No other stimuli are available when the judgment is made. In the *multiple-stimuli* methods, the entire series of stimuli is usually available and is allowed to influence directly the judgment of each member. *Limited-category* methods refer to those methods in which the subject is required to judge (rate or sort) on the basis of a specified number of discrete steps or categories. In the *unlimited-category* methods, either the subject may determine for himself the number of steps, or he may make his ratings directly on a linear continuum.

Single-Stimulus or Rating-Scale Methods

The method of single stimuli has been defined as "any psychophysical method in which the report follows the presentation of one stimulus only" (Volkmann, 1932, p. 809).

In the typical experimental procedure, the several stimuli are presented to the subject one at a time in random order. After the presentation of each stimulus, the subject rates the stimulus with respect to a particular defined attribute. Either he is explicitly instructed to make his ratings on the basis of an equal-interval scale, or the assumption is made that he will do so. Repeated judgments of each stimulus are obtained by either (*a*) presenting the series of stimuli many times to a single subject (to obtain the subjective scale of a single individual) or (*b*) presenting the series of stimuli once each to a sample drawn from a population of individuals (to obtain an average subjective scale of a population).

The two forms of the method differ in the way in which the rating is expressed. In one form the subject is instructed to express his rating in terms of a specified number of categories. The categories may be identified by numerals, letters, words, or phrases, or may be simply a series of *n* boxes or line segments on a sheet of paper. Combinations of boxes or line segments with numerals, letters, etc., are also used.

In the alternative procedure no limitation is placed by the experimenter on the number of categories. The subject may be asked to rate the stimuli in terms of physical units, such as grams, inches, or decibels, or simply to assign any numbers to the stimuli that seem appropriate to him. Alternatively, he may be instructed to indicate on a line segment the appropriate position of the stimulus as in the graphic rating method. We have as raw data a number of ratings for each stimulus. We can either divide the rating continuum arbitrarily into a number of equal categories (e.g., 10-gram steps or, for graphic rating, 1-inch segments), and treat the data as though ratings in a specified number of categories were made, or we can use the actual ratings directly.

Multiple-Stimuli Methods

In general the two alternative procedures parallel those of the single-stimulus methods. In the method of equal-appearing intervals, the subject is presented with the series of stimuli and instructed to sort the stimuli into a specified number of piles so that the intervals between the piles are subjectively equal. The subject is cautioned against assuming any particular distribution of stimuli. (This caution is relevant with any of the methods.) Note the slight difference in task: in the single-stimulus method, the subject is instructed to make his ratings on the basis of a scale whose intervals are subjectively equal; in the method of equal-appearing intervals, he makes his ratings (sortings) *so that* the intervals are subjectively equal. Though from an experimental viewpoint the results might differ, the two tasks from a formal point of view would seem to be just two ways of stating the same thing. A second difference between the single-stimulus and multiple-stimuli methods is that in the latter the subject ordinarily may rearrange the stimuli as much as he wishes until he is satisfied that the intervals between the piles are equal.

In the alternative multiple-stimuli procedure, the stimuli are presented to the subject with instructions to arrange them along a linear continuum so that they appear to be appropriately spaced. Again, he may readjust the positions of the stimuli until he is satisfied with the arrangement. As before, the data may be artificially categorized, or may be used directly.

Replication

We have mentioned before that repeated judgments might be obtained either by (*a*) presenting the stimulus series to a single judge a number of times (replication over trials) or (*b*) presenting the stimulus series once each to a number of judges (replication over subjects). In the former case, the result will be a subjective scale for an individual; in the latter, an average subjective scale for a group. Either alternative presents practical problems.

If replication is to be over trials, the problem of recognition of a particular stimulus by the subject is important. In general, those stimuli that have obvious identifying characteristics other than the particular attribute to be scaled do not lend themselves well to repetition over trials. For example, if the stimuli are a small group of individuals to be rated on executive ability by a superior, repetition over trials would accomplish little. After the first trial or two, the judge would simply remember what rating he gave John Doe on the previous trial and would be likely to make his rating on the present and on all subsequent trials agree.

The danger of the subject basing his present rating directly on the previous rating may even be present with a series of stimuli that vary only on the attribute of interest. It could occur, for example, with a short series of pure tones, all of the same pitch and rated with respect to loudness. If the subject is aware of the fact that the experimenter is presenting the same short series of tones over and over, and if they differ in loudness enough so that they are not easily confused, he is likely to recognize a particular stimulus each time it is presented and to remember his previous rating of that stimulus.

If replication is to be over subjects, the problem of sampling comes to the fore. In general, if an average subjective scale for a given population is desired, the subjects used should be an appropriate sample of that population.   If we are interested in a subjective scale of preferences for various musical compositions of high school freshmen, for example, the sample of subjects on which the scale is to be based should be an appropriate group of high school freshmen, and not, for instance, a group of music instructors or a group of college psychology students.

Specification of Origin and Unit

The problem of specification of an origin and unit, or more generally of any two points on the scale, is ordinarily not pressing when replication is over trials for a single subject.   As we shall see in the discussion of anchoring effects, the subject, even with no instructions to do so, settles down to a relatively constant unit and origin based on the particular stimulus series within a very few trials.

When replication is over subjects, however, specification of the origin and unit becomes extremely important.   If it is left to the subjects to choose their own reference values, then it is more than likely that they will differ from subject to subject.   Indeed with a method of single stimuli, each subject would be likely to change these parameters as he progresses through the stimulus series, so that, for a single subject, a rating of (say) 7 at the beginning of the series would have an entirely different meaning from the same rating at the end.   It would seem that at least with the single-stimulus methods, if replication is to be over subjects, then it is almost essential that procedures for establishing a fixed unit and origin be employed.   This could be accomplished either by specifying the unit and origin directly or by giving the subjects sufficient practice trials for them to become familiar with the nature of the stimulus series.

With the multiple-stimuli approach, somewhat more freedom might be allowed.   Since the subject is instructed to rearrange the stimuli as much as he wishes, there is less danger that different reference points will be used for different stimuli.   Without instructions which determine the unit and origin, however, it would still be possible that ratings of different subjects would not be directly comparable.   In this case, the averaging procedures described in the next section would have the effect of weighting the judgments of those subjects who used a small unit of measurement more than the judgments of those who used a larger unit.   The best procedure, in general, would still seem to be to specify a common unit and origin experimentally.

Order of Presentation of Stimuli

It is probably a good idea to present the stimuli in a random order.   In some experimental procedures, particularly the multiple-stimuli procedures, order of presentation *may* have no important effects on the final sorting or arrangement. On the other hand, it might, and it would seem foolish to take any chances when the effects are so easily eliminated. With replication over subjects, it is a good idea to present the stimuli in different orders for different subjects. Whether all orders are random or whether counterbalancing procedures are used would depend on the particular situation. When the replication is over trials for a single subject, different orders on successive trials would seem to be essential, not only to eliminate any ordinary order effect, but also to prevent the experiment from turning into an investigation of serial rote learning. Again, whether strict randomization on down the line or systematic counterbalancing procedures are used would depend on the specific experiment.

3. ANALYTICAL PROCEDURES

Basic Matrices

The data gathered by any of the experimental procedures outlined in the previous section consist of a number of ratings or sortings assigned to each stimulus. In general, each stimulus will have been rated the same number of times. If the ratings were made in terms of a limited number of categories, or if the data have been artificially categorized, they can be conveniently summarized in a frequency matrix such as that shown in Table 1. In this table, the rows ($j = 1, 2, \cdots, n$) stand for the stimuli

Table 1. CATEGORICAL JUDGMENTS

The element f_{jg} gives the number of times
stimulus j was rated in category g

Categories $g = 1, 2, \cdots, m+1$

		1	2	$\cdots$	g	$\cdots\cdots$	$m+1$
	1	f_{11}	f_{12}	$\cdots$	f_{1g}	$\cdots\cdots$	$f_{1,m+1}$
	2	f_{21}	f_{22}	$\cdots$	f_{2g}	$\cdots\cdots$	$f_{2,m+1}$
Stimuli	j	f_{j1}	f_{j2}		f_{jg}		$f_{j,m+1}$
$j = 1, 2, \cdots, n$							
	n	f_{n1}	f_{n2}	$\cdots$	f_{ng}	$\cdots\cdots$	$f_{n,m+1}$

and the columns ($g = 1, 2, \cdot \cdot \cdot, m+1$) for the categories. The element f_{jg} at the intersection of the jth row and gth column gives the number of times stimulus j was rated in category g.

In the unlimited-category procedures, where the raw data have not been artificially categorized, the ratings can be displayed directly as in Table 2.

Table 2. RAW DATA, UNLIMITED CATEGORIES

The element a_{ji} gives the rating assigned to stimulus j on trial i
(or by subject i)

Trials (or Subjects) $i = 1, 2, \cdot \cdot \cdot, N$

		1	2	$\cdots$	i	$\cdots\cdots$	N
	1	a_{11}	a_{12}	$\cdots$	a_{1i}	$\cdots\cdots$	a_{1N}
	2	a_{21}	a_{22}		a_{2i}		a_{2N}
	.	.	.		.		.
	.	.	.		.		.
	.	.	.		.		.
Stimuli	j	a_{j1}	a_{j2}		a_{ji}		a_{jN}
$j = 1, 2, \cdot\cdot\cdot, n$	.	.	.		.		.
	.	.	.		.		.
	.	.	.		.		.
	.	.	.		.		.
	n	a_{n1}	a_{n2}		a_{ni}		a_{nN}

In this table, the row again gives the stimulus ($j = 1, 2, \cdot \cdot \cdot, n$). The columns ($i = 1, 2, \cdot \cdot \cdot, N$), however, now correspond to the subject or trial, depending on whether replication is over subjects or trials. The element a_{ji} gives the rating of stimulus j by subject i (or on trial i).

In the discussion to follow we shall assume that precautions have been taken to insure that all ratings are made in the same unit and referred to the same origin. Ratings made by different subjects or on different trials by the same subject are thus assumed to be directly comparable. Differences in ratings of a given stimulus are attributed to unsystematic error. We shall first discuss the direct computation of scale values. Following this will be a discussion of procedures available when measures of each stimulus on a related continuum are known.

Direct Computation of Scale Values

The direct calculation of scale values is straightforward. The scale value of any stimulus is given by an average of the ratings assigned to it.

This average may be either a mean or a median, depending on the particular experiment. If the mean is used, the formula for computing scale values from raw data arranged as in Table 1 is simply

$$s_j = \frac{1}{N} \sum_{g=1}^{m+1} c_g f_{jg}$$

where s_j = observed mean scale value of stimulus j
    N = number of ratings of stimulus j
$m+1$ = number of categories
    c_g = value of category g
    f_{jg} = number of times stimulus j is sorted into category g

An idealized set of data is given in Table 3. The stimuli are weights, rated on a five-point scale. The mean scale value for each stimulus is given in the last column of the table.

Table 3. HYPOTHETICAL DATA: FREQUENCIES WITH WHICH EACH WEIGHT WAS RATED IN EACH CATEGORY

Stimuli in grams	Categories					Mean Scale Value
	1	2	3	4	5	
50	40	47	13			1.73
55	16	51	30	3		2.20
60	4	35	48	13		2.70
65	1	19	51	27	2	3.10
70		9	44	40	7	3.45
75		3	30	51	16	3.80
80		1	18	53	28	4.08
85			10	43	47	4.37
90			4	35	61	4.57

If the median is preferred, either numerical interpolation or graphical methods might be used. One graphical procedure would involve the steps indicated in Table 4 and Figure 1. Table 4 is a table of cumulative proportions derived from Table 3. In Table 4, the element in the jth row and gth column is the proportion of times that stimulus j was rated below the upper boundary of category g; i.e., the proportion of times stimulus j was sorted *in or below* category g. For example, the proportion of times the 60-gram weight was sorted below the upper boundary of category 3 is equal to 0.87. Given this table, we can easily construct the stimulus

Table 4. THE PROPORTION OF TIMES EACH STIMULUS WAS RATED
BELOW THE UPPER BOUNDARY OF EACH CATEGORY

| Stimuli | Category Boundaries | | | | Median |
in grams	1	2	3	4	Scale Value
50	0.40	0.87	1.00	1.00	1.20
55	0.16	0.67	0.97	1.00	1.70
60	0.04	0.39	0.87	1.00	2.18
65	0.01	0.20	0.71	0.98	2.60
70	0.00	0.09	0.53	0.93	2.95
75	0.00	0.03	0.33	0.84	3.29
80	0.00	0.01	0.19	0.72	3.60
85	0.00	0.00	0.10	0.53	3.94
90	0.00	0.00	0.04	0.39	(4.20)

functions shown in Figure 1. Here, the upper boundaries of the categories
are laid off in equal units on the abscissa. Category 5, the top category, of
course has no upper boundary. The ordinate indicates the proportion of

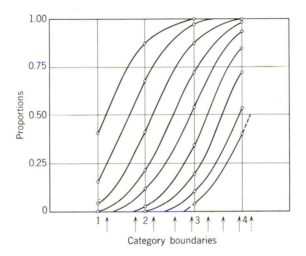

Figure 1. Estimated median scale values.

times stimulus j was rated below the upper boundary of category g. The
plot for each stimulus thus consists of m points, one for each category
boundary. The point on the abscissa where the curve for a given stimulus
crosses the 0.50 level on the ordinate indicates the median scale value of

that stimulus. The median scale values for the stimuli are indicated by arrows in Figure 1.

There are, of course, many procedures that might be used in fitting the curves. Under many circumstances, a simple free-hand fit such as was used in Figure 1 will give adequate results. More elaborate procedures for fitting such curves are discussed in Chapter 7.

For data arranged in the form of Table 2 the formula for the mean is simply

$$s_j = \frac{1}{N} \sum_{i=1}^{N} a_{ji}$$

That is, the scale value of the jth stimulus is simply the average of the ratings in the jth row of Table 2. For the median, counting and interpolation procedures would be used. Though the mean is the more stable of the two estimates, owing to a phenomenon called the *end effect*, the median is often the preferred measure. The end effect results from the artificial curtailing of the distribution of ratings of those stimuli near either extreme of the scale. It is assumed that ordinarily the ratings of a given stimulus will tend to distribute themselves more or less symmetrically about the mean as is shown in Figure 2. Suppose, however, that categories

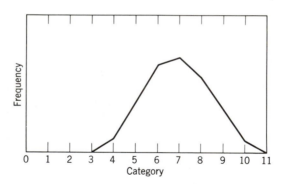

Figure 2. A typical, more or less symmetrical distribution of judgments for a single stimulus.

9 through 11 were not available to the subject, i.e., that he has been instructed to rate on a scale from 1 through 8. Consider now a stimulus whose "true" error distribution is somewhat as in Figure 2. We would expect roughly the same frequency of judgment for categories 1 through 7. Category 8, however, is now unbounded on its upper extreme. It includes not only the interval equivalent to that shown in Figure 2 but also

the intervals corresponding to categories 9 through 11 of that figure. Hence, if people behaved as expected, we would now obtain a frequency distribution such as illustrated in Figure 3. The reverse picture would occur if the "true" position of the stimulus were at the lower extreme of the scale. In either event it is easily seen that the mean will be displaced toward the center of the scale. The median is much less likely to be so influenced, and thus is a better measure to use in this situation.

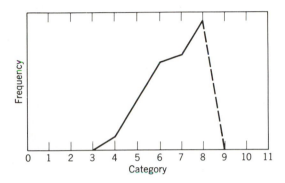

Figure 3.   Distribution of judgments of the same stimulus as shown in Figure 2 but now subject to an end effect.

Many times it is also desirable to obtain a measure of the variability of the ratings or sortings of each stimulus. Ordinarily either the standard deviation or the semi-interquartile range has been taken as the measure of dispersion. As we shall see in the discussion of the construction of master scales, and the discussion of attitude measurement by subjective estimate methods, measures of the dispersion of each stimulus on the subjective continuum become particularly important when we are dealing with complex stimuli which have no known related physical continuum.

The Relationship between the Subjective Continuum and a Related Physical Continuum

Often the stimuli are such that their values on a related physical continuum are known. In such cases, it is highly desirable to determine the functional relationship between the subjective and the physical magnitudes. If such a function has been derived from a relatively small set of stimuli, it can then be used along with physical measurements to determine the subjective scale value of any new stimulus within the range of the original set.

When a related physical continuum is known, the determination of the scale values of a set of stimuli may proceed in either of two ways. In the first (e.g., see Thurstone and Chave, 1929) which was outlined in the preceding section, we estimate *the scale value on the subjective continuum of each stimulus*. We can also obtain a measure of the precision of our estimate. In the alternative procedure (e.g., see Rogers, 1941), we can estimate *the location of a category boundary on the physical continuum*. Again, we can obtain a measure of the precision of our estimate.

The two procedures are indicative of somewhat different lines of thought concerning the characteristics of the subjective continuum.

In the first procedure, variability of judgment is attributed to the *stimulus being perceived at somewhat different locations on the subjective continuum* from trial to trial. For a given experimental situation, the category boundaries are assumed to remain fixed after the first few trials. Each *stimulus* is thus thought of as projecting a frequency distribution on the *subjective continuum*. Hence, we take the mean or median of the distribution as the scale value, and the standard deviation or interquartile range as a measure of variability. The related physical continuum is not used in determining these values except as a means of identifying the stimuli. If the stimuli have other identifying characteristics, it is im-material *for the scaling of this particular set of stimuli*, whether or not a related physical continuum is known. If the physical continuum is known, however, we can plot the subjective scale values against the physical scale values of the stimuli, fit a curve, and use this curve (along with the physical measurements) to estimate the scale value of any new stimulus located within the range of the original set.

In the second procedure, a given stimulus is treated as though it were always at the same place on the subjective continuum. The variability is ascribed to the *shifting of the set of categories up and down the subjective continuum* (i.e., the shifting, expanding, or contracting of the "subjective scale"; see section 4). With this viewpoint, neither the positions of the stimuli nor the distributions of the positions of the category boundaries can be determined directly from the subjective continuum alone. We can, however, determine for each of the boundaries separating adjacent categories the distribution on the related physical continuum, and can thus determine the median position on the *physical continuum* of each *category boundary*. These medians should also be equally spaced on the subjective continuum.

Determining the median position of the category boundary is computationally the same as determining any threshold by the psychophysical method of constant stimuli (see Chapter 7). One simple procedure is to plot a *psychometric function* for each category boundary. Psychometric functions of the four category boundaries for the data given in Table 4 are shown in Figure 4. In this figure, the physical continuum is indicated by the abscissa. The ordinate indicates the proportion of times stimulus j was sorted below category boundary g. Thus, the plot for each category boundary consists of n points, one for each of the n stimuli. Curves were fitted by eye to each of the four sets of n points (again, for more elaborate curve-fitting procedures, see the discussion in Chapter 7). The point on the abscissa where the curve crosses the 0.50 level of the ordinate gives the

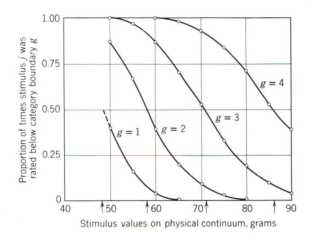

Figure 4. Plot of the psychometric function of the gth category boundary. The location of the arrows gives the median position on the physical continuum of the boundary between category g and $g + 1$.

value in physical units of the median position of the gth category boundary. In the present example, the median positions of the four category boundaries, as indicated by the arrows in Figure 4, are approximately at 48, 58, 71, and 86 grams. Note that for the lowest category boundary it was necessary to extrapolate the curve to obtain an estimate of the median.

Given estimates of the median value on the physical continuum of the category boundaries, and the assumption that the category boundaries are equally spaced on the subjective continuum, we can construct a function relating the two continua, such as is shown in Figure 5. Here, the ordinate corresponds to the subjective continuum, and the abscissa to the physical continuum. Category boundaries are spaced off in equal units on the subjective continuum, and a point is entered for each category boundary above the abscissa value of its median. When a curve has been fitted to the points, the subjective scale values of any stimulus within the range of the curve can be read directly from the graph, assuming that the physical value of the stimulus is known.

The curve of Figure 5 was constructed using the procedure outlined directly above. We can also construct an equivalent curve, however, using the mean or median subjective scale values of the stimuli as given in Tables 3 and 4. It is of some interest to see how the functions derived from the different procedures compare. The plot of median subjective scale values (given in Table 4) against the physical scale values of the stimuli

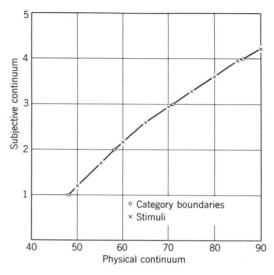

Figure 5.   Function relating the subjective to the physical continuum.

is shown by the small ×'s in Figure 5. We see that these two procedures give virtually identical results. (A similar plot of the mean subjective scale values would also give substantially the same results were it not that the arbitrary origin of the subjective scale in this instance differs from the others by 0.5 subjective unit, and that the means of the extreme stimuli were influenced very slightly by the end effect.) The equivalence of the two procedures is, of course, as it should be, since the two approaches are no more than two alternative ways of accomplishing the same thing. Although they may be affected somewhat differently by chance errors, we would not expect them to give results that differ greatly.

4. THE CONCEPT OF ANCHORING

In an experiment using any of the single-stimulus methods, where the experimenter does not specify two points (or one point, if a natural origin is implied), the subject's first judgment must, of course, either be made at random or be based on past experiences with the attribute which he brings into the experimental situation.   With each succeeding presentation, his judgment is modified so that, in a very short time, his judgments are largely made relative to the particular range of stimuli presented in the experiment.   For example, assume that a subject is required to rate a series of five weights ranging from 75 to 100 grams on a five-point scale. The number assigned to the first weight will depend on the past experiences and expectations that the subject brings into the experimental situation. After he becomes acquainted with the series, however, the judgments will distribute themselves so that the 100-gram weight is rated at the heavy end of the scale and the 75-gram weight at the light end.   What happens if, without the subject's knowledge, we now substitute a new series of stimuli ranging instead from 100 grams to 130 grams?   For the first few trials, ratings at the heavy end of the continuum will predominate.   Very soon, however, the ratings will tend to distribute themselves "appropriately" among the new set of stimuli (see, for example, Wever and Zener, 1928). Although some variation will remain, ratings of the 100-gram weight will now tend to stabilize at the light end of the scale while those of the 130-gram weight will continue to be rated at the heavy end.   In the usual terminology of psychophysics, this change in judgment is ascribed to a "shift in the position of the absolute scale."

In addition to shifting back and forth, the absolute scale is also spoken of as varying in width (expanding or contracting) to enable the ratings to coincide with the particular range of stimuli.   We can keep the midpoint of the scale constant and vary its width simply by adding (or substituting) new stimuli at both extremes.   While we recognize the fact that a good share of the psychophysical literature on absolute scales has made use of this terminology, it would seem that the problems will become clearer if, instead of speaking in terms of an absolute scale which shifts up or down and expands or contracts, we continue to conceive of a subjective continuum which stays put but with an *origin* (reference point) and *unit* that are functions of the particular experimental situation.   This is, of course, merely a change in terminology.   In this framework, we can simply say that the subject adjusts the origin and unit in which the judgments of the subjective magnitude are reported to the particular set of stimuli and to the rating categories allowed.   The "shift in the absolute scale" is simply a change in the origin, while the "expansion or contraction of the absolute scale" is simply a change in unit.

The concept of anchoring, in general, refers to those conditions that determine the origin and unit of the subjective continuum which the subject will use in reporting his judgments of magnitude.   The factors that determine the unit and origin are regarded as "anchors" or "anchoring agents."

Naturally, a change in these factors will cause a change in the judgments of the stimuli.

In making a judgment, the subject explicitly reports only the *magnitude* of the stimulus attribute. Since a report of a magnitude automatically implies a unit and a reference point (origin), anchoring effects are always present in an absolute judgment situation. This is true regardless of the attribute judged. What then, are the factors that determine the unit and reference point of the judgments when they have not been anchored *by the instructions*? Perhaps the most obvious are the range and distribution of the stimuli being judged along with the number (and units) of the categories of judgment allowed. We have seen that the subject tends to adjust his reports to the particular range of stimuli. If the stimuli in a weight-judging experiment range from 70 to 100 grams, the subject will tend to judge the heaviest stimulus in the "heaviest" category and the lightest stimulus in the "lightest" category. We would expect this to occur, within limits, regardless of the range, and, to perhaps a lesser extent, of the "average" weight of the stimuli. That is, if the subject is instructed to rate the weights on a scale from 1 to 6, we would expect him to do so, regardless of whether the range of stimuli in terms of physical weight goes from 70 to 100 grams, 100 to 130 grams, or 70 to 130 grams.

A second kind of anchoring effect arises from the past experiences of the subject. In a sense, he goes into the experimental situation with a pre-conceived notion of what reference point and unit to use. These factors, of course, are of primary importance for the first few judgments made. The degree to which these preconceived tendencies have a lasting influence is probably dependent on the attribute being judged as well as on the subject and the particular set of instructions (McGarvey, 1943, p. 15). This would seem to be particularly true for those attributes that seem to progress from one extreme through a zero or neutral to the opposite extreme when the instructions designate that the zero or neutral point lies somewhere between the extreme categories (see, for example, Cohen, 1937, pp. 94–95). Under these circumstances, the neutral point would be expected to continue to have a substantial anchoring effect throughout the experiment. This is not, of course, to say that the neutral point is com-pletely independent, but only that it is not completely dependent on the range of stimuli. For example, if a subject is instructed to rate a series of colors, on a seven-point scale ranging from extremely unpleasant through neutral to extremely pleasant, the chances are that the ratings will be stimulus-anchored; that all seven categories will be utilized. Whether or not a given color is judged as on the "pleasant" or "unpleasant" side will depend on the particular set of stimuli (see Cohen, 1937). If, however, the subject were judging the pleasantness associated with the drinking of various materials, it is doubtful whether any set of liquids would result in a swallow of concentrated sulfuric acid being judged "extremely pleasant."

If a stimulus is available that is outside of the range of the experimental stimulus series, it may exert an anchoring effect on the units in which the judgment is made, even though the subject is not explicitly instructed to make his ratings as though the stimulus were included in the judged series (Postman and Miller, 1945). The subject will, within limits, tend to increase the size of the unit in relation to the distance between the anchoring stimulus and the judged series. It has also been shown that, if standards are simply held in mind, either due to instructions from the experimenter (Hunt and Volkmann, 1937; Cohen, 1937) to do so or due to the subject's preconceived notion of what the range of the experimental stimuli is going to be (Rogers, 1941, p. 16), then these standards will also tend to determine the units in which the judgments are reported. For example, if a subject is instructed to judge a series of colors on a six-point scale with respect to pleasantness, and is told to assign 6 to the most pleasant color he can think of, he will tend to increase the size of his units even though this will result in few if any judgments of 6 being given.

Most of the experimental work on anchoring has been devoted either to demonstrating that anchoring effects (that is, that the origin and unit in which judgments are expressed are not *absolute*, but are determined by experimental conditions) are common to a great number of judgment situations, or to studying the effects, on the judgments, of the introduction of one or more new "anchoring stimuli." An excellent review of all but the most recent of this experimental literature has been given by McGarvey (1943). In these experiments the typical procedure is as follows: A subject is presented with a series of stimuli and asked to judge them on a scale of a given number of steps with regard to some attribute. Judgments are repeated until stable estimates of the parameters can be made. (The subject has now established an "absolute scale" which is "stimulus-anchored.") One or more new experimental series are run which are identical with the first except for the introduction of an *anchoring stimulus*. The subject is instructed that the anchoring stimulus is to define a particular category (e.g.: "This stimulus will define category 6"). In general, the effects of anchoring may be evaluated either on the subjective continuum (the mean or median judgment given to each stimulus) or on a functionally related "physical" continuum* (the median locations of the category boundaries).

---

* Actually any related continuum can be used whether physical or psychological. It is only necessary that the scale values of the stimuli be known on a related continuum.

The major conclusions arrived at in the experiments on anchoring effects might be summarized as follows:

1. Other things being equal, with no instructions the judgment unit and reference point tend to be determined by the particular range of stimuli. (The "width and position" of the "absolute scale" are largely determined by the range of stimuli; the absolute scale tends to become stimulus-anchored.)

2. If an anchoring stimulus is now introduced which lies beyond the range of the original set of stimuli, and the instruction is given that the anchoring stimulus is to define the extreme category, the judgment unit tends to increase. (The absolute scale extends toward the anchoring stimulus.)

3. The extent to which the judgment unit increases is a function of the distance between the stimulus series and the anchoring stimulus. According to Rogers, "up to a certain point, the anchoring effect is a rectilinear function of the remoteness of the anchoring stimulus" (1941, p. 17). Beyond this point the effects are variable.

5. EQUAL-INTERVAL PROPERTIES

In calculating scale values by any of the variations of the subjective-estimate methods discussed in this chapter, we have proceeded under the assumption that the subject is capable of rating or sorting stimuli on an equal-interval subjective scale. If the assumption is correct, the procedures discussed will give estimates of scale values of stimuli which have equal-interval properties. It should be noted, however, that the methods themselves make no explicit provision for *testing* the basic assumption. They do not have criteria built into them for rejecting the assumptions as do, for example, the methods to be presented in Chapters 8 to 10. From the data gathered in any single experiment we would have no basis for concluding whether or not the subject was judging on the basis of an equal-interval scale. We would always be able to calculate scale values and/or to relate the scale values to the physical stimulus values on the basis of an equal-interval assumption. It should also be noted that the consistency of the judgments is not by itself an adequate criterion on which to evaluate the assumption. It is, of course, true that, if the judgments are completely inconsistent, we have evidence that the subject is not judging on an equal-interval scale. However, even if the judgments are completely consistent, it does not necessarily follow that the subject is judging on an equal-interval scale. For example, the criterion of consistency does not distinguish between judgments in equal units and judgments of straight ordinal position of the stimuli.

The Primary Test of Equality of Intervals for Scales with No Related Physical Continuum

How, then are we to determine the adequacy of the approach? The answer would seem to lie in the invariance characteristics which an equal-interval scale must possess. We have seen that an equal-interval scale is a scale in which the numbers assigned to the stimuli are determined to within a linear transformation of the form $y = ax + b$. In an equal-interval scale, the ratios of differences between scale values are invariant. With respect to subjective-estimate scales, the minimum requirement would seem to be that the ratios of differences in scale values assigned to any three or more stimuli be invariant with respect to the values of the remaining stimuli in the set. For example, consider the four stimuli a, b, c, and d, common to several sets of stimuli shown in Figure 6. If

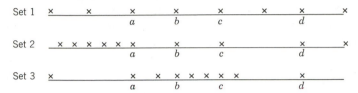

Figure 6.   Experimental demonstration of equality of units.

each of the three sets are scaled by the same method, a necessary condition for concluding that the scales have equal-interval properties in a fundamental sense is for the ratios of the form $(c - a)/(b - a)$ and $(b - a)/(d - c)$ to be invariant, within sampling error, for the three scales.

To put it another way, plots of the scale values of the four stimuli obtained when the four are members of one experimental series against the scale values obtained when members of any other experimental series should be linear.

Note that we do not require the scale values themselves to be invariant, or the ratios of scale values, or even the differences in scale values. Such requirements are necessary only for more restricted scales. Variations in scale values, ratios of scale values, and differences between scale values occur with changes in origin and unit, and thus do not negate the equal-interval property. In the three stimulus sets shown in Figure 6, the four stimuli common to each might have the following scale values:

Stimulus	Set 1	Set 2	Set 3
a	3	2	2.4
b	4	2.5	2.7
c	5	3	3
d	7	4	3.6

Since the plots are linear, we would conclude that the scales have equal-interval properties, and differ from one another only in unit and origin.

If on the other hand the subject were actually reporting only the ordinal position of the stimuli in each set, we would have obtained the following sets of scale values for the four stimuli:

Stimulus	Set 1	Set 2	Set 3
a	3	6	3
b	4	7	4
c	5	8	6
d	7	9	9

In this case, the plots are not linear, and we conclude that the scales do not have equal-interval properties.

A well-known phenomenon which might at first thought be taken as evidence that the difference ratios are dependent on the particular distribution of stimuli is Hollingworth's *law of central tendency*. This law states that "In all estimates of stimuli belonging to a given range or group, we tend to form our judgments around the median value of the series—toward this mean each judgment is shifted by virtue of a mental set corresponding to the particular range in question" (Hollingworth, 1913, p. 45). The point at or near the median which is neither over nor underestimated for this particular set of stimuli is called the indifference point. For example, given a series of weights, the stimuli below the indifference point will be overestimated and those above will be underestimated. In general, the greater the distance of a stimulus from the indifference point, the greater the error in estimation. This tendency has led to the suggestion that the subject has a permanent set to force any series of stimuli into a normal distribution (Guilford, 1936, pp. 255, 258).

If this were true, then scales constructed by these methods could not have equal-interval properties, taking as a criterion the independence of difference ratios of the particular set of stimuli. The phenomenon could also arise, however, if the amount of under- or overestimation were simply a linear function of the distance of the stimulus from the indifference point, as is implied by the linear-regression hypothesis put forth by Johnson (1952). Consider, for example, a series of stimuli which are actually rectangularly distributed on the subjective continuum. If the subject actually forces the distribution into the normal form, the relationship between the true and the obtained scale values is as shown in Figure 7a. If, on the other hand, the amount of under- or overestimation is linearly related to the distance from the indifference point, the relationship between true and obtained would be as shown in Figure 7b. Either case would give rise to the law of central tendency. In the latter event, however, the equal-interval properties of the scale are preserved, since the difference between true and obtained is simply a matter of unit. Little evidence one

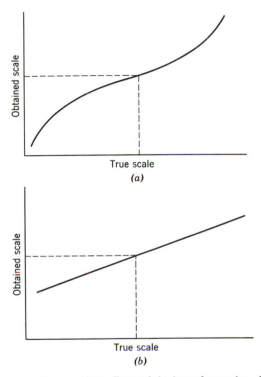

Figure 7. Two possible effects of the law of central tendency.

way or the other is available for those attributes for which no corresponding physical continuum is available.

Attributes for Which Scale Values on a Related Physical Continuum Are Available

When a related physical continuum is available, somewhat different and more efficient experimental procedures can be used to test the basic notion of invariance of difference ratios over changes in the distribution of stimuli. We need no longer base the test solely on the values of a subset of stimuli common to several distributions. The different stimulus distributions do not even need to have a subset of stimuli in common. For, if we construct for each distribution the function relating the subjective scale to the corresponding physical scale, we can then determine whether the scales resulting from use of the different distributions are linearly related.

Stevens and Galanter (1956) review the literature and report several of their own experiments dealing with the invariance characteristics of subjective-estimate scales. Their results indicate that, *for the limited-category methods at least*, the stimulus distribution does affect the scale form. In general, for these methods, stimulus sets which are linearly spaced on the physical continuum give scales which are not linearly related to those obtained using sets which are logarithmically spaced on the physical continuum. They also state that those subjective-estimate methods which require a direct numerical estimate of the magnitude of the stimulus are less susceptible to changes in spacing of the stimuli.

Additional Invariance Properties

We have stated that the minimum requirement of an equal-interval scale is invariance of difference ratios with respect to the remaining stimuli in the experimental series. In the narrow sense of the word, if this invariance characteristic has been experimentally demonstrated, we would then claim that we had established an equal-interval scale. There are further invariance characteristics, however, which, if not strictly necessary, would at least seem highly desirable in terms of usefulness or of practical application of the scale. These characteristics concern the invariance of difference ratios with respect to minor changes in experimental method.

In section 2, the subjective-estimate methods were divided into four types on the basis of the two-way classification: single versus multiple stimulus, and limited versus unlimited category. All four of these procedures require at least formally the same basic assumptions. Furthermore, within each class, variations in procedure are possible, such as variation in instructions to subject, in number of categories, in labeling of the categories. In view of the fact that the same broad rationale underlies all these methods and their variations, it would seem reasonable to expect that they would result in scales that are linearly related to one another. This is, of course, assuming that they all first meet the minimum requirement discussed above. In a practical situation it may well be that certain procedures are more susceptible to biasing effects of the particular distribution of stimuli used. In such cases, only those procedures that do meet the first test would be expected to show a linear relation to one another.

Again, the subjective-estimate methods discussed in this chapter should ideally result in scales that are linearly related to those constructed by the fractionation methods discussed in the following chapter as well as by the equisection methods discussed in Chapter 6. Both fractionation and equisection methods can be considered formally as special examples of the more general subjective-estimate methods, a point that will be discussed more fully in the next chapters.

It would thus seem that the primary requirement for an equal-interval scale as constructed by one of the subjective-estimate methods is the demonstration of invariance of difference ratios with respect to the form of the distribution of stimuli used in construction of the scale. Given satisfaction of this requirement, we can then inquire into the generality of the scale in terms of invariance with respect to number of categories, type of labeling, instructions to subject, class of method, and the like.

One further remark must be made. Strictly speaking, it is the particular scale which can meet the equal-interval requirements and not the method by which the scale is constructed. That is, we do not validate a *method* as such, but instead only the results of its use in a particular situation. The fact that an equal-interval scale of attribute Z can be constructed by a particular method which will meet all experimental tests does not validate the method itself, but only its use in relation to attribute Z. The method may be entirely inappropriate when applied to attribute Y. Hence, with each new attribute scaled, it is desirable to demonstrate experimentally any invariance characteristics which are to be attributed to that scale.

6. RELATED PROBLEMS

The Construction of a Master Scale

The discussion in Section 3 gave alternative procedures for obtaining scale values for a given set of stimuli on a subjective continuum. This is the scaling problem per se, and the procedures given are adequate for many purposes. Among these would be, first, those problems wherein it is desired to compare two or more scales on a given set of stimuli constructed from judgments of two or more individuals or groups of individuals. In this case, we would be using the scales to study the differences or similarities of different judges or groups of judges. "Does the subjective scale of subject or group X differ from that of Y, and, if so, how"? Second, the procedures would be adequate for investigation of those problems wherein we are interested in the scale values of the particular stimuli themselves for a given individual or group. Among these might be mentioned such practical problems as the grading of essay questions, the determination of preferences for different foods or equipment, and the determination of the attractiveness of advertisements, as well as a great number of theoretical problems wherein the subjective values of the set of stimuli must be determined.

Occasionally we wish to go beyond mere scaling of a given set of stimuli on some psychological continuum. We wish to have available a standard yardstick covering either the entire length or a given portion of the continuum. We have seen that, when there is a related physical continuum, this problem is solved by construction of a psychophysical function relating the two continua. Given this function, we can determine the psychological scale value of any new stimulus from knowledge of its value on the physical continuum.

When the psychological continuum has no related physical attribute, the equivalent procedure is to construct a scale of standards or a master scale. Given this scale, the psychological value of a new stimulus can be determined directly by comparing it with the scale of standards with respect to the attribute. These procedures have been used, for example, by Thorndike in construction of his handwriting scale, and by Hillegas with his scale of quality of English compositions (Thorndike, 1910; Hillegas, 1912).

Construction of a master scale presents additional problems which are concerned with the selection of the stimuli to serve as standards: i.e., stimuli which are to constitute the master scale. The usual procedure is to determine, initially, the scale values and dispersions of a very large number of stimuli. The stimulus series should be distributed over the entire range of the attribute, and, if possible, should extend beyond the extremes desired for the final scale. From this large group of stimuli, a relatively small subset is selected to comprise the master scale. Ideally, the standards would be selected so that they are evenly distributed over the range of interest. In addition, however, the dispersions of the stimuli must be considered. A small dispersion for a stimulus indicates a high degree of agreement among the judges with respect to the scale value of that stimulus. The larger the dispersion, the greater the ambiguity, and, obviously, the less desirable that stimulus is for serving as a standard. Hence, the final selection will ordinarily represent some compromise between selecting stimuli that are equally spaced over the continuum and selecting those stimuli that are the least ambiguous.

Attitude Measurement

The criteria used in the selection of items to constitute a master scale as described in the previous section are sufficient only if the application of the scale to the measurement of other objects is based on tasks falling within the judgment sphere. That is, given a master scale and a new stimulus whose scale value is to be determined, the new stimulus is located by comparison with the standards, with respect to the amount of the given attribute associated with each.

An entirely different method of application of a master scale is also used, particularly in attitude measurement (Thurstone and Chave, 1929). Here, instead of comparing a stimulus with the standards with respect to the attribute, a subject *responds* to each standard on the basis of whether or not he agrees with that stimulus. Typically, the master scale is administered to a group of subjects, each of whom is asked to *check those stimuli with which he is in agreement*.   In this particular application, it is assumed that the subject will endorse those opinion statements (items) that most nearly represent his own attitude.   The general idea is that, other things being equal, the probability that a subject will endorse an item decreases as the distance (amount of difference) between his own attitude and that reflected by the item increases.   He will thus be likely to reject items that reflect *more* favorable opinions as well as those that reflect *less* favorable opinions. The median or mean of the scale values of the items endorsed by a given subject is taken as the scale value of that subject on the attitude continuum.   In addition, an index of dispersion of the endorsed items gives an estimate of the range of opinions that he finds acceptable.

This type of application introduces problems concerned with dimensionality.   If the stimulus series is multidimensional, it is quite possible, and reasonable, for a subject to endorse one statement and reject another, even though the two statements have the same scale value *with respect to the attribute along which the stimuli have been scaled*.   The reason for this can perhaps be made most clear with an illustration using color stimuli. Assume that we have a series of color chips, all of the same hue but differing in saturation and brightness, such as is shown by the circles in Figure 8.   Assume further that scale values have been assigned to these stimuli with respect to the *saturation* dimension using, say, the method of equal-appearing intervals.   These stimuli are analogous to the attitude scale, and have saturations (scale values) as follows:

Standard	Saturation
a	1
b	4
c	5
d	6
e	6

Now, let us introduce two new color chips designated X and Y in the figure to represent two subjects.   We shall attempt to determine their saturations in a manner analogous to that used in attitude measurement. Instead of using the same general form of judgment as was used in scaling the standards, we now ask: Which standards are "close" to stimulus X; which are "close" to stimulus Y?   (X endorses only those items that represent his own attitude—which are close to him in the multidimensional space.)   For X, standards *a* and *e* will be checked; for Y, standards *b*, *c*, and *d*, giving mean saturation values of 3.5 and 5 for the two new stimuli. We might note the following points however.   First, X and Y are actually equal in saturation, and both have saturation scale values of 4.   Second,

X checked *a* and *e* as closest to him, leaving out *b*, *c*, and *d*, in spite of the fact that the latter three stimuli all have *saturations* more similar to his than the former.   Third, *Y* checked *d* and not *e*, even though *d* and *e* both have the same saturation scale value.   In like manner *X* checked *e* but not *d*.

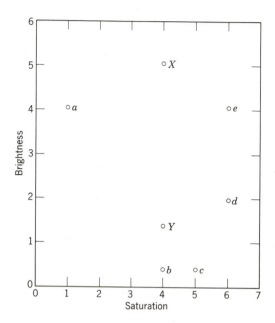

Figure 8.   Illustration of the fallacy involved in applying an attitude scale constructed by the judgment approach to the scaling of subjects by the response approach.

In attitude measurement, the situation is somewhat more complex, of course.   Instead of only one additional dimension, there may be several such dimensions common to the stimuli.   Furthermore, each stimulus will possess some specific variance, which probably accounts for their differences in popularity.   The statements also differ with respect to ambiguity.   Nevertheless, the essential nature of the difficulty outlined above is much the same when an attitude scale constructed by the judgment approach is applied to the scaling of subjects via the response approach.   Perhaps an even greater difficulty is this: It is not always clear that the general notion that the probability of endorsement of an item depends on the amount of difference between the attitude reflected by the item and that held by the subject, is an appropriate one.   Indeed, as we shall see in Chapters 12 and 13, responses to a good many types of items do not behave in this way at all.   Hence, it seems clear that further criteria, *based on data gathered by the response approach*, are necessary for both the selection of items and the scaling of subjects if such difficulties are to be controlled.

Thurstone and Chave (1929) when presenting this general procedure for attitude measurement recognized this state of affairs and provided a rough criterion based on responses.   After having scaled the series of attitude statements by the judgment method of equal-appearing intervals, they administered the series to a group of 300 subjects using the response approach: i.e., with instructions to check those statements with which they were in agreement.   From these responses, the following quantities were obtained:

N_j = number of subjects who endorsed item j
N_k = number of subjects who endorsed item k
N_{jk} = number of subjects who endorsed both items j and k

It is clear that, if items j and k have about the same scale values, those subjects who endorse one should also endorse the other.   If items j and k have widely different scale values, subjects who endorse one would not be expected to endorse the other.

It is also true that some items seem to be intrinsically more popular than others, a factor that can probably be attributed to their specific variances.   Hence N_{jk} alone is not sufficient to indicate similarity.   Two popular statements would be likely to be jointly endorsed by more subjects than two unpopular ones, even though the unpopular statements are closer together in the attitude space.   The index of similarity devised by Thurstone and Chave cancels out the effects of popularity by dividing N_{jk} by the product $N_j N_k$.

Since in actual use we are concerned with the distribution of the indices of similarity between any given statement j and each of the other statements ($k = 1, 2, \cdots, n$), the factor $1/N_j$ is common to all and may be ignored, leaving, for each stimulus j, computation of values for the following ($n - 1$) indices:

$$C_{jk} = \frac{N_{jk}}{N_k} \qquad (k = 1, 2, \cdots, n, \quad j = k),$$

where C_{jk} denotes the index of similarity.

For each statement j, a plot is made of the scale value of k against the value of C_{jk}.   Hypothetical examples of such plots are shown in Figures 9 to 11.   In each plot, the scale value of j is shown by the arrow.

The criterion of relevance for each statement *j* is the appearance of the plot as a whole. A relevant item will tend to have high indices for statements with similar scale values and decreasing indices as the difference between it and the other statements increases. Such items are represented

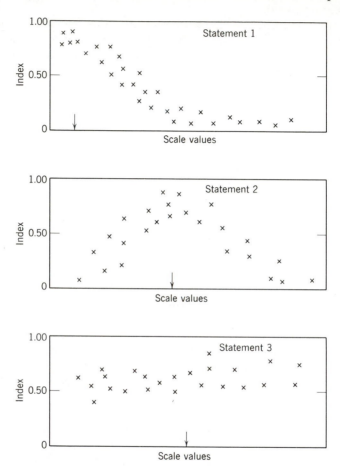

Figures 9, 10, and 11. The criterion of relevance.

by Figures 9 and 10. Figure 11 gives an example of an irrelevant item— one that is clearly unsatisfactory. Subjects who endorse this item are equally likely to endorse any of the other items, regardless of their scale values. In addition, if items of any subgroup have consistently higher indices with each other than would be expected, it is likely that they have in common a second dimension.

Thus, when constructing a master scale by a subjective-estimate method which is to be applied using the response approach, we have the following steps:

(a) Amass a large number of items thought to represent the continuum of interest.

(b) Determine the scale values of the items and their dispersions on the continuum through use of one of the subjective-estimate methods. Ordinarily, this has been the method of equal-appearing intervals using judgments of a large number of judges.

(c) Eliminate those items that are clearly too ambiguous to be useful, using the index of dispersion as the criterion.

(d) Adminster the remaining items to a representative sample of subjects with instructions to endorse those items with which they are in agreement.

(e) Compute and plot, for each statement, the indices of similarity between it and each other statement.

(f) Select items for the master scale on the basis of relevance, ambiguity, and distribution of scale values.

It should be noted that the criterion of relevance discussed here is admittedly rough. Since such criteria are not concerned with the scaling of the stimuli but only with the selection of a subset of stimuli which have already been scaled and which are to be applied through use of a response technique, alternative procedures or improvements will not be discussed at this time. We shall instead postpone discussion of these problems to the section of the monograph devoted to the response approach, where they most appropriately belong. It was felt desirable to include this one early technique to bring out and emphasize the fact that, when a scale is constructed by the judgment approach, and applied by the response approach, judgment procedures alone are not sufficient to insure that the final results will be at all meaningful, even assuming that the judges are capable of validly carrying out the task set for them. The fact that stimuli can be validly scaled with respect to some attribute is no guarantee that the resulting scale can be profitably used through the response approach to measure attitudes of subjects.

▶5

The Fractionation Methods ◀

1. INTRODUCTION

A considerable amount of activity since the early 1930's has been devoted to the construction of subjective scales by the fractionation methods. In the main, the use of these procedures has been limited to the subjective scaling of psychophysical attributes, although at least one experimenter (Reese, 1943) has attempted to extend the range of application to other domains. Examples of attributes that have been scaled by these methods are given in Table 1. In the examples given, the subjective scales are expressed in terms of their relations to the correlated physical attributes.

The logic of the fractionation methods can be stated quite simply: It is assumed that a subject is capable of directly perceiving and reporting the magnitude of a sense-ratio: i.e., the ratio between two subjective magnitudes. This assumption is, of course, subject to tests of internal consistency. Fractionation methods are found in two general forms. In one form, the subject is presented with two stimuli and instructed to report the subjective ratio between them with respect to the designated attribute. For example, two tones of the same pitch might be presented to the subject with instructions to report the ratio of loudness of the first tone to the second. We shall refer to methods that use this approach as *direct-estimate methods*. In the other form, the subject's task is to report when two stimuli stand in a prescribed ratio. One stimulus (the standard) is kept fixed, and the other (the variable) is adjusted. The subject's task is to report when the subjective ratio of the variable to the standard is equal to some prescribed ratio. For example, the subject might be instructed to

94

Table 1. Subjective Attributes Scaled Using
Fractionation Procedures

Subjective Attribute	Correlated Attribute	References
Loudness	Intensity	Richardson and Ross (1930)
		Ham and Parkinson (1932)
		Laird, Taylor, and Wille (1932)
		Geiger and Firestone (1933)
		Churcher (1935)
		Robinson (1953)
		Stevens and Poulton (1956)
Pitch	Frequency	Stevens, Volkmann, and Newman (1937)
		Stevens and Volkmann (1940a)
Numerousness	Physical number	Taves (1941)
Visual rate	Physical rate	Reese (1943)
Pain	Intensity	Hardy, Woelff, and Goodell (1948)
		Swartz (1953)
Weight	Physical weight	Harper and Stevens (1948)
		Guilford and Dingman (1954)
		Baker and Dudek (1955)
Saltiness	Concentration	Lewis (1948)
Sweetness	Concentration	Lewis (1948)
Sourness	Concentration	Lewis (1948)
Bitterness	Concentration	Lewis (1948)
Brightness	Intensity	Hanes (1949a)
Temporal intervals	Physical time	Greg (1951)

adjust the variable stimulus until it is *one half* as loud as the standard. We shall call these methods, the *prescribed-ratio methods*.

In either form, if it is assumed for the moment that the subject is actually capable of carrying out the instructions, it is easy to see that the problems concerned with obtaining a linear scale which is referred to a rational origin, i.e., a ratio scale, are solved. For, if the sense ratios among a series of stimuli are known, the assignment of a set of numbers to the stimuli which bear the same ratios to one another is straightforward. These numbers are then determined to within a linear transformation of the type $y = ax$. We are thus free to assign the value of one stimulus arbitrarily (to specify the unit), and the values of the remaining stimuli are then determined. As an illustration, assume that the following relations are known among stimuli a, b, c, d, and e:

$$\frac{a}{b} = \frac{1}{2}, \qquad \frac{b}{c} = \frac{1}{2}, \qquad \frac{c}{d} = \frac{1}{2}, \qquad \frac{d}{e} = \frac{1}{2}$$

Data of this form might be obtained through use of the prescribed-ratio approach. A number is assigned arbitrarily to one of the stimuli to determine the unit. For the purpose of illustration, let $a = 1$. Any other positive value assigned to this or any of the other stimuli would serve as well. Given $a = 1$, then $b = 2$, $c = 4$, $d = 8$, and $e = 16$ follow immediately. The numbers assigned are the scale values of the stimuli on a ratio scale of the attribute in question.

Since all of the properties necessary to construct a ratio scale are contained in the assumption that the subject can directly report the ratio between two values on a given psychological continuum, it might be well to examine the nature of this task more closely. We might ask how this task differs from that of the subjective-estimate methods discussed in the previous chapter. Upon examination we find that this task is a special case of that set in the subjective-estimate methods. A ratio judgment can be considered to be simply a subjective estimate with (a) the origin anchored at an absolute zero and (b) the value of one of the two nonzero stimuli specified. If the subject is capable of carrying out the instructions given in the subjective-estimate methods when two anchors are given, one of which is an absolute zero ("let zero stand for 'just not any' loudness") and the other specifies the unit ("let 16 stand for stimulus e"), then logically at least, he should be able to carry out the task set in the ratio methods, for the tasks would seem to require identical abilities. The particular experimental and analytical procedures differ somewhat, but, under these anchoring conditions, the requirements of the subject would seem to be the same.

There is one exception to this general statement. And that concerns the special case of halving or doubling. If the subject is not capable of reporting ratios in general or of estimating directly the scale values of a series of stimuli, he may still be capable of making valid half- or double-judgments. These judgments are unique among the ratios in that, if the subject is capable only of recognizing when one sense distance is greater than, equal to, or less than another, he can carry out these judgments. A ratio judgment of half or double is the same as a bisection judgment when one of the standards is zero. Actually, when making half- or double-judgments, a "zero" stimulus is often physically present. If we examine the list of sense magnitudes given in Table 1, we see, for example that "zero" loudness is probably background or ambient noise present between stimulation, "zero" brightness is the ground surrounding the two stimuli, and "zero" weight is the sensation when the hand is lifted without any stimulus.

Except, perhaps, for pitch, "zero" magnitudes of the attribute can all be either considered to be physically present or, at worst, easily envisaged (e.g., numerousness, visual rate). With pitch this may not be the case. "Zero" pitch is not easily envisaged by a good number of people. For this reason it is not too surprising that straight half- or double-judgments of pitch give results somewhat at variance with those obtained by bisection procedures (Stevens and Volkmann, 1940a). In any event, for those situations for which an absolute zero is readily available or conceived, it is apparent that the half- and double-judgments constitute a special case of the bisection judgment often used in the method of equisection discussed in the following chapter. However, since the experimental and analytical procedures are the same, regardless of the particular ratio used, the half- and double-judgment cases will be included here. It should be kept in mind, however, that the requirements of the subject when using half- or double-judgments are considerably less than those for making ratio judgments in general. While a person who is capable of making ratio judgments in general should be able to make half- or double-judgments, the reverse is not necessarily true.

As might be expected, the prescribed-ratio and direct-estimate forms of the fractionation methods differ both in the requirements of the data and in their experimental and analytical procedures. We shall first discuss the more popular, and also more restricting, prescribed-ratio approach.

2. THE PRESCRIBED-RATIO APPROACH

Requirements of the Variable to Be Scaled

In order to use the prescribed-ratio approach, it seems clear that the continuum to be scaled must be such as to meet the following two requirements: First, a stimulus must be available at any given point on the continuum between the extremes of the range to be scaled. We should be able to vary the value of the stimulus continuously, or at worst by small discrete steps, over the entire range of interest. Otherwise, the value of the stimulus which stands in the prescribed ratio might not be available to the subject. Second, the stimuli must have been previously scaled with respect to a related attribute. As we shall see, construction of a subjective scale by the prescribed-ratio methods is accomplished by the construction of the function relating the values on the subjective attribute to those on a related (usually physical) attribute. *If a related attribute is not available,* the function cannot of course be constructed, and scale values can be obtained for only a very limited number of stimuli. For example, if the prescribed ratio is $1/n$, only those stimuli whose scale values equal $k(n^a)$ could be determined (where $a = 1, 2, 3, \cdots$, and k is simply a multiplying constant). Specifically, if the prescribed ratio is $1/2$, stimuli standing only in the following relationships to one another can be scaled: 1, 2, 4, 8,

16, · · ·; if 1/3: 1, 3, 9, 27, 81, · · ·.   In actual practice, of course, these two requirements are likely to go together.

The procedures involved in the construction of a scale (more specifically, of the function relating the subjective attribute to the known, correlated attribute) by the prescribed-ratio method consist of two parts: first, the use of one of the psychophysical methods to obtain the estimate of that stimulus which stands in the prescribed ratio to the standard for each of a number of standard stimuli, and, second, the use of these estimates in constructing the function.   Systematic experimental procedures are necessary for the first step because of the problem of error or variability of judgments with respect to any standard.   The discussion will be facilitated if we first consider the construction of the psychophysical function from the estimates and then go back to a consideration of the various problems associated with the actual collection of the data.

The Construction of the Scale

To make the discussion of procedures specific, we shall follow through the procedures for a hypothetical example where one half is taken as the prescribed ratio.   Any other simple ratio could be used as well to illustrate the procedures, of course.

Let us assume, then, that we have selected a set of seven standard stimuli distributed over the range of interest of the magnitude to be scaled.   For each standard, we have obtained stable estimates of the stimulus which appears one half as great as that standard.   The physical values of the standards and of the stimuli judged half are as follows:

Standard (in Physical Units)	Stimulus Judged Half (in Physical Units)
10	7
20	13
30	19
40	24
50	30
60	35
70	40

The first step is to make the "half-judgment" plot shown in Figure 1 and to fit a smooth curve to the points.   Often it will be found convenient to use log–log paper when making this plot, since it is not unusual for the log–log function to be approximately linear.   Fitting a smooth curve to the observed points enables us to estimate that stimulus which would be judged half of any given stimulus within the experimental range.

The psychophysical function relating the subjective magnitude to the known physical magnitude may now be constructed as follows:

1. We first specify arbitrarily the unit of the subjective scale. Any positive number may be assigned to any one stimulus in order to specify the unit. We shall assign the value of unity to that stimulus which was judged half of the smallest standard; i.e., the stimulus having the value of 7 on the physical scale is arbitrarily designated as unity on the psychological

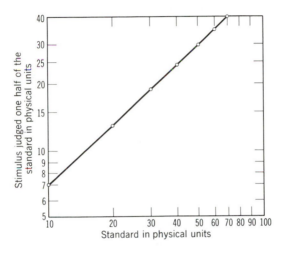

Figure 1. The "half-judgment" plot. Hypothetical data.

scale. Hence a point is entered at (7, 1) on the psychophysical function shown in Figure 2. Let us call this stimulus *A*.

2. On the half-judgment function we see that the stimulus of which stimulus *A* was judged half has a physical value of 10. Call this stimulus *B*. Stimulus *B* is thus subjectively twice as great as stimulus *A*. Since stimulus *A* has a subjective value of 1, the subjective value of stimulus *B* must be 2, and therefore we enter a point at (10, 2) in Figure 2. We now return to Figure 1 and find the physical value of the stimulus of which stimulus *B* was judged half. This stimulus is designated *C* and has a physical value of 14.9. Stimulus *C* is thus subjectively twice stimulus *B*, or four times as great as stimulus *A* and must, therefore, have a subjective scale value of 4. A point is thus plotted at (14.9, 4) on Figure 2. We return again to Figure 1 to find the value of stimulus *D*—the stimulus twice as great as *C*. Its physical value is 23.2, and so a point is entered at (23.2, 8) on Figure 2. This process is continued until the end of the

half-judgment function is reached. In the present example, additional points on Figure 2 will be entered at (38, 16) and (66, 32).

3. The points are connected by a smooth curve. (Since a smooth curve was used in Figure 1, the points in Figure 2 will always lie along a smooth curve.) This curve is the *psychophysical magnitude function*. From it the subjective scale value of any stimulus lying within the experimental range can be estimated, assuming only that the physical magnitude of the stimulus

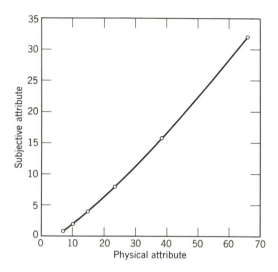

Figure 2. The psychophysical magnitude function constructed from the fitted half-judgment function given in Figure 1. The curve gives the subjective magnitude of a stimulus (ordinate) as a function of its physical magnitude (abscissa).

is known. Extrapolation beyond the ends of the function is also possible, of course, though we would have less confidence in the resulting estimates.

It should be noted that it is possible to use judgments of the reciprocal of the prescribed ratio in constructing the function shown in Figure 1 simply by considering the coordinates to be reversed. In this case, the curve fitted in Figure 1 could be based on both half- and double-judgments. The double judgments would be entered by plotting the value of the standard on the ordinate and the double-judgment on the abscissa. Both sets of points—the half and double estimates—should fall along the same curve. If they do not, the validity of the procedure is in doubt. It would seem desirable to use judgments of both the prescribed ratio and its reciprocal whenever constructing a scale by these procedures as a pre-liminary test of the basic assumptions.

Under some circumstances, it may be feasible or even possibly simpler to determine the psychophysical function from the half-judgments through use of algebraic instead of graphical procedures.   If a simple mathematical function can be fitted to the points in the half-judgment function, then algebraic procedures for determining the equation relating the two magnitudes might be considered.   Harper and Stevens (1948) have given such a procedure for the case where the log–log plot is linear.   Since this procedure would seem to be restricted to the case where the slope is equal to unity (Armington, 1953), it will not be discussed further in this monograph.   Readers interested in their approach are referred to the original paper.   A more general solution for the linear case has been given by Armington (1953).

It would also be possible, of course, to construct the psychophysical magnitude function directly, using a series of successive experiments. That is, we could select as the first standard the largest stimulus and obtain the stimulus that is subjectively half of it.   This new stimulus could then serve as the standard in the next experiment, etc.   An alternative procedure which would allow the direct construction of the psychophysical magnitude function would be to select a single standard and then obtain values for a number of different prescribed ratios.   Geiger and Firestone (1933), for example, had the subjects adjust a variable to the following ratios with the standard: 1/100, 1/10, 1/4, 1/2, 1, 2, 4, 10, and 100.   Given these estimates, a psychophysical magnitude function can be constructed directly.

Experimental Procedures

The preceding section was concerned with the analytical procedures used to construct the psychophysical magnitude function from estimates of the physical values of stimuli which are subjectively $1/a$th of the known standards.   The present section will be concerned with experimental procedures for obtaining these estimates.

Because of the variability of responses to any given standard, either within a single individual or between individuals, it is desirable to use one of the psychophysical methods to obtain a representative estimate of the quantity desired.   Perhaps the most popular method is the method of average error.   In this procedure, the subject adjusts the variable stimulus until it is subjectively $1/a$th of the standard, where $1/a$ is the prescribed ratio.   The following set of instructions, taken from Stevens, Volkmann, and Newman (1937), will serve as an illustration of the task:

> You will be presented with two tones which differ in pitch.   The pitch of one tone may be varied by turning a crank; you are to adjust this tone until its pitch is just *half* of the pitch of the fixed tone.   During the course of the adjustment, take care to produce values of the variable pitch which are plainly

higher than the desired half-value and other values which are plainly lower. If the fixed and the variable tones differ widely in loudness, report this fact.

A principal variant of the method which offers some advantages differs in that the experimenter adjusts the variable at the subject's direction until the subject is satisfied that the specified ratio has been obtained. A second variant consists of displaying a number of stimuli before the subject with instructions to select the one that appears to be half as great as the standard (see, for example, Harper and Stevens, 1948).

In either case, repeated judgments are obtained for each standard. The number of repetitions will depend on the nature of the attribute to be scaled and the level of precision desired by the experimenter. For each observation, the physical value of the stimulus judged $1/a$th of the standard is recorded. An average of the observations for each standard (such as the arithmetic mean, the geometric mean, or the median) is taken as the estimate of the stimulus which is subjectively $1/a$th of that standard.

Other procedures, based on the method of constant stimuli or perhaps on the method of limits might also be used. In the constant-stimuli methods, the task set for the subject would be to indicate whether the variable is greater or less than $1/a$th of the standard (or, in the three-category case, greater than, equal to, or less than). In the method of limits he would indicate when the variable is just noticeably greater than $1/a$th of the standard, and also when it is just noticeably less than $1/a$th of the standard. For both procedures the point analogous to the point of subjective equality is the value taken as the estimate. The reader is referred to Chapter 7 for further consideration of these methods. For more detailed discussion, see Guilford (1936, 1954) or Woodworth (1938).

A number of points will arise in designing and carrying out the experiment. Some of the most general are listed below.

SELECTION OF STANDARDS. The number of standards needed will vary with the particular situation and can be decided only by the experimenter. In general, they should be distributed throughout the range of interest and in sufficient number to enable accurate fitting of a smooth curve to the half-judgment function or to enable detection of any discontinuities should they occur.

REPLICATION. Repeated judgments might be obtained over judges, over trials for a single judge, or both, depending on the nature of the continuum and whether a scale for an individual or for a group of individuals is desired. In the latter case, if the scale is to be generalized beyond the particular set of subjects used, care must be taken to obtain a sample of subjects which is appropriate for the problem at hand. Among the factors to be considered is the question of whether experienced (trained) or naive subjects should be used, or whether subjects should be trained before obtaining the experimental data. Training a subject might decrease the variability of his responses: i.e., increase his reliability. It is also possible, however, that the training process will change the form of the psychophysical magnitude function. Further, different training procedures may result in different changes in the function. Here again, the answer would seem to lie in the use to which the scale is to be put. If, for example, the scale is to be used in conjunction with naive subjects, then the use of naive subjects in constructing the scale would seem most reasonable.

PREVENTION OF CONSTANT ERRORS OR BIAS DUE TO EXTRANEOUS FACTORS. Biasing effects can come from many sources. The well-known time and space errors resulting from a fixed temporal or spatial order of variable and standard are but two examples (see Woodworth, 1938). These errors can be controlled by appropriate counterbalancing procedures. A second type of bias arises from the characteristics of the particular set of variable stimuli employed. Consider first the case where the variable stimuli are presented to the subject in serial order. If the initial value of the variable is always greater than $1/a$th of the standard, the final results will more than likely differ from those obtained if the initial value was always less than $1/a$th. To minimize this effect, counterbalancing procedures again are used. Instead of the variable initially being always larger or always smaller than $1/a$th of the standard, care is taken to balance out this effect. One procedure is to equate the number of times it is larger and smaller, and then randomize the order. A further precaution is to vary the amount by which it is larger or smaller from trial to trial to keep the subject from tending to base his judgment on, say, the number of turns of the crank (see, for example, Stevens and Poulton, 1956).

Somewhat more difficult to control is the effect due to the particular distribution of variable stimuli used. Numerous studies have shown that, when a subject is presented with a range of stimuli, he tends to select one near the middle of the series (see, for example, Helson, 1947). Where the judgment required of the subject is difficult, as it is in the fractionation methods, the effect of context can be overpowering. Garner (1954a), for example, presents data which indicate that, under some circumstances at least, the stimulus which is judged one half as great as a given standard can be considered to be entirely dependent on the set of variable stimuli presented. He used the psychophysical method of constant stimuli in demonstrating the potency of this *context effect*. If, instead, the method of average error is used (where the value of the variable stimulus can be adjusted continuously by the subject), the context effect depends upon slightly different factors. Here, it is the function relating the rate of change of the magnitude of the subjective attribute to the rate of change of position of the control adjusted by the subject to produce this subjective change that can have a biasing effect. If, for different parts of the range, widely different changes in subjective magnitude result from a given amount of rotation of the crank, a bias can easily occur. According to Stevens and Poulton (1956), the ideal situation would be one where the crank is calibrated in terms of the unknown subjective attribute itself. In order to eliminate completely the bias due to context, one would thus carry out successive experiments. The information obtained in any given experiment could then be used in selecting variable stimuli or calibrating the controls for the following experiment.

When repetition is over trials for a single individual, the further problem arises of whether to obtain all of the judgments for a single standard before going on to the next or to obtain a single judgment for each standard and then repeat the series. The latter procedure would seem to offer the most promise for experimentally independent judgments, though it might be more difficult for the subject.

Another factor to be considered is the order of presentation of the standards. If possible, the order should be varied from trial to trial (or subject to subject) either systematically or haphazardly in order to eliminate any bias due to practice, learning, or any other factor which might result in an order effect. As usual, the particular experimental situation will determine the procedures used.

3. DIRECT ESTIMATION OF SENSE RATIOS

The chief advantages of this procedure over the prescribed-ratio methods lie in the requirements of the data. Stimuli do not need to be continuously variable, nor, for that matter, even ordered with respect to the magnitude to be scaled. Scale values on a related continuum are not necessary either, since the stimuli may be scaled directly without the necessity of constructing a psychophysical magnitude function such as given in Figure 2.

In the usual form of the method (see, for example, Ham and Parkinson, 1932; Richardson and Ross, 1930; Hardy, Woelff, and Goddell, 1948; Stevens, 1956c), it is essentially a special case of the subjective-estimate approach (with anchors, one of which is an absolute zero) discussed in the previous chapter. Assume that we have n stimuli which are to be scaled with respect to some attribute. One of the stimuli is selected as the standard (the anchoring stimulus). Ordinarily, this is either the largest or smallest stimulus of the group, though Stevens recommends a middle stimulus (1956c). Each of the remaining stimuli is presented with the standard, and an estimate of the ratio is obtained. If the standard is the smallest stimulus, the subject might be asked how many times the variable is larger than the standard; if the standard is the largest, he might be asked to report what fraction or per cent of the standard is the variable. As usual, repeated judgments are necessary in order to obtain a stable estimate of the ratio. Since the experimental problems concerning subjects, order of presentation, of stimuli, etc., are much the same as described earlier, they will not be repeated here.

The ratio of each stimulus to the standard is obtained from the judgments. When the unit of measurement is specified by assigning a number to one of the stimuli arbitrarily, the scale values of the remaining stimuli can be calculated directly from the ratios. If physical values of the stimuli are also known, construction of a psychophysical magnitude function such as is shown in Figure 2 will allow the estimation of scale values of other stimuli within the experimental range.

A considerably more complete procedure has been proposed by Comrey (1950b). In the earlier procedures, the presentation of stimuli is as in the psychophysical method of constant stimuli. With n stimuli, $n-1$ ratios, all referred to a single standard were obtained. In Comrey's procedure, the presentation of stimuli is as in the method of paired comparisons, where, instead of comparisons of each stimulus with a standard, all the stimuli serve in turn as standards, giving $n(n-1)/2$ independent observed ratios. Each stimulus is thus compared with each other stimulus. From these $n(n-1)/2$ ratios, the scale values of the n stimuli are computed. We turn now to a more detailed discussion of his procedure.

As usual, let there be n stimuli whose scale values on a ratio scale are to be determined. Stimuli are presented to the subject in pairs. (For a more detailed discussion of experimental problems involved in procedures requiring presentation of all possible pairs of stimuli, see Chapter 9.) The subject is instructed to "divide 100 points between them in accordance with the absolute ratio of the greater to the lesser" (Comrey, 1950b, p. 317). This method of reporting comparative judgments was earlier advocated by Metfessel (1947) and has come to be called the *constant-sum method*. For example, the assignment of 80 of the 100 points to one member and the remaining 20 to the other is to indicate that the former is four times as large as the latter. A split of 60–40 would in like manner indicate a ratio of three to two; 50–50, that the stimuli are of the same magnitude.

While Comrey speaks only in terms of obtaining repeated judgments of each pair of stimuli through use of a number of subjects (i.e., replication over subjects), it is apparent that the method might also be appropriate for replication over trials with a single subject. Let us assume that N judgments (from either N subjects or N trials with a single subject) have been obtained for each of the $n(n-1)/2$ pairs of stimuli.

If we wish, we can consider these judgments to be subjective estimates of the scale values of the pair of stimuli where the unit and origin are anchored as follows: Zero stands for the absolute origin, and 100 for the sum of the scale values of the two stimuli. The unit of measurement is thus peculiar to each pair of stimuli. When considered in this way, it is seen that, for each pair of stimuli, the arithmetic mean of the number of points assigned to each member of the pair by the different judges will give a reasonable estimate. We thus compute the average number of points assigned to each member of each stimulus pair as follows:

$$(1) \qquad v_{jk} = \frac{1}{N} \sum_{i=1}^{N} {}_i p_{jk} \qquad (j, k = 1, 2, \cdots, n, \quad j \neq k)$$

where v_{jk} = average number of points out of 100 assigned to stimulus k when compared to stimulus j

$\quad {}_i p_{jk}$ = number of points out of 100 assigned by subject i to stimulus k when compared with stimulus j

$\quad N$ = number of subjects

$\quad n$ = number of stimuli

If we now average v_{jk} over j ($j = 1, 2, \cdots, n$) for each value of k, the resulting averages will give an estimate of the rank order of the stimuli. The stimulus having the largest average is the largest stimulus, etc.

The values of v_{jk} can now be arranged in the $n \times n$ matrix $\mathbf{V}$ given in Table 2. In this table, rows and columns are ordered with respect to the

Table 2. Matrix $\mathbf{V}$ with Elements v_{jk} Denoting the Average Number of Points Assigned to Stimulus k When Compared with Stimulus j

	1	2	$\cdots\cdots$	k	$\cdots$	n
1	v_{11}	v_{12}	$\cdots\cdots$	v_{1k}	$\cdots$	v_{1n}
2	v_{21}	v_{22}	$\cdots\cdots$	v_{2k}	$\cdots$	v_{2n}
.	.	.		.		
.	.	.		.		
.	.	.		.		
j	v_{j1}	v_{j2}	$\cdots\cdots$	v_{jk}	$\cdots$	v_{jn}
.	.	.		.		.
.	.	.		.		.
.	.	.		.		.
.	.	.		.		.
.	.	.		.		.
n	v_{n1}	v_{n2}	$\cdots\cdots$	v_{nk}	$\cdots$	v_{nn}

stimuli. The first subscript of an element is the row indicator, and the second the column indicator. Thus, v_{jk}, the element in the jth row and kth column, is the average number of points assigned to stimulus k when compared with stimulus j.

The next step is to construct matrix **W** from the elements in matrix **V**. The entries in matrix **W** are the ratios of the stimulus values indicated by the column to those indicated by the row. For example, the entry in the jth row and kth column, w_{jk}, is the ratio of the value of the stimulus k to that of stimulus j. In general, if s_j denotes the scale value of stimulus j, then

$$(2) \qquad\qquad w_{jk} = \frac{v_{jk}}{v_{kj}}$$

is an estimate of the ratio s_k/s_j.

It is immediately apparent that the entry in the jth row and kth column is the reciprocal of that in the kth row and jth column. That is,

$$(3) \qquad\qquad w_{jk} = \frac{1}{w_{kj}}$$

We thus have $n(n-1)/2$ independent observed ratios from which to estimate the n scale values. Since these n scale values can be estimated from only $n-1$ ratios (the value of one stimulus is assigned arbitrarily), it is obvious that the data are considerably overdetermined. Any of a great number of sets of $n-1$ ratios could be used. Each would of course make use of only a fraction of the data available. In order to make better use of the data, it is clear that some sort of averaging procedure is indicated. The following procedure was used by Comrey (1950b) and has since been used by Guilford (1954), Guilford and Dingman (1954), and Baker and Dudek (1955).

Comrey observed that, in addition to w_{jk}, the direct estimate of the ratio s_k/s_j, we can also compute a number of additional estimates of this same ratio from other observations. Consider, for example, the ratio s_1/s_2. In addition to the directly observed estimate w_{21}, we have the following $n-2$ estimates of the same quantity: w_{31}/w_{32}, w_{41}/w_{42}, w_{51}/w_{52}, etc. In general, the ratios w_{j1}/w_{j2} ($j = 1, 2, \cdots, n$) are all estimates of the ratio s_1/s_2.

We can thus obtain $n-1$ estimates of the ratio s_1/s_2. In like manner $n-1$ estimates can be obtained for the ratios of each of the other adjacent pairs of stimuli: s_2/s_3, s_3/s_4, $\cdots$, s_j/s_{j+1}, $\cdots$, s_{n-1}/s_n. The arithmetic procedure consists of obtaining the ratios of corresponding elements of adjacent columns of matrix **W**. Comrey then takes the arithmetic average of the ratios for each pair of adjacent stimuli as the ratios to be used in estimating the scale values. When the scale value of one stimulus is specified arbitrarily (say, $s_1 = 1$) the solution for the remaining stimuli is straightforward. Let s'_j denote the final estimate of s_j. We then have $s'_1 = 1$. Since $\bar{w}_{12} = s_2/s_1$, $s'_2 = \bar{w}_{12}$. In like manner, $s'_3 = s'_2\bar{w}_{23}$, $s'_4 = s'_3\bar{w}_{34}, \cdot \cdot \cdot, s'_n = s'_{n-1}\bar{w}_{n-1,n}$.

A Modified Analytical Procedure

The procedure given above is somewhat analogous to one solution for scale values in the law of comparative judgment (discussed in Chapter 9). However, the use of the arithmetic mean of the derived ratios *in the present case* leads to inconsistencies. In the procedure given above, we saw that we could obtain $n-1$ estimates of the ratio s_1/s_2. But, in a similar manner, we could also obtain $n-1$ estimates of the reciprocal ratio s_2/s_1. If we were to do so, we would find that the arithmetic mean of the former is *not* equal in general to the reciprocal of the arithmetic mean of the latter; i.e., if $\bar{w}_{21}$ denotes the average of the estimates of the ratio s_1/s_2, and $\bar{w}_{12}$ denotes the average of the estimates of the reciprocal ratio s_2/s_1, then in general

$$(4) \qquad \bar{w}_{21} \neq \frac{1}{\bar{w}_{12}}$$

This is true in general for any pair of stimuli. We thus conclude that the arithmetic mean is not an especially good average to use here. If we had taken the *geometric* mean instead, this inconsistency would not have appeared. The reciprocal of the geometric mean of a series of ratios is equal to the geometric mean of the reciprocals of the ratios. The geometric mean would thus seem to be an appropriate average to use.

The notion of using geometric means suggests the use of logarithms. When the basic equations are written in terms of logarithms, however, an alternative solution based on the least-squares principle gives a computationally simple and straightforward procedure. Let us consider first the solution with error-free data. We can take as our starting point either matrix **V** with elements v_{jk} as given by equation 1 (the most appropriate place when data are obtained by the constant-sum method) or matrix **W** with elements w_{jk} as given in equation 2 (an appropriate place when data are obtained by direct estimates of ratios). From equation 2 it is apparent that

$$(5) \qquad \log w_{jk} = \log v_{jk} - \log v_{kj} \qquad (j, k = 1, 2, \cdot \cdot \cdot, n)$$

From equation 2 it is also apparent that

$$(6) \qquad \log w_{jk} = \log s_k - \log s_j \qquad (j, k = 1, 2, \cdot \cdot \cdot, n)$$

Hence, if we specify arbitrarily the scale value of one stimulus as before (say, $\log s_1 = 0$), we can then solve for the scale values of the remaining stimuli using equation 6.

Scaling with Fallible Data

When we are given fallible data, we have log w'_{jk} as estimates of the true log w_{jk}. Equation 6 no longer holds exactly because of errors in the estimates. Our task is to use the observed values (log w'_{jk}) to solve for a set of estimates (log s'_j) of the logs of the true scale values (log s_j).

Let the difference between pairs of derived estimates (log s'_k — log s'_j) be denoted by log w''_{jk}. If it were not for error, the *derived* values of log w''_{jk} would equal the *observed* values of log w'_{jk} for all values of j and k. With fallible data, however, they will be somewhat different. The solution for the logarithms of the scale values which we want is the one for which the sums of squares of these differences is a minimum; i.e., we wish to determine those values for the set of log s_j for which

$$(7) \qquad Q = \sum_{j=1}^{n} \sum_{k=1}^{n} (\log w''_{jk} - \log w'_{jk})^2$$

is a minimum.

The development will be simplified if we adopt the following notation:

$$u_{jk} = \log w_{jk} \qquad \text{(true value)}$$
$$u'_{jk} = \log w'_{jk} \qquad \text{(observed value)}$$
$$y_j = \log s_j \qquad \text{(true value)}$$
$$y'_j = \log s'_j \qquad \text{(estimated value)}$$

Equation 7 may now be rewritten

$$(8) \qquad Q = \sum_{j=1}^{n} \sum_{k=1}^{n} (u'_{jk} - y'_k + y'_j)^2$$

In order to solve for the values of y'_k (and y'_j, since j and k are alternative subscripts for the same set of stimuli) which will minimize Q, we take the partial derivative of Q with respect to each y'. Now, the elements summed over in equation 8 can be arrayed in an $n \times n$ square matrix with elements $(u'_{jk} - y'_k + y'_j)^2$ such as is shown in Table 3. Note that a particular value of y' (say y'_k) appears only in elements in the kth row and kth column of this matrix. Since the elements in any given row are identical with the elements in the corresponding column except for sign, we need be concerned only with the column. Differentiating with respect to y'_k, we get

$$(9) \qquad \frac{1}{2} \frac{\partial Q}{\partial y'_k} = -2 \sum_{j=1}^{n} (u'_{jk} - y'_k + y'_j) \qquad (k = 1, 2, \cdots, n)$$

Table 3. MATRIX E^2 WITH ELEMENTS $(u'_{jk} - y'_k + y'_j)^2$

	1	2	$\cdots\cdots$	k	$\cdots$	n
1	$(u'_{11} - y'_1 + y'_1)^2$	$(u'_{12} - y'_2 + y'_1)^2$	$\cdots\cdots$	$(u'_{1k} - y'_k + y'_1)^2$	$\cdots$	$(u'_{1n} - y'_n + y'_1)^2$
2	$(u'_{21} - y'_1 + y'_2)^2$	$(u'_{22} - y'_2 + y'_2)^2$	$\cdots\cdots$	$(u'_{2k} - y'_k + y'_2)^2$	$\cdots$	$(u'_{2n} - y'_n + y'_2)^2$
3	$(u'_{31} - y'_1 + y'_3)^2$	$(u'_{32} - y'_2 + y'_3)^2$	$\cdots\cdots$	$(u'_{3k} - y'_k + y'_3)^2$	$\cdots$	$(u'_{3n} - y'_n + y'_3)^2$
.						
j	$(u'_{j1} - y'_1 + y'_j)^2$	$(u'_{j2} - y'_2 + y'_j)^2$	$\cdots\cdots$	$(u'_{jk} - y'_k + y'_j)^2$	$\cdots$	$(u'_{jn} - y'_n + y'_j)^2$
.						
n	$(u'_{n1} - y'_1 + y'_n)^2$	$(u'_{n2} - y'_2 + y'_n)^2$	$\cdots\cdots$	$(u'_{nk} - y'_k + y'_n)^2$	$\cdots$	$(u'_{nn} - y'_n + y'_n)^2$

Setting the partial derivative equal to zero and dividing by two gives

$$(10) \qquad \sum_{j=1}^{n} y'_k = \sum_{j=1}^{n} u'_{jk} + \sum_{j=1}^{n} y'_j \qquad (k = 1, 2, \cdots, n)$$

Dividing through by n, we get

$$(11) \qquad y'_k = \frac{1}{n} \sum_{j=1}^{n} u'_{jk} + \frac{1}{n} \sum_{j=1}^{n} y'_j \qquad (k = 1, 2, \cdots, n)$$

In order to give a solution entirely in terms of the observed u'_{jk}, it is necessary to specify a unit of measurement for the scale values. There will be no loss in generality if we assign the unit so that the geometric mean of the estimated scale values s'_j is equal to unity: i.e., so that

$$(12) \qquad \frac{1}{n} \sum_{j=1}^{n} y'_j = 0$$

Equation 11 then becomes

$$(13) \qquad y'_k = \frac{1}{n} \sum_{j=1}^{n} u'_{jk} \qquad (k = 1, 2, \cdots, n)$$

Equation 13, then, is a least-squares solution for estimating the logarithms of the scale values ($y'_k = \log s'_k$) from the logarithms of the observed ratios

$(u'_{jk} = \log w'_{jk})$. The estimated scale values themselves are given, of course, by the antilogarithms of y'_k.

A numerical example using a portion of Comrey's (1950*b*) data is given in Tables 4 through 6. Comrey had 47 subjects judge ratios of line length

Table 4. MATRIX V

The element in the *j*th row and *k*th column gives the average number of points assigned to stimulus *k* when compared with stimulus *j*

Stimulus	1	3	5	7	9
1	—	44.91	36.09	28.74	11.00
3	55.09	—	41.04	34.51	12.79
5	63.91	58.96	—	41.34	16.00
7	71.26	65.49	58.66	—	21.06
9	89.00	87.21	84.00	78.94	—

Data from Comrey (1950*b*).

using the constant-sum method. The observed average values of $v_{j'k}$ for 5 of his stimuli are given in Table 4. The logarithms of these observed values are given in Table 5. Table 6 contains the observed values of $u_{j'k} = \log v_{k'j} - \log v_{j'k}$ along with the solutions for the y'_k, the estimates of

Table 5. MATRIX LOG V

The element in the *j*th row and *k*th column is the logarithm of the corresponding element in Table 2

Stimulus	1	3	5	7	9
1	—	1.65234	1.55739	1.45849	1.04139
3	1.74107	—	1.61321	1.53794	1.10687
5	1.80557	1.77056	—	1.61637	1.20412
7	1.85285	1.81617	1.76834	—	1.32346
9	1.94939	1.94057	1.92428	1.89730	—

the scale values s'_k, and the physical length of the lines in inches. Though not actually observed in this case, zeros have been entered in the diagonal cells of matrix **U** since these cells all represent the logarithms of the ratio of the scale value of the stimulus to itself. The psychophysical magnitude function relating subjective line length and physical line length for these data is given in Figure 3. The two attributes are very nearly linearly related over this range.

Table 6. Matrix U

The solution for the scale values y'_k and the physical scale
values of the stimuli in inches

Stimuli	1	3	5	7	9	Check sum
1	0	−0.08873	−0.24818	−0.39436	−0.90800	−1.63927
3	0.08873	0	−0.15735	−0.27823	−0.83370	−1.18055
5	0.24818	0.15735	0	−0.15197	−0.72016	−0.46660
7	0.39436	0.27823	0.15197	0	−0.57384	0.25072
9	0.90800	0.83370	0.72016	0.57384	0	3.03570
$\sum_j u'_{jk}$	1.63927	1.18055	0.46660	−0.25072	−3.03570	0.00000
$y'_k = \dfrac{1}{n} \sum_j u'_{jk}$	0.327854	0.236110	0.093320	−0.050144	−0.607140	0.00000
$s'_k = $ antilog y'_k	2.127	1.722	1.240	0.891	0.247	
Physical length in inches	9.95	7.97	5.72	4.23	1.25	

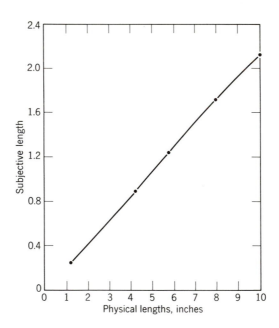

Figure 3. The psychophysical magnitude function for the data of Table 6.

4. VALIDATION PROCEDURES

With the exception of Comrey's method, which will be discussed separately, the fractionation procedures in this chapter have no built-in criteria for rejecting the basic assumptions. As was true of the subjective-estimate methods, we have no basis for concluding that the scale actually possesses the properties attributed to it from the data gathered in the scaling process itself. Scale values of the stimuli could always be computed, assuming only that the subject could make valid ordinal judgments, and that he behaved more or less consistently. While a certain amount of consistency of judgment is a necessary condition for a valid scale, it is by no means a sufficient condition. Suppose, for example, the subject was instructed to make "half-judgments" and instead he selected at random *any* ratio (less than unity) at the beginning of the experiment and behaved consistently thereafter. There is nothing in the analytical procedures which would indicate that the ratio was actually not one half but was instead a different ratio selected at random.

We thus must perform *additional* experiments in order to demonstrate whether or not the scale values do possess the ratio properties attributed to them.

It should again be mentioned that validation procedures are necessary for each attribute scaled. The scaling procedure itself cannot be validated (or invalidated) in general, but only with respect to the particular attribute. If, for example, it were shown that a loudness scale constructed by a particular procedure met all the tests of ratio properties that could be devised, there would still be no basis for concluding that a subjective weight scale constructed by the same procedure is therefore a valid ratio scale. Of course, if one procedure were found to be valid for a large number of different attributes, our confidence in the method itself would increase. Nevertheless, we would still have to carry out experimental checks when the procedure was applied to a new attribute before we could conclude that the new scale does in fact exhibit ratio properties.

In discussing experimental tests of the properties of the scale, we shall again be concerned with two problems: What are the properties to be tested, and how are they to be tested? The answer to the first problem will depend on the properties ascribed to the scale. The appropriate experimental procedures to test these properties will be determined by the nature of the attribute scaled. Here one important factor will be whether the scale is expressed as a psychophysical magnitude function or as simply the scale values of the stimulus series.

In the most narrow sense, we could hold that a ratio scale has been obtained if the scale value of any stimulus of the series has been determined to within a linear transformation of the form $y = ax$ under a very restricted experimental situation. We could hold, for example, that the only quantitative judgment a subject is capable of making is a "fourth-judgment"—that subjects were so constructed that they could recognize when one stimulus is one-fourth of another but could not necessarily make any other valid quantitative judgments.

What properties of the scale could then be tested? Let us assume that we have constructed a psychophysical magnitude function using this judgment. We might first ask: "Is this function independent of the particular set of stimuli used in its construction?" To answer the question, we could select another set of standards and obtain estimates of the stimuli judged one fourth of the standards. If the observed estimates agree within reasonable limits with those that we can calculate from the function, we would conclude that the function is in fact independent of the particular stimuli used. The scale values, then, have been determined to within a linear transformation of the form $y = ax$ under these very specific experimental conditions. Any other experimenter, when using the same experimental conditions, should obtain a function that is the same as the first except for the arbitrary unit. Is this then a ratio scale? It is certainly more than an ordinal scale, since the ratio of any two stimuli is independent of the values of the remaining stimuli in the series. For the same reason, it could be considered to be more than an equal-interval scale. On the other hand, we have experimentally demonstrated only one of the properties characteristic of a ratio scale. Other tests, such as equality of intervals, or consistency with subjective ratios other than one fourth, have been ruled out by the basic assumption. It would thus seem reasonable to assert that this is a ratio scale, not in any fundamental sense, but by definition only.

If we wish to define the ratio scale in this manner, then we can go ahead and determine experimentally the "constant errors" that a subject makes when estimating other ratios, such as one third or one fifth, or in making other quantitative judgments, such as bisecting a sense distance.

It is possible, of course, that other prescribed ratios could be used which would give scale values determined to within the same linear transformation also, but which would each differ in a nonlinear fashion among themselves and from those obtained when using "one-fourth judgments." Indeed, we could conceivably obtain a different "ratio" scale of a given magnitude for each prescribed ratio, each scale being valid by definition only. In the absence of a larger theoretical system, of which measures of the attribute are to play a part, we would have no logical procedure for choosing among them. Given such a larger system, however, our choice would likely be dictated by one of two factors, depending on how the attribute enters into the system. If a number of theoretical functional relationships between the attribute and other variables of the system have been deduced from the general theory, we would choose that scale of the attribute which agrees with the larger theory. If, instead, we were proceeding in an inductive manner in an attempt to relate the attribute to the variables already a part of the system, we would choose that scale which resulted in the simplest relationships, other things being equal.

If the scale were built on the assumption that the subject is capable of directly perceiving and reporting sense ratios in general instead of only a particular ratio, we would have additional properties subject to experimental test. Hitherto, we could test only whether the scale was independent of the particular set of stimuli used in its construction. With the broader assumption, we have the additional test of whether it is also independent of the particular ratio used in its construction. In this case, the ratio of the scale values assigned to any two stimuli would equal, within reasonable limits, the ratio that the subject would report when the two stimuli are presented to him. A scale constructed by "half-judgments" should allow us to predict the "one-fourth judgments" or "one-tenth judgments." If the scale is in the form of a psychophysical magnitude function, one procedure would be to select a series of stimuli distributed throughout the range, present all possible pairs of stimuli to the subject, and obtain direct estimates of the ratios between the members of each pair, much as is done in constructing a scale by Comrey's procedure. If the judged ratios agree with the ratios calculated from the magnitude function, it would be concluded that the scale has ratio properties of a more fundamental sort than that discussed in the previous paragraphs.

A further reasonable condition that might be required of the scale is that equal differences in scale values correspond to subjectively equal intervals. For example, given three stimuli, A, B, and C, with scale values of 7, 8, and 9 units, respectively, we could require that the subjective distance from A to B is equal to the subjective distance from B to C. The various forms of the method of equisection to be discussed in the next chapter would be appropriate to determine whether this is the case.

We could, of course, propose additional requirements of a more complex nature based on, for example, judgments of equality of ratios of differences and the like. Since these tasks become more and more complex, however, it is doubted that a disagreement between observed and calculated values would be interpreted as disproving the ratio properties of the scale. A more reasonable explanation of any disagreement would be that there is a limit to the complexity of judgment that the subject can make. On the other hand, if the observed values agreed with the calculated, this would be rightly interpreted as an additional verification of the scale.

In general, it would seem that the first three tests are sufficient for verifying that a scale constructed by the fractionation methods possesses ratio properties in a more than definitional sense. Of these three tests, the first would seem to be necessary before it could be concluded that the scale possesses ratio properties in *any* sense; the second and perhaps also the third before it could be concluded that the ratio characteristics had been experimentally demonstrated.

With Comrey's procedure demonstration of independence of the scale of the particular set of stimuli used would require additional experimentation. The data are overdetermined to such an extent, however, that additional experimentation would not seem to be necessary for the second test discussed. A separate experiment using equisection judgments would be necessary, of course, to demonstrate experimentally the property of subjective equality of intervals. However, we could also hold that any disagreement here results from a lack of ability to make valid judgments of sense distances, in which case we would retain the scale and consider the equisection results to be inappropriate.

The internal-consistency test of Comrey's procedure lies in the degree to which a matrix of ratios computed from the scale values agrees with the matrix of observed ratios. A rigorous statistical test for goodness of fit has yet to be devised. Until such a statistical test has been developed, the experimenter's own judgment must be used to determine whether the fit of the computed ratios to the observed ratios is adequate. Assuming a close agreement between theory and data, it is clear that the second test is satisfied at least in a preliminary way. For, if the $n(n-1)/2$ independent observed ratios can be reproduced from n scale values, it is reasonable to conclude that the scale is independent of any particular ratio.

▶ *Equisection Methods*

1. INTRODUCTION

The equisection methods are perhaps the least demanding of the quantitative-judgment methods from the standpoint of requirements of the subject. Both the subjective estimate and the fractionation methods present rather formidable tasks to the subject. In the one instance, he must be able to report directly the scale value of the stimulus, under some circumstances even selecting his own unit and origin, whereas, in the other, he must be able to report directly the numerical value of the sense ratio between pairs of stimuli. It is difficult to conceive how a subject could make these responses unless he had directly available to him, with all of its properties, a "ruler" of the attribute to be scaled. Indeed, we could consider these two scaling procedures to be merely practical ways of asking the subject to reproduce his ruler for us. Although the equisection methods could also be considered in the same fashion, a much simpler approach is also available. Let us consider this simpler approach.

The Basic Theory

We need assume only that the subject is capable of responding to ordinal characteristics of *sense distances*. For, if the subject can judge whether the interval between two stimuli is greater than, less than, or equal to a second interval (i.e., can make *ordinal judgments* of sense distances), a scale with equal-interval properties can be constructed. If one of the intervals is the interval between a "zero" stimulus and a stimulus with a finite value, the result would be a ratio scale.

The theory underlying the equisection procedures is thus simply that the subject is capable of reporting ordinal characteristics of sense distances, where a sense distance is defined as the interval separating two magnitudes in a given subjective continuum.   As usual, this assumption is subject to test by additional experimentation.

Although equisection is both the simplest and one of the oldest of the quantitative-judgment methods, it has not been used extensively as such in the construction of subjective scales.   It was originally of interest as a means of testing Fechner's law.   For the early history of the method, see Boring (1942, p. 42) and Titchener (1905, pp. 210–232).   More recently, the method has been applied by Judd (1933) in the construction of a saturation scale for yellow colors, by Stevens and Volkmann (1940a) in revising their scale of pitch, and by Garner (1954a) in experiments on loudness.

The applications of the method have all been in the field of sensation, where a corresponding physical scale has been available.   The subjective scales have, as a result, been expressed in terms of a psychophysical magnitude function relating the psychological attribute to the corresponding physical attribute.   It should be noted, however, that a related physical scale is by no means necessary for the application of the method.   The only requirement of the attribute to be scaled is that stimuli be available, either continuously or in small discrete steps, over the range of the attribute to be scaled.   This requirement is necessary to guarantee that stimuli which lie at equal intervals along the continuum will be available to the subject.

Relationship to Subjective Estimate Methods

The relationship between the equisection methods of the present chapter and the multiple-stimuli variety of the subjective estimate methods discussed in Chapter 4 should be made clear.   These two types of approach have often been considered as one.   As we shall see, however, the subjective estimate methods place demands on the subject that are not required in the equisection approach.

In illustrating the difference between the two approaches, we shall consider explicitly the multiple-stimuli, unlimited-category case of Chapter 4.   This we have called the "arrangement methods."   The conclusions reached, however, are equally applicable to the other multiple-stimuli case: i.e., the method of equal-appearing intervals.

In the arrangement method, the subject is presented with n stimuli. His task is to space out these n stimuli on a line segment so that the physical distances between the stimuli on the line segment represent the corresponding magnitudes of the intervals between the stimuli on the subjective continuum.   The positions of two of the stimuli may be specified in advance by the experimenter in order to determine the unit and origin of the scale. For example, the largest and the smallest stimuli might be specified as defining the ends of the scale. The subject's task is then to specify the position of each of the remaining stimuli within these two extremes. If s_a and s_b stand for the two anchor stimuli, something like the following might be obtained:

$$s_a \qquad s_1 \qquad s_2 \qquad\qquad\qquad s_3 \qquad s_b$$

The subject indicates the positions of s_1 through s_3.

In equisection, the problem is somewhat different. While there are several varieties of procedures, the one most similar to the arrangement example might be as follows. The subject has available an *unlimited* number of stimuli which are ordered with respect to the attribute. The experimenter designates the smallest s_a and the largest s_b as standards. The task set for the subject is to select $n-1$ of the remaining stimuli so that the $n-1$ stimuli divide the interval between the two standards into n subjectively equal intervals. Something like the following might be obtained in this experiment.

$$s_a \qquad s_1 \qquad s_2 \qquad s_3 \qquad s_b$$

The important thing to note is that the equisection task requires only that the subject be able to make valid ordinal judgments of sense distances. In the example, s_2 could be selected because the distance of any smaller stimulus from the standard s_b is greater than its distance from s_a, while for any stimulus larger than s_2 the reverse would be true. The other two variable stimuli, s_1 and s_3, could be selected on a like basis. With the arrangement method, however, the subject must not only be able to judge that one distance is greater than another, but also must be able to indicate *how much greater*. His task is to locate all stimuli, regardless of whether or not they fall at equal intervals. When considered this way, the multiple-stimuli, subjective estimate methods are seen to require what might be called interval judgments of sense distances, a task that would seem to be considerably more complex than the ordinal judgments required in the equisection methods.

2. THE SCALING PROCEDURES

Equisection methods all have in common the fact that their use in the construction of scales having equal-interval or ratio properties depends on the ability of the subject to make ordinal judgments of sense distances. The various procedures differ from one another in a number of ways.

The major differences involved center around the task set for the subject, the number of scale values solved for simultaneously, the requirement of a related physical attribute, the particular psychophysical procedure used to obtain estimates of the relevant parameters, and replication. We shall consider each in turn.

The Specific Task Set for the Subject

The experimental problem set for the subject can be formulated in three ways. The scale can be constructed by using any one of the three ways or by any combination.

Problem 1. Given two standard stimuli, i and j, the task set for the subject is to estimate the values of $n-1$ variable stimuli which will divide the interval between the standards into n subjectively equal intervals. As special cases, we have the methods of bisection ($n = 2$), trisection ($n = 3$), $\cdots$, n-section. The method of "half-judgments" discussed in the previous chapter can be considered to be a special example of the method of bisection where one of the standards is subjectively equal to zero.

Problem 2. In the simplest form, the subject is given two standard stimuli, i and j, and his task is to obtain an estimate of the value of a variable stimulus k which makes the interval between i and j (d_{ij}) subjectively equal to the interval between j and k (d_{jk}). More generally, we might have n variable stimuli and require the subject to adjust the entire set so that distances between adjacent stimuli are all subjectively equal to that between the two standards; i.e., so that $d_{ij} = d_{jk} = d_{kl} = d_{lm} = \cdots$. The method of "double-judgments" can be considered as a special case where a single variable stimulus is given and where one of the standards is subjectively equal to zero.

Problem 3. Given three standard stimuli, h, i, and j, the task set for the subject is to estimate the value of the variable k which makes the interval d_{hi} subjectively equal to the interval d_{jk}.

While the three forms all require the same ability of the subject—that he be able to make ordinal judgments of sense distances—we might surmise that the bisection case of the first along with the single variable case of the second would be found to be the easiest for the subject and perhaps also the most reliable. If recommendations were to be made it would be to use one or both of these to *construct* the scale, and the remaining procedures to check the validity of the scale.

Simultaneous versus Progressive Solution of Scale Values

Suppose we wish to divide a given segment of some continuum into eight equal steps. We could theoretically use two standards and seven variables, and solve for all scale values at once. Alternatively, we could solve for the scale values progressively, using two or three standards and one variable in each of seven successive experiments. We could also combine the two approaches, using fewer experiments with more variables in each. Some of the possible procedures are outlined schematically below. In these diagrams, S stands for standard stimuli, V for variable stimuli, the horizontal line for the subjective continuum, and each row for an experiment. In each experiment it is assumed that the value of the variable stimulus V is obtained by psychophysical procedures. For example, in the first diagram, the subject is presented with standards at the extremes of the segment of the continuum to be scaled, and with seven variables. He adjusts the variables until he is satisfied that the intervals are all equal to one another. The procedures schematically portrayed are of course only a few of those possible.

I. SIMULTANEOUS SOLUTIONS

    A. Using Problem 1:

             S V V V V V V V S
             ——————————————————————————————

    B. Using Problem 2:

             S S V V V V V V V
             ——————————————————————————————

II. PROGRESSIVE SOLUTIONS

    A. Using Problem 1, successive bisections:

Experiment 1	S			V			S
2				S	V		S
3	S	V	S				
4	S V S						
5		S V S					
6			S V S				
7				S V S			

    B. Using Problem 2:

Experiment 1	S S V		
2		S S V	
3			S S V

        etc.

C. Using Problem 3 (after the first step):

Experiment					
1	S	S	V		
2	S	S	S	V	
3	S	S		S	V

etc.

D. Using combinations:

Experiment								
1	S				V			S
2	S	V	V	V	S			
3					S	V	V	V	S

In each case, the assignment of scale values is straightforward. If one of the standards is a zero value, the experimenter is free to assign a number arbitrarily to one of the remaining stimuli. The rest of the stimuli are then assigned numbers so that the differences in numbers assigned to successive stimuli are all equal. Assuming that the judgments are valid, the result is a ratio scale. If no zero stimulus is used, the experimenter is free to assign arbitrarily any two numbers to any two stimuli. (The scale will, of course, be reversed unless he assigns the larger number to the larger stimulus.) The assignment of numbers to the remaining stimuli is carried out as before. In this case, however, assuming the judgments are valid, the result is an equal-interval scale.

Use of a Related Physical Attribute

The presence of a related physical continuum allows us to construct a psychophysical magnitude function relating the two attributes. Given this function, we can then estimate the subjective scale value of any stimulus, assuming only that its physical magnitude is known.

If the physical scale values of stimuli are available, an additional experimental scheme is also possible. The continuum can then be divided into several overlapping segments, each of which can be scaled separately. One such procedure is as follows:

Experiment								
1	S	V	V	V	S			
2			S	V	V	V	S	
3				S	V	V	V	S

Ordinarily the size of the interval in each scale will differ. When a psychophysical magnitude function can be plotted, however, the overlapping portions of the continuum can be used to establish a common unit and origin. For an example of the application of this type of procedure, see Stevens and Volkmann (1940*a*).

The Particular Psychophysical Method Used to Obtain Estimates of the Relevant Parameters

The application of psychophysical methods to obtain estimates of the values of the variable stimuli is necessary in order to minimize the effects of variable and constant errors. Any of the three basic psychophysical methods, as well as many of their variants, could be used to obtain estimates of the variables in conjunction with any of the three tasks discussed above. An exception to this statement would seem to be in those procedures that involve more than one variable stimulus. Here the method of average error would seem to be the appropriate procedure. The methods of limits and of constant stimuli would not be as easily adaptable.

With the method of average error, the subject adjusts the variable stimulus until he feels that the intervals are subjectively equal. Alternatively, he selects that stimulus out of a number of stimuli which makes the prescribed intervals equal. In the method of limits, the experimenter adjusts the variable, and the subject indicates, for each setting, whether one interval is greater or less than the other. With the constant-stimuli methods, pairs of distances are presented to the subject who judges whether one member of the pair is greater or less than the other (or, in the three-category case, greater than, equal to, or less than the other).

In all the psychophysical methods, it is the parameter analogous to the point of subjective equality that is taken as the best estimate of that stimulus which makes the intervals equal. For a somewhat more detailed discussion of the psychophysical methods themselves, the reader is referred to Chapter 7. For more detailed discussions, see Guilford (1954) or Woodworth (1938).

Replication

Replication is a fundamental requirement for any of the psychophysical methods. It is through replication that the variable errors and the more common constant errors (time, space, movement, etc.) are controlled. As is true of all the judgment methods, repeated judgments might be obtained either over trials with a single subject or over subjects, or over both. It should be kept in mind, however, that the scales obtained using the latter two procedures refer to a *population* of subjects and may not be characteristic of any *single* subject in the group.

3. ILLUSTRATIVE EXAMPLE: THE CONSTRUCTION OF A SCALE OF PITCH

The data for this example were taken from an experiment reported by Stevens and Volkmann (1940*a*). The purpose of their experiment was to construct a scale of pitch of pure tones over the range of 40 to 12,000 cycles per second, using equisection procedures.

The total range was divided into three overlapping segments of 40–1000 cycles, 200–6500 cycles, and 3000–12,000 cycles per second. For each segment, the procedure was as schematically portrayed in procedure I*A* of the preceding section. That is, the two extreme frequencies of each segment were taken as standards. The subject's task for each segment was to adjust three variable tones so that they divided that segment into four subjectively equal intervals. The psychophysical method used was thus a variant of the method of average error. Replication was over both subjects and trials; each of the ten subjects performing each task five times. The subjects were experienced observers. Precautions were taken in selecting the segments so that none could be divided so that the intervals were all octaves or fifths.

Table 1 gives the average of the 50 settings (five settings for each of ten subjects) when each of the three overlapping segments was divided into four subjectively equal intervals. Entries are expressed in terms of the frequencies of the tones. These means are taken as the "best" estimates of the stimuli which divide the segments into four equal steps.

Table 1. DATA ON EQUISECTION*

Entries give the mean of 50 settings (five settings for each of ten subjects) when dividing each of three overlapping segments into four subjectively equal intervals of pitch. Entries are expressed in terms of frequency

Segment	$\frac{1}{4}$ point	$\frac{1}{2}$ point	$\frac{3}{4}$ point
40–1000 cps	161	404	693
200–6500 cps	867	2022	3393
3000–12,000 cps	4109	5526	7743

* From Stevens and Volkmann (1940*a*).

From these data, Stevens and Volkmann constructed a scale extending from 40 cycles to 12,000 cycles per second. They first constructed the psychophysical function for the middle segment and second fitted by "purely graphical methods involving no small amount of trial and error" (p. 337) the two other segments to this function directly, under the requirement that the vertical distances between successive values in any given segment be equal, and that the stimuli in the overlapping portions fall on the same curve. They also used additional procedures to obtain a natural zero point, which was taken as the pitch of a 20-cycle-per-second tone. Their unit of pitch, the *mel*, was then specified by arbitrarily assigning the pitch value of 1000 mels to the 1000-cycle-per-second tone.

The scaling procedure described below differs slightly from that used by Stevens and Volkmann in that a more easily described analytical procedure has been substituted for the trial and error. In addition, we are not concerned here with the further problems of establishing a natural origin and standard kind of unit.

We first construct, for each of the three segments, a psychophysical magnitude function relating pitch to frequency. For each segment, the five stimuli (two standards and three variables) are plotted so that the successive vertical distances between adjacent stimuli are all equal on the vertical axis (the subjective continuum), and spaced according to frequency on the horizontal axis (the physical continuum). The plotted points for the three segments are given in Figures 1, 2, and 3.

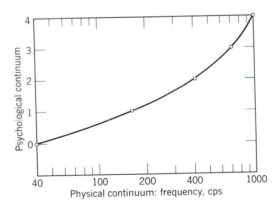

Figure 1. The lower segment of the psychophysical magnitude function. The five points are spaced in equal steps on the ordinate (psychological continuum) and according to frequency on the abscissa (physical continuum). Both unit and origin of the ordinate are arbitrary.

We next fit a curve to each plot. The curves of Figures 1, 2, and 3 were fitted by eye. We thus have three psychophysical functions relating pitch to frequency. Since the ranges of the two extreme segments overlap with that of the middle, these overlapping portions can be used to combine the three into a single scale extending from 40 to 12,000 cycles.

From the fitted curves of Figures 1, 2, and 3, we next read off the subjective scale values of several corresponding points on the overlapping

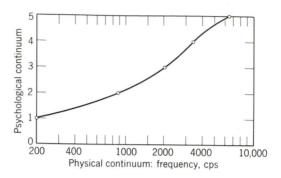

Figure 2.   The middle segment of the psychophysical magnitude function.

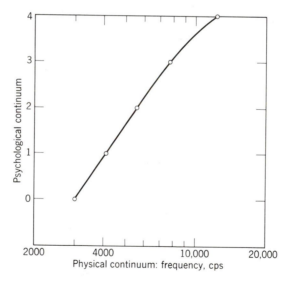

Figure 3.   The upper segment of the psychophysical magnitude function.

portions of the lower- and middle-range scales and of the middle- and upper-range scales, and construct the two plots shown in Figures 4 and 5. For the lower- versus middle-range scales, the frequencies selected were 200, 404, 693, 867, and 1000 cycles per second.   In Figure 4, the subjective

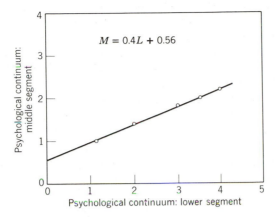

Figure 4. The subjective scale determined from the middle segment plotted against that determined from the lower segment. The straight line was fitted by eye. The equation of the line enables one to transform the scale values of the lower segment L to values expressed in terms of the unit and origin of the middle segment M.

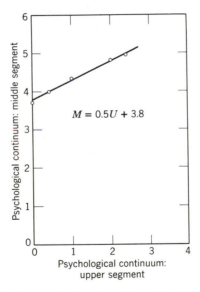

Figure 5. The subjective scale determined from the middle segment plotted against that determined from the upper segment. The equation of the line enables one to transform from the scale of the upper segment to that of the middle segment.

scale values for these stimuli for the lower segment (obtained from Figure 1) are plotted against the subjective scale values of these stimuli for the middle segment (obtained from Figure 2). Figure 5 contains the analogous plot of subjective scale values of the middle segment against those of the upper segment. The frequencies chosen for this plot were 3000, 3393, 4109, 5526, and 6500 cycles per second.

Linearity of these plots is a rough test of the equal-interval property of the scales. If these plots are linear, we can fit straight lines, and then use the result to combine the data into a single psychophysical function. If not, we have evidence that the procedures have not yielded an equal-interval scale. It should be noted, however, that slight departures from linearity could result from the procedures used in fitting the curves of Figures 1, 2, and 3 rather than directly from the data themselves. In the present example, the plots are actually slightly curvilinear. However, since the departure from linearity is very small, we can proceed with the next step.

Straight lines were fitted to the plots of Figures 4 and 5 by eye, and the equation of each line was determined. These equations are given in the corresponding figure. Using these equations, the subjective scales of the upper and lower segments can be transformed to the scale of the middle segment. For example, the equation relating the middle and lower segments is

$$M = 0.4L + 0.56$$

If we substitute the scale value of a stimulus expressed in terms of the unit and origin of the scale of the lower segment for L in this equation and then solve for M, the result will be the scale value of that stimulus referred to the unit and origin of the scale for the middle segment. Thus, substitution of subjective scale values of 0, 1, 2, 3, and 4, successively, for L gives the values 0.56, 0.96, 1.36, 1.76, and 2.16, respectively, for M. These then are the subjective scale values of the five observed points of the lower segment when referred to the scale of the middle segment.

The equivalent equation relating the upper and middle segments is

$$M = 0.5U + 3.8$$

The same procedure results in subjective scale values of the five observed points of the upper segment of 3.8, 4.3, 4.8, 5.3, and 5.8 when referred to the scale of the middle segment.

We now have the subjective scale values of each stimulus in terms of a common unit and origin, along with the physical frequency of each stimulus. Using these values, we can construct the final psychophysical magnitude function covering the entire range. This function is shown in

Figure 6. Here, the squares refer to the stimuli of the lower segment, the circles to stimuli of the middle segment, and the triangles to stimuli of the upper segment. It can be seen that the over-all fit is quite good.

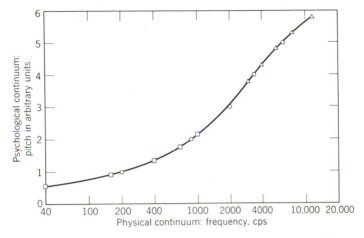

Figure 6. The final psychophysical magnitude function showing pitch as a function of frequency. The squares represent data obtained from the lower segment; the circles, the middle segment; and the triangles the upper segment. Data from Stevens and Volkmann (1940a).

4. EQUAL-INTERVAL PROPERTIES

As was true with the methods described in the previous two chapters, a scale can always be constructed through use of the equisection procedures discussed in section 2. The procedures themselves ordinarily have no built-in criteria for rejecting the hypothesis that the subject is capable of directly sectioning the continuum into equal intervals. Hence, additional experiments are necessary before we can conclude that the property of equality of intervals has been demonstrated.

Again, the experimental tests are concerned with the invariance of the difference ratios under various conditions. The primary condition that the scale constructed by these procedures must satisfy is invariance of difference ratios with respect to the particular stimuli used in its construction. Included in this condition is the requirement that the scale form be independent of the size of the interval which is sectioned. For example, a subjective scale of a given continuum constructed by sectioning the continuum directly into six equal intervals should be linearly related to the results that would be obtained if the continuum were directly sectioned into, say, three or eight equal intervals.

Given a psychophysical magnitude function constructed by one of the equisection procedures, one test of this condition would be to repeat the experiment, using precisely the same experimental procedures on different standard stimuli which are separated by an interval of different magnitude. If the results agree with what would be predicted from the function constructed from the data of the first experiment, i.e., if the subjective scales are linearly related, we would conclude that a scale with equal-interval properties has in fact been obtained. Stevens and Volkmann, for example, found that, in addition to their own overlapping segments, the results of bisection experiments of Pratt, of Münsterberg, and of Lorenz all agreed remarkably well with their pitch function, as did Münsterberg's experiment on equating nonadjacent pitch extents (Stevens and Volkmann, 1940*a*).

In like manner, Judd used standards separated by "from one to perhaps four 'least perceptible differences'" (Judd, 1933, p. 36) in constructing his saturation scale for yellow colors. Again, a high degree of consistency was found, indicating that the difference ratios are independent of the particular stimuli and intervals used.

In the subjective scale of loudness, however, the checks did not yield such clear results. Here, a bisection experiment carried out by Gage (1934) indicated that the results were dependent on the size of the interval bisected. His procedure was as follows:

(*a*) Bisect a given loudness interval to obtain the midpoint.

(*b*) Bisect again each half of the given interval, thus giving points at $\frac{1}{4}$ and $\frac{3}{4}$.

(*c*) Bisect the interval between the $\frac{1}{4}$ and $\frac{3}{4}$ points, and compare the value obtained with that of the initial bisection. The two should of course agree.

Actually, he found the second considerably louder than the first. He concluded as a result that the method was invalid. Later, the experiment was repeated by Newman, Volkmann, and Stevens (1937) under somewhat different conditions. In their results, the differences, though in the same direction, were considerably smaller. They concluded that consistent results would be obtained if constant errors could be minimized.

Invariance of difference ratios should also obtain between the different variants of the equisection procedure. Logically, this is perhaps not strictly necessary. However, the meaning of the scale would be drastically restricted if, for example, the results referred only to the method of bisection using the psychophysical method of constant stimuli. Rather, any of the equisection procedures outlined in section 2 should agree with any of the others to within a linear transformation, *provided that they both first meet the primary requirements given above.*

In the abstract, according to the rationale underlying the equisection procedures, all pairs of stimuli that are separated by equal intervals on the constructed scale should appear subjectively to be separated by equal intervals; i.e., equal distances on the constructed scale should appear subjectively to be equal. In the usual equisection procedures, only those intervals that are adjacent to one another are equated experimentally. However, direct procedures are also available for testing equality of non-adjacent intervals. The method would be essentially a paired-comparisons experiment on sense distances. As mentioned previously, one such procedure as used by Münsterberg gave results that agree very well with Stevens and Volkmann's pitch scale. It would seem that a direct test of this sort would be desirable for any of those scales that purport to represent subjectively equal intervals. This direct test would also seem to be appropriate for scales constructed by any of the quantitative-judgment methods discussed in the preceding two chapters.

►**7**

The Differential- ◄
Sensitivity Methods

1. EQUALLY OFTEN NOTICED DIFFERENCES

It is a well-known fact that there are limits to the resolving power of the subject. Given a series of stimuli which differ with respect to some discriminable aspect—some psychological attribute—it is possible to select two stimuli which are so close together on the continuum that the subject cannot report with any confidence which is the greater. An equally well-known fact is that the resolving power or sensitivity of subjects varies both between subjects and within a given subject momentarily over time. Hence, there is actually no dividing point such that any stimulus having a greater value, e.g., brighter, heavier, redder, will always be noticed as greater than a standard, and any stimulus having a smaller value be never noticed. Rather, as the difference between a standard stimulus and a variable increases, the probability that the greater stimulus will be judged to be greater increases. If two stimuli which are exceedingly close together on the continuum are presented to a subject who is required to judge which is the greater, the probability of his judging correctly will be little if any better than one half. As the difference increases, the probability of a correct response increases (Brown, 1910).

In spite of this fact, psychologists have long spoken, and still speak, of the "just noticeable difference," the *jnd*. The *jnd* or, as alternative terms, the difference limen, *DL*, or difference threshold, *DT*, is generally taken to mean that difference which is noticed a specified proportion of the time (usually half or halfway between pure chance and perfect). The precise definition depends on the particular set of procedures used (as we shall see, there are several different kinds of *DL*'s. Unfortunately, perhaps, the relationship among them is not always clear).

The scaling methods with which this chapter is concerned are those methods that are based on the concept of the *equality on the psychological continuum of just noticeable differences*. That is to say: If a stimulus *B* is "just noticeably greater" than stimulus *A*, and stimulus *C* is "just noticeably greater" than stimulus *B*, then the *distance* on the psychological continuum that separates *A* and *B* is equal to the distance separating *B* and *C*. This notion may be taken as an assumption, subject to further test, or as a definition of what is meant by equality of intervals on the psychological continuum (see, for example, Boring, 1942, p. 42). We shall consider it to be the latter.

This general approach to scaling marks the very beginnings of experimental psychology. Fechner's law, which is based on the notion of equality of *jnd*'s, represents an early attempt to express mathematically the relationship between the physical magnitude of the stimulus and the psychological magnitude of the sensation it arouses. Fechner's law, however, is only a special case of what can be called the differential sensitivity methods. The approach may be used when Fechner's law does not hold. As a matter of fact, it may even be used when no corresponding physical attribute of the stimuli is available.

Given the definition of what is to be meant by equality of intervals, i.e., equality of *jnd*'s, we have only to devise experimental methods for obtaining *jnd*'s in order to obtain a scale possessing a unit of measurement. Assuming that procedures can be devised which determine uniquely a stimulus that is just noticeably different from another, the scale values will be determined to within a linear transformation of the form $y = ax + b$. For example, if we can establish experimentally that stimulus *B* is just noticeably greater than *A*, *C* is just noticeably greater than *B*, *D* than *C*, etc., a scale possessing equal-interval properties in the sense of the definition can be constructed simply by assigning successive integers to the stimuli: $A = 1, B = 2, C = 3, D = 4$, etc. We could of course add any constant (e.g., $A = 3, B = 4, C = 5$, etc.) and/or multiply each scale value by a positive constant (e.g., $A = 6, B = 8, C = 10$, etc.) without disturbing the scale form.

In order to determine the values to within the $y = ax$ transform, an additional definition to specify an absolute zero point is needed. For many continua, particularly in the sensory domain, it is reasonable to ask: What is the stimulus that possesses the least perceptible amount of the attribute in question? For example, consider a series of colors extending from neutral gray to a highly saturated red.   We might wish to determine the stimulus that possesses the attribute "redness" to a just noticeable degree. Here again, variability is the rule, and we define the *absolute limen* or threshold as that stimulus which is judged as possessing the attribute just half of the time.   This definition would of course take different forms with different continua.   With loudness or other intensity dimensions, for example, we would define the *AL* as that stimulus which is just strong enough to be perceived half of the time.   In psychophysics, the absolute limen is usually taken as the natural origin of the psychological continuum.*

With these two definitions, the *jnd* specifying the unit and the *AL* specifying the origin, it is possible to obtain a scale with ratio properties.

As we shall see, to determine *jnd*'s or *DL*'s, only ordinal judgments of the stimuli are required of the subject.   That is to say, the subject need only to be able to judge whether one stimulus is greater than, less than, or equal to another.   Thus, the distinguishing characteristics of these differential sensitivity scaling methods are (1) the requirement of no more than ordinal judgments of the stimuli by the subject, and (2) the definition that just noticeable differences are psychologically equal.

2. TWO POINTS OF VIEW CONCERNING THE *jnd*

It should not be assumed from the forgoing discussion that the notion of the *jnd* is simple and straightforward.   The concept has generated an immense amount of controversy throughout the years.   Two rather different points of view concerning the *jnd* underlie much of the debate. Rather than discussing the resulting controversies, we shall instead present briefly the two points of view themselves.   Although, because of variability of responses, both views have led to statistical definitions of the *jnd*, the preferred definitions tend to differ both experimentally and analytically.

The View of Classical Psychophysics

The *jnd* or *DL* is defined in terms of the (average) size of the increment (or decrement) that must be added to (or subtracted from) a standard stimulus before the variable stimulus arouses a sensation which is noticeably different from (greater or less than) the standard.   In some procedures, it is one-half the difference between the point of transition from

---

* At first thought, it might seem that the origin ought to be located somewhat below the *AL*, since the *AL* corresponds to the stimulus that possesses the attribute to "a just noticeable degree."   The zero point ought to coincide with the stimulus that possesses the attribute to a "just not noticeable degree."   However, from the definition of the *AL* given above, it is clear that "just noticeable" and "just not noticeable" describe the same stimulus, since, if the attribute is judged to be present to a noticeable extent just half of the time, it necessarily follows that it is also judged to be not present just half of the time.

"less than" to "equal" and the equivalent point from "equal" to "greater than." The subject is supposed to report his *sensations*. He is not supposed to be judging, for example, whether one *stimulus* is greater than another, but instead whether one sensation is greater than the other. To judge the relative magnitude of the stimuli is to commit the *stimulus error*. Since he is supposed to be giving a straightforward report of his sensations, the experimental procedures must not be such as to keep him from doing so. In particular, procedures that do not allow reports of equality or doubt are not to be recommended. Since the average positions of the transition points are the things to be determined, the methods that get at these "directly," i.e., the methods that use an index of *central value* in the definition of the *jnd*, are to be preferred. The other procedures have only indirect validity. The absolute size of the *jnd* is an important quantity. It has a sort of uniqueness about it that reminds us more of enumeration than of measurement. The names of Titchener (1905), Urban (1950), and perhaps Stevens (1951b) can be associated with this general point of view.

The "Objective" View

The "objective" point of view seems to have had its beginnings with Jastrow (1888) and Cattell (Fullerton and Cattell, 1892). The *DL* is simply a measure of the differential sensitivity of the subject. The traditional notion of sensation is dispensed with entirely as far as the responses of the subject are concerned. He judges stimuli, not sensations. Restriction of available reports to two categories (such as greater or less) is desirable. Use of the category of equal or doubtful has been frowned on, since it has been found that the degree to which this category is used by the subject depends on his attitude. The *DL* as a measure of differential sensitivity is best stated in terms of the dispersion of his distribution of errors: e.g., the probable error, standard deviation, or, perhaps, in the case of ogive functions, the maximum slope. The absolute size of the *DL* does not have the peculiar status that it has in the other approach, since any of a number of different indices might be used. Thorndike (1910) and Thurstone (1948) might also be mentioned in connection with this point of view.

The discussion in the following section on experimental procedures for the construction of differential sensitivity scales is somewhat biased in favor of the "objective" view, especially in the section where we discuss various tasks set for the subject. Here we commit the "stimulus error" consistently, in that the discussion proceeds in terms of judgments of stimuli rather than reports of sensations. The parallel discussion appropriate for the latter view would have amounted to little more than a change in terminology.

3. EXPERIMENTAL PROCEDURES

Task Set for the Subject

The primary experimental problem is to devise procedures to enable us to determine the proportion of times one stimulus is judged as greater than another with respect to the given attribute; i.e., to determine a *jnd*. In order to arrive at a ratio scale, the further problem of determining the stimulus which is judged as *possessing* the attribute to a just noticeable degree also must be dealt with. Numerous procedures have been developed to enable us to determine these quantities. (See, for example, Woodworth, 1938; Guilford, 1936, 1954; and Titchener, 1905.)

In the determination of *jnd*'s, one or the other of the following tasks is generally required of the subject:

1. He is presented with two stimuli and is required to judge which is the greater. In some cases, judgments of equality or doubt are also allowed.

2. He is presented with *n* stimuli and required to sort or rate them into *r* ($r \leq n$) piles or categories such that the piles appear ordered with respect to the psychological attribute. For the special case where $r = n$, the subject places the stimuli in rank order.

3. He is presented with a standard stimulus and a continuously variable comparison stimulus. His task is to adjust the comparison stimulus until it appears equal to the standard.

4. He is presented with a standard and a discrete series of comparison stimuli. His task is to select that comparison stimulus which appears equal to the standard.

5. He is presented with two stimuli. His task is to judge whether they are the same or different.

6. He is presented with two standard stimuli and a comparison stimulus which is identical with one of the standards. His task is to select the standard which is the same as the comparison stimulus.

The situations in which any particular task can be applied in determination of *jnd*'s vary with the task. The first two would seem applicable to virtually any set of stimuli possessing the attribute. The third and fourth would seem limited to those attributes for which a continuous (or virtually continuous) series of stimuli is readily available. The stimuli should already be ordered with respect to the attribute under consideration. As a matter of fact, the analytical procedures accompanying these tasks further require not only that the stimuli be ordered on the attribute, but also that their values on a monotonically related continuum be known on an interval scale.

Much the same is true with the fifth and sixth tasks. Here, in addition, it is necessary that the stimulus series vary only with respect to the attribute of interest, since judgments of "same" or "different" are attributed to similarity or difference with *respect to the attribute under consideration*. If we were attempting to determine a *jnd* for *pitch* of pure tones, for example, neither task 5 nor 6 would be applicable if the various stimuli differed appreciably in loudness. For then, two tones with the same pitch might consistently be judged to be different if their loudness differed considerably.

In actual practice, of course, tasks 3, 4, 5, and 6 are used mainly in the sensory domain where, first, the order of the stimuli on the psychological attribute is already known; second, use can be made of a related physical continuum in the analysis of the data; and, third, variation of the stimuli on attributes other than the attribute of interest can be eliminated or controlled.

Regardless of the particular tasks used, the essence of all of the procedures is replication. Judgments are repeated until relatively stable estimates of the proportions can be obtained. Under some circumstances, replication may be over a sample of subjects from some defined population; under others, over trials within a single subject. Further, through replication, the various constant errors, such as space, time, movement, anticipation, habituation, and the like are controlled.

Procedures That Do not Require Availability of a Related Physical Continuum

The first two tasks, direct comparison of pairs, and sorting into ordered categories, are most adaptable to those discrete stimulus series, such as excellence of handwriting samples, which have no known physical correlate and which have not previously been ordered with respect to the attribute of interest. Ordinarily a very large number of stimuli must be available. In the ideal case, the analytical procedures would consist simply of, first, selecting from the initial set of stimuli a subset such that stimulus B is judged greater than stimulus A, stimulus C greater than stimulus B, stimulus D greater than stimulus C, etc., a given, fixed proportion of the time, and, second, assigning successive integers to the successive members of the subset. This procedure was used, for example, by Thorndike (1910, p. 40) in the construction of one of his handwriting scales.

Thorndike gives a standard scale made up of ten specimens of children's handwriting. Each specimen was judged, in direct comparison, to be better than the immediately preceding specimen by approximately 80 per cent of the judges. If one assigns the integers from one to ten to the ten stimuli, he will then have an interval scale of excellence of handwriting based on the notion of equality of equally often noticed differences.

While these proportions were obtained by direct comparison of pairs, they could equally well have been obtained through use of a sorting or ranking procedure. The proportion would then be the proportion of times that one stimulus was ranked or sorted above the other, with perhaps some adjustment for ties.

But suppose the first step is not possible—that there is no subset of stimuli (A, B, C, D, etc.) covering the range of the whole series such that the differences between the successive pairs are noticed equally often. Then, if an equal-interval scale is to be constructed, some sort of interpolation procedure is necessary.

Suppose stimulus B is judged greater than stimulus A 75 per cent of the time; and stimulus C is judged greater than stimulus B 85 per cent of the time. How are we to determine the relationship among the distances AB and BC? The rationale used by Thorndike and several of the other early workers at Columbia* was to use the integral of the normal curve in making the interpolation. The distance BC is assumed to exceed the distance AB by the amount that the unit normal deviate corresponding to a proportion of 0.85 exceeds that corresponding to the proportion 0.75. With this additional assumption, scale values may be assigned to the stimuli, even though they are not exactly equally often noticed.

With respect to the continua having no known related physical magnitude, the procedures based on the definition of equally often noticed differences have been largely supplanted by the more general judgment model developed by Thurstone (discussed in detail in Chapters 8–10). Thurstone's model was, as a matter of fact, developed out of this early work.

Procedures That Make Use of a Monotonically Related Attribute

The phrase "monotonically related physical attribute" automatically implies that a good share of the general problem has already been solved. In the first place, it implies that the *order* of the stimuli on the psychological continuum is already known. It implies further that a considerable degree of control exists over those variables other than the "monotonically related attribute" which are also related in some fashion to the psychological attribute of interest. For, if order on the psychological continuum were not known, we could not know that the two attributes were monotonically related, and if, in any experiment, other variables were not controlled or eliminated, the monotonic relation would not be likely to be obtained.

In view of these considerations, we need not be restricted to ordinal judgments, i.e., judgments of greater or less, rank order, or ordered categories, in obtaining the required proportions, but might instead make use of judgments of equality or difference. For example, we could define

* For a summary and bibliography see Hollingworth (1914).

the *jnd* or *DL* in terms of that comparison stimulus, *known to be greater than the standard*, which is judged *different* from the standard some designated proportion (e.g., 0.50) of the time.   Or it could be defined as the difference between two standard stimuli for which a third stimulus, identical with one of the two standards, is correctly identified a specified proportion of the time.   A third variation is to have the subject adjust a variable stimulus a large number of times until it appears equal to the standard, and then define the *DL* in terms of the probable error or standard deviation of the distribution of settings.

A further use to which the monotonically related attribute is put is in the specification and reproduction of particular stimuli.   For example, knowledge of the physical correlates of frequency and intensity enables us to reproduce a particular tone whenever we wish.

But the main utility of the monotonically related attribute is in enabling us to express the data in terms of the physical values of the stimuli, and, as a result, in enabling us to carry out various interpolations based on empirically obtained functions.   There are three principal problems in which these interpolation procedures are used.   In each case, they serve to eliminate a great deal of experimental labor.   They are the estimation of an individual *DL*, the estimation of *DL*'s over the entire range of stimuli, and the estimation of the scale value of a stimulus.   We shall consider each in more detail.

THE ESTIMATION OF A PARTICULAR *DL*.   With no known related attribute, either we must determine experimentally the comparison stimulus that is noticed as greater than the standard a specified proportion of the time, or we must *assume* some function to enable use of interpolation procedures.   We saw that Thorndike assumed that the proportions formed a normal ogive with fixed variance on the psychological continuum.   This enabled him to estimate the *distance*, in terms of *DL*'s, between the two stimuli.   With a related continuum, however, we can plot the empirical results (e.g., the proportion of times each comparison stimulus was judged greater than the standard against the physical value of that comparison stimulus), fit a curve, and estimate the *stimulus* that would be judged greater than the standard the specified proportion of the time.   In the one instance, we deal with an assumed function and use it to estimate a distance; in the other, we deal with an empirical function to select the stimulus satisfying the desired conditions.   We shall discuss this further in the next section.

ESTIMATION OF *DL*'S OVER THE ENTIRE RANGE.   We need not determine experimentally each and every *jnd* step when scale values of the stimuli on the related physical continuum are known.   Instead, we can select a rather small number of standard stimuli spread out over the entire range, determine the size of the *DL in physical units* for each standard, and plot *the physical size of the DL as a function of the physical size of the stimulus* as is shown in Figure 1. From a smooth curve fitted to the observed data, we can estimate the size (in physical units) of any *DL*, and hence can estimate, for any standard, that stimulus which is just noticeably greater.

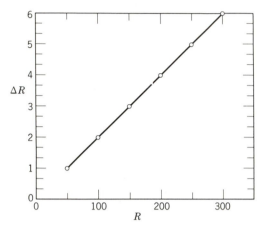

Figure 1. Plot of the size of the *jnd* in physical units, ΔR, as a function of the magnitude of the standard stimulus in physical units, *R*, based on observations of six hypothetical standard stimuli. The plotted points refer hypothetically to the observed data. From the fitted curve we can estimate the *jnd* for any other magnitude of *R* within the experimental range.

ESTIMATION OF THE SCALE VALUE OF ANY STIMULUS. From the curve in Figure 1 it is a straightforward matter to construct a psychophysical magnitude function showing the relationship of the value of the stimulus on the psychological attribute as a function of its corresponding value on the physical attribute. Figure 2 gives an example of such a curve. The psychological scale value of any stimulus in terms of the number of *jnd*'s from the origin can be read directly from this curve, assuming that its physical value is known. If the origin of the psychological attribute (zero on the ordinate) is the absolute limen, the scale values can be considered as measured on a ratio scale.

The Psychophysical Methods

In the beginning of this chapter we indicated that there are several different kinds of *DL*'s. We could speak of "the *DL*" in the discussion of the various uses of a related continuum only because the procedures considered were common to all. In the present section we consider several alternative operational procedures for determining (defining) a *DL* when a related physical continuum is available. These procedures are, of course, the well-known *psychophysical methods*. There are actually a great variety of psychophysical methods, differing from one another in either or both the particular way in which the data are obtained and the

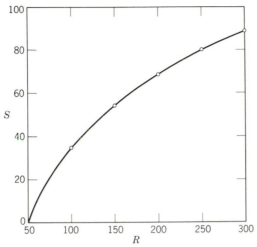

Figure 2. Psychophysical magnitude function.

particular analytical methods for determining the *DL*. For our purposes, we need only consider briefly examples of the three "classical" methods handed down from Fechner: the method of average error, the method of limits, and the method of constant stimuli. Of these methods, the first uses judgments of equality, and the second and third, judgments of greater or less, often along with judgments of equal or doubtful. We shall outline each of these methods briefly. For more detail on these methods, as well as others, see Woodworth (1938), Guilford (1936, 1954), or Titchener (1905).

4. THE METHOD OF AVERAGE ERROR

This method is also called the method of adjustment or the method of equivalents. The subject is presented with a standard stimulus and a variable comparison stimulus. His task is to adjust the variable until it is subjectively equal to the standard with respect to some given attribute. Repeated judgments are obtained. The initial value of the variable is randomized or systematically counterbalanced—sometimes above, below, and by greater or lesser amounts. For each judgment, the physical value of the variable judged to be equal to the standard is recorded. We thus have as raw data a large number of estimates of the value of the variable which is subjectively equal to the standard. Because of fluctuations within the subject, these estimates will not always be the same but will

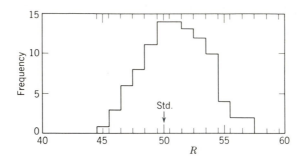

Figure 3. Frequency distribution showing the number of estimates of equality with the standard falling within the class interval indicated.

instead form a frequency distribution on the physical continuum, such as is shown in Figure 3. From the estimates, we compute

(*a*) A measure of central value: The median, arithmetic mean, or geometric mean are the most common.

(*b*) A measure of dispersion: The probable error, standard deviation, interquartile range, or average deviation might be used.

We can now define the following psychophysical quantities, all measured in terms of physical units:

(*a*) *PSE*, the point of subjective equality. The measure of central value is defined as the *PSE*. Note that the *PSE* is not necessarily equal to the standard.

(*b*) *CE*, the constant error. This quantity is the difference between the *PSE* and the physical value of the standard stimulus:

$$CE = PSE - \text{Std.}$$

(*c*) *DL* (or *jnd*). The *DL* is equated to the measure of dispersion. The measure which most closely corresponds to the general definition of a *DL* given earlier would be the upper quartile range $(Q_3 - Q_2)$. However, the standard deviation would seem to be as good a measure to use.

5. THE METHOD OF JUST NOTICEABLE DIFFERENCES

The method of just noticeable differences is also called the method of limits or method of serial exploration. We again have a standard and a variable comparison stimulus.   In this method, however, the experimenter adjusts the variable by small discrete steps, beginning one series with the variable clearly greater than the standard, and then decreasing its value (the descending series), and balancing this series with one where the variable is initially clearly less than the standard.   In one form of the method the subject's task is to judge whether the variable at each step is greater than, equal to, or less than the standard.   Judgments of "doubtful" might also be allowed.   Each series is ended the moment the two transitions are made.   A hypothetical set of raw data is given in Table 1.   In this table, + indicates a judgment of "variable greater than standard," = a judgment of equality, and − a judgment of "variable less than standard."   The column on the left gives the physical values of the variable.   The standard is indicated as having a physical value of 20.

Table 1. THE METHOD OF JUST NOTICEABLE DIFFERENCES

R = physical values of comparison stimuli
d = descending series of comparison stimulus values
a = ascending series of comparison stimulus values

Standard stimulus = 20

R	a	d	a	d	a	d	a	d	a	d	a	d	a	d
10	+								+					
12	+				+				+				+	
14	+	+			+		+		+		+		+	
16	+	+	+		=		+		+		+	+	+	
18	=	+	−	+	=		=		+	+	=	=	+	+
Std 20	=	=		=	=	+	=	+	=	=	=	=	=	=
22	−	−		=	−	=	=	=	−	=	−	−	=	=
24	−			−		−	−	−	−	−	−		−	−
26	−			−			−		−				−	−
28	−			−			−		−					−
30				−					−					
L_u	21	21	17	23	21	23	23	23	21	23	21	21	23	23
L_l	17	19	17	19	15	21	17	21	19	19	17	17	19	19

$$\Sigma L_l = 256 \qquad\qquad \Sigma L_u = 304$$
$$\bar{L}_l = 18.29 \qquad\qquad \bar{L}_u = 21.71$$
$$IU = \bar{L}_u - \bar{L}_l = 21.71 - 18.29 = 3.42$$
$$DL = \tfrac{1}{2}IU = \tfrac{1}{2}(\bar{L}_u - \bar{L}_l) = 1.71$$
$$PSE = \tfrac{1}{2}(\bar{L}_u + \bar{L}_l) = \tfrac{1}{2}(21.71 + 18.29) = 20$$
$$CE = PSE - \text{Std.} = 20 - 20 = 0$$

Each series gives an estimate of the upper limen and also the lower limen, where the former is defined as the transition point between $+$ and $=$, and the latter between $=$ and $-$. The physical values of both limens for each trial are entered at the bottom of the table.

The mean upper and lower limens, L_u and L_l, have been computed to be 21.71 and 18.29, respectively. The interval of uncertainty IU is defined as the difference between the mean upper limen and the mean lower limen: in this case, 3.42. The DL is equal to one-half the interval of uncertainty or 1.71. The point of subjective equality PSE is equal to the average of the values of L_u and L_l: in this case, 20.00. The constant error, $PSE -$ Std, is here equal to zero.

6. THE CONSTANT METHODS

As in the method of limits, a standard stimulus is paired with each of a number of comparison stimuli. The subject reports whether one member of the pair is greater or less than the other. Equal or doubtful judgments are often allowed also. The comparison stimuli, however, are presented not in serial order as in the method of limits, but instead in a prearranged order which is unknown to the subject. Usually only four to seven comparison stimuli are used, which have been selected through preliminary experimentation. A large number of repetitions is necessary.

From the responses we tabulate the frequency of times each comparison stimulus was judged greater than the standard, less than the standard, and, if allowed, equal to the standard or doubtful. These frequencies are converted to proportions. It is the proportions that are used in estimating the psychophysical constants.

We thus have as raw data, assuming n comparison stimuli, n independent proportions when only two categories of judgment are permitted (n, since $P_g + P_l = 1$), or $2n$ independent proportions when three categories of judgment are permitted ($P_g + P_l + P_= = 1$). Since n usually varies from four to seven, we will have somewhere in the neighborhood of four to fourteen independent proportions from which to compute the psychophysical constants.

We now ask: "Given these proportions, how do we proceed to analyze the data?" The reader who is unfamiliar with the psychophysical literature might suggest that we simply make up a plot with the value of the proportions on the ordinate and the physical value of the variable stimuli on the abscissa, fit smooth curves to the data, and pick off the desired quantities—a reasonable enough answer. If two categories of judgment are allowed, we need only plot one set of proportions, say P_g, and fit one curve, since the other will be its mirror image. Such a curve is shown in Figure 4. This curve, as well as that given in the following figure, is known in psychophysics as the *psychometric function*.

The point of subjective equality is simply the stimulus having an equal probability of being judged greater and less. The *DL* might best be the difference between the 75 per cent and the 50 per cent points on the curve,

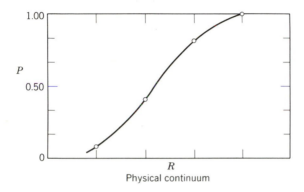

Figure 4. Psychometric function, two-category case. The plotted points correspond to the proportion of times the comparison stimulus indicated on the abscissa is judged to be greater than the standard stimulus.

or perhaps one-half the difference between the 75 per cent and 25 per cent points.

With three categories of judgment, we would plot both the P_g and P_l since they may vary somewhat independently. We would then obtain curves such as is shown in Figure 5. Here the *PSE* would seem most reasonably defined as the intersection of the two curves—i.e., that stimulus having an equal probability of being judged greater or less than the standard. The *DL* might reasonably be defined as one-half the distance between the 50 per cent points on the two curves, or perhaps the difference between the 50 per cent point on the greater curve and the *PSE*.

In each case, the alternative definitions of *DL* would theoretically depend on whether we wish to conceive of the *DL* as the increment that must be added to a stimulus, or the average of the increment added and the decrement that must be subtracted from a stimulus to be noticed half of the time.

Actually, of course, we have skipped over a number of problems, about which has centered a good bit of controversy. Perhaps the most basic controversy centers around the equal or doubtful judgments: should they be allowed, and, if so, what should be done with them? Here the field would seem to be split three ways: (1) Do not allow them. (2) Allow them but throw them away (treat the data as in Figure 4, for example). (3) Allow them, and use them in the analysis of the data (as in Figure 5, for example).

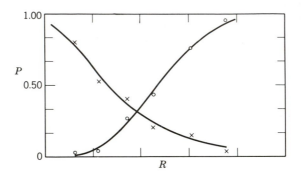

Figure 5. Psychometric function, three-category case. The small circles indicate the proportion of times each comparison stimulus (indicated by its value on the abscissa) was judged greater than the standard. The crosses indicate the corresponding proportion of times that it was judged less than the standard. One minus the sum of the two proportions for any given comparison stimulus is equal to the proportion of judgments of equality or doubt.

Regardless of how the "doubtful" judgment controversy is settled, we have the problem of how to "fit a smooth curve" to the data. Here we have, perhaps among others, the following:

1. Connect the points with straight lines—the linear interpolation method.
2. Make the plot on probability paper (or convert to normal deviates, and plot on ordinary paper), and connect the points with straight lines— the normal interpolation method.
3. Same as 2 above, but fit a straight line to the points—the normal graphic method.
4. Fit the integral of the normal curve to the points, using least-squares procedures.
5. Same as 4, only weight the proportions appropriately in the fitting process (Urban and Kelley's process).
6. Substitute the log of the stimulus values in any of the first five procedures.
7. Take pencil in hand, and fit a smooth ogive to the points.

We could also use Spearman's method (1908)—in which the psychometric curve is not employed at all—or the methods of probit analysis (Bliss, 1935*a*, 1935*b*; Finney, 1947). Functions other than the normal curve might also be tried. For example, the logistic function (see Berkson, 1953) might be fitted to the data, or a straight line might be fitted to angles resulting from the arcsin $\sqrt{p}$ transformation.

If the true form of the function is the integral of the normal curve, then method 5 would seem appropriate. If the function is the normal integral when measured on a logarithmic scale of the physical attribute, as we might expect if Weber's law were true, then the combination of 6 and 5 would be best. If neither is true, which is probably the case for many situations, we might do at least as well, and probably better, by simply fitting the curve by hand. This would seem to be particularly likely when the proportions are based on a large enough number of observations to be highly reliable.

With the three-category method, problems and controversies abound even after the curves have been fitted. Assume that we have fitted the curves in Figure 5 by method 5. Then the average *DL* suggested is identical with Urban's *DL* (1910). But this *DL* is to a great extent dependent on the attitude of the subject. All a subject need do to have a zero *DL*, i.e., to be "infinitely sensitive," is to give only "greater than" and "less than" judgments, since the *DL* depends on the equality judgments. Culler has suggested an alternative *DL* for the three-category case (1926*b*). He recommends that the average of the probable errors of the two curves be used. This is identical with taking the average of the differences between the 50 per cent and 75 per cent points of the two curves shown in Figure 5 when Urban's process is used for fitting the curves.

We shall not pursue the problems and controversies over the constant methods any further. A detailed discussion of these problems, as well as step-by-step procedures for most of the analytical methods outlined here, is available in Guilford (1936, 1954) and Woodworth (1938).

With but slight changes in experimental procedure, the three methods can also be used to obtain the absolute limen, the stimulus that is ordinarily assigned the value of zero on the psychological continuum. Of the three methods, the method of limits and the constant method would seem to be the most appropriate. The experimental procedures for determining the *AL* are the same as those corresponding to the *DL* except that

1. No standard is presented.
2. The subject judges in terms of presence or absence of the attribute instead of greater, equal, or less.
3. In each case, the *PSE* is taken as the absolute limen.

7. REMARKS ON THE PSYCHOPHYSICAL METHODS

The method of average error has never really been enthusiastically received as a procedure for obtaining a *DL*.   Its primary usefulness as a method has been in connection with other problems.   Among the troublesome things about this method, as far as its use in determination of the *DL* is concerned, are the unknown role played by motor factors in the adjustments, the lack of control over timing of each adjustment, and, where the standard and variable must be presented successively, the fact that the standard must be presented first.

The method of limits and Urban's procedure for the three-category method of constant stimuli are in line with the classical point of view outlined earlier.   Similarly, we can associate the two-category method of constant stimuli with what we have called the "objective" view.   Culler's *DL* for the three-category case might be considered to represent a compromise.

As stated earlier, these are only three out of a great number of psychophysical methods.   We have not covered the field in detail since, as we have noted, this material is readily available elsewhere.   Two recent developments in psychophysical theory which might be just mentioned, however, are the quantum theory advocated by Stevens and others (von Békésy, 1930;   Stevens and Volkmann, 1940*b*;   Stevens, Morgan, and Volkmann, 1941;   Volkmann, 1941;   Stevens, 1951*b*) and the application of signal detection theory to psychophysics (Peterson and Birdsall, 1953; Tanner and Swets, 1954;   Marill, 1956).

The quantum theory is closely related to the classical approach to psychophysics.   An assumption that the neural structures associated with the perception of differences along the sensory continuum are divided into functionally distinct units leads to predictions concerning the shape of the psychometric function.   Under one kind of closely controlled experimental condition, the theory predicts that the function will be linear with slope proportional to the differential sensitivity of the subject.   The authors cited report data in line with the theory.   For data that fit the theory, use of the quantum as a measure of differential sensitivity has been recommended, where the quantum is operationally defined as the difference between the smallest increment which is always noticed and the largest increment which is never noticed.

Signal-detection theory, as applied to psychophysics, represents an alternative approach to the logical derivation of the shape of the psychometric function.   Though the theory was developed independently outside the field of psychology, it is in agreement with the objective point of view discussed earlier.   Many of the notions involved parallel those of the scaling procedures discussed in Chapter 10. The approach of signal-detection theory seems to hold a great deal of promise for psychophysics in general.

8. WEBER'S LAW AND FECHNER'S LAW

It has been repeatedly demonstrated that, when *DL*'s are obtained for a number of stimuli which differ with respect to the attribute of interest, the size of the *DL* (in physical units) for any given attribute depends on the physical magnitude of the stimuli involved.   As a general rule, the greater the magnitude of the stimuli, the greater the size of the *DL*.   Weber's law is the most common mathematical statement of this empirical fact.   His law may be written as follows

(1)
$$\frac{\Delta r}{r} = k$$

where Δr is the increment that must be added to the standard stimulus r to be noticed a specified proportion of the time, and k is a constant called the Weber ratio.

Actually, Weber's law is only approximately true.   The most marked deviations are at the extremes of the psychological continuum.   This fact has led a number of writers to propose substitute laws.   The laws in all cases are simply alternative equations for fitting the function relating Δr to r.   For a discussion of these laws, and for further references, the reader is referred to Guilford (1954).

Fechner, using the definition of equality of intervals along with Weber's law, derived the relationship between the two psychophysical attributes. Let us follow through his derivation.

Taking Weber's law as given, and the definition of equality of *jnd*'s, we can write immediately

(2)
$$\Delta s = c\,\frac{\Delta r}{r}$$

where c is a unit-specifying constant of proportionality.   Equation 2 is Fechner's *fundamental formula*.   Since all Δs's are equal by definition, we need only to begin with the absolute limen and summate successive values to obtain the scale.   If we treat the Δ's in equation 2 as differentials and integrate, we get

(3)
$$s = c \ln r + C$$

where C is the constant of integration.   In order to solve for C, let $s = 0$. By definition, when $s = 0$, $r = r_0$, the absolute limen.   Hence,

$$0 = c \ln r_0 + C$$

and

$$C = -c \ln r_0$$

Substituting, we have

$$s = c \ln r - c \ln r_0 = c \ln \frac{r}{r_0}$$

Ordinarily, we convert from natural logarithms to common logarithms by making the appropriate changes in the constant. Doing this, we obtain

(4) $$s = K \log \frac{r}{r_0}$$

where

s = magnitude of the sensation
K = constant of proportionality
r = physical value of the stimulus
r_0 = absolute limen

Equation 4 is Fechner's measurement formula for relating the two psychophysical attributes.

The applicability of Fechner's law thus depends on two factors: the definition or assumption of equality of *jnd*'s and the validity of Weber's law for the particular attribute.* Of the two, only the second is subject to experimental test. The first is definitional in nature and thus out of reach of experimental evidence.

In general, if Weber's law is not applicable, then Fechner's law is not applicable. But the general approach can still be used. If any of the substitute laws referred to above hold for the attribute, these can be used in place of Weber's law for deriving an analogous measurement formula. More generally, if a function relating Δr to r is obtained empirically which fits none of the proposed laws, we saw that the empirical function can be used directly in constructing a curve relating the two continua.

9. EVALUATION

Two points should be emphasized. First, it is apparent that, as far as the general approach is concerned, it is not necessary to have previously measured the stimuli on a continuum which is monotonically related to the

---

* We could conceivably accept Fechner's law even though Weber's law were shown to be inapplicable. In such case we would simply consider equation 4 to be the definition of the psychological magnitude. From the standpoint of the derivation, the law could be valid only if the departure of Weber's law from the empirically true state of affairs was exactly balanced by a departure of the assumption of equality of *jnd*'s from the "true" state of affairs. See Thurstone (1927c) for a discussion of the two laws in terms of his scaling theories.

attribute being scaled. While the psychophysical methods in their usual form require such a continuum, it is not necessary in the general case. We saw that scales based on the notion of equality of equally often noticed differences can be and have been constructed for attributes having no known physical correlate. The same procedures used in the construction of these scales could, of course, be applied as well to those attributes that do have physical correlates, although the experimental labor would thereby be increased considerably.

Second, it is apparent that, regardless of whether the scale is expressed as a psychophysical magnitude function or simply in terms of the scale values of a series of standard stimuli, the numbers assigned to the stimuli are determined at least theoretically to within a linear transformation. Given a set of procedures for obtaining a just noticeable difference, and the definition of equality of just noticeable differences, the numbers assigned to the stimuli are determined to within the transformation $y = ax + b$. If, in addition, the absolute limen is specified as the origin, then the transformation becomes $y = ax$, and we could hold that ratio properties can be attributed to the scale.

Theoretically, any two experimenters who, having agreed on a method for obtaining *jnd*'s, on the psychological equality of *jnd*'s, and on the absolute limen as the natural origin, set out independently to scale a given attribute would obtain scales that are related by the equation $y = ax$.

It is important to note, however, that the interval or ratio properties are obtained by definition and not by experimentation. Furthermore, these properties are largely beyond direct experimentation. Given the definition, there are few experimental tests that are directly relevant in testing the "validity" of the scale. We are limited pretty much to the determination of whether or not a specific set of procedures determines a *jnd* uniquely and just how specific our definitions need be. Is the scale form invariant with time? Is it independent of the particular proportion chosen as defining the *jnd*? Is it independent of variations in instructions to the subject, of different methods of presenting the stimuli, of different experimental procedures for gathering the data? Such questions, which surprisingly enough remain largely unanswered, are of considerable importance. If the scale form is not invariant over these variations in procedure (i.e., if scales constructed using different variations in procedure are not linearly related), we find ourselves in the position of having not a *jnd* scale of a particular attribute, but as many *jnd* scales of that attribute as there are variations in procedure for determining a *jnd*. If, on the other hand, the scale form is invariant with respect to a wide number of variations in procedure of obtaining *jnd*'s, this fact alone would impart a certain amount of scientific respectability to the scale.

It should be noted that we are not concerned here with the variations in *size* of *jnd*'s obtained under different instructions, experimental methods, or analytical procedures.   Whether one procedure yields large *jnd*'s and another small ones has no bearing on the problem of determining whether or not the scales developed from the procedures are linearly related.   Nor are we concerned here with experiments designed to test whether the interval between two stimuli *N jnd*'s apart will be judged to be equal to the interval

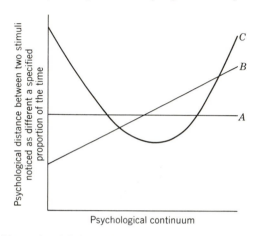

Figure 6.   Alternative definition functions relating proportions to distances.

between two other stimuli an equal number of *jnd*'s apart.   Such experiments are interesting and important but are not to be considered as tests of whether or not a *jnd* scale is an interval or ratio scale.   They are best interpreted as adding to (or subtracting from) the theoretical import of the scale, or the constitutive meaning of equality of intervals rather than testing the "validity" of the definition.

Since the interval properties are obtained by definition or stipulation, it might be well to consider the definition in somewhat more detail.   Consider Figure 6.   The definition upon which the scaling procedures discussed in this chapter is based implies that the proportion of times that a difference between two stimuli is noticed depends only on the magnitude of the psychological distance between them, and is thus invariant with respect to the order of magnitude of the stimuli themselves.   Curve *A* corresponds to this situation.   It should be noted, however, that we could equally well have defined the continuum so that any other function were true: e.g., curves *B* and *C*.   Curve *B* corresponds to an alternative definition stipulating that the scale is to be such that the psychological size of the *jnd* is a linear-increasing function of the psychological magnitude of the stimulus.

If curve *C* were chosen as the defining relation, *jnd*'s would be large at low and high magnitudes of the psychological attribute and small for medium values. The definition actually used specifies that, of the infinitely large number of possible curves, curve *A* is to be taken as the function relating the size of a *jnd* to the magnitude of the stimuli involved. It has a certain amount of pragmatic justification in that it is the simplest possible curve that could be used.

One further point should be noted. An additional implication of the definition "equally often noticed differences are equal" is that statements like the following should hold true:

If $$P_{c>b} = 0.75$$

and $$P_{b>a} > 0.50$$

then $$P_{c>a} > 0.75$$

That is, given three points arranged as indicated below,

$$a \quad b \qquad\qquad c$$

if the distance *bc* is one *jnd* ($P_{c>b} = 0.75$) and *b* is greater than *a* ($P_{b>a} > 0.50$), then the distance *ac* must be greater than one *jnd* ($P_{c>a} > 0.75$). If this condition is not satisfied, we may have a situation where several stimuli are one *jnd* less than a given stimulus, and yet these several stimuli do not have equal values on the continuum, a state of affairs clearly incompatible with the requirements of an interval scale.

There is perhaps small danger that this condition will not be met when the stimulus series is pure (that is, when the stimuli differ from one another only with respect to the attribute being scaled) or, when, if any irrelevant differences do occur, they are under experimental control. In the sensory domain, where control of the stimulus series is maximal, the problems arising from variations in the stimuli on irrelevant attributes can usually be solved. Even here, a certain amount of experimental ingenuity is often called for, however. For example, in the process of determining a *jnd* for lifted weights, we would want to determine the proportion of times one weight is judged heavier than another. We would take precautions to insure as far as possible that the two weights were indistinguishable except for the attribute of interest. For, if some weights were large and others small, or if some were made of wood and others steel, we would more or less expect to run into trouble. Even when the two weights seem indistinguishable, however, other less obvious attributes remain, some of which cannot be eliminated entirely and thus must be controlled experimentally. If two otherwise identical weights are placed before a subject, we might note that they differ with respect to *spatial position*.   And the well-known *space error* refers to the fact that, for some subjects, spatial position is a factor entering into the size of the obtained proportion.   We might eliminate this factor by blindfolding the subject and placing the weights on a turntable which is rotated so that both weights are lifted from the same position.   Now, however, a further factor becomes apparent: One of the two weights will be lifted before the other.   The great deal of work on the *time error* attests to the fact that this too is a factor which can enter into the size of the obtained proportion.   This factor cannot easily be eliminated, but it can be controlled experimentally by counterbalancing procedures: i.e., by insuring that each weight is lifted first as often as it is lifted second.

Elimination or control of extraneous variables is not always possible for those attributes, such as excellence of handwriting, attitude, beauty, eminence, and the like, which have no known single physical correlate. Handwriting specimens, attitude statements, and paintings each differ among themselves in a great many ways other than the relevant attributes of excellence, attitude, or beauty.   For attributes like these, it is not unreasonable to expect that the requirements of the definition underlying the methods discussed in this chapter will not always be met.   Some stimuli may be considerably more ambiguous or heterogeneous than others.   If so, it would not be unreasonable to expect several stimuli, differing from one another with respect to the attribute, all to be judged greater than a particular stimulus the same proportion of the time.

Under these circumstances, the *jnd* methods would not be appropriate, since they assume that the obtained proportions are dependent only on the psychological distance between the stimuli.   The methods discussed in the next chapters are more general in that they explicitly allow for the possibility that the stimuli will differ with respect to such factors as ambiguity or heterogeneity.

Thurstone's Judgment Scaling Model

1. INTRODUCTION

In Chapter 7, we saw that the approach of Fullerton and Cattell (1892) leads to the translation of the original notion of equality on the psychological continuum of "just noticeable differences" to the notion of equality on this continuum of "equally often noticed differences." Thorndike (1910) later applied this principle to the scaling of handwriting samples with respect to excellence, a psychological attribute for which there is no simple physical correlate. Lack of a physical correlate presented a new problem. If stimulus A is judged better than stimulus B 75 per cent of the time, and stimulus B is judged better than stimulus C 85 per cent of the time, how much greater than the distance AB is the distance BC? Thorndike solved this problem by assuming that the difference in distances is proportional to the difference in the *unit normal deviates* corresponding to the two proportions. The general notion "Equally often noticed differences are equal" is thus transformed to the notion that the psychological distance between stimuli is proportional to the normal deviate transform of the proportion of times the (directed) difference is noticed.

The next step was taken by Thurstone (1927a, 1927d). In 1927 he presented a mathematical model for relating scale values of a set of stimuli to observable proportions. In his model, the assumptions made by Thorndike are no longer necessarily true. They are rather deductions from a special case of the model, and the particular special case may or

155

may not fit a given set of data adequately. Thus the original *definition* of equality of *jnd*'s has been gradually transformed into a mathematical model where the notion itself becomes subject to empirical test.

This and the next two chapters deal almost entirely with Thurstone's basic mathematical model for judgment data. In the present chapter, we shall consider the model itself. In Chapter 9 we deal with its application to observations in the form of comparative judgments. Chapter 10 continues with a discussion of its application to categorical-judgment data. Some of the same notions are involved in the multidimensional extensions of the judgment approach to scaling discussed in Chapter 11.

2. THURSTONE'S JUDGMENT SCALING MODEL

The basic model underlying the Thurstone scaling methods is essentially as follows (see Thurstone, 1927*a*):

We take as given a series of stimuli to which the subject can respond differentially with respect to some given attribute. Our task is to locate these stimuli on a psychological continuum in such a way that we can account for the responses given by the observer. The psychological continuum can be considered to be a continuum of subjective or psychological magnitudes. In Thurstone's terminology, each psychological magnitude is mediated by a "discriminal process." Each discriminal process thus has a value on the psychological continuum. Thurstone defined the discriminal process as "that process by which the organism identifies, distinguishes, or reacts to stimuli." It should be noted immediately that the definition implies nothing about either the physiological or the experiential nature of the process. Its introduction does little more than to enable us to get around using the term "sensation." The latter term means too much to too many people for the purposes of the present model.

Each stimulus when presented to an observer gives rise to a discriminal process. Because of momentary fluctuations in the organism, a given stimulus does not always excite the same discriminal process, but may excite one with a higher or lower value on the psychological continuum. As a result, instead of a single discriminal process always associated with a given stimulus, we have a number of discriminal processes which may be associated with it. If we present the stimulus to the observer a large number of times, we can think of a frequency distribution on the psychological continuum of discriminal processes associated with that stimulus. The postulate is made that the frequencies with which discriminal processes are associated with any given stimulus form a normal distribution on the psychological continuum. This can always be done with a single stimulus, of course. However, once having defined the scale in this manner, it becomes a matter of experimental fact whether or not the remaining stimuli also project normal distributions on the psychological continuum.

The discriminal process most often associated with a given stimulus is defined as the *modal discriminal process*. The scale value of the stimulus on the psychological continuum is taken as the value of its modal discriminal process. Since in a normal distribution the mode, median, and mean coincide, the scale value of the stimulus can also be considered as value of the mean or median discriminal process associated with it.

The standard deviation of the distribution associated with a given stimulus is called the *discriminal disperson* of that stimulus. The discriminal dispersions, as well as the scale values, may be different for different stimuli.

The model thus postulates a psychological continuum upon which the values of the discriminal processes associated with each stimulus form a normal distribution. Figure 1 gives an illustration of such a continuum

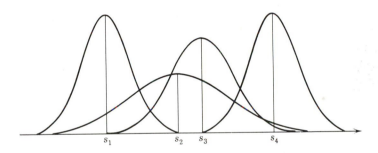

Figure 1. Distributions on the psychological continuum of discriminal processes associated with four stimuli.

along with the distributions associated with four stimuli: 1, 2, 3, and 4. The scale value of each stimulus is defined as the value of the modal discriminal process associated with it. Thus, the scale value of stimulus 1 is s_1, of stimulus 2 is s_2, etc. Each stimulus is also characterized by its discriminal dispersion. The discriminal dispersions of different stimuli are not necessarily all equal.

The observer cannot report directly the value of the discriminal process on the psychological continuum. Hence, we cannot obtain directly from the observer the frequency distribution associated with a stimulus. Scaling the stimuli must always be done indirectly.

We can, however, deduce equations relating judgments of *relations among stimuli* (which the observer can make) to the scale values and dispersions of the stimuli on the psychological continuum.   We can then use these equations to estimate the scale values and dispersions of the stimuli. Finally, we can test the model by determining the goodness of fit of the theory to the observed data.   One of these sets of equations is known as the *law of comparative judgment*.   The law of comparative judgment, which is discussed in detail in Chapter 9, is concerned with paired-comparisons judgments, that is, with judgments of the form "stimulus *A* is *X*'er than stimulus *B*."   A similar set of equations, which will here be called the *law of categorical judgment*, is concerned with judgments that require the observer to place (rate or sort) the stimuli into a number of ordered categories.   It is discussed in Chapter 10.

The Law
of Comparative Judgment

1. DERIVATION OF THE LAW OF COMPARATIVE JUDGMENT

The law of comparative judgment is a set of equations relating the proportion of times any given stimulus k is judged greater on a given attribute than any other stimulus j to the scale values and discriminal dispersions of the two stimuli on the psychological continuum. The set of equations is derived from the postulates presented in the preceding chapter. In brief, these postulates are:

1. Each stimulus when presented to an observer gives rise to a discriminal process which has some value on the psychological continuum of interest.

2. Because of momentary fluctuations in the organism, a given stimulus does not always excite the same discriminal process, but may excite one with a higher or lower value on the continuum. If any stimulus is presented to an observer a large number of times, a frequency distribution of discriminal processes associated with that stimulus will be generated. It is postulated that the values of the discriminal processes are such that the frequency distribution is normal on the psychological continuum. Each stimulus thus has associated with it a normal distribution of discriminal processes.

3. The mean and standard deviation of the distribution associated with

159

a stimulus are taken as its scale value and discriminal dispersion, respectively.

Consider the theoretical distributions of discriminal processes for any two stimuli j and k as shown in Figure 1. Let s_j and s_k correspond to the

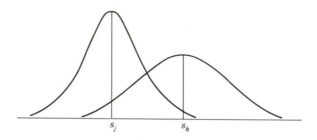

Figure 1.   Distributions of discriminal processes associated with stimuli j and k on the psychological continuum.

scale values of the two stimuli and σ_j and σ_k to their discriminal dispersions. If the two stimuli were presented together to the observer, each would excite a discriminal process: d_j and d_k. The difference in discriminal processes $(d_k - d_j)$ for any single presentation of the pair of stimuli is called a *discriminal difference*. If the two stimuli were presented together a large number of times, the discriminal differences themselves would form a normal distribution on the psychological continuum. The mean of this distribution is equal to the difference in scale values of the two stimuli, since the difference between means is equal to the mean of differences. In like manner, from the well-known formula for the standard deviation of differences, we know that

$$(1) \qquad \sigma_{d_k-d_j} = (\sigma_j^2 + \sigma_k^2 - 2r_{jk}\sigma_j\sigma_k)^{1/2}$$

where r_{jk} is the correlation between momentary values of discriminal processes associated with stimuli j and k.

Each time the two stimuli are presented to the observer, he is required to judge which is higher on the psychological continuum (e.g., which is *louder, heavier,* or *more beautiful*). It is assumed that the judgment "stimulus k is greater than stimulus j" occurs whenever the discriminal process for stimulus k is greater than that for stimulus j, that is, whenever the discriminal difference $(d_k - d_j)$ is positive. Whenever this discriminal difference is negative, the judgment "stimulus j is greater than stimulus k" will be obtained. When the two distributions overlap, as in Figure 1, it is possible for the discriminal difference to be negative for any particular trial even though the scale value s_k is greater than s_j. From a large number of judgments, the proportion of times stimulus k is judged greater than stimulus j can be determined.

The distribution of discriminal differences on the psychological continuum is illustrated in Figure 2. The shaded portion to the right of the

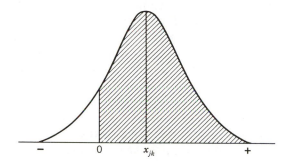

Figure 2. The distribution of discriminal differences on the psychological continuum. The shaded portion to the right of the zero point gives the proportion of times stimulus k was judged greater than stimulus j. The quantity x_{jk} is the difference in scale values measured in $\sigma_{d_k - d_j}$ units.

zero point corresponds to the proportion of times $(d_k - d_j)$ is positive, and hence, the proportion of times stimulus k is judged greater than stimulus j. The unshaded part to the left of the zero corresponds to the proportion of times $(d_k - d_j)$ is negative, or the proportion of times stimulus j is judged greater than stimulus k. The mean of the distribution is equal to the difference in scale values of the two stimuli $(s_k - s_j)$. From the theoretical proportion of times stimulus k is judged greater than stimulus j we can determine the difference $(s_k - s_j)$ from a table of areas under the unit normal curve. This difference is called x_{jk} and is measured in $\sigma_{d_k - d_j}$ units. We can thus write the equation:

$$(2) \qquad s_k - s_j = x_{jk}\sigma_{d_k - d_j}$$

Since we know the relation between the standard deviation of the differences and the discriminal dispersions of the two stimuli (equation 1), we can write

$$(3) \qquad s_k - s_j = x_{jk}(\sigma_j^2 + \sigma_k^2 - 2r_{jk}\sigma_j\sigma_k)^{1/2}$$

Equation 3 is the complete form of the law of comparative judgment, where

s_j, s_k denote the scale values of stimuli j and k.

σ_j, σ_k denote the discriminal dispersions of stimuli j and k.

r_{jk} is the correlation between the pairs of discriminal processes d_j and d_k.

x_{jk} is the normal deviate corresponding to the theoretical proportion of times stimulus k is judged greater than stimulus j.

The law of comparative judgment is not solvable in its complete form, since, regardless of the number of stimuli, there are always more unknowns than observation equations. For example, with n stimuli, there are n scale values, n discriminal dispersions, and $n(n-1)/2$ independent correlations which are unknown. The zero point of the scale can be set arbitrarily at the scale value of one stimulus, and the unit can be taken as one of the discriminal dispersions, leaving $2(n-1) + n(n-1)/2$ unknowns. Against this we have only $n(n-1)/2$ observation equations—one for each independently observable proportion. The number of equations is always $2(n-1)$ less than the number of unknowns. Simplifying hypotheses are thus necessary in order to make the law workable.

Thurstone (1927a) presented five cases of the law of comparative judgment. His *case I* referred to the complete form of the law as developed above. His *case II* referred to a parallel law obtainable by substitution of replication over individuals for replication over trials within a single individual. His *cases III, IV,* and *V* denoted three special sets of equations obtained from various simplifying assumptions. Since we are really dealing here with two kinds of variation rather than one, we shall abandon Thurstone's classification in favor of a two-way classification of our own. We shall, however, indicate where Thurstone's last three cases fit into the classification we use.

We shall use the term "class" to denote the kind of replication involved, and the term "condition" to denote particular sets of simplifying assumptions. Any condition might be paired with any class.

Three different classes have been used:

Class I: Models involving replication over trials within a single individual. The derivation given above is appropriate for this class.

Class II: Models involving replication over individuals, each pair of stimuli being compared once by each individual. The theoretical development of these models differs from those of class I in that an assumption that the discriminal processes associated with any given stimulus for a large number of individuals form a normal distribution on the psychological continuum is substituted for the corresponding assumption regarding the distribution obtained by replication over trials within a single individual. The resulting sets of equations are formally identical with those of the class I models.

Class III: Models involving replication over both individuals and trials. Each pair of stimuli is compared several times by each of several individuals. These mixed models would seem to involve an assumption that individuals and trials within individuals are interchangeable. Note that the class II models do not necessarily involve this assumption. Class II models can be appropriate even though some individuals are consistently better discriminators than others.

Simplifying Conditions

In order to arrive at a workable set of equations, i.e., one for which a large enough set of stimuli will give more observational equations than unknowns, it is necessary to specify additional restrictions. We shall consider three conditions which lead to solutions equivalent to Thurstone's cases III, IV, and V. Others, both more and less restrictive, are possible, of course.

Condition A. It is assumed that the covariance term in the complete law of comparative judgment (equation 3) is constant for all pairs of stimuli. With this assumption, equation 3 reduces to

$$(4) \qquad s_k - s_j = x_{jk}(a_j^2 + a_k^2)^{1/2}$$

where
$$a_j^2 \equiv \sigma_j^2 - c$$

and
$$a_k^2 \equiv \sigma_k^2 - c$$

Equation 4 is formally identical with the equation of Thurstone's case III, though the assumption of equal covariances is slightly less restricting than Thurstone's assumption of zero correlations between all pairs of stimuli. This would seem to be of academic interest only, however, since the only reasonable way in which the covariance would become constant even though the dispersions vary would be for the correlation term to vanish.

No practical solution has yet been devised for equation 4. It is solvable in theory, however. With n stimuli, there are n scale values and n values of a which are unknown. We can set the zero point of the scale at one scale value and use one value of a as the unit of measurement, leaving $2(n-1)$ unknowns. We have $n(n-1)/2$ observation equations, so, whenever $n(n-1)/2 \geq 2(n-1)$, a solution is possible. With four stimuli, the number of unknowns is equal to the number of observation equations and an exact solution may be possible:

Equations	Unknowns
$s_2 - s_1 = x_{21}(a_2^2 + a_1^2)^{1/2}$	Set the zero point of the
$s_3 - s_1 = x_{31}(a_3^2 + a_1^2)^{1/2}$	scale at s_1, and let the unit
$s_4 - s_1 = x_{41}(a_4^2 + a_1^2)^{1/2}$	of the scale be a_1. This
$s_3 - s_2 = x_{32}(a_3^2 + a_2^2)^{1/2}$	leaves as unknowns:
$s_4 - s_2 = x_{42}(a_4^2 + a_2^2)^{1/2}$	$s_2 \qquad a_2$
$s_4 - s_3 = s_{43}(a_4^2 + a_3^2)^{1/2}$	$s_3 \qquad a_3$
	$s_4 \qquad a_4$

An adequate test of the condition A model would require use of more than four stimuli. With five or more stimuli, there are more observation equations than unknowns. The system is overdetermined, and we can then evaluate experimentally the goodness of fit of the model to the data. With fallible data (observed proportions in place of theoretical proportions) some efficient system of estimating the unknowns is indicated. None has been devised thus far.

Condition B. It is assumed that the correlation terms are all equal and, in addition, that the differences between discriminal dispersions are small. In this case, an approximate equation for the law is

$$(5) \qquad s_k - s_j = x_{jk}[\tfrac{1}{2}(1 - r)]^{1/2}(\sigma_k + \sigma_j)$$

Equation 5 is formally identical with the equation of Thurstone's case IV. In obtaining the equation for case IV, however, Thurstone assumed zero correlations between pairs of stimuli. Since our equation is formally identical to his, his explicit assumption was unnecessarily restricting. One needs only to assume that the correlations are all equal.

Equation 5 was obtained in the following manner: Let

$$(6) \qquad \sigma_k - \sigma_j = d$$

where d is small compared with σ_j.

Substituting $(\sigma_j + d)$ for σ_k and the constant r for r_{jk} in equation 3 gives

$$(7) \qquad s_k - s_j = x_{jk}[\sigma_j^2 + (\sigma_j + d)^2 - 2r\sigma_j(\sigma_j + d)]^{1/2}$$

Expanding, and dropping the d^2 term, we get

$$(8) \qquad s_k - s_j = x_{jk}(2\sigma^2 - 2r\sigma_j^2 + 2d\sigma_j - 2rd\sigma_j)^{1/2}$$
$$= x_{jk}[2\sigma_j(1 - r)]^{1/2}(\sigma_j + d)^{1/2}$$

Expanding the quantity $(\sigma_j + d)^{1/2}$ and dropping the third term, we have

$$(9) \qquad (\sigma_j + d)^{1/2} = \sqrt{\sigma_j} + \frac{d}{2\sqrt{\sigma_j}} \cdots$$

Substitution in the preceding equation gives

$$(10) \qquad s_k - s_j = x_{jk}[2\sigma_j(1 - r)]^{1/2}\left[\sqrt{\sigma_j} + \frac{d}{2\sqrt{\sigma_j}}\right]$$
$$= x_{jk}\sigma_j[2(1 - r)]^{1/2} + \tfrac{1}{2}x_{jk}d[2(1 - r)]^{1/2}$$

Since $\sigma_k - \sigma_j = d$, we can write

$$s_k - s_j = x_{jk}[2(1 - r)]^{1/2}[\sigma_j + \tfrac{1}{2}(\sigma_k - \sigma_j)]$$

and, finally,

$$(11) \qquad s_k - s_j = x_{jk}[\tfrac{1}{2}(1 - r)]^{1/2}(\sigma_j + \sigma_k)$$

It is interesting to note that equation 11 is an exact expression for the general law if the correlation term is equal to minus one. That is, if we let $r_{jk} = -1$ in the general equation 3, we have

$$(12) \qquad s_k - s_j = x_{jk}[\sigma_k^2 + \sigma_j^2 - 2\sigma_j\sigma_k(-1)]^{1/2}$$

and

$$s_k - s_j = x_{jk}(\sigma_j + \sigma_k)$$

The only difference between equation 5 and equation 12 is in the factor $[\tfrac{1}{2}(1 - r)]^{1/2}$. Since this is a constant multiplying factor, and since the unit is arbitrary anyway, for all practical purposes the two equations are identical.

Condition C. It is assumed that the standard deviation of the distribution of discriminal differences is constant for all pairs of stimuli. If we denote this constant standard deviation by c, equation 3 reduces to

$$(13) \qquad s_k - s_j = cx_{jk}$$

Equation 13 is formally identical with Thurstone's case V. Thurstone's original equation was obtained by assuming zero correlations and equal discriminal dispersions. If we let $\sigma_j = \sigma_k = \sigma$ and $r = 0$, then equation 3 would reduce to

$$(14) \qquad s_k - s_j = x_{jk}\sigma\sqrt{2}$$

which is the equation of Thurstone's case V. Later, Mosteller (1951*a*) and, in connection with a somewhat different problem, Guttman (1946*b*) obtained equivalent equations by assuming equal discriminal dispersions and equal correlations. With this assumption and letting $\sigma_j = \sigma_k = \sigma$ and $r_{jk} = r$, equation 3 becomes

$$(15) \qquad s_k - s_j = x_{jk}\sigma[2(1 - r)]^{1/2}$$

Equations 13, 14, and 15 differ from one another only with respect to the multiplying constant. In each case, we can specify the unit of measurement so that the multiplying constant is equal to unity. Since the unit of measurement must be specified arbitrarily, the three equations are actually indistinguishable.

Summary

The nine versions of the law of comparative judgment resulting from the pairing of each *class* with each *condition* are given in Table 1. The first

Table 1. A Two-Way Classification of Special Cases of
the Law of Comparative Judgment

	Condition A (Assume constant covariance)	Condition B (Assume equal correlations, small differences in dispersions)	Condition C (Assume constant variance of distributions of discriminal differences)
Class I (within individual)	$\begin{aligned} s_k - s_j \\ = x_{jk}(a_j^2 + a_k^2)^{1/2} \end{aligned}$	$\begin{aligned} s_k - s_j \\ = x_{jk}[\tfrac{1}{2}(1-r)]^{1/2}(\sigma_j + \sigma_k) \end{aligned}$	$s_k - s_j = cx_{jk}$
Class II (between individuals)	$\begin{aligned} s_k - s_j \\ = x_{jk}(a_j^2 + a_k^2)^{1/2} \end{aligned}$	$\begin{aligned} s_k - s_j \\ = x_{jk}[\tfrac{1}{2}(1-r)]^{1/2}(\sigma_j + \sigma_k) \end{aligned}$	$s_k - s_j = cx_{jk}$
Class III (mixed)	$\begin{aligned} s_k - s_j \\ = x_{jk}(a_j^2 + a_k^2)^{1/2} \end{aligned}$	$\begin{aligned} s_k - s_j \\ = x_{jk}[\tfrac{1}{2}(1-r)]^{1/2}(\sigma_j + \sigma_k) \end{aligned}$	$s_k - s_j = cx_{jk}$

column of this table is of little practical importance at the present time
since workable analytical procedures for condition A are not yet available.
While the equations in any column are algebraically identical, it should be
kept in mind that the interpretation of the terms of the equations differs
according to the row.

The *experimental* procedures used in the collection of data depend on
the class variable. These procedures are discussed in the next section.
The *analytical* procedures used depend on the condition. Analytical
procedures for condition C are discussed in section 4, and for condition B
in section 5.

2. EXPERIMENTAL PROCEDURES: THE METHOD OF
PAIRED COMPARISONS

All forms of the law of comparative judgment assume that each stimulus
has been compared with each other stimulus a large number of times.
The law requires that data of the form "the proportion of times any
stimulus k is judged greater than any other stimulus j" are available. The
direct method for obtaining empirical estimates of these proportions is
known as the *method of paired comparisons.*

The method of paired comparisons is essentially a generalization of the
two-category case of the method of constant stimuli. In the method of
constant stimuli, each stimulus is compared with a single standard. In

paired comparisons, each stimulus serves in turn as the standard. Each stimulus is paired with each other stimulus. With n stimuli, there are thus $n(n-1)/2$ pairs. Each pair is presented to the subject, whose task is to indicate which member of the pair appears greater (*heavier, brighter, louder*) with respect to the attribute to be scaled. The subject must designate one of the pair as greater. No equality judgments are allowed. This is consistent with the derivation of the law, wherein the probability of a zero discriminal difference is vanishingly small.

In order to obtain data from which the proportions may be estimated, it is necessary for a large number of comparisons to be made of each pair of stimuli. We have seen that the necessary replication might be obtained by (1) having a single subject judge each pair a large number of times (class I models), (2) many subjects each judge each pair once (class II models), or (3) several subjects each judge each pair several times (class III models). The choice will depend on (*a*) the purpose of the experiment, (*b*) the extent of individual differences, and (*c*) the nature of the stimuli. If the experimenter is interested in obtaining the scale of a single individual, or in comparing scales between individuals, then the first alternative must be used. If individual differences are known or can be assumed to be negligible, any of the three alternatives may be used, whichever is the most convenient. If interest is in the "average" scale for a population, then the second alternative should be used, where the subjects are an appropriate sample from that population. In order to use either the first or third alternative, however, the stimuli should be such that no extraneous differentiating cues are available to the subject. If the subject can identify the stimulus pairs, there is the possibility that he will base his later judgments on his memory of his earlier judgments of the pair.

In the usual form of the method of paired comparisons, a stimulus is not compared with itself (or with an identical stimulus). It is assumed that, if such judgments were obtained, proportions of 0.50 would result. It is important to note, however, that there is nothing in the law or in the method itself that prohibits such judgments. With certain kinds of stimuli it may well be that the experimenter will wish to check this assumption experimentally. Other types of stimuli, however, do not lend themselves to experimental verification of the assumption. While it is reasonable to present a subject with two identical sounds and ask him which is the louder, a question such as "Which do you prefer, beef roast or beef roast?" is unreasonable.

No explicit provision is made for time or space errors in the law of comparative judgment. Nor is there provision for changes in performance due to fatigue or practice effects, or for judgments based in part on factors other than the relative magnitudes of the discriminal processes.

Consequently it is necessary to control experimentally the conditions that might introduce these biasing effects. Most of these factors can be controlled in the assignment of the relative positions (spatial or temporal) of the members of each stimulus pair and the order of presentation of the pairs themselves. Control by randomization of relative positions and of orders, though probably not the most efficient method, would seem to be adequate for many problems. More efficient methods use counterbalancing procedures. For example, time (or space) errors can be controlled by arranging the members of the pairs so that half the time each stimulus appears first (or to the right, above, etc.) and half the time second (to the left, below, etc.). Perhaps the best procedure is to counterbalance *each* pair of stimuli: e.g., with stimulus pair *j*, *k*, present *j* first half of the time, *k* first half of the time. Practice or fatigue effects can be controlled by reversing the order of presentation of the pairs for half of the subjects (or trials).

Additional precautions, some of which may or may not be relevant for any given experiment are:

1. Keeping pairs having one stimulus in common maximally separated in the order of presentation.

2. Arranging pairs so that "correct" responses are approximately evenly divided between first and second members of the pairs.

3. Arranging pairs so that there is no detectable systematic pattern of "correct" responses.

4. Arranging pairs so that there is no systematic variation in difficulty of judgment.

5. Varying the order of presentation from trial to trial to eliminate serial learning of a response pattern.

The reader is referred to Ross (1934) and Wherry (1938) for further discussion of this problem. Ross gives "optimal" orders for stimulus pairs for from five to seventeen stimuli as well as his general method for calculating orders of presentation. His orders are optimal in the sense that (*a*) each stimulus appears first in half the pairs of which it is a member, (*b*) pairs having one stimulus in common are maximally separated in the order of presentation, and (*c*) there is no detectable pattern of "correct" responses. Wherry discusses the problem of fatigue effects and their elimination through use of variants of a given list.

3. THE THREE BASIC MATRICES: F, P, AND X

After each of the $n(n-1)/2$ pairs of stimuli have been presented a large number of times, we have as raw data the number of times each stimulus was judged greater than each other stimulus.   These observed frequencies may be arranged in the $n \times n$ square matrix **F**.   Such a matrix is shown in Table 2.   The general element f'_{jk}, which appears at the intersection of the jth row and kth column, denotes the observed number of times stimulus k was judged greater than stimulus j.   (In this and the following sections, an unadorned lower case symbol denotes the *theoretical* value, the same symbol with a prime denotes the corresponding *sample estimate*, and, with a double prime, the corresponding *derived value*.)   The diagonal cells of matrix **F** will ordinarily be left vacant.   Since the symmetric cells (e.g., f'_{23} and f'_{32}) sum to the total number of judgments of the pair made, the matrix contains $n(n-1)/2$ independent cells.

Matrix **P** is constructed from matrix **F**.   The element p'_{jk} is the observed proportion of times stimulus k was judged greater than stimulus j. Diagonal cells are again left vacant ordinarily.   Symmetric cells now sum to unity (e.g., $p'_{23} + p'_{32} = 1$).

Table 2. THE RAW FREQUENCY MATRIX **F**

Stimuli $(k = 1, 2, \cdots, n)$

		1	2	$\cdots\cdots$	k	$\cdots$	n
	1	—	f'_{12}	$\cdots\cdots$	f'_{1k}	$\cdots$	f'_{1n}
	2	f'_{21}	—	$\cdots\cdots$	f'_{2k}	$\cdots$	f'_{2n}
	.	.	.		.		.
Stimuli	.	.	.		.		.
$(j = 1, 2, \cdots, n)$	j	f'_{j1}	f'_{j2}	$\cdots\cdots$	f'_{jk}	$\cdots$	f'_{jn}
	.	.	.		.		.
	.	.	.		.		.
	.	.	.		.		.
	n	f'_{n1}	f'_{n2}	$\cdots\cdots$	f'_{nk}	$\cdots$	—

From matrix **P** is constructed in turn matrix **X**, the basic transformation matrix.   The element x'_{jk} is the *unit normal deviate corresponding to the element* p'_{jk}, and may be obtained by referring to a table of areas under the unit normal curve.   The element x'_{jk} will be positive for all values of p'_{jk} over 0.50, and negative for all values of p'_{jk} under 0.50.   Proportions of 1.00 and 0.00 cannot be used since the x values corresponding to these proportions are unboundedly large.   When such proportions occur, the corresponding cells in matrix **X** are left vacant.   Zeros are entered in the diagonal cells since we can ordinarily assume that here $s_k - s_j = 0$.   The matrix is skew-symmetric: that is, the symmetric elements sum to zero, since, e.g., $x'_{23} = -x'_{32}$.

Matrix $\mathbf{X}$ contains the sample estimates x'_{jk} of the theoretical values found in the equation of the law of comparative judgment. The element x'_{jk} is an estimate of the difference $(s_k - s_j)$ between scale values of the two stimuli measured in units of the standard deviation of the distribution of discriminal differences $\sigma_{d_k - d_j}$. Each independent element of matrix $\mathbf{X}$ is an estimate of a value for one equation of the law. However, since the elements are observed quantities, each will be somewhat in error. Analytical procedures have been devised which tend to allow the errors to cancel one another and thus give reasonably good estimates of the unknowns. In the discussion of analytical procedures to which we now turn, it will be assumed that the raw data has been transformed into matrix $\mathbf{X}$.

4. ANALYTICAL PROCEDURES FOR CONDITION C

The Least-Squares Solution, Applicable to a Complete X Matrix

Mosteller (1951a) and Horst (1941) have shown that the usual procedure for obtaining estimates of scale values from a matrix $\mathbf{X}$ which contains no vacant cells is a least-squares solution. The derivation given below, in general, follows Mosteller's original treatment, although it does differ somewhat.

The set of equations of condition C is given by

$$(16) \qquad s_k - s_j = cx_{jk} \qquad (j, k = 1, 2, \cdots, n)$$

where s_j, s_k denote the scale values of stimuli j and k, respectively.

$\qquad x_{jk}$ is the unit normal deviate corresponding to the theoretical proportion of times stimulus k is judged greater than stimulus j.

$\qquad c$ denotes the constant standard deviation of the distribution of discriminal differences.

With fallible data, we have the x'_{jk} as estimates of the true x_{jk}, and equation 16 no longer holds exactly for all pairs of stimuli. We want to use the observed values x'_{jk} to solve for a set of estimates s'_j, s'_k of the true scale values s_j, s_k.

First let us specify the unit of measurement of the scale values. We shall let the unit be such that the constant c in equation 16 is equal to unity. Equation 16 then simplifies to

$$(17) \qquad s_k - s_j = x_{jk} \qquad (j, k = 1, 2, \cdots, n)$$

Let x''_{jk} denote the difference between pairs of estimates of scale values:

$$(18) \qquad x''_{jk} \equiv s'_k - s'_j \qquad (j, k = 1, 2, \cdots, n)$$

With errorless data, the derived x''_{jk} will equal the corresponding observed x'_{jk}. With fallible data, they will be somewhat different. Our task is to solve for the set of estimates of the scale values of the stimuli for which the sum of squares of these discrepancies is a minimum, i.e., which minimizes the quantity

$$(19) \qquad Q = \sum_{j=1}^{n} \sum_{k=1}^{n} (x'_{jk} - x''_{jk})^2$$

Since $x''_{jk} = s'_k - s'_j$, we can write

$$(20) \qquad Q = \sum_{j=1}^{n} \sum_{k=1}^{n} (x'_{jk} - s'_k + s'_j)^2$$

To minimize Q, we take the partial derivative of Q with respect to each s'. Note that a particular value of s' (say s'_2) appears only in the second row and second column of the matrix of squared errors (Table 3). Further,

Table 3. THE MATRIX OF SQUARED ERRORS

Stimuli k

		1	2	$\cdots$	k	$\cdots$	n
	1	0	$(x'_{12}-s'_2+s'_1)^2$	$\cdots$	$(x'_{1k}-s'_k+s'_1)^2$	$\cdots$	$(x'_{1n}-s'_n+s'_1)^2$
	2	$(x'_{21}-s'_1+s'_2)^2$	0	$\cdots$	$(x'_{2k}-s'_k+s'_2)^2$	$\cdots$	$(x'_{2n}-s'_n+s'_2)^2$
	.	.	.		.		.
Stimuli j	j	$(x'_{j1}-s'_1+s'_j)^2$	$(x'_{j2}-s'_2+s'_j)^2$	$\cdots$	$(x'_{jk}-s'_k+s'_j)^2$	$\cdots$	$(x'_{jn}-s'_n+s'_j)^2$
	.	.	.		.		.
	n	$(x'_{n1}-s'_1+s'_n)^2$	$(x'_{n2}-s'_2+s'_n)^2$	$\cdots$	$(x'_{nk}-s'_k+s'_n)^2$	$\cdots$	0

since $x'_{jk} = -x'_{kj}$ and $(s'_k - s'_j) = -(s'_j - s'_k)$, we need only be concerned with the columns. Differentiating the elements of each column with respect to s'_k, we get

$$(21) \qquad \frac{\partial Q}{\partial s'_k} = -2 \sum_{j=1}^{n} (x'_{jk} - s'_k + s'_j) \qquad (k = 1, 2, \cdots, n)$$

Setting the partial derivative equal to zero and rearranging terms gives

$$(22) \qquad \sum_{j=1}^{n} s'_k = \sum_{j=1}^{n} x'_{jk} + \sum_{j=1}^{n} s'_j \qquad (k = 1, 2, \cdots, n)$$

Table 4. Illustrative Example (Errorless Data): the Least-Squares
Solution for Condition C

Matrix P

The element p'_{jk} is equal to the proportion of times stimulus
k was judged greater than stimulus j.

Stimuli k

		1	2	3	4	5	
	1	—	0.6915	0.8413	0.8943	0.9594	
	2	0.3085	—	0.6915	0.7734	0.8943	
Stimuli j	3	0.1587	0.3085	—	0.5987	0.7734	
	4	0.1057	0.2266	0.4013	—	0.6915	
	5	0.0406	0.1057	0.2266	0.3085	—	
$\sum\limits_{j}^{n} p'_{jk}$		0.6135	1.3323	2.1607	2.5749	3.3186	10.0000 $\sqrt{}$

Matrix X

The element x'_{jk} is equal to the unit normal deviate corresponding
to element p'_{jk}

Stimuli k

		1	2	3	4	5	
	1	0.00	0.50	1.00	1.25	1.75	
	2	−0.50	0.00	0.50	0.75	1.25	
Stimuli j	3	−1.00	−0.50	0.00	0.25	0.75	
	4	−1.25	−0.75	−0.25	0.00	0.50	
	5	−1.75	−1.25	−0.75	−0.50	−0.00	
$\sum\limits_{j}^{n} p'_{jk}$		−4.50	−2.00	0.50	1.75	4.25	0.00 $\sqrt{}$
$\dfrac{1}{n}\sum\limits_{j}^{n} x'_{jk} = s'_k$		−0.90	−0.40	0.10	0.35	0.85	0.00 $\sqrt{}$

Dividing by n gives

$$(23) \qquad s'_k = \frac{1}{n} \sum_{j=1}^{n} x'_{jk} + \frac{1}{n} \sum_{j=1}^{n} s'_j \qquad (k = 1, 2, \cdots, n)$$

We have not yet specified an origin for the scale. It will be convenient to set the origin at the mean of the estimated scale values, i.e., so that

$$(24) \qquad \frac{1}{n} \sum_{j=1}^{n} s'_j = 0$$

With this specification, equation 23 reduces to

$$(25) \qquad s'_k = \frac{1}{n} \sum_{j=1}^{n} x'_{jk} \qquad (k = 1, 2, \cdots, n)$$

Thus, a least-squares estimate of the scale values can be obtained simply by averaging the columns of matrix X.

The least-squares solution presented above requires that all elements in the matrix X be present. Often, however, a number of these cells will be vacant. We have seen that, whenever an observed proportion p'_{jk} is 1.00 or 0.00, the transformation to the corresponding x'_{jk} cannot be made. Ordinarily the range of the stimuli will greatly exceed their discriminal dispersions, and, as a result, observed proportions of 1.00 or 0.00 will be obtained. Alternative procedures for incomplete matrices are discussed below.

Solutions for Condition C Applicable to an Incomplete Matrix X

Several procedures are available for obtaining estimates of the scale values when, for one reason or another, the matrix X contains unfilled cells. The traditional procedure will be presented first. While it has no elegant least-squares properties, the resulting estimates are probably adequate for most purposes.

THE TRADITIONAL PROCEDURE FOR INCOMPLETE MATRICES. If the unit of measurement is specified so that c is equal to unity, it follows that the theoretical equations for stimulus k and stimulus $k+a$ can be written, respectively,

$$(26) \qquad s_k - s_j = x_{jk} \qquad (j = 1, 2, \cdots, n)$$

and

$$(27) \qquad s_{k+a} - s_j = x_{j,k+a} \qquad (j = 1, 2, \cdots, n)$$

Subtracting equation 26 from equation 27, we have

$$(28) \qquad s_{k+a} - s_k = x_{j,k+a} - x_{jk} \qquad (j = 1, 2, \cdots, n)$$

It is thus seen that, for errorless data, the difference $(x_{j,k+a} - x_{jk})$ for any value of j is equal to the difference in scale values $(s_{k+a} - s_k)$. In like manner, the corresponding differences between *observed* x values $(x'_{j,k+a} - x'_{jk})$ is an *estimate* of this difference in scale values. For any two stimuli $(k$ and $k+a)$, there will be as many such estimates as there are filled pairs of cells in the k and $(k+a)$th columns of matrix **X**. The average of the estimates is taken as the estimate of the difference $d_{k,k+a}$:

$$(29) \qquad d'_{k,k+a} = s'_{k+a} - s'_k = \frac{1}{n_k} \sum_{j=1}^{n_k} (x'_{j,k+a} - x'_{jk})$$

where $n_k = $ the number of terms summed over.

Theoretically, a in equation 29 may take any value from 1 to $n-k$. In actual practice, however, differences are obtained only for stimuli that are adjacent on the attribute being scaled. Adjacent stimuli will ordinarily have more filled cells in common and will give more reliable estimates of differences. The usual procedure when constructing the matrix **X** is to arrange its columns in rank order with respect to the attribute. The rank order of the columns is given by the rank order of the sums of the columns of matrix **P**.

Given matrix **X** with columns arranged in rank order, the differences $d'_{k,k+1}$ are obtained using equation 29. If the zero point of the scale is now located arbitrarily (say $s'_1 = 0$), the scale values for all stimuli are obtained simply by cumulating the successive differences:

$$
\begin{aligned}
s'_1 &= 0 \\
s'_2 &= d'_{12} \\
s'_3 &= s'_2 + d'_{23}
\end{aligned}
$$

(30)
$$\cdot$$
$$\cdot$$
$$\cdot$$

$$s'_n = s'_{n-1} + d'_{n-1,n}$$

The differences $d'_{k,k+1}$ may also be obtained graphically. From equation 28 it is apparent that

$$(31) \qquad x_{j,k+1} = x_{jk} + d_{k,k+1}$$

which is the equation of a straight line with unit slope. If we make the $n-1$ plots of column $k+1$ $(x'_{j,k+1})$ against column k (x'_{jk}) of matrix **X**, where $k = 1, 2, \cdot\cdot\cdot, n-1$, and then fit a straight line with unit slope to each plot, the intercept on axis $k+1$ for each plot will be an estimate of the difference $d_{k,k+1}$. The number of points in each plot will be equal to the number of filled pairs of cells in the columns involved. Given the estimates of the differences, the scale values can be estimated as before.

Table 5. Illustrative Example (Errorless Data) Traditional Condition C Solution for Incomplete Matrices X

Matrix P

The element p'_{jk} is equal to the proportion of times stimulus k was judged greater than stimulus j

		\multicolumn{5}{c}{Stimulus k}	
		1	2	3	4	5	
	1	—	1.000	0.935	1.000	0.975	
	2	0.000	—	0.000	0.160	0.025	
Stimulus j	3	0.065	1.000	—	0.935	0.690	
	4	0.000	0.840	0.065	—	0.160	
	5	0.025	0.975	0.310	0.840	—	
$\sum_{j}^{n} p'_{jk}$		0.090	3.815	1.310	2.935	1.850	10.000 $\checkmark$

Matrix X

The element x'_{jk} is equal to the unit normal deviate corresponding to element p'_{jk}. The columns of X are arranged in increasing order of $\Sigma p'_{jk}$

		\multicolumn{5}{c}{Stimulus k}	
		1	3	5	4	2	
	1	0.0	1.5	2.0	—	—	
	2	—	—	−2.0	−1.0	0.0	
Stimulus j	3	−1.5	0.0	0.5	1.5	—	
	4	—	−1.5	−1.0	0.0	1.0	
	5	−2.0	−0.5	0.0	1.0	2.0	
$\sum_{j}^{n} x'_{jk}$		−3.5	−0.5	−0.5	1.5	3.0	0.00 $\checkmark$

Table 6. ILLUSTRATIVE EXAMPLE, CONTINUED. MATRIX
OF DIFFERENCES BETWEEN COLUMNS

The elements in the jth row are equal to $(x'_{j,k+1} - x'_{jk})$.

	d'_{13}	d'_{35}	d'_{54}	d'_{42}
1	1.5	0.5	—	—
2	—	—	1.0	1.0
3	1.5	0.5	1.0	—
4	—	0.5	1.0	1.0
5	1.5	0.5	1.0	1.0
$\sum\limits^{n_k} d'_{jk,k+1}$	4.5	2.0	4.0	3.0
n_k	3	4	4	3
$\dfrac{1}{n_k}\sum\limits_{j}^{n_k} d'_{jk,k+1}$	1.5	0.5	1.0	1.0

$$s'_1 = 0$$
$$s'_3 = 0 + 1.5 = 1.5$$
$$s'_5 = 1.5 + 0.5 = 2.0$$
$$s'_4 = 2.0 + 1.0 = 3.0$$
$$s'_2 = 3.0 + 1.0 = 4.0$$

GULLIKSEN'S LEAST-SQUARES SOLUTION FOR INCOMPLETE DATA. Gulliksen's solution makes use of the general procedure for incomplete data given by Horst (1941) and others. The discussion below follows Gulliksen (1956a) closely.

When matrix **X** is incomplete, we can take the quantity to be minimized as

(32) $$Q = \sum_{j,k}^{n_{jk}} (x'_{jk} - s'_k + s'_j)^2$$

where n_{jk} is used to indicate that we sum only over the filled cells of matrix **X**. Steps parallel to those of our equations 21 and 22 give

(33) $$n_k s_k - \sum_{j}^{n_k} s_j = \sum_{j}^{n_k} x_{jk} \qquad (k = 1, 2, \cdots, n)$$

where n_k corresponds to the number of filled cells in column k.

It is convenient to use matrix algebra for the remaining steps.   We first define the following matrices:

$S \equiv n \times 1$ column vector with elements s_k

$1 \equiv n \times 1$ column vector of ones

$D \equiv n \times n$ matrix, the *transpose* of matrix X with zeros entered for missing cells (both on and off the principal diagonal)

$M \equiv n \times n$ matrix differing from matrix X in that -1 is entered in each off-diagonal cell that is filled in matrix X, 0 is entered in each off-diagonal cell that is vacant in matrix X, and n_k, the number of filled cells in column k of matrix X, is entered into the diagonal cells

$Z \equiv D1 = n \times 1$ column vector with elements equal to the sum of the columns of matrix X

Equation 33 can now be written

$$(34) \qquad\qquad\qquad MS = Z$$

Matrix M has no inverse, since we have yet to specify an origin for the scale.   Let us define the origin so that the first element of S is equal to zero.   Then we can obtain a solution for the remaining scale values by deleting the first row from Z and S, and both the first row and column from matrix M, leaving the equation

$$(35) \qquad\qquad\qquad M_1 S_1 = Z_1$$

Since M_1 will ordinarily have an inverse, the solution for the remaining scale values is given by

$$(36) \qquad\qquad\qquad S_1 = M_1^{-1} Z_1$$

The solution indicated by equation 36 involves computation of the inverse of matrix M_1.   This is ordinarily a tedious process.   As an alternative, Gulliksen has also given an iterative procedure based on the same equations.

First, let us define the two matrices N and L:

$N \equiv n \times n$ diagonal matrix with elements $1/(n_k+1)$

$L \equiv n \times n$ matrix with zeros wherever there are zeros in M and 1 in all remaining cells

Then,

$$(37) \qquad\qquad\qquad M = N^{-1} - L$$

and equation 34 becomes

$$(38) \qquad \mathbf{Z} = \mathbf{N}^{-1}\mathbf{S} - \mathbf{LS}$$

The general rationale for the iterative procedure is as follows. If $\mathbf{T}_i$ designates the ith trial vector of scale values, then the difference between the *experimental* values $\mathbf{Z}$ and those *derived* from the trial scale values $\mathbf{MT}_i$ is

$$(39) \qquad \mathbf{ME}_i = \mathbf{Z} - \mathbf{MT}_i$$

If the average discrepancy for each scale value were used to correct that scale value, then the new trial vector would be given by

$$(40) \qquad \mathbf{T}_{i+1} = \mathbf{T}_i + \mathbf{NME}_i$$

and the next by

$$(41) \qquad \mathbf{T}_{i+2} = \mathbf{T}_{i+1} + \mathbf{NME}_{i+1}$$

However, Gulliksen indicates that $\mathbf{T}_{i+2}$ can also be expressed in terms of the elements of trial i:

$$(42) \qquad \mathbf{T}_{i+2} = \mathbf{T}_i + \mathbf{N(I + LN)ME}_i$$

Hence, one iteration based on equation 42 is equivalent to two based on equation 40. Before actually applying the trial value to compute the discrepancies, however, it is first necessary to adjust the variance of the trial values to agree with that of the observed values. Let the unadjusted vector of trial values now be denoted by $\mathbf{T}_{i'}$ and the corresponding adjusted vector by $\mathbf{T}_i$. Then, if we compute

$$(43) \qquad a^2 = \frac{\mathbf{Z'Z}}{\mathbf{T}_{i'}'\mathbf{M'MT}_{i'}}$$

the relation between $\mathbf{T}_{i'}$ and $\mathbf{T}_i$ is given by

$$(44) \qquad \mathbf{T}_i = a\mathbf{T}_{i'}$$

Thus, given the trial vector $\mathbf{T}_{i'}$ (for the initial trial vector, the scale values obtained from the traditional procedure might be used), the iterative routine involves the following cycle of steps:

    1. Computing $\mathbf{MT}_{i'}$.
    2. Adjusting the vector $\mathbf{T}_{i'}$ to $\mathbf{T}_i$, using equations 43 and 44.
    3. Computing the discrepancies, using equation 39 ($\mathbf{T}_i$ in equation 39 refers to the *adjusted* vector).
    4. Computing the next (unadjusted) trial vector by

$$\mathbf{T}_{(i+1)'} = \mathbf{T}_i + \mathbf{N(I + LN)ME}_i$$

Steps 1 through 4 are repeated until the discrepancies of equation 39 become negligible. If desired, a constant can be added to $T_{(i+1)}$, to adjust the origin of the trial vector.

We might ask what happens if we assume equality of discriminal dispersions when in fact some of the discriminal dispersions are not equal. Mosteller (1951b) has shown that, if condition C is assumed, and all discriminal dispersions are actually equal except for one, the stimuli will all be correctly spaced relative to one another except for the one stimulus with the aberrant discriminal dispersion. According to Mosteller, the following generalizations also hold: (a) If we have n stimuli, k of which have equal discriminal dispersions and the remaining $n-k$ each different from the rest, and apply the condition C solution to the data, the k stimuli with equal discriminal dispersions will remain correctly spaced relative to one another. (b) If we have n stimuli made up of a number of subsets with equal discriminal dispersions in each subset, the stimuli within each subset will be properly spaced relative to one another, but the subsets themselves will not.

5. ANALYTICAL PROCEDURES FOR CONDITION B

Of the analytical procedures for the law of comparative judgment, condition C has been used the most by far. There are, however, numerous situations where we might not wish to impose the condition C restriction. If the stimuli are complex, we would expect that their dispersions will differ somewhat from one another. Even with homogeneous stimuli, such as the loudness of pure tones, for example, it is not at all unlikely that the discriminal dispersions vary as a function of the loudness itself.

Condition B, as we have seen, is an approximate expression for the complete law when the correlation between pairs of discriminal processes is constant and when the discriminal dispersions are not widely different. It is also an exact expression when a perfect negative correlation obtains between the pairs of discriminal processes.

Thurstone (1932) has given an approximate solution for case IV (algebraically identical with our condition B) which is not unduly laborious. The following derivation conforms to his presentation closely. Similar condition B solutions which follow the same general approach have been given by Burros (1951) and Burros and Gibson (1954). Though the latter solution is designated by the authors as a solution for Thurstone's case III, it actually seems to involve much the same restrictions on the variance of the discriminal dispersions as underlie condition B. Gibson (1953) has also given formal equations for a least-squares solution for condition B. However, the computational labor that would be involved in obtaining a numerical solution is such that it has not yet been applied to data.

Consider the equations containing the theoretical deviates x_{jk} and $x_{j,k+1}$. We may write, from equation 5,

(45) $$A(s_k - s_j) = x_{jk}(\sigma_k + \sigma_j)$$

and

(46) $$A(s_{k+1} - s_j) = x_{j,k+1}(\sigma_{k+1} + \sigma_j)$$

where A in Thurstone's original article is equal to $\sqrt{2}$ and in our equation 5, to $[2/(1 - r)]^{1/2}$. Subtracting equation 45 from equation 46, we get

(47) $$A(s_{k+1} - s_k) = x_{j,k+1}(\sigma_{k+1} + \sigma_j) - x_{jk}(\sigma_k + \sigma_j)$$

Solving for $x_{j,k+1}$, we have

(48) $$x_{j,k+1} = \left(\frac{\sigma_k + \sigma_j}{\sigma_{k+1} + \sigma_j}\right) x_{jk} + \frac{A(s_{k+1} - s_k)}{\sigma_{k+1} + \sigma_j}$$

If we were to plot $x_{j,k+1}$ against x_{jk} for all values of j, the plot would be linear except for the variation in σ_j. Equation 48 can be approximated by assuming that the σ_j term is equal to unity, giving

(49) $$x_{j,k+1} = \left(\frac{\sigma_k + 1}{\sigma_{k+1} + 1}\right) x_{jk} + \frac{A(s_{k+1} - s_k)}{\sigma_{k+1} + 1}$$

Equation 49 is the equation of a straight line. The slope of the line of best fit is thus, approximately,

$$\frac{\sigma_k + 1}{\sigma_{k+1} + 1}$$

But the slope is also given by the ratio of the standard deviations of x_{jk} and $x_{j,k+1}$, where $j = 1, 2, \cdots, n$. That is, if we define

$$V_k^2 = \frac{1}{n} \sum_{j=1}^{n} (x_{jk} - \bar{x}_{.k})^2$$

$$V_{k+1}^2 = \frac{1}{n} \sum_{j=1}^{n} (x_{j,k+1} - \bar{x}_{.,k+1})^2$$

then the slope is equal to V_{k+1}/V_k, and we can write, approximately,

(50) $$\frac{V_{k+1}}{V_k} = \frac{\sigma_k + 1}{\sigma_{k+1} + 1} \qquad (k = 1, 2, \cdots, n-1)$$

In general, then

(51) $$V_k(\sigma_k + 1) = B \qquad (k = 1, 2, \cdots, n)$$

where B is a constant of proportionality. Rearranging and summing over k, we have

$$(52) \qquad B \sum_{k=1}^{n} \frac{1}{V_k} = \sum_{k=1}^{n} \sigma_k + n$$

If we now define the unit to be such that the average discriminal dispersion is unity (which is in line with the approximation of equation 49), then

$$(53) \qquad \sum_{k=1}^{n} \sigma_k = n$$

and we can solve for B:

$$(54) \qquad B = \frac{2n}{\sum_{k=1}^{n} \frac{1}{V_k}}$$

Given the value of B, the discriminal dispersions can be obtained from equation 51:

$$(55) \qquad \sigma_k = \frac{B}{V_k} - 1 \qquad (k = 1, 2, \cdots, n)$$

Given the values for σ_k, the scale values of the stimuli may be obtained as follows:

$$(56) \qquad A(s_k - s_j) = x_{jk}(\sigma_j + \sigma_k)$$

Summing over j $(j = 1, 2, \cdots, n)$, and setting the origin of the scale at the average scale value, we have

$$(57) \qquad Ans_k = \sigma_k \sum_{j=1}^{n} x_{jk} + \sum_{j=1}^{n} \sigma_j x_{jk}$$

or

$$(58) \qquad As_k = \frac{1}{n} \left(\sigma_k \sum_{j=1}^{n} x_{jk} + \sum_{j=1}^{n} \sigma_j x_{jk} \right) \qquad (k = 1, 2, \cdots, n)$$

Actual application of the procedure to fallible data differs from that given above only in that fallible estimates x'_{jk} are substituted for the theoretical values x_{jk} used in the derivation. The quantity A is an unknown stretching factor. We may follow Thurstone and set it equal to $\sqrt{2}$ or may equally well equate it to unity or some larger value.

If the observation matrix $\mathbf{X}$ contains vacant cells, the procedure given above cannot be used. The estimates of the standard deviations V'_k must all be based on the same values of j. Thus, if any cell of the jth row of matrix $\mathbf{X}$ is missing, the entire row must be omitted in calculation of the

Table 7. Illustrative Example (Errorless Data): Thurstone's
Approximate Solution for Case IV

Matrix X

		Stimuli k					
		1	2	3	4	5	
	1	0.0000	0.2778	0.6818	1.2500	1.2500	
	2	−0.2778	0.0000	0.5000	1.0714	1.1364	
Stimuli j	3	−0.6818	−0.5000	0.0000	0.2778	0.5769	
	4	−1.2500	−1.0714	−0.2778	0.0000	0.5000	
	5	−1.2500	−1.1364	−0.5769	−0.5000	0.0000	
$\Sigma x'_{jk}$		−3.4596	−2.4300	0.3271	2.0992	3.4633	0.0 ✓
$\Sigma x'^2_{jk}$		3.6670	2.7665	1.1248	3.0376	3.4367	
$n\Sigma x'^2_{jk}$		18.3350	13.8325	5.6240	15.1880	17.1835	
$(\Sigma x'_{jk})^2$		11.9688	5.9049	0.1070	4.4066	11.9944	
$n\Sigma x'^2_{jk} - (\Sigma x'_{jk})^2$		6.3662	7.9276	5.5170	10.7814	5.1891	
$nV'_k = [n\Sigma x'_{jk} - (\Sigma x'_{jk})^2]^{1/2}$		2.5231	2.8156	2.3488	3.2835	2.2780	
$\dfrac{1}{nV'_k}$		0.39634	0.35516	0.42575	0.30455	0.43898	

$$\sum_{k}^{n} \frac{1}{nV'_k} = 1.9208 \qquad nB = 5.2062$$

$\sigma'_k = \dfrac{nB}{nV'_k} - 1$	1.0634	0.8490	1.2165	0.5856	1.2854	5.0 ✓

values of V'_k. Often, there will be few if any rows that are completely
filled. When this occurs, a rough procedure would be as follows:

(a) Arrange the columns of matrix X in approximate order of increasing
scale values of the stimuli, and plot x'_{jk} (abscissa) against $x'_{j,k+1}$ for all
values of j for which both are present. This is the same graphical procedure as was suggested for the condition C solution for an incomplete
matrix X. There again will be $n-1$ plots.

(b) Fit a straight line to the points, and determine its slope.

If we define the slope as $c'_{k,k+1}$ and the unit of measurement to be such
that the average discriminal dispersion is equal to unity, then, from
equation 49, we have the approximate relation

(59)
$$c'_{k,k+1} = \frac{\sigma'_k + 1}{\sigma'_{k+1} + 1}$$

Table 8. ILLUSTRATIVE EXAMPLE, CONTINUED. MATRIX **Y**

The elements y'_{jk} are equal to $\sigma'_k x'_{jk}$

		Stimuli k					$\sum_k y'_{jk}$ $= -\sum_j \sigma'_j x'_{jk}$
		1	2	3	4	5	
	1	0.0000	0.2359	0.8294	0.7320	1.6068	3.4041
	2	−0.2954	0.0000	0.6083	0.6274	1.4607	2.4010
Stimuli j 3	3	−0.7250	−0.4245	0.0000	0.1627	0.7415	−0.2453
	4	−1.3293	−0.9096	−0.3379	0.0000	0.6427	−1.9341
	5	−1.3293	−0.9648	−0.7018	−0.2928	0.0000	−3.2887

		1	2	3	4	5	
$\Sigma y'_{jk}$		−3.6790	−2.0630	0.3980	1.2293	4.4517	
$\sqrt{} = \left(\sum_j x'_{jk}\right)\sigma'_k$		−3.6789	−2.0631	0.3979	1.2293	4.4517	

$$ns'_k = \sum_j y'_{jk} - \sum_k y'_{jk}$$

	−7.0831	−4.4640	0.6433	3.1634	7.7404	0.0000 $\sqrt{}$

s'_k	−1.417	−0.893	0.129	0.633	1.548	0.000 $\sqrt{}$

or

(60) $\sigma'_{k+1} = \dfrac{1}{c'_{k,k+1}}(\sigma'_k + 1) - 1 \qquad (k = 1, 2, \cdots, n-1)$

(c) Let $a \equiv \sigma'_1 + 1$. Then application of equation 60 enables us to solve for the estimates of the discriminal dispersions in terms of a:

$$\sigma'_1 = a - 1$$

$$\sigma'_2 = \frac{a}{c'_{12}} - 1$$

$$\sigma'_3 = \frac{a}{c'_{12}c'_{23}} - 1$$

(61)

$$\sigma'_4 = \frac{a}{c'_{12}c'_{23}c'_{34}} - 1$$

$$\vdots$$

$$\sigma'_n = \frac{a}{c'_{12}c'_{23}c'_{34}\cdots c'_{n-1,n}} - 1$$

If we now let

(62) $$G'_{1k} \equiv \frac{1}{c'_{12}c'_{23} \cdots c'_{k-1,k}} \qquad (k = 2, 3, \cdots, n)$$

then

(63) $$\sigma'_k = aG'_{1k} - 1 \qquad (k = 2, 3, \cdots, n)$$

Define $G'_{11} \equiv 1$. Then, summing over k and dividing by n gives

(64) $$\frac{1}{n} \sum_{k=1}^{n} \sigma'_k = \frac{a}{n} \sum_{k=1}^{n} G'_{1k} - 1$$

which, since the average discriminal dispersion is equal to unity, simplifies to

(65) $$\frac{a}{n} \sum_{k=1}^{n} G'_{1k} = 2$$

Solving explicitly for a, we get

(66) $$a = \frac{2n}{\sum_{k=1}^{n} G'_{1k}}$$

Equation 66 gives a solution for a in terms of observable data. Given the numerical value for a, the solution for the σ'_k is given by equations 61.

(d) To solve for the estimates of the scale values of the stimuli we use equation 47:

$$A(s'_{k+1} - s'_k) = x'_{j,k+1}(\sigma'_{k+1} + \sigma'_j) - x'_{jk}(\sigma'_k + \sigma'_j)$$

There are as many estimates of the difference $A(s_{k+1} - s_k)$ as there are filled pairs of cells in the k and $k+1$'th columns of matrix **X**. We take the average as the estimate wanted:

(67) $$A(s'_{k+1} - s'_k) = \frac{1}{n_k} \sum_{j}^{n_k} [x'_{j,k+1}(\sigma'_{k+1} + \sigma'_j) - x'_{jk}(\sigma'_k + \sigma'_j)]$$

where n_k is the number of terms summed over. The scale values themselves are obtained from the differences by arbitrarily setting the origin and then adding the successive differences. Since A is again an unknown stretching factor, we may equate it to unity or any larger value.

It should be emphasized that the solutions given for condition B are approximate solutions only. Even when the raw data are errorless, and completely satisfy equation 45, the solution obtained will be only approximately correct. As a matter of fact, matrix **X** in the illustrative example given in Tables 7 and 8 was constructed by first specifying values for σ_k and s_k, and then using these values in equation 45 to obtain values for x'_{jk}.

Thus, an exact solution of the values of σ'_k and s'_k would reproduce the given x values perfectly (within rounding error). Figure 3 gives plots of the true values of σ_k and s_k against the obtained values. The reason for

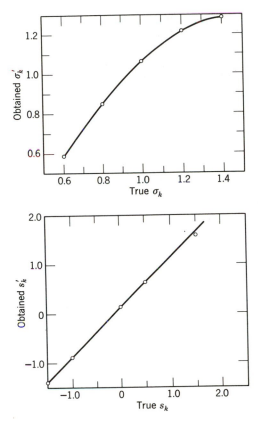

Figure 3. True values of σ_k and s_k against obtained values for the errorless illustrative example.

the discrepancy lies, of course, in the step taken in going from equation 48 to equation 49.

It might be noted that equation 58 is a least-squares solution for the scale values, *assuming* that the discriminal dispersions are correct.

6. GOODNESS OF FIT OF THE MODEL TO THE DATA

We have seen that, through the use of the law of comparative judgment, scale values of stimuli may be estimated from the observed proportions p'_{jk}.

Given these scale values, the procedure may be reversed; that is, derived proportions p''_{jk} can be obtained from the estimates of the scale values. For example, in condition C, the difference between any two scale values $(s'_k - s'_j)$ is equal to the fitted normal deviate x''_{jk}. By performing the subtraction for all values of j and k, a matrix of fitted normal deviates can be constructed. Actually, since $s'_k - s'_j = -(s'_j - s'_k)$, only those x''_{jk} below the principal diagonal need be computed. These fitted deviates may then be used to obtain a matrix of fitted proportions p''_{jk}. Again only those p''_{jk} below the principal diagonal need be computed.

The test of the applicability of the model used to the data is in how well the fitted proportions p''_{jk} correspond to the observed proportions p'_{jk}. A common procedure is simply to obtain the average absolute deviation:

$$(68) \qquad \overline{p''_{jk} - p'_{jk}} = \frac{1}{n(n-1)} \sum_{j>k} |p''_{jk} - p'_{jk}|$$

If the average discrepancy is "small," it is concluded that the model fits adequately. In addition the individual deviations are scanned and perhaps tested statistically to see if too many appear to be "too large."

A single over-all test of goodness of fit for condition C has been given by Mosteller (1951c). His test uses the inverse-sine transformation. If θ is an angle measured in degrees, and we define

$$\theta'_{jk} = \sin^{-1} \sqrt{p'_{jk}}$$

$$\theta''_{jk} = \sin^{-1} \sqrt{p''_{jk}}$$

$$N = \text{number of observations on which } p'_{jk} \text{ is based}$$

then

$$(69) \qquad \chi^2 = \frac{\sum_{j>k} (\theta''_{jk} - \theta'_{jk})^2}{821/N}$$

With n stimuli, there are $n(n-1)/2$ independent proportions to be fitted. Against this we have the n scale values. Two of these scale values are arbitrary, however, since we choose the origin and unit arbitrarily. This leaves $n-2$ parameters free for fitting the $n(n-1)/2$ entries. Hence the appropriate number of degrees of freedom is $\frac{n}{2}(n-1) - (n-2) - 1$ or $(n-1)(n-2)/2$.

The test can also be extended to condition B, the only difference being in the number of degrees of freedom. In condition B, in addition to the $n-2$ parameters free for fitting the data in condition C, there are the n discriminal dispersions, giving $2n-2$ in all. Hence, with condition B the appropriate number of degrees of freedom would seem to be

$$\frac{n}{2}(n-1) - 2n - 1.$$

Remarks on the Chi-Square Test for Condition C

It is important to keep in mind the efficiency of the analytical procedure used in obtaining the scale values. In the least-squares procedure, scale values that would minimize the sum of squares of the discrepancies between the observed and derived distances $(x''_{jk} - x'_{jk})$ were obtained. From the viewpoint of obtaining a scale, this would seem to be the reasonable procedure. However, these scale values are not necessarily the best estimates in the sense of minimizing sums of squares of $(\theta''_{jk} - \theta'_{jk})$. The alternative solutions presented would seem to be even less efficient in estimating the scale values to a minimum chi-square criterion. This means that the procedures actually used will be likely to give a value of chi-square that is somewhat higher than necessary. It would thus seem that, other things being equal, it would be wise to give the theory the benefit of the doubt in borderline cases.

One of the other things that may *not* be equal is the effect of time or space errors. Mosteller found that, when he applied the test to baseball data, the fit was usually too good rather than not good enough. It was suggested to him that the reason might lie in the fact that "the proportion of games won by any team from any other team involves an admixture of games played at home and away, and that, if these were separated, we might then not get such consistently good agreement" (1951c, p. 212). If, for example, at home $p_{jk} = 0.25$, away $p_{jk} = 0.75$, and the average $p_{jk} = 0.50$, then the variance based on $p_{jk} = 0.50$ is $n/4$ while that based on $p_{jk} = 0.25$ for half of the games and $p_{jk} = 0.75$ for the other half is $3n/16$.

Psychophysicists will immediately identify the "at home" or "away" effect as analogous to the space error, and the method of scheduling the games between any two teams so that half are at the home field of one team and half at the home field of the other as an example of counter-balancing by pairs.

The generalization to any situation involving the elimination of sizable time or space errors by counterbalancing in this way would seem reasonable. A proportion of a given magnitude obtained in this way will be more reliable than one of the same magnitude obtained where time or space errors are negligible. Since the chi-square test is based on the latter situation, the effect will be to overestimate the goodness of fit.

Mosteller has also discussed the behavior of the chi-square test in terms of the three major condition C postulates which may not hold.

1. *The Normality Postulate.* The test is very poor at detecting deviations from normality. Since a failure of normality is not very important in obtaining scale values, this would not seem to represent a weakness in the test.

2. *Lack of Unidimensionality or Additivity.* Since any deviation from additivity will tend to cause a discrepancy between x_{jk}'' and x_{jk}', it will result in an increased chi square. The test is therefore sensitive to a lack of additivity.

3. *Unequal Discriminal Dispersions* (more properly, unequal standard deviations of discriminal differences). Unequal discriminal dispersions may or may not cause high chi-square values. Mosteller states that "The best that can be said is that sometimes such aberrations will cause high values of chi square and sometimes not, depending on the nature of the case" (1951c, p. 217).

One kind of variation in discriminal dispersions which is of considerable interest in psychophysical theory is the case where the discriminal dispersions vary systematically as a function of the scale values. Especially interesting is the case where the discriminal dispersions and scale values of the stimuli are related by a simple monotonic function. It seems likely that the test will be rather insensitive to aberrations of this type, due to the fact that application of the condition C model results in a surprising close fit. This is unfortunate and somewhat disturbing, since the scale values estimated from the condition C model in situations of this type are *not* linearly related to the true scale values. There is a kind of trading relation between discriminal dispersions and scale values here. If the discriminal dispersion actually increases linearly with scale value, and a condition C analysis is applied to the data, the solution gives a scale that becomes more and more compressed toward its upper end, when compared with the true scale.

An example using errorless data which illustrates both the distortion of the scale and the degree to which the (inappropriate) condition C model can approximate the data is given in Tables 9 to 13 and Figure 4. Table 9 gives the true scale values and true discriminal dispersions for five stimuli. The values were chosen so that the relation between discriminal dispersion and scale value would be linear. Theoretical unit normal deviates, obtained from the values of Table 9 using the condition A equation,

$$x_{jk} = \frac{s_k - s_j}{(\sigma_j^2 + \sigma_k^2)^{1/2}} \qquad (j, k = 1, 2, \cdots, n)$$

are given in Table 10. The true proportions corresponding to these deviates are given in Table 11.

The bottom row of Table 10 contains the least-squares estimates s_k' of the scale values obtained using the condition C model.   The plot of these estimates s_k' against the true scale values of the stimuli is given in Figure 4 as an illustration of the degree and type of distortion that occurs.

Table 9. THEORETICAL SCALE VALUES s_k AND DISCRIMINAL DISPERSIONS σ_k FOR FIVE STIMULI

	1	2	3	4	5
s_k	0.00	0.50	1.00	1.50	2.00
σ_k	0.50	0.75	1.00	1.25	1.50

Table 10. THEORETICAL UNIT NORMAL DEVIATES x_{jk} AND CONDITION C ESTIMATES OF SCALE VALUES

	1	2	3	4	5
1	—	0.555	0.894	1.114	1.265
2	−0.555	—	0.400	0.686	0.894
3	−0.894	−0.400	—	0.312	0.555
4	−1.114	−0.686	−0.312	—	0.256
5	−1.265	−0.894	−0.555	−0.256	—
Σx_{jk}	−3.828	−1.425	0.427	1.856	2.970
$\dfrac{1}{n}\Sigma x_{jk} = s_k'$	−0.7656	−0.2850	0.0854	0.3712	0.5944

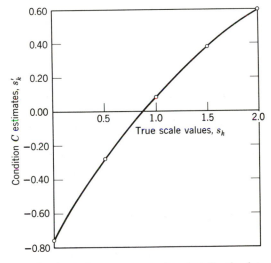

Figure 4.   Plot of estimated versus true scale values for the data of Table 10.

In spite of this distortion, or, perhaps, because of it, the proportions derived from the least-squares estimates correspond closely to the theoretical values. Table 12 contains the derived proportions p''_{jk} computed from these estimates according to the equations of condition C. The discrepancies $(p'_{jk} - p''_{jk})$ are shown in Table 13. The average of the absolute values of the discrepancies is equal to 0.0122.

Table 11. THEORETICAL PROPORTIONS p_{jk} CORRESPONDING
TO THE DEVIATES OF TABLE 10

	1	2	3	4	5
1	—	0.710	0.814	0.867	0.897
2	0.290	—	0.655	0.754	0.814
3	0.186	0.345	—	0.623	0.710
4	0.133	0.246	0.377	—	0.601
5	0.103	0.186	0.290	0.399	—

Table 12. DERIVED PROPORTIONS p''_{jk} COMPUTED FROM THE
CONDITION C LEAST-SQUARES ESTIMATES OF SCALE VALUES

	1	2	3	4	5
1	—	0.685	0.803	0.872	0.913
2	0.315	—	0.644	0.744	0.810
3	0.197	0.356	—	0.612	0.694
4	0.128	0.256	0.388	—	0.588
5	0.087	0.190	0.306	0.412	—

Table 13. DISCREPANCIES $(p_{jk} - p''_{jk})$

	1	2	3	4	5
1	—	0.025	0.011	−0.005	−0.016
2	−0.025	—	0.011	0.010	0.004
3	−0.011	−0.011	—	0.011	0.016
4	0.005	−0.010	−0.011	—	0.013
5	0.016	−0.004	−0.016	−0.013	—

$$\frac{1}{n(n-1)} \sum_j \sum_k |p_{jk} - p''_{jk}| = 0.0122$$

7. METHODS OF REDUCING EXPERIMENTAL LABOR

The greatest single criticism of the method of paired comparisons has been the large number of observations involved. Obtaining proportions for all pairs of stimuli becomes very tedious and time-consuming when the number of stimuli becomes large. The number of pairs increases much faster than the number of stimuli, of course. For example, with 10 stimuli there are 45 pairs, with 15 stimuli, 105 pairs, and with 20 stimuli, 190 pairs. As a result, the amount of overdetermination also increases much faster than the number of stimuli, and, hence, the number of degrees of freedom left after fitting the data. It would seem to be necessary to obtain only a sufficient number of observed proportions to enable us to evaluate the goodness of fit of the model to the data. Hence, for a large number of stimuli, satisfactory results can be obtained by filling only a part of the proportion matrix $\mathbf{P}$. Since proportions obtained from pairs of widely separated stimuli tend toward 1.00 or 0.00, there is often a considerable segment of matrix $\mathbf{P}$ which is not available in any event.

One method of reducing the number of observations is to select a limited number of stimuli as standards. Standards selected should be spaced out over the length of the scale. Each stimulus is then compared with each standard, giving $mn - m(m+1)/2$ independent proportions where $m =$ the number of standards. For example, with nine stimuli, four of which are taken as standards, matrix $\mathbf{P}$ would look like Figure 5a, where the shaded part indicates observed proportions.

A second procedure, which would seem to be particularly appropriate when the length of the scale greatly exceeds the discriminal dispersions, is shown schematically in Figure 5b. In this procedure it is necessary to know roughly the rank order of the stimuli. If a correlated physical variable is not known, the rank orders can be obtained roughly by some quick method such as the method of equal-appearing intervals. Given the stimuli in rank order, proportions are obtained only for those pairs that are close together in scale value. Each stimulus is compared with (say) only four or five others. The proportions that are not obtained are those involving widely separated stimuli, and thus would tend toward unity or zero anyway.

A modification of this procedure would be to divide the total matrix into several overlapping submatrices as in Figure 5c. In analyzing such a matrix, it would be possible to scale the submatrices separately, and then use the overlapping stimuli to join the subscales together.

A third procedure has been used by Uhrbrock and Richardson (1933). They divided the matrix into nonoverlapping submatrices. In addition they selected m standard stimuli as in the first procedure described. Figure 5d gives their procedure schematically. The separate submatrices are related to one another through the comparisons they all have with the m standards.

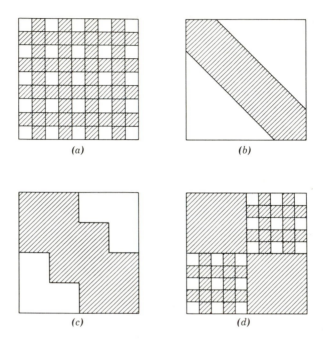

Figure 5.   Methods for reducing the number of proportions obtained in the method of paired comparisons.

It is also possible to use experimental methods other than paired comparisons to collect data for the law of comparative judgment. Two methods which have been suggested are the method of rank order and the method of choice. In both these methods the proportions p'_{jk} are *deduced* from the observed behavior of the subject rather than calculated directly.

In the method of rank order, the subject is instructed to rank the stimuli in order with respect to the attribute to be scaled. From these judgments is deduced the proportion of times stimulus k was perceived as greater than stimulus j. It is assumed that, in ranking the stimuli, the subject compares each stimulus with every other one. From each rank order of n stimuli is thus deduced $n(n-1)/2$ "judgments." For example, if on a certain trial the subject ranked four stimuli in the order $a < b < c < d$, we deduce that the following six judgments were made: $b > a$, $c > a$,

$d > a$, $c > b$, $d > b$, and $d > c$. With a large number of trials, the proportions p'_{jk} can be obtained, and the law of comparative judgment can be applied.

Hevner (1930) analyzed by the law of comparative judgment proportions obtained from a set of stimuli by both the method of paired comparisons and the method of rank order. The resulting scales were equivalent to within a linear transformation. She obtained comparative proportions from the method of rank order by actually tabulating each time one member of a pair was ranked above the other. This involved a great deal of labor. Later, Thurstone (1931a) showed how the proportions can be deduced from the frequency distributions of the rank order assigned to each stimulus. Although his procedures decrease the computational labor considerably, a substantial amount of labor remains.

Since it has been shown possible to analyze the rank-order data directly by the law of categorical judgment (discussed in the following chapter), it would now seem that the whole process of transforming the raw data into comparative proportions is unnecessary. As a result, his derivation and equations will not be presented here. The interested reader is referred to Thurstone's original paper for this material.

Guilford (1937b) has given a procedure for deducing paired-comparison proportions p'_{jk} from data collected by the *method of choices*. In this method, n stimuli are presented to each of a large number of subjects. Each subject merely indicates which stimulus appears greatest on the attribute of interest (e.g., *most beautiful*, *most preferred*, etc.). We thus have as raw data the frequency with which each stimulus was selected as greatest. Let f'_j and f'_k be the number of times stimulus j and stimulus k were selected, respectively. We know that each time stimulus j was selected it was perceived as greater than k. In like manner each time k was selected, it appeared greater than j. Whenever a different stimulus was selected, we have no information about the relative size of stimuli j and k. Therefore, the sum of the two frequencies gives the total number of observations in which we know the result of the comparison between stimuli j and k, and the proportion p'_{jk} of times we know that k appeared greater than j is given by

$$(70) \qquad p'_{jk} = \frac{f'_k}{f'_j + f'_k} \qquad \begin{aligned} &(j = 1, 2, \cdots, n) \\ &(k = 1, 2, \cdots, n) \end{aligned}$$

It also follows that

$$(71) \qquad p'_{jk} = 1 - \frac{f'_j}{f'_j + f'_k}$$

Using formula 70, the entire matrix **P** can be constructed, and the law of comparative judgment applied to the data. The method of choices suffers from a number of disadvantages, however. In the first place, each proportion is based on different subsets of subjects. For example, the subjects on which p'_{12} is based are not the same subjects as those on which p'_{34} is based. Furthermore, the number of observations on which the proportions are based will be different for different proportions. It would seem that the characteristics of the population would be of particular importance when this method is used. A second disadvantage is that some stimuli may never be selected as greater than the rest. When this occurs, those stimuli could not, of course, be scaled.

A third disadvantage, which would seem to be the most serious when first choices alone are obtained from the subjects, is that even condition C leaves no remaining degrees of freedom.

The raw data consist of n frequencies of which $n-1$ are independent. Against this, with condition C, are n scale values of which two are arbitrary. The degrees of freedom would thus seem to be $(n-1) - (n-2) - 1 = 0$. We ought, therefore, to be able to fit perfectly with condition C a matrix $\mathbf{P}$ derived from any set of frequencies f'_j, regardless of the characteristics of the stimuli being scaled. Since there are no degrees of freedom, we have no way of evaluating the goodness of fit of the law to the data. If the postulates involved in the law of comparative judgment do not actually apply to the set of stimuli (or the attribute), if gross errors are made in recording the frequencies with which each stimulus is picked, analysis by condition C should still yield a scale which would reproduce the proportions perfectly. Actually, it does not (Guilford, 1937b). The slight errors, however, are systematic, and probably result from the fact that equation 70 is not strictly appropriate for use in conjunction with the law of comparative judgment. Given equation 70 for estimating the proportions p_{jk}, a more appropriate model is that developed by Bradley and Terry and discussed in section 9 of this chapter. Their model would always fit data of this type perfectly. Indeed, with appropriate choice of unit, the "true ratings" solved for in the Bradley–Terry model would turn out to be identical with the raw frequencies (f'_j) used to generate the proportions in the first place.

It would appear that, when first choices alone are involved, little will be gained by applying the law of comparative judgment to the data. The scale values obtained can best be considered as ordinal numbers as are the original frequencies.

8. DETERMINATION OF A RATIONAL ZERO POINT

We have seen that the scale values derived through use of the law of comparative judgment locate the stimuli on the psychological continuum with respect to one another only. The zero point must be chosen arbitrarily. The method itself cannot determine an absolute zero point, since it operates only on judgments of differences between stimuli. The scale values are thus determined to within a linear transformation of the type $y = ax + b$.

Often it is advantageous to express the locations of the stimuli with reference to a rational rather than an arbitrary zero point: that is, to determine the scale values to within a linear transformation of the type $y = ax$.

Additional operations are necessary in order to obtain the location of an absolute zero point. These operations would seem to fall into two classes: those appropriate for use with single-ended continua and those appropriate for use with double-ended continua. By single-ended continua is meant those continua that progress in one direction only from an absolute zero. Examples that might be cited are pitch, loudness, brightness, saltiness, and perhaps socioeconomic status. By double-ended continua is meant those continua that seem to be most reasonably considered as progressing from one extreme through a zero or neutral point to the opposite extreme. In general, esthetic and affective continua, along with many attitude and personality-trait continua would seem to fall into this category. Examples are the progression from extremely pleasing through zero to extremely displeasing and from extremely favorable through zero to extremely unfavorable.

With single-ended continua, it would seem reasonable to equate the absolute zero point with the absolute limen as found by the standard psychophysical methods (see Chapter 7).

With double-ended continua, the problem is somewhat different although not necessarily more difficult. Perhaps the simplest approach would be to use judgments obtained from the two-category case of the method of single stimuli. In this method the judgment required of the subject is of the form: "Is stimulus k greater or less than zero?" For example, we might ask, "Is stimulus k pleasant or unpleasant?" or "Do you like or dislike stimulus k?," depending on the attribute being scaled. The judgment is repeated for each stimulus, and the raw data are in the form of the proportion of times any stimulus k was judged to be greater than zero. If we assume that the zero point has a definite, fixed location on the psychological continuum, and ascribe the variation in judgment entirely to the discriminal dispersion of the stimulus, then we may write the following equation:

$$(72) \qquad r_j = ax_j\sigma_j \qquad (j = 1, 2, \cdots, n)$$

where

r_j is the scale value of stimulus j referred to the rational zero point.

x_j is the unit normal deviate corresponding to p_j, the theoretical proportion of times j is judged greater than zero.

σ_j is the discriminal dispersion of the stimulus j.

a is a constant of proportionality to allow for the possibility that the dispersions are greater for this type of judgment than for the straight paired-comparison judgment.

Assume that the scale values of the stimuli referred to an arbitrary origin, along with the corresponding discriminal dispersions, are known. Then, the relation among s_j, r_j, and σ_j is given by

$$(73) \qquad\qquad s_j = ax_j\sigma_j + b \qquad (j = 1, 2, \cdot \cdot \cdot, n)$$

since r_j and s_j are linearly related. The location of the rational zero point on the s_j scale is given by b.

If we have obtained the empirical estimates x'_j, using the method of single stimuli, and have computed the values of s'_j and σ'_j from data gathered by the method of paired comparisons, we can estimate the location of the rational origin of the s'_j scale as follows: Plot s'_j against $x'_j\sigma'_j$ for all available values of j. (We would expect that proportions of 1.00 or 0.00 will be obtained for those stimuli at the extremes of the continuum. As a result, we will not have numerical estimates of x_j for all values of j.) The intercept on the s'_j axis of a straight line fitted to these points is an estimate of the location of the rational origin. To convert the original estimates to the new zero point, simply subtract the value of the intercept from each value of s'_j:

$$s'_j - b' = \text{scale value of stimulus } j \text{ referred to a rational origin}$$

The procedure given above applies to scales derived from any of the workable conditions of the law of comparative judgment. For scales derived from condition C, however, a shorter and somewhat more general procedure is available. In this event, we can assume that the zero point itself projects a normal distribution on the psychological continuum. The relation between r_j and x_j is then given by

$$(74) \qquad\qquad r_j = x_j c_0 \qquad (j = 1, 2, \cdot \cdot \cdot, n)$$

where c_0 denotes the (constant) standard deviation of the distribution of discriminal differences $(d_j - d_0)$. For an empirical estimate of the rational origin of the s'_j scale, we might plot the x'_j obtained from the method of single stimuli against the s'_j computed from condition C, fit a straight line to the points, and take the intercept on the s'_j axis as the estimate of the location of the rational origin. An alternative procedure would be to plot the p'_j against the s'_j. If probability paper is used, the points should fall along a straight line, except for error; if linear graph paper is used, the points should fall along a normal ogive. When the appropriate curve is fitted to the data, the point on the s'_j axis corresponding to a proportion of 0.50 gives the location of the new origin.

Horst (1932) has given a more complex procedure for dealing with double-ended scales. In his procedure one solves directly for scale values which are referred to a rational origin. His procedure, which again stems directly from Thurstone's original model, combines the analysis of comparative judgments with the analysis of a new kind of judgment, which might be called a *summative* judgment.

In making a comparative judgment, the subject is required to judge whether stimulus k is greater than stimulus j. It is assumed that this judgment is determined by whether the *discriminal difference* is positive or negative on that trial. In making a summative judgment, the subject is required to judge whether stimulus k is more positive than stimulus j is negative. For example, in an affective situation, where the stimuli range from very pleasant through neutral (zero) to very unpleasant, the subject might be presented with two stimuli and asked, "If you could have stimulus k, would you be willing to take stimulus j?" It is assumed that an affirmative answer means that, on that trial, stimulus k was perceived as being more pleasant than stimulus j was unpleasant—that the *sum* of the values of the discriminal processes associated with the two stimuli was greater than zero. In like manner, a negative response would indicate that the sum was less than zero. It is assumed that the discriminal distribution associated with any stimulus is the same, regardless of whether the task set for the subject is to make comparative judgments or summative judgments.

We have seen that the complete form of the equation for comparative judgments may be written:

$$s_k - s_j = x_{jk}(\sigma_j^2 + \sigma_k^2 - 2r_{jk}\sigma_j\sigma_k)^{1/2}$$

In an analogous manner, the complete form of the equation for summative judgments is found to be

(75) $$s_k + s_j = z_{jk}(\sigma_j^2 + \sigma_k^2 + 2r_{jk}\sigma_j\sigma_k)^{1/2}$$

where all terms are the same as before except for z_{jk}, which is here defined as the unit normal deviate corresponding to the proportion obtained by the summative judgments.

Horst makes the following simplifying assumptions: (*a*) the discriminal dispersions are all equal, and (*b*) the correlation term is zero.*   With these assumptions, the two equations simplify to

(76) $$s_k - s_j = x_{jk} \sigma \sqrt{2}$$

and

(77) $$s_k + s_j = z_{jk} \sigma \sqrt{2}$$

Since $\sigma \sqrt{2}$ is constant for all equations, we may choose the unit to make this quantity equal to unity, thus further simplifying the equations to

(78) $$s_k - s_j = x_{jk}$$

and

(79) $$s_k + s_j = z_{jk}$$

Theoretically, we could obtain $n(n-1)/2$ independent proportions for each kind of judgment. These proportions could then be used to construct a matrix **X** for comparative judgments, and an analogous matrix **Z** for summative judgments. (The diagonal cells of both matrices are left vacant.)   If all off-diagonal cells were filled for both matrices, a least-squares solution for scale values which are referred to a rational origin is straightforward.   First, if we add equations 78 and 79, we get

(80) $$s_k - s_j + s_k + s_j = x_{jk} + z_{jk}$$

or

(81) $$2s_k = x_{jk} + z_{jk}$$

With fallible data and n stimuli, we take as our problem the estimation of the values of s_k' which minimizes the quantity

(82) $$Q = \sum_{\substack{j=1}}^{n} \sum_{\substack{k=1 \\ j \neq k}}^{n} (x_{jk}' + z_{jk}' - 2s_k')^2$$

Taking the partial derivative of Q with respect to s_k' and equating to zero, we have the n equations:

(83) $$\frac{1}{4} \frac{\partial Q}{\partial s_k} = - \sum_{\substack{j=1 \\ j \neq k}}^{n} (2s_k' - x_{jk}' - z_{jk}') = 0 \qquad (k = 1, 2, \cdots, n)$$

---

* We saw that Thurstone originally made the same assumptions for his case V, but that Mosteller showed that the assumption of equal r was all that was necessary. In the present case, however, we must continue to assume that $r = 0$. Horst's solution is thus somewhat more restricting than our condition *C*.

Rearranging and summing each term separately, we get

$$(84) \qquad 2(n-1)s'_k = \sum_{\substack{j=1 \\ j \neq k}}^{n} (x'_{jk} + z'_{jk}) \qquad (k = 1, 2, \cdots, n)$$

and, finally, dividing through by $2(n-1)$, we have the solution for s'_k in terms of observed quantities

$$(85) \qquad s'_k = \frac{1}{2(n-1)} \sum_{\substack{j=1 \\ j \neq k}}^{n} (x'_{jk} + z'_{jk}) \qquad (k = 1, 2, \cdots, n)$$

In the usual experimental situation, however, proportions of unity or zero will be obtained for numerous pairs of stimuli in both judgmental situations. Hence, both matrix **X** and matrix **Z** will have numerous vacant off-diagonal cells. Actually, it is apparent from equations 78 and 79, that cells that are filled in **X** will tend to be vacant in **Z** and vice versa. Hence, the solution given above would seem to be of theoretical interest only. For a practical solution, we must allow for the fact that vacant off-diagonal cells will be present in both matrices. The procedure developed by Horst is essentially as follows. We first define the errors e_{jk} and i_{jk} for the two situations:

$$(86) \qquad e_{jk} \equiv x'_{jk} - s'_k + s'_j$$

$$(87) \qquad i_{jk} \equiv z'_{jk} - s'_k - s'_j$$

We wish to determine the scale values that minimize the sum of the quantities U and V, where

$$(88) \qquad U = \sum_{j,k} (x'_{jk} - s'_k + s'_j)^2$$

$$(89) \qquad V = \sum_{j,k} (z'_{jk} - s'_k - s'_j)^2$$

In equation 88, the summation is only over cells that are filled in matrix **X**; in equation 89, the summation is only over cells that are filled in matrix **Z**.

Differentiating U and V with respect to a particular stimulus s_g $(g = 1, 2, \cdots, n)$, and setting the partial derivatives equal to zero, we have the two sets of equations

$$(90) \qquad \frac{1}{2} \frac{\partial U}{\partial s'_g} = \sum_{k} (x'_{gk} - s'_k + s'_g) - \sum_{j} (x'_{jg} - s'_g + s'_j) = 0$$
$$(g = 1, 2, \cdots, n)$$

and

(91) $\qquad \dfrac{1}{2}\dfrac{\partial V}{\partial s'_g} = -\sum_k (z'_{gk} - s'_k - s'_g) - \sum_j (z'_{jg} - s'_g - s'_j) = 0$

$$(g = 1, 2, \cdots, n)$$

Again, summation is only over cells that are filled in the corresponding observation matrix.

Since $\mathbf{X}$ is skew-symmetric and $\mathbf{Z}$ is symmetric, it is apparent that

(92) $\qquad \displaystyle\sum_k (x'_{gk} - s'_k + s'_g) = -\sum_j (x'_{jg} - s'_g + s'_j)$

and

(93) $\qquad \displaystyle\sum_k (z'_{gk} - s'_k - s'_g) = \sum_j (z'_{jg} - s'_g - s'_j)$

we can therefore rewrite equations 90 and 91, respectively (returning to the subscript k in place of g)

(94) $\qquad \displaystyle\sum_j (x'_{jk} - s'_k + s'_j) = 0 \qquad (k = 1, 2, \cdots, n)$

and

(95) $\qquad \displaystyle\sum_j (z'_{jk} - s'_k - s'_j) = 0 \qquad (k = 1, 2, \cdots, n)$

In equation 94 the summation will be over only those values of j for which cell x'_{jk} is filled. In like manner, in equation 95, the summation will be over only those values of j for which cell z'_{jk} is filled. In order to simplify the algebra, let us define the following four matrices:

$\mathbf{1} \equiv 1 \times n$ row vector with elements equal to unity

$\mathbf{S} \equiv 1 \times n$ row vector with elements equal to s'_j

$\mathbf{A} \equiv n \times n$ symmetric matrix with off-diagonal cells equal to -1 whenever the corresponding cell of matrix $\mathbf{X}$ is filled, and equal to zero whenever the corresponding cell of matrix $\mathbf{X}$ is vacant. The diagonal cells have elements equal to the number of (-1)'s in their respective columns (or rows).

$\mathbf{B} \equiv n \times n$ symmetric matrix with off-diagonal cells equal to $+1$ whenever the corresponding cell of matrix $\mathbf{Z}$ is filled, and equal to zero whenever the corresponding cell of matrix $\mathbf{Z}$ is vacant. Diagonal cells have elements equal to the number of $(+1)$'s in their respective columns (or rows).

In the notation of matrix algebra, equations 94 and 95 become, respectively,

(96) $\qquad\qquad\qquad \mathbf{1X} - \mathbf{SA} = 0$

and

(97) $$1Z - SB = 0$$

Rearranging and adding equation 96 to equation 97, we have

(98) $$S(A + B) = 1(X + Z)$$

Solving for S, we have

(99) $$S = 1(X + Z)(A + B)^{-1}$$

Since **X**, **Z**, **A**, and **B** can be constructed from observational data and since the matrix (**A**+**B**) will ordinarily have an inverse, equation 99 gives the least-squares solution for double-ended scales.

9. ALTERNATIVE DISTRIBUTION FUNCTIONS FOR CONDITION C

The restriction that the standard deviation of discriminal differences be constant in condition C leaves us with the following relation:

(100) $$p_{jk} = \frac{1}{\sqrt{2\pi}} \int_{-\infty}^{x_{jk}} \exp\left(-\tfrac{1}{2}x^2\right) dx$$

where $x_{jk} = s_k - s_j$, and p_{jk} is the proportion of times stimulus k is judged to be greater than stimulus j.

If we wish, we can eliminate entirely from our thinking the theoretical development given in Chapter 8 (which led to the deduction of equation 100), and instead simply take equation 100 as the basic postulate of the condition C model. That is, we might simply postulate that equation 100 gives the transformation necessary to convert a proportion p_{jk} into a difference in scale values.

When looked at this way, it becomes clear that other transformations specifying the relation of p_{jk} to s_k and s_j might be considered in place of the normal ogive. Two such alternative transformations are briefly considered below.

The Bradley–Terry Model

One of the more interesting alternative transformations has been given by Bradley and Terry (1952; see also Terry et al., 1952). They specify that

(101) $$p_{jk} = \frac{p_k}{p_j + p_k}$$

where p_{jk} is defined as before and where p_j and p_k denote the "true rating" of stimuli j and k, respectively.

Actually, the log of the "true ratings" corresponds more closely to the scale values of condition C, since, as the authors have pointed out, if we substitute the "squared hyperbolic secant" function for the normal ogive, then, letting $\log_e p_k \equiv r_k$, the scale value of stimulus k, we can write

(102)
$$p_{jk} = \frac{1}{4} \int_{-\infty}^{r_k - r_j} \text{sech}^2 \frac{y}{2} \, dy$$

The values of r_k are thus directly analogous to the scale values of condition C, the only difference being that the transformation of equation 102 is substituted for that of equation 100. Actually, the two transformations do not differ greatly, being virtually linearly related over the range of proportions ordinarily used. The function relating $(r_k - r_j)$ to $(s_k - s_j)$ for various values of p_{jk} is given in Figure 6.

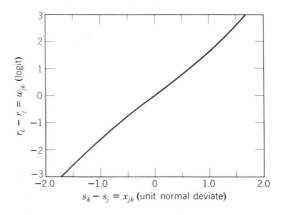

Figure 6. Illustration of the relation between logits and normal deviates.

Procedures for obtaining maximum-likelihood estimates of the parameters p_j from observed proportions have been given by Bradley and Terry (1952).

The relation between the Bradley–Terry model and the general logistic function advocated for use in bioassay by Berkson and others (e.g., see Berkson, 1953) might be pointed out. The logistic function is given by

(103)
$$p = \frac{1}{1 + \exp\left[-(a + bx)\right]}$$

If we define

$$\text{logit } p \equiv \log_e \frac{p}{1 - p}$$

then

(104) $\text{logit } p = a + bx$

In the Bradley–Terry model, if we define

$$w_{jk} \equiv r_k - r_j$$

then it is easy to show that

(105) $\text{logit } p_{jk} = \log_e \dfrac{p_{jk}}{p_{kj}} = w_{jk}$

or

(106) $p_{jk} = \dfrac{1}{1 + \exp(-w_{jk})}$

which is identical with equation 103 under the condition that $a = 0$ and $b = 1$.

For a discussion of the application of the logistic function to frequency data, along with an extensive set of references, see Berkson (1953). Additional references for the Bradley–Terry model include Bradley (1953, 1954) and Hopkins (1954).

The Arcsine Transformation

Mosteller has suggested using the arcsine transformation in place of the normal ogive (personal communication). If we let t_j and t_k denote the

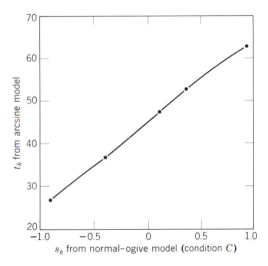

Figure 7.   Illustration of similarity of scales obtained from the normal-ogive and the arcsine models.

scale values of stimuli j and k respectively, then we might take $\theta_{jk} = t_k - t_j$ as our basic postulate, where θ_{jk}, measured in degrees, is given by

(107) $$\theta_{jk} = \sin^{-1}\sqrt{p_{jk}}$$

The least-squares solution for estimating t'_k, given empirical estimates θ'_{jk}, is directly analogous to that given earlier for condition C, since, once the transformation of observed p'_{jk} values has been carried out, the equations are formally identical.

The arcsine transformation also does not differ greatly from the normal ogive, particularly in the middle of the range. As a result, scales obtained by the two methods will again be very nearly linearly related. Figure 7 shows the relation between the two scales obtained from the application of the normal-ogive model and the arcsine model to the data of the illustrative example given in Table 4.

10 ◀

▶ *The Law*

of Categorical Judgment

1. THEORETICAL DEVELOPMENT

The "law of categorical judgment" is a set of equations relating parameters of stimuli and category boundaries to a set of cumulative proportions derived from the proportion of times each stimulus is judged to be in each category of a set of categories which are ordered with respect to a given attribute.

Like the law of comparative judgment, which it parallels, it is based on Thurstone's general judgment model. The basic notions common to the two laws are discussed in Chapter 8. We can summarize them here as follows:

A psychological continuum of the attribute of interest is postulated. Each time a stimulus is presented to a subject, it brings about some sort of a discriminal process which has a value on this continuum. Owing to various and sundry factors, upon repeated presentation, the stimulus is not always associated with a particular value, but may be associated with one higher or lower on the continuum. It is postulated that the values associated with any given stimulus project a normal distribution on the continuum. Different stimuli may have different means (scale values) and different standard deviations (discriminal dispersions).

In Chapter 9 it was shown that the additional assumption, that, when two stimuli are presented to the subject, he judges one to be greater than the other whenever the first has a higher value on the continuum than the second, leads to the general law of comparative judgment:

(1) $s_k - s_j = x_{jk}(\sigma_j^2 + \sigma_k^2 - 2r_{jk}\sigma_j\sigma_k)^{1/2}$ $(j, k = 1, 2, \cdots, n)$

where j,k = alternative subscripts for stimuli

$\quad n$ = number of stimuli

$\quad s_k$ = scale value of stimulus k

$\quad \sigma_k$ = discriminal dispersion of stimulus k

$\quad r_{jk}$ = correlation between momentary values associated with stimuli j and k

$\quad x_{jk}$ = unit normal deviate corresponding to the proportion of times stimulus k was judged greater than stimulus j

To derive the law of categorical judgment, we replace the additional assumption of Chapter 9 with the following assumptions (Torgerson, 1954):

1. The psychological continuum of the subject can be divided into a specified number of ordered categories or steps.

2. Owing to various and sundry factors, a given category boundary is not necessarily always located at a particular point on the continuum. Rather, it also projects a normal distribution of positions on the continuum. Again, different category boundaries may have different mean locations and different dispersions.

3. The subject judges a given stimulus to be below a given category boundary whenever the value of the stimulus on the continuum is less than that of the category boundary.

Essentially, this amounts to the assumption that the boundaries between adjacent categories behave like stimuli. Procedures directly analogous to those used in deriving the law of comparative judgment lead to the following set of equations for the categorical-judgment situation:

(2) $t_g - s_j = x_{jg}(\sigma_j^2 + \sigma_g^2 - 2r_{jg}\sigma_j\sigma_g)^{1/2}$ $\begin{array}{l}(j = 1, 2, \cdots, n) \\ (g = 1, 2, \cdots, m)\end{array}$

where the new terms are defined as follows:

$m+1$ = number of categories

$\quad t_g$ = mean location of the gth category boundary

$\quad \sigma_g$ = dispersion of the gth category boundary

$\quad r_{jg}$ = correlation between momentary positions of stimulus j and category boundary g

$\quad x_{jg}$ = unit normal deviate corresponding to the proportion of times stimulus j is sorted below boundary g

Equation 2 is the complete form of the law of categorical judgment. It is not solvable in its complete form, since there are again always more unknowns than equations. With n stimuli sorted into $m+1$ categories, we have as unknowns the $2n$ parameters of the stimuli, the $2m$ parameters of the category boundaries, and the mn correlation terms. Two parameters (e.g., the origin and unit) can be specified arbitrarily, leaving us with $2(n+m-1) + mn$ unknowns. Against this we have only mn equations, one for each independently observable proportion. Hence, simplifying hypotheses are again necessary.

In Chapter 9, we set up a two-way classification of special cases of the general law to make clear the distinction between the special parallel *classes* of models resulting from variations in *kind of replication* used to generate the proportions and the *special conditions* resulting from various *simplifying assumptions*. This scheme will also be used here.

Classes of Models

Class I: models involving replication over trials within a single subject. The derivation of equation 2 involved this type of replication.

Class II: models involving replication over individuals, each stimulus being judged once by each subject. The theoretical development leading to a parallel equation 2 involves the substitution of individuals for trials.

Class III: mixed models, involving replication over both individuals and trials. Each stimulus is judged several times by each subject. Interchangeability of individuals and trials is assumed.

Simplifying Conditions

Several sets of additional restrictions which lead to solvable versions of the general equation might be developed. We shall limit the presentation to the following four:

Condition A. It is assumed that the covariance term of equation 2 is constant over all values of j and g. With this additional assumption, equation 2 reduces to

$$(3) \qquad t_g - s_j = x_{jg}(a_j^2 + b_g^2)^{1/2} \qquad \begin{matrix} (j = 1, 2, \cdots, n) \\ (g = 1, 2, \cdots, m) \end{matrix}$$

where

$$a_j \equiv (\sigma_j^2 - c)^{1/2}$$
$$b_g \equiv (\sigma_g^2 - c)^{1/2}$$

For all practical purposes, of course, the assumption is that r_{jg} is equal to zero, since this is the only reasonable way for the covariance to be constant when the variances vary. Condition A is solvable only in theory. Even then the fit would remain invariant if a constant k were added to each a_j

and subtracted from each b_g. Since no practical analytical procedures are available, we shall not discuss it further.

Condition B. It is assumed that σ_g is constant for all values of g ($\sigma_g^2 = c$), and that the correlation term vanishes (perhaps more precisely, that the value under the radical in equation 2 is constant for a fixed value of j). Then, if we define $a_j^2 \equiv \sigma_j^2 + c$, equation 2 reduces to

$$
(4) \qquad t_g - s_j = x_{jg} a_j \qquad \begin{aligned} (j &= 1, 2, \cdots, n) \\ (g &= 1, 2, \cdots, m) \end{aligned}
$$

Equation 4 is formally identical with the equation underlying the general method of successive intervals (see, for example, Saffir, 1937; Mosier, 1940a; Gulliksen, 1954; Burros, 1955; Rimoldi and Hormaeche, 1955; and Diederich, Messick, and Tucker, 1955). In the general method of successive intervals, however, it has been assumed, either explicitly or implicitly, that the category boundaries are *fixed* throughout the experiment, resulting in the general equation

$$
(5) \qquad t_g - s_j = x_{jg} \sigma_j
$$

Since equations 4 and 5 are formally identical, this assumption of fixed category boundaries is unnecessarily restricting. We need only assume that the dispersions of the category boundaries are all equal and that all correlation terms vanish.

This is a considerably more lenient condition. It would seem so especially in the class II situation, where the proportions are obtained from responses of a group of *subjects.* Here, the requirement of fixed category boundaries means that all subjects divide the continuum into exactly the same steps, even though the different steps may be unequal in size. The good fit of the model to empirical data probably results from the fact that the restriction of equation 5 is not really necessary.

Condition C. Under some circumstances, it may be reasonable to assume that σ_j is constant for all stimuli ($\sigma_j^2 = k$) and that all correlation terms vanish. Then, defining $b_g^2 \equiv \sigma_g^2 + k$, we have the set of equations

$$
(6) \qquad t_g - s_j = x_{jg} b_g \qquad \begin{aligned} (j &= 1, 2, \cdots n) \\ (g &= 1, 2, \cdots, m) \end{aligned}
$$

In this equation, the dispersions of the category boundaries are left free to vary. Strictly speaking, this model requires independently observed proportions, p'_{jg}. In the usual sorting or rating procedures (see section 2), however, these proportions are not completely independent—the cumulative process used in estimating p_{jg} artificially prevents the result $p'_{jg} > p'_{j,g+1}$. Such a result is theoretically implied, however, by equation 6, assuming that the values of b_g actually do vary. Under any reasonable situation, however, a reversal such as this would occur theoretically only for proportions in the immediate neighborhood of zero or unity. Since, for a number of reasons (e.g., extreme unreliability of estimates of x_{jg}, along with high sensitivity of the model to departures from normality in these regions), proportions in the region of zero and unity are not used anyway, the requirement is of no practical importance.

Condition D. It is assumed that σ_j is constant, σ_g is constant, and r_{jg} is constant for all values of j and g (or, equivalently, simply that the value under the radical in equation 2 is constant). Equation 2 then reduces to

$$(7) \qquad t_g - s_j = x_{jg}c \qquad \begin{matrix} (j = 1, 2, \cdots, n) \\ (g = 1, 2, \cdots, m) \end{matrix}$$

Equation 7 is essentially the equation involved in Attneave's method of graded dichotomies (1949), Garner and Hake's equidiscriminability scaling procedure (1951), and Edwards' special case of the method of successive intervals (1952). Again, it should be pointed out that assumption of fixed category boundaries is unnecessary; it is only necessary that they be equal to a constant (which, in turn, is not necessarily equal to the constant of the dispersions of the stimuli).

Summary

The various combinations of classes and conditions gives the twelve versions of the law of categorical judgment shown in Table 1. It should

Table 1.   A Two-Way Classification of Special Cases of
the Law of Categorical Judgment

	Condition A	Condition B	Condition C	Condition D
Assumptions	$r_{jg}\sigma_j\sigma_g = c$	$\sigma_g^2 = c$ $r_{jg} = 0$	$\sigma_j^2 = c$ $r_{jg} = 0$	$\sigma_j^2 = k_1$ $\sigma_g^2 = k_2$ $r_{jg} = r$
Class I (within individual)	$t_g - s_j = x_{jg}(a_j^2 + b_g^2)^{1/2}$	$t_g - s_j = x_{jg}a_j$	$t_g - s_j = x_{jg}b_g$	$t_g - s_j = x_{jg}c$
Class II (between individuals)	$t_g - s_j = x_{jg}(a_j^2 + b_g^2)^{1/2}$	$t_g - s_j = x_{jq}a_j$	$t_g - s_j = x_{jg}b_g$	$t_g - s_j = x_{jg}c$
Class III (mixed)	$t_g - s_j = x_{jg}(a_j^2 + b_g^2)^{1/2}$	$t_g - s_j = x_{jg}a_j$	$t_g - s_j = x_{jg}b_g$	$t_g - s_j = x_{jg}c$

be emphasized that, though the equations are identical in form within each column, the meaning of the terms varies according to the row.

In the next section, we discuss briefly the various experimental procedures used in the collection of data. Following this, we discuss the analytical problem in general and present several alternative solutions for various of the special conditions.

2. EXPERIMENTAL PROCEDURES

The law was developed for the case where the stimuli have been placed into categories which are ordered with respect to the attribute being investigated. In particular, it assumes that the proportion of times each stimulus is sorted below each category boundary is known. There are a number of procedures available for obtaining estimates of these proportions. In general, they can be classified as *sorting* procedures, *rating* procedures, or *rank-order* procedures.

Sorting Procedures—the Method of Successive Intervals

The subject's task is to sort the stimuli into $m+1$ piles so that the first pile contains those stimuli that are most positive with respect to the attribute; the second pile, the stimuli next most positive; etc. It is only necessary that the piles be in rank order with respect to the attribute. There is no requirement that the subject sort the stimuli so that the intervals between piles are equal. Often the piles may be identified with adjectives which progress from extremely positive to zero or extremely negative, depending on the particular attribute.

Rating Procedures

Instead of presenting all stimuli to the subject at once, the stimuli are presented one at a time. The subject's task is to rate each stimulus with respect to the attribute. The rating may be expressed on a numerical scale (e.g., rate on a scale from 1 to 10, 10 being most positive), an adjective scale, or a graphic scale. In the last case the graphic scale is arbitrarily divided into as many categories as desired by the experimenter.

Rank-Order Procedures

In the method of rank order, the subject is required to place the stimuli in rank order with respect to the attribute. Each rank may be taken as a category, or several adjacent ranks may be combined to make up each category.

With any of these procedures, repeated judgments are necessary in order to obtain estimates of the proportions. The necessary replication, as we have seen, might be obtained by having a single subject repeat the procedure a large number of times (class I models), many subjects each carry out the procedure once (class II models), or several subjects each carry out the procedure several times (class III models).   The alternative used will again depend on the nature of the stimuli and the purpose of the experiment (see Chapter 9 for a discussion of some of the factors that must be taken into consideration).

3. THE FOUR BASIC MATRICES

Regardless of the particular experimental method used, the immediate raw data will be in the form of the frequency with which each stimulus is sorted (rated, ranked) into each category.   These observed frequencies may be arranged in the $n \times m+1$ matrix F, where the rows represent the stimuli ($j = 1, 2, \cdots, n$) and the columns, the categories ($g = 1, 2, \cdots, m+1$).   An artificial example is given in Table 2.   The element f'_{jg} is the number of times stimulus j was sorted into category g.   (As in Chapter 9, a prime indicates an estimate, and a double prime indicates a value derived from such estimates.)

Table 2.   THE RAW FREQUENCY MATRIX F
(HYPOTHETICAL DATA)

The element in the jth row and gth column is the number
of times stimulus j was placed in category g

Categories ($g = 1, 2, \cdots, m+1$)

		1	2	3	4	5
	1	100	38	49	11	2
	2	84	27	47	23	19
Stimuli	3	13	32	110	39	6
($j = 1, 2, \cdots, n$)	4	62	14	32	23	69
	5	4	9	49	58	80

In order to obtain the x values which are found in the equations of the law of categorical judgment, the following three matrices are constructed.

Matrix Φ

Matrix Φ is an $n \times m+1$ matrix whose elements, ϕ'_{jg} are equal to the number of times stimulus j was sorted below the gth category boundary (the gth category boundary being defined as the upper boundary of the gth category).   Matrix Φ is constructed from F by cumulating from the left.

In general,

$$(8) \qquad \phi'_{jg} = \sum_{g=1}^{g} f'_{jg}$$

The elements in the last $(m+1)$ column of matrix $\boldsymbol{\Phi}$ should be equal to the total number of times the jth stimulus was sorted, and thus may be used to check the computation. An example is given in Table 3.

Table 3. THE CUMULATIVE FREQUENCY MATRIX $\boldsymbol{\Phi}$

The element in the jth row and gth column is the number of times stimulus j was sorted below the gth category boundary (Below the upper boundary of category g)

Category Boundaries ($g = 1, 2, \cdots, m+1$)

		1	2	3	4	5
	1	100	138	187	198	200
Stimuli	2	84	111	158	181	200
$(j = 1, 2, \cdots, n)$	3	13	45	155	194	200
	4	62	76	108	131	200
	5	4	13	62	120	200

Matrix P

Matrix $\mathbf{P}$ is an $n \times m$ matrix whose elements give the proportion of times stimulus j was judged to be below the gth category boundary (Table 4). In general,

$$(9) \qquad p'_{jg} = \frac{\phi'_{jg}}{\phi'_{j,m+1}}$$

The $(m+1)$th column of matrix $\mathbf{P}$, which would always contain all cells of unity, is dropped from the matrix.

Table 4. THE CUMULATIVE PROPORTION MATRIX $\mathbf{P}$

The element in the jth row and gth column is the proportion of times stimulus j was sorted below the gth category boundary

Category Boundaries ($g = 1, 2, \cdots, m$)

		1	2	3	4
	1	0.500	0.690	0.935	0.990
Stimuli	2	0.420	0.555	0.790	0.905
$(j = 1, 2, \cdots, n)$	3	0.065	0.225	0.775	0.970
	4	0.310	0.380	0.540	0.655
	5	0.020	0.065	0.310	0.600

Matrix X

Matrix **X** (Table 5) is an $n \times m$ matrix whose elements are the unit normal deviates corresponding to the elements of matrix **P**. Element x'_{jg} will be negative for all proportions below 0.50 and positive for all above 0.50. Any cells of matrix **P** that contain proportions of zero or unity cannot be transformed into x values, and therefore the cells of matrix **X** corresponding to such cells must be left vacant. Matrix **X** contains the empirical estimates x'_{jg} of the theoretical values x_{jg} of the equations of the law of categorical judgment.

Table 5. THE BASIC TRANSFORMATION MATRIX **X**

The element in the jth row and gth column is the unit normal deviate corresponding to p'_{jg}

Category Boundaries ($g = 1, 2, \cdots, m$)

		1	2	3	4
	1	0.0000	0.4959	1.5141	2.3262
Stimuli	2	−0.2019	0.1383	0.8064	1.3106
($j = 1, 2, \cdots, n$)	3	−1.5141	−0.7554	0.7554	1.8808
	4	−0.4959	−0.3055	0.1004	0.3989
	5	−2.0537	−1.5141	−0.4959	0.2533

With experimentally obtained data, the x values will each be somewhat in error. A number of procedures have been devised to obtain estimates from fallible data of the scale values and discriminal dispersions of the stimuli, and of the locations of the category boundaries. All the solutions have in common the four basic matrices presented above. In the discussion of analytical procedures in the next sections, it will be assumed that the data have previously been transformed into the basic matrix **X**.

4. ANALYTICAL PROCEDURES: GENERAL CONSIDERATIONS

The general problem dealt with in this and the following two sections is the problem of obtaining adequate estimates of the parameters of the stimuli and category boundaries when given observed data in the form of matrix **X**.

Conditions B, C, and D all lead to workable solutions. However, we need not consider conditions B and C separately, since a mathematical duality exists between them. If we multiply both sides of equation 6 by (-1), we get

$$(10) \qquad s_j - t_g = (-x_{jg})b_g \qquad \begin{array}{l} (j = 1, 2, \cdots, n) \\ (g = 1, 2, \cdots, m) \end{array}$$

which, in form, is identical with equation 4.   Hence any solution developed for condition B is also a solution for condition C.   The solutions presented in the following section are given in terms of condition B, since this condition corresponds to the standard method treated in the literature.   We have only to reverse the signs of the elements in matrix X and remember that an operation on j becomes an operation on g, and vice versa, in order to use any condition B solution for condition C.

A great number of analytical procedures dealing specifically with the categorical-judgment situation have been devised (Saffir, 1937; Guilford, 1938, 1954; Mosier, 1940a; Attneave, 1949; Garner and Hake, 1951; Edwards, 1952; Gulliksen, 1954; Burros, 1955; Rimoldi and Hormaeche, 1955; Diederich, Messick, and Tucker, 1955; Messick, Tucker, and Garrison, 1955).   In addition, several procedures have been developed for mathematically parallel problems in related fields (Thurstone, 1925, 1927f; Tucker, 1952).   Some of the procedures relate to condition B while others are restricted to condition D.   While the terminology used in all the procedures has implied fixed category boundaries, this is unnecessary as we have seen.

We shall first present various alternative solutions for condition B. Several simpler solutions appropriate for the more restricting condition D are presented in section 6.

5. ANALYTICAL PROCEDURES: CONDITION B

The General Problem

In this section we deal with procedures for obtaining estimates of scale values s_j' and dispersion parameters a_j' of the stimuli and locations of the category boundaries t_g' from data in the form of the elements of matrix X. It will be worth while to examine the matrix X more closely before going into the various analytical procedures themselves.

Consider first a matrix X composed of errorless elements x_{jg} which fit the condition B model exactly.   Then each element is a term in one equation of the following set:

$$(11) \qquad t_g = a_j x_{jg} + s_j \qquad \begin{matrix} (j = 1, 2, \cdots, n) \\ (g = 1, 2, \cdots, m) \end{matrix}$$

Notice that *each row of the matrix gives directly the positions of the category boundaries*.   However, the unit and origin to which they are referred differs from one row to the next, the values in the jth row being referred to an origin at s_j and in the unit a_j ("t_g is x_{jg} a_j-units above the point s_j"). With fallible data in place of the true values, of course, the situation becomes more complex.   Some efficient procedure for using the available data for estimating the unknowns is indicated.

Two rather elaborate least-squares approaches are available. One (Gulliksen, 1954) will be presented in this chapter. The other (Tucker, 1952) is outlined briefly in Chapter 13 in connection with a parallel problem of one of the response methods. The basic difference between the two approaches has been pointed out by Diederich, Messick, and Tucker (1955). First, notice that equation 11 is the equation of a straight line in t_g and x_{jg}. It can also be written

$$(12) \qquad x_{jg} = \left(\frac{1}{a_j}\right) t_g - \left(\frac{s_j}{a_j}\right)$$

Equations 11 and 12 can be considered to be the equations of the two regression lines of the plot of x_{jg} against t_g $(g = 1, 2, \cdots, m)$. The basic difference between Gulliksen's and Tucker's approaches can now be stated quite simply: Gulliksen solves for the values of a'_j, s'_j, and t'_g which minimize the sum of squares of the errors made in estimating t'_g from x'_{jg}:

$$(13) \qquad Q_1 = \sum_{j=1}^{n} \sum_{g=1}^{m} (x'_{jg} a'_j - t'_g + s'_j)^2$$

His approach thus involves the regression lines indicated by equation 11. Tucker's solution involves the other regression lines, since he solves for the values of $(1/a_j)'$, $(s_j/a_j)'$, and t'_g which minimize the sums of squares of the errors made in estimating x'_{jg} from t'_g:

$$(14) \qquad Q_2 = \sum_{j=1}^{n} \sum_{g=1}^{m} \left[x'_{jg} - \left(\frac{1}{a_j}\right)' t'_g + \left(\frac{s_j}{a_j}\right)' \right]^2$$

Now, if the correlation between x'_{jg} and t'_g were perfect, the slope of equation 11 would be equal to the ratio of the standard deviations of t and x_j, while the slope of equation 12 would be equal to the reciprocal ratio. Hence, the two procedures would give the same result. The estimates will differ, however, when the correlation is less than perfect, for then both slopes are reduced by multiplication with the correlation factor r'_{tx_j}. It should be noted, incidentally, that, when the x'_{jg} are obtained from *cumulated* proportions, the correlations will be very nearly one in any event, since monotonicity of the relation between the two variables is artificially imposed by the experimental procedure.

The remaining solutions to condition B have been derived algebraically and use "common-sense" averaging procedures (either numerical or graphical) in obtaining the estimates. Differences between the two general types of algebraic solutions parallel the differences between the two least-squares solutions.

Gulliksen's Least-Squares Solution for Condition _B_

As stated earlier, the problem is to solve for the values of a'_j, s'_j, and t'_g which minimize the error Q_1 defined by equation 11. The solution given below follows Gulliksen (1954) closely, differing only in our explicit choice of origin and unit of the scale.

Let us specify the origin and unit so that

(15)
$$\sum_{g=1}^{m} t'_g = 0$$

and

(16)
$$\sum_{g=1}^{m} t'^2_g = m$$

Using the Lagrange multipliers γ and 2λ to impose the conditions of equations 15 and 16, we can write the function to be minimized as follows:

(17) $\quad Q = \sum_{j=1}^{n} \sum_{g=1}^{m} (a'_j x'_{jg} - t'_g + s'_j)^2 - 2\lambda \left(\sum_{g=1}^{m} t'_g \right) - \gamma \left(\sum_{g=1}^{m} t'^2_g - m \right)$

Taking the partial derivative of Q with respect to each s'_j in turn, we get the n equations:

(18)
$$\frac{1}{2} \frac{\partial Q}{\partial s'_j} = \sum_{g=1}^{m} (a'_j x'_{jg} - t'_g + s'_j) \qquad (j = 1, 2, \cdots, n)$$

Setting the partial derivative equal to zero and simplifying gives

(19)
$$ms'_j + a'_j \sum_{g=1}^{m} x'_{jg} - \sum_{g=1}^{m} t'_g = 0$$

Let

(20)
$$\frac{1}{m} \sum_{g=1}^{m} x'_{jg} = \bar{x}'_j.$$

Using equation 15, we can then write equation 19 as follows:

(21)
$$s'_j = -a'_j \bar{x}'_j. \qquad (j = 1, 2, \cdots, n)$$

Taking the partial derivative of Q with respect to each t'_g in turn gives

(22) $\quad \dfrac{1}{2} \dfrac{\partial Q}{\partial t'_g} = - \sum_{j=1}^{n} (a'_j x'_{jg} - t'_g + s'_j) - \lambda - \gamma t'_g \qquad (g = 1, 2, \cdots, m)$

Equating to zero and simplifying gives

$$(23) \qquad (n - \gamma)t'_g - \lambda - \sum_{j=1}^{n} s'_j - \sum_{j=1}^{n} a'_j x'_{jg} = 0$$

Using equation 21, we can write

$$(24) \qquad (n - \gamma)t'_g - \lambda - \sum_{j=1}^{n} a'_j(x'_{jg} - \bar{x}'_{j.}) = 0$$

If we sum equation 24 over g and use equation 15, we see that

$$(25) \qquad\qquad\qquad \lambda = 0$$

Equation 24 now becomes

$$(26) \qquad (n - \gamma)t'_g = \sum_{j=1}^{n} a'_j(x'_{jg} - \bar{x}'_{j.}) \qquad (g = 1, 2, \cdots, m)$$

We now square both sides of equation 26, giving

$$(27) \qquad (n - \gamma)^2 t'^2_g = \left[\sum_{j=1}^{n} a'_j(x'_{jg} - \bar{x}'_{j.}) \right]^2$$

Using k as an alternative subscript for stimuli, we can write equation 27 in the following form:

$$(28) \qquad (n - \gamma)^2 t'^2_g = \sum_{j=1}^{n} \sum_{k=1}^{n} a'_j a'_k (x'_{jg} - \bar{x}'_{j.})(x'_{kg} - \bar{x}'_{k.})$$

Summing over g, and letting $\tilde{x}'_{j.}$ and $\tilde{x}'_{k.}$ denote the standard deviations of x'_{jg} and x'_{kg} respectively, and r'_{jk} the correlation between them gives

$$(29) \qquad (n - \gamma)^2 = \sum_{j=1}^{n} \sum_{k=1}^{n} a'_j \tilde{x}'_j . a'_k \tilde{x}'_k . r'_{jk} \qquad (r'_{jj} = r'_{kk} = 1)$$

We next differentiate Q with respect to each of the a'_j in turn, giving

$$(30) \qquad \frac{1}{2} \frac{\partial Q}{\partial a'_j} = \sum_{g=1}^{m} (a'_j x'_{jg} - t'_g + s'_j) x'_{jg} \qquad (j = 1, 2, \cdots, n)$$

Equating to zero and summing each term separately gives

$$(31) \qquad \sum_{g=1}^{m} a'_j x'^2_{jg} + \sum_{g=1}^{m} s'_j x'_{jg} - \sum_{g=1}^{m} t'_g x'_{jg} = 0$$

Substituting from equation 21 gives

(32)
$$a'_j \sum_{g=1}^{m} x'^2_{jg} - m a'_j \bar{x}'^2_{j\cdot} = \sum_{g=1}^{m} t'_g x'_{jg}$$

Since

(33)
$$\sum_{g=1}^{m} x'^2_{jg} - m\bar{x}'^2_{j\cdot} = m\bar{x}'^2_{j\cdot}$$

substitution of equation 26 into equation 32 gives

(34)
$$a'_j m\bar{x}'^2_{j\cdot} = \frac{1}{n-\gamma} \sum_{g=1}^{m} x'_{jg} \left[\sum_{k=1}^{n} a'_k(x'_{kg} - \bar{x}'_{k\cdot}) \right]$$

Since

(35)
$$\sum_{g=1}^{m} x'_{jg}(x'_{kg} - \bar{x}'_{k\cdot}) = \sum_{g=1}^{m} (x'_{jg} - \bar{x}'_{j\cdot})(x'_{kg} - \bar{x}'_{k\cdot}) = m r'_{jk} \bar{x}'_j \bar{x}'_k.$$

equation 34 becomes

(36)
$$(n-\gamma)a'_j \bar{x}'^2_{j\cdot} = \sum_{k=1}^{n} a'_k r'_{jk} \bar{x}'_{j\cdot} \bar{x}'_k.$$

which simplifies to

(37)
$$(n-\gamma)a'_j \bar{x}'_{j\cdot} = \sum_{k=1}^{n} a'_k r'_{jk} \bar{x}'_k.$$

If we now define the element

(38)
$$z'_j = a'_j \bar{x}'_j.$$

and the matrices

$\mathbf{Z}$ = row vector with elements z'_j

$\mathbf{R}$ = $n \times n$ correlation matrix with elements r'_{jk}, where $r'_{jj} = r'_{kk} = 1$

then equation 37 can be written

(39)
$$\mathbf{ZR} = (n-\gamma)\mathbf{Z}$$

Let $\theta = n - \gamma$. Equation 39 then becomes

(40)
$$\mathbf{Z}(\mathbf{R} - \theta\mathbf{I}) = 0$$

Using the same notation, equation 29 becomes

(41)
$$\theta^2 = \mathbf{ZRZ'}$$

If we postmultiply equation 40 by $\mathbf{Z}'$, we get

(42) $$\mathbf{ZRZ}' - \mathbf{Z}\theta\mathbf{Z}' = 0$$

Substituting from equation 41 gives

(43) $$\theta^2 - \theta\mathbf{ZZ}' = 0$$

or

(44) $$\theta = \mathbf{ZZ}'$$

We can now obtain numerical values for the vector $\mathbf{Z}$. Equation 40 can be solved by finding the latent vector corresponding to the largest latent root of matrix $\mathbf{R}$. The elements of the latent vector are proportional to the elements of the vector $\mathbf{Z}$. The proportionality constant is chosen so that equation 44 is satisfied.

Once the values of z_j' are obtained, equation 38 can be used to solve for the a_j', equation 26 for the t_g', and equation 21 for the s_j'. Equations 21, 26, 38, 40, and 44 thus constitute the least-squares solution for condition B.

The principal computational difficulty in the solution is in solving for the latent vector, ordinarily a very laborious process. Gulliksen (1954) noted that the off-diagonal entries in matrix $\mathbf{R}$ are all very high and very nearly equal. He suggested, as an approximation to the least-squares solution, that it be assumed that the true value of the correlations is constant ($r_{jk} = r$). If we then take the average of the observed r_{jk}' as an estimate of the constant, the problem simplifies considerably.

Let us denote by $\bar{r}'$ the average of the observed correlations. Then, the largest latent root of $\overline{\mathbf{R}}$ (where $\overline{\mathbf{R}}$ is the matrix with unity in the diagonal cells and $\bar{r}'$ in the off-diagonal cells) is

(45) $$\theta = 1 + (n - 1)\bar{r}'$$

The elements of the latent vector $\mathbf{Z}$ are all equal to c, where

(46) $$c = z_j' = \left[\frac{1 + (n - 1)\bar{r}'}{n}\right]^{1/2}$$

Using equations 21, 26, and 38, we can write

(47) $$a_j' = \frac{1}{\bar{x}_{j.}'}\, c$$

(48) $$s_j' = -\frac{\bar{x}_{j.}'}{\bar{x}_{j.}'}\, c$$

and

$$(49) \qquad t'_g = \frac{1}{nc} \sum_{j=1}^{n} \frac{x'_{jg} - \bar{x}'_{j\cdot}}{\tilde{x}'_{j\cdot}}$$

We need not actually compute all values of r'_{jk} in order to obtain the value of c. Gulliksen shows that, if we define

$$(50) \qquad u'_g = \sum_{j=1}^{n} \frac{x'_{jg} - \bar{x}'_{j\cdot}}{\tilde{x}'_{j\cdot}}$$

then the variance ($\tilde{u}'^2$) of the u'_g, which can readily be computed from the data, is related to the $\bar{r}'$ by

$$(51) \qquad \tilde{u}'^2 = n[1 + (n-1)\bar{r}']$$

Multiplying by n/n and substituting from equation 46 gives

$$(52) \qquad \tilde{u}'^2 = n^2 c^2$$

or

$$(53) \qquad c = \frac{\tilde{u}'}{n}$$

We can simplify things slightly by changing the (arbitrary) unit of measurement by a factor of $n/\tilde{u}'$. Then equation 47 becomes

$$(54) \qquad a'_j = \frac{1}{\tilde{x}'_{j\cdot}}$$

equation 48 becomes

$$(55) \qquad s'_j = -\frac{\bar{x}'_{j\cdot}}{\tilde{x}'_{j\cdot}}$$

and equation 49 becomes

$$(56) \qquad t'_g = \frac{nu'_g}{\tilde{u}'^2}$$

Equations 54, 55, and 56 give the values of the unknowns, a'_j, s'_j, and t'_g, in terms of observable data. These equations correspond to Gulliksen's approximation to his least-squares solution.

Both the least-squares solution and the approximation to it require that the matrix **X** contain no vacant cells. It has been seen that, whenever the range of the stimuli greatly exceeds their dispersion parameters, proportions of zero or unity are likely to be obtained. As a result, the cells of matrix **X** which correspond to these proportions will be vacant. Actually, in most scaling situations, vacant cells will be present, and, hence, the procedures given above cannot be used without modification.

Diederich, Messick, and Tucker (1955) give an iterative procedure which generalizes Gulliksen's least-squares solution to the incomplete data case. Their procedure also provides for weighting the observation equations. In Messick, Tucker, and Garrison (1955) this latter procedure is adapted to punched-card routines. Alternative procedures are discussed in the next sections.

Thurstone-Type Solutions for Condition *B*

These solutions, as well as those following, differ from the former in that the solutions are obtained in terms of the population parameters. Application of the procedures to fallible data involves substitution of the observed estimates for the population values, and use of simple averaging or curve-fitting procedures. The approach discussed below stems more or less directly from Thurstone's original method (presented by Saffir, 1937).

Consider first a matrix **X** composed of true values of x_{jg}. Let k be an alternative subscript for stimuli. We can then write, for stimuli j and k, the two sets of equations

$$(57) \qquad t_g - s_j = x_{jg}a_j \qquad (g = 1, 2, \cdots, m)$$

and

$$(58) \qquad t_g - s_k = x_{kg}a_k \qquad (g = 1, 2, \cdots, m)$$

Subtracting equation 58 from 57, we have

$$(59) \qquad s_k - s_j = x_{jg}a_j - x_{kg}a_k$$

Solving for x_{jg}, we obtain

$$(60) \qquad x_{jg} = \frac{a_k}{a_j} x_{kg} + \frac{s_k - s_j}{a_j} \qquad (g = 1, 2, \cdots, m)$$

Equation 60 is the equation of a straight line. The x values of stimulus j can be plotted against those of stimulus k (the jth row against the kth row of matrix **X**). In the errorless case, the points all fall along a straight line. The slope of the line is equal to the ratio of the dispersion parameters, a_k/a_j, and the intercept, to $(s_k - s_j)/a_j$.

If we specify the unit of the scale so that $a_j = 1$, and the origin so that $s_j = 0$, we can solve for a_k and s_k.

Any two stimuli might be plotted against each other. Each plot, in the errorless case, would have m points, one for each column of matrix **X**. A theoretical solution could be obtained by plotting the x values of stimulus j against those of each of the remaining stimuli, and using the slope and intercept relations given above to solve for the remaining scale values. The category boundaries would be given directly by the elements of row j.

In actual practice, we have the observed estimates x'_{jg} in place of the theoretical values x_{jg}. Further, each plot may have less than m points, since matrix X may have vacant cells. In addition, owing to error, the points will not fall exactly along a straight line.

The procedure followed in the actual construction of the scale is to work with only the adjacent pairs of stimuli (since these will in general have the most points in common). A numerical example is given in Table 6. The routine is outlined below.

1. Arrange the rows of X in approximate order of increasing magnitude of scale value. This is accomplished by first summing matrix P over g for each row ($j = 1, 2, \cdots, n$), and then arranging the rows in order of increasing magnitudes of the sums.

2. Plot against each other the adjacent rows:

$$x'_{1g} \text{ against } x'_{2g} \qquad \text{(stimulus 1 vs. stimulus 2)}$$
$$x'_{2g} \text{ against } x'_{3g} \qquad \text{(stimulus 2 vs. stimulus 3)}$$
$$\cdot \qquad\qquad \cdot$$
$$\cdot \qquad\qquad \cdot$$
$$\cdot \qquad\qquad \cdot$$
$$x'_{n-1,g} \text{ against } x'_{ng} \qquad \text{(stimulus } n-1 \text{ vs. stimulus } n)$$

There are thus $n-1$ plots for n stimuli. Fit a straight line to the points for each plot.

3. Define the unit and origin so that $a'_1 = 1$, and $s'_1 = 0$. Then, from equation 60, if the obtained slope of the plot of the jth stimulus against the $(j+1)$th stimulus is defined as $C'_{j,j+1}$ and the intercept as $I'_{j,j+1}$, we have, from the definition of the origin and unit, and from the first plot,

$$a'_1 = 1, \qquad\qquad s'_1 = 0$$
$$a'_2 = C'_{12}, \qquad\qquad s'_2 = I'_{12}$$

4. These values are then used in solving for a'_3 and s'_3. From the second plot

$$C'_{23} = \frac{a'_3}{a'_2}$$

or

$$a'_3 = C'_{23}a'_2$$

and

$$I'_{23} = \frac{s'_3 - s'_2}{a'_2}$$

or

$$s'_3 = s'_2 + a'_2 I'_{23}$$

5. This process is repeated in like manner until all dispersions and scale values are obtained. In general,

(61) $$a'_{j+1} = C'_{j,j+1} a'_j$$

and

(62) $$s'_{j+1} = s'_j + I'_{j,j+1} a'_j$$

6. Once the scale values and discriminal dispersions of the stimuli have been determined, the basic equation 4 can be used to estimate the locations of the category boundaries t_g:

$$t'_g = s'_j + x'_{jg} a'_j$$

For each category boundary there are as many estimates as there are filled cells in the corresponding column of matrix **X**. The average of these estimates can be taken as the value wanted, and may be written

(63) $$t'_g = \frac{1}{q} \sum_{j}^{n} (s'_j + x'_{jg} a'_j) \qquad (g = 1, 2, \cdots, m)$$

where $q =$ the number of nonvacant cells summed over in the gth column of matrix **X**.

Numerical procedures can be used in place of the graphical solution presented above. (Saffir actually used the method of averages for fitting the lines.)   If the matrix **X** contains no vacant cells, numerical procedures are particularly straightforward.   From equation 60, since $(s_k - s_j)/a_j$ is an additive constant for particular values of j and k $(g = 1, 2, \cdots, m)$, it is clear that

(64) $$\frac{\tilde{x}_{k.}}{\tilde{x}_{j.}} = \frac{a_j}{a_k}$$

or

(65) $$a_j \tilde{x}_{j.} = a_k \tilde{x}_{k.} = C$$

It is convenient (with no loss in generality) to specify the unit so that $C = 1$.   Then, in the errorless case,

(66) $$a_j = \frac{1}{\tilde{x}_{j.}}$$

Table 6. ILLUSTRATIVE EXAMPLE (ERRORLESS DATA).
THURSTONE'S GENERAL SOLUTION

MATRIX X

Category Boundaries g

		1	2	3	4
	1	0.000	0.500	1.500	2.250
	2	−0.200	0.133	0.800	1.300
Stimuli j	3	−1.500	−0.750	0.750	1.875
	4	−0.500	−0.300	0.100	0.400
	5	−2.000	−1.500	−0.500	0.250

1. Define $s_1' = 0$, $a_1' = 1$.

2. To solve for s_2' and a_2', plot x_{1g}' against x_{2g}'.

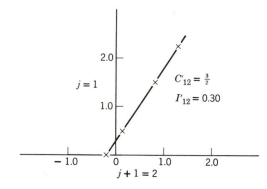

$$C_{12}' = \frac{a_2'}{a_1'} = \frac{3}{2}$$

$$a_2' = \frac{3}{2}$$

$$I_{12}' = \frac{s_2' - s_1'}{a_1'} = 0.30$$

$$s_2' = 0.30$$

3. To solve for s_3' and a_3', plot x_{2g}' against x_{3g}'.

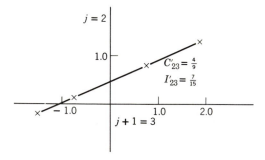

$$a_3' = C_{23}' a_2'$$
$$= \left(\tfrac{4}{9}\right)\left(\tfrac{3}{2}\right)$$
$$= \tfrac{2}{3}$$

$$s_3' = s_2' + a_2' I_{23}'$$
$$= 0.30 + \left(\tfrac{3}{2}\right)\left(\tfrac{7}{15}\right)$$
$$= 1.0$$

Table 6. ILLUSTRATIVE EXAMPLE CONTINUED.

4. To solve for s_4' and a_4', plot x_{3g}' against x_{4g}'.

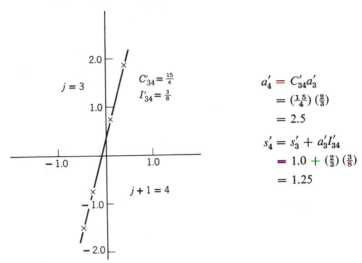

$j = 3$

$C_{34}' = \frac{15}{4}$
$I_{34}' = \frac{3}{8}$

$j + 1 = 4$

$a_4' = C_{34}' a_3'$
$= \left(\frac{15}{4}\right)\left(\frac{2}{3}\right)$
$= 2.5$

$s_4' = s_3' + a_3' I_{34}'$
$= 1.0 + \left(\frac{2}{3}\right)\left(\frac{3}{8}\right)$
$= 1.25$

5. To solve for s_5' and a_5', plot x_{4g}' against x_{5g}'.

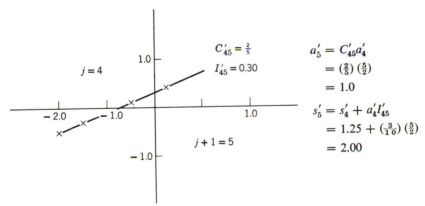

$j = 4$

$C_{45}' = \frac{2}{5}$
$I_{45}' = 0.30$

$j + 1 = 5$

$a_5' = C_{45}' a_4'$
$= \left(\frac{2}{5}\right)\left(\frac{5}{2}\right)$
$= 1.0$

$s_5' = s_4' + a_4' I_{45}'$
$= 1.25 + \left(\frac{3}{10}\right)\left(\frac{5}{2}\right)$
$= 2.00$

6. To solve for the values of t_g', use equation 63.

$$t_1' = \frac{1}{5}\sum_{j=1}^{5}(x_{j1}'a_j' + s_j') = 0.00$$

$$t_2' = \frac{1}{5}\sum_{j=1}^{5}(x_{j2}'a_j' + s_j') = 0.50$$

$$t_3' = \frac{1}{5}\sum_{j=1}^{5}(x_{j3}'a_j' + s_j') = 1.50$$

$$t_4' = \frac{1}{5}\sum_{j=1}^{5}(x_{j4}'a_j' + s_j') = 2.25$$

If we next average equation 57 over j, we get

$$(67) \qquad t_g = \frac{1}{n} \sum_{j=1}^{n} x_{jg} a_j + \frac{1}{n} \sum_{j=1}^{n} s_j$$

If we now define the origin so that $\frac{1}{n} \sum_{j=1}^{n} s_j = 0$, equation 67 reduces to

$$(68) \qquad t_g = \frac{1}{n} \sum_{j=1}^{n} x_{jg} a_j$$

To solve for the values of s_j, we average equation 57 over g:

$$(69) \qquad s_j = \bar{t}_{.} - a_j \bar{x}_{j.}$$

Table 7. ILLUSTRATIVE EXAMPLE (ERRORLESS DATA)
ALGEBRAIC SOLUTION BASED ON EQUATION 11
COMPLETE MATRICES **X**

MATRIX **X**

		Category Boundaries g				$\bar{x}'_{j.}$	$\tilde{x}'_{j.}$	$a'_j = \dfrac{1}{\tilde{x}'_{j.}}$
		1	2	3	4			
	1	0.000	0.500	1.500	2.250	1.06250	0.87278	1.1458
Stimuli	2	−0.200	0.133	0.800	1.300	0.50825	0.58190	1.7185
j	3	−1.500	−0.750	0.750	1.875	0.09375	1.30915	0.7638
	4	−0.500	−0.330	0.100	0.400	−0.07500	0.34910	2.8645
	5	−2.000	−1.500	−0.500	0.250	−0.93750	0.87278	1.1458

	1	2	3	4	$\bar{t}'_{.}$
$t'_g = \dfrac{1}{5} \sum_{j}^{5} a'_j x'_{jg}$	−1.0426	−0.4699	0.6760	1.5353	0.1747

$$s'_j = \bar{t}'_{.} - a'_j \bar{x}'_{j.}$$

Stimuli j		
	1	−1.043
	2	−0.699
	3	0.103
	4	0.390
	5	1.249

Equations 66, 68, and 69 give an algebraic solution for the unknowns in terms of the elements of the matrix $\mathbf{X}$. With fallible data we merely substitute the observed x'_{jg} for the theoretical x_{jg}, and use the averaging procedures indicated to solve for the estimates s'_j, a'_j, and t'_g. A numerical example is given in Table 7.

Equation 66 is the same as equation 54 of Gulliksen's approximation procedure discussed earlier. Equation 69 differs from the corresponding equation 55 only in the arbitrary choice of the origin. The estimates of t_g given by equation 68 will be linearly related to the corresponding estimates of equation 56, but their spacing relative to the scale values of the stimuli will differ, since Gulliksen's formulation includes the regression effect caused by the lack of perfect correlation.

Burros (1955) and Rimoldi and Hormaeche (1955) have also presented equations equivalent to our equation 66, except that a slight amount of computational labor is added by their defining the unit so that $\sum_{j=1}^{n} a_j = n$.

With this unit, we must compute

$$(70) \qquad C = \frac{n}{\sum_{j=1}^{n} \tilde{x}'_j.}$$

before using equation 65 to solve for the values of a'_j.

The solutions for t'_g presented thus far involve, essentially, the average over j of the values of x'_{jg}, *weighted by the corresponding dispersion parameters a'_j*. In an alternative approach, this weighting factor disappears. The solutions presented above all use equation 11 as their starting point. In the alternative approach, to be presented below, we begin with the condition B model expressed in the form of equation 12 instead.

Alternative Approach to the Condition B Model

We begin with the condition B model expressed in the form of equation 12:

$$(71) \qquad x_{jg} = \frac{1}{a_j} t_g - \frac{1}{a_j} s_j \qquad \begin{array}{l} (j = 1, 2, \cdots, n) \\ (g = 1, 2, \cdots, m) \end{array}$$

With error-free data and no vacant cells in matrix $\mathbf{X}$, the values of t_g are given by the *unweighted* average of the corresponding columns of matrix $\mathbf{X}$. For, if we sum equation 71 over j, we get the m equations,

$$(72) \qquad t_g \sum_{j=1}^{n} \frac{1}{a_j} - \sum_{j=1}^{n} \frac{s_j}{a_j} = \sum_{j=1}^{n} x_{jg} \qquad (g = 1, 2, \cdots, m)$$

There will be no loss in generality if we specify the origin and unit of the scale to be such that

(73)
$$\sum_{j=1}^{n} \frac{s_j}{a_j} = 0$$

and

(74)
$$\sum_{j=1}^{n} \frac{1}{a_j} = n$$

Substituting these values into equation 72 and dividing through by n, we have

(75)
$$t_g = \frac{1}{n} \sum_{j=1}^{n} x_{jg} \qquad (g = 1, 2, \cdots, m)$$

To solve for the values of a_j, we note first that, for a given value of j, the quantity $(1/a_j)s_j$ in equation 71 is constant over varying values of g. Hence, we have the following relation between the a_j and the standard deviations of t and x_{jg}:

(76)
$$\frac{1}{a_j} \tilde{t}. = \tilde{x}_j. \qquad (j = 1, 2, \cdots, n)$$

Solving explicitly for a_j, we get

(77)
$$a_j = \frac{\tilde{t}.}{\tilde{x}_j.} \qquad (j = 1, 2, \cdots, n)$$

To solve for the s_j, we average equation 71 over g and multiply through by a_j, giving

(78)
$$s_j = \bar{t}. - a_j \bar{x}_j. \qquad (j = 1, 2, \cdots, n)$$

Equations 75, 77, and 78 give the values of the unknowns in terms of the theoretical values of x_{jg}. With fallible data, we can again simply substitute the observed estimates x'_{jg} for the theoretical values and use the averaging procedures indicated to solve for the estimates t'_g, s'_j, and a'_j. A numerical example is given in Table 8.

The solution given above requires that matrix **X** contain no vacant cells. If vacant cells are present in but a few rows of the matrix, the method can be used to solve for t'_g if these rows are omitted from the calculations. Often, however, few if any of the stimuli will be represented in all categories. When this occurs, the method cannot be used. A procedure

Table 8. ILLUSTRATIVE EXAMPLE (ERRORLESS DATA)
ALTERNATIVE SOLUTION BASED ON EQUATION 12
COMPLETE MATRICES **X**

MATRIX **X**

	Category Boundaries g				$\sum_g x'_{jg}$	$\bar{x}'_{j.}$	$\tilde{x}'_{j.}$
	1	2	3	4			
Stimuli j 1	0.000	0.500	1.500	2.250	4.250	1.06250	0.87278
2	−0.200	0.133	0.800	1.300	2.033	0.50825	0.58190
3	−1.500	−0.750	0.750	1.875	0.375	0.09375	1.30915
4	−0.500	−0.300	0.100	0.400	−0.300	−0.07500	0.34910
5	−2.000	−1.500	−0.500	0.250	−3.750	−0.93750	0.87278
$\sum_j x'_{jg}$	−4.200	−1.917	2.650	6.075	2.608 $\checkmark$	$\bar{i}'_.$	$\tilde{i}'_.$
$\bar{x}'_{.g} = t'_g$	−0.840	−0.3834	0.530	1.215	0.5216 $\checkmark$	0.1304	0.79712

$$a'_j = \frac{\bar{i}'_.}{\tilde{x}'_{j.}} \quad s'_j = \bar{i}'_. - a'_j \bar{x}'_{j.}.$$

Stimuli j		
1	0.9133	−0.840
2	1.3699	−0.566
3	0.6089	0.073
4	2.2834	0.302
5	0.9133	0.987

somewhat in the same spirit which can be used with an incomplete matrix **X** is given below.

Consider the three category boundaries t_g, t_{g+1}, and t_{g+2}. We can write the three sets of equations ($j = 1, 2, \cdots, n$)

$$(79) \qquad \frac{1}{a_j} t_g - \frac{1}{a_j} s_j = x_{jg}$$

$$(80) \qquad \frac{1}{a_j} t_{g+1} - \frac{1}{a_j} s_j = x_{j,g+1}$$

$$(81) \qquad \frac{1}{a_j} t_{g+2} - \frac{1}{a_j} s_j = x_{j,g+2}$$

If we subtract equation 79 from 80, and equation 80 from 81, and then take the ratio, we get

$$(82) \qquad \frac{t_{g+1} - t_g}{t_{g+2} - t_{g+1}} = \frac{x_{j,g+1} - x_{jg}}{x_{j,g+2} - x_{j,g+1}}$$

Equation 82 may be rewritten as follows:

$$(83) \quad x_{j,g+2} - x_{j,g+1} = \left(\frac{t_{g+2} - t_{g+1}}{t_{g+1} - t_g} \right) (x_{j,g+1} - x_{jg}) \qquad (j = 1, 2, \cdots, n)$$

Equation 83 is the equation of a straight line through the origin. Let $C_{g,g+2}$ denote the slope of the line. Then,

$$(84) \qquad C_{g,g+2} = \frac{t_{g+2} - t_{g+1}}{t_{g+1} - t_g} \qquad (g = 1, 2, \cdots, m-2)$$

Again we must specify an origin and unit for the scale. We will set the origin and unit so that $t_1 = 0$ and $t_2 = 1$. Equation 84 may now be used to solve for the values of t_g.

$$t_1 = 0$$
$$t_2 = 1$$
$$t_3 = C_{13}(t_2 - t_1) + t_2 = C_{13} + t_2$$
$$t_4 = C_{24}(t_3 - t_2) + t_3$$
$$.$$
$$.$$
$$.$$
$$t_m = C_{m-2,m}(t_{m-1} - t_{m-2}) + t_{m-1}$$

With fallible data, we have the x'_{jg} as observed estimates of the population values x_{jg}. We again simply substitute the one for the other. We therefore plot $(x'_{j,g+2} - x'_{j,g+1})$ against $(x'_{j,g+1} - x'_{jg})$—there will be a separate plot for each value of g from $g = 1$ to $g = m-2$. For any given plot, a point will be entered for each value of j for which cells $x'_{jg}, x'_{j,g+1}$, and $x'_{j,g+2}$ are all filled. If we now fit a straight line through the origin to the points, and take the obtained slope as an estimate of the true slope, we can use the procedure outlined above to solve for the values of t'_g. A numerical example is given in Table 9 and Figure 1.

Given values for the t'_g, we can use a procedure devised by Mosier (1940a) to estimate the scale values and dispersion parameters of the stimuli. Mosier's procedure involved, essentially, using a limited number of stimuli to construct the scale and to locate the category boundaries, and then using the estimates t'_g to solve for values of s'_j and a'_j for the remaining stimuli.

Table 9. ILLUSTRATIVE EXAMPLE (ERRORLESS DATA)
ALTERNATIVE PROCEDURE FOR OBTAINING VALUES OF t'_g:
INCOMPLETE MATRICES **X**

1. Construct matrix **X**.

MATRIX **X**

Category Boundaries g

		1	2	3	4
	1	0.000	0.500	1.500	—
	2	−0.200	0.133	0.800	1.300
	3	−1.500	−0.750	0.750	1.875
Stimuli j	4	−0.500	−0.300	0.100	0.400
	5	−2.000	−1.500	−0.500	0.250
	6	—	−2.000	0.000	1.500
	7	−1.500	−0.500	1.500	—

2. Construct a matrix of differences between corresponding cells of adjacent columns.

MATRIX $\|x'_{j,g+1} - x'_{jg}\|$

		$x'_{j2} - x'_{j1}$	$x'_{j3} - x'_{j2}$	$x'_{j4} - x'_{j3}$
	1	0.500	1.000	—
	2	0.333	0.667	0.500
	3	0.750	1.500	1.125
Stimuli j	4	0.200	0.400	0.300
	5	0.500	1.000	0.750
	6	—	2.000	1.500
	7	1.000	2.000	—

3. Plot column 1 against column 2, column 2 against column 3, and fit straight lines through the origin of each plot. The slopes of the lines, as shown in Fig. 1 are found to be $C'_{13} = 2.0$ and $C'_{24} = 0.75$.

4. Define origin and unit so that $t'_1 = 0$ and $t'_2 = 1$. Then

$$t'_3 = C'_{13}(t'_2 - t'_1) + t'_2 = 2.0 + 1.0 = 3.0$$

$$t'_4 = C'_{24}(t'_3 - t'_2) + t'_3 = (0.75)(2.0) + 3.0 = 4.5$$

It is the last step that is of interest here. Given the estimates of the category-boundary locations, a plot such as that shown in Figure 2 is made. In this plot, the ordinate and abscissa are laid off in the units selected in constructing the scale.

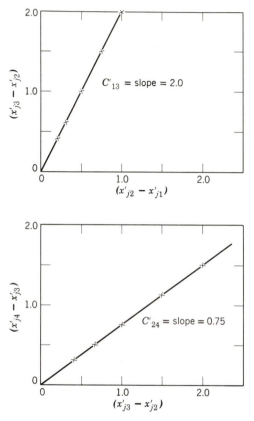

Figure 1. Plots of $(x'_{j,g+1} - x'_{jg})$ against $(x'_{j,g+2} - x'_{j,g+1})$.

The category boundaries are spaced off on the abscissa. For each stimulus in turn, the values of x'_{jg} are plotted. If the law holds, the points will fall on a straight line except for error variation. The slope of the line is equal to the reciprocal of the dispersion parameter a'_j, while the scale value s'_j is given by the point on the abscissa below the place where the line crosses the ordinate value of zero. For example, assume that the values of t'_g for four category boundaries to be $t'_1 = 0.00$, $t'_2 = 0.50$, $t'_3 = 1.50$, and $t'_4 = 2.25$. In Figure 2 these values are laid off on the abscissa. Assume that the x values associated with stimulus j were $x'_{j1} = -1.00$,

$x'_{j2} = -0.75$, $x'_{j3} = -0.25$, and $x'_{j4} = +0.125$. To determine the scale value and dispersion parameter of stimulus j, points have accordingly been entered at $(0, -1.00)$, $(0.50, -0.75)$, $(1.50, -0.25)$, and $(2.25, 0.125)$, and a straight line fitted. The line crosses zero on the ordinate at an abscissa

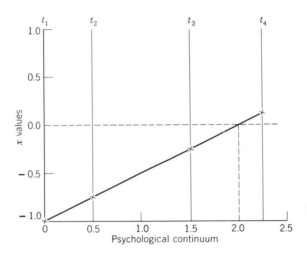

Figure 2. Mosier's procedure. The scale value of stimulus j is equal to 2.0 (the abscissa value of the point where the line crosses zero on the ordinate). The dispersion parameter is equal to 2.0 (the reciprocal of the slope).

value of 2.00. Hence, $s'_j = 2.00$. The slope of the line is 0.50, and therefore $a'_j = 1/0.50 = 2.00$.

Summary

The most elegant solutions for condition B (and, with appropriate changes, condition C) are Gulliksen's least-squares procedure, the extension of his procedure to incomplete matrices by Diederich, Messick, and Tucker (1955), and the alternative least-squares solution developed by Tucker (presented in Chapter 13). These solutions are "best" in the sense of minimizing the error terms specified (equation 13 for Gulliksen's solution and equation 14 for Tucker's solution). However, the least-squares procedures involve a substantial amount of labor. Ordinarily, we would not expect much difference between the results of either least-squares solution and those of the more straightforward algebraic procedures. Furthermore, those differences that do occur might almost as well be ascribed to special characteristics of the particular least-squares solution as to inadequacies in the algebraic procedure. Hence, the algebraic solutions seem more useful for most purposes.

Several straightforward procedures are available for a matrix X that contains no vacant cells. Perhaps the quickest and easiest solution is, first, to sum the columns of matrix X to obtain estimates of the spacing of the category boundaries (equation 75), and, second, to use Mosier's graphical procedure (Figure 2) to solve for the s_j' and a_j'.

The quickest, purely numerical procedure for a complete matrix would be to compute the column means, the standard deviation of the column means, and the row means and standard deviations. The t_g', a_j', and s_j' are then given by equations 75, 77, and 78, respectively. The estimates of t_g obtained using this procedure are the unweighted column means.

Equations 66, 68, and 69 represent an alternative numerical procedure that employs weighted averages instead of simple averages for estimates of the t_g. The weighting procedure has the effect of transforming the rows of matrix X to a common unit before averaging. The estimates of the s_j and a_j in the two procedures are identical except for unit and origin.

In Gulliksen's approximation procedure (equations 54, 55, and 56), the estimates of the s_j and a_j are identical with those given above, again except for unit and origin. The t_g' are linearly related to the t_g' of equation 68, but the spacing of the t_g' *relative to* the s_j' is altered by a factor that depends on the average correlation between rows of matrix X. The difference results from Gulliksen's definition of error in his least-squares procedure (equation 13). Unless one is particularly interested in this definition of error, the additional adjustment would not seem to be especially desirable.

Ordinarily, the matrix X will contain vacant cells. Often, however, it is possible to divide the matrix into a small number of overlapping, completely filled matrices. When this can be done, it is probably best to use one of the procedures given above on the individual submatrices. The overlapping segments can be used to transform the resulting subscales to a single over-all scale. Two progressive solutions were also discussed, one based on equation 60 and the other on equation 83. The choice between them depends on the number of stimuli, the number of categories, and the amount of overlap between successive rows and successive columns of matrix X. Other things being equal, the solution that requires the fewest plots with the most points per plot is best.

6. ANALYTICAL PROCEDURES: CONDITION D (CONSTANT VARIANCE OF DISCRIMINAL DIFFERENCES)

A Least-Squares Solution for Condition D

When we assume that the variance of the discriminal differences is constant, the general equation of the law of categorical judgment reduces to

$$t_g - s_j = c x_{jg} \qquad \begin{array}{l} (j = 1, 2, \cdots, n) \\ (g = 1, 2, \cdots, m) \end{array}$$

Since the scale is determined only to within a linear transformation, there is no loss in generality when we specify the unit of the scale so that $c = 1$, giving

$$(85) \qquad t_g - s_j = x_{jg} \qquad \begin{array}{l} (j = 1, 2, \cdots, n) \\ (g = 1, 2, \cdots, m) \end{array}$$

With fallible data, we have the observed estimates x'_{jg} of the true values x_{jg}. The task is to use these observations to solve for estimates t'_g and s'_j of the locations of the category boundaries and the scale values of the stimuli. If we define the derived values $x''_{jg} \equiv t'_g - s'_j$, a least-squares approach would be to solve for the values of t'_g and s'_j which minimize the following quantity:

$$(86) \qquad Q = \sum_{j=1}^{n} \sum_{g=1}^{m} (x'_{jg} - x''_{jg})^2$$

or, equivalently,

$$(87) \qquad Q = \sum_{j=1}^{n} \sum_{g=1}^{m} (x'_{jg} - t'_g + s'_j)^2$$

Taking the partial derivative of Q with respect to each s'_j and t'_g in turn gives the two sets of equations

$$(88) \qquad \frac{1}{2} \frac{\partial Q}{\partial s'_j} = \sum_{g=1}^{m} (x'_{jg} - t'_g + s'_j) \qquad (j = 1, 2, \cdots, n)$$

$$(89) \qquad \frac{1}{2} \frac{\partial Q}{\partial t'_g} = -\sum_{j=1}^{n} (x'_{jg} - t'_g + s'_j) \qquad (g = 1, 2, \cdots, m)$$

Setting the partial derivatives equal to zero and rearranging terms, we get

$$(90) \qquad ms'_j = \sum_{g=1}^{m} t'_g - \sum_{g=1}^{m} x'_{jg} \qquad (j = 1, 2, \cdots, n)$$

$$(91) \qquad nt'_g = \sum_{j=1}^{n} s'_j + \sum_{j=1}^{n} x'_{jg} \qquad (g = 1, 2, \cdots, m)$$

We have not yet set an origin for the scale. It will be convenient to specify the origin so that

$$(92) \qquad \sum_{j=1}^{n} s'_j = 0$$

Then, dividing equation 91 through by n gives

(93) $$t'_g = \frac{1}{n} \sum_{j=1}^{n} x'_{jg} \qquad (g = 1, 2, \cdots, m)$$

Substituting equation 93 into equation 90 and dividing through by m gives

(94) $$s'_j = \frac{1}{mn} \sum_{j=1}^{n} \sum_{g=1}^{m} x'_{jg} - \frac{1}{m} \sum_{g=1}^{m} x'_{jg} \qquad (j = 1, 2, \cdots, n)$$

Equations 93 and 94 give the scale values of the stimuli and the locations of the category boundaries in terms of the observed data. The computations for condition D are seen to be very simple. Given the matrix $\mathbf{X}$, we obtain the row, column, and grand averages. The column averages are the least-squares estimates of the locations of the category boundaries. The row averages subtracted from the grand average are least-squares estimates of the scale values of the stimuli.

The least-squares procedure given above requires that matrix $\mathbf{X}$ contain no vacant cells. For the incomplete case, we might use an iterative procedure analogous to that presented by Gulliksen for condition C of the law of comparative judgment (see Chapter 9, section 4). Alternatively, either of the two algebraic-type solutions presented below can be used.

Algebraic Solutions for Condition D, Applicable to the Incomplete Data Case

We have the choice of solving for the t'_g first, and then using the obtained values to determine the s'_j, or of solving for the s'_j first, and then using the obtained values to determine the t'_g. In either case, the procedures are straightforward.

Consider an errorless matrix $\mathbf{X}$, which may or may not have vacant cells. If we specify the unit so that $c = 1$, we can write the two sets of equations involving categories g and $g+1$, respectively, as follows

(95) $$t_g - s_j = x_{jg} \qquad (j = 1, 2, \cdots, n)$$

(96) $$t_{g+1} - s_j = x_{j,g+1}$$

Subtracting equation 95 from equation 96, we have

(97) $$t_{g+1} - t_g = x_{j,g+1} - x_{jg} \qquad (j = 1, 2, \cdots, n)$$

If we specify the origin so that $t_1 = 0$, equation 97 enables us to solve for the t_g when given the theoretical values of x_{jg}.

With fallible data, an averaging procedure is indicated. If we substitute estimates for theoretical values in equation 97, it is clear that there will be as many estimates of the difference $(t_g - t_{g+1})$ as there are pairs of filled cells in the g and $(g+1)$th columns of matrix $\mathbf{X}$. The average is taken as the value wanted:

$$(98) \quad t'_{g+1} - t'_g = \frac{1}{q} \sum_{j}^{n} (x'_{j,g+1} - x'_{jg}) \qquad (g = 1, 2, \cdots, m-1)$$

where q is equal to the number of terms summed over. Given the differences between the boundaries, the values of t'_g can be obtained by assigning an origin (say $t_1 = 0$) and adding the successive differences to obtain the remaining values.

The scale values s'_j can be obtained by Mosier's procedure (discussed in section 5) once the t'_g have been obtained. The best fitting line *with unit slope* would be used. Alternatively, the s'_j can be obtained by translating the elements in each column to the common origin ($t'_1 = 0$) numerically. In the latter procedure, a new matrix is constructed with elements $(t'_g - x'_{jg})$. Vacant cells in the original matrix $\mathbf{X}$ will remain vacant, of course. Each filled cell in the jth row of the new matrix is an estimate of s_j. The average of these estimates is taken as the value wanted:

$$(99) \quad s'_j = \frac{1}{q} \sum_{g}^{m} (t'_g - x'_{jg}) \qquad (j = 1, 2, \cdots, n)$$

where q again is equal to the number of terms summed over.

Attneave's *method of graded dichotomies* (1949) is essentially equations 98 and 99. He cumulates his frequencies from the right instead of from the left as we have done. The result is that his matrix $\mathbf{X}$ is equal to the negative of our $\mathbf{X}$. Though this makes some difference between the arithmetical operations presented here and those presented by Attneave, the two procedures are the same in principle. He also presents a method for correcting the scale values when discriminal dispersions are different, but, in general, the logic of the method requires equality of discriminal dispersions.

Garner and Hake's *scale of equidiscriminability* (1951) consists of equation 98 for estimating t'_g, along with Mosier's procedure for obtaining scale values of the stimuli.

If we wish, we can reverse the procedure and solve first for the s'_j. The first step is to arrange the rows of matrix $\mathbf{X}$ so that they are approximately in order of magnitude of s'_j. This is accomplished by first summing the rows of matrix $\mathbf{P}$ and then arranging the rows of $\mathbf{X}$ in order of magnitude of the sums. Procedures directly analogous to those leading to equations 98 and 99 then give the following two equations:

$$(100) \quad s'_{j+1} - s'_j = \frac{1}{q} \sum_{g}^{m} (x'_{jg} - x'_{j+1,g}) \qquad (j = 1, 2, \cdots, n-1)$$

$$(101) \qquad t'_g = \frac{1}{q} \sum_j^m (x'_{jg} + s'_j) \qquad (g = 1, 2, \cdots, m)$$

where q, in each case, again refers to the number of terms summed over. Given the differences $(s'_{j+1} - s'_j)$ from equation 100, the values of s'_j can be obtained by assigning the origin (say $s_1 = 0$) and adding the successive differences to obtain the remaining values. Once the s'_j have been determined, equation 101 can be used to solve for the t'_g.

Numerical examples for condition D are given in Table 10.

Table 10. ILLUSTRATIVE EXAMPLES (ERRORLESS DATA)
SOLUTIONS FOR CONDITION D

1. *The Least-Squares Solution for a Complete Matrix* **X.**

MATRIX **X**

	Category Boundaries g				$\sum_g x'_{jg}$	$\frac{1}{m}\sum_g x'_{jg}$	$\frac{1}{nm}\sum_j\sum_g x'_{jg} - \frac{1}{n}\sum_g x'_{jg} = s'_j$
	1	2	3	4			
Stimuli i 1	0.1	1.0	1.4	1.6	4.1	1.025	−0.960
2	−0.5	0.4	0.8	1.0	1.7	0.425	−0.360
3	−1.0	−0.1	0.3	0.5	−0.3	−0.075	0.140
4	−1.2	−0.3	0.1	0.3	−1.1	−0.275	0.340
5	−1.7	−0.8	−0.4	−0.2	−3.1	−0.775	0.840
$\sum_j$	−4.3	0.2	2.2	3.2	1.3 √	0.325 √	0.000 √
$\frac{1}{n}\sum_j = t'_g$	−0.86	0.04	0.44	0.64	0.26 √	0.065 √	

2. *Solving for t'_g First: Incomplete Matrix* **X.**

(*a*) Construct matrix **X**:

MATRIX **X**

	Category Boundaries g			
	1	2	3	4
Stimuli j 1	0.5	1.5	2.0	—
2	−0.5	0.5	1.0	1.8
3	−1.3	−0.3	0.2	1.0
4	−2.0	−1.0	−0.5	0.3
5	—	−1.7	−1.2	−0.4

Table 10. ILLUSTRATIVE EXAMPLES CONTINUED.

(b) Construct a matrix of differences between corresponding cells of adjacent columns.

$$\text{MATRIX } \|x'_{j,g+1} - x'_{jg}\|$$

	$x'_{j2} - x'_{j1}$	$x'_{j3} - x'_{j2}$	$x'_{j4} - x'_{j3}$
1	1.0	0.5	—
2	1.0	0.5	0.8
Stimuli j 3	1.0	0.5	0.8
4	1.0	0.5	0.8
5	—	0.5	0.8
Σ	4.0	2.5	3.2
$t'_{g+1} - t'_g = \dfrac{1}{q}\Sigma$	1.0	0.5	0.8

(c) Set the origin at $t'_1 = 0$. Then cumulate the average differences.

$$t'_1 = 0 \qquad\qquad t'_3 = 0.5 + 1.0 = 1.5$$
$$t'_2 = 1.0 + 0 = 1.0 \qquad\qquad t'_4 = 0.8 + 1.5 = 2.3$$

(d) To solve for s'_j, construct a matrix with elements $(t'_g - x'_{jg})$.

$$\text{MATRIX } \|t'_g - x'_{jg}\|$$

	$t'_1 - x'_{j1}$	$t'_2 - x'_{j2}$	$t'_3 - x'_{j3}$	$t'_4 - x'_{j4}$	Σ	$\dfrac{1}{q}\Sigma = s'_j$
1	−0.5	−0.5	−0.5	—	−1.5	−0.5
Stimuli 2	0.5	0.5	0.5	0.5	2.0	0.5
j 3	1.3	1.3	1.3	1.3	5.2	1.3
4	2.0	2.0	2.0	2.0	8.0	2.0
5	—	2.7	2.7	2.7	8.1	2.7

3. *Solving for s'_j First: Incomplete Matrix X:*

(a) Construct matrix **X** with stimuli in approximate rank order (order of magnitude of $\sum\limits_{g}^{m} p'_{jg}$). Matrix **X** for this example is that presented in part 2 above.

(b) Construct a matrix of differences between corresponding cells of adjacent rows.

Table 10. Illustrative Examples Continued.

Matrix $\|x'_{jg} - x'_{j+1,g}\|$

	Boundaries g					
	1	2	3	4	Σ	$\frac{1}{q}\Sigma = s'_{j+1} - s'_j$
$x'_{1g} - x'_{2g}$	1.0	1.0	1.0	—	3.0	1.0
$x'_{2g} - x'_{3g}$	0.8	0.8	0.8	0.8	3.2	0.8
$x'_{3g} - x'_{4g}$	0.7	0.7	0.7	0.7	2.8	0.7
$x'_{4g} - x'_{5g}$	—	0.7	0.7	0.7	2.1	0.7

(c) Set the origin at $s'_1 = 0$. Then cumulate average differences.

$$s'_1 = 0 \qquad\qquad s'_4 = 0.7 + 1.8 = 2.5$$
$$s'_2 = 1.0 + 0 = 1.0 \qquad\qquad s'_5 = 0.7 + 2.5 = 3.2$$
$$s'_3 = 0.8 + 1.0 = 1.8$$

(d) To obtain values of t'_g, construct a matrix with elements $(x'_{jg} + s'_j)$.

Matrix $\|x'_{jg} + s'_j\|$

	Category Boundaries g			
	1	2	3	4
$x'_{1g} + s'_1$	0.5	1.5	2.0	—
$x'_{2g} + s'_2$	0.5	1.5	2.0	2.8
$x'_{3g} + s'_3$	0.5	1.5	2.0	2.8
$x'_{4g} + s'_4$	0.5	1.5	2.0	2.8
$x'_{5g} + s'_5$	—	1.5	2.0	2.8
Σ	2.0	7.5	10.0	11.2
$\frac{1}{q}\Sigma = t'_g$	0.5	1.5	2.0	2.8

7. GOODNESS OF FIT OF THE MODEL TO THE DATA

Through use of any of the special conditions, the relevant parameters of the stimuli and category boundaries can be estimated, given the observed proportion p'_{jg} of times each stimulus is judged below each category boundary. In evaluating goodness of fit, the procedure is reversed—the estimates of the parameters of the stimuli and category boundaries are used to obtain corresponding *derived* or fitted proportions p''_{jg}. The quantity p''_{jg} is the proportion corresponding to the unit normal deviate x''_{jg}, where, for condition B,

$$x''_{jg} = \frac{1}{a'_j}(t'_g - s'_j)$$

for condition C,

$$x''_{jg} = \frac{1}{b'_g}(t'_g - s'_j)$$

and for condition D,

$$x''_{jg} = t'_g - s'_j$$

We can thus obtain, for any of the conditions, a derived proportion corresponding to each observed proportion. Evaluation of the applicability of the model to the data is based on how well the two sets of proportions agree.

Edwards and Thurstone (1952) suggest the average absolute discrepancy as an index of the degree of agreement:

$$\overline{p''_{jg} - p'_{jg}} = \frac{1}{mn}\sum_{j=1}^{n}\sum_{g=1}^{m}|p''_{jg} - p'_{jg}|$$

An additional check on the model can be obtained by plotting *rows* of matrix **X** against each other (for condition B), *columns* of matrix **X** against each other (for condition C), or both rows against rows and columns against columns (for condition D). Systematic departures from *linearity* would indicate that the assumptions underlying the procedure used have not been met.

Guilford (1954) has suggested applying Mosteller's (1951c) chi-square test for the law of comparative judgment (see Chapter 9) to the categorical-judgment situation. However, the experimental procedure for obtaining the observed proportions p'_{jg} forces the proportions within any row to increase monotonically (i.e., p'_{jg} can never be greater than $p'_{j,g+1}$, owing to the cumulative procedure used). Hence the observed proportions are not completely independent, and the test would not seem to be strictly appropriate.

8. REMARKS ON THEORETICAL TRADING RELATION-SHIPS AMONG CONDITIONS B, C, AND D

One of the disturbing things about the law of categorical judgment (and, for that matter, the law of comparative judgment as well) is its ability to give what seems to be a very close fit to the data even though the assumptions involved are not correct. Actually, two things need to be considered here.   If the model were to fit well *and the resulting scales were linearly related to the true scales*, we would be more pleased than disturbed. Situations such as this seem likely to occur when the *normality* assumption is violated.   Since most common S-shaped curves are very nearly linearly related to the normal ogive over the range of interest, violation of the normality assumption has little effect on either the fit of the model or the resulting scale.

It is when the model seems to fit the data at the expense of distorting the scale form that the problem becomes serious.   In Chapter 9, we saw how well condition C of the law of comparative judgment fit data derived from condition B when the dispersion parameters were linearly related to the scale values.   A substantial distortion occurred in the resulting scale.

Much the same kind of trading relations exist among conditions B, C, and D of the present model.   It is instructive to look at the solutions for the unknown parameters in the three conditions.   We shall limit the discussion to the case where matrix X contains no vacant cells.   Table 11

Table 11.   Observational Quantities Proportional to Unknown Parameters for Conditions B, C, and D

		Condition	
	B	C	D
s'_j	$-\dfrac{\bar{x}'_{j.}}{\bar{x}'_{j.}}$	$-\bar{x}'_{j.}$	$-\bar{x}'_{j.}$
t'_g	$\bar{x}'_{.g}$	$\dfrac{\bar{x}'_{.g}}{\tilde{x}'_{.g}}$	$\bar{x}'_{.g}$
a'_j	$\dfrac{1}{\bar{x}'_{j.}}$	Constant	Constant
b'_g	Constant	$\dfrac{1}{\bar{x}'_{.g}}$	Constant

(Parameters label at left spanning rows s'_j, t'_g, a'_j, b'_g.)

gives, for each of the conditions, the observational quantities to which each of the unknown parameters is proportional.   (We have used the algebraic solutions here, since the least-squares adjustments only complicate things without really adding anything different.)   Note that for conditions B and D the t'_g are proportional to the same quantity.   The same is true with conditions C and D for the s'_j.   Hence, if condition B is appropriate and a condition D solution is applied to the data, the t'_g will be appropriately spaced but the s'_j will not.   In like manner, if condition C is appropriate and a condition D solution is used, the s'_j will be spaced appropriately but the t'_g will not.   If either condition B or C is appropriate and the other is applied, estimates for both scales will be distorted.

It is interesting to see what kind of distortion occurs in one particular case which is of interest in psychophysical theory.   This is the case where the dispersion parameters are related in a simple manner to the corresponding location parameters.   We shall consider here a hypothetical case where the relation is linear.   Let us use condition B to construct a set of artificial data, where the s_j and a_j are related by a linear equation, and then apply condition C and D solutions to the data.   The reverse procedure, that of using condition C to generate the data and then applying condition B and D solutions, would give equivalent results (except for the interchange of roles of boundaries and stimuli) due to the duality between the two conditions.

A set of true scale values and dispersion parameters for five stimuli and true positions of four category boundaries are given in Table 12.   Matrix X (Table 13) was constructed by using these values in equation 5 to solve for each of the x_{jg}.   The results of the condition C solution (the condition C versions of equations 75, 77, and 78 were used) and the condition D solution (equations 93 and 94) are given in Table 14.   Figures 3 and 4 indicate the amount and type of distortion that occurs to the estimates of s_j and t_g respectively.

While for the condition C solution a large degree of distortion occurs in both the t_g and s_j values, nonetheless *for this particular example condition C fits the data exactly*.   (A perfect fit ordinarily would not occur even with errorless data, but a *good* fit in the sense of Thurstone and Edwards' criterion seems quite likely.)

The condition D solution distorts only the scale values of the stimuli, the locations of the category boundaries being spaced correctly.   In this

Table 12.   HYPOTHETICAL TRUE VALUES USED
TO GENERATE MATRIX X

Stimuli

	1	2	3	4	5
s_j	1.0	2.0	3.0	4.0	5.0
a_j	$\frac{2}{3}$	1.0	$1\frac{1}{3}$	$1\frac{2}{3}$	2.0

Category Boundaries

	1	2	3	4
t_g	1	2	3	4

particular example, it does not reproduce the data especially well, however. The average absolute discrepancy between the derived and observed proportions is in the neighborhood of 0.05.

Table 13. MATRIX X GENERATED BY APPLICATION OF THE CONDITION B EQUATION TO THE DATA OF TABLE 12

		Category Boundaries g				$\sum_{g} x_{jg}$	$\bar{x}$
		1	2	3	4		
	1	0.00	1.50	3.00	4.50	9.00	2.250
	2	−1.00	0.00	1.00	2.00	2.00	0.500
Stimuli j	3	−1.50	−0.75	0.00	0.75	−1.50	−0.375
	4	−1.80	−1.20	−0.60	0.00	−3.60	−0.900
	5	−2.00	−1.50	−1.00	−0.50	−5.00	−1.250
$\sum_{j} x_{jg}$		−6.30	−1.95	2.40	6.75		0.225
$\bar{x}_{.g}$		−1.26	−0.39	0.48	1.35	$\bar{x}_{..}$	0.045
$\tilde{x}_{.g}$		0.7144	1.0716	1.4288	1.7861	$\sigma_{\bar{x}_j}$	1.2502

Table 14. CONDITION B, C, AND D SOLUTIONS FOR DATA OF TABLE 13

		a'_j	s'_j		
		B	B	C	D
	1	$\frac{2}{3}$	1.0	−2.250	−2.205
	2	1	2.0	−0.500	−0.455
Stimuli j	3	$1\frac{1}{3}$	3.0	0.375	0.420
	4	$1\frac{2}{3}$	4.0	0.900	0.945
	5	2	5.0	1.250	1.295

		b'_g	t'_g		
		C	B	C	D
	1	$\frac{7}{4}$	1	−2.250	−1.26
Category Boundaries	2	$\frac{7}{6}$	2	−0.500	−0.39
g	3	$\frac{7}{8}$	3	0.375	0.48
	4	$\frac{7}{10}$	4	0.900	1.35

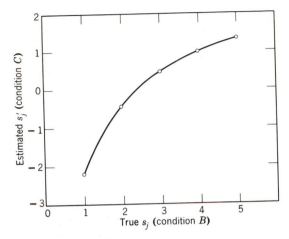

Figure 3. The relation between the true s_j and the condition C estimates. The condition D estimates differ from those of condition C only by an additive constant. Hence the plot of condition C estimates against true values would appear the same as that given above.

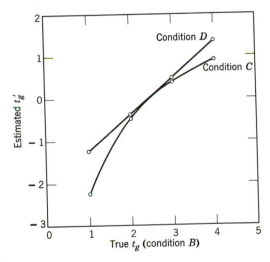

Figure 4. The relations between the true t_g and the conditions C and D estimates.

9. THE METHOD OF PAIRED COMPARISONS, AND THE SPECIAL CONDITIONS OF THE LAW OF CATEGORICAL JUDGMENT

The rationale of the law of categorical judgment is actually as appropriate for comparative judgments as it is for the categorical judgment situation. Since the law was derived by treating the boundaries between categories as though they were stimuli, it is clear that stimuli can actually be used in place of the boundaries. We can select a subset of stimuli to serve in place of the category boundaries and then obtain observations of the proportions p'_{jg} *directly*, using the method of paired comparisons. In some respects, this would be a more satisfactory procedure than those that involve sorting or rating. Since the p'_{jg} would each be determined independently, the formal limitation on the condition C model would be eliminated. In addition, Mosteller's chi-square test could be used, since the dependency conditions introduced by the cumulating process would no longer be present.

The method of paired comparisons is thus an appropriate experimental method for the models given in this chapter. For some purposes, the present models are superior to those given in Chapter 9. In the usual comparative-judgment situation, each stimulus is compared with every other stimulus. With the present models, we would first divide the total set of stimuli into two subsets. Each stimulus in a given subset would then be compared only with the stimuli in the other subset. Thus, in place of the $\frac{1}{2}n(n-1)$ pairs, we only need $m(n-m)$.

The rationale lends itself well to the notion of studying a small set of standards intensively and then using these standards to scale a much larger set of stimuli. In the larger experiment, each new stimulus would need only be compared with each standard.

One further point might be mentioned. In the usual method of paired comparisons, space and time errors present a problem. We saw in Chapter 9 how we ordinarily attempt to eliminate their effects by counterbalancing procedures. Harris (1957), however, has shown that use of a procedure equivalent to the condition D model of this chapter, in conjunction with the method of paired comparisons, enables us not only to get around the bothersome aspects of these effects, but also to study the effects themselves. If we let g denote a particular stimulus when it is on the left of the pair (or first, or on top), and j denote the same stimulus (for $j = g$) when it is on the right, application of the condition D model results in two scales for the same set of stimuli, with both scales referred to the same origin and in the same unit. The effect of the space error can be determined by comparing the two scales.

► *Multidimensional Scaling**

1. INTRODUCTION

The methods discussed in the preceding chapters presuppose knowledge of the dimensions of the area being investigated. They all require judgments with respect to a particular defined attribute: stimulus *i* is *heavier*, *higher in pitch*, *twice as salty*, or *more conservative* than stimulus *j*. Further, the attribute is presumed to be unidimensional: i.e., to be such that all quantities possessing the attribute can be represented by a single rank order. This is implied by the task set for the subject. Comparative concepts such as brighter, heavier, and more conservative are intended to refer to a single dimension.

The observer, of course, is expected to know what the experimenter means by brighter or heavier. His task is to abstract out the particular attribute of interest and make his judgment accordingly. Ideally, the method itself provides a test of one sort or another to determine whether in fact the attribute can be represented by a unidimensional continuum. The primary test for *unidimensionality* in the judgment methods is the transitivity requirement on the ordering relation (see Chapter 2).

The multidimensional-scaling models to be discussed in this chapter represent more or less direct extensions of the notions underlying unidimensional scaling models to deal with situations where the stimuli may vary simultaneously with respect to several dimensions. The typical problem to be handled by the multidimensional-scaling procedures might be roughly stated as follows: Given a set of stimuli which vary with respect

---

* Portions of this chapter have appeared previously in Torgerson (1951, 1952).

to an unknown number of dimensions, determine (*a*) the minimum dimensionality of the set, and (*b*) projections of the stimuli (scale values) on each of the dimensions involved.

In the multidimensional-scaling models, the notion of a single, unidimensional, underlying continuum is replaced by the notion of an underlying multidimensional space. Instead of considering the stimuli to be represented by points along a single dimension (i.e., a unidimensional space) the stimuli are represented by points in a space of several dimensions. Instead of assigning a single number (scale value) to represent the position of the point along the dimension, as many numbers are assigned to each stimulus as there are independent dimensions in the relevant multidimensional space. Each number corresponds to the projection (scale value) of the point on one of the axes (dimensions) of the space.

In the preceding chapters, the terms attribute, dimension, and continuum could be used more or less interchangeably, since the attribute, if it existed, could be represented by a unidimensional continuum. We also did not make a special point of distinguishing carefully between a quantity of an attribute and the object that possesses the attribute. In the present chapter, it will be desirable to make finer distinctions. In particular, we shall want to keep in mind the distinction between a quantity and an object on the one hand, and to make a distinction between an attribute and a dimension on the other.

In our terminology, an *object* refers to the "thing" that possesses or carries the *attribute*. For example, it might be a particular color chip. The object itself possesses a great many *attributes*: color, size, position, length, shape, weight, texture, etc. The term *quantity* refers to a particular amount or degree of a given attribute possessed by a particular object. The color chip with regard to color is a particular quantity of color. The color chip with regard to its size is a particular quantity of size, etc. We shall use the term "stimulus" when referring to a quantity and the term "stimulus-object" when referring to the object itself.

It will also be convenient to set up a formal distinction between an attribute and a dimension, even though in many empirical situations the distinction will seem artificial. Briefly, we shall consider attributes to belong to objects and dimensions to belong to attributes.

An attribute refers to a particular kind of property of an object. It is a property of an object that is capable of further subdivision. *Length, color, position,* and *weight* are attributes of objects. (*Triangular* and *male* are also properties of objects, but in our terminology are not attributes, since these properties are not capable of further subdivision—an object is triangular, or it is not; a person is a male or he is not.)

We shall use the term "dimension" in characterizing a particular attribute. Some attributes of objects are unidimensional. *Length* and *weight* are clear-cut examples. Others are multidimensional. *Spatial position* and *color* are perhaps the two most well-known examples of multidimensional attributes.

Thus, in the present terminology, a set of *stimulus-objects* may vary with respect to several *attributes*, whereas a set of *stimuli* would vary with respect to the several *dimensions* of the particular complex attribute. In many practical situations, of course, a given mode of variation can be considered either in terms of a unidimensional attribute of the stimulus-objects or in terms of a dimension of a more complex attribute. Thus, *brightness* can be considered by itself as a unidimensional attribute or as one dimension of the more complex attribute of *color*.

However, in the formal development of the multidimensional models to be discussed in this chapter, it is desirable to consider multidimensional scaling as concerned only with determining the *dimensionality and projections on dimensions of a multidimensional attribute for the set of stimuli*.

Perhaps the most practical reason for this is the following: Multidimensional methods do not in general attempt to determine scale values with respect to all the aspects in which the stimulus-objects vary, but rather only with respect to a selected domain. (The "selected domain" here corresponds to our use of the term "complex attribute.") For example, in the multidimensional scaling of attitude statements, the investigator will ordinarily be interested in the attitude reflected by the statement and the dimensionality of the complex attitude attribute. He will not be interested in other aspects with respect to which the statements vary, such as grammatical quality, length of statement, or number of adjectives, for example.

If the stimulus-objects vary with respect to numerous attributes or properties which, owing either to explicit instruction or to assumption, are ignored by the subject as irrelevant to the problem, *these attributes will not be represented as dimensions in the space*.

Suppose, for example, the experiment deals with dimensionality of meaning of words like the following: exquisite, lovely, beautiful, fair, gorgeous, glamorous, pretty, and comely. Do these words all mean the same thing to the subject, or do the meanings vary? If the latter, do they vary along a single dimension or are several dimensions necessary? In one of the models to be discussed, the stimuli are presented to the subject in triads. His task is to judge whether a stimulus *A* is more like stimulus *B* than like stimulus *C*. In the present example, even with no explicit instructions to do so, we would expect the subject to ignore such irrelevant attributes of the *stimulus-objects* as number of letters, number of letters in common, vowel–consonant ratio, difficulty of spelling, number of pages apart in the dictionary, along with virtually an infinite number of similar variables. Yet, these are clearly all perfectly respectable, easily discriminable attributes of the words themselves. In the present example, the stimulus-object corresponds to the word, while the stimulus corresponds to the meaning of the word. Though the complex attribute involved perhaps has no single name, it is clear that it is concerned with the general domain of beauty. It is with this complex attribute that the multidimensional-scaling procedure would deal, and not with the modes of variation of the stimulus-objects themselves. The dimensions obtained would refer to dimensions of beauty with respect to which these word meanings vary and would not refer to the "dimensionality" of the set of words themselves.

General Notions Involved in Multidimensional-Scaling Models

The complex attribute is represented by a postulated psychological space. The dimensionality of the space corresponds to the (unknown) dimensionality of the attribute. Individual stimuli are represented by points in the space. The position of a stimulus in the space corresponds to the amount or degree of the complex attribute possessed by the stimulus.

It is postulated that the distance between any two points in the space is a function of the degree of similarity of the two stimuli. If the two stimuli are identical, the distance between their corresponding points in the space is zero. As the degree of similarity decreases, the distance between their corresponding points increases. The distance between any two stimuli in turn is related to the projections or scale values of the two stimulus points on each of the dimensions of the space.

Thus a particular multidimensional-scaling procedure involves two steps:

1. A theory concerning the characteristics of the multidimensional space. This theory relates the dimensionality of the space and the projections of points on axes of the space to the distances between the points.

2. A theory relating distances between the points to observable relations between the stimuli. In the procedures to be considered here, distances are related to observations on the relative *similarity* of stimuli.

The first step can be considered in terms of a spatial or geometric model which specifies the formal characteristics of the postulated psychological space. The second step can be considered in terms of a unidimensional-scaling model for scaling distances on a psychological distance continuum (or, equivalently, scaling stimulus pairs on a similarity continuum).

We may thus consider the problem in terms of two distinct models: a *distance model* for obtaining distances between all pairs of stimuli, and a *spatial model* for obtaining the dimensionality of the space and the projections of the stimulus points on axes of the space.

The two models can be considered somewhat independently. Thus a particular spatial model, combined with any of several different distance models for determining distances between stimuli, generates a special multidimensional-scaling model. In like manner, a particular distance model might be combined with any of several spatial models in order to create a new multidimensional-scaling procedure.

We shall not attempt to discuss, or for that matter even enumerate, the many multidimensional-scaling models that can result from different combinations of the two problems. Rather, in section 2, we shall discuss the two different kinds of spatial models that have been suggested, showing how interpoint distances between all pairs of stimuli can be used to determine the dimensionality of the space and the projections of the stimuli on axes of the space. Following this, section 3 will be devoted to a discussion of various distance models that have been proposed for determining distances between all pairs of stimuli from observable data. Since in certain of these methods, distances are determined on an *interval* scale, i.e., with respect to an arbitrary origin, whereas the spatial models require that distances be given on a *ratio* scale, the next section (4) will deal with procedures for converting an interval scale of distances to a ratio scale of distances. This is the "additive constant problem" of multidimensional scaling. A brief discussion of procedures for evaluating goodness of fit of model to data in section 5 will complete the formal development of the methods.

In section 6 we shall use an empirical example in following through in detail a particular multidimensional-scaling procedure. The procedure used involves an extension of Thurstone's model (Chapter 8) for determining distances on an interval scale from judgments of similarity obtained by the experimental method of triads, along with the Euclidean spatial model for relating interpoint distances to dimensionality and scale values along the several dimensions.

In section 7 we shall mention several empirical checks that have been carried out on multidimensional-scaling procedures and finally, in section 8, we shall discuss briefly a number of additional approaches to the problem of obtaining distances between stimuli.

2. SPATIAL MODELS

Any of a large number of different geometric spaces could conceivably be used as the basic spatial model for a multidimensional-scaling procedure. However, except for Attneave's (1950) "city-block" model (suggested earlier by Householder and Landahl, 1945), the Euclidean model is the only one that has been considered at all seriously. Even Attneave's model can perhaps be best considered in terms of Cartesian coordinates of a Euclidean space, as we shall see. While there is no reason for ruling out other non-Euclidean spaces as formal models for multidimensional scaling, the Euclidean space does have a number of distinct advantages. It is familiar; graphical representation is convenient; it has a good deal of theoretical and conceptual simplicity; and it has particularly neat and simple mathematical properties.

The difference between the Euclidean model and Attneave's model is easily seen by comparing their respective equations which relate the distance between two stimulus points to the projections of the points on axes of the space. We shall use the following notation:

j, k = alternative subscripts for stimuli ($j, k = 1, 2, \cdots, n$)

d_{jk} = distance between stimuli j and k

m = subscript for orthogonal axes of the space ($m = 1, 2, \cdots, r$)

a_{jm} = projection of stimulus j on axis m

Then, in the Euclidean model,

$$(1) \qquad d_{jk} = \left[\sum_{m=1}^{r} (a_{jm} - a_{km})^2 \right]^{1/2} \qquad (j, k = 1, 2, \cdots, n)$$

That is, the distance between any two points in a Euclidean space is equal to the square root of the sum of squares of the differences in projections over all orthogonal axes of the space. Equation 1 is a direct application of the Pythagorean theorem. This is easily seen in Figure 1 where the two

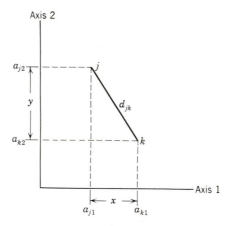

Figure 1. The relation between the distance between two points and their projections on coordinate axes: $d_{jk} = \sqrt{x^2 + y^2}$.

coordinates represent orthogonal axes of a two-dimensional Euclidean space. The difference in projections on the abscissa is equal to x, and the corresponding difference on the ordinate is equal to y. Since these are the two legs of a right triangle with hypotenuse equal to d_{jk}, it follows that $d_{jk} = (x^2 + y^2)^{1/2}$. Note that this remains true, regardless of the location of the origin of the axes, and regardless of their orientation, as long as the two axes are orthogonal to one another. Figure 2 gives the same two

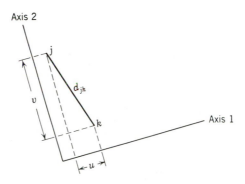

Figure 2. Invariance of the relation between distance and projections under a Euclidean transformation.

points, but the axes have been translated to a new origin and have been rotated (orthogonally) to give a different orientation. Equation 1 still remains true. In a Euclidean space the distances between points are invariant over a translation and orthogonal rotation of the axes: i.e., over a *Euclidean transformation*. Hence, as we shall see, when we are given the distances between all pairs of stimuli and use the distances to solve for the projections on axes of the space, the solution will be determined only to within an arbitrary translation and rotation of axes. Without additional criteria, one set of axes is as good as another.

The model proposed by Attneave postulates the following relationship between distances and projections:

$$(2) \qquad d_{jk} = \sum_{m=1}^{r} |a_{jm} - a_{km}| \qquad (j, k = 1, 2, \cdots, n)$$

That is, the "distance" between any two points is equal to the sum of the absolute differences of their projections on the r axes of the space. Thus in Figure 1, according to this model, the distance between points j and k would simply be equal to $(x + y)$. Note that $(x + y)$ in Figure 1 is not equal to the corresponding $(u + v)$ in Figure 2.   In this model, the distances are *not* invariant over a rotation of axes.   Hence, Attneave's model implies a fixed, unique set of axes for the space.   This runs counter to our usual notions of how distances should behave.   Distances "ought" to stay put, regardless of how we choose to describe the positions of the points.   However, under a good many situations, equation 2 describes a reasonable state of affairs.   For example, suppose one were in a city which is laid out in square blocks.   A point three blocks away in one direction and four blocks away in the other would quite reasonably be described as seven blocks away.   Few people, if asked, would describe the point as five blocks distant.   Further, if new streets were put in at an angle to the old, the "distance" between the two points would change.   This is directly analogous to Attneave's model.   In a city laid out in square blocks, the axes or dimensions of the space are fixed.   They correspond to the directions of the streets and avenues.   If we interpret distance between two points to mean how far we must travel to get from one point to the other, then the total distance is equal to the sum of the distances in each of the two permissible directions.

It seems not at all unlikely that in certain multidimensional-scaling situations much the same thing might occur.   For example, if a subject is required to rate a set of stimulus pairs with respect to their similarity, and the stimuli differ with respect to obvious and compelling dimensions, his ratings might very well behave as though they were a straight sum of the differences on the separate dimensions: that is, as though the subject were saying "These two stimuli differ this much with respect to brightness, plus this much with respect to size, plus this much with respect to shape."

On the other hand, if separate dimensions are not obvious, the subject might be more likely to judge the over-all difference directly.   In this event, we would expect the Euclidean model to show more promise. Since the primary contributions of multidimensional scaling would seem to be in those areas where the separate dimensions are not only not obvious to the subject, but also not even known to the experimenter, an emphasis on the Euclidean model seems reasonable.

Determining the Dimensionality and Projections on Axes of a Euclidean Space from the Interpoint Distances between All Pairs of Stimuli

Let us assume that we have applied a model for scaling the psychological distances between n stimuli.   Some of the possible models for accomplishing this are described in the next section.   For the present, we shall assume this has been done, and we have available as data the $n(n-1)/2$ independently determined distances between the n stimuli.   Assume for the moment that the distances are exactly correct; no error is involved.

Then the problem is, first of all, to determine whether the mutual inter-point distances between stimuli can be considered as the distances between points in a real Euclidean space. If so, the second problem is to determine the dimensionality of the space and the projections of the points on axes of the space.

Equation 1, given earlier, relates the interpoint distances to the projections in a real, Euclidean space. Given the projections, it is easy enough to apply equation 1 to determine the interpoint distances. The reverse is not so true, however. Hence, some additional theorems will be necessary to enable us to determine the answers to the questions given above. These theorems have been provided by Young and Householder (1938).

Let i, j, and k be alternative subscripts for stimuli ($i, j, k = 1, 2, \cdots, n$), and d_{ij}, d_{ik}, and d_{jk} be the distances between the points, where $d_{ij} = d_{ji}$, $d_{ik} = d_{ki}$, and $d_{jk} = d_{kj}$. Then, let us define the matrix $\mathbf{B}_i$. $\mathbf{B}_i$ is an $(n-1) \times (n-1)$ symmetric matrix with elements

(3) $\qquad b_{jk} = \frac{1}{2}(d_{ij}^2 + d_{ik}^2 - d_{jk}^2) \qquad \begin{array}{l} (j, k = 1, 2, \cdots, n) \\ (j, k \neq i) \end{array}$

The element b_{jk} can be interpreted as the scalar product of the vectors from point i to points j and k. This can easily be seen from the cosine law, where, for any three points,

$$d_{jk}^2 = d_{ij}^2 + d_{ik}^2 - 2d_{ij}d_{ik}\cos\theta_{jik}$$

Rearranging terms gives

(4) $\qquad d_{ij}d_{ik}\cos\theta_{jik} = \frac{1}{2}(d_{ij}^2 + d_{ik}^2 - d_{jk}^2)$

Hence, from equations 3 and 4 it is seen that $b_{jk} = d_{ij}d_{ik}\cos\theta_{jik}$, the scalar product of vectors from point i to points j and k. Any of the n points may be taken as point i. There are thus n possible matrices $\mathbf{B}_i$. Each of these matrices can be considered as a matrix of scalar products of vectors from an origin at point i.

The following theorems from Young and Householder hold for any of the $\mathbf{B}_i$ matrices:

1. *If a matrix $\mathbf{B}_i$ is positive semidefinite, the distances between the stimuli may be considered as distances between points lying in a real, Euclidean space.* In terms of the latent roots of matrix $\mathbf{B}_i$, this means that the points can be considered as lying in a real, Euclidean space if the latent roots are all either positive or zero. Negative latent roots imply an imaginary space.

2. *The rank of any positive semidefinite matrix $\mathbf{B}_i$ is equal to the dimensionality of the set of points.* The number of positive latent roots is equal

to the number of dimensions necessary to account for the mutual interpoint distances.   For a given set of stimuli, matrix $\mathbf{B}_i$ will have the same rank, regardless of which stimulus is selected as the origin.

3. Any positive semidefinite matrix $\mathbf{B}_i$ may be factored to obtain a matrix $\mathbf{A}$, where

$$(5) \qquad\qquad\qquad \mathbf{B}_i = \mathbf{A}\mathbf{A}'$$

If the rank of matrix $\mathbf{B}_i$ is equal to r, where $r \leqslant (n-1)$, then matrix $\mathbf{A}$ is an $(n-1) \times r$ rectangular matrix whose elements are the projections of the points on r orthogonal axes with origin at the ith point of the r-dimensional, real Euclidean space.   Assuming that error-free interpoint distances are given for a set of stimuli, and a matrix $\mathbf{B}_i$ has been constructed at a given origin, different procedures for factoring matrix $\mathbf{B}_i$ will result in different $\mathbf{A}$ matrices, which, however, will all be related by orthogonal rotations of the axes. $\mathbf{B}_i$ matrices constructed by using different points as the origin will give corresponding $\mathbf{A}$ matrices which differ from one another with respect to both translation and orthogonal rotation of the axes.   The configuration of the points remains the same, of course.   The solutions differ only because the location of the origin and the direction of the axes are arbitrary within the Euclidean space.

The three theorems given above constitute a solution to the problems of determining dimensionality of the space and projections of the stimuli on axes when true interpoint distances are given.   The first theorem enables us to decide whether the positions of the stimuli can be represented by a real, Euclidean space.   The second theorem gives a criterion for determining the (minimal) dimensionality of the space.   The third gives a procedure for solving for projections (scale values) on an arbitrary set of axes of the space.

However, in a practical problem, we do not have error-free interpoint distances given.   When fallible estimates are used in place of the parameter values, each point will be somewhat in error.   Hence, in this case, assuming that the true dimensionality is substantially less than the number of stimuli, each $\mathbf{B}_i$ matrix will, when factored, yield results that differ somewhat above and beyond differences due to orientation of axes and location of origin.   In placing the origin at a particular point i, the implicit assumption is that this particular point is without error.   We would thus have the problem of choosing among the n different factor matrices that could be obtained.

One solution to this problem is to place the origin at the centroid of all of the stimuli rather than at a particular point (Torgerson, 1952).   This procedure gives a unique solution and tends to allow the errors in the individual points to cancel one another.   On the average, we would expect an origin at the centroid of all of the points to be less in error than an origin at one of the points selected arbitrarily.

It is first necessary, however, to find a convenient procedure for obtaining a matrix **B*** of scalar products from an origin at the centroid of all of the stimuli. According to equation 5,

$$\mathbf{B}_i = \mathbf{A}\mathbf{A}'$$

where **B**$_i$ is an $(n-1)\times(n-1)$ matrix referred to an origin at point i. From this equation it is apparent that the general element of **B**$_i$ is

$$(6) \qquad b_{jk} = \sum_{m=1}^{r} a_{jm}a_{km}$$

We shall, however, consider **B**$_i$ to be an $n \times n$ matrix with the ith row and column composed of zero elements. In like manner **A** is $n \times r$ with the ith row composed of zero elements.

We wish to translate the axes from an origin at point i to an origin at the centroid of all n points.

Let **A*** $= \|a_{jm*}\|$ be the desired matrix of projections of points j on axis m* of the new coordinate system with origin at the centroid of the n points. Then

$$(7) \qquad a_{jm*} = a_{jm} - c_m$$

where

$$c_m = \frac{1}{n}\sum_{j=1}^{n} a_{jm} = \frac{1}{n}\sum_{k=1}^{n} a_{km} = \text{the average projection of points on axis } m$$

$$= \text{projection of centroid on axis } m$$

$$(8) \qquad \mathbf{B}^* = \mathbf{A}^*\mathbf{A}^{*'} = \|b_{jk}^*\|$$

and, shortening the summational notation by letting $\sum_{m}^{r}$ denote $\sum_{m=1}^{r}$,

$$(9) \qquad b_{jk}^* = \sum_{m}^{r} a_{jm*}a_{km*}$$

Substituting from equation 7 into equation 9, we have

$$(10) \qquad b_{jk}^* = \sum_{m}^{r} (a_{jm} - c_m)(a_{km} - c_m)$$

$$= \sum_{m}^{r} a_{jm}a_{km} - \sum_{m}^{r} a_{jm}c_m - \sum_{m}^{r} a_{km}c_m + \sum_{m}^{r} c_m c_m$$

From the definition of c_m it is seen that

$$(11) \quad b_{jk}^* = \sum_m^r a_{jm}a_{km} - \frac{1}{n}\sum_m^r a_{jm}\sum_k^n a_{km} - \frac{1}{n}\sum_m^r a_{km}\sum_j^n a_{jm}$$

$$+ \frac{1}{n^2}\sum_m^r \left(\sum_j^n a_{jm}\right)\left(\sum_k^n a_{km}\right)$$

But

$$(12) \quad \sum_j^n b_{jk} = \sum_m^r a_{jm}\sum_k^n a_{km} = \sum_m^r a_{km}\sum_j^n a_{jm}$$

and

$$(13) \quad \sum_k^n\sum_j^n b_{jk} = \sum_m^r\left(\sum_j^n a_{jm}\right)^2$$

Substituting, we have

$$(14) \quad b_{jk}^* = b_{jk} - \frac{1}{n}\sum_j^n b_{jk} - \frac{1}{n}\sum_k^n b_{jk} + \frac{1}{n^2}\sum_j^n\sum_k^n b_{jk}$$

But, from equation 3, the element

$$b_{jk} = \tfrac{1}{2}(d_{ij}^2 + d_{ik}^2 - d_{jk}^2)$$

Substituting this value into equation 14 gives

$$(15) \quad b_{jk}^* = \tfrac{1}{2}(d_{ij}^2 + d_{ik}^2 - d_{jk}^2) - \frac{1}{2n}\sum_j^n (d_{ij}^2 + d_{ik}^2 - d_{jk}^2)$$

$$- \frac{1}{2n}\sum_k^n (d_{ij}^2 + d_{ik}^2 - d_{jk}^2) + \frac{1}{2n^2}\sum_j^n\sum_k^n (d_{ij}^2 + d_{ik}^2 - d_{jk}^2)$$

Summing each term separately and simplifying gives

$$(16) \quad b_{jk}^* = \frac{1}{2}\left(\frac{1}{n}\sum_j^n d_{jk}^2 + \frac{1}{n}\sum_k^n d_{jk}^2 - \frac{1}{n^2}\sum_j^n\sum_k^n d_{jk}^2 - d_{jk}^2\right)$$

Equation 16† gives a routine method for computing directly from the interpoint distances a matrix **B*** of scalar products between points referred to an origin at the centroid of all of the points. Given estimates of the psychological distance between all pairs of stimuli, equation 16 is used to compute matrix **B***. This matrix is then factored by any of the usual factoring procedures to obtain the projections of the stimuli on the r

---

† The transformation from equation 14 to equation 16 was pointed out by Drs. L. R. Tucker, B. F. Green, and R. Abelson (see Messick and Abelson, 1956).

orthogonal axes of the space. (See Thurstone, 1947, for a discussion of factor-analysis methods.)

The orientation of the axes will depend on both the configuration of points and the particular factor method used. Once the factor matrix **A** has been obtained, it may be rotated and translated to a psychologically meaningful set of dimensions, if criteria for such are available.

Determining Projections on Axes from Interpoint Distances, Assuming Attneave's Spatial Model

It will be recalled that, in this model, the distance between two points is assumed to be equal to the sum of the absolute differences in their projections on the r fixed dimensions of the system:

$$d_{jk} = \sum_{m}^{r} |a_{jm} - a_{km}| \qquad (j, k = 1, 2, \cdots, n)$$

Again, while this set of equations serves well for determining distances between stimuli when their projections on the axes are given, the reverse is not true. Computing projections when only the interpoint distances are given is no easy matter.

Unfortunately, as is so often the case with procedures that involve absolute differences, no neat, compact procedure such as was given in the preceding section for the Euclidean model is available.

Applications of the model have been limited to those sets of stimuli for which the dimensionality—and the fixed dimensions—is known to a high level of certainty by the experimenter. In Attneave's experiments (1950), the stimuli used varied along such dimensions as size, color, and brightness. In this case, where we can assume that the stimuli which vary along a single physical dimension vary along a single corresponding psychological dimension, we can locate the stimuli in the space rather easily. Subsets of stimuli that vary on only one dimension should fall along a straight line parallel to one of the axes in the space. Given these subsets, we can then assign positions to the remaining stimuli on the basis of their distances from the stimuli included within the subsets, using trial and error procedures.

For the general case, however, where both dimensionality and the particular dimensions themselves are not known, no systematic procedure is yet available.

3. DISTANCE MODELS

The spatial models discussed in the preceding section require that the distances between all pairs of stimuli be given. They are not concerned with the question of how the distances are to be determined.   For example, we *could* apply the Euclidean model mechanically to the results of *any* procedure that yields a number for each pair of stimuli.   Whether it would be worth while to do so is another matter.

In the context of the present discussion of multidimensional scaling, the numbers characterizing each pair of stimuli are determined by one or another of several *distance models*.   The models all depend on the psychological similarity of the pairs of stimuli.   A psychological distance as determined through use of one of the models is a quantitative measure of the degree of similarity between the two stimuli.   Application of one of the spatial models to the psychological distances gives information as to whether such distances can be considered to be distances between stimuli in a multidimensional space of the complex attribute of interest.   It further gives the projections on axes of this multidimensional space.

The models for scaling psychological distance are for the most part directly analogous to corresponding unidimensional-scaling methods. Most of the methods discussed in earlier chapters can be extended (at least theoretically) to the scaling of psychological distance.   In each case, however, a somewhat more complex judgment is required of the subject. The direct extensions of the unidimensional models require the following substitutions:

1. Where the judgment before was concerned with the amount of a particular attribute possessed by *each stimulus*, the judgment now will concern the degree of similarity of a *pair* of stimuli with respect to some complex attribute.   In the method of equal-appearing intervals, for example (Chapter 4), the subjects sorted the stimuli into piles which were defined to be equally spaced with respect to some defined attribute.   In the direct multidimensional extension, the subject would sort *pairs of stimuli* into piles which have been defined to be equally spaced on a *similarity* continuum.

2. Where before, the scale value was assigned to represent the amount of the attribute possessed by the *stimulus*, now the scale value represents the *psychological distance* between the pair of stimuli on a similarity or distance continuum.   In the method of equal-appearing intervals again, the average position is taken as the scale value of the stimulus.   In the multidimensional extension, the average position into which the pair of stimuli was sorted is taken as the psychological distance between them.

Where before, the scale values of the stimuli may have been determined on a *ratio scale* (i.e., with respect to a natural origin) or on an *interval scale* (i.e., with respect to an arbitrary origin), so in the corresponding multidimensional extensions the distances may be determined on a ratio scale or an interval scale. Henceforth, we shall use the unmodified term "distance" when referring to distances on a ratio scale and the term "comparative distance" when referring to distances referred to an interval scale.

Among the direct extensions of the unidimensional methods which either have been used for determining distances or which might be so used are those listed below.

1. *The Method of Equal-Appearing Intervals.* This procedure has been used by Abelson (1954) in a multidimensional investigation of attitudes. In this particular case, the similarity of two attitude statements was represented by the judged amount of agreement they reflected. (Suppose two people are having a discussion. One person says statement *A*. The other says statement *B*. How much in agreement are they?) The subjects rated the pairs of stimuli on a scale anchored at a natural origin—one of the categories denoted "in perfect agreement." Average ratings were interpreted directly as psychological distances.

2. *The Law of Categorical Judgment in Conjunction with the Experimental Method of Successive Intervals.* This procedure has been used by Attneave under the name of the method of graded dichotomies (1950) and by Messick (1954). Attneave's stimuli were geometric figures which varied with respect to such dimensions as brightness, size, color, and shape. The task set for the subject was to rate the pairs of stimuli on a seven-point scale varying from "identical" to "extremely different" with respect to how much alike they seemed to be. Messick carried out two experiments with the method; one on color and one on perception of attitudes. In the color experiment, the subjects' task was to sort pairs of Munsell color chips into piles which were ordered in terms of the similarity continuum. In the attitude experiment, his stimuli were attitude statements taken from three different Thurstone attitude scales. The task set for the subject was to consider a person who would strongly agree with statement *A* and then rate in terms of the amount of agreement such a person would have with each of the remaining stimuli. Each stimulus in turn was taken to define the attitude of the imagined person, and the remaining stimuli were rated accordingly. Each pair of stimuli was thus rated twice on an agreement continuum. Attneave and Messick both treated the ratings by the categorical-judgment model discussed in Chapter 10, ending up with the comparative distances between all pairs of stimuli (comparative distances, since the categorical-judgment model gives scale values referred to an arbitrary origin).

3. *The Method of Tetrads* would be a direct extension of the method of paired comparisons discussed in Chapter 9. Here, pairs of stimulus pairs

would be presented to the subject. He would be required to indicate the pair for which the two members were the more similar. Analytical procedures would parallel those discussed in Chapter 9. The method would again result in the comparative distances between each pair of stimuli, since the law of comparative judgment yields scale values with respect to an arbitrary origin.

In addition to the direct extension of the unidimensional-scaling methods, a number of distance models have been developed which, though based on the same generalization in rationale, use somewhat different experimental procedures. Chief among these are the method of triadic combinations as used by Richardson (1938) in his pioneering work with multidimensional scaling, the complete method of triads (Torgerson, 1951, 1952; Messick, 1954) and the multidimensional method of rank order (Klingberg, 1941).

These methods are all based on a direct generalization of condition C of the law of comparative judgment (though it should be noted that Klingberg himself used the short-cut procedure given by Guilford (1928) in his actual computation of comparative distances). The salient feature of the methods is the relative simplicity of judgment required of the subject.

The experimental procedures are briefly outlined below. (A whole system of similar experimental procedures has recently been discussed by Coombs, 1954.)

In the *method of triadic combinations*, the stimuli are presented to the subject in triads. The subject decides which two of the three are most alike and which two are most different. For example, given a triad of the three stimuli *A*, *B*, and *C*, the subject might respond with the following *two judgments*:

A and B are most alike.
B and C are most different.

Given these judgments, we deduce the following *three relationships*:

A appeared more like B than C.
B appeared more like A than C.
C appeared more like A than B.

Thus, for a given triad, *three relationships* are deduced from *two judgments*. All possible triads are presented to the subject. From the deduced relationships, the proportion of times each stimulus appeared more like one of each other pair is obtained. These proportions are then converted into *differences in distances* in the same manner as proportions in the law of comparative judgment are converted into differences in scale values.

From the observed differences in distances is obtained the scale of comparative distances.

One basic difference distinguishes the *complete method of triads* from Richardson's method of triadic combinations. In the complete method of triads, instead of deducing three relationships from two judgments, judgments of the relationships themselves are obtained directly. The method requires three separate presentations of each triad. At each presentation, one of the judgments is obtained. For example, consider a particular triad with elements A, B, and C in a series of triads. The first time the series is presented, the subject is required to judge whether A is more like B or C; the second time the series is presented, he is required to judge whether B is more like A or C; and the third time whether C is more like A or B. This would seem to involve the simplest and most natural task of all of the different procedures.

Let the stimuli be designated as i ($i = 1, 2, \cdots, n$). Then, in the *method of multidimensional rank order*, the subject is required to rank, in order of degree of similarity to a given stimulus i, the $n-1$ remaining stimuli. This is repeated for each value of i. There are thus obtained n rank orders from each subject. From these rank orders, the proportion of times each stimulus is judged more like one of each other pair of stimuli may be obtained. The same procedures may then be used to obtain the scale of comparative distances.

The three different methods differ only in the experimental procedure used for obtaining data. The underlying model is the same for all three, as are the form and amount of data collected. In each instance the experimental procedure ends with proportions of the form $_kp_{ij}$, where $_kp_{ij}$ refers to the proportion of times stimulus k was judged to be more like stimulus i than like stimulus j.

Since comparisons are not made between all pairs of stimulus pairs, but only between those that have one stimulus in common, the usual analytical procedures as presented in Chapter 9 are not particularly appropriate. A least-squares solution, developed primarily for the complete method of triads, but equally appropriate to either of the other two procedures is given below.‡

The Complete Method of Triads for Obtaining Comparative Distances between Stimuli

The stimuli are presented to the subject in triads. The judgment required of the subject is of the form: "Stimulus k is more similar to

---

‡ This derivation differs from an earlier version (Torgerson, 1952) only in that the present matrices $_k\mathbf{P}_{ij}$ correspond to the *transpose* of the equivalent matrices in the earlier discussion.

stimulus i than to stimulus j." With n stimuli, there are $n(n-1)(n-2)/6$ triads. In each triad, each stimulus is compared with each other pair, making a total of $n(n-1)(n-2)/2$ judgments for each subject. From these judgments we obtain the proportion of times any stimulus k is judged more similar to stimulus i than to j.

These proportions can be arranged in the n matrices $_k\mathbf{P}_{ij}$, where k, i, and j are alternative subscripts for the stimuli. k gives the number of the matrix, i is a row index, and j is a column index. The element $_kp_{ij}$ is the proportion of times stimulus k is judged closer to stimulus i than to j. The matrices $_k\mathbf{P}_{ij}$ have vacant cells in the principal diagonal, and in the kth row and column.§ The matrices are such that the sum of symmetric elements is unity—e.g., $_kp_{gh} + {_kp_{hg}} = 1$. For example, given four stimuli, 1. 2, 3, and 4, there are four $_k\mathbf{P}_{ij}$ matrices. The second matrix ($k = 2$) is illustrated below:

$$_2\mathbf{P}_{ij}$$

$$j$$

		1	2	3	4
	1	·	·	$_2p_{13}$	$_2p_{14}$
i	2	·	·	·	·
	3	$_2p_{31}$	·	·	$_2p_{34}$
	4	$_2p_{41}$	·	$_2p_{43}$	·

Consider first the errorless case. Let a circumflex indicate a true value. It is postulated that the true proportion $_k\hat{p}_{ij}$ is a function of the corresponding difference in distance $(\hat{d}_{kj} - \hat{d}_{ik})$. The same rationale that underlies condition C of the law of comparative judgment (Chapter 9) leads to the transformation function

(17)
$$_k\hat{p}_{ij} = \int_{-\infty}^{_k\hat{x}_{ij}} \frac{1}{\sqrt{2\pi}} \exp\left(-\tfrac{1}{2}x^2\right) dx$$

where

$$_k\hat{x}_{ij} = \hat{d}_{kj} - \hat{d}_{ik}$$

The $_k\hat{x}_{ij}$ are thus the unit normal deviates corresponding to the proportions $_k\hat{p}_{ij}$.

In the errorless case, the solution is straightforward. We could simply define an arbitrary origin by setting one of the distances equal to zero: e.g., $\hat{d}_{ik} = 0$. Then the numerical solution for the remaining distances is

---

§ It might be noted that the elements in the kth row and column *could* be obtained experimentally. However, since the method would ordinarily be used in connection with supraliminal distances, the experimentally determined proportions would be either 0.00 or 1.00. As in paired comparisons, proportions of 0.00 and 1.00 cannot be utilized.

given directly. Since there are $\frac{1}{2}n(n-1)(n-2)$ differences in distances $_k\hat{x}_{ij}$ and only $\frac{1}{2}n(n-1)-1$ unknown distances, the solution is considerably overdetermined. In the errorless case it would make no difference which subset of $\frac{1}{2}n(n-1)-1$ equations were used. They would all give the same solution.

For fallible data, we are given experimentally the $\frac{1}{2}n(n-1)(n-2)$ elements $_kp_{ij}$ as estimates of $_k\hat{p}_{ij}$. Using the same transformation as in equation 17, we obtain the equivalent set of $_kx_{ij}$ as estimates of the true differences $(\hat{d}_{kj} - \hat{d}_{ik})$. These estimates can be arranged in the n matrices $_k\mathbf{X}_{ij}$. The matrices are skew symmetric $(_kx_{gh} + _kx_{hg} = 0)$, have zero diagonal elements, and have vacant cells in the kth row and column.

The problem is to devise an efficient procedure for obtaining estimates of the $\frac{1}{2}(n)(n-1)$ distances from the $\frac{1}{2}(n)(n-1)(n-2)$ observed estimates, $_kx_{ij}$. The derivation of a least-squares solution to the problem is given below.

In the errorless case, $_k\hat{x}_{ij} = \hat{d}_{kj} - \hat{d}_{ik}$. A reasonable procedure would thus seem to be to solve for the values of the distances which minimizes the following function:

$$(18) \qquad 2F = \sum_{\substack{k}}^{n} \sum_{\substack{j \\ j \neq k}}^{n} \sum_{\substack{i \\ i \neq j \\ i \neq k}}^{n} [_kx_{ij} - (d_{kj} - d_{ik})]^2$$

If we define a set of matrices $_k\mathbf{E}_{ij}$ with elements $(_kx_{ij} + d_{ik} - d_{kj})$, it is seen that $2F$ is equal to the sum of squares of elements of the matrices $_k\mathbf{E}_{ij}$.

Let g and h correspond to two particular stimuli with $d_{gh} = d_{hg}$, the distance between them. The term d_{gh} (or d_{hg}) occurs only in the error matrices $_g\mathbf{E}_{ij}$ and $_h\mathbf{E}_{ij}$ as follows:

In $_g\mathbf{E}_{ij}$ the hth column contains the elements $_gx_{ih} + d_{ig} - d_{gh}$.
$\qquad$ the hth row contains the elements $_gx_{hj} + d_{hg} - d_{gj}$.
In $_h\mathbf{E}_{ij}$ the gth column contains the elements $_hx_{ig} + d_{ih} - d_{hg}$.
$\qquad$ the gth row contains the elements $_hx_{gj} + d_{gh} - d_{hj}$.

To minimize $2F$, we first take the derivative of F with respect to d_{gh}. We shall designate this derivative as F'. It is apparent that the derivatives of all terms of F except those containing the element d_{gh} vanish. Therefore,

$$(19) \qquad F' = -\sum_{\substack{i \\ i \neq g,h}}^{n} (_gx_{ih} + d_{ig} - d_{gh}) + \sum_{\substack{j \\ j \neq g,h}}^{n} (_gx_{hj} + d_{hg} - d_{gj})$$

$$- \sum_{\substack{i \\ i \neq g,h}}^{n} (_hx_{ig} + d_{ih} - d_{hg}) + \sum_{\substack{j \\ j \neq g,h}}^{n} (_hx_{gj} + d_{gh} - d_{hj})$$

But, since matrices $_g\mathbf{E}_{ij}$ and $_h\mathbf{E}_{ij}$ are skew-symmetric,

$$-\sum_{\substack{i \\ i \neq g,h}}^{n} (_g x_{ih} + d_{ig} - d_{gh}) = \sum_{\substack{j \\ j \neq g,h}}^{n} (_g x_{hj} + d_{hg} - d_{gj})$$

and

$$-\sum_{\substack{i \\ i \neq g,h}}^{n} (_h x_{ig} + d_{ih} - d_{hg}) = \sum_{\substack{j \\ j \neq g,h}}^{n} (_h x_{gj} + d_{gh} - d_{hj})$$

Therefore, we may write

$$(20) \quad F' = -2\sum_{\substack{i \\ i \neq g,h}}^{n} (_g x_{ih} + d_{ig} - d_{gh}) - 2\sum_{\substack{i \\ i \neq g,h}}^{n} (_h x_{ig} + d_{ih} - d_{hg})$$

Setting F' equal to zero, and summing over each term, we find

$$(21) \quad \sum_{\substack{i \\ i \neq g,h}}^{n} {_g x_{ih}} + \sum_{\substack{i \\ i \neq g,h}}^{n} d_{ig} - (n-2)d_{gh} + \sum_{\substack{i \\ i \neq g,h}}^{n} {_h x_{ig}} + \sum_{\substack{i \\ i \neq g,h}}^{n} d_{ih} - (n-2)d_{hg} = 0$$

Remembering that $d_{gg} = d_{hh} = 0$, and that the diagonals and kth row and column of all $_k\mathbf{X}_{ij}$ matrices are vacant, we can write

$$(22) \quad \sum_{i}^{n} {_g x_{ih}} + \sum_{\substack{i \\ i \neq h}}^{n} d_{ig} - (n-2)d_{gh} + \sum_{i}^{n} {_h x_{ig}} + \sum_{\substack{i \\ i \neq g}}^{n} d_{ih} - (n-2)d_{hg} = 0$$

Adding d_{gh} to $\displaystyle\sum_{\substack{i \\ i \neq h}}^{n} d_{ig}$ and to $\displaystyle\sum_{\substack{i \\ i \neq g}}^{n} d_{ih}$, subtracting d_{gh} from $-(n-2)d_{gh}$

and $-(n-2)d_{hg}$, and remembering that $d_{gh} = d_{hg}$, we have

$$(23) \quad \sum_{i}^{n} {_g x_{ih}} + \sum_{i}^{n} d_{ig} - (n-1)d_{gh} + \sum_{i}^{n} {_h x_{ig}} + \sum_{i}^{n} d_{ih} - (n-1)d_{hg} = 0$$

Summing over g, $g \neq h$, we have

$$(24) \quad \sum_{\substack{g \\ g \neq h}}^{n} \sum_{i}^{n} {_g x_{ih}} + \sum_{\substack{g \\ g \neq h}}^{n} \sum_{i}^{n} d_{ig} - (n-1)\sum_{\substack{g \\ g \neq h}}^{n} d_{gh} + \sum_{\substack{g \\ g \neq h}}^{n} \sum_{i}^{n} {_h x_{ig}}$$

$$+ (n-1)\sum_{i}^{n} d_{ih} - (n-1)\sum_{\substack{g \\ g \neq h}}^{n} d_{hg} = 0$$

But

$$\sum_{\substack{g \\ g \neq h}}^{n} \sum_{i}^{n} {}_h x_{ig} = 0$$

and, since $d_{hh} = 0$,

$$\sum_{i}^{n} d_{ih} = \sum_{\substack{g \\ g \neq h}}^{n} d_{hg}$$

therefore,

$$(25) \qquad \sum_{\substack{g \\ g \neq h}}^{n} \sum_{i}^{n} {}_g x_{ih} + \sum_{\substack{g \\ g \neq h}}^{n} \sum_{i}^{n} d_{ig} - (n-1) \sum_{g}^{n} d_{gh} = 0$$

Adding $\sum_{i}^{n} d_{ih}$ to $\sum_{\substack{g \\ g \neq h}}^{n} \sum_{i}^{n} d_{ig}$ and subtracting $\sum_{g}^{n} d_{gh}$ from $-(n-1)\sum_{g}^{n} d_{gh}$,

we see that

$$(26) \qquad \sum_{\substack{g \\ g \neq h}}^{n} \sum_{i}^{n} {}_g x_{ih} + \sum_{g}^{n} \sum_{i}^{n} d_{ig} - n \sum_{g}^{n} d_{gh} = 0$$

Rearranging, dividing by $n(n-1)$, and remembering that cells ${}_g x_{ig}$ are vacant, we find

$$(27) \qquad \frac{1}{n(n-1)} \sum_{g}^{n} \sum_{i}^{n} {}_g x_{ih} = \frac{1}{n-1} \sum_{g}^{n} d_{gh} - \frac{1}{n(n-1)} \sum_{g}^{n} \sum_{i}^{n} d_{ig}$$

Also, if we divide equation 23 by $2(n-1)$ and rearrange, we obtain

$$(28) \quad d_{gh} - \frac{1}{2(n-1)} \left(\sum_{i}^{n} d_{ig} + \sum_{i}^{n} d_{ih} \right) = \frac{1}{2(n-1)} \left(\sum_{i}^{n} {}_g x_{ih} + \sum_{i}^{n} {}_h x_{ig} \right)$$

It will be convenient to denote the averages in equations 27 and 28 by replacing the index summed over by a dot, e.g.,

$$d_{.h} \equiv \frac{1}{n-1} \sum_{i}^{n} d_{ih} = \frac{1}{n-1} \sum_{g}^{n} d_{gh}$$

$$d_{..} \equiv \frac{1}{n(n-1)} \sum_{i}^{n} \sum_{g}^{n} d_{ig}$$

$$_g x_{.h} \equiv \frac{1}{n-1} \sum_{i}^{n} {}_g x_{ih}$$

$$_. x_{.h} \equiv \frac{1}{n(n-1)} \sum_{i}^{n} \sum_{g}^{n} {}_g x_{ih}$$

After substitutions have been made for the appropriate terms, equation 28 becomes

(29) $$d_{gh} - \tfrac{1}{2}(d_{.g} + d_{.h}) = \tfrac{1}{2}({}_g x_{.h} + {}_h x_{.g})$$

and equation 27 becomes

(30) $$x_{.h} = d_{.h} - d_{..}$$

and, when $h = g$,

$$x_{.g} = d_{.g} - d_{..}$$

Substituting for $d_{.g}$ and $d_{.h}$ in equation 29, we have

(31) $$d_{gh} - \tfrac{1}{2}(d_{..} + x_{.g} + d_{..} + x_{.h}) = \tfrac{1}{2}({}_g x_{.h} + {}_h x_{.g})$$

which rearranged becomes

(32) $$d_{gh} - d_{..} = \tfrac{1}{2}({}_g x_{.h} + x_{.g} + {}_h x_{.g} + x_{.h})$$

When $g = j$, $h = k$, the comparative distance $h_{jk} = d_{gh} - d_{..}$. Since the x values are functions of the observed proportions (equation 17), equation 32 gives the comparative distances as functions of the observed data. Equation 32, then, gives a rather straightforward method for obtaining the best estimate, in a least-squares sense, of the matrix of comparative distances.

4. THE "ADDITIVE-CONSTANT" PROBLEM

Both the Euclidean model and the city-block model require as given the *absolute* distances between all pairs of stimuli. Several of the distance models, including those that require the simpler type of judgment, yield distances which are determined only with respect to an arbitrary origin. Such *comparative* distances are related to the absolute distances required by the spatial models by an equation of the form

(33) $$d_{jk} = h_{jk} + c$$

where d_{jk} is the required absolute distance, h_{jk} is the comparative distance given by the distance model, and c is an unknown additive constant. Comparative distances as such cannot be used directly in conjunction with a spatial model, since the dimensionality, projections, and the configuration itself will be functions of the arbitrarily selected zero point to which the comparative distances are referred. Hence it is necessary to consider procedures for converting comparative distances to the corresponding absolute distances. We shall consider in detail only those procedures that have been worked out in connection with the Euclidean spatial model.

Equivalent analytical procedures for other spatial models remain to be developed. Except where otherwise noted, then, the remainder of this section is concerned with procedures for estimating the additive constant which are appropriate for the Euclidean model.

The basic assumption involved is that the appropriate value of the additive constant is that value which will allow the stimuli to be fitted by a real, Euclidean space of the smallest possible dimensionality. Consider, for example, five points having the following comparative interpoint distances h_{jk} ($j, k = 1, 2, \cdots, 5$; $j \neq k$):

$$h_{12} = 0.2, \quad h_{14} = 0.2, \quad h_{25} = -0.8, \quad h_{15} = -1.8, \quad h_{35} = -1.8$$
$$h_{13} = 1.2, \quad h_{24} = 3.2, \quad h_{34} = \quad 0.2, \quad h_{23} = \quad 0.2, \quad h_{45} = -0.8$$

With these comparative distances the value of the additive constant which will allow the stimuli to be fitted by a real, Euclidean space of the smallest possible dimensionality is 4.8. If we add 4.8 to each of the comparative distances to convert them into absolute distances, we obtain

$$d_{12} = 5, \quad d_{14} = 5, \quad d_{25} = 4, \quad d_{15} = 3, \quad d_{35} = 3$$
$$d_{13} = 6, \quad d_{24} = 8, \quad d_{34} = 5, \quad d_{23} = 5, \quad d_{45} = 4$$

The five stimuli can be plotted in a two-dimensional space as shown in Figure 3.

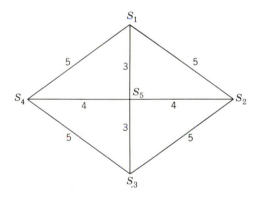

Figure 3

Note that for any smaller value of the additive constant the points do not exist in a real Euclidean space. For example, if 1, 2, or 3 is added, then $d_{45} + d_{25} < d_{24}$, an impossible relationship in real Euclidean space. Also, for any larger value of the additive constant, the points lie in a real space of dimensionality greater than two.

In theory, where we are dealing with errorless comparative distances, the computation of the value of the additive constant which permits the location of the stimuli in a real, Euclidean space of the smallest possible dimensionality is straightforward but tedious. What is needed is the value of the additive constant which results in a positive semidefinite matrix $\mathbf{B}^*$ of the lowest possible rank: i.e., a matrix $\mathbf{B}^*$ with the largest possible number of zero latent roots under the restriction that the remaining latent roots are all positive. One procedure for accomplishing this would be as follows: First, construct the $\mathbf{B}^*$ matrix from the available data ($d_{jk} = h_{jk} + c$). Next, evaluate the determinant of $\mathbf{B}^*$. This determinant will be a polynomial in c. If this polynomial is set equal to zero, one of the solutions for c is the value of the additive constant desired. The appropriate value of c is the one that meets the conditions given above.

In a practical scaling problem, however, we are given only fallible estimates of comparative distances. In this case, the strict mathematical criterion of a positive semidefinite matrix $\mathbf{B}^*$ should not be taken too seriously. Several points might be noted here. (For a more detailed discussion, see Torgerson, 1952.) It is always possible to make the constant large enough to guarantee that the matrix $\mathbf{B}^*$ contains no negative roots, and hence to guarantee that the points can be fitted into a real Euclidean space. More particularly, it would seem to be always possible to make the constant such that the points fit into a real, Euclidean space whose dimensionality is at least two less than the number of points. We might further surmise that for fallible data we would probably never obtain a positive semidefinite matrix $\mathbf{B}^*$ with a rank that was less than the number of stimuli minus two, due to the errors involved. Further, the value of the additive constant which gives a positive semidefinite matrix $\mathbf{B}^*$ with rank equal to two less than its order is probably not the "best" estimate possible. A procedure that gives this result assumes implicitly that any error in the comparative distances would be such as to change the zero latent roots to positive values. It would seem more reasonable to assume that errors in estimates of comparative distances would be equally likely to change some of the zero roots to negative values. Consider three points on a line, for example, such that the true interpoint distances are related by the equation $\hat{d}_{12} + \hat{d}_{23} = \hat{d}_{13}$. The former assumption would mean that any error in estimation would be such as to make the left-hand term greater than the right, whereas the latter assumption would hold that the reverse is equally likely. Hence, in the practical situation, we probably do not want a matrix $\mathbf{B}^*$ which is strictly positive semidefinite, but rather one that we can assume would have been so had it not been for error. As a practical criterion, we want to estimate that value of the additive constant which results in a $\mathbf{B}^*$ matrix with the smallest possible number of large positive latent roots (the "true" dimensions of the system), under the condition that the remaining roots are all small and distributed about zero (the "error" dimensions of the system), providing, of course, that such a value exists.

Three procedures for estimating the additive constant from fallible data will be given here. The first (Torgerson, 1952) is a least-squares estimate of the additive constant under the hypothesis that the true dimensionality of the points is equal to unity: i.e., that except for error, the points all fall along a straight line. It is the method that would be appropriate if the procedures of the present chapter were to be used as a unidimensional-scaling method. The second procedure is a general iterative solution developed by Messick and Abelson (1956). While their solution is by far the most elegant, it also involves a considerable amount of labor. Finally, we shall present a rougher method which has been found to give good results (Torgerson, 1952) and which is considerably easier and more rapid.

Estimating the Additive Constant—Unidimensional Case

Ideally, in the unidimensional case, the true distances $\hat{d}_{ij}$ between any three points are related by the equation

$$(34) \qquad \hat{d}_{ij} + \hat{d}_{jk} = \hat{d}_{ik} \quad \text{where} \quad i < j < k$$

and, since $\hat{d}_{ij} = \hat{h}_{ij} + \hat{c}$,

$$\hat{h}_{ij} + \hat{c} + \hat{h}_{jk} + \hat{c} = \hat{h}_{ik} + \hat{c}$$

or

$$(35) \qquad \hat{c} = \hat{h}_{ik} - \hat{h}_{ij} - \hat{h}_{jk}$$

Any set of three stimuli could thus be used to determine the true additive constant $\hat{c}$. Where we are given only fallible comparative distances h_{ij}, each triplet of the form $(h_{ik} - h_{ij} - h_{jk})$ may be taken as an estimate of $\hat{c}$. These estimates will differ from one another due to the fallible nature of the available data. If we define the following error term

$$(36) \qquad e = c - h_{ik} + h_{ij} + h_{jk} \qquad (i < j < k)$$

the estimate, c, which minimizes the sum of squares of these errors is simply the average of the estimates from each of the $\frac{1}{6}(n)(n-1)(n-2)$ triplets:

$$(37) \quad c = \frac{6}{n(n-1)(n-2)} \sum_{i < j < k} (h_{ik} - h_{ij} - h_{jk}), \quad \begin{array}{l} (i = 1, 2, \cdots, n-2) \\ (j = 2, 3, \cdots, n-1) \\ (k = 3, 4, \cdots, n) \end{array}$$

This solution for the additive constant c requires that the order of the stimuli be known on the underlying dimension. This order can ordinarily be obtained from the matrix of comparative distances $\mathbf{H}$. When the comparative distances are referred to an origin such that the average of all of the comparative distances between different stimuli is equal to zero, as in the solution given for the method of triads in the preceding section, for example, then the sum of any column k of $\mathbf{H}$ divided by $n-1$ gives the average distance from point k to all of the other points minus the average distance of all points from each other:

$$(38a) \qquad \frac{1}{n-1} \sum_{\substack{j \neq k}}^{n} h_{jk} = \frac{1}{n-1} \sum_{\substack{j \neq k}}^{n} d_{jk} - c \qquad (k = 1, 2, \cdots, n)$$

Hence, large values of $\displaystyle\sum_{j}^{n} h_{jk}$ indicate that k is near one end of the scale, and small values indicate that k is near the center of the scale. Inspection of individual elements will ordinarily suffice to determine which side of the scale k is on. For example, if two points j and k both have large values of Σh, they will be on the same side of the scale if the comparative distance between them is small, and will be on opposite sides if it is large. In the final ordering, values of Σh will begin large, decrease to a minimum, and then increase.

Given a matrix $\mathbf{H}$ with stimuli in the proper order, a short-cut procedure for obtaining the additive constant c is as follows:

1. Obtain the diagonal sums S_g of the elements above the principal diagonal:

$$(38b) \qquad S_g = \sum_{j=1}^{n-g} h_{j(j+g)} \qquad (g = 1, 2, \cdots, n-1)$$

2. Multiply each S_g by $(2g - n)$; sum the products, and divide by $\frac{1}{6}n(n-1)(n-2)$. The result is the estimate of c. That is, if we let $t_g \equiv 2g - n$,

$$(39) \qquad c = \frac{6}{n(n-1)(n-2)} \sum_{g=1}^{n-1} S_g t_g$$

Given the estimate of the additive constant, c, the matrix of comparative distances $\mathbf{H}$ can be converted into a matrix of absolute distances $\mathbf{D}$. Given these distances, two alternative procedures are available. We could, of course, proceed with the multidimensional analysis, converting the distances into scalar products, and then obtaining the first principal component (or, as an approximation, the first centroid). The factor loadings would correspond to the scale values of the stimuli on the underlying dimension. The amount and kind of variance remaining in the residual matrix after extraction of the first factor would give one indication of the adequacy of the hypothesis of unidimensionality.

A second procedure would involve taking note of the fact that, under the hypothesis of unidimensionality, the elements of the **D** matrix are estimates of the absolute difference in scale values of the two stimuli involved. That is, d_{jk} is an estimate of $|s_k - s_j|$. In order to give the appropriate sign to the differences so that $d_{jk} = s_k - s_j$, it is only necessary to make all of the elements below the principal diagonal negative. Given this change, a least-squares solution for the scale values of the stimuli is simply the averages of the columns of matrix **D***, the matrix of signed differences in scale values:

$$(40) \qquad s_k = \frac{1}{n} \sum_{j=1}^{n} d_{jk}^* \qquad (k = 1, 2, \cdots, n)$$

where

$$d_{jk}^* = d_{jk} \quad \text{for} \quad k > j$$
$$d_{jk}^* = -d_{jk} \quad \text{for} \quad j > k$$

and

$$d_{jj}^* = 0$$

This follows directly from the discussion of condition C of the law of comparative judgment given in Chapter 9.

Messick and Abelson's General Solution

The solution given above is limited to the application of multidimensional-scaling methods to unidimensional-scaling problems, since the estimate of the additive constant was appropriate for only that case. The general solution to be described here is relevant to the general problem, with no restrictions on the dimensionality.

The basic notion, which was mentioned earlier, is that the estimate of c which is desired is the one that gives a relatively small number of large latent roots, with the remaining roots small and distributed about zero, providing, of course, that such a value of c exists. The rationale is that the large roots will then correspond to the "true" dimensions of the system, and the remaining small roots will correspond to error.

The procedure is based on the theorem that the sum of the diagonal elements of any symmetric matrix is equal to the sum of its latent roots. Since matrix **B***** is a symmetric matrix,

$$(41) \qquad \sum_{j=1}^{n} b_{jj}^* = \sum_{m=1}^{r} \beta_m$$

where β_m is the mth root of matrix **B***** $(m = 1, 2, \cdots, r)$. Since the elements b_{jj}^* are known functions of available data h_{jk} and the unknown additive constant c, if the latent roots of $\mathbf{B}^*$ were known, we could set the sum of the large latent roots equal to the sum of the diagonals of $\mathbf{B}^*$ and solve for the additive constant c. This procedure would insure that the remaining roots summed to zero. The roots themselves, however, are functions of the additive constant c. Hence, it would seem that we cannot determine the latent roots without c, and we need the latent roots to solve for c. What is needed is a method for pulling ourselves up by our own bootstraps. Messick and Abelson's procedure does just this. Their equations are given below.

We take as given the comparative distance matrix $\mathbf{H}$, with off-diagonal cells equal to h_{jk}, and diagonal cells h_{jj} defined to be equal to zero. Let a period replacing a subscript denote an average over that subscript: e.g.,

$$h_{j.}^2 = \frac{1}{n} \sum_{k=1}^{n} h_{jk}^2 \quad \text{and} \quad h_{..} = \frac{1}{n^2} \sum_{j=1}^{n} \sum_{k=1}^{n} h_{jk}$$

The general element of matrix $\mathbf{B}^*$ was expressed in terms of the absolute distances d_{jk} in equation 16. If we substitute $(h_{jk} + c)$ for d_{jk} in this equation and then simplify, we obtain

$$b_{jk}^* = \tfrac{1}{2}(h_{j.}^2 + h_{.k}^2 - h_{..}^2 - h_{jk}^2) + (h_{j.} + h_{.k} - h_{..} - h_{jk})c$$

$$(42) \qquad\qquad + \tfrac{1}{2}\left(\delta_k^j - \frac{1}{n}\right)c^2$$

where $\delta_k^j = 1$ for $j = k$ and zero otherwise.

In matrix notation, equation 42 can be written

$$(43) \qquad\qquad \mathbf{B}^* = \mathbf{U} + c\mathbf{W} + \tfrac{1}{2}c^2\mathbf{V}$$

where the elements of matrices $\mathbf{U}$, $\mathbf{W}$, and $\mathbf{V}$ are, respectively,

$$u_{jk} \equiv \tfrac{1}{2}(h_{j.}^2 + h_{.k}^2 - h_{..}^2 - h_{jk}^2)$$
$$w_{jk} \equiv (h_{j.} + h_{.k} - h_{..} - h_{jk})$$
$$v_{jk} \equiv -\frac{1}{n} \quad \text{for} \quad j \neq k \quad \text{and} \quad v_{jj} = 1 - \frac{1}{n} \quad \text{for} \quad j = k.$$

From equation 42 it is apparent that the diagonal elements

$$(44) \qquad b_{jj}^* = h_{j.}^2 - \tfrac{1}{2}h_{..}^2 + (2h_{j.} - h_{..})c + \frac{1}{2}\left(1 - \frac{1}{n}\right)c^2$$

The sum of the diagonal elements of $\mathbf{B}^*$ is given by

$$(45) \qquad\qquad \sum_{j=1}^{n} b_{jj}^* = \frac{n}{2}h_{..}^2 + nh_{..}c + \tfrac{1}{2}(n-1)c^2$$

Equation 45 gives the sum of the diagonal elements of $\mathbf{B}^*$ as a function of the observed comparative distances and the unknown additive constant.

Consider now the latent roots and vectors of $\mathbf{B}^*$. Let $\mathbf{X}_m$ denote the normalized latent vector corresponding to the mth latent root β_m. Then,

$$(46) \qquad \mathbf{X}_m' \mathbf{B}^* \mathbf{X}_m = \beta_m$$

Let r equal the "true rank" of matrix $\mathbf{B}^*$; i.e., r equals the number of large latent roots of $\mathbf{B}^*$. Then, the sum of the large latent roots can be expressed in terms of the matrix $\mathbf{B}^*$ and the latent vectors as follows:

$$(47) \qquad \sum_{m=1}^{r} \beta_m = \sum_{m=1}^{r} (\mathbf{X}_m' \mathbf{B}^* \mathbf{X}_m)$$

Substituting for $\mathbf{B}^*$ in equation 47 from equation 43, we have

$$(48) \qquad \sum_{m=1}^{r} \beta_m = \sum_{m=1}^{r} [\mathbf{X}_m' (\mathbf{U} + c\mathbf{W} + \tfrac{1}{2}c^2\mathbf{V})\mathbf{X}_m]$$

or, summing each term separately,

$$(49) \qquad \sum_{m=1}^{r} \beta_m = \sum_{m=1}^{r} (\mathbf{X}_m' \mathbf{U} \mathbf{X}_m) + c\sum_{m=1}^{r} (\mathbf{X}_m' \mathbf{W} \mathbf{X}_m) + \tfrac{1}{2}c^2 \sum_{m=1}^{r} (\mathbf{X}_m' \mathbf{V} \mathbf{X}_m)$$

It can be shown that the last term of equation 49 simplifies to $\tfrac{1}{2}rc^2$. The points involved in the proof are listed below.

1. Matrix $\mathbf{V}$ has elements $v_{jj} = 1 - 1/n$; $v_{jk} = -1/n$. Hence, the first $n-1$ roots of $\mathbf{V}$ are equal to unity, and the remaining root is equal to zero.

2. Any vector with the proper number of terms and whose terms sum to zero is a permissible latent vector corresponding to one of the unit roots of $\mathbf{V}$, since, for any such vector $\mathbf{X}$, $\mathbf{X}'\mathbf{V}\mathbf{X} = 1$.

3. Since $\mathbf{B}^*$ is a centroid matrix, one root at least is always equal to zero, and, as a result, all latent vectors corresponding to the remaining roots are composed of elements that sum to zero. Hence the latent vectors of $\mathbf{B}^*$ are permissible latent vectors of $\mathbf{V}$, and we can write

$$\sum_{m=1}^{r} (\mathbf{X}_m' \mathbf{V} \mathbf{X}_m) = r$$

With this simplification, equation 49 becomes

$$(50) \qquad \sum_{m=1}^{r} \beta_m = \sum_{m=1}^{r} (\mathbf{X}_m' \mathbf{U} \mathbf{X}_m) + c\sum_{m=1}^{r} (\mathbf{X}_m' \mathbf{W} \mathbf{X}_m) + \tfrac{1}{2}rc^2$$

Equation 50 gives the sum of the large latent roots as a function of the corresponding latent vectors, the unknown constant, and the available comparative distances.

The actual computation procedure can now be given as follows:

1. Choose a trial estimate of c. An overestimate is better than an underestimate according to Messick and Abelson, since the $\mathbf{X}_m$ vectors are less sensitive to overestimates than to underestimates.

2. Compute a trial matrix $\mathbf{B}^*$, using the trial value of c in equation 42 or equation 43.

3. Obtain the first r latent vectors of $\mathbf{B}^*$, stopping when the latent vectors become sufficiently "small" (see Hotelling, 1933, for numerical procedures for obtaining latent vectors).

4. Normalize the latent vectors so that the sums of squares of elements of each vector is equal to unity.

5. Substitute these vectors into equation 50. Then, this equation will contain only the two powers of c as an unknown quantity on the right-hand side.

6. Enter the available data into equation 45. Then the right-hand term of this equation will contain only the two powers of c as an unknown quantity.

7. Since by definition the left-hand terms of equations 45 and 50 are equal, set the right-hand terms equal to each other, and solve the resulting quadratic for c. The root of the quadratic which gives the larger value of $\sum\limits_{m}^{r} \beta_m$ is the value wanted.

If desired, further cycles can be run, using the value of c obtained from a given trial as the initial estimate for the following trial. However, Messick and Abelson (1956) and Messick (1954) found that, at least for the case where the initial guess is not an underestimate, the $\mathbf{X}_m$ vectors are sufficiently insensitive to changes in c so that a single trial is ordinarily sufficient. It might also be noted that they suggest that centroid vectors might be used as an approximation to the latent vectors $\mathbf{X}_m$.

Estimating c from a Unidimensional Subspace

If the number of stimuli substantially exceeds the dimensionality (i.e., if $n \gg r$), there will often be subsets of stimuli that fall very nearly along a straight line in the space. If such a one-dimensional subspace of four or more points exists in the data, it can be used to estimate the additive constant. It is relatively easy to determine whether or not such a subspace exists. Let c_{ijk} be the value of the additive constant that would be required to locate stimuli i, j, and k along a straight line in the space. Then

$$(51) \qquad c_{ijk} = h_{ik} - h_{jk} - h_{ij} \quad \text{where} \quad h_{ik} > h_{ij}, h_{jk}$$

Given the $\frac{1}{6}n(n-1)(n-2)$ values of c_{ijk} (one for each stimulus triplet), the following points may be noted:

1. Points most nearly in a straight line in the total space will give the largest value of c_{ijk}, except for error.

2. If any subset of four or more stimuli exists such that all combinations of three give the same "highest" value of c_{ijk}, that value is a good estimate of the unknown additive constant c.

3. If no such subset exists, the largest value of c_{ijk} would still be likely to be an adequate estimate of the unknown constant. Using this value is equivalent to assuming that, of the n points in the space, at least three lie approximately along a straight line.

When we bear in mind the fact that the configuration of points actually changes very little with a considerable change in the additive constant (see, for example, Torgerson, 1951; Messick and Abelson, 1956; Messick, 1954) it is apparent that some such procedure as this would ordinarily give adequate results. If a more refined estimate is needed, Messick and Abelson's solution should be used.

5. EVALUATION OF GOODNESS OF FIT

In those multidimensional-scaling procedures discussed in the preceding three sections, the problems concerning goodness of fit can be considered either in terms of the procedure as a whole or in terms of the goodness of fit of the two models separately. We might ask the two separate questions: Do the observed judgments behave in the manner required by the distance model? If so, do the interpoint distances behave in the manner required by the spatial model? Alternatively, we could combine the two into a single question: Do the original judgments behave in the manner required by the over-all multidimensional scaling procedure? We shall consider each separately.

Goodness of Fit of Distance Models to Data

Procedures for evaluation of goodness of fit of the distance model to the observations are essentially the same as the procedures used in the corresponding unidimensional-scaling models. In those methods which involve generalization of Thurstone's judgment model, such as the method of triads, for example, the usual procedure would consist of checking the observed proportions against an equivalent set of proportions derived from the fitted distances. In the method of triads, $n(n-1)/2$ (comparative) distances are estimated from $n(n-1)(n-2)/2$ independently observed proportions $_kp_{ij}$. These distances can in turn be used to derive $n(n-1)(n-2)/2$ derived proportions $_k\tilde{p}_{ij}$. We might then, for example, compute the average discrepancy between the corresponding pairs, and, if it is small, conclude that the model fits adequately.

Alternatively, a generalization of Mosteller's chi-square test for goodness of fit would seem appropriate (Chapter 9). It will be recalled that, in this procedure, the arcsin $\sqrt{p}$ transformation is applied to the proportions. In the present case, chi-square would be computed as follows:

$$(52) \qquad \chi^2 = \frac{\displaystyle\sum_{k}^{n} \sum_{j>i}^{n} (_k\theta_{ij} - _k\tilde{\theta}_{ij})^2}{\dfrac{821}{N}}$$

where $_k\theta_{ij}$ and $_k\tilde{\theta}_{ij}$ are measured in degrees, and

$$_k\theta_{ij} = \sin^{-1}\sqrt{_kp_{ij}} \qquad \text{(observed proportions)}$$

$$_k\tilde{\theta}_{ij} = \sin^{-1}\sqrt{_k\tilde{p}_{ij}} \qquad \text{(derived proportions)}$$

$$n = \text{number of stimuli}$$

$$N = \text{number of subjects}$$

$$\text{d.f.} = \tfrac{1}{2}n(n-1)(n-2) - [\tfrac{1}{2}n(n-1) - 2] - 1$$
$$= \tfrac{1}{2}n(n-1)(n-3) - 1$$

Goodness of Fit of the Spatial Model to the Observed Distances

If the distance model yields absolute distances directly, it is meaningful to ask whether the distances exist (within reasonable allowances for experimental error) in a *real* space. In the Euclidean model, this would be answered by determining whether the matrix **B*** contained any substantial negative latent roots. If the distance model yields only comparative distances, however, this is no longer a testable hypothesis, since in this case the additive constant can be determined with this in mind. We can always choose an additive constant that guarantees that all points can be represented by a real, Euclidean space. (It should be noted, however, that such a procedure would ordinarily result in locating the points in a space of $n-2$ dimensions.)

The question of the "true" dimensionality of the space is appropriate, regardless of whether the given data are in the form of absolute distances or comparative distances. For the Euclidean model, the question is essentially the standard factor-analysis question of when to stop factoring. Ordinarily, we extract factors until the cells in the residual matrix appear to contain no more systematic variance. One procedure which has been used in multidimensional-scaling experiments (Torgerson, 1951; Messick,

1954) is to compare the total variance in the original **B*** matrix with the total variance of a **B̃*** matrix derived from the first r factors according to the equation

$$\tilde{b}_{jk} = \sum_{m}^{r} a_{jm} a_{km}$$

In a two-dimensional space, for example, if it were not for error, the following relation would hold:

$$\sum_{j}^{n} \sum_{k}^{n} b_{jk}^{*2} = \left(\sum_{j}^{n} a_{j1}^2\right)^2 + \left(\sum_{j}^{n} a_{j2}^2\right)^2 + 2\left(\sum_{j}^{n} a_{j1} a_{j2}\right)^2$$

The left-hand term gives the sum of squares of the elements of the observed matrix **B***, while the right-hand term is equal to the sum of squares of elements in the **B̃*** matrix derived from the first two factors. In the empirical case, we can compute each side separately, and, if the two are about the same size, conclude that the space is of dimensionality equal to two. An equivalent procedure would be to compute the residual matrix with elements

(53) $$\rho_{jk} = b_{jk}^* - \sum_{m}^{r} a_{jm} a_{km}$$

and then sum the squares of the elements in this matrix. The sum of squares of the residuals will be equal to the difference between the sum of squares of the observed scalar products b_{jk}^* and the sum of squares of the derived scalar products $\tilde{b}_{jk}^*$.

Over-all Evaluation of Goodness of Fit

For a single, over-all evaluation of goodness of fit, the procedure would involve the following two steps:

1. Computation of derived distances between stimuli from the final factor loadings. For example, with the Euclidean model we have the $\frac{1}{2}n(n-1)$ derived distances

(54) $$\tilde{d}_{jk} = \left[\sum_{m}^{r} (a_{jm} - a_{km})^2\right]^{1/2}$$

2. Using these values as the derived distances, evaluate the goodness of fit of distances to observed data by whatever procedure is appropriate for the distance model. In the method of triads again, the procedure would involve computation of derived differences in distances $(\tilde{d}_{jk} - \tilde{d}_{ik} = {}_k\tilde{x}_{ij})$, conversion of the resulting normal deviates into derived proportions ${}_k\tilde{p}_{ij}$,

and comparison of the observed proportions with those derived in this manner from the final results.

6. AN EMPIRICAL EXAMPLE

The following empirical example is taken from Torgerson (1951). It involves use of the complete method of triads for obtaining comparative distances, and the Euclidean spatial model for determining projections of stimuli on axes of the space. The additive constant is estimated from linear subsets of stimuli.

Nine Munsell colors all of the same red hue but differing from each other in brightness and saturation were presented to 38 subjects. We wish to determine (*a*) whether the multidimensional method will give a configuration of points lying in two dimensions and (*b*) how this configuration compares with the Munsell system from which the colors were selected.

The nine Munsell colors selected are listed below with the stimulus numbers assigned to them for this experiment.

Stimulus Number	Munsell Designation*
1	5R/7/4
2	5R/6/6
3	5R/6/10
4	5R/5/4
5	5R/5/8
6	5R/5/12
7	5R/4/6
8	5R/4/10
9	5R/3/4

* In the Munsell notation the first term gives the designator for hue, the second for value (brightness), and the third for chroma (saturation).

The Munsell system is arranged so that, theoretically, steps along the value and chroma scales represent equal sense distances along the respective psychological dimensions. Two chroma steps represent approximately a sense distance equivalent to one value step. A plot of the stimuli according to the Munsell system appears in Figure 4.

Eighty-four color triads were constructed from nine Munsell colors, one for each set of three stimuli. Two easy triads were selected for the first two judgments. The remaining 82 cards were added in random orientation and order. The triads were then numbered. For the triad judgments, the 84 cards were first presented in order, giving judgments 1 to 84. The stack was then rotated and presented again, giving judgments 85 to

168, and then rotated and presented again, giving judgments 169 to 252. Thus each stimulus was judged closer to one of each other pair of stimuli. The same order and procedure was used for all 38 subjects.

From the raw data, nine matrices, $_k\mathbf{P}_{ij}$, were constructed. The element $_kp_{ij}$ gives the proportion of times stimulus k was judged more like stimulus i than j. Using $\sqrt{2}$ times the normal deviate, the proportions were converted to differences in distances, giving the nine matrices $_k\mathbf{X}_{ij}$.

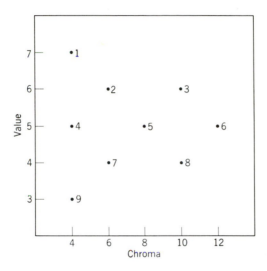

Figure 4.   Value and chroma of the Munsell stimuli.
(1 value unit = 2 chroma units)

In transforming the proportions to differences in distances, however, a difficulty was encountered—how to transform proportions of 0.00 or 1.00 into x values. It was decided to estimate these x values by using all available one-step computations. For example, if $_1p_{23} = 1.00$, we can estimate $_1x_{23}$ from $n-2$ other pairs of x values:

$$_1x_{24} - {}_1x_{34} = {}_1x_{23} \quad (\text{i.e., } d_{14} - d_{12} - d_{14} + d_{13} = d_{13} - d_{12})$$
$$_1x_{25} - {}_1x_{35} = {}_1x_{23}$$
$$\begin{array}{ccc} \cdot & \cdot & \cdot \\ \cdot & \cdot & \cdot \end{array}$$
$$_1x_{29} - {}_1x_{39} = {}_1x_{23}$$

and also

$$_2x_{13} - {}_3x_{12} = {}_1x_{23}$$

A number of these equations may, of course, also contain "infinite" elements. The procedure used was to obtain the average estimate of $_k x_{ij}$ from those of the seven possible equations that contained only finite observed elements. Estimates were thus based on from two to seven equations. x values estimated in this way are underlined in the nine matrices $_k \mathbf{X}_{ij}$. These matrices are given in Table 1.

Table 1. $_k \mathbf{X}_{ij}$. EXPERIMENTAL DIFFERENCES IN DISTANCES $(d_{kj} - d_{ik})$

TABLE 1A. $_1 \mathbf{X}_{ij}$

	1	2	3	4	5	6	7	8	9
1									
2			+2.74	+2.74	+3.00	+3.16	+3.76	+2.29	+4.00
3		−2.74		−0.68	+0.90	+1.67	+1.27	+2.00	+2.66
4		−2.74	+0.68		+1.58	+2.29	+2.29	+2.64	+3.57
5		−3.00	−0.90	−1.58		+1.42	+1.58	+2.74	+2.29
6		−3.16	−1.67	−2.29	−1.42		−0.48	+1.01	+0.48
7		−3.76	−1.27	−2.29	−1.58	+0.48		+1.01	+1.77
8		−2.29	−2.00	−2.64	−2.74	−1.01	−1.01		+0.68
9		−4.00	−2.66	−3.57	−2.29	−0.48	−1.77	−0.68	

TABLE 1B. $_2 \mathbf{X}_{ij}$

	1	2	3	4	5	6	7	8	9
1			+2.00	+1.01	+2.74	+3.46	+2.00	+2.74	+2.29
2									
3	−2.00			−0.78	+0.58	+1.77	+0.28	+2.00	+1.27
4	−1.01		+0.78		+1.77	+2.29	+2.74	+3.02	+2.80
5	−2.74		−0.58	−1.77		+2.00	+1.27	+2.29	+1.77
6	−3.46		−1.77	−2.29	−2.00		−2.00	+0.28	−0.19
7	−2.00		−0.28	−2.74	−1.27	+2.00		+1.27	+2.29
8	−2.74		−2.00	−3.02	−2.29	−0.28	−1.27		−0.68
9	−2.29		−1.27	−2.80	−1.77	+0.19	−2.29	+0.68	

TABLE 1C. $_3X_{ij}$

	1	2	3	4	5	6	7	8	9
1		−0.90		+0.68	−0.48	−0.58	+1.42	+0.68	+2.00
2	+0.90			+2.74	0.00	+0.09	+1.42	+2.00	+3.80
3									
4	−0.68	−2.74			−2.29	−1.42	+1.58	−0.28	+2.74
5	+0.48	0.00	+2.29			+0.48	+2.74	+2.74	+3.94
6	+0.58	−0.09	+1.42	−0.48			+2.29	+2.74	+2.74
7	−1.42	−1.42	−1.58	−2.74	−2.29			−0.48	+0.73
8	−0.68	−2.00	+0.28	−2.74	−2.74	+0.48			+1.64
9	−2.00	−3.80	−2.74	−3.94	−2.74	−0.73	−1.64		

TABLE 1D. $_4X_{ij}$

	1	2	3	4	5	6	7	8	9
1		−1.29	+0.90		+0.90	+0.90	−1.42	+0.68	−0.58
2	+1.29		+2.29		+1.58	+3.03	+0.68	+1.58	+0.38
3	−0.90	−2.29			−2.29	+0.78	−2.00	−1.27	−1.77
4									
5	−0.90	−1.58	+2.29			+2.74	−1.77	+1.42	0.00
6	−0.90	−3.03	−0.78	−2.74			−2.74	−1.58	−1.27
7	+1.42	−0.68	+2.00		+1.77	+2.74		+2.09	+2.00
8	−0.68	−1.58	+1.27		−1.42	+1.58	−2.09		−0.90
9	+0.58	−0.38	+1.77		0.00	+1.27	−2.00	+0.90	

TABLE 1E. $_5X_{ij}$

	1	2	3	4	5	6	7	8	9
1		−1.77	−1.58	−0.90		−1.14	−1.42	−2.00	+0.38
2	+1.77		−0.48	−0.19		−0.48	+0.78	−0.78	+1.27
3	+1.58	+0.48		+0.90		−0.19	−0.58	−0.28	+2.29
4	+0.90	+0.19	−0.90			+0.38	−0.58	−1.01	+1.58
5									
6	+1.14	+0.48	+0.19	−0.38			0.00	−0.38	+0.90
7	+1.42	−0.78	+0.58	+0.58		0.00		−0.19	+1.72
8	+2.00	+0.78	+0.28	+1.01		+0.38	+0.19		+2.29
9	−0.38	−1.27	−2.29	−1.58		−0.90	−1.72	−2.29	

TABLE 1F. $_6X_{ij}$

	1	2	3	4	5	6	7	8	9
1		−2.29	−1.88	−0.68	−2.29		−1.14	−1.58	+0.19
2	+2.29		−1.44	+0.28	−1.73		−0.48	−1.77	+1.14
3	+1.88	+1.44		+2.00	−0.78		+0.78	−0.09	+2.00
4	+0.68	−0.28	−2.00		−2.74		−1.58	−2.00	+1.14
5	+2.29	+1.73	+0.78	+2.74			+1.77	−0.19	+2.74
6									
7	+1.14	+0.48	−0.78	+1.58	−1.77			−2.29	+1.50
8	+1.58	+1.77	+0.09	+2.00	+0.19		+2.29		+2.57
9	−0.19	−1.14	−2.00	−1.14	−2.74		−1.50	−2.57	

TABLE 1G. $_7X_{ij}$

	1	2	3	4	5	6	7	8	9
1		−2.74	−0.68	−2.29	−2.74	0.00		−0.78	−1.77
2	+2.74		+1.58	−1.26	−1.01	+1.27		−0.58	−1.77
3	+0.68	−1.58		−2.38	−2.23	−0.09		−1.77	−1.77
4	+2.29	+1.26	+2.38		+0.78	+2.29		+0.90	−0.09
5	+2.74	+1.01	+2.23	−0.78		+1.58		−0.48	+0.68
6	0.00	−1.27	+0.09	−2.29	−1.58			−1.79	−1.58
7									
8	+0.78	+0.58	+1.77	−0.90	+0.48	+1.79			−0.68
9	+1.77	+1.77	+1.77	+0.09	−0.68	+1.58		+0.68	

TABLE 1H. $_8X_{ij}$

	1	2	3	4	5	6	7	8	9
1		−2.00	−2.00	−2.00	−3.80	−2.74	−2.74		−1.01
2	+2.00		−0.78	−1.42	−2.90	−1.42	−2.74		−0.38
3	+2.00	+0.78		−0.28	−2.74	−1.58	−0.58		−0.09
4	+2.00	+1.42	+0.28		−2.74	−1.27	−2.74		−0.19
5	+3.80	+2.90	+2.74	+2.74		+0.90	−0.58		+1.77
6	+2.74	+1.42	+1.58	+1.27	−0.90		−1.58		+0.28
7	+2.74	+2.74	+0.58	+2.74	+0.58	+1.58			+1.85
8									
9	+1.01	+0.38	+0.09	+0.19	−1.77	−0.28	−1.85		

TABLE 1 I. $_9X_{ij}$

	1	2	3	4	5	6	7	8	9
1		−2.74	+0.28	−2.24	−1.42	+0.09	−2.74	−1.01	
2	+2.74		+2.74	−2.25	−1.58	+0.58	−2.27	−0.58	
3	−0.28	−2.74		−3.80	−2.74	−0.48	−3.61	−2.29	
4	+2.24	+2.25	+3.80		+1.01	+2.74	−1.27	+1.42	
5	+1.42	+1.58	+2.74	−1.01		+1.58	−2.12	−1.42	
6	−0.09	−0.58	+0.48	−2.74	−1.58		−2.74	−1.47	
7	+2.74	+2.27	+3.61	+1.27	+2.12	+2.74		+2.29	
8	+1.01	+0.58	+2.29	−1.42	+1.42	+1.47	−2.29		
9									

From the matrices $_kX_{ij}$, the following matrices were constructed.

$_kX_{.j}$ Rows k, columns j.   Each row contains the average of elements of columns of the corresponding $_kX_{ij}$ matrix.

$.X_{.j}$ A row vector consisting of the averages of the columns of the matrix $_kX_{.j}$.

G_{kj} Rows k, columns j.   The entry in the gth row, hth column is $(_gx_{.h} + .x_{.g})$.

H Rows j, columns k, with elements $h_{jk} = d_{jk} - c$.

This is the final stage in the method of triads as outlined in section 3. These matrices appear in Tables 2 to 5.   The unknown constant c is equal to the (unknown) average distance between stimulus pairs.

Table 2. $_kX_{.j}$.   AVERAGES OF COLUMNS OF THE n MATRICES $_kX_{ij}$

	1	2	3	4	5	6	7	8	9
1		−2.71125	−0.63500	−1.28875	−0.31875	+0.94125	+0.70500	+1.37625	+1.93125
2	−2.03000		−0.39000	−1.54875	−0.28000	+1.42875	+0.09125	+1.53500	+1.19375
3	−0.35250	−1.36875		+0.38625	−1.58375	−1.15000	+1.15000	+0.72000	+2.19875
4	−0.01125	−1.35375	+1.21750		−0.27500	+1.63000	−1.41750	+0.47750	−0.26750
5	+1.05374	−0.23625	−0.52500	−0.07000		−0.24375	−0.41625	−0.86625	+1.30375
6	+1.20875	+0.21375	−0.90375	+0.84750	−1.48250		+0.01750	−1.31125	+1.41000
7	+1.37500	−0.12125	+1.14250	−1.22625	−0.87250	+1.05250		−0.47750	−0.87250
8	+2.03625	+0.95500	+0.31125	+0.40500	−1.78375	−0.60125	−1.60125		+0.27875
9	+1.22250	+0.07750	+1.99250	−1.52375	−0.34625	+1.09000	−2.13000	−0.38250	

Table 3. $.X_{.j}$. AVERAGES OF COLUMNS OF MATRIX $_kX_{.j}$

	1	2	3	4	5	6	7	8	9
1	+0.50028	−0.50500	+0.24556	−0.44653	−0.77139	+0.46083	−0.40014	+0.11903	+0.79736

Table 4. G_{kj}. Nonsymmetric Comparative Distances

	1	2	3	4	5	6	7	8	9
1		−2.21097	−0.13472	−0.78847	+0.18153	+1.44153	+1.20528	+1.87653	+2.43153
2	−2.53500		−0.89500	−2.05375	−0.78500	+0.92375	−0.41375	+0.10300	+0.68875
3	−0.10694	−1.12319		+0.63181	−1.33819	−0.90444	+1.39556	+0.96556	+2.44931
4	−0.45778	−1.80028	+0.77097		−0.72153	+1.18347	−1.86403	+0.03097	−0.71403
5	+0.28236	−1.00764	−1.29639	−0.84139		−1.01514	−1.18764	−1.63764	+0.53236
6	+1.66958	+0.67458	−0.44292	+1.30833	−1.02167		+0.47833	−0.85042	+1.87083
7	+0.97486	−0.52139	+0.74236	−1.62639	−1.27264	+0.65236		−0.87764	−1.27264
8	+2.15528	+1.07403	+0.43028	+0.52403	−1.66472	−0.48222	−1.48222		+0.39778
9	+2.01986	+0.87486	+2.78986	−0.72639	+0.45111	+1.88736	−1.33264	+0.41486	

Table 5. H. Comparative Distances

	1	2	3	4	5	6	7	8	9
1		−2.37	−0.12	−0.62	0.23	1.56	1.09	2.02	2.23
2	−2.37		−1.01	−1.93	−0.90	0.80	−0.47	1.05	0.78
3	−0.12	−1.01		0.70	−1.32	−0.67	1.07	0.70	2.62
4	−0.62	−1.93	0.70		−0.78	1.25	−1.75	0.28	−0.72
5	0.23	−0.90	−1.32	−0.78		−1.02	−1.23	−1.65	0.49
6	1.56	0.80	−0.67	1.25	−1.02		0.57	−0.67	1.88
7	1.09	−0.47	1.07	−1.75	−1.23	0.57		−1.18	−1.30
8	2.02	1.05	0.70	0.28	−1.65	−0.67	−1.18		0.42
9	2.23	0.78	2.62	−0.72	0.49	1.88	−1.30	0.42	

The next step is to estimate the additive constant c. It was decided to attempt to find one or more one-dimensional subspaces to use in obtaining an estimate of c, the unknown additive constant. This procedure was described in section 4. First, the values of c_{ijk} were calculated which would place each set of three stimuli in a straight line. These values are shown in Table 6. Examining this table, we see that two subsets of four points seem to give high values in a consistent manner. One set is composed of stimuli 1, 2, 5, and 8; the other of 1, 2, 4, and 9. The values are listed below:

1, 2, 5, 8		1, 2, 4, 9	
i, j, k	c_{ijk}	i, j, k	c_{ijk}
1, 2, 5 = 3.50		1, 2, 4 = 3.68	
1, 2, 8 = 3.34		1, 2, 9 = 3.82	
2, 5, 8 = 3.60		1, 4, 9 = 3.57	
1, 5, 8 = 3.44		2, 4, 9 = 3.48	

Other high values found in Table 6 are:

i, j, k	c_{ijk}
1, 2, 7 = 3.93	
2, 3, 4 = 3.64	
1, 2, 3 = 3.26	
3, 5, 8 = 3.67	

Table 6. VALUES OF c_{ijk}

ijk	c_{ijk}	ijk	c_{ijk}	ijk	c_{ijk}	ijk	c_{ijk}
123	3.26	159	1.51	259	1.19	389	1.50
124	3.68	167	−0.10	267	0.70	456	3.05
125	3.50	168	1.13	268	0.92	457	2.20
126	3.13	169	−1.21	269	0.30	458	2.71
127	3.93	178	2.11	278	2.70	459	1.99
128	3.34	179	2.44	279	2.55	467	2.43
129	3.82	189	−0.21	289	−0.15	468	1.64
134	1.44	234	3.64	345	2.80	469	1.35
135	1.67	235	1.43	346	1.22	478	3.21
136	2.35	236	2.48	347	2.12	479	2.33
137	0.14	237	2.55	348	−0.28	489	0.86
138	1.44	238	1.36	349	2.64	567	2.82
139	0.51	239	2.85	356	1.67	568	2.00
145	1.63	245	2.05	357	3.62	569	2.41
146	0.93	246	2.38	358	3.67	578	1.70
147	3.46	247	3.21	359	3.45	579	3.02
148	2.36	248	2.70	367	1.17	589	1.72
149	3.57	249	3.43	368	2.04	678	2.42
156	2.35	256	2.72	369	1.41	679	2.61
157	2.09	257	1.66	378	1.55	689	2.13
158	3.44	258	3.60	379	2.85	789	2.90

From examination of the two four-point subspaces and keeping in mind the other high estimates of c_{ijk}, it was decided that 3.60 would be a good estimate. Using this estimate, the matrix of comparative distances **H** was converted into a matrix of absolute distances **D**. This matrix is given in Table 7. Matrix **D** in turn can be converted into matrix **B***, the matrix of scalar products referred to an origin at the centroid of all of the stimuli using equation 16. Matrix **B*** is given in Table 8.

Table 7. D_{jk}. ABSOLUTE DISTANCES

	1	2	3	4	5	6	7	8	9
1		1.23	3.48	2.98	3.83	5.16	4.69	5.62	5.83
2	1.23		2.59	1.67	2.70	4.40	3.13	4.65	4.38
3	3.48	2.59		4.30	2.28	2.93	4.67	4.30	6.22
4	2.98	1.67	4.30		2.82	4.85	1.85	3.88	2.88
5	3.83	2.70	2.28	2.82		2.58	2.37	1.95	4.09
6	5.16	4.40	2.93	4.85	2.58		4.17	2.93	5.48
7	4.69	3.13	4.67	1.85	2.37	4.17		2.42	2.30
8	5.62	4.65	4.30	3.88	1.95	2.93	2.42		4.02
9	5.83	4.38	6.22	2.88	4.09	5.48	2.30	4.02	

Table 8. B*. Scalar Products with Origin at Centroid

	1	2	3	4	5	6	7	8	9
1	10.3527	6.0905	3.1148	2.4146	−1.6181	−3.5498	−3.9893	−7.1180	−5.6975
2	6.0905	3.3412	2.3102	1.9546	−1.4344	−3.4227	−1.3954	−5.6428	−1.8010
3	3.1148	2.3102	7.9873	−3.5729	1.9345	4.2879	−5.0784	−1.7535	−9.2299
4	2.4146	1.9546	−3.5729	3.3569	−1.7577	−5.4961	1.7996	−2.3509	3.6519
5	−1.6181	−1.4344	1.9345	−1.7577	1.0800	1.7985	−0.4360	2.1366	−1.7034
7	−3.5498	−3.4227	4.2879	−5.4961	1.7985	9.1733	−2.2754	3.7921	−4.3079
6	−3.9893	−1.3954	−5.0784	1.7996	−0.4360	−2.2754	3.6648	2.4021	5.3080
8	−7.1180	−5.6428	−1.7535	−2.3509	2.1366	3.7921	2.4021	6.9957	1.5383
9	−5.6975	−1.8010	−9.2299	3.6519	−1.7034	−4.3079	5.3080	1.5383	12.2412

Table 9. A. Centroid Factor Matrix

	1	2	3	4	5	6	7	8	9
I	−3.118	−1.944	−1.396	−0.589	0.408	1.161	1.229	2.393	1.856
II	0.178	0.488	−2.445	1.778	−0.900	−2.450	1.302	−0.767	2.814

Matrix **B*** was then factored by the centroid method (Thurstone, 1947). Two factors were extracted (Table 9).   It might be well to consider whether two factors are sufficient.   If a matrix **B** is of rank 2:

$$b_{jk} = a_{j1}a_{k1} + a_{j2}a_{k2}$$

$$\sum_j \sum_k b_{jk}^2 = \sum_j \sum_k (a_{j1}a_{k1} + a_{j2}a_{k2})^2$$

$$\sum_j \sum_k b_{jk}^2 = \left(\sum_j a_{j1}^2\right)^2 + \left(\sum_j a_{j2}^2\right)^2 + 2\left(\sum_j a_{j1}a_{j2}\right)^2$$

If we assume that the centroids are good approximations to the principal axes and then compare the right- and left-hand sides of the equation, we obtain 1523.9 for the left-hand number, and 1495.7 for the right.   Since these values are very nearly equal, we shall conclude that matrix **B*** is of rank 2 except for variable errors.   The residuals are given in Table 10.

Table 10. R_{jk}. Residuals

	1	2	3	4	5	6	7	8	9
1	0.5991	−0.0578	−0.8027	0.2616	−0.1858	0.5063	−0.3891	0.4799	−0.4114
2	−0.0578	−0.6760	0.7896	−0.0581	−0.2020	0.0299	0.3584	−0.6165	0.4339
3	−0.8027	0.7896	0.0605	−0.0479	0.3036	−0.0816	−0.1793	−0.2882	0.2413
4	0.2616	−0.0581	−0.0479	−0.1513	0.0828	−0.4562	0.2085	0.4223	−0.2582
5	−0.1858	−0.2020	0.3036	0.0828	0.1035	−0.8802	0.2344	0.4700	0.0720
6	0.5063	0.0299	−0.0816	−0.4562	−0.8802	1.8229	−0.5124	−0.8654	0.4316
7	−0.3891	0.3584	−0.1793	0.2085	0.2344	−0.5124	0.4592	0.4597	−0.6368
8	0.4799	−0.6165	−0.2882	0.4223	0.4700	−0.8654	0.4597	0.6810	−0.7448
9	−0.4114	0.4339	0.2413	−0.2582	0.0720	0.4316	−0.6368	−0.7448	0.8779

Table 11. V. Rotated Factor Matrix

	1	2	3	4	5	6	7	8	9
A	2.709	1.520	2.342	−0.268	0.038	0.057	−1.681	−1.797	−2.918
B	−1.554	−1.306	1.563	−1.854	0.987	2.710	−0.615	1.756	−1.687

Factor matrix **A** was rotated orthogonally so as to orient the two axes in directions comparable to the value and chroma dimensions of the Munsell system. The rotated factor matrix **V** is given in Table 11. The transformation matrix **Λ** is given in Table 12. A plot of matrix **V** is given in

Table 12. Λ. Transformation Matrix

	A	B
I	−0.8944	0.4472
II	−0.4472	−0.8944

Figure 5. In this plot factor *A* corresponds to brightness and factor *B* to saturation. The zero points of both scales are located at the centroid of

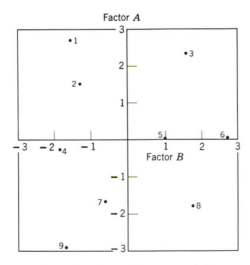

Figure 5. Rotated factor matrix V.

the stimuli. We could, of course, easily translate the axes to a new zero point which would result in all scale values being positive. If we compare Figure 5 with Figure 4, the plot of value and chroma according to the Munsell system, we see that the two configurations are quite similar.

Figure 6 gives a plot of Munsell value with factor A, and Figure 7 a plot of Munsell chroma with factor B. These plots show that, in general, the empirical results agree very well with the Munsell system.

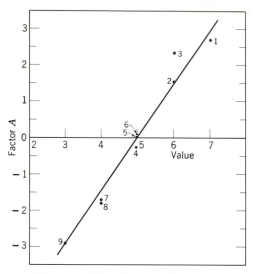

Figure 6.   Munsell value with factor A.

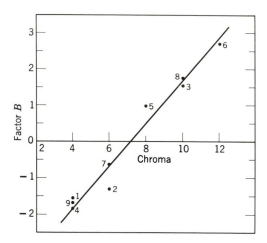

Figure 7.   Munsell chroma with factor B.

7. EMPIRICAL TESTS OF MULTIDIMENSIONAL METHODS

The models based on generalizations of Thurstone's judgment model for obtaining distances, along with the Euclidean model for obtaining projections, have undergone a considerable amount of empirical evaluation. In the earliest multidimensional-scaling experiment, Richardson (1938) used Munsell color chips varying in brightness and saturation. Even though efficient computational procedures had not yet been developed, he obtained results reported to be in close agreement with the corresponding Munsell dimensions of value and chroma. Much the same experiment was repeated by Torgerson (1951) using more efficient procedures, with the results given in section 6 of this chapter. At the same time the method was applied to a set of nine gray stimuli which differed only in brightness. Several checks on the method were made in this experiment. The stimuli were scaled by the multidimensional method of triads, and also by using the experimental method of paired comparisons along with condition C of the law of comparative judgment. Both scaling procedures were carried out twice on the same set of subjects. It was found that the multi-dimensional method yielded a unidimensional scale in both trials. The scales were linearly related to each other, and to the scales resulting from the unidimensional method of paired comparisons.

More recently, Messick (1954) applied the same procedures to eight of the same colors on a different sample of subjects, using the general analytical procedure for estimating the additive constant discussed in section 4 of this chapter. The resulting configuration of stimuli agreed closely with both the Munsell system and the results given in Figure 5 though slightly more closely with the latter than with the former. He also applied the method of successive intervals along with a generalization of the law of categorical judgment to a larger set of color stimuli (the same eight plus eight additional colors of the same red hue). Here, however, three factors were obtained. The first two factors were clearly the same as the brightness and saturation factors obtained by the method of triads. The remaining factor, on which three stimuli have fairly high loadings, is more difficult to interpret. Though Messick does suggest a tentative interpretation, he also notes that it may be instead an artifact due to the particular method used.

More than that, it may indicate a general tendency for procedures based on the generalization of Thurstone's judgment model to underestimate large distances slightly. A suspicion that this might be so in the case of the method of triads has been noted previously (Torgerson, 1951). It is apparent in Messick's solution that it is the stimuli at the greatest distances from the centroid of all the points that make it necessary to extract the additional factor. (In his successive-intervals experiment, he used stimuli over a wider range of brightness and saturation than had been used previously, which could explain why the additional factor did not turn up before.) More experimental work is necessary, however, before we can tell. It is clear in any event that the general procedure works well when the distances are kept within reasonable bounds.

Incidentally, the same eight or nine color chips have recently been used by Wilson (ditto) in conjunction with a multidimensional-scaling approach based on a simple distance index and also by Shepard (1955) in conjunction with a distance model based on confusions during learning. Both report substantial agreement with the results given above.

Comparison of Spatial Models

Attneave (1950) found that his "city-block" spatial model fitted closely distances obtained from application of his method of graded dichotomies (see Chapter 10). The investigators mentioned above found a similarly good fit when the distances were interpreted in terms of a Euclidean space. The two opposing results cannot be accounted for on the basis of the procedures used for obtaining distances, since the procedures used by Attneave, Torgerson, and Messick are all just different varieties of the same model. It is suspected that the difference lies in the nature of the "complex attribute" investigated in the two cases. Earlier, it was suggested that Attneave's model might be appropriate in those situations where the different dimensions are obvious and compelling, whereas the Euclidean model might be appropriate otherwise. Attneave's choice of dimensions and of the stimuli along these dimensions presented very favorable conditions for obtaining the "simple sum" type of judgment required by his model. The dimensions varied were simple, obvious, and compelling—form and size, size and reflectance, and form, size, and color. In addition, the stimulus pattern itself would emphasize the "given dimensions." His stimuli were always arranged to form a "plus" when plotted on the physical dimensions, as shown in Figure 8.

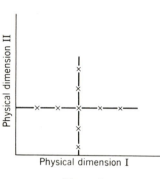

Figure 8

This arrangement itself would tend to emphasize to the subject the "given" dimensions. It would be interesting to see if this sort of judgment would be obtained even with obvious physical dimensions, if instead of the above pattern a more or less random scattering of points were used.

Experimentation is needed in order to determine the conditions under which one or the other model is the more appropriate. It may be that, in many situations, the subject's judgment falls somewhere in between, with the distance between two points equal to more than the square root of the sum of squares of differences in projections as required by the Euclidean model, but less than the simple sum of differences in projections as required by Attneave's model. In this case, some more general equation for relating distances to projections might be needed. One such equation, which contains both spatial models as special cases is given below:

$$(55) \qquad d_{jk} = \left[\sum_m^r (|a_{km} - a_{jm}|)^c \right]^{1/c}$$

When $c = 1$, equation 55 is equivalent to Attneave's model; when $c = 2$, it is equivalent to the Euclidean model. Values of c between 1 and 2 would correspond to various transitional models in between the two.

8. OTHER APPROACHES TO THE PROBLEM OF DETERMINING DISTANCES BETWEEN STIMULI

The preceding discussion has dealt entirely with distance models based on judgments of similarity. Further, the distance models discussed were all generalizations of Thurstone's scaling procedures: in particular, the method of equal-appearing intervals, and the various extensions of his general judgment model. These particular approaches to scaling of distances between stimuli are not the only ones possible, of course. In the present section we shall discuss briefly several alternative approaches which either have been used or which seem promising. The first two procedures to be mentioned remain within the "judgment" realm in the sense in which we have been using the term. The remaining possibilities discussed all deal with somewhat different approaches.

A Generalization of the Ratio Judgment Methods of Chapter 5 to the Scaling of Distances

In some situations the subject may be able to give not only judgments of the form "stimulus A is more like stimulus B than like stimulus C," but may also be able to indicate *how much* more stimulus A is like stimulus B than stimulus C. Possible tasks might include the following:

1. The subject might be told to assume that on some scale the distance (or amount of difference) between stimuli A and B is ten units. His task would then be to report the distance (or amount of difference) between stimuli A and C on the same scale.

2. Since any three points define a plane, the experimenter could fix two stimuli on a surface and then require that the subject indicate the appropriate position of a third stimulus on this surface. Measurement of the

ratios of the physical distances could then give estimates of the corresponding ratios of psychological distances.

Other possible procedures for obtaining more or less direct estimates of the ratio of distances d_{ij}/d_{jk} for all sets of three or four stimuli could be devised.

In case any such experimental procedures were used, a fairly efficient procedure for obtaining estimates of distances between stimulus pairs from the observed ratios would be to convert the observed ratios to logarithms and then apply the least-squares procedures devised for the corresponding extensions of Thurstone's judgment model. For example, in the second experimental procedure given above, we would obtain $\frac{1}{2}n(n-1)(n-2)$ direct estimates of ratios of the form d_{jk}/d_{ik}. When converted to logarithms, these estimates would become

$$(56) \qquad \log \frac{d_{jk}}{d_{ik}} = \log d_{jk} - \log d_{ik} \equiv {}_{k}y_{ij}$$

The estimates ${}_{k}y_{ij}$ could then be treated exactly in the same manner as the normal deviates ${}_{k}x_{ij}$ of the method of triads, as discussed in section 3 of this chapter. The final solution corresponding to matrix **H** of section 3 would consist of the $\frac{1}{2}n(n-1)$ estimates of the logarithms of the distances between the stimuli. These estimates could then be converted to distances, and the procedures of section 2 applied to determine the configuration of stimuli.

Two points might be noted here. First, the solution suggested above is a "best" solution in the sense of obtaining estimates of the distances which minimize the quantity

$$(57) \qquad \sum_{k} \sum_{j>i} ({}_{k}y_{ij} - \log d_{kj} + \log d_{ik})^2$$

Second, there is here no "additive-constant problem," since the procedure gives estimates of absolute distances directly. On the other hand, of course, the task may ordinarily be too difficult for the subject, since it involves judgments of a fairly high level of complexity.

Use of Simple Indices of Distances

Several investigators (Osgood and Suci, 1952; Rowan, 1954; Wilson, ditto) have applied multidimensional-scaling procedures to simple, more or less arbitrary indices of similarity. For example, Rowan has used the index

$$(58) \qquad d_{ij} = 1 - \frac{N_{ij}}{2m(n-2)}$$

where

d_{ij} is the defined distance between stimuli i and j,

n is the number of stimuli,

m is the number of subjects,

N_{ij} is the total number of times stimuli i and j are picked as most similar when appearing in triads with the remaining $n-2$ stimuli.

Wilson modified Rowan's index slightly and then equated it to the *square* of the distance between the two stimuli. He also used the complete method of triads, thus obtaining separate frequencies for judgments of the form "*i* is more like *j* than like *k*" and "*j* is more like *i* than like *k*" when summed over all values of k. His definition is given below:

$$(59) \qquad\qquad d_{ij}^2 = 1 - \frac{N_{ij} + N_{ji} + 2m}{2mn}$$

where

N_{ij} is the number of times i was judged more like j than like k for all k

N_{ji} is the number of times j was judged more like i than like k for all k

Osgood and Suci use an index of the general form

$$d_{ij}^2 = \sum_a (x_{aj} - x_{ai})^2$$

They have applied such an index in several ways. In the triad situation we have been discussing, it would become

$$(60) \qquad\qquad d_{ij}^2 = \sum_k (p_{jk} - p_{ik})^2$$

where

p_{jk} = the proportion of times j was judged more like k

p_{ik} = the proportion of times i was judged more like k

Several points might be noted concerning the use of such indices. First of all, they are indices of distance and not scaled distances. Since indices are simply a matter of definition, there is no internal basis for selecting one definition over another. Any of the three mentioned above could be applied to a given set of triad data. Others, of course, could easily be devised.

In the distance *models* discussed previously, some provision is made for evaluating goodness of fit of the distance model to the data. An internal criterion is available for deciding whether or not the judgments of similarity can be accounted for (in the manner specified by the model) in terms of the estimated distances between stimuli. In the triad method of section 3, for example, a basic notion is that relations like the following exist:

$$(d_{ig} - d_{ih}) + (d_{ih} - d_{ij}) = (d_{ig} - d_{ij})$$

Separate estimates of each difference in distance are obtained from the observations. The extent to which such differences in distances are additive in this sense is a matter of experimental fact and not simply a matter of definition. No such notions are available with the simple indices given above.

A second point concerns the general notion that the relations between quantities measured on an interval or ratio scale should be independent of the remaining stimuli in the set. The relative distances among any three stimuli, for example, should remain the same regardless of what other stimuli are included in the experiment. If a distance *model* fits the data, this invariance should hold (whether it does or not can be determined experimentally). With the simple indices, on the other hand, the relative distances between stimuli are clearly functions of the remaining stimuli in the set.

It should be noted, however, that in many situations simple indices such as these might give good results. The difficulty, of course, is that, unless a great deal is known about the particular complex attribute being investigated, it is not easy to tell.

Other Approaches to Scaling Distances between Stimuli

All the experimental procedures discussed thus far have been based on direct *judgments* concerning similarity of stimuli. The general multi-dimensional approach, however, is not necessarily restricted to judged similarity. Procedures might be devised instead for relating different kinds of observables to distances between stimuli.

Many kinds of behavior other than direct judgment could be interpreted in terms of the degree of similarity of stimuli. One such kind of behavior would concern the intrusion errors in paired-associates learning (Attneave, 1950; Shepard, 1955). Other things being equal, we would expect that, the greater the degree of similarity between two stimuli, the larger the number of confusions between the two.

Similarity in meaning of concepts could be investigated in terms of the number of times different concepts are applied to the same situation. In experiments on the facial expression of emotion, for example, where several pictures are described by subjects in terms of the emotion represented in each picture, similar concepts like "happiness" and "mirth" are applied to the same picture considerably more often than widely different ones such as "happiness" and "contempt," for example. (See Wood-worth, 1938.)

Other procedures which result in what can be called "confusion" matrices could be devised. The general notion would be to present the subject with n stimuli, one at a time, and require him to make one of n different categorical responses, where one particular response is appropriate for each stimulus. The confusion matrix would then have the elements $p_{i|j}$, the proportion of time the subject gives j as a response when i is presented. Green (ditto) has reported some progress on development of a model for relating such proportions to distances between stimuli.

►12

Deterministic Models ◄
for Categorical Data

1. INTRODUCTION

In Chapter 3, it will be recalled. the scaling methods were divided into two broad approaches: the judgment approach and the response approach. Chapters 4 through 11 have dealt with various judgment methods. With the present chapter we turn to a consideration of some of the different *response* methods.

The response methods differ from those methods discussed in Chapters 4 through 11 in that the systematic variability of responses of subjects to stimuli is ascribed to variability both in the subjects and in the stimuli, rather than to variability in the stimuli alone. Both subjects and stimuli can ordinarily be assigned scale values in the response methods, whereas in the judgment methods only the stimuli are scaled.

The task set for the subject also differs in general between the two approaches. In the judgment methods with which we have been concerned up to the present, the subject's task was to evaluate a stimulus with respect to an attribute possessed by the stimulus. This task took two main forms: the categorical-judgment procedures, where the subject simply sorted or rated stimuli into categories with respect to amount or degree of the attribute, and the various kinds of comparative judgments, where the subject judged whether one stimulus was greater than another, was twice as great, or was halfway between a pair of stimuli, always, of course, with respect to the designated attribute. In the response methods, with which we will be concerned from this point on, the subject's task is such as to give an indication of the relation of the stimulus to the subject himself. Again, this might take the form of a categorical response, where the subject agrees with, passes, or in some other fashion is characterized by the stimulus, or it may take the form of a comparative response, where the subject indicates that he agrees with or prefers one stimulus over another. In either form, the response is considered to depend not only on the nature of the stimulus but also on the nature of the subject himself.

A primary distinction between the two approaches is in the procedures for determining the ordinal characteristic of the scale. In the judgment methods, order presented few theoretical problems. It involved substantially a direct test of the postulates of order given in Chapter 2. In the response methods, however, the problem of order is more complex, involving derivative procedures provided by more elaborate ordinal models. Indeed, whereas in our discussion of the judgment methods we were concerned almost exclusively with problems of distance and origin, in the present and subsequent chapters we shall be concerned primarily with problems of order.

Actually, the central problem of the response methods might be stated thus: Without first determining for *all* pairs of elements whether element *a* is greater than, less than, or equal to another element *b* with respect to some specified attribute, how can we (1) decide whether the attribute can be represented by an ordinal scale, and (2) establish the rank order of the stimuli or subjects or both with respect to the attribute.

Different response methods are different models for answering these questions. All the unidimensional models begin with properties of an ordinal (or even, interval or ratio) scale. All are similar in that the relevant elements can be divided into two subgroups (e.g., *subjects* and *stimuli*) with the observable relations between elements restricted to those involving elements of different subgroups. That is, observations are made concerning whether a *subject* passes a *stimulus*, or whether a *subject* prefers one *stimulus* to another, but the equivalent observations within a subgroup are never obtained—a *subject* does not pass another *subject*, nor does one *stimulus* prefer a second *stimulus* to a third. Thus, a great block of information is not directly observable. For example, given n subjects and m stimuli, all considered as elements, we would obtain only nm observations of the form $a > b$ out of the $(n+m)(n+m-1)/2$ possible, leaving $n(n-1)/2 + m(m-1)/2$ unobserved.

From these common beginnings, the response methods branch out in a number of directions. Considering for the moment only the unidimensional methods, i.e., those that postulate and in some way or other provide a test for a single underlying continuum, the differences center around, first, the nature of the response and its theoretical interpretation, and, second, the provision for unsystematic or error variance.

Considering the latter first, we may classify the method according to whether the model is *deterministic* or *probabilistic*. In the deterministic approach, the model itself is stated in terms of the ideal case, where all the variation in responses is accounted for by the variation in subjects and stimuli. No provision for unsystematic or error variance is made *in the model itself*. Since things are virtually never ideal, the practical problem in this approach consists not of determining whether or not the model fits any particular set of data—it almost never will—but rather whether the model can serve as an adequate approximation to the data. In contrast, the probabilistic models have built into them provision of one sort or another for a certain amount of unsystematic variance. Since the models are probabilistic, they lend themselves to the setting up of statistical criteria for goodness of fit of the model to the data, and thus give a somewhat more satisfactory procedure for acceptance or rejection of the particular scaling hypothesis.

Considering the nature of the response and its interpretation, we divide the methods into those appropriate for categorical responses and those appropriate for comparative responses. Further subdivisions can in some cases be made in terms of differing theoretical interpretations of the response.

In the present chapter, we shall consider deterministic unidimensional models appropriate for categorical responses. We shall next take up the corresponding probabilistic approaches to the same sort of data. Finally, we shall consider something of the models developed for handling comparative data.

The Nature of the Problem

Throughout this and the following chapter, we shall be concerned with the analysis of data in the form of categorical responses of subjects to items. In general, each item may contain several response alternatives, and hence may serve to divide the subjects into several categories. The raw-data matrix will thus be of the form shown in Table 1. In this table, an × indicates the category of the item which characterizes the particular subject. Each subject is characterized by one category of each item.

We shall use the term "item" in its broadest sense. In general, it will refer to anything that can serve to divide the respondents into two or more mutually exclusive and exhaustive categories. It may, for example, be a typical mental test question, which divides the subjects into two categories —those who answered it correctly, and those who did not. It may be a typical questionnaire item, dealing with such things as attitude or opinion, biographical information, or beliefs.   It may also refer to overt behaviors, as when a person is observed in a controlled situation and his actions are classified into one of a number of possible categories.   In short, "item" will refer to anything that results in a classification of the subjects into categories, with the restriction that each subject must be in one and only one category of the item.

Table 1. The Raw-Data Matrix

Items and Item Categories

Subjects	1			2		3				· · ·	n		
	a	*b*	*c*	*a*	*b*	*a*	*b*	*c*	*d*	· · ·	*a*	*b*	*c*
1	×					×			×			×	
2		×		×					×		×		
3			×			×	×						×
4		×		×				×				×	
5			×	×				×				×	
·													
·													
·													
·													
·													
·													
·													
·													
N	×				×			×					×

The subjects will ordinarily be persons.   However, it should be noted that this is not necessary.   A more general definition might be "that which is characterized or categorized by the items."   Under some circumstances, for example, the term "subject" might correspond to a defined group of persons (see, for example, Riley et al., 1954) or a state of the Union (Shapiro, 1948).

The primary problem will be to determine whether the set of items and the set of individuals together "form a scale."   Can we order the subjects and/or the items along a continuum in such a way that the responses of subjects to items can be accounted for by this order?   Can we consider the responses to the items to be dependent on a single (though perhaps complex) attribute? Can the responses to the items be considered as indicating a relationship, with respect to a single attribute, between the "position" of the subject and that of the item categories? Can the alternative response categories within an item be ordered? If so, we shall say that the items form a scale for this group of subjects, or that the attribute to which all of the items refer is a *scalable attribute*.

2. THE GENERAL DETERMINISTIC APPROACH

We begin with some attribute in which we are interested—say, attitude toward war, socioeconomic status, or spelling ability. Our first postulate or assumption is that people can be ordered with respect to this attribute on a single continuum (we shall postpone a discussion of the multi-dimensional generalizations until later). We develop or select in some fashion a set of items whose content is concerned with the attribute of interest. We attempt to select items which are such that the responses of subjects to the item vary appropriately with respect to their positions on the underlying continuum. This is, of course, a complicated and important step. For the present, however, let us assume that we have given a set of items related to the attribute.

The second basic notion concerns the relation of the item to the postulated continuum. The particular notion used will, in general, involve certain requirements concerning the behavior of the item. We shall first consider the rationale used by Guttman (1941, 1944, 1950a) for items with any number of categories. Next, we shall consider the special case of dichotomous items, dealing first with alternative ways of looking at dichotomous items which behave as required by a Guttman scale, and then with a second major type of dichotomous item which behaves quite differently.

Guttman's Formulation

Each item is assumed to divide the underlying continuum into as many segments as there are response alternatives to the item, with a one-to-one relation existing between the segments and the alternatives. For example, a five-alternative item divides the continuum into five nonoverlapping contiguous segments, with one segment corresponding to each alternative, as is illustrated in Figure 1. All individuals characterized by positions in the continuum within a particular segment respond positively to the corresponding item alternative. Thus, in the figure, individual number 1 checks response alternative *a*, individual 2 checks *b*, individuals 3 and 4 check *c*, individual 5 checks *d*, and individual 6 checks *e*. Note that the item can be characterized completely by the locations of the boundaries between categories. An item with k response alternatives will have $k-1$ category boundaries.

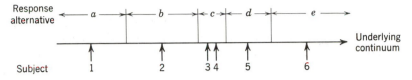

Figure 1. Schematic representation of a five-category item.

Different items will, of course, divide up the continuum in different ways. Figure 2 refers to a second item, this one having three response alternatives. Considering the same six individuals, individuals 1 and 2 check response alternative a of the second item, individuals 3 and 4 check alternative b, and individuals 5 and 6 check alternative c.

When considered in this way, it is clear that the items themselves cannot be ordered with respect to the continuum, since each item in a sense covers

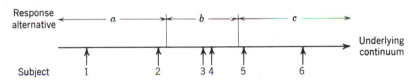

Figure 2. Schematic representation of a three-category item.

the entire continuum and simply divides the continuum into as many steps as the item has response alternatives. With such multiple-category items, it is the *boundaries between the categories* that can be considered to have positions on the continuum. Thus, with multiple-category items, we are concerned with ordering the subjects and/or the boundaries between the item categories.

Not all items fall within this scheme, even assuming that the responses are entirely determined by the attribute of interest. For example, consider the following two items dealing with the simple attribute of height.

Check the correct alternative:

1. My height is
    (*a*) Five feet ten inches or more.
    (*b*) Between five feet and five feet ten inches.
    (*c*) Five feet or under.

2. My height is

(*a*) Between five feet ten inches and six feet.
(*b*) Between five feet and five feet six inches.
(*c*) Neither of these.

Item 1 is clearly of the form required.   The three alternatives divide the continuum of height into three segments, the boundaries occurring at five feet and at five feet ten inches.   Item 2, however, does not fulfill the requirements, *even though it too is clearly concerned only with the attribute of height*.   Alternative *c* does not have a one-to-one relation with a single segment of the underlying continuum.   Individuals under five feet, between five feet six inches and five feet ten inches, and over six feet would all check alternative *c*.   Thus it is worth noting that not only the content of the item, but also the item form, is important in determining the appropriateness of the item for a particular model.

This factor is perhaps not too important when we are dealing with multicategory items.   Those multicategory items that do not behave in the manner prescribed by the model would simply seem to be bad items. However, with dichotomous items, i.e., items with but two response categories, this is not so.   Here we have two ideal item forms, both of which lead to simple, yet somewhat different, models.   Consider the two following dichotomous items.

1. I am over five feet six inches tall.
2. I am between five feet six inches tall and five feet ten inches tall.

The form of the first item corresponds to the form prescribed above for the multicategory items.   The item divides the continuum of height into two segments or categories with the separating boundary at the point corresponding to five feet six inches.   All individuals below this point will answer the item negatively—they are all in the "negative" category.   All individuals over five feet six inches tall will answer the item affirmatively, and are all in the "positive" category.   The usual Guttman scaling procedures require a dichotomous item to be in this form.   Dichotomous items having this form have been called *increasing probability* (Thurstone and Chave, 1929), *cumulative* (Loevinger, 1948; Mosteller, 1949), or *monotone* (Coombs, 1952) items.   We shall use the last term.

The second item represents an ideal type which does not fit into the usual Guttman procedure.   It is discussed below.

An Alternative Formulation

Dichotomous monotone items permit a very simple rule of interpretation for relating individuals, items, and responses to the underlying continuum.

For this particular situation, we can assume that the items and individuals are both elements located in the continuum.   The response of an individual to an item can be interpreted simply as indicating a direction relation between the individual and the item.   Thus a positive response might indicate that the individual is above or greater than the item with respect to the continuum, and a negative response that the item is greater than the individual.   The scaling task could then be conceived as obtaining the joint order of subjects and items on the underlying continuum; i.e., constructing a joint scale (Coombs, 1952).

The form of the second item corresponds to that used in the Thurstone attitude scales (Thurstone and Chave, 1929).   In this form of item, the positive response indicates, within limits, the position of the subject directly.   Items of this general form are called variously *nonmonotone* (Coombs), *differential* (Loevinger), *point* (Mosteller), or *maximum probability* (Thurstone and Chave) items.   Note that individuals who are taller than five feet ten inches as well as individuals who are shorter than five feet six inches will respond in the negative category.   There is thus no simple *one-to-one* relation between the response categories and the underlying continuum.   Though items having this general form will not fit into the usual Guttman scheme, a deterministic model in the same spirit which essentially parallels that for the cumulative items has been developed by Mosteller (1949).

The Trace Line or Operating Characteristic of Dichotomous Items

The relationship of the dichotomous item to the underlying continuum can also be considered in terms of a curve known as the item trace line

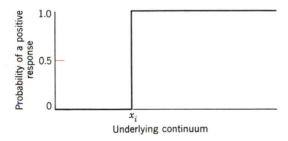

Figure 3.   An example of the trace line of a perfect monotone item.   For all subjects below point x_i, the probability of a positive response to the item is zero.   For all subjects above point x_i, the probability is unity.

(Lazarsfeld, 1950) or item operating characteristic (Green, 1954).   In this way of looking at the problem, only the subjects are considered to have positions in the underlying continuum. The relation of the item to the underlying continuum is described in terms of its trace line, which, for dichotomous items, can be presented as a curve relating the probability of a positive response to the item to position on the underlying continuum. Actually, this particular notion will be of more value in the following chapter when we discuss various probability models. The deterministic *models*, dealing as they do with the ideal case, require the probability of a

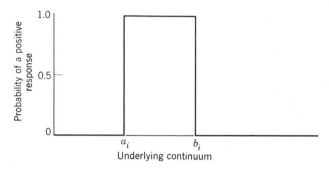

Figure 4.   An example of the trace line of a perfect point item. The probability of a positive response to the item is unity for all subjects between points a_i and b_i, and is zero for all subjects below point a_i or above point b_i.

positive response to the item to be either 1 or 0 at any particular point on the underlying continuum. An example of the trace line of a perfect monotone item is shown in Figure 3, while Figure 4 gives an example of the trace line of a perfect point item.

Summary Statement

We thus have at least three alternative ways of looking at the relation of the item to the postulated underlying continuum: the notion that the item divides the continuum into segments, with each segment corresponding to a category of the item and each person as a point; the notion (for dichotomous items) that both subjects and items can be represented as points in the continuum with the response of subject to item interpreted as a direction or ordering relation; and finally, the notion of the item trace line. In addition, we have seen that there are two main item forms of dichotomous items, the monotone and the point. Since the two behave quite differently, somewhat different procedures are required in each case for determining whether a set of items forms a scale. We shall discuss each in turn.

3. SCALOGRAM ANALYSIS—THEORY

The general deterministic procedure for determining whether or not the responses of subjects to items *form a scale* is known as *scalogram analysis* (Guttman, 1950*a*). Scalogram analysis is based on an analysis of the *response patterns* of the subjects to the set of items, where a *response pattern* denotes the set of responses to items given by a subject. For example, with n dichotomous monotone items there are 2^n response patterns that are possible. If the items form a scale, only $n+1$ of these patterns will occur. It is the nonoccurrence (or relative nonoccurrence) of the deviant patterns that enables the scalogram procedure to recover the order of the individuals and/or category boundaries on the underlying continuum from the observed data.

We shall consider separately examples of the scale analysis of a set of perfect multicategory items, a set of perfect dichotomous monotone items, and, finally, sets of perfect dichotomous nonmonotone items. The exact form of the scalogram differs somewhat in each case, although the general principle remains the same. For our examples, we shall continue to use the attribute of height.

Scale Analysis of a Set of Three Multicategory Items

Assume that the three questions given below are administered to N subjects:

1. With respect to height, which of the following is true?

    (*a*) I am over six feet tall.
    (*b*) I am between six feet and five feet six inches tall.
    (*c*) I am between five feet six inches and five feet tall.
    (*d*) I am under five feet tall.

2. Are you

    (*a*) Over five feet eight inches tall.
    (*b*) Under five feet four inches tall.
    (*c*) Neither over five feet eight inches tall nor under five feet four inches.

3. I believe my height to be

    (*a*) Five feet two inches or less.
    (*b*) Between five feet two inches and five feet ten inches.
    (*c*) Five feet ten inches or more.

Assume for the sake of argument that the subjects knew their own heights, were not careless, and did not lie. There are $4 \times 3 \times 3 = 36$ possible patterns of response to these three items. Of these, we would find only eight occurring. (Eight, since there are $3+2+2 = 7$ category boundaries and hence, assuming no identical boundaries, eight nonoverlapping categories. In general, with n items having a total of m categories in all, the number of response patterns equals $m-n+1$.) The remaining 28 possible patterns would represent nonscale types, and do not occur in a perfect scale. The eight response patterns divide the subjects into eight classes or types. Table 2 shows these eight response patterns. In this

Table 2. SCALOGRAM PATTERN FOR THREE
MULTICATEGORY ITEMS

Item Categories

		1a	3c	2a	1b	2c	3b	1c	2b	3a	1d
	I	×	×	×							
	II		×	×	×						
	III			×	×		×				
Subject	IV				×	×	×				
Types	V					×	×	×			
	VI						×	×	×		
	VII							×	×	×	
	VIII								×	×	×

table, called a *scalogram*, the columns correspond to item *categories* and the rows to subject types (a row for each response pattern occurring). An × indicates a positive response of the subject type indicated by the row to the item category indicated by the column. Since there are three questions, each row has three ×'s. For example, individuals of type II checked categories 1b, 2a, and 3c. The most important thing to note about Table 2 is the "parallelogram pattern" of the responses. If the responses form a perfect scale, we can always arrange the categories and the subject types to create a parallelogram pattern analogous to that seen in Table 2. This is in fact a necessary and sufficient condition for a perfect scale. The order of subject types necessary to create this pattern gives the order of the subject types on the underlying continuum. Furthermore, categories *within* an item are also ordered, but this is not necessarily true of categories of *different* items. This is easily seen in an examination of categories 2c and 3b. Category 3b is both above and below category 2c. The segment of the underlying continuum corresponding to category 3b completely encloses that corresponding to category 2c. Hence it is immaterial whether 2c precedes 3b or whether 3b precedes 2c in the scalogram. The *category boundaries*, however, are completely ordered. Since the boundary between each subject type corresponds to a boundary between two categories of one of the items, the order of the category boundaries is easily read from the parallelogram. In the present example, the order is 1*ab*, 3*cb*, 2*ac*, 1*bc*, 2*cb*, 3*ba*, and 1*cd*, where the digit refers to the item number and the two letters to the categories involved (e.g., 1*ab* is the boundary between categories *a* and *b* of item 1).

Scale Analysis of a Set of Four Dichotomous Monotone Items

Assume that the following four items have been administered to a sample of subjects:

		Yes	No
1.	Are you over six feet tall?	____	____
2.	Are you over five feet eight inches tall?	____	____
3.	Are you over five feet four inches tall?	____	____
4.	Are you over five feet tall?	____	____

If we again assume that the subjects behave as they ought, we would find that the responses to the four items divide the sample of subjects into five subject types. That is, of the 2^4 possible response patterns, only five will occur. By choosing the appropriate order of item categories and of subject types, the scalogram shown in Table 3 can be formed. As before,

Table 3. SCALOGRAM PATTERN FOR FOUR DICHOTOMOUS MONOTONE ITEMS

		Yes				No				Number of Subjects of Each Type
		1	2	3	4	1	2	3	4	
	I	×	×	×	×					N_1
	II		×	×	×	×				N_2
Type	III			×	×	×	×			N_3
	IV				×	×	×	×		N_4
	V					×	×	×	×	N_5

an × indicates the category of the item that was checked. Thus individuals of type II checked the "yes" category of items 2, 3, and 4, and the "no" category of item 1. Again, the scalogram pattern forms a parallelogram. For the dichotomous monotone items, however, the last half of the scalogram is completely redundant. The order of the negative-response categories is exactly the same as that of the positive-response categories.

Furthermore, the two halves are exact opposites of each other, since a response in the positive category automatically implies no response in the negative category. The parallelogram is simply two right triangles (one inverted) placed side by side.

As was true of the multicategory items, the order of the subject types necessary to give the scalogram pattern is the order of the types with respect to the attribute of height. (Note: Reversing the order of *both* subjects and items would also give a scalogram pattern. In this case, the order would correspond to the attribute of *shortness*. There is nothing in the scale pattern itself which gives the direction of the ordering. However, other considerations will ordinarily make this obvious.)

Since we are now dealing with dichotomous items, we may speak of scaling the item itself. This is of course identical with scaling the category boundaries, since there is but a single category boundary characterizing each item. We find that the order of the items in either half of the scalogram necessary to create the parallelogram pattern corresponds to the order of the items (category boundaries) on the underlying continuum.

We can further speak of the joint scale of subjects and items. In the present case the joint order is obviously type I, item 1, type II, item 2, $\cdots$, type IV, item 4, type V. Note that we have five subject types for four items. In general, a scale of n dichotomous monotone items orders the subjects into $n+1$ ordered types.

We might note further that the order of the subject types is perfectly correlated with the number of positive item categories checked by the type. Thus, the subjects in the tallest class (type I) checked four positive categories, those in the next tallest class checked three positive categories, and so on down to the shortest class (type V) who checked no positive categories at all. Further, these positive categories are checked in such a fashion that all subjects having a higher rank than a given subject responded positively to all items to which the given subject responded positively, *plus* one or more additional items. We can thus say the subject i has more of the attribute than subject j because he has all that subject j has plus some more. One implication of this is that, from rank position, or total score (the number of positive responses), we can reproduce exactly the response of the subject to every item.

It might also be noted that the order of the items is perfectly (inversely) correlated with the item marginal: i.e., the number of subjects responding positively to each item. Thus,

Item 1 was responded positively to by N_1 subjects.
Item 2 was responded positively to by N_1+N_2 subjects.
Item 3 was responded positively to by $N_1+N_2+N_3$ subjects.
Item 4 was responded positively to by $N_1+N_2+N_3+N_4$ subjects.

Individuals who respond positively to a given item all have higher rank scores than those who respond negatively to that item. Further, if an individual responds positively to an item of a given rank, he will respond positively to all items of a lower rank.

It is of some interest to examine the fourfold tables between dichotomous monotone items of a perfect scale. These fourfold tables will always have one zero cell. Furthermore, this zero frequency always occurs in the array having the lowest marginal frequency, and, within this array, in the cell representing a positive response on the less popular item and a negative response on the more popular item. In Table 4 are shown two of the fourfold tables between items on the perfect scale illustrated in Table 4.

Table 4. FOURFOLD TABLES SHOWING THE RELATION BETWEEN TWO PAIRS OF ITEMS OF THE PERFECT SCALE SHOWN IN TABLE 3

Item 1

		+	−	Total
Item 4	+	N_1	$N_2 + N_3 + N_4$	$N_1 + N_2 + N_3 + N_4$
	−	0	N_5	N_5
	Total	N_1	$N_2 + N_3 + N_4 + N_5$	$N = N_1 + N_2 + N_3 + N_4 + N_5$

Item 2

		+	−	Total
Item 3	+	$N_1 + N_2$	N_3	$N_1 + N_2 + N_3$
	−	0	$N_4 + N_5$	$N_4 + N_5$
	Total	$N_1 + N_2$	$N_3 + N_4 + N_5$	N

In the first, the zero frequency occurs in the cell representing a positive response to item 1 and a negative response to item 4—no one who says he is over six feet tall says he is not over five feet tall. In the second, it occurs in the cell indicating a positive response to item 2 and a negative response to item 3. That these zero cells must occur is obvious from the basic notion that, in a perfect scale, all individuals who respond positively to an item of a given rank also respond positively to all items of lower rank. This notion also implies that, given any two items j and k, with popularities p_j and p_k, if $p_j \leqslant p_k$, then $p_j = p_{jk}$, where p_{jk} refers to the proportion of subjects responding positively to both items j and k.

Since each fourfold table has the zero cell, it is clear that in a perfect scale the tetrachoric correlation between items is always unity. When all items are scored in the same direction, the matrix of interitem tetrachorics is a matrix of positive ones. Thus a factor analysis of such a matrix would yield a single factor (with loadings of items all equal to unity, and correspondingly with unit communalities).

Such cannot be said, however, of the matrix of *point* correlations between items. Even though the items form a perfect scale, the point correlations may range from almost zero to unity. In general, if the items are ordered with respect to the attribute, any array of the matrix of inter-item point correlations will have the characteristic that the size of the coefficients decreases on each side of the principal diagonal. Barring items with identical marginals, the rank of the matrix of point correlations will be equal to its order, and hence a multiple factor analysis would yield as many factors as there are items. This results from the fact that the size of the point correlation between two items depends in part on the marginal distributions of the items. The point correlation can be unity only when the two items have identical marginals. The dependence of various correlation indices on the marginal distributions of the items has been discussed in more detail by Ferguson (1941), Wherry and Gaylord (1944), and Smith (1950*b*).

Scale Analysis of Point Dichotomous Items

Construction of scales from point items is a bit more complex. The general notion is that a positive response of a subject to an item indicates that the subject and item are both at the same place on the continuum. Roughly speaking, with the point items, a positive response means "I am here," and a negative response means "I am not here," whereas, with the corresponding monotone items, the positive response means "I am above this," and a negative response means "I am below this."

While this may be the general notion, by itself it would not be sufficient to test the scale hypothesis. Given a set of point items, the subject would endorse at most only one of them—the one that coincides with his own position on the underlying continuum. If no item were included which corresponded with his position, he might endorse none at all. Even if all subjects endorsed one item each, we still could not test for the presence of a scale, nor could we determine the order of subjects or individuals. The scalogram pattern would not be overdetermined. If each subject responded to a single item, we could always arrange the data in the form of Table 5. This would be true, regardless of the nature of the items. Furthermore, through appropriate manipulation of subject types, we could obtain such a pattern for every possible order of the items. Hence, if we hypothesize that a positive response of a subject to an item means that the positions of the subject and item coincide *exactly*, the scalogram pattern cannot contain sufficient information to enable us to order either the subjects or items.   What is needed is a model that will allow, or require, the subject to respond positively to more than one item.

Table 5. SCALOGRAM PATTERN OBTAINED WHEN EACH
SUBJECT RESPONDS POSITIVELY TO A SINGLE ITEM ONLY

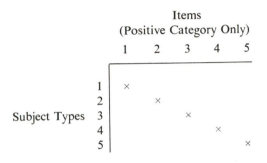

There would seem to be at least three reasonable ways of setting up an ideal error-free model for dealing with the point dichotomous items. First, we might consider the positive category of an item to correspond to a *segment* of the underlying continuum.   An item in this case would be rather directly analogous to a single category of a multicategory item. Here, the *item* could be characterized by two parameters—the upper and lower boundaries of the positive category—and the subject by a single parameter corresponding to his location.   Consider the following six items.

1. I am over five feet ten inches tall.
2. I am between six feet and five feet eight inches.
3. I am between five feet ten inches and five feet four inches.
4. I am between five feet six inches and five feet nine inches.
5. I am between five feet eight inches and five feet.
6. I am under five feet two inches.

We might first note that items 1 and 6 are actually dichotomous *monotone* items (though in opposite directions).   However, they can also be considered to be equivalent to point items with one category boundary beyond the range of the subjects.   The statement "I am over five feet ten inches tall" is for all practical purposes synonymous with the statement "I am between five feet ten inches and twelve feet tall."

The perfect scalogram for the six items given above (for the positive categories only) appears in Table 6.

Table 6. SCALOGRAM PATTERN FOR SIX POINT ITEMS

Each item is represented by two parameters and each subject by one parameter

		Items (Positive Category Only)					
		1	2	3	4	5	6
	1	×					
	2	×	×				
	3		×	×			
	4		×	×	×		
Subject Types	5			×	×	×	
	6			×		×	
	7					×	
	8					×	×
	9						×

We might note the following points:

1. The items and subjects have been arranged to form a "parallelogram," though even in this perfect errorless case the parallelogram is not regular. The real criterion in testing the scale hypothesis with this model (as it was with the multicategory items) is the solid string of ×'s in each column. With this model, if the items and subject types can be arranged so that in every column the ×'s appear in a single group, then the data form a scale. Note that this is not true of the *rows* in the present example.   Subjects of type 4 respond positively to items 3 and 5, but negatively to item 4.   If we attempt to remedy this by interchanging items 3 and 4, then the same sort of thing happens to subjects of type 3.   In this particular model, a perfect scale implies that the rows and columns can be arranged so that the positive responses form solid segments in the columns but not necessarily in the rows.

2. The arrangement necessary to create the solid segments in the columns gives the order of the subject types with respect to the underlying continuum.   Items, of course, are not simply ordered.   The order of the upper and lower boundaries of the positive category of each item is determined, however, and can be obtained directly from the scalogram pattern.

3. The characteristics of the scalogram in Table 6 are nearly identical with those of the scalogram for the multicategory items given in Table 2. The only difference in the *errorless* case is that, for the multicategory items, the upper boundary of one category necessarily corresponds to the lower boundary of another whenever the boundary occurs within the scale range.

In actual application, the difference might be more marked, however, since the multicategory items artificially eliminate one source of variance— within any multicategory item a subject is allowed to respond positively to but a single category, whereas, if these categories corresponded to separate questions, he might endorse more than one.

As a second general model, we might consider the items to correspond to a point in the continuum and assume that the *subjects* are best charac- terized by segments of the continuum.   That is, each subject ideally will endorse all items within a given range on the continuum.   Subjects might differ both in the general location of the items they will endorse and in the spread of items they will endorse.   The net result of this general approach would be precisely the same as that discussed above if the role of items and subjects were interchanged.   In this case, we would arrange rows and columns so that the positive responses form solid segments in the arrays corresponding to subjects rather than items.   It might be noted paren- thetically that this particular notion is present in the method of equal- appearing intervals as applied to attitude measurement (Thurstone and Chave, 1929).   In this scheme, subjects ideally can be characterised not only by median position with respect to the attitude, but also by the range of the statements they are willing to endorse.   Nevertheless, as an ideal model for scaling in what might be called the Guttman spirit, this model would not seem very worth while.   Since we are ordinarily dealing with many subjects and rather few items, allowing the subject two parameters and the items one might cause practical difficulties.

There is also the possibility of allowing two parameters for both subjects and items.   However, in this case solid groups of ×'s would not necessarily occur in either rows or columns, even though the model fits the data perfectly.   The scalogram notion would thus not be particularly approp- riate here.   We shall not consider it further.

A third general model is perhaps the most appropriate.   Consider both subjects and items as points in the continuum.   Let the task set for the subject be to endorse the r items with which he is in closest agreement. This particular procedure has been suggested and tried out by Mosteller (1949).   Let us see what would be expected to happen if the following six items were presented to the group of subjects along with instructions to endorse the three items that are most nearly true.

1. I am about six feet five inches.
2. I am about six feet.
3. I am about five feet nine inches.
4. I am about five feet six inches.
5. I am about five feet three inches.
6. I am about five feet.

Table 7 gives the scalogram we would expect if all subjects responded the way they ought to respond. (Again the positive categories only are included in the scalogram.) The scalogram in Table 7 is similar to that

Table 7. SCALOGRAM FOR SIX PERFECT POINT ITEMS WITH
SUBJECTS INSTRUCTED TO ENDORSE EXACTLY THREE ITEMS EACH

Items
(Positive Category Only)

		1	2	3	4	5	6
	1	×	×	×			
Subject Types	2		×	×	×		
	3			×	×	×	
	4				×	×	×

for the dichotomous *monotone* items (Table 3) in that, when columns and rows are arranged optimally, any departure from a *perfect* parallelogram pattern implies a departure from a perfect scale. In the perfect scale, both rows and columns are characterized by solid blocks of ×'s. The arrangement necessary to create the parallelogram gives the order of the subjects and also the order of the items on the underlying continuum.

Similarities and Differences

The characteristics of the final scales constructed from any of the item forms—multicategory, monotone dichotomous, or point dichotomous—that have been discussed are essentially the same. The scales are all ordinal scales, and, if they all deal with the same attribute, will order the subjects in the same way.

In each case, the items are also characterized by the scale, but here it is necessary to keep in mind exactly what it is that is being ordered. In the multicategory items it is the category boundaries. This is also true of the dichotomous monotone items, since these are but a special case of the former, although here, since each item is characterized by a single boundary, we can speak of scaling the item itself. With the point dichotomous items, the order may relate either to the item itself, considered as a point, or to the upper and lower boundaries of the positive category in a manner directly analogous to that for the multicategory items.

It is perhaps worth noting that multicategory items could be easily converted into either monotone or point dichotomous items before analysis. If we simply consider each category as a separate item, we would have a set of point items appropriate for the first point model discussed above.   To convert to monotone dichotomous items, it is only necessary to combine adjacent categories until but two remain for each item, assuming that order of the categories within any given item is known.

Most of the differences in the raw data of the different item forms are obvious from a consideration of the nature of the item forms themselves. In any of the perfect cases, the responses of a subject to the items can be reproduced from knowledge of his rank position only, although somewhat different rules are appropriate for each item form.

There is at least one difference between the monotone and point items which ought to be emphasized, however.   This has to do with the behavior of inter-item correlation coefficients.   It was mentioned earlier that, with monotone items, while the fourfold point coefficient computed between items is less than unity, even though the items form a perfect scale, the *tetrachoric* correlation would be unity if the items formed a perfect scale. With point items forming a perfect scale, *neither* the fourfold point nor the tetrachoric between items will be unity.   Factor analysis of correlations between items which form a perfect scale will in general yield more than one factor, regardless of whether point or tetrachoric correlation coefficients are used.

4. ANALYTICAL PROCEDURES

In the preceding section, the discussion dealt with various deterministic *models* and some of the properties of each.   We were concerned almost exclusively with the models themselves and with data that fitted the models perfectly.   We saw that in a perfect scale, among all of the possible response patterns, the only ones that occur are those corresponding to the perfect scale types.   In a perfect scale of four dichotomous monotone items, only five of the sixteen possible patterns occur.   With the items ordered, and $+$ and $-$ indicating positive and negative responses, respectively, the five patterns corresponding to the perfect scale types are as follows: $(+ + + +)$, $(- + + +)$, $(- - + +)$, $(- - - +)$, and $(- - - -)$. Nonscale patterns of the form $(+ + + -)$, $(+ - + -)$, $(+ - - +)$, and the like, simply do not occur in a perfect scale.

The absence of these nonscale patterns was actually the condition that enabled us to arrange the rows and columns of the scalogram to give the appropriate parallelogram picture.   Once this was accomplished, the task was finished.   The subjects were classified into ordered scale types.   The items or item categories were also ordered on the underlying continuum.

In actual practice, of course, the nonscale patterns do occur to some extent.   There will be, in general, no way of ordering rows and columns of the scalogram to create exactly the parallelogram appropriate for the particular model. Errors will occur, regardless of which set of response patterns is taken as the perfect scale types.

Virtually all the practical problems of scalogram analysis are brought about by the presence of these nonscale patterns. Primary among these problems are the following:

1. Devising a means of measuring the amount of error in any particular scalogram picture, i.e., for any particular arrangement of rows and columns.

2. Ordering the data so that the perfect scale model is approximated as closely as possible. This amounts to selection of that set of perfect scale types or response patterns which gives the least amount of error.

3. Evaluating the degree to which the obtained data approximates the ideal perfect scale.

4. Devising rules for assigning scale positions to subjects whose response patterns do not correspond to one of the perfect scale types.

5. Devising ways to improve the scalability of the items.

We shall discuss each briefly. Since virtually all the material on the scalogram techniques deals with items of multicategory or monotonic form, the remainder of this section will be presented in that context. Actually, Guttman's own development of scalogram analysis limits itself entirely to items of this form. Although several authors have noted that the same general technique could be used with point items as well (see, for instance, Stouffer, 1950; Mosteller, 1949; Loevinger, 1948; Green, 1954), no one seems to have made a serious attempt to use this form in the scalogram context. Perhaps the main reason for this is the difficulty of constructing point items with characteristics approaching those required by the model. In any event it should be emphasized that the remainder of this section applies strictly only to items of the general monotone form. Though in most instances the general ideas discussed below could be applied rather directly to analysis of point items, some modifications in the specific procedures would often be necessary.

The Measurement of Error

In a Guttman scale, reproducibility is a key concept. In a perfect scale, the responses of a subject to all of the items can be reproduced from knowledge of his rank position alone. Guttman takes this notion as the basis for his definition of error. Individuals with nonscale patterns are first given the rank positions of the most similar perfect scale types. An error is then simply a response made by a subject which would have been predicted wrongly on the basis of his assigned rank position (Guttman, in Stouffer et al., 1950, p. 77). An error is thus an *error in reproducibility*.

In the four item scale mentioned above, for example, a subject with a response pattern of $(+ + - +)$ would be given the rank corresponding to the pattern $(+ + + +)$. Since a pattern of $(+ + + +)$ would be predicted from his rank, one error would be made. In like manner, nonscale patterns such as $(+ + + -)$, $(- - + -)$, and $(+ - - +)$ each contain one error. Patterns such as $(+ - + -)$ or $(+ + - -)$ each contain two errors.

Guttman's basic over-all measure of error for the entire scale is the coefficient of reproducibility (Rep), and is defined by the following formula:

(1) $$\text{Rep} = 1 - \frac{\text{total number of errors}}{\text{total number of responses}}$$

It is equal to the proportion of responses to the items that can be correctly reproduced. Since each subject responds once to each item, regardless of the number of categories per item, it is apparent that

(2) $$\text{Rep} = 1 - \frac{\text{total number of errors}}{\text{number of items} \times \text{number of subjects}}$$

We can also evaluate the reproducibility of each item separately. In this case, the Rep for an item would be simply one minus the ratio of the number of errors on that item to the number of subjects in the sample. Rep for an *item* gives the proportion of responses to that item which can be correctly reproduced. It is clear that the over-all reproducibility for the scale of all items as defined above is simply the average of the individual item reproducibilities.

Ordering the Data

The primary problem here is to arrange the item categories (columns) and the subjects (rows) so that the scalogram picture is as much like the corresponding ideal as possible. In general, an error shows up in the scalogram picture as an × which is separated from the main body of ×'s in the column in which it occurs. Thus the scalogram picture for any particular arrangement of subjects and item categories gives a clear picture of the number of errors occurring in that arrangement. In the present context, the particular arrangement of rows and columns which is "most like" the ideal is taken to be the one that has the fewest errors, or, in other words, the one that gives the highest value of Rep. Since the arrangement of rows and columns defines the set of response patterns which are to be considered as the perfect scale types, we may define the problem as one of selecting the set of perfect scale types which maximizes the value of Rep.

Several techniques have been developed to aid in obtaining this arrangement. Except for Guttman's least-squares procedure, a discussion of which is reserved for a later section, the procedures are largely based more or less directly on the properties of the scalogram diagram.

The *scalogram board technique*, devised by Guttman and described in great detail by Suchman (1950*b*, Ch. 4) reproduces the raw response matrix through use of boards holding removable slats. Two boards are used. In one, the slats run vertically, corresponding to item categories. In the other, the slats run horizontally, corresponding to subjects. Small depressions or pits in the slats correspond to individual cells in the response matrix. Pellets are dropped in the appropriate pits to indicate a positive response in that particular cell. When the pellets have been placed in appropriate positions in the board containing the vertical slats, rearrangement of the slats corresponds to rearrangement of the columns of the response matrix: i.e., to rearrangement of the categories. With the pellets in the board with the horizontal slats, the equivalent procedure corresponds to a rearrangement of the subjects. The two boards are so designed that we can transfer the pellets from one board to the other simply by superimposing the two boards and then turning them over. In this way we can switch at will from rearranging categories to rearranging subjects. Since each subject occupies one row (slat) in this technique, it can easily be seen that it is limited to rather small samples. The scalogram board illustrated by Suchman makes provision for 100 subjects and a like number of item categories.

The usual procedure used assumes a rough knowledge of the order of the categories within each item though this assumption is not strictly necessary. This enables us to establish an initial rough rank order for both the categories and the subjects. The initial rank order of the "most positive" categories and also the "most negative" categories of the items is given by the relative popularities of the categories; the order of the "most positive" categories goes from the least popular to the most popular, while the reverse holds for the order of the "most negative" categories. The initial order (between items) of the "neutral" categories is not given, but this order is not important at this stage.

The initial order of the subjects is given either by simply the number of positive responses given by each subject or by a total score where the ordered categories of each item are given simple weights (e.g., 4, 3, 2, 1, 0 for a five-category item). At this stage of the game it is usually obvious that the data in their present form are not going to scale. Hence the next step is to combine categories in order to reduce the total amount of error. We shall discuss this later. Following this, the new item categories are once again ordered, primarily according to their marginal frequencies, and the subjects once again ordered according to total score (weighted or unweighted as the case may be). Further shifting, particularly of "neutral" categories and of subjects that have the same total score, might be necessary before the best arrangement is obtained.

The *Cornell technique* of scalogram analysis (Guttman, 1947c) is largely a paper and pencil analog of the same general procedure, except that here categories belonging to each item are kept together throughout. Guttman (1947c) has given a step-by-step outline of this procedure. Again, knowledge of the rough order of the categories within any one item is assumed, although this is not strictly necessary. Simple weights are assigned to the ordered categories of each item. Each subject is then given an initial total score, equal to the sum of the weights of the categories he checked. The total scores give an initial idea of the rank order of the subjects. The next step is to construct a table which differs from the response matrix given in Table 1 at the beginning of this chapter only in that the subjects are placed in rank order according to their total scores (within any given total score, the order of the subjects is immaterial). There will again be as many rows as there are subjects, and as many columns as there are item categories. Categories of each item are placed adjacent to one another and in their proper order. As before, an × indicates the category of the item checked by the subject. If the scale were perfect, the responses of the subjects to each item would show a pattern similar to that given in Table 8. Different items could of course have different numbers of categories, and the cutting points for the category boundaries would ordinarily occur at different places.

Since the table ordinarily will show entirely too much error at this stage (when multicategory items are used) the next step is again usually one of combining of adjacent categories. Following this, new simple weights are assigned to the combined categories, new total scores are computed, and a second trial table is constructed. This process can be repeated if necessary.

To evaluate the amount of error, cutting points are established at the boundaries of the categories for each item in such a fashion that the number of responses occurring outside of the boundaries of the categories is a minimum. The total error of reproducibility is then simply the number of responses falling outside of the boundaries.

In the Cornell technique, as in the scalogram board technique, practical considerations limit both the size of the sample of subjects and the total number of item categories used. Guttman suggests about a hundred subjects and a dozen items as adequate for testing scalability.

Goodenough (1944) and Marder (1952) have presented alternative paper and pencil techniques. In addition, various techniques which make use of IBM equipment have been developed and described by Noland (1945), Ford (1950), Kahn and Bodine (1951), and Toby (in Riley et al., 1954).

Table 8. Perfect Multicategory Items

	Categories (in order) of Item j				Categories (in order) of Item k		
	a	b	c	d	a	b	c
1	×				×		
2	×				×		
3	×				×		
4		×			·		
·		×			·		
·		×			×		
·		·			×		
·		×				×	
·		×				×	
·			×			×	
·			×			·	
·			×			·	
·			·			×	
·			×			×	
·			×				×
·				×			×
·				×			×
·				×			·
·				·			·
·				·			·
·				×			×
N				×			×

Ford's procedures, including a special procedure applicable to six or fewer dichotomous items, and also a more general IBM adaptation of the Cornell technique, along with Toby's procedure are both described in detail in Riley et al. (1954).

Evaluation of the Degree to Which the Obtained Data Approximates the Perfect Scale

As was mentioned before, the problem here is not one of testing whether or not a perfect scale exists. Ordinarily it does not, since with a deterministic model of this sort one variant observation is sufficient to reject the hypothesis. The problem is rather to set up some criterion that will indicate whether the approximation is close enough to enable us to treat the data as if it were a perfect scale without being too far off. Obviously, if the deviant observations are few in number, the data considered over-all must have very nearly the properties of a perfect scale.

Rep is the primary criterion of scalability. Originally a Rep of 0.85 was arbitrarily selected as the dividing line separating scales from nonscales (Guttman, 1947c). More recently, a Rep of 0.90 or better has been taken as the standard. A value of Rep equal to 0.90 or more means that, of all of the responses of all of the subjects to all of the items, no more than 10 per cent correspond to errors of reproducibility.

Though a Rep of 0.90 is a primary and necessary criterion for scalability, it is by no means a sufficient one. Various auxiliary criteria must be met. This is due primarily to the fact that Rep by itself has several rather unfortunate properties.

One of the difficulties with Rep is that it depends to a considerable extent on the values of the item marginals. Here, we might note two things: First, Rep itself is equal to the average of the individual item reproducibilities. Second, the reproducibility of an item can never be less than the proportion of subjects in its largest category. With respect to reproducibility, an item can never do worse than to assign all subjects to its largest category. Hence, any set of items breaking at 0.90–0.10 or 0.10–0.90 will be guaranteed to give an over-all value of Rep of 0.90 or higher, even though the items are entirely independent.

A second difficulty with Rep is that its expected value is often high, even when the items are known to be completely independent. This is especially true when the total number of categories is small. Festinger (1947), Guttman (1950a), and Green (1954) have given illustrative examples. For example, the expected Rep for four independent dichotomous items with popularities of 0.2, 0.4, 0.6, and 0.8 is slightly over 0.90; for five independent dichotomous items with popularities of 0.2, 0.4, 0.5, 0.6, and 0.8, the expected Rep is 0.85; with nine independent dichotomous items having popularities of 0.1, 0.2, 0.3, 0.4, 0.5, 0.6, 0.7, 0.8, and 0.9, the expected Rep drops down to 0.83. Three independent trichotomous items with category popularities of 0.1, 0.6, 0.3; 0.2, 0.6, 0.2; and 0.3, 0.6, 0.1 give an expected value of Rep of 0.84.

Thus, in evaluating Rep, at least three factors would need to be taken into account: the proportion of people in the most popular category for each of the items, the number of items, and the number of categories per item. Further difficulties arise because the scalogram procedures ordinarily used allow one to capitalize on chance variability. This would seem to be particularly true with small samples of subjects.

The coefficient of reproducibility has remained the primary criterion in spite of the limitations mentioned above. The various auxiliary criteria listed below are mostly in the nature of checks to insure that the value of

Rep actually obtained is not spuriously high (see Guttman, pp. 78–80, 287–288, and Suchman, pp. 117–119, in Stouffer et al., 1950; also Green, 1954).

1. *Number of Answer Categories.* For dichotomous items, at least ten items should be used. With multicategory items, a smaller number might suffice. In general, the more categories, the more confidence we can place in the value of Rep.

2. *Range of Marginal Frequencies.* While it is desirable to have a considerable range of marginals, items with extreme marginals tend to make the value of Rep spuriously high. Hence, few, if any, items should have more than 80 per cent of the subjects in their most popular category. If it is desired to include extreme items to enable us to order the extreme subjects, these items should be ignored when computing Rep.

3. *The Pattern of Errors.* The pattern of errors should be "random." Practically, this means that no large number of subjects should be found who all have the same nonscale pattern of responses. If this does occur, it is evidence that more than one variable is involved.

4. *Item Reproducibility.* The individual items should all have reproducibilities of 0.85 or more.

5. *Improvement.* Each item category should have more nonerror than error. In the scalogram diagram, or in a diagram such as Table 8, the number of errors in any particular category is the sum of the number of responses outside the boundaries (cutting points) in that column plus the number of blank cells occurring within the boundaries. The number of nonerrors equals the number of responses occurring within the boundaries.

Thus the criteria in use are mostly of a common-sense, intuitive nature. This would seem to be a necessary consequence of the deterministic approach. Until a theory of error is incorporated into the scaling model in some way or other, statistical tests of goodness of fit would not seem to be possible. As we shall see, the models discussed in the next chapter do incorporate theories of error, and thus, theoretically at least, do not have this difficulty.

If all of the criteria are met by a particular set of data, Guttman concludes that the area is scalable, and that the properties of a perfect scale may be attributed to the area. If the criteria are met except for a value of Rep that is too low, he uses the term "quasiscale." There is more error in a quasiscale than in a scale, but the error is unsystematic. Hence the quasiscale retains many of the desirable properties of a scale. In particular, the (curvilinear) correlation of a quasiscale with any other variable is equal to the multiple correlation of the items with that variable (see Guttman, p. 79, and Suchman, pp. 159–163, in Stouffer et al., 1950).

Alternative Coefficients and Procedures for Evaluating Goodness of Fit for Dichotomous Monotone Items

Loevinger (1947, 1948) presented a theory of homogeneous tests which is essentially the same as Guttman's scale analysis. A homogeneous test in Loevinger's terminology corresponds to a perfect scale. The degree of homogeneity corresponds roughly to the reproducibility. Two of her coefficients are of interest here—the coefficient of homogeneity for a pair of items, and the coefficient of homogeneity for the test. The homogeneity of a pair of items is given by the ratio of phi, the fourfold point correlation between the items, to the maximum possible phi that could be obtained from items having the same marginals as the pair. The formula for the homogeneity of two items is given below.

$$(3) \qquad H_{ij} = \frac{p_{i|j} - p_i}{1 - p_i} \quad \text{where} \quad p_j \leqslant p_i$$

In this formula,

H_{ij} is the homogeneity index.

$p_{i|j}$ is the proportion of subjects endorsing item j who also endorse item i, (p_{ij}/p_j).

p_i is the popularity of item i.

When $H_{ij} = 1$, the items are perfectly homogeneous; when $H_{ij} = 0$, the items are completely independent.

The coefficient of homogeneity for the complete test is essentially a weighted average of the indices of all of the pairs of items in the test:

$$(4) \qquad H_t = \frac{\displaystyle\sum_{i>j}^{\frac{1}{2}n(n-1)} p_j q_i \left(\frac{r_{ij}}{r_{ij\,\text{max}}}\right)}{\displaystyle\sum_{i>j}^{\frac{1}{2}n(n-1)} p_j q_i} = \frac{\displaystyle\sum_{i>j}^{\frac{1}{2}n(n-1)} p_j q_i H_{ij}}{\displaystyle\sum_{i>j}^{\frac{1}{2}n(n-1)} p_j q_i}$$

where n = the number of items

p_i = the popularity of item i

$q_i = 1 - p_i$

r_{ij} = point correlation between items i and j

$r_{ij\,\text{max}}$ = maximum possible point correlation between items i and j

According to Loevinger, it is related to the total test variance (where a subject's score is given by the number of correct responses) as follows:

$$(5) \qquad H_t = \frac{V_x - V_{\text{het}}}{V_{\text{hom}} - V_{\text{het}}}$$

where V_x denotes the observed test variance, V_{het} denotes the variance of a completely heterogeneous test made up of items having the same marginals, and V_{hom} denotes the variance of a completely homogeneous test made up of items with the same marginals. The coefficient H_t would seem to have a number of advantages over Rep, since it would appear that a good share of the dependency on item marginals has been eliminated. As was the case with Rep, however, its sampling characteristics are unknown. It has not been used a great deal.

The usual procedures for determining Rep, as we have seen, involve a great deal of direct manipulation of the raw data. Little use is made of summary statistics. As a result, most of the procedures are limited to a rather small number of subjects and items. Green (1954, 1956) has given a method for estimating Rep which is based on summary statistics and which thus does not become unmanageable with large samples. It is also a completely objective procedure, requiring none of the judgmental skills involved in the somewhat subjective methods ordinarily used in determining the optimal arrangement of subjects and items.

Green shows how the number of errors in any response pattern can be broken down into the sum of the number of first-order errors, the number of second-order errors, third-order errors, etc., where the order of the error is defined as follows.

Consider any particular response pattern where the items are in their proper serial order, such as $(+----+++--+++)$. The perfect scale pattern to which this is most similar is $(-----++++++++)$. The pattern thus contains three errors. The first-order errors correspond to pairs of adjacent items with responses in reverse order $(+-)$. There are two first-order errors in the pattern given above: i.e., two places where the sequence $(+-)$ occurs. If we count two errors, and eliminate the two corresponding pairs of items, the pattern remaining becomes $(---++-+++)$. This residual pattern contains one pair of adjacent items in the reverse order $(+-)$. This corresponds to a second-order error. Counting this error and eliminating the corresponding pair of items leaves the residual pattern $(---++++)$ which has no reversals. If further reversals had occurred, we would continue on, obtaining the number of third-order errors, fourth-order errors, etc. The total number of errors in the pattern is equal to the sum of the number of errors of each order. In the present example, two first-order errors plus one second-order error gives the appropriate total of three errors.

It should be noted that a second-order error appears in the *original* response pattern as the sequence of responses to adjacent items $(++--)$. Thus, from the original response pattern, we can count the number of second-order errors as the number of sequences of adjacent items having the pattern $(++--)$.

Green's computing procedure capitalizes on two important empirical properties of approximately perfect scales (or quasiscales). First, the order of the items on the basis of a complete scalogram analysis is either the same or very nearly the same as the order determined simply from the item popularities. (In a perfect scale, of course, the orders are identical.) Second, errors of order higher than two occur very infrequently, particularly when the number of items is not extremely large. Hence, they can be ignored in the estimation of Rep with very little loss in precision.

The total number of first-order errors in the entire response matrix is given by the total number of sequences of $(+-)$, which equals

$$(6) \qquad \sum_{i=1}^{n-1} N_{i+1,\bar{i}} \qquad (i+1 > i)$$

where the bar over the subscript indicates a negative response (i.e., $N_{i+1,\bar{i}}$ indicates the number of subjects who responded *positively* to item $i+1$ and *negatively* to item i), and where item $i+1$ has a higher scale rank (and therefore lower popularity) than item i. In like manner, the total number of second-order errors in the entire response matrix is equal to the total number of sequences of $(++--)$, or

$$(7) \qquad \sum_{i=2}^{n-2} N_{i+2,i+1,\bar{i},\overline{i-1}}$$

Since Rep is equal to one minus the total number of errors divided by the total number of responses (equation 2), we can write

$$(8) \qquad \text{Rep}_A = 1 - \frac{1}{Nn} \sum_{i=1}^{n-1} N_{i+1,\bar{i}} - \frac{1}{Nn} \sum_{i=2}^{n-2} N_{i+2,i+1,\bar{i},\overline{i-1}}$$

as Green's first method for estimating Rep. Rep_A differs from the true sample Rep for items in popularity order only in that the infrequent third-order and higher-order errors are ignored. A second formula, which involves the assumption that the two errors involved in any second-order pattern are independent, is given by the formula

$$(9) \qquad \text{Rep}_B = 1 - \frac{1}{Nn} \sum_{i=1}^{n-1} N_{i+1,\bar{i}} - \frac{1}{N^2n} \sum_{i=2}^{n-2} N_{i+2,i} N_{i+1,\overline{i-1}}$$

The routine procedure would thus be, first, to determine the order of the items in terms of their popularities; second, to tabulate $N_{i+1,\bar{i}}$ for each of the $n-1$ pairs of adjacent items; third, to tabulate either $N_{i+2,i+1,\bar{i},\overline{i-1}}$

or $N_{i+2,i}$; and, fourth, to apply either formula 8 or 9 to obtain the estimate of Rep. It is, of course, not necessary to construct separate tables with items or subjects in their proper order. We can work directly with the raw answer sheets. In applying the method to ten scales reported by Suchman, Green found the average discrepancies between the true sample Rep and the estimates to be 0.002 and 0.003 for Rep_A and Rep_B, respectively. Rep_A has some advantage over Rep_B in that it is known that it can never underestimate the true sample Rep.

As a single, over-all index of the reproducibility of the scale, Green suggests the following, which he calls the index of consistency:

$$(10) \qquad\qquad C = \frac{\text{Rep} - \text{Rep}_I}{1 - \text{Rep}_I}$$

where C is the index, Rep is the estimate computed from either equation 8 or 9, and Rep_I is the reproducibility of a completely independent set of items computed from the following formula:

$$(11) \qquad \text{Rep}_I = 1 - \frac{1}{N^2 n} \sum_{i=1}^{n-1} N_{i+1}N_i - \frac{1}{N^4 n} \sum_{i=2}^{n-2} N_{i+2}N_{i+1}N_i N_{i-1}$$

Since higher-order errors are neglected in both the computation of Rep_A or Rep_B and Rep_I, the index C should be relatively independent of number of items. It is essentially equivalent to Loevinger's coefficient of homogeneity in that, when items are all sensed in the same direction, it varies between zero and unity and is relatively insensitive to distribution of item marginals. According to Green, a value of the index equal to 0.50 or more corresponds roughly to a "scale" as distinguished from a "quasi-scale," or "nonscale."

Ordering the Subjects

The problem here is to assign scale positions to those subjects that do not have perfect scale patterns. These subjects may comprise a considerable proportion of the total sample, even though reproducibility is high. For example, Stouffer et al. (1952) have indicated that, with a four-item scale having a Rep of 0.90, as many as 40 per cent of the subjects might have nonscale patterns. With a 90 per cent reproducible scale composed of ten items, this can be true for nearly 90 per cent of the subjects.

We have already stated that one procedure used is to assign the subject to the rank associated with the perfect scale pattern most similar to his own: i.e., to the scale pattern that minimizes his error. However, under many circumstances, this by itself does not yield an unambiguous answer— the nonscale pattern can be assigned to any of several scale types without changing the error. For example, with a four-item scale, the pattern $(+-+-)$ could be classified with $(++++)$, $(--++)$, or $(----)$, in each case with two errors. Several suggestions have been made for dealing with these ambiguous cases. Henry (1952) suggests assignment to the most popular of the alternative scale types. Borgatta and Hays (1952) suggest an average of the alternatives. Ford (in Riley et al., 1954) used the following criteria: If the number of alternative types is odd, assign it to the middle type; if the number is even, assign it to the type closest to the middle of the scale, or, if two are equidistant from the middle, to the most negative of the two.

In actual practice, with scales composed of dichotomous items, the straight number of positive responses is often used for ordering all of the subjects. With multiple-category items a similar simple procedure, such as total score as used to obtain a trial order of the subjects in the scaling techniques discussed above, could be used, since it would correlate highly with the more involved procedures.

Improving Scalability

A typical procedure followed in the scalogram approach is to begin with around a dozen multicategory items. Two such items, taken from different Guttman scales (reported in Stouffer et al., 1950, pp. 102, 281), are reproduced below. The first is from a scale entitled "attitude toward the army," the second from a scale entitled "attitude toward officers."

On the whole, do you think the Army gives a man a chance to show what he can do? (Check one.)

1. ——— A very good chance
2. ——— A fairly good chance
3. ——— Not much of a chance
4. ——— No chance at all
5. ——— Undecided

How many of the officers in your company (battery, squadron, troop) are the kind you would want to serve under in combat?

1. ——— All of them are.
2. ——— Most of them are.
3. ——— About half of them are.
4. ——— Few of them are.
5. ——— None of them are.

It is usually not expected that so many items with so many categories in each will meet the scale criteria set up. One reason for this is the likelihood that the various modifiers differentiating between the alternatives ("very good," "fairly good," "not much," etc.) have different meanings for different subjects.   One subject, for example, who checks "fairly good" might have as favorable an attitude as another who checks "very good," but might simply have more conservative verbal habits.   A second reason might be that there are simply too many categories, that it is difficult to find areas which permit such precise ordering of subjects while still meeting the scale criteria.   In any event the expectation is ordinarily born out— the items do not form a scale in their present form.

The primary procedure for improving scalability is the combining of categories.   In combining categories, a number of cautions should be kept in mind: No combined category should have in it a large proportion (over 0.8) of the subjects; no combined category should have more error than nonerror; category boundaries of different items should differ from one another as much as possible; other things being equal, that particular combination should be used which eliminates the greatest amount of error. The usual procedure is perhaps to use a scalogram setup such as that given in Table 8 when deciding on which categories to combine.   A more elaborate procedure, involving the cross tabulation of every item against every other item followed by examination of the consequences of all possible dichotomizations is discussed in detail by Toby and Toby (in Riley et al., 1954, Ch. 15.   The procedure is attributed to Stouffer).

Stouffer et al. (1952; also in Riley et al., 1954) have given a technique involving combination of categories of *different* items.   Since responses to categories of different items are not mutually exclusive, the procedure also enables us to decide what is going to be considered a positive response in the new contrived category.   For example, three dichotomous items might be combined into a single contrived item by defining a positive response to the new contrived item as a positive response to at least two of the original three items.   A negative response would then be equivalent to no more than one positive response to the original three.   Stouffer indicates that both reproducibility and reliability can be improved through use of contrived items, providing the items are not too bad (e.g., have item Reps of at least 0.80) to start with.

If certain of the items cannot be improved enough to meet the scale criteria, a further way to increase "scalability" is simply to discard or revise the offending items.   While Guttman in general frowns on this procedure (1950a, p. 85), it would seem to be necessary in many cases. Guttman's disapproval stems mainly from his notions concerning a "universe of content."   We shall discuss this further in the section on sampling problems.

Under some circumstances, it might also be possible—and reasonable— to improve the scalability by discarding *subjects*, a procedure that would involve a redefinition of the subject population. For example, if we were interested in attitude toward a particular radio program, elimination of all subjects who have never heard of the program would seem reasonable. Filter questions to accomplish this are actually used in survey work.

If the problem becomes one of selecting for scalogram analysis the best out of a larger number of items, various techniques become available. Edwards and Kilpatrick (1948a, 1948b) discuss a procedure which begins with judgments of experts in the manner of the method of equal-appearing intervals (Chapter 4), progresses to the item-analysis techniques as developed by Likert for the attitude context (1932) and finally ends up with a scalogram analysis. Regular item-analysis procedures (see Gulliksen, 1950; Davis, 1951, 1952) can easily be used for this purpose as long as we take into account any different behavior they might have for items with different marginals. Factor-analysis procedures would probably give a good selection as long as the coefficients that are factored do not depend unduly on item marginals. Where chance success is not an element, tetrachoric correlations or the ratio of the phi coefficient to the maximum possible phi for the item marginals seem appropriate. A procedure for adding on items one at a time is included in the cross-tabulation procedure for dichotomizing items referred to above (Riley et al., 1954).

5. SAMPLING PROBLEMS

In the preceding sections, the discussion has been almost entirely in terms of the responses of a particular group of subjects to a particular set of items at a particular time. This is probably as it should be, since problems of sampling are not necessarily a part of the scaling problem itself when we are dealing with deterministic models. In those situations where interest is only in those subjects and items actually used in the experiment, sampling problems need not arise at all. For example, it is of interest of and by itself that the forty-eight states form a Guttman scale with respect to certain regulative functions assigned to their state boards of education (Hagood and Price, 1952) or to their laws dealing with Negroes (Shapiro, 1948).

In Guttman's own theoretical development, concepts of "population of subjects" and "universe of content" (items) play a central role. The meaning of population of subjects is clear. By "universe of content" is meant, essentially, all the possible items that could be constructed which deal with the topic of interest. Thus, to Guttman, "The universe consists of all the attributes that define the concept." (1950a, p. 80.) (Our use of the term "item" corresponds closely to Guttman's use of the term "attribute.") Again, "Another way of describing the universe is to say it consists of all the attributes of interest to the investigation which have a common content, so that they are classified under a single heading which indicates that content." (1950*a*, p. 80.)   Later, he states, "It is, therefore essential to inquire into the nature of the *universe of all possible questions of the same content*, and to determine what inferences can be made about that universe that will not depend on the particular sample of questions used." (1950*a*, p. 81.)

Furthermore, in Guttman's theorizing, it is the *universe* whose scalability for a given *population* is being "tested" and not the particular group of items (for either the population or the specific group of subjects).   Thus, both subject- and item-sampling problems are important considerations. We shall discuss each separately.

Subjects

It is clear that in many scaling problems the particular population of subjects that we are interested in is too large to be included in any one scaling experiment.   Hence there will be many situations where we will wish to select a sample of subjects in such a way that inferences concerning the behavior of the parent population can be made.   This is the usual sampling situation and involves no new problems of a theoretical nature.

In actual practice, of course, problems exist owing to the fact that little is known of the sampling distribution of the major scale criteria.   This fact has led Green (1954, p. 356) to suggest that the common use of subject samples as small as 100 might be a dangerous extravagance.   This would seem particularly true in view of the facts (*a*) that the expected value of Rep is often high, assuming complete independence of items, so that there is often not a great many percentage steps between expected chance reproducibility and "acceptable" reproducibility, and (*b*) that the scalogram procedures in common use allow one to capitalize on the chance variability.

Items

The notion of a universe of items does present some knotty problems. As Guttman says, items are constructed by the experimenter and are not drawn at random from the universe.   Furthermore, even if the experimenter finds himself with more items than he needs, he does not usually take a random subset of the size needed.   He ordinarily uses whatever means are at his disposal to pick the "best" items from the lot.   Hence the usual random sampling theory is not ordinarily appropriate.

It is clear that, if a universe has been defined, and if it forms a perfect scale, then any sample of items from that universe will scale perfectly, regardless of how the sample of items is drawn.   Further, the order of subjects will be invariant over item samples (except for ties) and will be the same as would have been obtained if the entire universe of items had been used.

Guttman feels that, if the criteria are set high enough (e.g., as high as those given earlier in this chapter), we can reverse this reasoning without much danger. If the criteria do not leave much room for variation, then it will make little difference whether the sample drawn is random or not (1950a, p. 287). Earlier he states:

> It seems quite safe to infer in general that, if a sample of items is selected without knowledge of their empirical interrelationships and is found to form a scale for any sizable random sample of individuals, then the universe from which the items are selected is scalable for the entire population of individuals. (1950a, p. 82).

Are we really justified in inferring that the universe is scalable when the particular sample of items is found to meet the scale criteria? For several reasons, it does not seem that such an inference is justified. Indeed, we might go back further and question the whole idea of a universe of items from which a sample is drawn. In many respects the concept seems artificial and forced. Before such a concept would become useful, it would seem to be necessary to devise some rigid procedure which would enable us to determine whether a particular item is or is not a member of the universe. Until this is done, we would have no clear-cut notion of what it is that we are generalizing to.

With respect to the inference itself, the trouble is that we can conceive of a great many situations—some of them reasonable—where the "universe" itself is not scalable but where certain samples from the universe are. Consider the following example of three calculus items given by Stouffer (1950) as an illustration of the cumulative characteristic in measurement of ability.

1. Integrate $\quad \dfrac{dy}{dx} = xy(y - a)$

2. Integrate $\quad \dfrac{dy}{dx} = x^2$

3. Differentiate $\quad y = x^2$

It would seem likely that these three items would form a scale with very little error indeed. Yet it is clear that we would not expect all samples of calculus items to scale. The reason why it seems likely that these three items would form a scale is primarily because they appear to differ widely in difficulty.

The idea here can perhaps be best illustrated if we return to the notion of the trace lines of a perfectly scalable set of dichotomous items. It will be recalled that the trace line refers in this case to the probability of a correct (or positive) response as a function of position on the underlying continuum. The trace line of a perfectly scalable item is zero up to a particular point (the "position" of the item, or the location of the boundary between the two categories). At this point it jumps to unity and remains unity

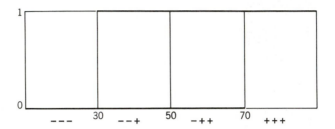

Figure 5.   Three perfect monotone items.

thereafter. Three perfect items might appear as in Figure 5, where the underlying continuum is spaced off in terms of percentiles. Between the various breaking points is given the response patterns of all subjects located therein. The point here is that there are a great many other varieties of item trace lines which in this case would also yield a perfect

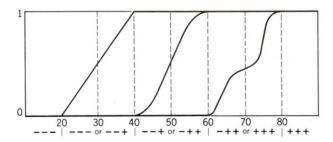

Figure 6.   Three imperfect items which nevertheless give a perfect scale.

scalogram pattern. Indeed, the only requirement is that the trace line of one item becomes unity before the trace line of the other leaves zero. Figure 6 gives examples of trace lines with approximately the same expected popularities as those in the previous figure. Note that, while this set of items must always form a perfect scalogram pattern, the order of the subjects will contain a certain amount of error. A person whose "true" ability is at, say, the 39th percentile might find himself in subject type IV $(---)$, while one at the 21st percentile might be in subject type III $(--+)$. This, of course, would be all the more true if we speak in terms of only *approximately perfect* reproducibility.

If we make the usual assumption that the correlation between items is determined entirely by the underlying variable, then the following points can be made:

1. If the item were of the same form as in Figure 6, but their popularities were more nearly alike, the items would not yield a scale pattern. Hence in this case, obtaining a scale was contingent on selection of items that were widely spaced in popularity.

2. Adding any item having an operating characteristic similar to one of the three and having a popularity between 0.20 and 0.80 will decrease the reproducibility (and, incidentally, increase the reliability).

Now it seems quite likely that a situation somewhat like this actually occurs, at least a good share of the time, in the practical business of scaling. The experimenter does his best to construct items relating to a particular area which he thinks will have steep trace lines. He tries to space these out as much as possible (within the limits dictated by the dependence of Rep on item popularity), if not when actually constructing the items, then when combining categories. In other words, he tries to do better than chance. It is quite possible that he sometimes succeeds. Hence, if the universe were actually made up of items having trace lines like these, the actual procedures used would be such as to enable him to obtain a scalable sample of items, even though the universe itself were not scalable.

Since, in many respects, item trace lines similar to some of those in Figure 6 seem intuitively quite reasonable, there is some justification for saying that the sample of items actually used in a scalogram analysis is probably much more likely to meet the scale criteria than would be either the "universe" itself or a random sample drawn from it.

As a matter of fact, empirical evidence might tend to support this. According to Stouffer (Riley et al., 1954, pp. 373–374), though hundreds of Guttman scales have been constructed, a good share of them are down to four or five items by the time the scaling procedure is through. Guttman, of course, specifies at least ten items if the items are dichotomous. But again, as Stouffer says, "A ten- or twelve-item cumulative-type scale is easier to talk about than to accomplish." (In Riley et al., 1954, p. 374.) One might wonder about accomplishing a 50- or 100- or 200-item scale. It should not be too difficult to construct that many items which all seem related to the content of interest. (This has long been routine in the Thurstone procedure, for example.) If we may legitimately generalize to the universe of content from such a sample of ten or so items, then we would expect that larger samples such as these would be no less likely to meet the scale criteria. However, to our knowledge, none have been reported, or for that matter, even attempted.

6. USE OF INTENSITY TO DEFINE A ZERO POINT

It will be recalled that the type of scale achieved when the data are found meet the criteria set up is an ordinal scale. Only the *order* of the subjects is determined. In many applications of the method, particularly in the fields of attitude and morale, the continuum appears to be bipolar. That is, it progresses from strongly negative through neutral to strongly positive. In these situations, it is often important to have a means of specifying the dividing point between the pros and cons, the favorable and unfavorable, or the good and the bad, as the case may be. Guttman (1947c) and Suchman (1950b) have suggested the use of intensity of feeling with which an attitude is held as a rational means for locating this zero point.

In general, the relation between intensity of feeling and scale value on the attitude itself is found to have a U or J shape. People with extreme attitudes (either pro or con) tend to have intense feelings on the subject, while those near the middle of the attitude scale are more indifferent. A definition of a zero point—the point dividing the pros from the cons—as the point where the subjects are most indifferent seems intuitively reasonable. Although this notion was developed in the context of the Guttman scale, it would equally apply to scales developed by any of the response methods.

To obtain a zero point in this way, we need a means for measuring intensity that is independent of the measure of the attitude variable itself. In the Guttman–Suchman *theory*, if intensity and the attitude were both measurable without error, a perfect curvilinear relation between the two would be found. In actual practice, of course, the relationship is found to be far from perfect, a circumstance ascribed to the lack of precise means for measuring intensity (Suchman, 1950b, p. 217). (It might be noted that the procedure would still seem to be a reasonable one, even though the theoretical relation were not perfect, as long as the regression of intensity on the attitude has the desired U or J shape.)

A number of techniques have been developed for measuring intensity (Katz, 1944; Cantril, 1946; Guttman, 1947c; Suchman, 1950b). Perhaps the most satisfactory is the "two-part" technique. Here, each regular attitude item is followed by an intensity question, such as "How strongly do you feel about this?", "How sure are you of your answer?", or "How hard was it for you to answer this question?" According to Suchman

(1950*b*), it makes little difference which of these question forms are used—they all give essentially the same result. The answers to the intensity questions are then subjected to a regular scalogram analysis. Although there is usually too much error for them to qualify as scales, the errors generally appear to be sufficiently unsystematic so that they may be classified as quasiscales.

A second procedure, called the *fold-over* technique has also been suggested. Here, the response alternatives to each regular question combine both intensity and attitude. For example, the alternatives might be *strongly agree, agree, undecided, disagree, strongly disagree*. We can use the items in the usual way to obtain attitude scores and then, as a second step, combine *strongly agree* and *strongly disagree* into a single high-intensity category, *agree* and *disagree* as a single moderate-intensity category, and leave *undecided* as the least intense category. However, both theoretical and empirical factors argue against this procedure as a basic method. There is first the point that experimental independence of the two variables no longer exists. Furthermore, according to Suchman (1950*b*, p. 253) the procedure sometimes does not give U-shaped curves in situations where the longer two-part procedure does. It does, however, represent a considerable saving in time, since the number of questions that must be answered by the respondent is cut in half.

Given intensity scores and attitude scores for all subjects, we might determine the zero point in a number of ways. Perhaps the simplest is to use the *median of the attitude ranks (or the corresponding percentile) of those subjects who were assigned the lowest-intensity score.* This procedure is recommended by Guttman (1954, p. 232), provided that at least 100 subjects are included in this lowest-intensity group.

Theoretically, the zero point thus obtained should be independent of particular biases in the questions used. This is an especially important consideration in those problems where it is desired to compare proportions of "favorable" and "unfavorable," between different groups of subjects, between different scales, or between different times. Suchman (1950*b*, pp. 266–275) has presented evidence that substantiates this desirable theoretical property. For two different 12-item scales, he took the six most favorable items and the six least favorable items and administered them as separate scales of the same attribute, along with appropriate intensity questions. While the distribution of subjects (using scale types as the base line) differed widely in each case, the zero points obtained through use of intensity divided the subjects into very nearly the same proportion of favorable and unfavorable. For one scale, the first six items gave a zero point at about the 69th percentile while the last six gave the 68th percentile. For the other scale, the equivalent percentile points were about 83 and 77. Thus the zero points remained virtually constant in each case, in spite of the extreme bias in the two subsets of items.

7. THE PRINCIPAL COMPONENTS

The discussion of the solution to the scale problem as presented in an earlier part of this chapter dealt almost entirely with more or less cut-and-try procedures, based on rearrangement of rows and columns of the scalogram diagram. In the present section, we shall give the least-squares solution developed by Guttman (1941, 1950a) for the problem.

Actually, the least-squares procedure has not been used to any great extent, perhaps primarily because it requires considerably more labor than the more usual scalogram procedures. Nevertheless, it does give a "best" solution in the sense of the specific problem posed, and hence could serve as a criterion against which to evaluate other more rapid procedures. It has also served as the basis for the theory of attitudes developed by Guttman (1950a, 1954).

The problem as originally posed by Guttman (1941) concerned the responses of subjects to multicategory items (and also, of course, dichotomous monotone items). More recently, Mosteller (1949) has shown that precisely the same reasoning can be applied to the nonmonotone or point item, the only difference being that, with the monotone items considered by Guttman, *each* category is included in the analysis, whereas, with the point items, only the *positive* category is included. Other than this, the solutions are equivalent.

The problem posed, and the solution of the problem, is equivalent to the maximum-variance solutions dealt with earlier by Horst (1935, 1936), Edgerton and Kolbe (1936), and Wilks (1938).

The problem is to develop a procedure for assigning values to subjects and item categories which are the best in some sense. To distinguish between values assigned to categories and those assigned to subjects, we shall follow Guttman in using the term "weight" when referring to categories and "score" when referring to subjects.

Actually, we can consider two problems separately:

1. Saying nothing at all about scores, solve for the set of weights for the categories that is most internally consistent in the sense that, for every person simultaneously, categories checked by a person have weights as much alike as possible and as different as possible from weights assigned to categories not checked by that person. This is equivalent to maximizing the ratio of the variance between people to the total variance. Since this ratio, in turn, is equivalent to the square of the correlation ratio, the

problem is one of choosing the weights that will maximize the correlation ratio.

2. Saying nothing about weights, solve for the set of scores for the subjects which is most internally consistent in the sense that, for every category simultaneously, all persons checking a category have scores as much alike as possible and as different as possible from scores of subjects who do not check that category. This amounts to maximizing the ratio of the variance between categories to the total variance.

However, it turns out that the two procedures are essentially equivalent —the most internally consistent score for an individual turns out to be proportional to the mean of the weights of the categories he checks, and, in like manner, the most internally consistent weight of a category is proportional to the mean of the scores of the subjects who checked it (Guttman, 1941). Hence, we need only carry through one solution here. We shall solve for the weights. Then, given the weights, the score of a subject is simply the mean of the weights of the categories he checks.

We shall follow Mosteller's (1949) derivation mostly, rather than Guttman's, since it seems easier. As we said earlier, if we keep in mind that, with point items, only the positive category is considered, while, with monotone items, all categories are included, the mathematical procedures are the same.

We use the following notation:

i an index for the ith subject

j, k alternative indices for categories

N total number of subjects

n total number of categories

r total number of responses for any given subject
     (For monotone items, r = number of items; for point items, r is the number of items the experimenter decides the subject must check. In each case it is constant over subjects.)

x_k weight assigned to category k

The task is to find the set of weights x_k $(k = 1, 2, \cdots, n)$ which maximizes the ratio of the variance between individuals to the total variance, or, since this ratio is equivalent to the square of the correlation ratio, which maximizes the correlation ratio.

Let us define

$$e_{ik} = \begin{cases} 1 & \text{if subject } i \text{ checks category } k \\ 0 & \text{if subject } i \text{ does not check category } k \end{cases}$$

Since each subject checks exactly r categories,

$$(12) \qquad \sum_{k=1}^{n} e_{ik} = r \qquad (i = 1, 2, \cdots, N)$$

We will assume that each category gets checked at least once (otherwise we throw it away). Thus,

$$(13) \qquad \sum_{i=1}^{N} e_{ik} > 0 \qquad (k = 1, 2, \cdots, n)$$

The score of subject i is given by t_i, where

$$(14) \qquad t_i = \frac{1}{r} \sum_{k=1}^{n} e_{ik} x_k$$

Let W denote the total sum of squares. Then

$$(15) \qquad W = \sum_{i}^{N} \sum_{k}^{n} e_{ik} x_k^2 - rN \left(\frac{\sum_{i}^{N} \sum_{k}^{n} e_{ik} x_k}{rN} \right)^2$$

From equation 14 this becomes

$$(16) \qquad W = \sum_{i} \sum_{k} e_{ik} x_k^2 - rN \left(\frac{\sum_{i} t_i}{N} \right)^2$$

Let R denote the sum of squares between individuals. Then

$$(17) \qquad R = \sum_{i} \left(t_i - \frac{1}{N} \sum_{i} t_i \right)^2$$

The variance ratio to be maximized is

$$(18) \qquad c^2 = r \frac{R}{W}$$

where c is the corresponding correlation ratio.

Differentiating equation 18 with respect to x_j gives

$$(19) \qquad \frac{\partial c^2}{\partial x_j} = \frac{r}{W^2} \left(W \frac{\partial R}{\partial x_j} - R \frac{\partial W}{\partial x_j} \right)$$

Setting the derivative equal to zero and rearranging terms, we have

$$(20) \qquad \frac{\partial R}{\partial x_j} = \frac{R}{W} \frac{\partial W}{\partial x_j}$$

Substituting from equation 18 gives

$$(21) \qquad \frac{\partial R}{\partial x_j} = \frac{c^2}{r} \frac{\partial W}{\partial x_j}$$

Since c^2 is invariant with respect to the origin of measurement for the values of x_j, we can specify that this origin shall be such that the mean score for individuals is equal to zero. Thus, we shall locate the x_j so that

$$(22) \qquad \frac{1}{N} \sum_i t_i = \frac{1}{rN} \sum_k \sum_i e_{ik} x_k = 0$$

Then equations 16 and 17 become, respectively,

$$(23) \qquad W = \sum_i \sum_k e_{ik} x_k^2$$

and

$$(24) \qquad R = \sum_i t_i^2 = \frac{1}{r^2} \sum_i \left(\sum_k e_{ik} x_k \right)^2$$

Differentiating equation 23 with respect to x_j, we get

$$(25) \qquad \frac{\partial W}{\partial x_j} = 2 \sum_i e_{ij} x_j = 2 x_j \sum_i e_{ij}$$

Differentiating equation 24 with respect to x_j, we get

$$\frac{\partial R}{\partial x_j} = \frac{2}{r^2} \sum_i \sum_k e_{ik} e_{ij} x_k$$

or

$$(26) \qquad \frac{\partial R}{\partial x_j} = \frac{2}{r^2} \sum_k x_k \sum_i e_{ij} e_{ik}$$

Substituting into equation 21 from equations 25 and 26 gives

$$(27) \qquad \sum_k x_k \sum_i e_{ij} e_{ik} = r c^2 x_j \sum_i e_{ij} \qquad (j = 1, 2, \cdot \cdot \cdot, n)$$

Dividing through by Σe_{ij} gives

$$(28) \qquad \sum_k x_k \left(\frac{\displaystyle\sum_i e_{ij} e_{ik}}{\displaystyle\sum_i e_{ij}} \right) = r c^2 x_j$$

If we now define

(29)
$$h_{jk} \equiv \frac{\sum_i e_{ij}e_{ik}}{\sum_i e_{ij}}$$

Equation 28 can be written

(30)
$$\sum_k h_{jk}x_k = rc^2x_j \qquad (j = 1, 2, \cdots, n)$$

which is a set of linear homogeneous equations.   The solution desired can be obtained from equation 30, using Hotelling's iterative procedure (1933). If this procedure is used, care should be taken so that the trial vectors of weights meet the condition imposed in equation 22.   As we shall see, the vector corresponding to the largest latent root of the system is an artifact. It is a constant vector which does not meet the restriction imposed by equation 22.   By keeping the trial vectors within this restriction, we iterate to the solution corresponding to the second largest latent root, which is the solution that maximizes the variance ratio.

The equation is more familiar if put into matrix notation.   Let us define the following matrices:

$\mathbf{X}$ = a $1 \times n$ row vector with elements x_k

$\mathbf{H}$ = an $n \times n$ square matrix with elements h_{jk} where the subscript j refers to rows and k to columns

Then in matrix notation equation 30 becomes

(31)
$$\mathbf{HX}' = rc^2\mathbf{X}'$$

Transposing, we get

(32)
$$\mathbf{X}(\mathbf{H}' - rc^2\mathbf{I}) = 0$$

which is the characteristic equation in its familiar form.   The latent vector desired is the vector corresponding to the second largest latent root of the matrix $\mathbf{H}'$.

Guttman ends up with a slightly different equation.   For his solution, let us return to equation 27.   If we define the following additional matrices

$\mathbf{M}$ = an $n \times N$ matrix with elements e_{ij}

$\mathbf{D}$ = an $n \times n$ diagonal matrix with the jth diagonal cell equal to $\sum_i e_{ij}$

then we can write equation 27 as follows:

(33) $$\mathbf{XMM'} = rc^2\mathbf{XD}$$

or

(34) $$\mathbf{X}(\mathbf{MM'} - rc^2\mathbf{D}) = 0$$

which is Guttman's (1941) equation 6.

To obtain a characteristic equation, define

(35) $$\bar{\mathbf{X}} = \mathbf{XD}^{1/2}$$

(36) $$\bar{\mathbf{M}} = \mathbf{D}^{-1/2}\mathbf{M}$$

Substituting these values in equation 34 and simplifying gives

(37) $$\bar{\mathbf{X}}(\bar{\mathbf{M}}\bar{\mathbf{M}}' - rc^2\mathbf{I}) = 0$$

which is Guttman's equation 12.

It might be noted that the latent roots of $\mathbf{H}'$ are exactly the same as those of $\bar{\mathbf{M}}\bar{\mathbf{M}}'$. Actually it can be shown that

(38) $$\bar{\mathbf{M}}\bar{\mathbf{M}}' = \mathbf{D}^{-1/2}\mathbf{H}'\mathbf{D}^{1/2}$$

Hence it is immaterial which is used in obtaining the solution. If we define

N_j = number of subjects responding to category j
N_k = number of subjects responding to category k
N_{jk} = number of subjects responding to both categories j and k

then the general element of $\mathbf{H}'$ is

$$h_{jk} = \frac{N_{jk}}{N_j}$$

where j now refers to the column and k to the row, and the general element of $\bar{\mathbf{M}}\bar{\mathbf{M}}'$ is equal to

$$\frac{N_{jk}}{(N_j N_k)^{1/2}}$$

There are in general $n-r+1$ latent roots, and hence the same number of latent vectors. Guttman (1941) has shown that the largest root of $\bar{\mathbf{M}}\bar{\mathbf{M}}'$ is equal to r, giving a latent vector $\bar{\mathbf{X}}$ equal to a row of unities. As was mentioned above, this is an artifact, since it does not meet the condition imposed in equation 22. The solution to the problem posed is thus the latent vector corresponding to the second largest latent root. This gives the weights which maximize the variance ratio subject to the conditions imposed. Given the weights of the categories, the optimal scores for the subjects are proportional to the average of the weights of the categories they checked.

Both Guttman and Mosteller have suggested that this procedure gives scores on an interval scale. It should be noted, however, that this would not be true in our use of the term, since the relative spacing is a function of both the particular sample of subjects and the particular set of items.

What of the remaining $n-r-1$ solutions? First of all, they are all orthogonal to one another. Second, succeeding solutions account for smaller and smaller proportions of the variance of the matrix. Third, they are all extraneous solutions *as far as the problem posed is concerned*.

However, for the case of a *perfect scale*, Guttman feels that the remaining components are more than simply extraneous solutions. Actually, they form the basis of his theory of the principal components of scalable attitudes. (1950*a*, 1954.)

The idea is that, at least for certain attitudes, the remaining solutions— principal components—represent various components of the attitude.

Guttman has shown, for the case of a perfect scale of dichotomous monotone items, that, if the sets of scores corresponding to each principal component are plotted against original scale rank, the following occurs: The scores corresponding to the first nontrivial component are a monotonic function of the original scale ranks. The scores on the second are a U-shaped function of the ranks; i.e., the curve has one inflection point. In like manner, the scores on the third give two inflection points, on the fourth, three inflection points, and so on. Further, while the linear correlation between the different components is always zero, the non-linear correlation is perfect for a perfect scale.

Guttman interprets the first nontrivial principal component as the *metric component*, since it is monotonically related to the scale ranks.

The second nontrivial component gives a U-shaped curve when plotted against original scale ranks. So does the empirically determined intensity of feeling about the attitude discussed in the immediately preceding section. Hence, the second component is interpreted as the *intensity* component.

More recently, both the third and fourth principal components have also received psychological interpretation—the third as the *closure* com-ponent and the fourth as the *involution* component. Through asking new kinds of questions about the attitude of interest, empirical indices have been developed for the subjects which, when plotted against original scale ranks, show two inflection points in the one case and three in the other. Hence, they are identified with the third and fourth principal components, respectively.

We have already seen that intensity questions are of the general form "How strongly do you feel about this?" Closure questions deal with topics like "How sure are you that you have made up your mind about this?" or "Are you likely to change your mind about this?" Involution questions deal with whether or not the person is putting forth much effort thinking about the problem—"Do you spend much time wondering about it?".

Now the investigation of the relations between these and perhaps other different aspects of attitudes is both interesting and important. But we might wonder whether or not the indices developed in this way have anything to do with the extraneous vectors resulting from the maximization problem posed earlier. In a rather trivial sense, of course, they do—the scatter diagrams of each of the three indices mentioned above with the scale ranks apparently give regressions with the appropriate number of bending points—this is what brings about the identification in the first place. Actually, as we shall see, the question is really a meaningless one, since, in Guttman's theoretical development, the *mathematical* principal components are forever beyond actual determination.

This is because Guttman poses the maximization problem in terms of the "infinite universe of content" and the "infinite population of subjects." The principal components he is talking about refer to the principal components determined from the *universe* and *population* and not from a *sample* therefrom. The *mathematical* principal components are *not invariant* over samples of either items or subjects (Guttman, 1954, p. 233) and, since in the case of the items, we have no way of knowing the characteristics of the "sample" with respect to the infinite "universe" of items, the *mathematical* principal components of any set of real data will not, in general, either correspond to or provide much information about the universe parameters. Since the crucial thing about the *empirical* intensity function (and presumably also the empirical closure and involution functions) is that it *is* invariant over samples of items, it follows that any close correspondence between the mathematical components for any real set of data and the analogous empirical components must be purely fortuitous.

We can, of course, still identify the empirical functions with the corresponding parameters of the infinite universe. However, since infinite universes of items can neither be observed nor analyzed, identification of the empirical functions and the universe parameters would be more a matter of definition or assumption than of experimental fact.

8. MULTIDIMENSIONAL EXTENSIONS

Coombs and his students (Coombs and Kao, 1954, 1955; Bennett, 1951, 1956; Milholland, 1953; Hays, 1954) have been working on extensions of the Guttman model to the multidimensional case. In the unidimensional model for dichotomous monotone items, it will be recalled that, with n stimuli, only $n+1$ of the possible 2^n response patterns could occur in a perfect scale. If nonscale patterns occur to such an extent that the data do not meet the requirements for a unidimensional scale, the experimenter might take any of several alternative courses. He might, first of all, simply conclude that the items (or "universe") are not scalable and let it go at that. He might instead reject certain items or certain individuals, if, by so doing, those remaining meet the criteria. A further alternative would be to attempt to apply one of the probability models discussed in the following chapter. Finally, he might wish to generalize the deterministic model to several dimensions. It is this latter alternative which is of interest in the present section.

In the multidimensional models to be considered here, the responses to items are considered to be determined by several attributes. The precise manner in which the responses are related to the dimensionality, the subject parameters, and the item parameters depends on the particular model.

Several different models have been devised by Coombs and his co-workers. We shall consider here the two classes particularly relevant to monotone dichotomous items—the conjunctive and disjunctive models on the one hand, and the compensatory models on the other.

The Conjunctive and Disjunctive Models

In the Guttman scale, items and subjects can be considered as points on a single dimension. The response of a subject to an item can be given a direct interpretation in terms of the ordering relation $>$; i.e., if subject i "passes" item j, then $i > j$, and, if subject i "fails" item j, then $j > i$, with respect to the single underlying dimension.

In the multidimensional models, subjects and items can be again considered as points, only this time in a multidimensional space. The interpretation of the response of a subject to an item is a generalization of the $>$ relation in the unidimensional case. Coombs has called it a "dominance" relation.

In the *conjunctive* model, the subject passes an item if he is as great or greater than that item on each and every one of the dimensions of the space. He fails the item if the item is greater than the subject on any *one* or more of the dimensions. Bennett has given an example of a case where we would expect this kind of situation to apply (in Coombs and Kao, 1954): He considered a subject taking a history test in French. In order to pass, the subject must know enough French to enable him to translate the questions. He must also know enough history before he can pass. If he does not know enough French, he will fail, regardless of how good a historian he is. In like manner, he will fail if he is a poor historian, regardless of how well he can translate the questions. In this situation, an excess of ability in one dimension does not compensate for a shortage in another.

In the *disjunctive* model, a positive response is interpreted as indicating that the subject is as great or greater than the item on any *one* or more dimensions, and a negative response as indicating that the subject is below the item on *every one* of the dimensions. As a possible example, consider a learning problem that can be solved in either of two ways—by learning an underlying principle, or by learning to answer the items by rote. If we assume two underlying attributes, "ability for rote learning" and "ability to stumble onto underlying principles," we have the disjunctive situation. A subject can pass if he has either enough rote-learning ability or enough stumbling-onto-principles ability. However, again, the two do not compensate for each other. A person with "just not enough" of both dimensions fails, whereas a person with just enough of either passes, even though his ability on the second dimension is virtually nil.

As might be suspected, a duality exists between the conjunctive and disjunctive models which makes them *mathematically* equivalent (even though psychologically they are quite dissimilar). If in the conjunctive case we reverse our terminology and call people "items" and items "people," then the problem immediately transforms to the disjunctive case. That is, if the subject must have as much or more of *all* dimensions to pass an item, then the item must have as much or more of any *one* dimension to pass the subject. The same is true of the disjunctive case: Reversing the role of items and subjects transforms the disjunctive case into the conjunctive.

We also have a duality with respect to pass and fail. If we reverse the roles of pass and fail, we convert from one model into the other, for, if the subject must exceed the item on all dimensions to *pass* the item, then it follows that, if the subject does not exceed the item on any one dimension, he will *fail*. Again, the same is true for the disjunctive case.

Hence, we have the two-way duality between pass and fail on the one hand, and subjects and items on the other. Any procedures or theorems developed for any one of the situations must necessarily apply to all the others, assuming that the appropriate transformations are made in the original data matrix. (For a set-theoretical proof of this duality, the reader is referred to Coombs and Kao.) From a *mathematical* standpoint, therefore, the models are identical, and we need consider only one. We shall choose the conjunctive-subjects-pass case first discussed.

The general problem can be stated as follows: Given the response patterns of the subjects to the items, can we (*a*) determine the dimensionality of the space: i.e., the number of underlying attributes, and (*b*) obtain the order of the subjects and items along each of the attributes, or perhaps, determine the position of subjects and items in the multidimensional space.

The space with which the model deals might be called an ordinal space. Orthogonal axes of this space correspond to the underlying attributes. Subjects and items can be considered as points in the ordinal space. The subject passes the item if he is above the item on every relevant dimension; he fails the item if he is below it on any dimension. Thus, in the two-dimensional illustration shown in Figure 7, an individual located at

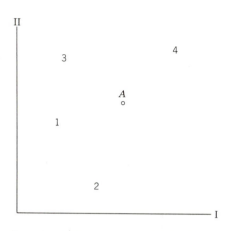

Figure 7. Two-dimensional illustrative example for the conjunctive model.
An individual at point *A* passes items 1 and 2 and fails items 3 and 4.

point *A* passes items 1 and 2 since he is above each on both dimensions. He fails item 3 because he is lower than this item on dimension II (even though above it on dimension I). Since he is lower than item 4 on both dimensions, he fails this item also.

The concept of "relevant dimensions" is of some importance. The questions asked must be such that the same set of attributes determine the responses in all cases (though any given item may require a zero amount of any attribute). Coombs and Kao give the following example where the requirement of relevance is not met. Consider two underlying attributes —one dealing with spelling ability and the other with ability to find synonyms. Assume two of the items are the following:

1. Spell "intermediate."
2. Give a synonym for "perspicuity."

The word intermediate may be both easier to spell and easier to find a synonym for. Yet the questions asked are such that a subject could easily fail item 1 and pass item 2, an inadmissible situation for this model. This is because "difficulty of finding a synonym for" is not *relevant* in question 1, and "difficulty of spelling" is not relevant in question 2.   In the subsequent discussion, we shall assume that the items are such that the same set of attributes is relevant for all items.

This, then, gives a brief picture of the model.   Let us see what sort of conclusions can be drawn from a set of raw data.   We shall consider only the completely deterministic case.   Procedures that allow for error variance have not yet been devised.

One of the first theorems of interest (given by Bennett) is that any item failed by any subject must be higher on at least one dimension than any item passed by that subject.

This theorem is of importance both in solving for the configuration and in giving a lower bound of the dimensionality.   The lower bound can be gotten as follows: Consider only those response patterns in which a single item is failed.   Then the dimensionality must be at least as great as the number of different failed items, since each failed item must be highest on at least one dimension.

A second estimate of the dimensionality is given by consideration of the number of possible response patterns having a given number of fails for a given number of stimuli in a given number of dimensions.   Let n equal the number of items, n_e the number of errors (i.e., the number of failed items or number of negative responses) in a given response pattern, and d the number of dimensions.   Then the maximum number of different response patterns having exactly n_e errors out of a total of n items for a space of dimensionality d is equal to

$$
(39) \qquad \binom{d + n_e - 1}{d - 1} = \frac{(d + n_e - 1)!}{(d - 1)!(n_e)!}
$$

(Coombs and Kao attribute this formula to Milholland.)

In order to estimate the minimum dimensionality of n stimuli, we would first count the number of different response patterns in the empirical data having exactly one error, two errors, three errors, $\cdots$, $n-1$ errors. (For any dimensionality, there is always only one possible pattern having no errors, and one having all errors, of course.)   We can then compute, for any assumed dimensionality, the maximum number of possible patterns of n stimuli having exactly one error, two errors, three errors, $\cdots$, $n-1$ errors.   If any of the $n-1$ empirical values exceeds its corresponding maximum possible value, then the assumed dimensionality is too low. Hence, the lower bound of the dimensionality would be equal to the smallest assumed value of d for which no empirical value exceeds the theoretically maximum possible.

An Example of Five Stimuli Which Fit the Conjunctive Model in Two Dimensions

Table 9 gives a hypothetical set of raw data. As before, an × indicates a positive response to the item, an ○ a negative response. Figure 8 gives

Table 9. Hypothetical Data Matrix for the Conjunctive Model

		A	B	C	D	E
	1	×	○	○	○	○
	2	×	×	○	○	○
	3	×	×	○	×	○
	4	×	×	×	×	○
	5	×	×	×	×	×
	6	○	×	×	×	×
Subject Types	7	○	○	×	×	×
	8	○	○	○	×	×
	9	○	○	○	×	○
	10	○	×	○	○	○
	11	○	×	○	×	○
	12	○	×	×	×	○
	13	○	○	×	×	○
	14	○	○	○	○	○

Figure 8. Two-dimensional configuration corresponding to the data of Table 9. Numbered regions in the figure correspond to response patterns of like numbered subject types in Table 9.

the corresponding configuration. The numbered regions in Figure 8 correspond to the similarly numbered response patterns in Table 9. In order to reconstruct the configuration, given only the raw data, more or less cut-and-try procedures are used—no neat, compact solution is yet available. We can first obtain a lower bound for the dimensionality, using Milholland's formula. We first count the number of patterns having exactly n_e errors ($n_e = 1, 2, \cdots, n-1$). The observed values are given in the first row of Table 10. Using the formula, we compute corresponding theoretical values for one dimension and for two dimensions. These are given in rows 2 and 3 of Table 10. It is apparent that at least

Table 10. OBSERVED AND MAXIMUM POSSIBLE PATTERNS HAVING EXACTLY n_e ERRORS FOR A ONE- AND A TWO-DIMENSIONAL SPACE

		n_e			
		1	2	3	4
Observed		2	3	4	3
Maximum,	$d = 1$	1	1	1	1
Maximum,	$d = 2$	2	3	4	5

two dimensions are necessary. Then, using Bennett's theorem, we proceed to reconstruct the configuration. From patterns 4 and 6 we see that items E and A are each highest on one dimension. We next look at the patterns with two errors (patterns 3, 7, 12). In pattern 3, C and E were failed, in 7, A and B were failed, and, in 12, A and E were failed. This suggests that on one dimension the order is $EC(ABD)$ and on the other $AB(CDE)$. Proceeding in the same fashion, we next look at those patterns with three errors, with four errors, etc. In general, before we can obtain a complete ordering on the two dimensions, it will be necessary to assume that in the final configuration there are no empty regions: e.g., that a response pattern occurs if it is possible for it to occur. With this assumption, the procedure yields the order $ECDBA$ for one dimension and $ABCED$ for the other.

It should be noted that, although we can locate the individuals in their proper region according to their response pattern, it is not always possible to order them with respect to the two underlying dimensions. Thus, individuals in regions 1, 2, 3, 4, and 5 cannot be ordered with respect to dimension 2, although with respect to dimension 1 we know that all individuals in region 5 are greater than those in region 4, who in turn are all greater than those in region 3, etc. Individuals in region 14, those who failed all of the items, cannot be ordered on either dimension.

The Compensatory Models

In the conjunctive situation, an excess of one dimension was of no help to the subject if he was short on another. He failed the item regardless of how high he was on the others. The compensatory models deal with the case where an excess on one dimension *can* compensate for shortages on another. In the compensatory models, passing or failing is considered to be determined by whether or not a weighted composite of amounts of the relevant dimensions exceeds a particular value. This is the usual notion dealt with, for example, in the construction of indices, in analysis of variance, and in factor analysis. Ordinarily the *linear* case is assumed: i.e., the case where the subject passes the item if a simple weighted sum of his amounts of the attributes exceeds a particular value.

Two kinds of compensatory models will be differentiated here—the *stimulus* compensatory and the *individual* compensatory. The difference between the two concerns whether the weights are considered to be characteristic of the item or of the individual. In the stimulus compensatory model, the weights are characteristic of the items. For any given item, the weighting function is fixed and constant for all subjects. This is the case ordinarily dealt with. For example, consider an arithmetic item that involves both reasoning and number ability. The item itself is considered to determine the relative weights of the two attributes. If the weighted sum for an individual exceeds the minimum required, he passes the item; otherwise he fails.

In the individual compensatory model, the situation is reversed. Here, it is the individual that determines the weighting function, which then must be considered as constant over items for that individual. This is the sort of situation involved when a group of English readers score a set of essays, and an inverse factor analysis is performed on the results. Assume that there are a number of attributes underlying quality of essays. Each reader determines for himself the relative importance of the various attributes. It is assumed that the score he gives any particular essay is determined by this weighting function. Different individuals may use different weighting functions, but it is assumed that each individual keeps his own weighting function constant over all of the essays.

Again, there is a duality situation here which makes the two mathematically equivalent even though psychologically different. Reversing the roles of subject and item converts from one model into the other. Hence we will consider only the stimulus compensatory model in any detail.

In the compensatory model, the underlying space is assumed to correspond to the positive segment of an r-dimensional, real, Euclidean space.

We will consider the subjects as points in this space, and the items as vectors. The basic notion is that a positive response of subject i to item j (i passes j) implies that the point corresponding to subject i is on the positive side of the hyperplane normal to the vector corresponding to item j. Consider two items, j and k, in two dimensions, as illustrated in Figure 9. The two items are represented by vectors j and k. The hyperplanes normal to these vectors divide the space into four regions, numbered 1 through 4. The positive side of each hyperplane is the side away from

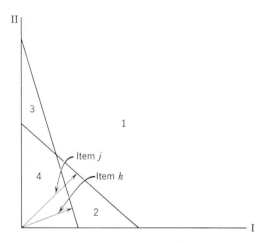

Figure 9. Vectors and hyperplanes corresponding to two stimuli. The hyperplanes divide the space into four regions, each corresponding to a given response pattern.

the origin. Hence, individuals in region 1 pass both items, individuals in region 2 pass item k and fail item j, those in region 3 pass item j and fail item k, while those in region 4 fail both items. We can define several additional concepts:

Generalized item difficulty = length of the vector corresponding to the item. It should be noted that this will not in general equal the proportion of people passing the item, since this will depend on the distribution of subjects.

Generalized ability of a subject = distance of the point corresponding to that subject from the origin.

Relative factor loading of an item on the underlying dimension = cosine of the angle between the direction of the dimension and the direction of the vector.

It is the relative factor loadings of the items on an ordinal scale that Coombs solves for. It is important to note that the relative factor loading does *not* correspond to the projection of the end of the vector onto the dimension, which is the usual notion of a factor loading. Actually, if we could obtain relative factor loadings and difficulties on a ratio scale, then the relative factor loading times the difficulty of the item would equal the projection of the terminus of the vector on the underlying dimension.

This gives a brief summary of the model itself. Two further steps have been taken: A procedure has been devised for obtaining a lower bound of the dimensionality in the general case, and procedures have been devised for determining the relative factor loadings (and hence the general form of the configuration) for the two-dimensional case. Solutions for more than two dimensions have yet to be devised.

Coombs gives the following recursion formula for estimating the maximum number of distinct response patterns p for n stimuli in r dimensions:

$$(40) \qquad\qquad p = \sum_{a=0}^{r} \binom{n}{a}$$

where $a =$ an index which takes on successive values from 0 to r

$$\binom{n}{0} \equiv 1 \text{ for any value of } n$$

$$\binom{n}{a} \equiv 0 \text{ for any value of } a \text{ greater than } n$$

$$\binom{n}{a} \equiv \frac{n!}{a!(n-a)!} \text{ for all other values of } a$$

As an example, consider the number of possible response patterns for four stimuli in two dimensions. Then

$$p = \sum_{a=0}^{2} \binom{4}{a} = \binom{4}{0} + \binom{4}{1} + \binom{4}{2} = 1 + 4 + 6 = 11$$

Hence there are eleven possible distinct response patterns which could occur, given four stimuli lying in two dimensions.

To obtain a lower bound for the dimensionality of n stimuli, we would thus first count up the number of different response patterns which occurred empirically, and, second, use the formula given above to determine the smallest number of dimensions which permits that many patterns to occur.

Procedures which are exact, though tedious, have been given by Coombs and Kao for solving for the relative factor loadings, and, hence, the configuration, for the special case of two dimensions. The procedure given below differs somewhat from that of Coombs, although it is based on the same general principle.

Consider any three stimuli in two dimensions. Assuming that all possible patterns occur (i.e., the three hyperplanes intersect with one

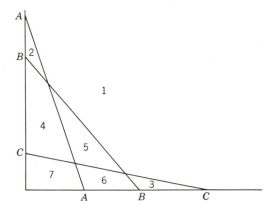

Region	Pattern A B C		
1	×	×	×
2	o	×	×
3	×	×	o
4	o	o	×
5	×	o	×
6	×	o	o
7	o	o	o

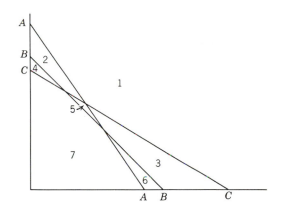

Region	Patterns A B C		
1	×	×	×
2	o	×	×
3	×	×	o
4	o	o	×
5	o	×	o
6	×	o	o
7	o	o	o

Figure 10. Illustration of the two possible configurations for three items in two dimensions assuming items all intersect with one another.

another), only two general configurations can occur. These are diagramed in Figure 10. The difference between the two is whether the hyperplane corresponding to the middle stimulus passes above or below the intersection of the hyperplanes of the other two stimuli. Note that in each case the three stimuli divide the space into seven regions. Now, in general, the number of possible response patterns for three stimuli is 2^n, or, in this case, eight. One of the response patterns is ruled out in each of the two possible cases. In the first case, it is the response pattern $\circ \times \circ$. In the second, it is the reverse, $\times \circ \times$. Note further, that the remaining six patterns occur as three pairs, with one member of the pair being the reverse of the other. Thus we have

<blockquote>
Patterns 1 and 7—$\circ \circ \circ$ and $\times \times \times$
Patterns 2 and 6—$\times \circ \circ$ and $\circ \times \times$
Patterns 3 and 4—$\times \times \circ$ and $\circ \circ \times$
</blockquote>

The information-giving pattern is the one that is left over—the one for which the reverse pattern does not occur. It will either have two passes and a fail, or two fails and a pass. In each case, *the item to which the odd response was given is between the other two on both dimensions.* Since the relative loadings on one dimension must, in the two-dimensional case, be the exact reverse of the relative loadings on the other dimension, the pattern gives us the order of the three items on the two dimensions.

Table 11. HYPOTHETICAL RAW-DATA MATRIX FOR THE
COMPENSATORY MODEL

		Items				
		A	B	C	D	E
	1	×	×	×	×	×
	2	×	×	○	×	×
	3	×	×	×	○	×
	4	×	○	×	○	×
	5	×	○	×	×	×
	6	×	×	×	×	○
	7	×	○	×	×	○
Subject Types	8	○	○	×	×	○
	9	○	○	×	×	×
	10	○	×	×	○	×
	11	×	×	○	○	×
	12	○	×	○	○	×
	13	○	○	○	○	×
	14	○	○	×	○	×
	15	○	○	×	○	○
	16	○	○	○	○	○

Further, *if the odd response is negative, the hyperplane corresponding to the middle stimulus passes above the intersection of the hyperplanes corresponding to the other two stimuli; if the odd response is positive, the hyperplane passes below that intersection.*   This alone gives us enough information to solve for the relative factor loadings, and to reconstruct the configuration to some extent.   We say "to some extent" because no information is available concerning the relative difficulties of the items.   The configuration we obtain will divide the space into the proper number of regions with the proper response pattern in each, but will not give us much information about the relative lengths of the different item vectors.

Consider the raw-data matrix presented in Table 11.   We shall find the pattern for which no reverse pattern is present for all subsets of three items. These patterns are listed in Table 12, along with the corresponding deductions from each concerning the order of the relative factor loadings

Table 12

Items	Unique Pattern	Order on Dimension I	Order on Dimension II
ABC	○ × ×	*BAC*	*CAB*
ABD	× ○ ○	*BAD*	*DAB*
ABE	× ○ ×	*EBA(CD)*	*(CD)ABE*
BCD	× × ○	*EBADC*	*CDABE*
BCE	○ × ×	*EBADC*	*CDABE*
CDE	× ○ ×	*EBADC*	*CDABE*

on the two dimensions.   The order on each dimension is completely determined by the time the fourth pattern is reached.   The remaining two patterns serve only to confirm the two orders.   Taking the additional information given in the sign of the odd response in each pattern, we can obtain a reconstruction of the configuration such as is illustrated in Figure 11.

If we consider the case where some of the hyperplanes do not intersect (in the positive segment of the space which we are considering) with every other item, the problem becomes a little less straightforward.   In this case, a subset of three items may yield anywhere from four patterns through seven patterns.   In all cases, however, the configuration can be reconstructed to the extent of determining (*a*) the order in which the hyperplanes intersect on the axes, and (*b*) the proper number of regions, each of which has a one-to-one relation with one of the observed response patterns. The order of the relative factor loadings, on the other hand, may not be completely determined.

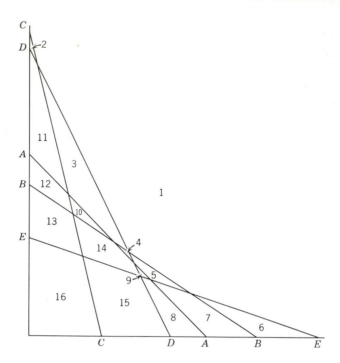

Figure 11. Two-dimensional configuration corresponding to the data of Table 11. Numbered regions correspond to similarly numbered subject types of Table 11.

Summary Statement

It is immediately apparent that a considerable amount of work needs to be done on these models before they will become of much practical use. Several of the primary problems are listed below, most of which have been noted previously by Coombs and Kao.

1. No compact solution is available for either the conjunctive or the compensatory case.

2. The models are completely deterministic. No error is tolerated. Some procedure for dealing with error would appear to be essential before the models will become of practical importance.

3. The solutions may not be unique. This is particularly true where the data are incomplete—where regions occur with no corresponding empirical response pattern. According to Coombs and Kao, Milholland found that, in the conjunctive case, even a complete set of response patterns may not yield a unique solution when the dimensionality is greater than two.

4. Any of the models can be applied to any set of data, and each will fit perfectly if the dimensionality is raised high enough. As a criterion for choosing among models, Coombs and Kao suggest that the appropriate model would have no more dimensions than an inappropriate one, and would involve fewer empty regions.

It might be noted here that, if we allow for the possibility that non-parallel hyperplanes in the compensatory model might not intersect

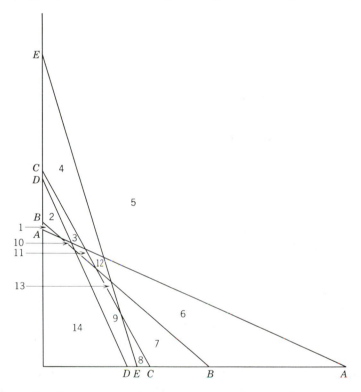

Figure 12. Compensatory solution to the conjunctive data given in Table 9.

within the positive quadrant, the conjunctive model becomes a special case of the compensatory model, at least for two-dimensional configurations. That is, any two-dimensional conjunctive solution can be transformed in a one-to-one manner into a corresponding compensatory solution. The reverse is not true, however. This is apparent from Figure 10. The first of the two patterns cannot occur in the conjunctive situation. Hence, the compensatory model is the more general of the two. A compensatory solution for the conjunctive data given in Table 9 is shown in Figure 12.

▶13

Probability Models ◀
for Categorical Data

1. INTRODUCTION

In this chapter we shall continue the discussion of response models designed for application to categorical data. The models considered in the previous chapter were completely deterministic; that is, the models themselves made no provision for variation in responses of subjects to items above and beyond that due to the separate relation of each subject and each item to the underlying variable. Few if any sets of empirical data fit the deterministic models exactly. Hence, the task became one of evaluating the degree to which the model approximated the data, the general notion being that, if there were not a great deal of difference between the empirical response patterns and those generated from the model, then use of the model could not lead one far astray. The difficulties arose in deciding what degree of approximation was necessary, and in devising means of specifying closeness of approximation. Statistical notions of goodness of fit were not applicable. The actual procedure used involved setting up and applying a number of interlocking, rule-of-thumb criteria.

In the present chapter, we shall be concerned with the probabilistic approach to the same general problem. In general, the basic notion is pretty much the same—the assumption of an underlying variable in terms of which the subjects and items are characterized. The probability models differ from the deterministic models in that they introduce explicitly notions which account for variation in responses above and beyond that determined by the subject and item parameters. In the deterministic models, the response is completely determined by the parameters associated with the subject and the item. In the probabilistic models, this complete determinism is replaced by a probability statement. The parameters associated with the subject and item determine the probability with which he will respond in a given way. In general, statistical notions of goodness of fit are applicable, at least theoretically. We can ask whether empirically obtained proportions differ from corresponding theoretical probabilities more than would be expected by chance alone.

We shall consider several different probability models in this chapter. The next section will deal with Lazarsfeld's general latent-structure theory. We shall find that the general model is completely abstract, and that additional postulates are necessary before the model can be applied to actual data. The additional postulates can take any of several different forms, leading to different special cases of the general model. Sections 3 and 4 are concerned with two of these cases developed by Lazarsfeld and his associates—the linear model and the latent-distance model. Section 5 is concerned with the normal-ogive model developed by Tucker and Lord. Though developed in a different context, the normal-ogive model can be considered as a third special case of the general latent-structure model. Section 6 gives an alternative way of looking at the normal-ogive model, relating Tucker's work to Thurstone's early mental-age model and to the law of categorical judgment. Finally, we shall consider Thurstone's method of similar reactions.

2. THE GENERAL LATENT-STRUCTURE MODEL

The latent-structure model represents one very general way of conceptualizing the measurement problems ordinarily encountered in the assessment of attitudes, abilities, and personality traits. It provides a framework for stating explicitly the assumptions ordinarily involved in such measurement, and, at the same time, provides the framework for developing the means of testing the adequacy of these assumptions.

The situation might be summarized as follows: A unidimensional continuum of the variable of interest to the investigator is assumed to exist. Subjects are assumed to be distributed along this continuum according to some (unknown) probability distribution. The investigator collects or devises a set of items, the responses to which he feels will be related to this variable. He then administers the items to a group of subjects, with the idea of using the information thus obtained to describe the subjects and perhaps the items in terms of the underlying variable.

We shall not concern ourselves at this time with how the investigator goes about selecting either the items or the subjects, but shall instead take these as given. We shall further find it advantageous to restrict ourselves to the case where the items are all dichotomous, though, as both Lazarsfeld (1950) and Green (1954) point out, this is not strictly a necessary restriction. The raw data, then, will consist of the responses of N subjects to n dichotomous items.

Three basic notions are involved in the general latent-structure model: The notion of a unidimensional continuum of the variable of interest, with the subjects distributed along this continuum according to some unknown probability distribution; the notion of the trace line for characterizing the item in terms of the underlying continuum; and the notion of independence of items at any given point on the underlying continuum. The meaning of the first notion is clear. We shall discuss the others in somewhat more detail.

The notion of the item trace line was introduced briefly in the preceding chapter. For the case of dichotomous items, the trace line for an item gives the probability of a positive response to the item from subjects located at any given value of the underlying variable. It is thus a curve giving the probability of a positive response as a function of position on the underlying variable. In the preceding chapter, we were limited to a consideration of perfect items—items for which the probability of a positive response at any given point is either zero or unity. In the more general case, the probabilities may take on values between zero and unity as well. Figure 1 gives some examples of the sorts of trace lines that might occur.

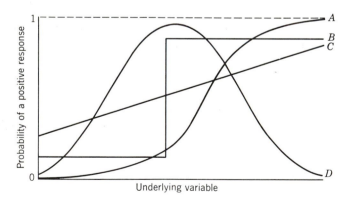

Figure 1. Examples of different types of trace lines. Trace lines A, B, and C correspond to different types of monotone items. Trace line D corresponds to a point item.

Since each item is related to the underlying variable, it follows that the items are related to each other.   In the latent-structure model, it is postulated that no two items have any relationship to each other above and beyond that which can be accounted for by their separate relations to the underlying variable.   That is, if the underlying variable is held constant, or partialed out, the items are all mutually independent of one another. For a group of subjects at any fixed value on the underlying variable, the items are uncorrelated.   This is perhaps the most important single notion in latent-structure analysis.   Most of our discussion of the model will depend directly on this postulate.

The General Accounting Equations

Let

x denote the underlying variable.

$f_i(x)$ represent the trace line of item i as a function of variable x.

$g(x)$ be the density function of the total population of subjects along the underlying variable x.   Thus, $g(x)\,dx$ gives the proportion of subjects within the small interval $(x, x+dx)$.

Then $f_i(x)\,g(x)\,dx$ gives the proportion of people who are within this interval and who respond positively to item i.   If we now integrate over all possible values of x, we obtain p_i, the proportion of people in the total population who respond positively to item i: i.e.,

$$(1) \qquad\qquad p_i = \int_{-\infty}^{+\infty} f_i(x)\, g(x)\, dx$$

Let us now consider the proportion of people who respond positively to both items i and j.   Since we have postulated that, for any fixed value of x, the items are independent, the probability of a positive response to both items for a given x is equal to the product of the separate probabilities. Hence, $[f_i(x)\, f_j(x)]$ gives the probability of a positive response to both items for a given value of x.   Similarly, $[f_i(x)\, f_j(x)\, g(x)\, dx]$ gives the proportion of people who are in the interval $(x, x+dx)$ and who respond positively to both items, and, integrating as before over x, we have

$$(2) \qquad\qquad p_{ij} = \int_{-\infty}^{+\infty} f_i(x)\, f_j(x)\, g(x)\, dx$$

where p_{ij} is equal to the proportion of people in the population who respond positively to both items i and j.

We can proceed in the same way to obtain the proportion of people in the population who respond positively to any three given items, $i, j,$ and k:

$$(3) \qquad p_{ijk} = \int_{-\infty}^{+\infty} f_i(x) \, f_j(x) \, f_k(x) \, g(x) \, dx$$

In general, since we can proceed in a similar fashion for any number of items,

$$(4) \qquad p_{ijkm\cdots} = \int_{-\infty}^{+\infty} f_i(x) \, f_j(x) \, f_k(x) \, f_m(x) \cdots g(x) \, dx$$

The complete set of these equations (one equation for each single item, one for each pair of items, one for each triplet, etc.) completely describes the interrelationships among the items: i.e., the frequency distribution of the response patterns to the items. Lazarsfeld calls them the accounting equations (1950, p. 370).

The terms on the left-hand side of equations 1 through 4 are (theoretically) observable. The terms on the right-hand side, i.e., the "latent" parameters of the items and the distribution of subjects, are unknown. An initial problem of the latent-structure approach is to derive from the relations given in equations 1–4 a set of equations that will enable us to solve for the unknown latent parameters when given the joint proportions.

Actually, the model in the form given by equations 1–4 is completely general. By specifying sufficiently complex functions for the trace lines, $f_i(x)$, any frequency distribution over the 2^n possible patterns could be fitted by the equations. We could reproduce the joint proportions exactly. Hence, additional restrictions or modifications are necessary before the model can rightly be called a scaling theory.

There are two general ways in which the additional restrictions (postulates) have been introduced:

1. Specification of something about the distribution function $g(x)$: i.e., the distribution of subjects on the underlying variable.

2. Specification of the form of the functions $f_i(x)$: e.g., specifying that the items all have trace lines of a given form.

The first procedure has led to the development of the latent-class model. In this model, it is assumed that the function $g(x)$ is a point or discrete distribution: that the subjects are all concentrated at m points. Individuals concentrated at a single point form a *latent class*. Within each latent class, the items are independent. If we let N_s equal the proportion of individuals in class s, and v_{is} equal the probability of a positive response to item i for class s, then, in the general accounting equations, N_s can be substituted for $g(x)$, v_{is} for $f_i(x)$, and a summation over finite classes for the integration over a continuous distribution, giving

$$1 = \sum_{s=1}^{m} N_s \tag{5}$$

$$p_i = \sum_{s=1}^{m} v_{is} N_s \tag{6}$$

$$p_{ij} = \sum_{s=1}^{m} v_{is} v_{js} N_s \tag{7}$$

and, in general,

$$p_{ijk\ldots} = \sum_{s=1}^{m} v_{is} v_{js} v_{ks} \cdots N_s \tag{8}$$

In the latent-class model, observed proportions of the form $\hat{p}_i$, $\hat{p}_{ij}$, and $\hat{p}_{ijk}$ (throughout this chapter, a carat over a symbol denotes a sample estimate) are used to estimate the number of latent classes m, the proportion of subjects within each latent class N_s, and the probability of a positive response to each item for each class v_{is}.

It is important to note that through the assumption that the subjects are concentrated into m classes, with independence of items within each class, we have lost the notion of an underlying unidimensional continuum. There is nothing in the summation equations given above which requires that the classes be ordered in any sense. Actually, the rationale here can be described as one that hypothetically partitions the total population of people into m homogeneous classes, such that within any single class the items are independent. It is thus concerned with *classification into categories or types* rather than with measurement or scaling along some attribute of interest. The parameters N_s and v_{is} which are estimated from the data are parameters that serve to describe the characteristics of the categories rather than to specify the scale values of subjects or items with respect to an underlying continuum.

For this reason, the latent-class model will not be considered further in the present monograph. Computational procedures for estimating the latent parameters have been given by Lazarsfeld and Dudman (1951), Green (1951a, b), Gibson (1951), and Anderson (1954). A large sample theory for the model has been developed by Anderson (1954). The most general procedures readily available at the present time are those given by Green and by Anderson. The model itself is discussed in detail by Lazarsfeld (1950, 1954).

Specification of the form of the trace lines, $f_i(x)$, leads to special cases of the general model which are more relevant to the present discussion. Three special cases will be considered in some detail: The linear model and the latent-distance model, which have been developed by Lazarsfeld (1950, 1951) in the context of latent-structure analysis, and the normal-ogive model, treated by Tucker (1952) and Lord (1953), and which stems out of the area of mental testing. Figure 2 gives examples of the form of the item trace lines postulated by each of three special cases.

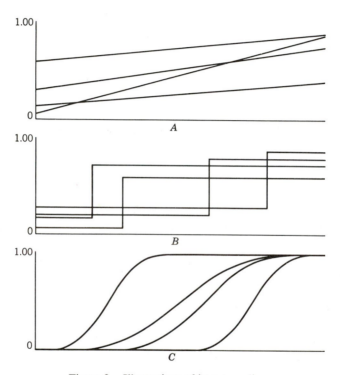

Figure 2.   Illustrations of item trace lines.

A.   The linear model.
B.   The latent-distance model.
C.   The normal-ogive model.

It is, of course, possible to postulate other forms of trace lines. One general equation, suggested by Lazarsfeld (1954) is the equation $y = a + b(x - c)^d$. It would also be desirable to have a solution for the case where the trace lines are normal curves, to serve as a probability model analogous to the deterministic model for point items discussed in the preceding chapter. Thurstone's method of similar reactions (1929*b*) can perhaps be considered as an approximate solution to this latter problem.

General Analytical Procedures

It is convenient to consider the analytical work on latent-structure analysis in terms of three separate, though related problems.

The first problem has already been mentioned: deriving, from the initial postulates of a specific model, sets of equations that enable us to solve for the latent parameters in terms of the theoretically observable joint proportions. Here the problem is treated entirely in terms of population values. The result is a solution that would be adequate if we were given errorless data: i.e., data not subject to sampling fluctuations. Since, in the special cases of the general latent-structure model, the number of equations exceeds the number of parameters to be solved for (given a sufficient number of items), we could use one subset of equations to obtain solutions for the unknown parameters and then use the remaining equations to test the validity of the particular theory.

Actually, of course, we never obtain errorless data. Instead, we observe only fallible estimates of the population joint proportions. With fallible data, use of different subsets of equations will, owing to error, result in somewhat different values being assigned to the latent parameters. Hence, the second problem is one of devising procedures that make efficient use of the available data in estimating the latent parameters.

Finally, we have the problem of evaluating the goodness of fit of the model to the data. For each specific model, we can derive relationships which must obtain between the observable data on the one hand, and the parameters of the items and subject population on the other, if the theory is appropriate. Different special models, of course, imply different relationships. In general, there will be many more observation equations than there are item and subject parameters to be estimated. As a result, the degrees of freedom left over after estimating the latent parameters can be used in evaluating the goodness of fit of the model to the data.

3. THE LINEAR MODEL

In the linear model, it is assumed that all trace lines are straight lines, that is, for any item i the trace line can be expressed by an equation of the form

$$(9) \qquad\qquad f_i(x) = a_i + b_i x$$

At first thought, it would seem impossible for items to have trace lines of this general form. If the parameter b_i is other than zero, the equation says that there will be regions on the underlying continuum for which the probability of a positive response is greater than unity. There will also be regions where the probability is less than zero. Hence, an additional assumption must be made. The assumption made is that the distribution of individuals is limited to that region of the continuum for which the values of $f_i(x)$ for all items range between zero and unity. Thus, trace lines can be linear for the region of the continuum in which individuals occur. And this is the region of interest—it is immaterial whether or not the trace lines depart from linearity outside of the region which contains all of the people. It should be noted, however, that this assumption puts a real limitation on the model. Very sensitive or sharply discriminating items cannot be represented very well. A linear trace line of this type, for example, cannot adequately represent an item that is failed by the bottom 25 per cent and passed by the upper 25 per cent of the subjects. The model thus is limited to relatively insensitive items. It is unique among the scaling models in this respect. Other trace-line models, such as the latent-distance model or the normal-ogive model, can accommodate items of any level of discriminability. The linear model cannot.

The analytical problem is to recover the item parameters and parameters of the distribution of subjects when given the joint proportions (p_i, p_{ij}, p_{ijk}, etc.). Let the distribution of subjects be denoted by $g(x)$ as before, and let us consider proportions rather than frequencies, so that the total area under the distribution curve is equal to unity. Let M_r denote the rth moment of $g(x)$, where

$$(10) \qquad M_r = \int_H x^r \, g(x) \, dx$$

and H indicates that the integration is only over the region for which $f_i(x)$ is between zero and unity.

There will be no loss in generality if we define the unit and origin of x so that

$$(11) \qquad M_1 = 0$$

and

$$(12) \qquad M_2 = 1$$

that is, so that the mean and variance for subjects are zero and one, respectively.

The first problem is to obtain expressions for the item parameters in terms of the marginal proportions for the population. That is, we wish to express the trace-line parameters a_i and b_i as functions of the proportions p_i, p_{ij}, p_{ijk}, etc. It should be noted that we are dealing here with population parameters throughout.

From equation 1, we have

$$p_i = \int_{-\infty}^{+\infty} f_i(x) \, g(x) \, dx$$

which, for the linear model, becomes

(13)
$$p_i = \int_H (a_i + b_i x) \, g(x) \, dx$$

$$= a_i \int_H g(x) \, dx + b_i \int_H x \, g(x) \, dx$$

$$= a_i + b_i M_1$$

and, since $M_1 = 0$ by definition,

(14)
$$p_i = a_i$$

From equation 2, we have

$$p_{ij} = \int_{-\infty}^{+\infty} f_i(x) f_j(x) \, g(x) \, dx$$

which, for the linear case, becomes

(15)
$$p_{ij} = \int_H (a_i + b_i x)(a_j + b_j x) \, g(x) \, dx$$

$$= a_i a_j \int_H g(x) \, dx + a_i b_j \int_H x \, g(x) \, dx + a_j b_i \int_H x \, g(x) \, dx$$

$$+ b_i b_j \int_H x^2 \, g(x) \, dx$$

Since $M_0 = 1$, $M_1 = 0$, and $M_2 = 1$, this simplifies to

(16)
$$p_{ij} = a_i a_j + b_i b_j$$

Since $p_i = a_i$ and $p_j = a_j$,

(17)
$$p_{ij} = p_i p_j + b_i b_j$$

Let us define the cross-product term c_{ij} where

(18)
$$c_{ij} = p_{ij} - p_i p_j$$

From equation 17 it is clear that

(19)
$$c_{ij} = b_i b_j$$

Considering any three items, i, j, and k, we can now solve for the values of b as follows:

(20) $$\frac{c_{ij}c_{ik}}{c_{jk}} = \frac{b_i^2 b_j b_k}{b_j b_k} = b_i^2$$

or

(21) $$b_i = \left(\frac{c_{ik}c_{ij}}{c_{jk}}\right)^{1/2}$$

The equation for the trace line of the ith item thus becomes

(22) $$f_i(x) = p_i + x \left(\frac{c_{ij}c_{ik}}{c_{jk}}\right)^{1/2}$$

Thus, if theoretical proportions were available, equation 18 could be used to determine the cross products, and then equations 14 and 21 could be used to determine the trace line of the ith item, as given by equation 22. In order to solve for the coefficients of the trace lines, only proportions of the form p_i and p_{ij} are needed. Higher-order joint proportions (such as p_{ijk}) are not necessary for this solution.

Determination of the Higher Moments of the Density Function $g(x)$

It is also possible to solve for the higher-order moments of the distribution of subjects in terms of the theoretical joint-occurrence proportions. To do so, it will be desirable to define what Lazarsfeld calls the *symmetric parameters* (1951, part II, paper 1). The symmetric parameter is a generalization to r stimuli of the cross-product term c_{ij} defined in equation 18. Let the symmetric parameter for any r stimuli be denoted $c_{i_1 j_2 \cdots t_r}$. (The first subscripts, i, j, $\cdots$, t, denote the particular stimuli; the second subscripts are added where necessary to keep track of the number of stimuli involved. We shall use the second subscript whenever the number of stimuli itself is a parameter and shall omit it whenever the number of stimuli is specified.) Then define

(23) $$c_{i_1 j_2 \cdots t_r} = \int_{-\infty}^{+\infty} [f_{i_1}(x) - p_{i_1}][f_{j_2}(x) - p_{j_2}] \cdots [f_{t_r}(x) - p_{t_r}] g(x)\, dx$$

The symmetric parameter can be expressed directly in terms of the joint proportions. Thus, for example,

(24) $$\begin{aligned} c_{ij} &= \int [f_i(x) - p_i][f_j(x) - p_j]\, g(x)\, dx \\ &= \int f_i(x) f_j(x)\, g(x)\, dx - p_i \int f_j(x)\, g(x)\, dx - p_j \int f_i(x)\, g(x)\, dx \\ &\quad + p_i p_j \int g(x)\, dx \\ &= p_{ij} - p_i p_j - p_i p_j + p_i p_j \\ &= p_{ij} - p_i p_j \end{aligned}$$

which is the same as equation 18. In like manner,

$$(25) \quad c_{ijk} = \int [f_i(x) - p_i][f_j(x) - p_j][f_k(x) - p_k]g(x)\, dx$$
$$= \int f_i(x) f_j(x) f_k(x) g(x)\, dx - \Sigma p_i \int f_j(x) f_k(x) g(x)\, dx$$
$$+ \Sigma p_i p_j \int f_k(x) g(x)\, dx - p_i p_j p_k \int g(x)\, dx$$
$$= p_{ijk} - \Sigma p_i p_{jk} + \Sigma p_i p_j p_k - p_i p_j p_k$$

where Σ indicates a summation over all combinations of subscripts with no duplication (e.g., $\Sigma p_i p_j p_k \equiv p_i p_j p_k + p_j p_k p_i + p_k p_i p_j$ and $\Sigma p_i p_{jk} \equiv p_i p_{jk} + p_j p_{ik} + p_k p_{ij}$).

The general expression,

$$c_{i_1 j_2 k_3 \cdots t_r} = \int [f_{i_1}(x) - p_{i_1}][f_{j_2}(x) - p_{j_2}][f_{k_3}(x) - p_{k_3}] \cdots$$
$$[f_{t_r}(x) - p_{t_r}]\, g(x)\, dx$$

after expansion and substitution, becomes

$$(26) \quad c_{i_1 j_2 k_3 \cdots t_r} = p_{i_1 j_2 k_3 \cdots t_r} - \Sigma p_{i_1} p_{j_2 k_3 \cdots t_r}$$
$$+ \Sigma p_{i_1} p_{j_2} p_{k_3 \cdots t_r} - \cdots \pm p_{i_1} p_{j_2} p_{k_3} \cdots p_{t_r}$$

But we can also express $c_{i_1 j_2 k_3 \cdots t_r}$ in terms of the moments of $g(x)$. For the linear case, since $f_i(x) = a_i + b_i x$, and since $p_i = a_i$, the general equation for any r items becomes

$$(27) \quad c_{i_1 j_2 k_3 \cdots t_r} = \int (b_{i_1} x)(b_{j_2} x)(b_{k_3} x) \cdots (b_{t_r} x)\, g(x)\, dx$$

or

$$c_{i_1 j_2 \cdots t_r} = b_{i_1} b_{j_2} \cdots b_{t_r} \int x^r g(x)\, dx$$

and finally

$$(28) \quad c_{i_1 j_2 \cdots t_r} = b_{i_1} b_{j_2} \cdots b_{t_r} M_r$$

Thus, for any two stimuli, i and j,

$$(29) \quad c_{ij} = b_i b_j M_2$$

and, since the second moment is defined to be equal to unity, equation 29 is identical with equation 19.

In like manner, for any three stimuli, i, j, and k,

$$(30) \quad c_{ijk} = b_i b_j b_k M_3$$

Solving for M_3, we have

$$(31) \quad M_3 = \frac{c_{ijk}}{b_i b_j b_k}$$

In general, for any r stimuli, the rth moment is given by

$$(32) \quad M_r = \frac{c_{i_1 j_2 k_3 \cdots t_r}}{b_{i_1} b_{j_2} b_{k_3} \cdots b_{t_r}}$$

Thus, given the joint proportions for n stimuli, we can solve for the first n moments of the distribution function.

Problems of Estimation

The preceding equations have dealt entirely in terms of population parameters. Solutions for the two parameters for each item (equations 14 and 21) and the moments of the distribution function (equation 32) were given in terms of the population joint proportions. Little has been done thus far on the problem of estimation of these parameters from observed proportions obtained from a sample of observations. One procedure, suggested by Lazarsfeld (1951, part II, paper 1) would be simply to apply the same equations, using observed proportions in place of the corresponding population values. Thus the observed proportion, $\hat{p}_i$ can be taken as an estimate of the item parameter a_i (equation 13).

Several procedures are available for estimating the item slope parameter b_i. We could, of course, use equation 21. There would be as many estimates of a given b_i as there are combinations of i, j, and k ($i \neq j \neq k$). An average of the estimates would be taken as the value wanted.

A more interesting procedure makes use of the techniques of factor analysis. In the errorless case, the matrix of cross products, i.e., the table giving the cross products of item i ($i = 1, 2, \cdots, n$) and item j ($j = 1, 2, \cdots, n, j \neq i$) is a symmetric matrix of rank one with diagonal cells vacant. The problem of estimation of the item parameters b_i from the cross products c_{ij} is thus precisely equivalent to the analytical problem of Spearman's single-factor theory (Spearman, 1927). It is worth noting that the cross product of any two items c_{ij} is identical to the *covariance* of the two items. Hence, the matrix of cross products of pairs of items is a matrix of covariances. It differs from the correlation matrix (of phi coefficients) usually used in factor analysis only in that the elements of the rows and columns have not been multiplied by the reciprocals of the standard deviations of the items concerned. The cross products c_{ij} and slope parameters b_i, b_j are analogous, respectively, to the correlations between tests and the factor loadings of tests on the single common factor. Hence, any of the solutions developed for the single common-factor model are also applicable here. One of the simplest and quickest of the estimation procedures (see Spearman, 1927, p. xvi, or Thurstone, 1947, p. 276), when translated to the present problem, becomes

$$(33) \qquad \hat{b}_i = \left(\frac{A_i^2 - B_i}{C - 2A_i} \right)^{1/2}$$

where A_i = the sum of the $n-1$ entries in column i of the observed cross-product matrix (the vacant diagonal cell is omitted)

A_i^2 = the square of A_i

B_i = sum of the *squares* of the $n-1$ entries in column i of the observed cross-product matrix (again omitting the vacant diagonal cell)

C = the sum of all $n(n-1)$ entries in the observed cross-product matrix (again omitting the vacant diagonal cells)

The moments of the distribution of subjects can be estimated through use of equation 32. Since there are $\binom{n}{r}$ estimates available for the rth moment $(r = 3, 4, \cdot \cdot \cdot, n)$, an average would be taken in each case as the value wanted.

Scoring the Subjects

Nothing has been said thus far about assigning scale values to the subjects. Although inverse-probability procedures could be used, the labor involved would seem to be prohibitive with more than a very few items. Lazarsfeld has given an illustration of the procedure, using response patterns to three stimuli (1951, part II, paper 1).

If the stimuli are all sensed in the same direction, which in the present case means that they are sensed so that the slopes of the trace lines are all positive, then the expected number of positive responses is monotonically related to the scale value on the underlying continuum. Hence, if a respectable number of items is used, the total number of positive responses given by a subject would be highly correlated with the scale values assigned by more elaborate procedures. This simple index would seem to be adequate for most purposes, though it would have only ordinal properties. However, since the first n moments of the distribution can be computed, we could presumably transform the raw-score distribution into one with moments equal to those computed from the data, and then consider the transformed scores to be referred to an interval scale.

Goodness of Fit of the Model to the Data

A preliminary test of goodness of fit can be obtained by using the estimated slope parameters, $\hat{b}_i$, in equation 19 to obtain a matrix of derived or fitted cross products $\hat{\hat{c}}_{ij}$. We can then examine the degree to which the fitted matrix $\|\hat{\hat{c}}_{ij}\|$ approximates the observed matrix $\|\hat{c}_{ij}\|$. A close fit would suggest that the model is appropriate.

In Lazarsfeld's models in general, a basic "test" of goodness of fit is the comparison of how closely the observed joint proportions $(\hat{p}_{ij}, \hat{p}_{ijk}, \cdot \cdot \cdot)$ are approximated by corresponding proportions derived from the fitted item and distribution parameters. Given the values of $\hat{a}_i$, $\hat{b}_i$, and $\hat{M}_r$, for all items and for all moments ($r = 1, 2, \cdots, n$) we can derive the proportions ($\hat{\hat{p}}_{ij}, \hat{\hat{p}}_{ijk}, \cdots$) which would be expected if the model fit the data perfectly. Equation 16 can be used to derive the proportion $\hat{\hat{p}}_{ij}$ (the fit of $\hat{\hat{p}}_i$ to the observed $\hat{p}_i$ is trivial, of course, since it must necessarily be perfect). An extension of the procedure for obtaining equation 16 gives the following equation for the general case for any r items ($i, j, k, \cdots, s, t = 1, 2, \cdots, n; \ i \neq j \neq k \neq \cdots \neq s \neq t$):

(34)
$$
\begin{aligned}
p_{i_1 j_2 k_3 \cdots s_{r-1} t_r} = \ & a_{i_1} a_{j_2} a_{k_3} \cdots a_{s_{r-1}} a_{t_r} + 0 + \\
& \Sigma b_{i_1} b_{j_2} a_{k_3} \cdots a_{s_{r-1}} a_{t_r} + \\
& M_3 \Sigma b_{i_1} b_{j_2} b_{k_3} \cdots a_{s_{r-1}} a_{t_r} + \\
& \cdots\cdots\cdots\cdots\cdots + \\
& M_{r-1} \Sigma b_{i_1} b_{j_2} b_{k_3} \cdots b_{s_{r-1}} a_{t_r} + \\
& M_r b_{i_1} b_{j_2} b_{k_3} \cdots b_{s_{r-1}} b_{t_r}
\end{aligned}
$$

where, as before, the Σ indicates a summation over all combinations of the subscripts with no duplication. This equation can be used to compute the remaining derived joint proportions.

The extent to which the derived joint proportions approximate the corresponding observed proportions gives an indication of the goodness of fit of the model to the data.

4. THE LATENT-DISTANCE MODEL

The latent-distance model is usually considered to be the probability analog of the Guttman scale (Green, 1954; Lazarsfeld, 1950) or quasiscale. It should be noted, however, that it is not the only probability analog of this scale. Actually, any model that requires monotonic trace lines and that permits items having sufficiently good discrimination could be so considered. One such model, for example, is the normal-ogive model discussed in the next section.

The latent-distance model, in addition to the postulates of general latent-structure analysis (equations 1–4), includes the assumption that the trace lines are all of the following form: The probability of a positive response is some constant value ($a_i - b_i$) up to a particular point x_i. At this point it jumps to another value ($a_i + b_i$) and remains constant at ($a_i + b_i$) thereafter. The general form of the latent-distance trace line is illustrated in Figure 3. The equation for the trace line of item i may thus be written

(35)
$$
\begin{aligned}
f_i(x) &= a_i - b_i \quad \text{for} \quad x \leqslant x_i \\
f_i(x) &= a_i + b_i \quad \text{for} \quad x > x_i
\end{aligned}
$$

Each item therefore has three parameters: a_i, b_i, and the breaking point x_i.

A more restricted version of the latent-distance model allows only two free parameters per item. In the restricted version, it is assumed that the

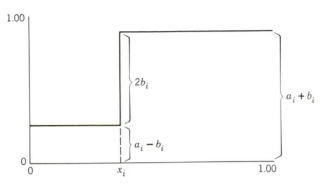

Figure 3. Trace line and parameters of item i: three-parameter version of the latent-distance model.

parameter a_i is equal to one half for all items. Specification of this value for the a_i gives *symmetric* trace lines for all items. Examples are given in Figure 4.

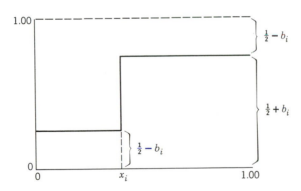

Figure 4. Symmetric trace line and parameters of item i: two-parameter version of the latent-distance model.

We shall use the more general three-parameter case in developing the basic latent-distance equations. Following this, we shall present separate solutions for the two-parameter and the three-parameter versions.

General Latent-Distance Equations

From equations 35 it is apparent that the shape of the density function of the subjects $g(x)$ will remain unknown. The shape of the trace line of any item will be invariant over any monotonic transformation of the function $g(x)$. If x_i is expressed in terms of the proportion of subjects occurring below x_i, then it is clear that none of the three parameters of the trace line will be affected by such a transformation. Hence, for convenience and without loss of generality we suppose $g(x) = 1$ for $0 \leqslant x \leqslant 1$ and $g(x) = 0$ otherwise.

If we so desire, we can thus consider the underlying continuum of the attribute to be spaced off in percentile units.

Given this assumption, we can write immediately

$$p_i = \int_0^{x_i} (a_i - b_i)\, dx + \int_{x_i}^1 (a_i + b_i)\, dx$$
$$= (a_i - b_i)x_i + (a_i + b_i)(1 - x_i)$$

If we define $\bar{x}_i \equiv 1 - x_i$, this reduces to

(36) $$p_i = a_i + b_i(\bar{x}_i - x_i)$$

We shall again need expressions for the symmetric parameters c_{ij} and c_{ijk}. It will be remembered that, in terms of the joint proportions,

(37) $$c_{ij} = p_{ij} - p_i p_j$$

and

(38) $$c_{ijk} = p_{ijk} - \Sigma p_i p_{jk} + 2p_i p_j p_k$$

where, as before, Σ indicates a summation over all combinations of subscripts with no duplication ($\Sigma p_i p_{jk} = p_i p_{jk} + p_j p_{ik} + p_k p_{ij}$). It is also worth noting at this time that, when $(c_{jk} + p_j p_k)$ is substituted for p_{jk}, equation 38 simplifies to

(39) $$c_{ijk} = p_{ijk} - \Sigma p_i c_{jk} - p_i p_j p_k$$

We next need to relate the symmetric parameters to the item parameters of the latent-distance model. In general, for any r items,

$$c_{i_1 j_2 \cdots t_r} \equiv \int_{-\infty}^{+\infty} [f_{i_1}(x) - p_{i_1}][f_{j_2}(x) - p_{j_2}] \cdots [f_{t_r}(x) - p_{t_r}]\, g(x)\, dx$$

In the present case, from equations 35 and 36, we see that

$$f_i(x) - p_i = a_i - b_i - a_i + b_i(x_i - \bar{x}_i) = 2b_i(x_i - 1) \quad \text{for} \quad x \leqslant x_i$$

and

$$f_i(x) - p_i = a_i + b_i - a_i + b_i(x_i - \bar{x}_i) = 2b_i x_i \quad\quad \text{for} \quad x > x_i$$

Since $g(x)$ is considered to be a unit rectangular distribution varying from zero to unity, we can write the symmetric function for any two *ordered* stimuli, $x_i < x_j$, as

$$c_{ij} = \int_0^{x_i} 2b_i(x_i - 1)2b_j(x_j - 1)\, dx + \int_{x_i}^{x_j} 2b_i x_i 2b_j(x_j - 1)\, dx$$
$$+ \int_{x_j}^1 2b_i x_i x_j 2b_j\, dx$$

which simplifies to

(40) $$c_{ij} = 4b_i b_j x_i \bar{x}_j$$

In like manner, for any three ordered stimuli $x_i < x_j < x_k$,

(41) $$c_{ijk} = \int_0^{x_i} 2b_i(x_i - 1)2b_j(x_j - 1)2b_k(x_k - 1)\, dx$$

$$+ \int_{x_i}^{x_j} 2b_i x_i 2b_j(x_j - 1)2b_k(x_k - 1)\, dx$$

$$+ \int_{x_j}^{x_k} 2b_i x_i 2b_j x_j 2b_k(x_k - 1)\, dx$$

$$+ \int_{x_k}^1 2b_i x_i 2b_j x_j 2b_k x_k\, dx$$

which, in turn, simplifies to

(42) $$c_{ijk} = 8b_i b_j b_k x_i(x_j - \bar{x}_j)\bar{x}_k$$

Equation 36 gives the observed proportion p_i as a function of the latent parameters of item i. Equations 37 through 39 give c_{ij} and c_{ijk} as functions of observable joint proportions. Hence, given the joint proportions p_i, p_{ij}, and p_{ijk}, we can compute the values of the c_{ij} and c_{ijk}. Equations 40 and 42, in turn, give c_{ij} and c_{ijk} as functions of the latent parameters of the latent-distance model.

The next step is to use equations 36, 40, and 42 to obtain solutions for the item parameters in terms of the observable p_i, c_{ij}, and c_{ijk}. Several different solutions for the item parameters have been developed (Lazarsfeld, 1950, ditto; Hays and Borgatta, 1954). While Lazarsfeld's (ditto) approach shows considerable promise, the simplest and most straightforward solution available at the present time is that given in Hays and Borgatta (1954). They give routine procedures for both the two- and three-parameter versions of the latent-distance model.

We shall present here only the Hays–Borgatta solutions. The derivations for each version of the latent-distance model are first carried out in terms of population parameters and, hence, are strictly appropriate only

for errorless data.   The various averaging and fitting procedures suggested
in Hays and Borgatta for dealing with fallible data are presented separately.

The Two-Parameter Version of the Latent-Distance Model

In the two-parameter version of the latent-distance model, a_i is assumed
equal to one half for all items.   Hence, equation 36 reduces to

(43) $$p_i = \tfrac{1}{2} + b_i(\bar{x}_i - x_i) \qquad (i = 1, 2, \cdots, n)$$

We can also write

(44) $$1 - p_i = \tfrac{1}{2} - b_i(\bar{x}_i - x_i)$$

and the product,

(45) $$p_i(1 - p_i) = \tfrac{1}{4} - b_i^2 + 4b_i^2 x_i \bar{x}_i$$

Now consider any three items i, j, and k for which $x_i < x_j < x_k$.
Using equation 40, we can write

$$\frac{c_{ij}c_{jk}}{c_{ik}} = \frac{(4b_i b_j x_i \bar{x}_j)(4b_j b_k x_j \bar{x}_k)}{4b_i b_k x_i \bar{x}_k}$$

which simplifies to

(46) $$\frac{c_{ij}c_{jk}}{c_{ik}} = 4b_j^2 x_j \bar{x}_j$$

Substituting equation 46 into equation 45 (and using the subscript j in
place of i) gives

$$p_j(1 - p_j) = \tfrac{1}{4} - b_j^2 + \frac{c_{ij}c_{jk}}{c_{ik}}$$

Solving for b_j, we get

(47) $$b_j = \left[\frac{c_{ij}c_{jk}}{c_{ik}} - p_j(1 - p_j) + \tfrac{1}{4} \right]^{1/2}$$

Given that the items are ordered in terms of the values of their breaking
points x_j, equation 47 gives the solution for b_j for all items except the first
and last items in the order.

Once the values of b_j have been determined for the middle items, the
corresponding values of x_j can be easily computed using equation 43.
Solving this equation explicitly for x_j, we get

(48) $$x_j = \frac{\tfrac{1}{2} - p_j}{2b_j} + \frac{1}{2}$$

Equations 47 and 48 thus give a solution for the two parameters of all
items except the first and last.   There will be, in general, as many solutions

for the parameters of item j ($j = 2, 3, \cdots, n-1$) as there are ordered combinations of items having j as the middle term.

We can compute the values of the parameters of the first and last items easily, once those of the remaining items have been obtained. From equation 40, we have, for the first and nth items, respectively,

(49)
$$c_{1i} = 4b_1 b_i x_1 \bar{x}_i$$

and

(50)
$$c_{in} = 4b_i b_n x_i \bar{x}_n$$

Rearranging terms, we get

(51)
$$b_1 x_1 = \frac{c_{1i}}{4b_i \bar{x}_i}$$

and

(52)
$$b_n \bar{x}_n = \frac{c_{in}}{4b_i x_i}$$

Equation 43 can be rewritten, for the first and last items, respectively, as

(53)
$$p_1 = \tfrac{1}{2} + b_1 - 2b_1 x_1$$

and

(54)
$$p_n = \tfrac{1}{2} - b_n + 2b_n \bar{x}_n$$

Substituting equations 51 and 52 in equations 53 and 54, respectively, and solving explicitly for b_1 and b_n, we get

(55)
$$b_1 = \frac{c_{1i}}{2b_i \bar{x}_i} + p_1 - \tfrac{1}{2}$$

and

(56)
$$b_n = \frac{c_{in}}{2b_i x_i} - p_n + \tfrac{1}{2}$$

Given b_1 and b_n, Equation 48 can be used to obtain values for x_1 and x_n. Again, several alternative solutions are available, one for each item for which values of b_i and x_i are available. With errorless data, they would all give identical results.

Averaging Procedures for Fallible Data. Two-Parameter Case

In equations 47, 48, 55, and 56, the item parameters are expressed (indirectly) as functions of the population joint proportions. The equations are appropriate only for errorless data. With fallible data, the alternative solutions available for a given item parameter will ordinarily give somewhat different results owing to sampling variation. The following averaging procedure is suggested by Hays and Borgatta for adapting the solution given above to fallible data.

We first obtain estimates $\hat{c}_{ij}$ of the cross-product terms as in equation 37, using the empirically obtained proportions $(\hat{p}_i, \hat{p}_{ij})$ in place of the theoretical values:

(57) $$\hat{c}_{ij} = \hat{p}_{ij} - \hat{p}_i\hat{p}_j$$

For a given value of j, there will be as many estimates of the ratio $c_{ij}c_{jk}/c_{ik}$ as there are values of i and k for which $x_i < x_j < x_k$. The average is taken as the estimate wanted. Let the average be denoted $\hat{c}_{jj}$. Then,

(58) $$\hat{c}_{jj} = \frac{1}{q} \sum_{\substack{i,k \\ x_i < x_j < x_k}} \frac{\hat{c}_{ij}\hat{c}_{jk}}{\hat{c}_{ik}}$$

where q denotes the number of terms summed over. This value is then used in the empirical analogs of equations 47 and 48 to obtain estimates of the parameters of the middle items for the restricted model:

(59) $$\hat{b}_j = [\bar{c}_{jj} - \hat{p}_j(1 - \hat{p}_j) + \tfrac{1}{4}]^{1/2}$$

(60) $$\hat{x}_j = \frac{\tfrac{1}{2} - \hat{p}_j}{2\hat{b}_j} + \frac{1}{2}$$

Empirical analogs of equations 55 and 56, along with equation 60, are used in estimating the two parameters of the end items. Several estimates are available for b_1 and b_n, one for each nonextreme value of i. The average of the estimates is taken as the value wanted:

(61) $$\hat{b}_1 = \hat{p}_1 - \tfrac{1}{2} + \frac{1}{2(n-2)} \sum_{i=2}^{n-1} \frac{\hat{c}_{1i}}{\hat{b}_i\hat{x}_i}$$

(62) $$\hat{b}_n = \tfrac{1}{2} - \hat{p}_n + \frac{1}{2(n-2)} \sum_{i=2}^{n-1} \frac{\hat{c}_{in}}{\hat{b}_i\hat{x}_i}$$

The Three-Parameter Version of the Latent-Distance Model

The solution for the three-parameter model requires use of the third-order symmetric parameter c_{ijk}. We first define the quantity u_j, where, for any three items ordered in terms of x_i,

(63) $$u_j \equiv \frac{c_{ijk}}{c_{ik}} \qquad (x_i < x_j < x_k)$$

Again, u_j will be computable only for the middle items. From equations 40 and 42, we see that

$$u_j = \frac{8b_ib_jb_kx_i(x_j - \bar{x}_j)\bar{x}_k}{4b_ib_kx_i\bar{x}_k}$$

which simplifies to

(64) $$u_j = 2b_j(x_j - \bar{x}_j) = -2b_j(\bar{x}_j - x_j)$$

Substituting equation 64 into equation 36, we get

(65) $$p_j = a_j - \tfrac{1}{2}u_j$$

Finally, solving explicitly for a_j, we have

(66) $$a_j = p_j + \tfrac{1}{2}u_j$$

To solve for the b_j, we note from equation 36 that, in the three-parameter model,

(67) $$p_j(1 - p_j) = a_j(1 - a_j) + (1 - 2a_j)b_j(\bar{x}_j - x_j) - b_j^2(\bar{x}_j - x_j)^2$$

Substituting from equations 46 and 64, we get

(68) $$p_j(1 - p_j) = a_j(1 - a_j) + \tfrac{1}{2}(2a_j - 1)u_j - b_j^2 + \frac{c_{ij}c_{jk}}{c_{ik}}$$

Rearranging and solving for b_j gives

(69) $$b_j = \left[\frac{c_{ij}c_{jk}}{c_{ik}} - p_j(1 - p_j) + a_j(1 - a_j) + \tfrac{1}{2}(2a_j - 1)u_j\right]^{1/2}$$

To solve for the x_j we need only rearrange terms in equation 36:

(70) $$x_j = \frac{a_j - p_j}{2b_j} + \frac{1}{2}$$

Equations 65, 69, and 70 give the three item parameters for all items, except the first and last in the x_i order, as functions of quantities that can be computed from the theoretical joint proportions.

Without further assumptions, no unique solution is possible for the two extreme items. One common procedure is to assume that the extreme items are symmetric: i.e., that $a_1 = a_n = \tfrac{1}{2}$. With this assumption, the solution for b_1 and b_n is given by equations 55 and 56, respectively. The solution for x_1 and x_n, once the b values have been computed, is given by equation 48.

Averaging Procedures for Fallible Data: Three-Parameter Case

Equations 57 and 58 are used to compute the $\hat{c}_{ij}$ and $\hat{c}_{jj}$, as in the two-parameter model. In addition, the three-parameter model requires one further averaging procedure. Equation 63 defines the quantity u_j in terms of the symmetric parameters c_{ij} and c_{ijk}. There will be as many direct empirical estimates for a given value of j ($j = 2, 3, \cdots, n-1$) of u_j as there are values of i and k for which $x_i < x_j < x_k$. Hays and Borgatta suggest using the average of these estimates:

$$\text{(71)} \qquad \hat{u}_j = \frac{1}{q} \sum_{\substack{i,k \\ x_i < x_j < x_k}} \frac{\hat{c}_{ijk}}{\hat{c}_{ik}}$$

where q denotes the number of terms summed over.

The empirical estimates of the three parameters of the $n-2$ nonextreme items are then given by

$$\text{(72)} \qquad \hat{a}_j = \hat{p}_j + \tfrac{1}{2}\hat{u}_j$$

$$\text{(73)} \qquad \hat{b}_j = [\hat{c}_{jj} - \hat{p}_j(1 - \hat{p}_j) + \hat{a}_j(1 - \hat{a}_j) + \tfrac{1}{2}(2\hat{a}_j - 1)\hat{u}_j]^{1/2}$$

and

$$\text{(74)} \qquad \hat{x}_j = \frac{\hat{a}_j - \hat{p}_j}{2\hat{b}_j} + \frac{1}{2}$$

The two parameters of the first and last items are estimated using equations 61, 62, and 60.

Thus, given sample estimates of the joint proportions of the forms $\hat{p}_i$, $\hat{p}_{ij}$, and $\hat{p}_{ijk}$, and the order of the items in terms of their breaking points,

Table 1. LATENT STRUCTURE OF THE GENERAL LATENT-DISTANCE MODEL

Class Interval	Proportion of Subjects within Class Interval	Item Number				
		1	2	3 $\cdots$	$n-1$	n
1	x_1	$\tfrac{1}{2}-b_1$	a_2-b_2	$a_3-b_3 \cdots$	$a_{n-1}-b_{n-1}$	a_n-b_n
2	x_2-x_1	$\tfrac{1}{2}+b_1$	a_2-b_2	$a_3-b_3 \cdots$	$a_{n-1}-b_{n-1}$	a_n-b_n
3	x_3-x_2	$\tfrac{1}{2}+b_1$	a_2+b_2	$a_3-b_3 \cdots$	$a_{n-1}-b_{n-1}$	a_n-b_n
4	x_4-x_3	$\tfrac{1}{2}+b_1$	a_2+b_2	$a_3+b_3 \cdots$	$a_{n-1}-b_{n-1}$	a_n-b_n
.	.	.	.	.	.	.
.	.	.	.	.	.	.
.	.	.	.	.	.	.
n	x_n-x_{n-1}	$\tfrac{1}{2}+b_1$	a_2+b_2	$a_3+b_3 \cdots$	$a_{n-1}+b_{n-1}$	a_n-b_n
$n+1$	$1-x_n$	$\tfrac{1}{2}+b_1$	a_2+b_2	$a_3+b_3 \cdots$	$a_{n-1}+b_{n-1}$	a_n+b_n

estimates of the three parameters of the $n-2$ nonextreme items and the two parameters of the two extreme items can be computed. The general solution for n stimuli would appear as in Table 1. It should be noted that, since the solution for $\hat{x}_i$ corresponds to the proportion of subjects below the position of x_i on the underlying continuum, by taking differences of adjacent stimuli we can obtain the proportions of cases within each interval. It is these values that are indicated in Table 1.

Ordering the Items in Terms of the Breaking Points x_i

All solutions of the latent-distance model developed thus far require that the items be ordered with respect to the breaking point of their trace lines. In the deterministic Guttman model, the order of the item breaking points x_i is given by the order of the marginal proportions p_i. From equations 36 and 43, it is apparent that, in the latent-distance models, even with perfect data, the two orders need no longer coincide exactly (though in any practical case the deviation is not likely to be large). Hence, even in the error-free case, additional information may be needed.

Consider the cross-product matrix $\|c_{ij}\|$. It is a symmetric matrix with vacant cells along the principal diagonal. Lazarsfeld (ditto) has pointed out that, with perfect data, while the rank of the matrix is equal to its order, *all minors of order greater than one, composed entirely of elements on one side of the principal diagonal, vanish.* For example, when $x_1 < x_2 < x_3 < x_4 < x_5 < x_6$, determinants of the form given below vanish:

$$\begin{vmatrix} c_{13} & c_{14} \\ c_{23} & c_{24} \end{vmatrix} = 0$$

$$\begin{vmatrix} c_{14} & c_{15} & c_{16} \\ c_{24} & c_{25} & c_{26} \\ c_{34} & c_{35} & c_{36} \end{vmatrix} = 0$$

Minors involving elements on both sides of the principal diagonal do not vanish in general. This fact gives us an additional lever on the ordering problem. If we consider only the minors of order two (tetrads), we get the following rule: "The more distant two rows (or columns) in the cross-product matrix are, the fewer of their tetrads vanish" (Lazarsfeld, ditto, p. 11). With errorless data this rule leaves indeterminate only the order of the first two items and the last two items (none of these items are contained in any tetrad composed solely of elements on one side of the principal diagonal).

With fallible data, the ordering procedure recommended by Lazarsfeld, (ditto, p. 11) is as follows: First, order the items according to their marginals ($\hat{p}_i$). Then inspect the tetrads of matrix $\|\hat{c}_{ij}\|$ to see if any of the positions of the items should be interchanged. Finally, order the first and last pairs of items so that, for as many of the rows and columns of $\|\hat{c}_{ij}\|$ as possible, the values of $\hat{c}_{ij}$ decline from the diagonal to the borders of the matrix.

Evaluation of Goodness of Fit of the Model to the Data

An initial test of goodness of fit is given by checking the degree to which the empirically observed cross-product matrix can be approximated by one computed from the estimates of b_i and x_i. Let $\hat{\hat{c}}_{ij}$ denote the derived cross product, where

$$\hat{\hat{c}}_{ij} = 4\hat{b}_i\hat{b}_j\hat{x}_i\hat{x}_j \qquad \begin{array}{l} (i = 1, 2, \cdots, n-1) \\ (j = 2, 3, \cdots, n) \\ (i < j) \end{array}$$

Then the elements of the matrix of differences $\|\hat{\hat{c}}_{ij} - \hat{c}_{ij}\|$ should all be close to zero.

As in all of Lazarsfeld's latent-structure models we can also evaluate the fit of the model to the data by comparing the observed proportions with those that can be derived from the fitted parameters. Equations 1 through 4 can be used to compute derived values of p_i, p_{ij}, p_{ijk}, etc., from the estimates of a_i, b_i, and x_i. If the derived values deviate very little from the observed values, we would accept the model. Eventually, when efficient estimation procedures are devised, a more rigorous test of goodness of fit would be appropriate. Green (1954) has suggested using a chi-square test along the lines of that developed by Mosteller for case V of the law of comparative judgment.

It should be noted here that we can also compute the expected proportion of subjects having a particular response pattern from the estimates of the item parameters. Hence, we could also compare these derived values with those observed. The procedure for computing the expected proportion of subjects having a particular response pattern from the values of the item parameters can be seen rather directly from Table 1. The general element of the main body of the table gives the probability that a person in the class indicated by the row will respond positively to the item indicated by the column. Let us call this element p_{gi}, where g ($g = 1, 2, \cdots, n+1$) is a row index indicating the class, and i is the usual item index (corresponding to the column). It is clear that the probability of a subject in class g responding negatively to item i is given by $1 - p_{gi} = q_{gi}$. Now consider any particular response pattern, for example, the pattern ($\times \times \circ \circ \times \cdots \circ \times$). The probability of a person in class g having this response pattern is equal to the product of the corresponding probabilities: in this case, $p_{g1}p_{g2}q_{g3}q_{g4}p_{g5} \cdot \cdot \cdot q_{g,n-1}p_n$. Hence, the expected proportion of subjects in the entire population having this response pattern would be equal to

$$(75) \qquad \sum_{g=1}^{n+1} x_g p_{g1}p_{g2}q_{g3}q_{g4}p_{g5} \cdot \cdot \cdot q_{g,n-1}p_n$$

where x_g gives the proportion of subjects in the class interval g as given in the second column of Table 1.

Scoring the Subjects

As was the case with the linear model, inverse-probability procedures could be used to estimate the scale values of the subjects. Here, however, the scale values would provide ordinal information only, since the latent-distance model makes no real requirements with respect to the underlying continuum other than that the subjects are ordered thereon.

A more practical procedure again would be simply to use total number of items answered positively. The rationale here is essentially the same as before: If items are all monotonic, and if they are all sensed in the same direction (here, sensed so that $b_i > 0$ for all values of i), then the expected total score is monotonically related to the scale value. Hence, given more than a very few items, total score would seem to be adequate as a means of determining the rank order of the subjects with respect to the underlying continuum.

5. THE NORMAL-OGIVE MODEL

Although the normal-ogive model is formally a special case of the general latent-structure analysis, it should be noted that the general notions have been developed independently and along somewhat different lines. The general notions of normal-ogive trace lines and independence of items except for the relationship due to their separate relations with the underlying continuum have been in use in the field of test theory for quite some time. Lord (1953), for example, gives 13 references ranging back to 1936 which make use of the assumption of normal-ogive trace lines.

In the present section, we will discuss the model somewhat in terms of the latent-structure approach; i.e., we will *begin* with the postulates of an underlying attribute, upon which subjects are distributed in an unknown fashion, and of independence of items at any given point on the underlying continuum, and the postulate that the trace line of each item is of the normal-ogive form. In the following section, we will see that, if we wish to begin our theorizing one step further removed from the data, so that the normal-ogive trace line results as a *deduction* from more primitive postulates, then a number of interesting relationships can be seen with respect to the present model, Thurstone's mental-age model, and the mathematics of the law of categorical judgment discussed in Chapter 10. For the present, however, we shall simply begin by postulating that the trace lines of the items are normal ogives.

The Normal-Ogive Trace Line

It is assumed that the trace line of item i is of the following form:

$$(76) \qquad f_i(x) = \frac{1}{\sqrt{2\pi}} \int_{-\infty}^{(x-M_i)/\sigma_i} \exp\left(-\tfrac{1}{2}z^2\right) dz$$

Consider a particular subject g having a scale value on the attribute of s_g, as is illustrated in Figure 5. Then p_{ig} gives the probability that subject g will respond positively to item i. In general,

$$(77) \qquad p_{ig} = \frac{1}{\sqrt{2\pi}} \int_{-\infty}^{z_{ig}} \exp\left(-\tfrac{1}{2}z^2\right) dz$$

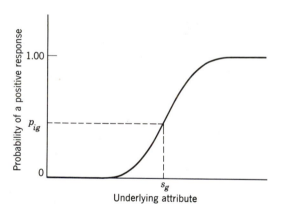

Figure 5.   Normal-ogive trace line of item i.

where z_{ig} is the unit normal deviate corresponding to p_{ig}, and is a function of the scale value of the subject s_g and of the two parameters necessary to specify the item trace line. There are, of course, a great number of alternative pairs of parameters which could serve to describe the normal ogive. Consider the transformation of the trace line of item i as shown in Figure 6 which occurs when p_{ig} is transformed into the unit normal deviate z_{ig}. (The quantity z_{ig} is thus the unit normal deviate corresponding to the probability that an individual at the point s_g will respond positively to item i.)   The normal ogive of Figure 5 then becomes the straight line of Figure 6.

Three alternative equations for this line are of interest.   First, let

(78)
$$z_{ig} = \frac{1}{\sigma_i}(s_g - M_i)$$

This is perhaps the most usual form.   Here, M_i gives the point on the attribute continuum corresponding to a z value of zero.   Hence, an

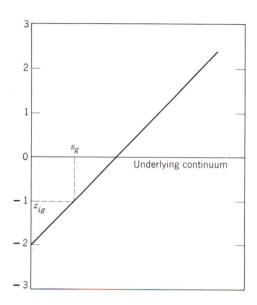

Figure 6.   Trace line of item i with the ordinate expressed in terms of z_{ig}, the unit normal deviate corresponding to p_{ig}.

individual at this point would have a probability of 0.50 of responding positively to the item.   The parameter M_i can therefore be considered to be a *location* parameter for the item.   The slope of the line is equal to the reciprocal of σ_i.   Thus, σ_i can be considered to be a *discrimination* parameter for the item.   A large value of σ_i indicates low discrimination for the item, while a small value of σ_i indicates high discrimination.

Although we are dealing here simply with the equation of a particular assumed form of the trace line, and not explicitly with a cumulated normal frequency function, it might be noted that M_i and σ_i can be considered to be the usual mean and standard deviation of that normal curve which, if integrated, would give the equation of the trace line of item i.

The second equation to be considered here for describing the straight line of Figure 6 is the equation used by Tucker (1952):

$$(79) \qquad\qquad z_{ig} = a_i s_g + b_i$$

The meaning of s_g is the same as before. The two parameters chosen to describe the item now correspond to the slope and to the intercept on the ordinate of the line. Tucker's item parameters, a_i and b_i, are related to the M_i and σ_i given above as follows:

$$\sigma_i = \frac{1}{a_i}$$

and

$$M_i = -\frac{b_i}{a_i}$$

The third form of the equation is that used by Lord (1953):

$$(80) \qquad\qquad z_{ig} = \frac{R_i s_g - h_i}{(1 - R_i^2)^{1/2}}$$

where the parameters h_i and R_i are related to M_i and σ_i as follows:

$$M_i = \frac{h_i}{R_i}$$

and

$$\sigma_i = \frac{(1 - R_i^2)^{1/2}}{R_i}$$

Lord's form of the equation has several advantages in *test theory*, where one often finds it convenient to assume that the population of individuals is distributed normally. With this additional assumption, R_i is the biserial correlation between the item and the underlying continuum, and h_i is the unit normal deviate corresponding to p_i, the proportion of individuals who respond positively to item i.

Solutions to the Problem

Lord (1953) has given the equations which constitute the formal maximum-likelihood solution to the normal-ogive model. He solves for the values of the unknown parameters h_i, R_i, and s_g, which maximize the likelihood of the observed responses of the subjects to the items. Unfortunately, the equations that constitute the formal solution to the problem are very complex. The maximum-likelihood procedure apparently does not lead to a practical, workable solution for the general case. Hence, we shall not give it here. Interested readers are referred to Lord's original paper (1953, pp. 60–63).

Tucker (1952) has given an approximate least-squares solution to the same problem, which, though it requires iterative procedures, is not prohibitively difficult or time-consuming. As we shall see, however, when the problem is seen in the light of Tucker's approach, other approximations which are both easy and rapid immediately suggest themselves.

Let us assume that the values of p_{ig} are given. These values can then be transformed into the unit normal deviates z_{ig}, thus giving (for $i = 1, 2, \cdots, n; \ g = 1, 2, \cdots, m$) the nm equations

$$z_{ig} = a_i s_g + b_i$$

If we define a unit and origin of our scale (say by setting $a_1 = 1$ and $b_1 = 0$), the *algebraic* solution follows immediately. For example, then

$$(81) \qquad\qquad s_g = \frac{z_{1g}}{a_1} = z_{1g} \qquad (g = 1, 2, \cdots, m)$$

Given s_g and z_{1g}, we can plot for each item, the trace line in the normal deviate form as given in Figure 6. The slope of the line is then equal to a_i, and the intercept on the ordinate to b_i.

Actually, of course, neither p_{ig} nor satisfactory estimates of p_{ig} are directly given by the data ordinarily. For the case we are dealing with here, each subject responds once only, either positively or negatively, to each item.

Tucker gets around this limitation in the observed data by taking advantage of the fact mentioned earlier that, for items with monotonic increasing trace lines, the expected total score of a subject is monotonically related to his scale score on the underlying continuum. In Tucker's *experimental* procedure the total sample of subjects is divided into m relatively homogeneous subgroups on the basis of total score. For example, the subgroups might correspond to the usual class intervals in the usual raw-score distribution. The proportion of people in the gth subgroup who respond positively to the ith item, $\hat{p}_{ig}$, is taken as an empirical estimate of the population proportion p_{ig}.

It is thus assumed that, within any subgroup, the subjects all have (approximately) the same amount of the attribute. Hence $\hat{p}_{ig}$ can be considered as an estimate of p_{ig}. Given this assumption, the mn observed values of $\hat{p}_{ig}$ can be converted into unit normal deviates $\hat{z}_{ig}$. These may then be used to estimate s_g (where now s_g refers to the scale value of the gth *subgroup* of subjects), and the two item parameters a_i and b_i (or, alternatively, either the parameters h_i and R_i used by Lord or the more familiar parameters M_i and σ_i).

It is of considerable interest to note that, when estimates $\hat{p}_{ig}$ are available, and when item parameters to be estimated are taken to be M_i and σ_i, the mathematical problem of estimation is formally identical with that of condition B of the law of categorical judgment discussed in detail in Chapter 10—i.e., with the usual form of the law of categorical judgment. In the present problem, we have the mn equations,

$$(82) \qquad S_g - M_i = z_{ig}\sigma_i \qquad \begin{array}{l} (i = 1, 2, \cdot \cdot \cdot, n) \\ (g = 1, 2, \cdot \cdot \cdot, m) \end{array}$$

In condition B of the categorical-judgment problem, we have the mn equations

$$t_g - S_j = x_{jg}a_j \qquad \begin{array}{l} (g = 1, 2, \cdot \cdot \cdot, m) \\ (j = 1, 2, \cdot \cdot \cdot, n) \end{array}$$

Hence, any of the solutions presented for condition B in Chapter 10 is also a solution for the present problem.

Tucker's own solution differs somewhat from those offered in Chapter 10. In the first place, of course, his item parameters differ, since he is concerned with the parameters a_i and b_i instead of our M_i and σ_i. He also weights his observation equations to take account of differences in the reliability of the estimates $\hat{z}_{ig}$. His solution is given below.

From equation 79, we have

$$z_{ig} = a_i S_g + b_i \qquad \begin{array}{l} (i = 1, 2, \cdot \cdot \cdot, n) \\ (g = 1, 2, \cdot \cdot \cdot, m) \end{array}$$

Tucker estimates the values of s_g, a_i, and b_i which will minimize the quantity F, where

$$F = \sum_i \sum_g w_{ig}(\hat{z}_{ig} - a_i s_g - b_i)^2$$

i.e., the weighted sum of squares of the differences $(\hat{z}_{ig} - z_{ig})$. The weights w_{ig} are given by

$$(83) \qquad w_{ig} = \frac{10}{p_{ig}(1 - p_{ig})} e^{-z_{ig}^2}$$

which are proportional to the usual y^2/pq weights, where y is the ordinate of the unit normal curve at the point that divides the total area of the curve into proportions of p and q.

The minimization procedure yields the following three equations, which form the basis for the iterative procedure:

$$(84) \quad a_i \sum_g w_{ig}s_g^2 + b_i \sum_g w_{ig}s_g = \sum_g w_{ig}\hat{z}_{ig}s_g \qquad (i = 1, 2, \cdot \cdot \cdot, n)$$

$$(85) \quad a_i \sum_g w_{ig}s_g + b_i \sum_g w_{ig} = \sum_g w_{ig}\hat{z}_{ig} \qquad (i = 1, 2, \cdot \cdot \cdot, n)$$

and

(86) $$s_g = \frac{\sum_i w_{ig}\hat{z}_{ig}a_i - \sum_i w_{ig}a_ib_i}{\sum_i w_{ig}a_i^2} \qquad (g = 1, 2, \cdots, m)$$

The quantities $\hat{z}_{ig}$ and w_{ig} are known. As a first step, assume a trial set of scale values of the m subgroups s_g. Using this set of trial values, solve equations 84 and 85 for estimates of the item parameters a_i and b_i. These values of a_i and b_i are then substituted into equation 86 to obtain a new set of trial values of s_g, which are in turn substituted into equations 84 and 85 for more refined estimates of a_i and b_i. The cycle is repeated until the estimates from one trial to the next stabilize to as many decimal points as desired.

6. AN ALTERNATIVE GENERAL NORMAL-OGIVE MODEL

The direct analogy between Tucker's approach and condition B of the law of categorical judgment suggests setting the problem up in such a way that further analogies suggest themselves. Let us therefore discuss the problem in terms of the following set of postulates:

1. Assume as before an underlying continuum of the attribute of interest.
2. Assume that *both* the items and the subjects can be represented as points in this continuum at any given instant of time.
3. Assume that the position of any given item is not fixed, but, for miscellaneous reasons, varies about some fixed point. Thus, we can consider each item to be represented by a frequency distribution of points on the continuum. In like manner, assume that each subject is represented by a frequency distribution of points on the continuum. We shall assume that the frequency distribution for any given item and the frequency

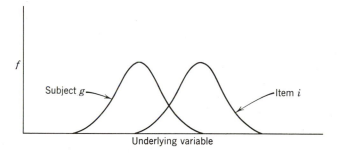

Figure 7.   Frequency distributions of positions for subject g and item i.

distribution for any given subject are both of the normal form. This is
illustrated in Figure 7. Let M_i and σ_i denote the mean and standard
deviation of the distribution for the ith item, and s_g and σ_g denote the
mean and standard deviation of the distribution for subject g.

4. Assume that a positive response of subject g to item i occurs when the
position of subject g is above that of item i, and a negative response occurs
when the reverse is true.

5. Assume that the positions of the subject and item are uncorrelated:
i.e., that the variation of any subject g about his mean is independent of
the variation of any item i about its mean.

Given these assumptions, it follows directly, along the line of reasoning
developed in Chapter 10, that

$$(87) \qquad p_{ig} = \frac{1}{\sqrt{2\pi}} \int_{-\infty}^{z_{ig}} \exp\left(-\tfrac{1}{2}z^2\right) dz$$

where

$$(88) \qquad z_{ig} = \frac{s_g - M_i}{(\sigma_g^2 + \sigma_i^2)^{1/2}} \qquad \begin{array}{l}(g = 1, 2, \cdots, m) \\ (i = 1, 2, \cdots, n)\end{array}$$

Rearranging, this becomes

$$(89) \qquad s_g - M_i = z_{ig}(\sigma_g^2 + \sigma_i^2)^{1/2}$$

Equation 89 might be taken as the general equation for the normal-ogive
model. (The even more general equation which includes the covariance
term $r_{ig}\sigma_g\sigma_i$ under the radical does not seem useful.)

We have developed equation 89 in terms of single subjects ($g = 1, 2,$
$\cdots, m$). Estimates of p_{ig} would theoretically refer to the proportion
obtained by presenting item i to subject g a large number of times, carefully wiping out any memory factors between presentations.

The model is not particularly useful in this form, since we are primarily
interested in the case where each subject responds once only, either
positively or negatively, to each item. We will therefore need to modify
the model in such a way that reasonable estimates of the p_{ig}'s become
available.

Recall the theoretical development of Chapter 10. Two distinct classes
of models were discussed (along with a third which was a mixture of the
two). In one class, distributions were generated by replication over trials
within a single subject. In the other, the distributions were generated
through replication over subjects. Both led to algebraically identical sets
of equations. Much the same thing can be developed for the present
model.

Let us assume that we can *partition the total sample of subjects into m subgroups, each of which projects a normal distribution of subject positions on the underlying continuum.* Distributions for different subgroups may differ in both mean and standard deviation. Let us further assume that, *within any subgroup*, the positions of subjects are uncorrelated with the positions of any items. One operational procedure for obtaining m subgroups is that based on total score as used by Tucker and described in the preceding section.

With this modification, the distribution for a single *subject* is replaced by a distribution for a *subgroup* of subjects. The parameters s_g and σ_g will thus, henceforth, refer to the mean and standard deviation on the underlying continuum of the gth subgroup. The meaning of the item parameters, M_i and σ_i, is unchanged. The estimate of the proportion p_{ig} will refer to the proportion of subjects within subgroup g who respond positively to item i.

Let us now consider two special cases of equation 89.

Constant Subgroup Variances—the Normal-Ogive Model

Assume that $\sigma_g^2 = K =$ constant for all values of g. Then, if we define $\alpha_i \equiv (\sigma_i^2 + K)^{1/2}$, equation 89 can be written

$$(90) \qquad s_g - M_i = z_{ig}\alpha_i \qquad \begin{matrix} (i = 1, 2, \cdots, n) \\ (g = 1, 2, \cdots, m) \end{matrix}$$

But equation 90 is identical in form with equation 82 of the preceding section. Hence, the model considered here is formally the same as the normal-ogive model considered by Tucker (1952). When viewed in this way, however, it is seen that in the problem presented by Tucker it is not necessary that all subjects in a given subgroup have the same scale value, but rather only that the distribution of subjects within a subgroup be normal, and that the variance of the distributions be constant over subgroups.

Constant Item Variances—Thurstone's Mental-Age Model

Assume that the item variances $\sigma_i^2 = C =$ constant for all items. Then, defining $\beta_g \equiv (\sigma_g^2 + C)^{1/2}$, equation 89 becomes

$$(91) \qquad s_g - M_i = z_{ig}\beta_g \qquad \begin{matrix} (i = 1, 2, \cdots, n) \\ (g = 1, 2, \cdots, m) \end{matrix}$$

Equation 91 is identical in form with equation 6 of Chapter 10. It is also formally identical with Thurstone's procedure for scaling of intelligence (1925).

Thurstone developed this scaling procedure in the context of the measurement of intelligence or achievement. In the case of intelligence, he makes the following assumptions:

1. Intelligence is normally distributed for individuals at a given age level.

2. The test items are perfectly correlated with the underlying continuum of intelligence.

Figure 8 gives an illustration for two age groups and one item of the model. The two age groups are represented by unit normal frequency

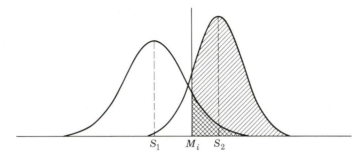

Figure 8. The normal distributions refer to age groups 1 and 2. M_i gives the position of item i. The proportion of the total area under each curve which is shaded indicates the proportion of subjects in the group who answer the item positively.

distributions having different means and different variances. The item is represented by a point. In terms of the trace-line notion, the item could be characterized as a normal ogive with an infinite slope, which, in turn, corresponds to a perfect Guttman-type item. The proportion of the area under the normal curve of each group which lies to the right of the point corresponding to the item (i.e., the shaded portion) corresponds to the proportion of subjects in that group who pass the item.

Thus we can write

$$(92) \qquad p_{ig} = \frac{1}{\sqrt{2\pi}} \int_{z_{ig}}^{\infty} \exp\left(-\tfrac{1}{2}z^2\right) dz$$

where

$$(93) \qquad z_{ig} = \frac{1}{\sigma_g}\left(s_g - M_i\right)$$

which rearranged becomes

$$(94) \qquad s_g - M_i = z_{ig}\sigma_g$$

Again, equation 94 is identical in form with equation 91. Hence, we conclude that in Thurstone's model the requirement of perfectly discriminating items is unnecessarily restricting. The model will fit the data, assuming only that the trace lines of the items are normal ogives with equal discrimination parameters—i.e., that the correlation of the item with the underlying continuum is constant over all items.

Since both equations 90 and 91 are identical in form with the corresponding equations 5 and 6 of the law of categorical judgment, it is evident that the solutions for that case discussed in Chapter 10 are also solutions to the present problem.

Summary Comments

To complete the analogy between the present model and the law of categorical judgment, we could consider the case where both item variances and group variances are constant. Then, with appropriate definition of unit, equation 89 would become simply

$$(95) \qquad\qquad s_g - M_i = z_{ig}$$

which is equivalent to condition *D*. This special case would probably be found too restrictive to be of general use however.

The general form of the model, as given by equation 89, perhaps deserves further comment. This too corresponds to one of the special conditions of the law of categorical judgment. Even though a solution for this problem has not been explicitly worked out for the general case of *m* groups and *n* items, the basic procedures for the solution have been given by Tucker (1948). In connection with a somewhat different problem, he showed, first, how to solve for the parameters of the items in terms of the mean and variance of a single group, and, second, given parallel solutions for two groups, how to use the item parameters to express the mean and variance of one group in terms of the mean and variance of the other. A generalization to *m* subgroups involving efficient estimates of the subgroup parameters has not as yet been developed.

7. THE METHOD OF SIMILAR REACTIONS

The method of similar reactions is an early model developed by Thurstone (1929b) in the field of attitude measurement. It has not received a great deal of use in spite of the fact that it seems to be the only probability-type model developed for point items. In terms of the general latent-structure theory, the model might be considered as dealing with the special case that assumes the trace lines are of the normal form. It should be noted, however, that the model does not fit into the latent-structure theory exactly.

The Basic Notions

An underlying continuum of the attribute is postulated. Items have positions on this continuum. The general idea is that the distance between the scale values of any two items is related to the number of people who respond positively to both items compared to the numbers of people who respond positively to each item separately. In particular, it is assumed that, if responses to the items were perfectly reliable, i.e., if everyone responded positively when he ought to, then we could write

$$(96) \qquad \frac{N_{ij}}{(N_i N_j)^{1/2}} = f(|S_j - S_i|)$$

where

$i, j =$ alternative subscripts for items
$S_i =$ scale value of item i
$N_i =$ number of subjects who (ought to) respond positively to item i
$N_{ij} =$ number of subjects who (ought to) respond positively to both items i and j

However, items are not perfectly reliable. It is assumed that this lack of reliability attenuates the frequencies of subjects who respond positively to each item. We shall denote the "reliability" parameter of each item as r_i ($0 < r_i < 1$), and then assume that

$$97) \qquad N_i = \frac{n_i}{r_i}$$

where n_i denotes the number of subjects who would respond positively to item i, taking the reliability of the item into account. We shall assume further that r_i and r_j are uncorrelated, so that

$$(98) \qquad N_{ij} = \frac{n_{ij}}{r_i r_j}$$

Then, substituting equations 97 and 98 into equation 96, we get

$$(99) \qquad \frac{n_{ij}/r_i r_j}{(n_i n_j/r_i r_j)^{1/2}} = f(|S_j - S_i|)$$

which simplifies to

$$(100) \qquad \frac{n_{ij}}{(r_i r_j n_i n_j)^{1/2}} = f(|S_j - S_i|)$$

Let us now define

(101)
$$K_{ij} \equiv \frac{n_{ij}}{(r_i r_j n_i n_j)^{1/2}}$$

where K_{ij} is the *coefficient of similarity*. K_{ij} varies between zero and unity as a function of the distance between items i and j on the underlying continuum. When the two items are at the same point, K_{ij} is equal to unity. As the distance between the two items increases, K_{ij} decreases, presumably becoming zero when the items are infinitely separated.

In order to tie things down, it is necessary to specify the nature of the function relating K_{ij} to the distance $|S_j - S_i|$. Thurstone makes the following assumption:

(102)
$$K_{ij} = \exp\left[-\tfrac{1}{2} \left(\frac{z_{ij}}{\sigma} \right)^2 \right]$$

where

(103)
$$z_{ij} = \pm(S_j - S_i) \qquad (i, j = 1, 2, \cdots, m)$$

The parameter K_{ij} is thus the *ordinate* of the normal curve *which has a maximum ordinate equal to unity*. Hence, if we are given K_{ij}, reference to an appropriate table of the normal curve will enable us to obtain the value of z_{ij}, which will be the abscissa value corresponding to an ordinate equal to K_{ij}. If we know z_{ij}, the solution for the scale values S_i can be obtained from equation 103.

Estimating K_{ij}, the Index of Similarity, from Observed Data

The preceding section gives the basic notions of the model in terms of the errorless population parameters. The empirical problem to be dealt with in the present section consists of, first, obtaining estimates of K_{ij} from observed data, and, second, using these estimates in an efficient manner to estimate the scale values S_i.

In order to estimate K_{ij}, we need estimates of r_i, r_j, n_i, n_j, and n_{ij}. The observed frequencies, $\hat{n}_i$, $\hat{n}_j$, and $\hat{n}_{ij}$ are taken as estimates of the corresponding theoretical frequencies. Thurstone suggests two alternative procedures for estimating the values of r_i, one of which is analogous to the usual test–retest reliability of test theory, and the other analogous to the usual parallel-form reliability.

THE TEST-RETEST METHOD. In this method, the items are administered to the same group of subjects on two different occasions. We thus have as observed data, for each item i, the estimates $\hat{n}_{i1}$, $\hat{n}_{i2}$, and $\hat{n}_{i12}$, where the arabic subscripts refer to the first and second administration. Since the scale value of the item is a constant, K_{ii} equals unity, and equation 101 can be written

$$1 = \frac{n_{i12}}{(r_i^2 n_{i1} n_{i2})^{1/2}}$$

Solving for r_i in terms of the observed frequencies gives

(104) $$\hat{r}_i = \frac{\hat{n}_{i12}}{(\hat{n}_{i1} \hat{n}_{i2})^{1/2}}$$

as the test–retest estimate of the "reliability" parameter.

THE PARALLEL-FORM METHOD. Assume that the order of the items is known. This order could be determined to an adequate approximation by various judgment methods, such as the method of equal-appearing intervals, for example. We next assume that adjacent items have approximately the same position on the underlying continuum. Then, we have, approximately

$$N_{i,i+1} = N_i = N_{i+1}$$

From equation 98 and the equality expressed above,

(105) $$N_{i,i+1} = \frac{n_{i,i+1}}{r_i r_{i+1}} = N_i = N_{i+1}$$

Since $N_i = n_i/r_i$, we can write

$$\frac{n_i}{r_i} = \frac{n_{i,i+1}}{r_i r_{i+1}}$$

or

(106) $$r_{i+1} = \frac{n_{i,i+1}}{n_i}$$

In like manner,

(107) $$r_i = \frac{n_{i,i+1}}{n_{i+1}}$$

The observed estimates, $\hat{n}_i$, $\hat{n}_{i+1}$, $\hat{n}_{i,i+1}$ can be substituted into equations 106 and 107 to give parallel form estimates of the reliability terms, $\hat{r}_i$ and $\hat{r}_{i+1}$.

Thus either the test–retest method (equation 104) or the parallel-form method (equations 106 and 107) can be used to estimate the reliability terms from the observed frequencies. These in turn, along with the observed frequencies themselves, can be substituted into equation 101 in place of the theoretical values to give estimates of K_{ij}:

(108) $$\hat{K}_{ij} = \frac{\hat{n}_{ij}}{(\hat{r}_i \hat{r}_j \hat{n}_i \hat{n}_j)^{1/2}} \qquad (i, j = 1, 2, \cdots, m)$$

The estimate $\hat{K}_{ij}$ can be transformed into $\hat{z}_{ij}$, using a table of the normal curve. ($\hat{z}_{ij}$ is the abscissa value corresponding to an ordinate of $\hat{K}_{ij}$ in a table of the normal curve set up to have a maximum ordinate equal to unity. If such a table is not available, we can divide $\hat{K}_{ij}$ by $\sqrt{2\pi}$ and then enter this value into the more usual table which is set up so that the total *area* under the normal curve is equal to unity.)

Estimating the Scale Values S_j from the Observed z_{ij}

We do not yet know what sign to give the normal deviate $\hat{z}_{ij}$; i.e., we do not yet know whether a positive value of $\hat{z}_{ij}$ should correspond to the difference $(S_i - S_j)$ or $(S_j - S_i)$. In order to determine this it is necessary to define the direction of the underlying continuum which is to be considered positive, and to order the items along this continuum. With m stimuli, we can obtain the $m(m-1)/2$ independent estimates of the differences $|S_j - S_i|$. These differences can be arranged in the $m \times m$ symmetric matrix shown in Table 2. In this table, $\hat{z}_{ij} = \hat{z}_{ji}$, and the diagonal elements $\hat{z}_{ii}$ are entered as zeros. Table 2 can thus be considered to be a table of nondirected distances between the item represented by the row and the item represented by the column.

Table 2. Normal Deviates Corresponding to Ordinates Equal to $\hat{K}_{ij}$

	1	2	3	$\cdots$	j	$\cdots$	m
1	0	$\hat{z}_{12}$	$\hat{z}_{13}$	$\cdots$	$\hat{z}_{1j}$	$\cdots$	$\hat{z}_{1m}$
2	$\hat{z}_{21}$	0	$\hat{z}_{23}$	$\cdots$	$\hat{z}_{2j}$	$\cdots$	$\hat{z}_{2m}$
3	$\hat{z}_{31}$	$\hat{z}_{32}$	0	$\cdots$	$\hat{z}_{3j}$	$\cdots$	$\hat{z}_{3m}$
$\vdots$							
i	$\hat{z}_{i1}$	$\hat{z}_{i2}$	$\hat{z}_{i3}$	$\cdots$	$\hat{z}_{ij}$	$\cdots$	$\hat{z}_{im}$
$\vdots$							
m	$\hat{z}_{m1}$	$\hat{z}_{m2}$	$\hat{z}_{m3}$	$\cdots$	$\hat{z}_{mj}$	$\cdots$	0

Thurstone does not discuss the problem of ordering the items. However, it seems that the following method is one that would suffice. First, the sum of any column of Table 2 is equal to m times the average distance of the item represented by that column from all of the items in the set. In general, items all on one side of the mean scale position of the entire set will be ordered with respect to each other in terms of their distance from the mean, as will all the items on the other side of the mean. Examination of the distances between items having about the same column sum will ordinarily suffice to determine whether they are on the same or opposite sides of the mean. The column sums, plus examination of individual cells, will thus ordinarily enable us to order the stimuli.

Given the order of the stimuli, Table 2 can be transformed into a table of directed distances $(S_j - S_i)$ as shown in Table 3 by, first, rearranging the columns and rows to correspond to the order of the items, and, second, placing a minus sign in front of all terms below the principal diagonal. In Table 3, the items are in increasing order from left to right and from top to bottom. Thus, the element in the ith row and jth column gives the estimate of the difference $(S_j - S_i)$.

At this point, the problem becomes identical with that of condition C of the law of comparative judgment which was discussed in detail in Chapter 9. If all cells are filled, the least-squares estimate of the scale values S_j is simply the sums of the columns. This solution gives the scale values in an arbitrary unit, referred to an origin at the mean value of all the stimuli. If some cells are vacant, or if it is desired to omit any distance greater than, say, 2σ, on the grounds of instability of estimates of distances of that size,

Table 3. TABLE OF DIRECTED DISTANCES, $z_{ij} = S_j - S_i$

The items are in increasing order from left to right and from top to bottom

	1	2	3	$\cdots$	j	$\cdots\cdots$	m
1	0	$S_2 - S_1$	$S_3 - S_1$	$\cdots$	$S_j - S_1$	$\cdots\cdots$	$S_m - S_1$
2	$S_1 - S_2$	0	$S_3 - S_2$	$\cdots$	$S_j - S_2$	$\cdots\cdots$	$S_m - S_2$
3	$S_1 - S_3$	$S_2 - S_3$	0	$\cdots$	$S_j - S_3$	$\cdots\cdots$	$S_m - S_3$
.							
.							
.							
i	$S_1 - S_i$	$S_2 - S_i$	$S_3 - S_i$	$\cdots$	$S_j - S_i$	$\cdots\cdots$	$S_m - S_i$
.							
.							
m	$S_1 - S_m$	$S_2 - S_m$	$S_3 - S_m$	$\cdots$	$S_j - S_m$	$\cdots\cdots$	0

or of possible inadequacy of the transformation function for such extreme values, then the alternative solutions to condition C which are discussed in Chapter 9 could be used.

The order of the scale values should be the same as the order of the columns of Table 3. If the scale values are not in exactly the same order as the columns, then it will be necessary to reconstruct Table 3 with the items in the order given by the first solution. Carrying out of subsequent steps would then give a better estimate of the scale values.

Evaluating the Goodness of Fit of the Model to the Data

Given the m scale values for the items, we can reverse the procedure and use these scale values to obtain derived distances between all pairs of stimuli. These $m(m-1)/2$ derived distances can then be compared with the observed distances given in Table 3. If the discrepancies are small relative to the range of the total scale, we would accept the model. If not, the model would be rejected, and we would conclude that either the items cannot be considered as located along a single continuum, or the procedures for relating the observations to the distances between stimuli are incorrect.

An Alternative Multidimensional Approach

Since the elements of Table 2 are the mutual interpoint distances between all pairs of stimuli, the multidimensional-scaling procedures discussed in Chapter 11 would be appropriate. If these procedures were used, it would be unnecessary to attempt to determine the order of the items as a separate preliminary step. In order to obtain estimates of the scale values using the multidimensional approach, we would simply convert the distances into scalar products and perform a factor analysis. If the hypothesis of a single underlying continuum is correct, the matrix of scalar products will be of unit rank (except for residual error) and the loadings on the first factor will correspond to the scale values of the items. Preferably, the first principal axis would be used, although for most purposes the first centroid would be expected to give a close enough approximation.

It might further be noted that there has really been nothing postulated in the model which requires that the underlying continuum be unidimensional. Equations 96, 99, 100, and 103, for example, could as well have been written in terms of d_{ij}, the distance between two items in a multidimensional space, instead of $|S_j - S_i|$, the absolute difference in scale values along a unidimensional underlying continuum. Hence, it would seem that the model is as appropriate for the multidimensional case as it is for the unidimensional case for which it was first developed. If systematic variance remains in the matrix of scalar products after the first factor has been extracted, it would therefore seem appropriate to extract further factors, precisely as is done in the multidimensional judgment model of Chapter 11. The factor loadings would correspond to the projections of the items on arbitrary axes of the multidimensional space occupied jointly by the items. These axes might be rotated or translated as desired in order to enable psychological interpretation of the dimensions of the particular attribute underlying the set of m items.

Models for Comparative Response Data

1. INTRODUCTION

Chapters 12 and 13 dealt with various models appropriate for categorical responses. The type of data to which these models were applicable consisted of the categorical response of each subject to each separate item. Subject i agreed with, passed, or in some other manner, was categorized by item j. Within the general response approach to scaling, by far the most attention has been devoted to development of models that require this type of data. Recently, however, Coombs and his students (Coombs, 1950, 1952, 1953; Bennett, 1951, 1956; Hays, 1954) have been concerned with the development of more or less parallel procedures within the general response approach which require data in the form of comparative responses rather than categorical responses. The raw data required consist of a rank order of some or all of the stimuli for each subject in terms of *his own preference or agreement*. For example, if the stimuli were attitude statements, the subject might be required to indicate the statement he agrees with most, the statement he agrees with next most, etc., down to the statement he agrees with least (or perhaps to order in this manner only r of the total n items). The data are thus explicitly comparative: Subject i prefers to endorse stimulus j more than stimulus k.

In the present chapter, we shall consider the scaling procedures developed by Coombs and his students for this type of data. The procedures are within the general response approach, since the preferences are assumed to be determined by the characteristics of both the subject and the stimuli. At the present stage of development, they are completely deterministic, in that in the model itself no provision is made for any variation in responses above and beyond that which can be accounted for by the relation of the subject and the stimuli to the underlying attribute. The discussion in sections 2 and 3 follows closely that given in Coombs (1950, 1953).

The General Unfolding Model

It is postulated that the preferences of the subjects for the stimuli can be accounted for by a single underlying attribute. This attribute can be represented by a unidimensional continuum analogous to a segment of a straight line. Subjects and stimuli can both be represented as points along this underlying continuum. It is postulated that the distance of any given stimulus from a particular subject is directly related to the extent to which the subject is willing to endorse or choose that stimulus. Thus, a stimulus located at the same point as the subject is the stimulus with which the subject is in perfect agreement or which he would prefer above all others. As the distance increases, the amount of agreement or "preferability" with the stimulus decreases. Thus, subject i will prefer stimulus j to stimulus k if the position of stimulus j is closer than that of stimulus k to the position of subject i (or equivalently, to the stimulus that represents the *ideal* of subject i). If we let s_i, s_j, and s_k denote the scale values of subject i and stimuli j and k, respectively (as measured on an interval scale), then the response "stimulus j preferred to stimulus k" made by subject i implies that

(1)
$$|s_j - s_i| < |s_k - s_i|$$

or

$$d_{ij} < d_{ik}$$

where d denotes the corresponding nondirected distances.

Equation 1 is the basic equation of the model. It implies that the rank order of preferences for a given subject corresponds to the rank order of the distances of the stimuli from the position of the subject on the underlying continuum. Different subjects can, of course, give different rank orders, since the subjects might be located at differing positions along the continuum. Coombs has called the rank order of the stimuli for any given subject a *qualitative I scale*, or more briefly, simply an I scale (1950, p. 146).

Consider the four stimuli (A, B, C, D) depicted in Figure 1. According to equation 1, a person at point X with respect to the underlying attribute would give the preference order $ABCD$, a person at point Y would give the order $BCAD$, and a person at point Z, the order $CDBA$. These orders correspond to three of the seven different I scales which could be obtained from the situation indicated. Each I scale can be considered as a simple rank order of the stimuli which would be obtained if the underlying continuum of Figure 1 were simply folded over at the point occupied by the

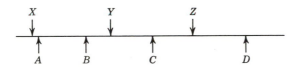

Figure 1. Illustrative example of the model. The line represents the underlying attribute. The letters A, B, C, and D denote the positions of four stimuli. The letters X, Y, and Z denote the positions of three subjects.

subject. The scaling task can be considered in terms of unfolding the obtained rank orders of preferences onto the single underlying continuum. Hence, Coombs calls the procedure "the unfolding technique."

2. ANALYTICAL PROCEDURES

We shall first consider the case where the experimental procedure has given us the complete rank order of all of the stimuli for each subject. For example, we might simply assume that each of N subjects has been required to place the n stimuli in rank order according to his preferences or his willingness to endorse them. This particular procedure assumes transitivity and consistency in the subjects' judgments. More complex experimental methods such as the methods of paired comparisons or triads allow for checks on either or both of these properties. The analytical procedures developed thus far for this approach, however, require that the data be perfectly transitive. Hence we shall not consider these more searching experimental procedures any further.

We shall also consider briefly an application of the unfolding technique to data gathered by a somewhat less searching procedure called by Coombs the "order k" methods (1952). In these procedures the subject is required to order only the first k stimuli in terms of his preferences, where $k < n-1$. That is, given n stimuli, each subject is required to indicate his first choice, second choice, third choice, etc., down to the kth choice. When $k = n-1$, of course, the method becomes identical with the usual complete rank order.

An Illustrative Example

Let us assume that each of a large number of subjects has indicated his rank order of preference for four samples of ice cream, which differ from one another only with respect to easily discernible differences in sweetness. We will thus have as raw data an I scale for each subject. Let us assume that the stimuli are located along the underlying continuum as indicated in Figure 2.

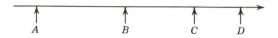

Figure 2.   Location of ice cream samples for illustrative example.

There are 4! ways in which the four stimuli might be ranked. If the ranks are determined in the manner required by the model, however, we shall see that only seven of these orders can occur. As was the case in the deterministic models of Chapter 12, it is the nonoccurrence of the deviant response patterns that enables recovery of the order on the underlying continuum.

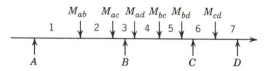

Figure 3.   Location of midpoints between all pairs of ice cream samples. M_{ab} denotes the midpoint between stimuli A and B.

The point halfway between any pair of stimuli divides the subjects into two groups or classes. All subjects on one side of the midpoint will rank the two stimuli in one order, and all subjects on the other side will rank the two stimuli in the reverse order. In Figure 2, for example, all subjects on the A side of the midpoint between stimuli A and B will give the order AB, while all those on the B side will give the order BA. The midpoint between any two stimuli thus serves as a boundary between ordered categories or classes of subjects. Since there are $\frac{1}{2}n(n-1)$ midpoints for n stimuli, there are $\frac{1}{2}n(n-1) + 1$ ordered classes of subjects. Figure 3 gives the positions of the $\frac{1}{2}(4)(3) = 6$ midpoints of our example, along with the ordered classes of subjects into which they divide the sample of subjects.

All subjects within a particular class give the same rank order of stimuli. The rank orders corresponding to the classes of Figure 3 are given below:

1. *ABCD*
2. *BACD*
3. *BCAD*
4. *BCDA*
5. *CBDA*
6. *CDBA*
7. *DCBA*

Thus, if the stimuli are located as in Figure 2, and the preferences of the subjects behave in the manner required by the model, only the seven rank orders given above will be obtained.

In actual practice, of course, we would be given the rank orders and would attempt to use them to recover as far as possible the order and spacing in the figures. Let us see what there is about these seven rank orders which would enable us to carry out the unfolding procedure.

Note, first of all, that of the seven rank orders only two are the exact reverse of each other (orders 1 and 7). These orders give immediately the order of the stimuli along the underlying continuum. (Either order may be used, of course, since there is nothing in the procedure to define a positive or negative direction on the attribute.) Once the order of the stimuli is known, the determination of the order of the six midpoints is straightforward. The orders given by adjacent classes of subjects differ from one another only by the interchange in rank of two adjacent stimuli. The boundary between the two adjacent classes is the midpoint of the two stimuli interchanged. Thus, the orders of class 1 (*ABCD*) and class 2 (*BACD*) differ only in that the ranks of stimuli *A* and *B* are reversed. Hence the boundary between class 1 and class 2 is the midpoint M_{ab}. In like manner, for classes 2 and 3, stimuli *A* and *C* are adjacent to each other and are reversed in the two classes, whereas the order of the remaining stimuli is the same. Hence the boundary between classes 2 and 3 is the midpoint M_{ac}.

In actually determining the order of the midpoints, we would therefore begin with the order for one of the two extreme classes, and find the one class that has an order which differs only in interchange of two adjacent stimuli. Given this class, we would find that class of those remaining whose order differed only by interchange of two adjacent stimuli, and so on, until we reach the final class.

Assuming that the model fits the data (as it did in our illustrative example), the procedures given thus far enable us to determine

1. The order of the stimuli.

2. The order of the midpoints between pairs of stimuli.
3. The order of the classes of subjects.

One further item of information remains. This has to do with the relative size of the intervals between some of the stimuli. In general, any four stimuli in a given order on the underlying continuum might give rise to two different internally consistent sets of rank orders, depending on the

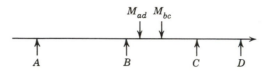

Figure 4. Illustration of the relation of midpoint order to size of interval. M_{ad} precedes M_{bc} when the distance d_{ab} is greater than the distance d_{cd}.

relative spacing of the four stimuli. For any four stimuli in order, the crucial bit of information is the order of the midpoint of the first and last stimuli as against that of the middle two stimuli. If the midpoint of the extreme stimuli precedes that of the middle stimuli, it follows that the distance between the first and second stimulus is greater than the distance between the third and fourth. This is easily seen in Figure 4. In the

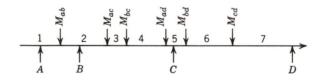

Figure 5. Spacing of four stimuli which gives a reversal in midpoint order. Here, since $d_{ab} < d_{cd}$, M_{bc} precedes M_{ad}.

illustrative example, the stimuli were spaced so that the midpoint M_{ad} came before the midpoint M_{bc}. If it had been set up instead with spacing as in Figure 5, we would have obtained the following set of rank orders:

1. *ABCD*
2. *BACD*
3. *BCAD*
4. *CBAD*
5. *CBDA*
6. *CDBA*
7. *DCBA*

The rank order given by the fourth class in the present example, *CBAD*, differs from that given in the original example, *BCDA*.   Determination of the order of the midpoints shows that M_{bc} now precedes M_{ad}, and, consequently, we know that the interval d_{ab} is here less than the interval d_{cd}.

Thus, in addition to the three kinds of information given above, Coombs' unfolding procedure also yields information concerning the relative size of some of the distances between the stimuli (beyond that given directly by the order of the stimuli themselves such as, for example, that, for any three stimuli in order *ABC*, d_{ac} is greater than either d_{ab} or d_{bc}).   Since some of the distances are ordered, Coombs calls the resulting scale an "ordered metric" scale.

Since each subset of four stimuli gives one item of information concerning the relative size of two of the distances, there will be, in general, as many items of information of this type as there are combinations of four stimuli, i.e., $\binom{n}{4}$ such comparisons.   Not all will necessarily be independent, however.   For example, with five stimuli, *ABCDE*, we might obtain the following set of rank orders:

1. *ABCDE*
2. *BACDE*
3. *BCADE*
4. *CBADE*
5. *CBDAE*
6. *CDBAE*
7. *DCBAE*
8. *DCBEA*
9. *DCEBA*
10. *DECBA*
11. *EDCBA*

When unfolded, the order of stimuli, order of midpoints, and order of subject classes would appear as illustrated in Figure 6.   The metric

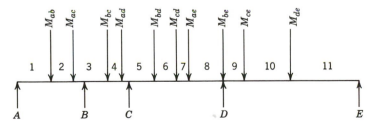

Figure 6.   An unfolded scale for five stimuli.

information, beyond that given directly by the rank order of the stimuli on the joint continuum is given in Table 1. Here, several of the metric deductions are redundant. For example, from the fact that $d_{ac} < d_{de}$, we can deduce directly that both d_{ab} and d_{bc} must be less than d_{de}.

Table 1. METRIC INFORMATION IN UNFOLDED
SCALE OF FIGURE 6

Subset of 4 Stimuli	Order of Midpoints	Metric Deduction
$ABCD$	M_{bc} precedes M_{ad}	$d_{ab} < d_{cd}$
$ABCE$	M_{bc} precedes M_{ae}	$d_{ab} < d_{ce}$
$ABDE$	M_{bd} precedes M_{ae}	$d_{ab} < d_{de}$
$ACDE$	M_{cd} precedes M_{ae}	$d_{ac} < d_{de}$
$BCDE$	M_{cd} precedes M_{be}	$d_{bc} < d_{de}$

Coombs's Parallelogram Procedure

It is also possible to set up the unfolding procedure in a manner directly analogous to the scalogram procedures discussed in Chapter 12. Indeed, one of the models discussed in that chapter (see section 3 of Chapter 12) is quite similar to the present models, and, as a matter of fact, could almost as well have been classified as a model for comparative data instead of as a categorical-response model. We refer, of course, to the model discussed for dealing with point or nonmonotone dichotomous items, where the subject was required to endorse or pick r out of the total set of n stimuli. It could be argued that responses of this form are more comparative than categorical, owing to the requirement that the subject "agree" with exactly r out of the n items. For data of this type, the scalogram analysis would give a scalogram of the form shown in Table 2. In this particular example $r = 3$ and $n = 5$; i.e., each subject is required to check three out of the five items. An × indicates a positive response to the item.

Table 2. SCALOGRAM FOR $r = 3$, $n = 5$

		Items 1	2	3	4	5
	I	×	×	×		
Subject Types	II		×	×	×	
	III			×	×	×

Suppose, instead of requiring only that the subject indicate the r items which he prefers to endorse, we also require that he indicate the rank order of these r items in terms of his willingness to endorse them. In the special case where $r = n-1$, this procedure would give a complete I scale for each subject. For values of r from 2 to $n-2$, only the first r stimuli would be so ordered for each subject. The responses can be arranged in a table analogous to the scalogram diagram where the *rank number* is entered in the appropriate cell instead of the ×. Table 3 illustrates such a diagram

Table 3. PARALLELOGRAM DIAGRAM FOR $r = 3$, $n = 5$

		Stimuli				
		A	B	C	D	E
	1	1	2	3		
	2	2	1	3		
	3	3	1	2		
	4	3	2	1		
Subject Classes	5		2	1	3	
	6		3	1	2	
	7		3	2	1	
	8			2	1	3
	9			3	1	2
	10			3	2	1

for $r = 3$, $n = 5$. The analytical procedure would consist of permuting rows and columns until the following criteria have been met (from Coombs, 1953):

1. The entries in each row and column form solid strings—i.e., there must be no blank cells separating the rank numbers in any row or column.
2. Entries in the first row must increase monotonically from left to right, and entries in the last row must decrease from left to right.
3. Entries in the first column must increase from top to bottom, and entries in the last column must decrease from top to bottom.
4. Entries in all other columns must first decrease monotonically and then increase again.

The finding of a permutation of rows and of columns which meets these four criteria is a necessary and sufficient test of the hypothesis that a single underlying attribute can be considered to underlie the preference responses of the subjects to the stimuli.

Note that the "order three out of five" type of data contains considerably more information than the "pick three out of five" type of data. In Table 2, the scalogram divided the subjects into but three ordered classes, whereas the analogous parallelogram of Table 3 divided the subjects into ten ordered classes (as against the eleven that would be obtained if the complete I scales had been given).   In addition, of course, the "order r" type of data contains the distance information previously discussed, provided that $r \geqslant 3$.   In general, the larger the value of r, the more information becomes available concerning distances between stimuli.

3. GENERAL COMMENTS ON THE UNFOLDING PROCEDURE

The Nature of the Underlying Continuum

As is true of all of the response methods, nothing in either the task set for the subject or the subsequent analytical procedures specifies the nature of the underlying attribute.   The procedures indicate whether or not the preference responses can be considered as having been generated from a single underlying attribute in the manner specified by the model; and, if so, they indicate the order of the stimuli, the stimulus midpoints, and the subject classes with respect to this underlying attribute.   But they indicate nothing about the nature of the attribute itself.

This is, of course, one of the primary differences between the judgment methods and the response methods.   In the judgment methods, it will be recalled, the nature of the attribute is given by the task set for the subject. He judges with respect to *brightness, conservatism,* or *sweetness,* for example.   The particular task is thus specific to the particular attribute. In the response methods, this is not the case.   Here, the task is more or less general.   A response of "agree" or "disagree" implies nothing ex-plicitly about any particular attribute, nor does a response of the form "subject i prefers stimulus j to stimulus k" give any explicit notion of the attribute or attributes that determine that response.

It should be noted, incidentally, that this is not true of the *individual I scales.*   The attribute corresponding to any particular I scale is simply an attribute of preference for that particular subject.   It is essentially an ordinal judgment scale.   The *joint scale* of subjects and stimuli which results from the unfolding process, however, is clearly not a scale of preferences.   In the ice cream example, the attribute presumably was one of *sweetness of ice cream.*   The samples of ice cream were ordered with respect to sweetness; the subjects were ordered on the same continuum in terms of the degree of sweetness of vanilla ice cream which they considered to be ideal.   We know this to be so, however, primarily because we set up. the hypothetical example to make it so.   In the general case, of course, we would not have this information.   Since there is nothing in either the task or the analysis that suggests the attribute, additional procedures would be necessary to determine its nature.

Under some circumstances (perhaps most) the experimenter will have a particular attribute in mind when selecting the set of stimuli. The "additional procedures" referred to above would then consist of whatever criteria were used in selecting the stimuli thought to represent this attribute. In such a situation, the unfolding procedure would be aided considerably if the subject not only indicated the *rank order* of the stimuli but also indicated the *direction* of each stimulus from his own position. For example, if the stimuli were a set of attitude statements chosen to reflect attitude toward the church, the subject could be asked to rank the statements in the order in which he would prefer to endorse them, and also to indicate for each statement whether it was more favorable or less favorable to the church than his own attitude. With this additional item of information, the unfolded scale would be given directly. (It would also further subdivide n of the subject classes into two ordered parts each, incidentally. For example, subjects who gave the rank order $ABCD$ would be subdivided into those who considered stimulus A to be somewhat too "pro" and those who considered A to be somewhat too "con.") In the general case, however, this would not be feasible, since, when the attribute is not known, the direction of deviation could not be indicated.

Treatment of "Error"

The model itself is an exceedingly stringent one. No extraneous variation is permitted. At the same time, the task set for the subject is at a fairly high level of difficulty (in many respects similar to the equisection judgment discussed in Chapter 6), since, for some stimuli at least, the subject must decide whether the degree that stimulus A is too far in one direction from the ideal is greater or less than the degree that stimulus B is too far in the other direction. (In the ice cream example: "Is sample A as much too sweet as sample B is too dry?") Hence, it is not surprising that few if any sets of data have been found that fit the model exactly.

Unfortunately, at the present stage of development, neither indices for evaluating degree of approximation of model to data (analogous to the coefficient of reproducibility of Chapter 12, for example) nor corresponding probability models (analogous to the procedures of Chapter 13, for example) are available. Until such procedures have been developed, the unfolding procedure will likely remain of more theoretical than practical interest.

Comparison with Group Preferability Scales or Indices

The experimental methods for gathering data for the unfolding procedure closely parallel those used for the various special cases of Thurstone's judgment model (Chapters 8 to 10).   As a general rule, we could attempt to fit either the unfolding model or the Thurstone model to a set of data collected by these methods.   While the attempt might be made to fit either model, it should be noted that, if one of the models fits the data, the other ordinarily will not.   The only time that both models would be expected to fit the same set of data would be in the degenerate case where all subjects gave the same rank order.   In general, the Thurstone model would require that either all subjects had the same "ideal" or that the "ideals" of all subjects were either all above or all below all of the stimulus points with respect to the underlying attribute.   In addition, if a scale with interval properties were to be obtained, it would also be necessary that the stimuli not be perfectly discriminable with respect to the attribute of preferability; i.e., a certain amount of "error" in the judgments is required.   The unfolding technique, on the other hand, requires that the stimuli be perfectly discriminable, and is more appropriate for the case where the "ideals" of the subjects are distributed throughout the range of the underlying attribute.

Where the Thurstone model is applied mechanically to data that fit the unfolding model, a comparison of the resulting scales is of interest. Coombs (1951) has indicated that in this case the "scale of preferability" obtained by the Thurstone model is approximately equivalent to the scale that would be obtained if the underlying attribute of his model were folded in the middle.   The "scale of preferability" is thus approximately equivalent to the average of the individual I scales.

It should again be emphasized, however, that the Thurstone model itself is not strictly appropriate in this case, and that a sufficiently sensitive test would indicate a lack of fit of the model to the data.   Hence, the numbers assigned to the stimuli would perhaps be best considered in terms of an index of preferability for the particular group rather than as scale values of the stimuli referred to an interval scale of preferability.

For an alternative procedure which gives a similar preferability index and which was designed specifically for the situation where the subjects differ systematically with respect to their preferences, see Guttman (1946*b*). Guttman's procedure gives index numbers which are "best," in a least-squares sense, for reproducing the judgment of each individual on each comparison.

4. MULTIDIMENSIONAL EXTENSIONS

Bennett (1951, 1956) and Hays (1954) have made considerable progress toward generalization of the unfolding model to the multidimensional case. Since this work is still very much in the developmental stage, we will give only the very basic notions here. For more detail the reader is referred to the original sources.

In the unidimensional unfolding model, the underlying attribute could be conceptualized as a segment of a straight line (i.e., a one-dimensional Euclidean space). In the multidimensional extension, the straight line is replaced by a space of dimensionality d. Bennett conceives of this multidimensional space as essentially Euclidean in nature (though he points out that he does not actually need *all* of the properties of a Euclidean space, since most of the procedures used in unfolding are at a more primitive level). Thus, in place of representing stimuli and subjects as points along a straight line, in the multidimensional extension we represent the stimuli and subjects as points in a real, Euclidean space of unknown dimensionality d.

As before, it is postulated that the order of preference for the stimuli given by a particular subject is monotonically related to the distances from that subject to the stimuli in the space. The greater the distance, the less the preference.

In unidimensional unfolding, a basic notion was the midpoint between each pair of stimuli. We saw that the midpoint between any two stimuli served as a boundary between classes of subjects, or, equivalently, between two *regions* of the underlying continuum. All subjects in one region placed the two stimuli in one rank order; all those in the other region placed the stimuli in the reverse order. Midpoints of more and more pairs of stimuli subdivided the continuum into more and more regions. The midpoints of all pairs of stimuli in the sample finally divided the continuum into $\frac{1}{2}n(n-1) + 1$ regions. Subjects within a given region all gave the same rank order.

In the multidimensional extension, the notion of a midpoint between a pair of stimuli is generalized to that of a hyperplane of equidistance between the pair of stimuli. In general, the locus of all points that are equidistant from a given pair of stimuli is a subspace with dimensionality equal to one less than the dimensionality of the total space. Thus, for a one-dimensional space, the locus is simply a point (i.e., the midpoint between the stimulus pair); for a two-dimensional space, the locus is a straight line (the perpendicular bisector of a line segment joining the two points); for a three-dimensional space, the locus is a plane; etc. We shall use the term "boundary hyperplane" to refer to these loci. The boundary hyperplane between any two stimuli thus divides the total space into two regions, with all subjects in one region ordering the two stimuli in one way and all those in the other region giving the reverse order.

The complete set of hyperplanes, i.e., the hyperplanes between all pairs of stimuli, divides the total space into a number of *elementary regions*.

All subjects within a given elementary region give the same rank order to the set of stimuli. Subjects in different regions give different rank orders. Thus, there will be one elementary region for each different rank order.

The task of multidimensional unfolding is essentially to determine the dimensionality of the space and the location of the stimulus points and the regions within this space, when given only the rank orders of the stimuli from the subjects.

We shall consider briefly here only the first of these problems: that of estimating the dimensionality. Although some progress has been made toward a deterministic solution for the configuration of the stimuli and regions within the space (Bennett, 1951, 1956; Hays, 1954), the work is still largely in the developmental stage.

Estimation of Dimensionality

We might ask: "How many regions can occur for n stimuli in a space of dimensionality d?" We have already seen that, for a unidimensional space, the maximum number of regions is equal to $\frac{1}{2}n(n-1) + 1$. Since each region is associated with a rank order, if the number of different rank orders returned by the subjects is greater than this value, we would know that the minimum dimensionality of the space would have to be greater than one. Thus, the total number of different rank orders returned can be used under some circumstances to set a lower bound for the dimensionality. This particular procedure would not be of great use ordinarily, however, since the number of different rank orders increases rapidly with both an increase in the dimensionality and an increase in the number of stimuli.

Bennett (1956) gives a table showing the number of possible rank orders for n stimuli in d dimensions ($n = 1, 2, \cdots, 40; d = 1, 2, \cdots, 5$). We have already seen that five stimuli in a unidimensional space can generate eleven different rank orders. According to Bennett's table, for the same number of stimuli in a two-dimensional space, this increases to 46; in a three-dimensional space, to 96. By the time we reach ten stimuli in a three-dimensional space, the number of different rank orders is somewhat over 10,000. Thus, unless both dimensionality and number of stimuli are small, we would likely find that the number of possible rank orders exceeds the number of subjects in the sample.

A more sensitive procedure for setting a lower bound to the dimensionality utilizes subsets of stimuli. The basic fact used is that all possible orders of any $d+1$ stimuli can occur in a space of dimensionality d. (This is implied directly from the fact that any r points *determine* a space of dimensionality $r-1$ or less.) For example, for two stimuli in a unidimensional space, both orders can occur, AB and BA. For any three stimuli in a two-dimensional space, all six possible orders can occur: *ABC*, *ACB*, *BAC*, *BCA*, *CAB*, *CBA*. All six orders *cannot* occur in a unidimensional space, however, since three stimuli divide a unidimensional space into no more than four regions. In general, the complete set of permutations of $d+2$ stimuli cannot occur in a space of dimensionality d. Hence the largest subset of stimuli for which all possible permutations in rank order occur sets a lower bound to the dimensionality of the space. The dimensionality cannot be smaller than one less than the largest number of stimuli for which a complete set of rank orders is obtained. For example, if the complete set of $5! = 120$ rank orders is obtained for any subset of five stimuli, we would know that the dimensionality must be at least four.

▶15

Summary ◀

1. INTRODUCTION

It seems desirable to conclude with a brief review of the distinguishing characteristics of the three major classes of scaling methods considered in this monograph and, in addition, an equally brief discussion of some of the key questions concerning progress to date for each.

Nearly all the methods discussed can be considered as examples of fundamental measurement, some perhaps to a greater degree than others. We have not, in general, attempted to deal with those procedures that fall into the derived or defined measurement categories. We have used the term "fundamental" in the monograph simply to designate those scaling methods whose general rationale involves the construction and application of a self-contained testable theory. This implies automatically that notions of goodness of fit are involved in one sense or another. It also implies that one possible outcome of a scaling experiment is the conclusion that the procedure is inappropriate or that the attribute under consideration cannot be represented by the particular number system implied by the scaling procedure. The net result of this general approach when it *does* fit the data adequately is that the numbers assigned to the various quantities of the attribute under consideration have meaning which is based upon the operation of empirical laws. A scale constructed through use of a fundamental scaling procedure which has been demonstrated to fit the data adequately can thus never be entirely trivial. Even if subsequent experimentation fails to reveal any lawful relations of the attribute with other variables, there is still the experimental fact that it does represent a set of lawful relations among different quantities of the attribute itself. It seems reasonable to assume, however, that attributes initially measured in this way *will* enter into lawful relations with other variables, or, at least, will stand a greater chance of doing so than would those scales whose meaning derives entirely from definition alone.

Within this general framework, we found that the scaling methods could be separated into two major classes, which we call the *judgment* methods and the *response* methods. These two great classes of methods differ from each other in a variety of ways. Some of these ways are listed below.

Assignment of "Cause" of Systematic Variability of Responses of Subjects to Stimuli

In the judgment methods, the systematic variability is ascribed to variation of the stimuli along a subjective continuum. Stimuli alone are given scale values. The procedure is analogous to a one-way classification in analysis of variance. In the response methods, the systematic variability is ascribed to both subjects and stimuli. Either or both may be assigned scale values. The analogy with analysis of variance here is a two-way classification with no interaction.

Task Set for the Subject

In the judgment methods, the task set for the subject involves specification of the attribute. His task is directed toward the amount of a specified attribute possessed by the stimulus. Thus, he might judge, for example, whether stimulus *A* is *heavier* than stimulus *B*, or twice as *bright* as stimulus *B*. Or, he may be required to rate, sort, or rank the stimuli with respect to *excellence* or *beauty* or *loudness*. In each instance, the attribute of interest is specified. In the response methods, the particular attribute is not specified. The subject only indicates whether he *agrees with* or *endorses* stimulus *A*, whether he *prefers* stimulus *A* to stimulus *B*, or whether he can *solve* stimulus *A* correctly, for example. His task can thus be formally the same, regardless of the attribute being investigated.

Specification of the Class of Elements to Which the Attribute Applies

In the judgment methods, the class of elements is specified more or less directly by the task set for the subject. For example, the attribute "redness" is associated with an object if the judgment "object *A* is redder than object *B*" or "object *B* is redder than object *A*" is appropriate. Electrons and pure tones are not members of the class of elements possessing the attribute "redness" since here the empirical operations would have no meaning.

In the response methods, the task set for the subject gives no indication of whether or not a given attribute is relevant to all of the elements (items). Other procedures are necessary to specify the class of elements. In general, the class of elements has been delimited either by the subjective judgment of the experimenter, or, after the fact, by selection of those items that happen to fit the particular scaling procedure used.

Determination of Order.   The Problem of Dimensionality

In the judgment methods, the postulates of order can be tested directly. The question asked can be phrased: "Is this attribute (which is specified in the task by the comparative relation: e.g., *brighter than, redder than*, or in general, *X'er than*) a unidimensional attribute?" In the response methods the ordinal characteristic is determined indirectly through use of derivative procedures. Here, the question might be phrased: "Do the responses to these items behave as though they were generated by a single unidimensional attribute?" Or, perhaps, "Does the same unidimensional attribute underlie the responses to all of these items?" In the one case, we are given an attribute and we question its dimensionality; in the other, we are given a set of items and we ask whether they all refer to a single (unidimensional) attribute. In both approaches multidimensional extensions have been devised.

The remaining major subdivision of the scaling methods is concerned with the distinction between the quantitative-judgment methods and the variability-of-judgment methods. This distinction has to do with the way in which the interval and ratio characteristics of the final scale are obtained. The quantitative-judgment methods obtain these characteristics more or less directly through quantitative judgments made by the subjects. The subject is required to judge equality of *sense distances*, as in the method of equisection; to judge *sense ratios*, as in the method of fractionation; or to estimate directly the magnitude of the attribute for a stimulus, as in the subjective-estimate methods. In the variability methods, the subject is not required to make responses more complex than ordinal judgments: i.e., judgments requiring that he be able to indicate when one stimulus is greater or less than another with respect to the designated attribute. He thus *ranks* the stimuli, or sorts them into *ordered* classes, or perhaps compares two stimuli directly and reports which is the *greater*. In these methods, the characteristics above and beyond order are derived from the variability of the responses to a given stimulus situation.

We thus have, as the two major types of scaling methods, the judgment methods and the response methods, with the judgment methods further subdivided into those that depend on quantitative judgments and those that depend upon variability of judgment in order to obtain interval or ratio properties.   In the remaining sections, we shall consider some key questions relevant to each.

2. THE JUDGMENT METHODS

Among the many questions that might be considered concerning these methods, three seem to stand out as basic.   All three actually have to do with the problem of invariance in one form or another.   The first question has to do with invariance within a particular technique.   The second has to do with invariance with respect to related techniques: i.e., techniques that derive from the same general scaling approach.   The third has to do with broader invariance characteristics concerning the relations of scales constructed by a particular approach to other variables.

Invariance within a Particular Technique

The use of the term "fundamental" to describe the majority of the methods discussed in this monograph implies that the assignment of numbers is not entirely arbitrary but is rather based, to some degree at least, on empirical laws.   We are interested here in whether or not the theory is ever applicable.   Does it fit the data adequately?   We are further interested in the extent to which the relations among scale values assigned to a given subset of stimuli depend on the remaining stimuli in the set, and also in the extent to which these obtained relations depend on minor variations in scaling technique.   Invariances of this type are of basic importance, since, if the *scale form* (i.e., the relations among scale values assigned to the stimuli) depends on the specific set of stimuli used, or on minute details of technique, the scale does not have a great deal to recommend for itself.   Indeed, if this is the case, we have actually progressed little if any beyond mere arbitrary assignment of numbers to the stimuli.   We could not expect that such scales would lead to discovery of stable relations of the attribute with other variables.

In the quantitative-judgment realm, the results are equivocal.   On the negative side there is first of all the effect of *context*, i.e., the distribution of stimuli chosen by the experimenter to be presented to the subject.   Garner (1954b), for example, showed that, under some conditions, the stimulus which is judged to be one half as great as a given standard can be considered to be entirely a function of the variable stimuli presented to the subject.   This result alone renders suspect a good share of the scales that have been constructed by the "prescribed-ratio" version of the fractionation methods.   There is also the fact that different investigators have obtained different results when using the same method on the same attribute (see, for example, Garner, 1954a, and Stevens, 1955, on loudness; Baker and Dudek, 1955, on subjective weight). With the subjective-estimate methods, the principal problem seems to be due to anchoring effects. The scale form apparently varies, depending on the particular anchoring conditions that exist.

In spite of these difficulties, however, much consistency remains in both of these methods. It is clear that the subjects are often able to use numbers or ratios in meaningful ways, although perhaps not quite to within the restrictions required by these methods. Garner's results (1954a) seem to indicate that subjects can and do judge ratios consistently, but that the ratio judged may not be the one prescribed by the experimenter. Scales of the same attribute obtained under these circumstances will not be linearly related to one another. However, linear plots will result if made in log–log coordinates. Results of subjective-estimate experiments also indicate that this may often be the case (Stevens, 1956b). If this is so, scales constructed for a given attribute would be invariant over a log–linear transformation of the form

$$\log y = a \log x + b$$

Although the equisection methods have not yet been investigated to as large an extent, the results seem a bit more favorable. Results for the attribute of pitch, for example, seem to show sufficient consistency, both among minor variations in method and also among different experimenters.

In general, it would seem reasonable to conclude that the construction of meaningful scales using the quantitative-judgment methods is considerably more difficult than was formerly supposed. For this reason, the validity of most presently available scales is in doubt. More experimental work is needed, especially on the effects on the scale form of context, of instruction, and of training.

The situation with respect to the variability models is also not clear. The scaling procedures based on Thurstone's judgment model do seem in general to fit the data closely. Actually, the fit tends to be very good, even when the rationale does not seem particularly appropriate: e.g., when the methods are used in experiments on *preferences* based on data gathered from a heterogeneous set of subjects. Very little, however, has been done concerning the effect on the scale form of the distribution of stimuli scaled. Work by Garner (1952a) indicated that, at least for the most restrictive case of the categorical-judgment version of the model, a certain amount of distortion occurs at the extremes of the scale in a given experiment, owing to the fact that discriminability at the extremes is better than at the center of the set. More careful experimental work on those attributes that lend themselves to precise experimental control is needed.

Invariance with Respect to Related Techniques

There is a sense in which different methods within a type or class "ought" to yield scales that are linearly related to one another. If they do not, we have an uncomfortable feeling that all is not well. This is not the case where we compare results of methods across classes, where the rationale is different, where the task set for the subject might be different, and where often the purpose itself is different. The results of the three varieties of *quantitative*-judgment methods ought, in this sense, to agree with one another with respect to both ordinal and interval properties of the resulting scales. In like manner, both the comparative and the categorical versions of Thurstone's judgment model ought to give results that are in agreement.

This is in general what happens when we consider the Thurstone model. Plots of the results of the comparative-judgment version against those of the categorical-judgment version have been found to be linear, though the number of experimental comparisons has not been large. With the quantitative-judgment methods, the results are more complex. Recent experimental evidence (see Stevens and Galanter, 1956) seems to indicate that those quantitative-judgment methods which emphasize the *interval* relation among stimuli (e.g., the limited-category methods of Chapter 4 and the equisection methods of Chapter 6) form one closely related subgroup of scales, while those that emphasize the *ratio* relation among stimuli (e.g., the direct numerical estimation procedures of Chapter 4 and the fractionation methods of Chapter 5) form another. The two subgroups of scales are not always linearly related to each other.

Relations between the Variability and the Quantitative-Judgment Approaches

We would expect the two approaches to give scales that are monotonically related to each other, since they both depend ultimately on the same operations to determine order. Beyond this, however, various results obtain. For certain attributes (e.g., pitch), the two approaches have yielded scales that are linearly related. For others (e.g., loudness, weight), the relation is more complex. Results of Stevens and Galanter (1956) seem to indicate that the scales resulting from the variability approach will be linearly related to quantitative-judgment scales when the two subgroups of quantitative-judgment scales are linearly related to each other. When the two subgroups of quantitative-judgment scales are not linearly related to each other, the variability scales will be more nearly linearly related to the scales obtained from those quantitative-judgment methods that emphasize the interval relation than to those that emphasize the ratio relation. More experimental evidence is needed. That the variability and the quantitative-judgment approaches, in general, arrive at somewhat different results is perhaps most clearly shown by the results of Kelley et al. (mimeo) on the influence of judges' attitudes on the obtained scale values of attitude items. The relative *discriminability* of the stimuli remained more or less invariant across the two groups, whereas the *judged distance* between stimuli varied as a function of the attitude of the group. Hence, scales obtained using the method of equal-appearing intervals, a quantitative-judgment method, varied as a function of the attitude of the judges. Judges with extreme attitudes tended to space out stimuli reflecting attitudes similar to their own, and bunch together stimuli at the other end of the scale. Scales of the same items constructed using the variability approach, on the other hand, were more nearly invariant.

Relations with Other Variables

The final question concerns the extent to which the scales have been used. Has the construction of scales by the judgment procedures led to the discovery of laws relating the scaled attributes to other variables? This is, of course, a primary reason for attempting to measure a variable in the first place. It should be noted, however, that it is not the only reason for experimentation in this area. Within the psychophysical tradition, much of the work on scaling reflects an interest in the judgment process itself. Here, interest is not so much in using the scale to establish laws relating the attribute to other variables as it is in studying directly the invariance characteristics and lawful changes in the judgments of the subject which accompany various changes in experimental conditions. Many of the experiments on central tendency, adaptation level, and anchoring are best viewed in this light.

Nevertheless, the construction of a scale of an attribute in order to use it remains a primary reason for scaling. As might be expected, the scales have found most use in those areas where no corresponding physical attribute is readily available. Judgment scales have long been used routinely in the investigation of personality traits, attitudes, abilities, preferences, and esthetics. It is in these very areas, however, that the precision of measurement is generally the smallest. As a result, the investigations are ordinarily limited to correlational analyses and to the testing of significance of group differences or group changes, rather than the specification of more precise functional relationships. It is perhaps unfortunate that, in the very areas where precision and experimental control are the highest, the scales have been least used. In the experimental laboratories, the uses to which the scales have been put are few indeed, though some beginnings have been made. For example, Hull and his associates (1947) have used the rationale of paired comparisons in the measurement of reaction potential in connection with his learning theory; Stevens and Volkmann (1940a) have reported a linear relation between pitch and distance along the basilar membrane; and Guttman and Kalish (1956) have investigated the relationship between generalization and discrimination in pigeons. In general, however, little has been done to date.

3. THE RESPONSE METHODS

Progress to date with the response methods has been mainly limited to developing the models themselves and to devising workable analytical procedures for solving the estimation problems. Very little experimental work has been done, especially with the probabilistic models. Here, applications to empirical data have been almost entirely restricted to illustrative examples presented primarily to demonstrate a particular analytical technique.

Guttman's deterministic model has had fairly wide application. When goodness of fit of the approach is evaluated in terms of the coefficient of reproducibility and auxiliary criteria, the conclusion that the items are "approximately scalable" has often been found to hold. Two factors should be noted, however. The first is that the scales have usually been based on a very few items. The second is that the coefficient of reproducibility is a deceptive index. According to Green (1956) the usual minimum standards for "scalability" correspond roughly to a minimum value of 0.5 for his coefficient I. This means that, in general, a set of items with a coefficient of reproducibility halfway between unity and that expected by chance under the hypothesis of complete independence of items will likely be considered as scalable. Hence it seems clear that the ideal Guttman scale does not actually describe empirical data very closely. Items in general have a considerable portion of their variance which is not attributable to their relation to the underlying attribute. This would be a serious factor indeed if perfect reproducibility (or nearly so) were really a necessary condition for measurement using the response approach. The more realistic criterion is that underlying the methods of Chapter 13: that the *covariance* among items be attributable to their separate relations to the underlying attribute. Much more experimental and analytical work on these methods is needed.

▶ *Appendix A*

THE CUMULATIVE NORMAL DISTRIBUTION FUNCTION: UNIT NORMAL DEVIATES TO CUMULATIVE PROPORTIONS

$$P_x = \int_{-\infty}^{x} e^{-(z^2/2)} \, dz \quad \text{for} \quad -4.99 \le x \le 0.00$$

x	.00	.01	.02	.03	.04	.05	.06	.07	.08	.09
−.0	.5000	.4960	.4920	.4880	.4840	.4801	.4761	.4721	.4681	.4641
−.1	.4602	.4562	.4522	.4483	.4443	.4404	.4364	.4325	.4286	.4247
−.2	.4207	.4168	.4129	.4090	.4052	.4013	.3974	.3936	.3897	.3859
−.3	.3821	.3783	.3745	.3707	.3669	.3632	.3594	.3557	.3520	.3483
−.4	.3446	.3409	.3372	.3336	.3300	.3264	.3228	.3192	.3156	.3121
−.5	.3085	.3050	.3015	.2981	.2946	.2912	.2877	.2843	.2810	.2776
−.6	.2743	.2709	.2676	.2643	.2611	.2578	.2546	.2514	.2483	.2451
−.7	.2420	.2389	.2358	.2327	.2297	.2266	.2236	.2206	.2177	.2148
−.8	.2119	.2090	.2061	.2033	.2005	.1977	.1949	.1922	.1894	.1867
−.9	.1841	.1814	.1788	.1762	.1736	.1711	.1685	.1660	.1635	.1611
−1.0	.1587	.1562	.1539	.1515	.1492	.1469	.1446	.1423	.1401	.1379
−1.1	.1357	.1335	.1314	.1292	.1271	.1251	.1230	.1210	.1190	.1170
−1.2	.1151	.1131	.1112	.1093	.1075	.1056	.1038	.1020	.1003	.09853
−1.3	.09680	.09510	.09342	.09176	.09012	.08851	.08691	.08534	.08379	.08226
−1.4	.08076	.07927	.07780	.07636	.07493	.07353	.07215	.07078	.06944	.06811
−1.5	.06681	.06552	.06426	.06301	.06178	.06057	.05938	.05821	.05705	.05592
−1.6	.05480	.05370	.05262	.05155	.05050	.04947	.04846	.04746	.04648	.04551
−1.7	.04457	.04363	.04272	.04182	.04093	.04006	.03920	.03836	.03754	.03673
−1.8	.03593	.03515	.03438	.03362	.03288	.03216	.03144	.03074	.03005	.02938
−1.9	.02872	.02807	.02743	.02680	.02619	.02559	.02500	.02442	.02385	.02330
−2.0	.02275	.02222	.02169	.02118	.02068	.02018	.01970	.01923	.01876	.01831
−2.1	.01786	.01743	.01700	.01659	.01618	.01578	.01539	.01500	.01463	.01426
−2.2	.01390	.01355	.01321	.01287	.01255	.01222	.01191	.01160	.01130	.01101
−2.3	.01072	.01044	.01017	$.0^2 9903$	$.0^2 9642$	$.0^2 9387$	$.0^2 9137$	$.0^2 8894$	$.0^2 8656$	$.0^2 8424$
−2.4	$.0^2 8198$	$.0^2 7976$	$.0^2 7760$	$.0^2 7549$	$.0^2 7344$	$.0^2 7143$	$.0^2 6947$	$.0^2 6756$	$.0^2 6569$	$.0^2 6387$
−2.5	$.0^2 6210$	$.0^2 6037$	$.0^2 5868$	$.0^2 5703$	$.0^2 5543$	$.0^2 5386$	$.0^2 5234$	$.0^2 5085$	$.0^2 4940$	$.0^2 4799$
−2.6	$.0^2 4661$	$.0^2 4527$	$.0^2 4396$	$.0^2 4269$	$.0^2 4145$	$.0^2 4025$	$.0^2 3907$	$.0^2 3793$	$.0^2 3681$	$.0^2 3573$
−2.7	$.0^2 3467$	$.0^2 3364$	$.0^2 3264$	$.0^2 3167$	$.0^2 3072$	$.0^2 2980$	$.0^2 2890$	$.0^2 2803$	$.0^2 2718$	$.0^2 2635$
−2.8	$.0^2 2555$	$.0^2 2477$	$.0^2 2401$	$.0^2 2327$	$.0^2 2256$	$.0^2 2186$	$.0^2 2118$	$.0^2 2052$	$.0^2 1988$	$.0^2 1926$
−2.9	$.0^2 1866$	$.0^2 1807$	$.0^2 1750$	$.0^2 1695$	$.0^2 1641$	$.0^2 1589$	$.0^2 1538$	$.0^2 1489$	$.0^2 1441$	$.0^2 1395$
−3.0	$.0^2 1350$	$.0^2 1306$	$.0^2 1264$	$.0^2 1223$	$.0^2 1183$	$.0^2 1144$	$.0^2 1107$	$.0^2 1070$	$.0^2 1035$	$.0^2 1001$
−3.1	$.0^3 9676$	$.0^3 9354$	$.0^3 9043$	$.0^3 8740$	$.0^3 8447$	$.0^3 8164$	$.0^3 7888$	$.0^3 7622$	$.0^3 7364$	$.0^3 7114$
−3.2	$.0^3 6871$	$.0^3 6637$	$.0^3 6410$	$.0^3 6190$	$.0^3 5976$	$.0^3 5770$	$.0^3 5571$	$.0^3 5377$	$.0^3 5190$	$.0^3 5009$
−3.3	$.0^3 4834$	$.0^3 4665$	$.0^3 4501$	$.0^3 4342$	$.0^3 4189$	$.0^3 4041$	$.0^3 3897$	$.0^3 3758$	$.0^3 3624$	$.0^3 3495$
−3.4	$.0^3 3369$	$.0^3 3248$	$.0^3 3131$	$.0^3 3018$	$.0^3 2909$	$.0^3 2803$	$.0^3 2701$	$.0^3 2602$	$.0^3 2507$	$.0^3 2415$
−3.5	$.0^3 2326$	$.0^3 2241$	$.0^3 2158$	$.0^3 2078$	$.0^3 2001$	$.0^3 1926$	$.0^3 1854$	$.0^3 1785$	$.0^3 1718$	$.0^3 1653$
−3.6	$.0^3 1591$	$.0^3 1531$	$.0^3 1473$	$.0^3 1417$	$.0^3 1363$	$.0^3 1311$	$.0^3 1261$	$.0^3 1213$	$.0^3 1166$	$.0^3 1121$
−3.7	$.0^3 1078$	$.0^3 1036$	$.0^4 9961$	$.0^4 9574$	$.0^4 9201$	$.0^4 8842$	$.0^4 8496$	$.0^4 8162$	$.0^4 7841$	$.0^4 7532$
−3.8	$.0^4 7235$	$.0^4 6948$	$.0^4 6673$	$.0^4 6407$	$.0^4 6152$	$.0^4 5906$	$.0^4 5669$	$.0^4 5442$	$.0^4 5223$	$.0^4 5012$
−3.9	$.0^4 4810$	$.0^4 4615$	$.0^4 4427$	$.0^4 4247$	$.0^4 4074$	$.0^4 3908$	$.0^4 3747$	$.0^4 3594$	$.0^4 3446$	$.0^4 3304$
−4.0	$.0^4 3167$	$.0^4 3036$	$.0^4 2910$	$.0^4 2789$	$.0^4 2673$	$.0^4 2561$	$.0^4 2454$	$.0^4 2351$	$.0^4 2252$	$.0^4 2157$
−4.1	$.0^4 2066$	$.0^4 1978$	$.0^4 1894$	$.0^4 1814$	$.0^4 1737$	$.0^4 1662$	$.0^4 1591$	$.0^4 1523$	$.0^4 1458$	$.0^4 1395$
−4.2	$.0^4 1335$	$.0^4 1277$	$.0^4 1222$	$.0^4 1168$	$.0^4 1118$	$.0^4 1069$	$.0^4 1022$	$.0^5 9774$	$.0^5 9345$	$.0^5 8934$
−4.3	$.0^5 8540$	$.0^5 8163$	$.0^5 7801$	$.0^5 7455$	$.0^5 7124$	$.0^5 6807$	$.0^5 6503$	$.0^5 6212$	$.0^5 5934$	$.0^5 5668$
−4.4	$.0^5 5413$	$.0^5 5169$	$.0^5 4935$	$.0^5 4712$	$.0^5 4498$	$.0^5 4294$	$.0^5 4098$	$.0^5 3911$	$.0^5 3732$	$.0^5 3561$
−4.5	$.0^5 3398$	$.0^5 3241$	$.0^5 3092$	$.0^5 2949$	$.0^5 2813$	$.0^5 2682$	$.0^5 2558$	$.0^5 2439$	$.0^5 2325$	$.0^5 2216$
−4.6	$.0^5 2112$	$.0^5 2013$	$.0^5 1919$	$.0^5 1828$	$.0^5 1742$	$.0^5 1660$	$.0^5 1581$	$.0^5 1506$	$.0^5 1434$	$.0^5 1369$
−4.7	$.0^5 1301$	$.0^5 1239$	$.0^5 1179$	$.0^5 1123$	$.0^5 1069$	$.0^5 1017$	$.0^6 9680$	$.0^6 9211$	$.0^6 8765$	$.0^6 8339$
−4.8	$.0^6 7933$	$.0^6 7547$	$.0^6 7178$	$.0^6 6827$	$.0^6 6492$	$.0^6 6173$	$.0^6 5869$	$.0^6 5580$	$.0^6 5304$	$.0^6 5042$
−4.9	$.0^6 4792$	$.0^6 4554$	$.0^6 4327$	$.0^6 4111$	$.0^6 3906$	$.0^6 3711$	$.0^6 3525$	$.0^6 3348$	$.0^6 3179$	$.0^6 3019$

Example: $P_{(-3.57)} = .0^3 1785 = 0.0001785$

APPENDIX A Continued

$$P_x = \int_{-\infty}^{x} e^{-(z^2/2)} \, dz \quad \text{for} \quad 0.00 \le x \le 4.99$$

x	.00	.01	.02	.03	.04	.05	.06	.07	.08	.09
.0	.5000	.5040	.5080	.5120	.5160	.5199	.5239	.5279	.5319	.5359
.1	.5398	.5438	.5478	.5517	.5557	.5596	.5636	.5675	.5714	.5753
.2	.5793	.5832	.5871	.5910	.5948	.5987	.6026	.6064	.6103	.6141
.3	.6179	.6217	.6255	.6293	.6331	.6368	.6406	.6443	.6480	.6517
.4	.6554	.6591	.6628	.6664	.6700	.6736	.6772	.6808	.6844	.6879
.5	.6915	.6950	.6985	.7019	.7054	.7088	.7123	.7157	.7190	.7224
.6	.7257	.7291	.7324	.7357	.7389	.7422	.7454	.7486	.7517	.7549
.7	.7580	.7611	.7642	.7673	.7703	.7734	.7764	.7794	.7823	.7852
.8	.7881	.7910	.7939	.7967	.7995	.8023	.8051	.8078	.8106	.8133
.9	.8159	.8186	.8212	.8238	.8264	.8289	.8315	.8340	.8365	.8389
1.0	.8413	.8438	.8461	.8485	.8508	.8531	.8554	.8577	.8599	.8621
1.1	.8643	.8665	.8686	.8708	.8729	.8749	.8770	.8790	.8810	.8830
1.2	.8849	.8869	.8888	.8907	.8925	.8944	.8962	.8980	.8997	.90147
1.3	.90320	.90490	.90658	.90824	.90988	.91149	.91309	.91466	.91621	.91774
1.4	.91924	.92073	.92220	.92364	.92507	.92647	.92785	.92922	.93056	.93189
1.5	.93319	.93448	.93574	.93699	.93822	.93943	.94062	.94179	.94295	.94408
1.6	.94520	.94630	.94738	.94845	.94950	.95053	.95154	.95254	.95352	.95449
1.7	.95543	.95637	.95728	.95818	.95907	.95994	.96080	.96164	.96246	.96327
1.8	.96407	.96485	.96562	.96638	.96712	.96784	.96856	.96926	.96995	.97062
1.9	.97128	.97193	.97257	.97320	.97381	.97441	.97500	.97558	.97615	.97670
2.0	.97725	.97778	.97831	.97882	.97932	.97982	.98030	.98077	.98124	.98169
2.1	.98214	.98257	.98300	.98341	.98382	.98422	.98461	.98500	.98537	.98574
2.2	.98610	.98645	.98679	.98713	.98745	.98778	.98809	.98840	.98870	.98899
2.3	.98928	.98956	.98983	$.9^2 0097$	$.9^2 0358$	$.9^2 0613$	$.9^2 0863$	$.9^2 1106$	$.9^2 1344$	$.9^2 1576$
2.4	$.9^2 1802$	$.9^2 2024$	$.9^2 2240$	$.9^2 2451$	$.9^2 2656$	$.9^2 2857$	$.9^2 3053$	$.9^2 3244$	$.9^2 3431$	$.9^2 3613$
2.5	$.9^2 3790$	$.9^2 3963$	$.9^2 4132$	$.9^2 4297$	$.9^2 4457$	$.9^2 4614$	$.9^2 4766$	$.9^2 4915$	$.9^2 5060$	$.9^2 5201$
2.6	$.9^2 5339$	$.9^2 5473$	$.9^2 5604$	$.9^2 5731$	$.9^2 5855$	$.9^2 5975$	$.9^2 6093$	$.9^2 6207$	$.9^2 6319$	$.9^2 6427$
2.7	$.9^2 6533$	$.9^2 6636$	$.9^2 6736$	$.9^2 6833$	$.9^2 6928$	$.9^2 7020$	$.9^2 7110$	$.9^2 7197$	$.9^2 7282$	$.9^2 7365$
2.8	$.9^2 7445$	$.9^2 7523$	$.9^2 7599$	$.9^2 7673$	$.0^2 7744$	$.9^2 7814$	$.9^2 7882$	$.9^2 7948$	$.9^2 8012$	$.9^2 8074$
2.9	$.9^2 8134$	$.9^2 8193$	$.9^2 8250$	$.9^2 8305$	$.9^2 8359$	$.9^2 8411$	$.9^2 8462$	$.9^2 8511$	$.9^2 8559$	$.9^2 8605$
3.0	$.9^2 8650$	$.9^2 8694$	$.9^2 8736$	$.9^2 8777$	$.9^2 8817$	$.9^2 8856$	$.9^2 8893$	$.9^2 8930$	$.9^2 8965$	$.9^2 8999$
3.1	$.9^3 0324$	$.9^3 0646$	$.9^3 0957$	$.9^3 1260$	$.9^3 1553$	$.9^3 1836$	$.9^3 2112$	$.9^3 2378$	$.9^3 2636$	$.9^3 2886$
3.2	$.9^3 3129$	$.9^3 3363$	$.9^3 3590$	$.9^3 3810$	$.9^3 4024$	$.9^3 4230$	$.9^3 4429$	$.9^3 4623$	$.9^3 4810$	$.9^3 4991$
3.3	$.9^3 5166$	$.9^3 5335$	$.9^3 5499$	$.9^3 5658$	$.9^3 5811$	$.9^3 5959$	$.9^3 6103$	$.9^3 6242$	$.9^3 6376$	$.9^3 6505$
3.4	$.9^3 6631$	$.9^3 6752$	$.9^3 6869$	$.9^3 6982$	$.9^3 7091$	$.9^3 7197$	$.9^3 7299$	$.9^3 7398$	$.9^3 7493$	$.9^3 7585$
3.5	$.9^3 7674$	$.9^3 7759$	$.9^3 7842$	$.9^3 7922$	$.9^3 7999$	$.9^3 8074$	$.9^3 8146$	$.9^3 8215$	$.9^3 8282$	$.9^3 8347$
3.6	$.9^3 8409$	$.9^3 8469$	$.9^3 8527$	$.9^3 8583$	$.9^3 8637$	$.9^3 8689$	$.9^3 8739$	$.9^3 8787$	$.9^3 8834$	$.9^3 8879$
3.7	$.9^3 8922$	$.9^3 8964$	$.9^4 0039$	$.9^4 0426$	$.9^4 0799$	$.9^4 1158$	$.9^4 1504$	$.9^4 1838$	$.9^4 2159$	$.9^4 2468$
3.8	$.9^4 2765$	$.9^4 3052$	$.9^4 3327$	$.9^4 3593$	$.9^4 3848$	$.9^4 4094$	$.9^4 4331$	$.9^4 4558$	$.9^4 4777$	$.9^4 4988$
3.9	$.9^4 5190$	$.9^4 5385$	$.9^4 5573$	$.9^4 5753$	$.9^4 5926$	$.9^4 6092$	$.9^4 6253$	$.9^4 6406$	$.9^4 6554$	$.9^4 6696$
4.0	$.9^4 6833$	$.9^4 6964$	$.9^4 7090$	$.9^4 7211$	$.9^4 7327$	$.9^4 7439$	$.9^4 7546$	$.9^4 7649$	$.9^4 7748$	$.9^4 7843$
4.1	$.9^4 7934$	$.9^4 8022$	$.9^4 8106$	$.9^4 8186$	$.9^4 8263$	$.9^4 8338$	$.9^4 8409$	$.9^4 8477$	$.9^4 8542$	$.9^4 8605$
4.2	$.9^4 8665$	$.9^4 8723$	$.9^4 8778$	$.9^4 8832$	$.9^4 8882$	$.9^4 8931$	$.9^4 8978$	$.9^5 0226$	$.9^5 0655$	$.9^5 1066$
4.3	$.9^5 1460$	$.9^5 1837$	$.9^5 2199$	$.9^5 2545$	$.9^5 2876$	$.9^5 3193$	$.9^5 3497$	$.9^5 3788$	$.9^5 4066$	$.9^5 4332$
4.4	$.9^5 4587$	$.9^5 4831$	$.9^5 5065$	$.9^5 5288$	$.9^5 5502$	$.9^5 5706$	$.9^5 5902$	$.9^5 6089$	$.9^5 6268$	$.9^5 6439$
4.5	$.9^5 6602$	$.9^5 6759$	$.9^5 6908$	$.9^5 7051$	$.9^5 7187$	$.9^5 7318$	$.9^5 7442$	$.9^5 7561$	$.9^5 7675$	$.9^5 7784$
4.6	$.9^5 7888$	$.9^5 7987$	$.9^5 8081$	$.9^5 8172$	$.9^5 8258$	$.9^5 8340$	$.9^5 8419$	$.9^5 8494$	$.9^5 8566$	$.9^5 8634$
4.7	$.9^5 8699$	$.9^5 8761$	$.9^5 8821$	$.9^5 8877$	$.9^5 8931$	$.9^5 8983$	$.9^6 0320$	$.9^6 0789$	$.9^6 1235$	$.9^6 1661$
4.8	$.9^6 2067$	$.9^6 2453$	$.9^6 2822$	$.9^6 3173$	$.9^6 3508$	$.9^6 3827$	$.9^6 4131$	$.9^6 4420$	$.9^6 4696$	$.9^6 4958$
4.9	$.9^6 5208$	$.9^6 5446$	$.9^6 5673$	$.9^6 5889$	$.9^6 6094$	$.9^6 6289$	$.9^6 6475$	$.9^6 6652$	$.9^6 6821$	$.9^6 6981$

Example: $P_{(3.57)} = .9^3 8215 = 0.9998215$

Reproduced from Table II of A. Hald, *Statistical Tables and Formulas*, John Wiley & Sons, 1952.

► *Appendix B*

THE CUMULATIVE NORMAL DISTRIBUTION FUNCTION: CUMULATIVE PROPORTIONS TO UNIT NORMAL DEVIATES

$$\frac{1}{\sqrt{2\pi}} \int_{-\infty}^{x_p} e^{-(z^2/2)} \, dz = P \text{ for } 0.500 \leq P \leq 0.999$$

$$(\text{for } P < 0.500, \, x_{1-P} = -x_P)$$

100 P	.0	.1	.2	.3	.4	.5	.6	.7	.8	.9
50	0.000	0.003	0.005	0.008	0.010	0.013	0.015	0.018	0.020	0.023
51	0.025	0.028	0.030	0.033	0.035	0.038	0.040	0.043	0.045	0.048
52	0.050	0.053	0.055	0.058	0.060	0.063	0.065	0.068	0.070	0.073
53	0.075	0.078	0.080	0.083	0.085	0.088	0.090	0.093	0.095	0.098
54	0.100	0.103	0.105	0.108	0.111	0.113	0.116	0.118	0.121	0.123
55	0.126	0.128	0.131	0.133	0.136	0.138	0.141	0.143	0.146	0.148
56	0.151	0.154	0.156	0.159	0.161	0.164	0.166	0.169	0.171	0.174
57	0.176	0.179	0.181	0.184	0.187	0.189	0.192	0.194	0.197	0.199
58	0.202	0.204	0.207	0.210	0.212	0.215	0.217	0.220	0.222	0.225
59	0.228	0.230	0.233	0.235	0.238	0.240	0.243	0.246	0.248	0.251
60	0.253	0.256	0.259	0.261	0.264	0.266	0.269	0.272	0.274	0.277
61	0.279	0.282	0.285	0.287	0.290	0.292	0.295	0.298	0.300	0.303
62	0.305	0.308	0.311	0.313	0.316	0.319	0.321	0.324	0.327	0.329
63	0.332	0.335	0.337	0.340	0.342	0.345	0.348	0.350	0.353	0.356
64	0.358	0.361	0.364	0.366	0.369	0.372	0.375	0.377	0.380	0.383
65	0.385	0.388	0.391	0.393	0.396	0.399	0.402	0.404	0.407	0.410
66	0.412	0.415	0.418	0.421	0.423	0.426	0.429	0.432	0.434	0.437
67	0.440	0.443	0.445	0.448	0.451	0.454	0.457	0.459	0.462	0.465
68	0.468	0.470	0.473	0.476	0.479	0.482	0.485	0.487	0.490	0.493
69	0.496	0.499	0.502	0.504	0.507	0.510	0.513	0.516	0.519	0.522
70	0.524	0.527	0.530	0.533	0.536	0.539	0.542	0.545	0.548	0.550
71	0.553	0.556	0.559	0.562	0.565	0.568	0.571	0.574	0.577	0.580
72	0.583	0.586	0.589	0.592	0.595	0.598	0.601	0.604	0.607	0.610
73	0.613	0.616	0.619	0.622	0.625	0.628	0.631	0.634	0.637	0.640
74	0.643	0.646	0.650	0.653	0.656	0.659	0.662	0.665	0.668	0.671
75	0.674	0.678	0.681	0.684	0.687	0.690	0.693	0.697	0.700	0.703
76	0.706	0.710	0.713	0.716	0.719	0.722	0.726	0.729	0.732	0.736
77	0.739	0.742	0.745	0.749	0.752	0.755	0.759	0.762	0.765	0.769
78	0.772	0.776	0.779	0.782	0.786	0.789	0.793	0.796	0.800	0.803
79	0.806	0.810	0.813	0.817	0.820	0.824	0.827	0.831	0.834	0.838
80	0.842	0.845	0.849	0.852	0.856	0.860	0.863	0.867	0.871	0.874
81	0.878	0.882	0.885	0.889	0.893	0.896	0.900	0.904	0.908	0.912
82	0.915	0.919	0.923	0.927	0.931	0.935	0.938	0.942	0.946	0.950
83	0.954	0.958	0.962	0.966	0.970	0.974	0.978	0.982	0.986	0.990
84	0.994	0.999	1.003	1.007	1.011	1.015	1.019	1.024	1.028	1.032
85	1.036	1.041	1.045	1.049	1.054	1.058	1.063	1.067	1.071	1.076
86	1.080	1.085	1.089	1.094	1.098	1.103	1.108	1.112	1.117	1.122
87	1.126	1.131	1.136	1.141	1.146	1.150	1.155	1.160	1.165	1.170
88	1.175	1.180	1.185	1.190	1.195	1.200	1.206	1.211	1.216	1.221
89	1.227	1.232	1.237	1.243	1.248	1.254	1.259	1.265	1.270	1.276
90	1.282	1.287	1.293	1.299	1.305	1.311	1.317	1.323	1.329	1.335
91	1.341	1.347	1.353	1.359	1.366	1.372	1.379	1.385	1.392	1.398
92	1.405	1.412	1.419	1.426	1.433	1.440	1.447	1.454	1.461	1.468
93	1.476	1.483	1.491	1.499	1.506	1.514	1.522	1.530	1.538	1.546
94	1.555	1.563	1.572	1.580	1.589	1.598	1.607	1.616	1.626	1.635
95	1.645	1.655	1.665	1.675	1.685	1.695	1.706	1.717	1.728	1.739
96	1.751	1.762	1.774	1.787	1.799	1.812	1.825	1.838	1.852	1.866
97	1.881	1.896	1.911	1.927	1.943	1.960	1.977	1.995	2.014	2.034
98	2.054	2.075	2.097	2.120	2.144	2.170	2.197	2.226	2.257	2.290
99	2.326	2.366	2.409	2.457	2.512	2.576	2.652	2.748	2.878	3.090

Based on Table IX of R. A. Fisher and F. Yates, *Statistical Tables*, Oliver and Boyd, by permission of the authors and publishers.

Bibliography ◄

Abelson, R. P. (1954) A technique and a model for multidimensional attitude scaling. *Amer. Psychologist*, **9**, 319 (abs).

Allport, F. H., and D. A. Hartman (1925) The measurement and motivation of a typical opinion in a certain group. *Amer. Pol. Sci. Rev.*, **19**, 735–760.

Anderson, T. W. (1954) On estimation of parameters in latent structure analysis. *Psychometrika*, **19**, 1–11.

Andrews, T. G. (ed.) (1948) *Methods of Psychology*. New York: Wiley.

Angoff, W. H. (1949) An empirical approach to a problem of psychophysical scaling. *J. Appl. Psychol.*, **33**, 59–68.

Armington, J. C. (1953) A note concerning the *veg* scale of apparent weight. *Amer. J. Psychol.*, **66**, 304–306.

Attneave, F. (1949) A method of graded dichotomies for the scaling of judgments. *Psychol. Rev.*, **56**, 334–340.

Attneave, F. (1950) Dimensions of similarity. *Amer. J. Psychol.*, **63**, 516–556.

Asch, S. E., H. Block, and M. Hertzman (1938) Studies in the principles of judgment and attitudes: I. Two basic principles of judgment. *J. Psychol.*, **5**, 219–251.

Bain, R. (1930) Theory and measurement of attitudes and opinions. *Psychol. Bull.*, **27**, 357–379.

Baker, K. E., and F. J. Dudek (1955) Weight scales from ratio judgments and comparisons of existent weight scales. *J. Exp. Psychol.*, **50**, 293–308.

Ballin, M. R., and P. R. Farnsworth (1941) A graphic rating method for determining the scale values of statements in measuring social attitudes. *J. Soc. Psychol.*, **13**, 323–327.

Barnhart, E. N. (1936) A comparison of scaling methods for affective judgments. *Psychol. Rev.*, **43**, 387–395.

Barnhart, E. N. (1939) A computational short cut in determining scale values for ranked items. *Psychometrika*, **4**, 241–242.

Barrett, M. (1914) A comparison of the order of merit method and the method of paired comparisons. *Psychol. Rev.*, **21**, 278–294.

Bartlett, R. J. (1940) Measurement in psychology. Address to Section J, Psychology. Report of the Brit. Assoc. Adv. Sci., **1**, 422–441.

Beebe-Center, J. G. (1929) The law of affective equilibrium. *Amer. J. Psychol.*, **41**, 54–69.

Beebe-Center, J. G. (1932) *The Psychology of Pleasantness and Unpleasantness.* New York: D. Van Nostrand.

Beebe-Center, J. G. (1949) Standards for use of the gust scale. *J. Psychol.*, **28**, 411–420.

Beebe-Center, J. G., and D. Waddell (1948) A general psychological scale of taste. *J. Psychol.*, **26**, 517–524.

Békésy, G. von (1930) Über das Fechner'sche Gesetz und seine Bedeutung für die Theorie der akustischen Beobachtungsfehler und die Theorie des Hörens. *Ann. Physik.*, **7**, 329–359.

Bendig, A. W. (1952) Inter-judge *vs* intra-judge reliability in the order of merit method. *Amer. J. Psychol.*, **65**, 84–88.

Bendig, A. W. (1953) The reliability of self ratings as a function of the amount of verbal anchoring and of the number of categories on the scale. *J. Appl. Psychol.*, **37**, 38–41.

Bendig, A. W. (1954) Reliability and the number of rating scale categories. *J. Appl. Psychol.*, **38**, 38–40.

Bendig, A. W. (1955) Rater reliability and the heterogeniety of the scale anchors. *J. Appl. Psychol.*, **39**, 37–39.

Bennett, J. F. (1951) A method for determining the dimensionality of a set of rank orders. Ph.D. Thesis, University of Michigan.

Bennett, J. F. (1956) Determination of the number of independent parameters of a score matrix from the examination of rank orders. *Psychometrika*, **21**, 383–395.

Benson, P. H. (1955) A model for the analysis of consumer preference and an exploratory test. *J. Appl. Psychol.*, **39**, 375–381.

Bergmann, G., and K. W. Spence (1944) The logic of psychophysical measurement. *Psychol. Rev.*, **51**, 1–24.

Berkson, J. (1953) A statistically precise and relatively simple method of estimating the bio-assay with quantal response, based on the logistic function. *J. Amer. Stat. Assn.*, **48**, 565–600.

Bishop, Ruth (1940) Points of neutrality in social attitudes of deliquents and non-deliquents. *Psychometrika*, **5**, 35–45.

Bittner, R. H., and E. A. Rundquist (1950) The rank-comparison rating method. *J. Appl. Psychol.*, **34**, 171–177.

Bliss, C. I. (1935a) The calculation of the dosage-mortality curve. *Ann. Appl. Bio.*, **22**, 134–167.

Bliss, C. I. (1935b) The comparison of dosage-mortality data. *Ann. Appl. Bio.*, **22**, 307–333.

Borgatta, E. F., and D. G. Hays (1952) Some limitations on the arbitrary classification of non-scale response patterns in a Guttman scale. *Pub. Opin. Quart.*, **16**, 410–416.

Boring, E. G. (1916) The number of observations upon which a limen may be based. *Amer. J. Psychol.*, **27**, 315–319.

Boring, E. G. (1917a) Urban's tables and the method of constant stimuli. *Amer. J. Psychol.*, **28**, 280–293.

Boring, E. G. (1917b) A chart of the psychometric function. *Amer. J. Psychol.*, **28**, 465–470.

Boring, E. G. (1920a) The logic of the normal law of error in mental measurement. *Amer. J. Psychol.*, **31**, 1–33.

Boring, E. G. (1920*b*) The control of attitude in psychophysical experiments. *Psychol. Rev.*, **27**, 440–452.

Boring, E. G. (1921) The stimulus-error. *Amer. J. Psychol.*, **32**, 449–471.

Boring, E. G. (1924) Is there a generalized psychometric function? *Amer. J. Psychol.*, **35**, 75–78.

Boring, E. G. (1929) *A History of Experimental Psychology*. New York: Appleton-Century.

Boring, E. G. (1935) The relation of the attributes of sensation to the dimensions of the stimulus. *Phil. Sci.*, **2**, 236–245.

Boring, E. G. (1942) *Sensation and Perception in the History of Experimental Psychology*. New York: Appleton-Century.

Bradley, R. A. (1953) Some statistical methods in taste testing and quality evaluation. *Biometrics*, **9**, 22–38.

Bradley, R. A. (1954) Incomplete block rank analysis: on the appropriateness of the model for a method of paired comparisons. *Biometrics*, **10**, 375–390.

Bradley, R. A., and M. E. Terry (1952) The rank analysis of incomplete block designs. I. The method of paired comparisons. *Biometrika*, **39**, 324–345.

Bressler, J. (1933) Judgment in absolute units as a psychophysical method. *Arch. Psychol.*, no. 152.

Bridgman, P. W. (1927) *The Logic of Modern Physics*. New York: Macmillan.

Brotemarkle, R. A., and S. W. Fernberger (1934) A method for investigating the validity of the categories of a judgment test. *J. Educ. Psychol.*, **25**, 579–584.

Brown, C. W., P. Bartelme, and G. M. Cox (1933) The scoring of individual performance on tests scaled according to the theory of absolute scaling. *J. Educ. Psychol.*, **24**, 654–662.

Brown, D. R. (1953) Stimulus similarity and the anchoring of subjective scales. *Amer. J. Psychol.*, **66**, 199–214.

Brown, W. (1910) The judgment of difference. *Univ. Calif. Publ. Psychol.*, **1**, no. 1.

Brown, W. (1914) The judgment of very weak sensory stimuli. *Univ. Calif. Publ. Psychol.*, **1**, no. 3, 199–268.

Brown, W., and G. H. Thomson (1925) *The Essentials of Mental Measurement*. London: Cambridge University Press.

Burke, C. J. (1953) Additive scales and statistics. *Psychol. Rev.*, **60**, 73–75.

Burnham, R. W. (1942) A study of auditory "brightness". *J. Exp. Psychol.*, **30**, 490–494.

Burros, R. H. (1951) The application of the method of paired comparisons to the study of reaction potential. *Psychol. Rev.*, **58**, 60–66.

Burros, R. H. (1955) The estimation of the discriminal dispersion in the method of successive intervals. *Psychometrika*, **20**, 299–305.

Burros, R. H., and W. A. Gibson (1954) A solution for Case III of the Law of Comparative Judgment. *Psychometrika*, **19**, 57–64.

Burt, C. (1951) Test construction and the scaling of items. *Brit. J. Psychol., Stat. Sect.*, **4**, 95–129.

Burt C. (1953) Scale analysis and factor analysis. *Brit. J. Stat. Psychol.*, 6, 5–23.

Campbell, N. R. (1920) *Physics, The Elements*. Cambridge: The University Press.

Campbell, N. R. (1928) *An Account of the Principles of Measurement and Calculation*. London: Longmans Green.

Campbell, N. R. (1938) Symposium: Measurement and its importance for philosophy. *Proc. Arist. Soc. Suppl.*, **17**, 121–142. London: Harrison.

Canter, R. R., and J. Hirsch (1955) An experimental comparison of several psychological scales of weight. *Amer. J. Psychol.*, **68**, 645–649.

Cantril, H. (Ed.) (1944) *Gauging Public Opinion*. Princeton, N.J.: Princeton University Press.

Cantril, H. (1946) The intensity of an attitude. *J. Abn. Soc. Psychol.*, **41**, 129–135.

Carnap, R. (1950) *Logical Foundations of Probability*. Chicago: University of Chicago Press.

Cattell, R. B. (1944) Psychological measurement: normative, ipsative, interactive. *Psychol. Rev.*, **51**, 292–303.

Chapin, F. S. (1935) *Contemporary American Institutions*. New York: Harper.

Cheatham, P. G., and C. T. White (1952) Temporal numerosity: I. Perceived number as a function of flash number and rate. *J. Exp. Psychol.*, **44**, 447–451.

Cheatham, P. G., and C. T. White (1954) Temporal numerosity: III. Auditory perception of number. *J. Exp. Psychol.* **47**, 425–428.

Churcher, B. G. (1935) A loudness scale for industrial noise measurements. *J. Acoust. Soc. Amer.*, **6**, 216–226.

Churcher, B. G., A. J. King, and H. Davis The minimum perceptible change of intensity of a pure tone. *Phil. Mag.*, **18**, 927–939.

Churchman, C. W., R. L. Ackoff, and M. Wax (Eds.) (1947) *Measurement of Consumer Interest*. Philadelphia: University of Pennsylvania Press.

Clark, K. E., and P. H. Kriedt (1948) An application of Guttman's new scaling techniques to an attitude questionnaire. *Educ. Psychol. Msmt.*, **8**, 215–223.

Cobb, P. W. (1932) Webers law and the Fechnerian muddle. *Psychol. Rev.*, **39**, 533–551.

Cohen, M. R., and E. Nagel (1934) *An Introduction to Logic and Scientific Method*. New York: Harcourt Brace.

Cohen, N. E. (1937) The relativity of absolute judgments. *Amer. J. Psychol.*, **49**, 93–100.

Comrey, A. L. (1950a) An operational approach to some problems in psychological measurement. *Psychol. Rev.*, **57**, 217–228.

Comrey, A. L. (1950b) A proposed method for absolute ratio scaling. *Psychometrika*, **15**, 317–325.

Comrey, A. L. (1951) Mental testing and the logic of measurement. *Educ. Psychol. Msmt.* **11**, 323–334.

Conklin, E. S., and J. W. Sutherland (1923) A comparison of the scale of values method with the order of merit method. *J. Exp. Psychol.*, **6**, 44–57.

Conrad, H. S. (1932a) The bogey of the "personal equation" in ratings of intelligence. *J. Educ. Psychol.*, **23**, 147–149.

Conrad, H. S. (1932)b The personal equation in ratings: I. An experimental determination. *J. Genet. Psychol.*, **41**, 267–293.

Conrad, H. S. (1933) The personal equation in ratings: II. A systematic evaluation. *J. Educ. Psychol.*, **24**, 39–46.

Conrad, H. S. (1946) Some principles of attitude measurement: A reply to "Opinion-attitude methodology". *Psychol. Bull.*, **43**, 570–589.

Coombs, C. H. (1948a) Some hypotheses for the analysis of qualitative variables. *Psychol. Rev.*, **55**, 167–174.

Coombs, C. H. (1948b) A rationale for the measurement of traits in individuals. *Psychometrika*, **13**, 59–68.

Coombs, C. H. (1950) Psychological scaling without a unit of measurement. *Psychol. Rev.*, **57**, 145–158.

Coombs, C. H. (1951) Mathematical models in psychological scaling. *J. Amer. Stat. Assn.*, **46**, 480–489.

Coombs, C. H. (1952) A theory of psychological scaling. *Eng. Res. Bull.* no. 34, Ann Arbor: University of Michigan Press.

Coombs, C. H. (1953) The theory and methods of social measurement. In L. Festinger, and D. Katz (Eds.) *Research Methods in the Behavioral Sciences.* New York: Dryden Press, 471–535.

Coombs, C. H. (1954) A method for the study of interstimulus similarity. *Psychometrika*, **19**, 183–195.

Coombs, C. H. (1956) The scale grid: some interrelations of data models. *Psychometrika*, **21**, 313–330.

Coombs, C. H., and Beardslee, D. C. (1954) Social choice and strength of preference. In C. H. Coombs, R. M. Thrall, and R. L. Davis (Eds.) *Decision Processes.* New York: Wiley.

Coombs, C. H., and R. C. Kao (1954) On the multidimensional analysis of monotonic single stimuli data (ditto).

Coombs, C. H., and R. C. Kao (1955) Non-metric factor analysis. *Engng. Res. Bull.* no. 38., Ann Arbor, University of Michigan Press.

Coombs, C. H., H. Raiffa, and R. M. Thrall (1954) Some views on mathematical models and measurement theory. *Psychol. Rev.*, **61**, 132–144.

Corso, J. F. (1951) The neural quantum in discrimination of pitch and loudness. *Amer. J. Psychol.*, **64**, 350–368.

Corso, J. F. (1956) The neural quantum theory of sensory discrimination. *Psychol. Bull.*, **53**, 371–393.

Cowdrick, M. (1917) The Weber–Fechner law and Sanford's weight experiment. *Amer. J. Psychol.*, **28**, 585–588.

Cronbach, L. J. (1949) *Essentials of Psychological Testing.* New York: Harper.

Cross, L. (1949) The use of class concepts in social research. *Amer. J. Sociol.*, **55**, 409–421.

Culler, E. A. (1926a) Thermal discrimination and Weber's law. *Arch. Psychol.*, no. 81.

Culler, E. A. (1926b) Studies in psychometric theory. *Psychol. Monog.*, **35**, no. 163, 56–137.

Culler, E. A. (1926c) Studies in psychometric theory. *J. Exp. Psychol.*, **9**, 169–194.

Culler, E. A. (1926d) Studies in psychometric theory. *J. Exp. Psychol.*, **9**, 271–298.

Culler, E. A. (1927) Studies in psychometric theory. *J. Exp. Psychol.*, **10**, 463–477.

Davis, F. B. (1951) Item selection techniques. In E. F. Lindquist (Ed.) *Educational Measurement.* Washington, D.C.: Amer. Council on Education.

Davis, F. B. (1952) Item analysis in relatlon to educational and psychological testing. *Psychol. Bull.*, **49**, 97–119.

Diederich, G. W., S. J. Messick, and L. R. Tucker (1955) A general least squares solution for successive intervals. *Res. Bull.* 55–24. Princeton: Educational Testing Service.

Doughty, J. M. (1949) The effect of psychophysical method and context on pitch and loudness functions. *J. Exp. Psychol.*, **39**, 729–745.

Droba, D. D. (1932) Methods for measuring attitude. *Psychol. Bull.* **29**, 309–329.

Dudycha, G. J. (1942) Attitudes toward war. *Psychol. Bull.*, **39**, 846–860.

Dushnik, B. (1950) Concerning a certain set of arrangements. *Proc. Amer. Math. Soc.*, **1**, 788–796.

Edgerton, H. A., and L. E. Kolbe (1936) The method of minimum variation for the combination of criteria. *Psychometrika*, **1**, 183–187.

Edwards, A. L. (1946) A critique of neutral items in attitude scales constructed by the method of equal appearing intervals. *Psychol. Rev.*, **53**, 159–169.

Edwards, A. L. (1948) On Guttman's scale analysis. *Educ. Psychol. Msmt.*, **8**, 313–318.

Edwards, A. L. (1951) *Psychological Scaling by Means of Successive Intervals.* Chicago: University of Chicago Psychometric Laboratory.

Edwards, A. L. (1952) The scaling of stimuli by the method of successive intervals. *J. Appl. Psychol.*, **36**, 118–122.

Edwards, A. L., and K. C. Kenny (1946) A comparison of the Thurstone and Likert techniques of attitude scale construction. *J. Appl. Psychol.* **30**, 72–83.

Edwards, A. L., and F. P. Kilpatrick (1948a) Scale analysis and the measurement of social attitudes. *Psychometrika*, **13**, 99–114.

Edwards, A. L., and F. P. Kilpatrick (1948b) A technique for the construction of attitude scales. *J. Appl. Psychol.*, **32**, 374–384.

Edwards, A. L., and L. L. Thurstone (1952) An internal consistency check for scale values by the method of successive intervals. *Psychometrika*, **17**, 169–180.

Edwards, Ward. (1954) The theory of decision making. *Psych. Bull.* **51**, 380–417.

Engen, T. (1956) An evaluation of a method for developing ratio-scales. *Amer. J. Psychol.*, **69**, 92–95.

Engen, T., and N. Levy (1956) Constant sum judgments of facial expressions. *J. Exp. Psychol.*, **51**, 396–398.

Entwisle, D. Intensity and zero-point analysis in psychological scaling. Rep. no. 11. Lab. of Soc. Relations, Harvard University.

Eysenck, H. J., and S. Crown (1949) An experimental study in opinion-attitude methodology. *Int. J. Opin and Att. Res.*, **3**, 47–86.

Farnsworth, P. R. (1945a) Further data on the obtaining of Thurstone scale values. *J. Psychol.*, **19**, 69–74.

Farnsworth, P. R. (1945b) Attitude scale construction and the method of equal appearing intervals. *J. Psychol.*, **20**, 245–249.

Fehrer, E. (1952) Shifts in scale values of attitude statements as a function of the composition of the scale. *J. Exp. Psychol.*, **44**, 179–188.

Ferguson, A., C. S. Myers, R. J. Bartlett, et. al. (1938) Quantitative estimation of sensory events. Report of the Brit. Assoc. Adv. Sci., Cambridge, 108th year, 277–334.

Ferguson, A., C. S. Myers, R. J. Bartlett, et al. (1940) Quantitative estimation of sensory events. Final Report, *Adv. of Sci.*, **2**, 331–349.

Ferguson, G. A. (1941) The factorial interpretation of test difficulty. *Psychometrika*, **6**, 323–349.

Ferguson, G. A. (1942) Item selection by the constant process. *Psychometrika*, **7**, 19–29.

Ferguson, L. W. (1941) A study of the Likert technique of attitude scale construction. *J. Soc. Psychol.*, **31**, 51–58.

Fernberger, S. W. (1913) On the relation of the methods of just perceptible differences and constant stimuli. *Psychol. Monog.*, **14**, no. 61.

Fernberger, S. W. (1914) The effect of the attitude of the subject upon the measure of sensitivity. *Amer. J. Psychol.*, **25**, 538–543.

Fernberger, S. W. (1930) The use of equality judgments in psychophysical procedures. *Psychol. Rev.*, **37**, 107–112.

Fernberger, S. W. (1931) On absolute and relative judgments in lifted weight experiments. *Amer. J. Psychol.*, **43**, 560–578.

Festinger, L. (1943*a*) Studies in decision: I. Decision time, relative frequency of judgment and subjective confidence as related to physical stimulus difference. *J. Exp. Psychol.*, **32**, 291–306.

Festinger, L. (1943*b*) Studies in decision: II. An empirical test of a quantitative theory of decision. *J. Exp. Psychol.*, **32**, 411–423.

Festinger, L. (1947) The treatment of qualitative data by "scale analysis". *Psychol. Bull.*, **44**, 149–161.

Finney, D. J. (1947) *Probit Analysis. A Statistical Treatment of the Sigmoid Response Curve.* London: Cambridge University Press.

Fletcher, H. (1934) Loudness, pitch, and timbre of musical tones and their relation to the intensity, the frequency, and the overtone structure. *J. Acoust. Soc. Amer.*, **6**, 59–69.

Fletcher, H. (1935) New concepts of pitch, loudness and timbre of musical tones. *J. Frank. Inst.*, 405–429.

Fletcher, H., and W. A. Munson (1933) Loudness, its definition, measurement and calculation. *J. Acoust. Soc. Amer.*, **5**, 82–108.

Fletcher, H., and W. A. Munson (1937) Relation between loudness and masking. *J. Acoust. Soc. Amer.*, **9**, 1–10.

Foa, Uriel G. (1950*a*) The use of scale and intensity analysis in opinion research. *Int. J. Opin. and Att. Res.*, **4**, 192–208.

Foa, Uriel G. (1950*b*) Scale and intensity analysis in sociometric research. *Sociometry*, **4**, 358–362.

Ford, R. N. (1950) A rapid scoring procedure for scaling attitude questions. *Pub. Opin Quart.*, **14**, 507–532.

Freyd, Max (1923) The graphic rating scale. *J. Educ. Psychol.*, **14**, 83–102.

Fullerton, G. S., and J. McK. Cattell (1892) *On the Perception of Small Differences.* Philadelphia: Pub. Univ. of Penn.. no. 2.

Furfey, P. H. (1926) An improved rating scale technique. *J. Educ. Psychol.*, **17**, 45–48.

Gage, F. H. (1934) The measureability of auditory sensations. *Proc. Roy. Soc.*, **116b**, 103–119.

Galanter, E. H. (1956) An axiomatic and experimental study of sensory order and measure. *Psychol. Rev.*, **63**, 16–28.

Garner, W. R. (1952*a*) An equidiscriminability scale for loudness judgments. *J. Exp. Psychol.*, **43**, 232–238.

Garner, W. R. (1952*b*) Some statistical aspects of half-loudness judgments, *J. Acoust. Soc. Amer.*, **24**, 153–157.

Garner, W. R. (1953) An informational analysis of absolute judgments of loudness. *J. Exp. Psychol.*, **46**, 373–380.

Garner, W. R. (1954*a*) A technique and a scale for loudness measurement. *J. Acoust. Soc. Amer.*, **26**, 73–88.

Garner, W. R. (1954*b*) Context effects and the validity of loudness scales. *J. Exp. Psychol.*, **48**, 218–224.

Garner, W. R., and H. W. Hake (1951) The amount of information in absolute judgments. *Psychol. Rev.*, **58**, 446–459.

Geiger, H. E., H. H. Remmers, and R. J. Greenly (1938) Apprentices attitudes toward their training and the construction of a diagnosis scale. *J. Appl. Psychol.*, **22**, 32–41.

Geiger, P. H., and F. A. Firestone (1933) The estimation of fractional loudness. *J. Accoust. Soc. Amer.*, **5**, 25–30.

Ghiselli, E. E., and C. W. Brown (1955) *Personnel and Industrial Psychology*. New York: McGraw-Hill.

Gibson, J. J. (1937) Adaptation with negative after effect. *Psychol. Rev.*, **44**, 222–244.

Gibson, W. A. (1951) Applications of the mathematics of multiplefactor analysis to problems of latent structure analysis. Part V of Lazarsfeld, et al. (1951), The use of mathematical models in the measurement of attitudes. RAND Research Memorandum no. 455. Santa Monica: The RAND Corporation.

Gibson, W. A. (1953) A least squares solution for Case IV of the Law of Comparative Judgment. *Psychometrika*, **18**, 15–21.

Gibson, W. A. (1955) An extension of Anderson's solution for the latent structure equations. *Psychometrika*, **20**, 69–73.

Goheen, H. W., and S. Kavruck (1950) *Selected References on Test Construction, Mental Test Theory, and Statistics*, 1929–1949. Washington, D.C.: U.S. Government Printing Office.

Goodenough, W. H. (1944) A technique for scale analysis. *Educ. Psychol. Msmt.*, **4**, 179–190.

Gordon, K. (1912) Esthetics of simple color arrangements. *Psychol. Rev.*, **19**, 352–363.

Gordon, K. (1923) A study of esthetic judgments. *J. Exp. Psychol.*, **6**, 36–43.

Gordon, K. (1924) Group judgments in the field of lifted weights. *J. Exp. Psychol.*, **7**, 398–400.

Graham, C. H. (1934) Psychophysics and behavior. *J. Gen. Psychol.*, **10**, 299–310.

Graham, C. H. (1951) Behavior and the psychophysical methods: an analysis of some recent experiments. *Psychol. Rev.*, **59**, 62–70.

Green, Bert F. Jr. (1951*a*) Latent class analysis: A general solution and an empirical evaluation. Ph.D. Thesis, Princeton University.

Green, Bert F. Jr. (1951*b*) A general solution for the latent class model of latent structure analysis. *Psychometrika*, **16**, 151–166.

Green, Bert F. Jr. (1954) Attitude measurement. In Lindzey, G. (Ed.) *Handbook of Social Psychology*. Cambridge, Mass.: Addison-Wesley.

Green, Bert F. Jr. (1956) A method of scalogram analysis using summary statistics. *Psychometrika*, **21**, 79–89.

Green, Bert F. Jr. (ditto) Notes on a multidimensional scale for absolute judgments.

Greenwood, J. A. (1943) A preferential matching problem. *Psychometrika*, **8**, 185–191.

Gregg, L. W. (1951) Fractionation of temporal intervals. *J. Exp. Psychol.*, **42**, 307–312.

Gridgeman, N. T. (1955) The Bradley–Terry probability model and preference tasting. *Biometrics*, **11**, 335–344.

Grossnickel, Louise T. (1942) The scaling of test scores by the method of paired comparisons. *Psychometrika*, **7**, 43–64.

Guilford, J. P. (1928) The method of paired comparisons as a psychometric method. *Psychol. Rev.*, **35**, 494–506.

Guilford, J. P. (1931*a*) Racial preferences of a thousand American university students. *J. Soc. Psychol.*, **2**, 179–204.

Guilford, J. P. (1931*b*) Some empirical tests of the method of paired comparisons. *J. Gen. Psychol.*, **5**, 64–76.

Guilford, J. P. (1932) A generalized psychophysical law. *Psychol. Rev.*, **39**, 73–85.

Guilford, J. P. (1933) An examination of a typical test of introversion by means of the method of similar reactions. *J. Soc. Psychol.*, **4**, 430–443.

Guilford, J. P. (1936) *Psychometric Methods.* New York: McGraw-Hill.

Guilford, J. P. (1937a) The psychophysics of mental test difficulty. *Psychometrika,* **2,** 121–133.

Guilford, J. P. (1937b) Scale values derived from the method of choices. *Psychometrika,* **2,** 139–150.

Guilford, J. P. (1938) The computation of psychological values from judgments in absolute categories. *J. Exp. Psychol.,* **22,** 32–42.

Guilford, J. P. (1939) A study in psychodynamics. *Psychometrika,* **4,** 1–23.

Guilford, J. P. (1954) *Psychometric Methods.* Second Edition. New York: McGraw-Hill.

Guilford, J. P., and K. M. Dallenbach (1925) The determination of memory span by the method of constant stimuli. *Amer. J. Psychol.,* **36,** 621–628.

Guilford, J. P., and H. F. Dingman (1954) A validation study of ratio-judgment methods. *Amer. J. Psychol.,* **67,** 395–410.

Guilford, J. P., and H. F. Dingman (1955) A modification of the method of equal-appearing intervals. *Amer. J. Psychol.,* **68,** 450–454.

Gulliksen, H. (1946) Paired comparisons and the logic of measurement. *Psychol. Rev.,* **53,** 199–213.

Gulliksen, H. (1950) *Theory of Mental Tests.* New York: Wiley.

Gulliksen, H. (1954) A least squares solution for successive intervals assuming unequal standard deviations. *Psychometrika,* **19,** 117–139.

Gulliksen, H. (1956a) A least squares solution for paired comparisons with incomplete data. *Psychometrika,* **21,** 125–134.

Gulliksen, H. (1956b) Measurement of subjective values. *Psychometrika,* **21,** 229–244.

Guttman, L. (1941) The quantification of a class of attributes: A theory and method of scale construction. In Horst, Paul, et al., *The Prediction of Personal Adjustment.* New York: Social Science Research Council.

Guttman, L. (1942) A revision of Chapin's social status scale. *Amer. Sociol. Rev.,* **7,** 362–369.

Guttman, L. (1944) A basis for scaling qualitative data. *Amer. Sociol. Rev.,* **9,** 139–150.

Guttman, L. (1945) A basis for analyzing test-retest reliability. *Psychometrika,* **10,** 255–282.

Guttman, L. (1946a) The test–retest reliability of qualitative data. *Psychometrika,* **11,** 81–95.

Guttman, L. (1946b) An approach for quantifying paired comparisons and rank order. *Ann. Math. Statist.,* **17,** 144–163.

Guttman, L. (1947a) Suggestions for further research in scale and intensity analysis of attitudes and opinions. *Int. J. Opin. and Att. Res.,* **1,** 30–35.

Guttman, L. (1947b) On Festinger's evaluation of scale analysis. *Psychol. Bull.,* **44,** 451–465.

Guttman, L. (1947c) The Cornell technique for scale and intensity analysis. *Educ. Psychol. Msmt.,* **7,** 247–280.

Guttman, L. (1950a) Chapters 2, 3, 6, 8, and 9 in Stouffer, et al. *Measurement and Prediction.* Princeton, N.J.: Princeton University Press.

Guttman, L. (1950b) The third component of scalable attitudes. (abs.) *Int. J. Opin. and Att. Res.,* **4,** 285–287.

Guttman, L. (1951) Scale analysis, factor analysis and Dr. Eysenck. *Int. J. Opin. and Att. Res.,* **5,** 103–120.

Guttman, L. (1953) On Smith's paper on " 'randomness of error' in reproducible scales." *Educ. Psychol. Msmt.*, **13**, 505–511.

Guttman, L. (1954) The principal components of scalable attitudes in Lazarsfeld, P. F. (Ed.), *Mathematical Thinking in the Social Sciences*. Glencoe, Ill.: The Free Press.

Guttman, L., and U. G. Foa (1951) Social contact and an intergroup attitude. *Pub. Opin. Quart.*, **15**, 43–53.

Guttman, L., and E. A. Suchman (1947) Intensity and a zero point for attitude analysis. *Amer. Sociol. Rev.*, **12**, 57–67.

Guttman, N., and H. I. Kalish (1956) Discriminability and stimulus generalization. *J. Exp. Psychol.*, **51**, 79–88.

Hagood, M. J., and D. O. Price (1952) *Statistics for Sociologists*. New York: Holt.

Ham, L. B., and J. S. Parkinson (1932) Loudness and intensity relations. *J. Acoust. Soc. Amer.*, **3**, 511–534.

Hanes, R. M. (1949a) A scale of subjective brightness. *J. Exp. Psychol.*, **39**, 438–452.

Hanes, R. M. (1949b) The construction of subjective brightness scales from fractionation data: a validation. *J. Exp. Psychol.*, **39**, 719–728.

Hardy, J. D., and C. T. Javert (1949) Studies on pain: measurement of pain intensity in childbirth. *J. Clin. Invest.*, **28**, 153–162.

Hardy, J. D., H. G. Wolff, and H. Goodell (1947) Studies on pain: discrimination of differences in intensity of a pain stimulus as a basis of a scale of pain intensity. *J. Clin. Invest.*, **26**, 1152–1158.

Hardy, J. D., H. G. Wolff, and H. Goodell (1948) Studies on pain: an investigation of some quantitative aspects of the dol scale of pain intensity. *J. Clin. Invest.* **27**, 380–386.

Harper, R. S., and S. S. Stevens (1948) A psychological scale of weight and a formula for its derivation. *Amer. J. Psychol.*, **61**, 343–351.

Harris, W. P. (1957) A revised law of comparative judgment. *Psychometrika*, **22**, 189–198.

Harrison, S., and M. J. Harrison (1951) A psychophysical method employing a modification of the Muller–Urban weights. *Psychol. Bull.*, **48**, 249–256.

Hays, D. G., and E. F. Borgatta (1954) An empirical comparison of restricted and general latent distance analysis. *Psychometrika*, **19**, 271–279.

Hays, W. L. (1954) An extension of the unfolding technique to *r*-dimensions. Ph.D. Thesis, University of Michigan.

Heintz, R. K. (1950) The effect of remote anchoring points upon the judgment of lifted weights. *J. Exp. Psychol.*, **40**, 584–591.

Helson, H. (1947) Adaptation level as a frame of reference for prediction of psychophysical data. *Amer. J. Psychol.*, **60**, 1–29.

Helson, H. (Ed.) (1951) *Theoretical Foundations of Psychology*. New York: D. Van Nostrand.

Helson, H., and W. C. Michels (1954) A reconciliation of the VEG scale with Fechner's law. *Amer. J. Psychol.*, **67**, 677–683.

Helson, H., W. C. Michels, and A. Sturgeon (1954) The use of comparative rating scales for the evaluation of psychophysical data. *Amer. J. Psychol.*, **67**, 321–326.

Hempel, C. G. (1952) Fundamentals of Concept formation in empirical science. In O. Neurath and others (Eds.) *Inter. Encyclopedia of Unified Science*, Vol. 2, no. 7. Chicago: University of Chicago Press.

Henmon, V. A. C. (1911) The relation of the time of a judgment to its accuracy. *Psychol. Rev.*, **18**, 186–201.

Henry, A. F. (1952) A method of classifying non-scale response patterns in a Guttman scale. *Pub. Opin. Quart.*, **16**, 94–106.

Hevner, K. (1930) An empirical study of three psychophysical methods. *J. Gen. Psychol.*, **4**, 191–212.

Hillegas, M. B. (1912) A scale for the measurement of quality in English compositions. *Teach. Coll. Rec.*, **13**, no. 4.

Hollingworth, H. L. (1911) Judgments of persuasiveness. *Psychol. Rev.*, **18**, 234–256.

Hollingworth, H. L. (1913) Experimental studies in judgment. *Arch. Psychol.*, no. 29.

Hollingworth, H. L. (1914) Professor Gattell's studies by the method of relative position. *Arch. Psychol.*, no. 30, 75–91.

Holway, A. H., and C. C. Pratt (1936) The Weber-ratio for intensitive discrimination. *Psychol. Rev.*, **43**, 322–340.

Hopkins, J. W. (1954) Incomplete block rank analysis: some taste test results. *Biometrics*, **10**, 391–399.

Horst, A. P. (1932) A method for determining the absolute value of a series of stimulus situations. *J. Educ. Psychol.*, **23**, 418–440.

Horst, A. P. (1935) Measuring complex attitudes. *J. Soc. Psychol.*, **6**, 369–374.

Horst, A. P. (1936) Obtaining a composite measure from different measures of the same attribute. *Psychometrika*, **1**, 53–60.

Horst, A. P. (1941) The prediction of personal adjustment. *Soc. Sci. Res. Coun. Bull.*, no. 48.

Hotelling, H. (1933) Analysis of a complex of statistical variables into principal components. *J. Educ. Psychol.*, **24**, 417–441.

Householder, A. S., and H. D. Landahl (1945) Mathematical biophysics of the central nervous system. *Math. Bioph. Monog.*, no. 1.

Householder, A. S., and G. Young (1940) Weber laws, the Weber law, and psychophysical analysis. *Psychometrika*, **5**, 183–193.

Hovland, C. I. (1938) A note on Guilford's generalized psychophysical law. *Psychol. Rev.*, **45**, 430–434.

Hovland, C. I., and M. Sherif (1952) Judgmental phenomena and scales of attitude measurement: item displacement in Thurstone scales. *J. Abn. Soc. Psychol.*, **47**, 822–832.

Howes, D. H. (1951) The loudness of multicomponent tones. *Amer. J. Psychol.*, **63**, 1–31.

Hull, C. L., J. M. Felsinger, A. I. Gladstone, and H. G. Yamaguchi (1947) A proposed quantification of habit strength. *Psychol. Rev.*, **54**, 237–254.

Hunt, W. A. (1941) Anchoring effects in judgment. *Amer. J. Psychol.*, **54**, 395–403.

Hunt, W. A., and J. Flannery (1938) Variability in affective judgment. *Amer. J. Psychol.*, **51**, 507–513.

Hunt, W. A., and J. Volkmann (1937) The anchoring of an affective scale. *Amer. J. Psychol.*, **49**, 88–92.

Hurst, P. M., and S. Siegel (1956) Prediction of decisions from a higher ordered metric scale of utility. *J. Exp. Psychol.*, **52**, 138–144.

Information and Educational Division (Research Branch, Army Service Forces) (1943) The desire of enlisted men for post-war full-time schooling: an example of a scale (mimeo.).

Information and Educational Division (Research Branch, Army Service Forces) (1944*a*) The screen of neurotics. Report B–104.

Information and Educational Division (Research Branch, Army Service Forces) (1944*b*) A study of psychoneurotics in the army. Report B–107.

Information and Educational Division (Research Branch, Army Service Forces) (1945*a*) Experiments on the measurement of the intensity function and zero point in attitude analysis. Report D-1 (mimeo.).

Information and Educational Division (Research Branch, Army Service Forces) (1945*b*) Questions and answers about scale analysis. Report D-2 (mimeo.).

Irwin, F. (1935) Psychophysical measurement methods. *Psychol. Bull.*, **32**, 140–171.

Jahn, J. A. (1951) Some further contributions to Guttman's scale analysis. *Amer. Soc. Rev.*, **16**, 233–239.

Jahoda, M., M. Deutch, and S. Cook (1951) *Research Methods in the Study of Social Relations.* New York: Dryden Press.

Jastrow, J. (1888) Critique of psychophysic methods. *Amer. J. Psychol.*, **1**, 271–309.

Jensen, E. M., E. P. Reese, and T. W. Reese (1950) The subitizing and counting of visually presented fields of dots. *J. Psychol.*, **30**, 363–392.

Johannsen, D. E. (1941) *The Principles of Psychophysics.* Tufts College, Mass.: Author.

Johnson, D. M. (1945) A systematic treatment of judgment. *Psychol. Bull.*, **42**, 193–224.

Johnson, D. M. (1949*a*) Generalization of a reference scale for judging pitch. *J. Exp. Psychol.*, **39**, 316–321.

Johnson, D. M. (1949*b*) Learning function for a change in the scale of judgment. *J. Exp. Psychol.*, **39**, 851–860.

Johnson, D. M. (1952) The central tendency of judgment as a regression phenomenon. *Amer. Psychologist*, **7**, 281, (abs.).

Johnson, H. M. (1930) Some properties of Fechner's intensity of sensation. *Psychol. Rev.*, **37**, 113–123.

Johnson, H. M. (1936) Pseudo-mathematics in the mental and social sciences. *Amer. J. Psychol.*, **48**, 342–351.

Johnson, H. M. (1945) Are psychophysical problems genuine or spurious? *Amer. J. Psychol.*, **58**, 189–211.

Johnson, P. O., and F. Tsao (1944) Factorial design in the determination of differential limen values. *Psychometrika*, **9**, 107–144.

Jones, L. A. (1917) The fundamental scale of pure hue and retinal sensibility to hue differences. *J. Opt. Soc. Amer.*, **1**, 63–77.

Jones, L. A., and E. M. Lowry (1926) Retinal sensibility to saturation differences. *J. Opt. Soc. Amer.*, **13**, 25–34.

Jones, L. V., and W. W. Rozenboom (1956) The validity of the successive intervals method of psychometric scaling. *Psychometrika*, **21**, 165–183.

Jones, L. V., and L. L. Thurstone (1955) The psychophysics of semantics: an experimental investigation. *J. Appl. Psychol.*, **39**, 31–36.

Judd, D. B. (1933) Saturation scale for yellow colors. *J. Opt. Soc. Amer.*, **23**, 35–40.

Jurgensen, C. E. (1942) A two dimensional rating scale. *Amer. J. Psychol.*, **55**, 255–260.

Jurgensen, C. E. (1949) A fallacy in the use of median scale values in employee check lists. *J. Appl. Psychol.*, **33**, 56–58.

Kahn, L. A., and A. J. Bodine (1951) Guttman scale analysis by means of IBM equipment. *Educ. Psychol. Msmt.*, **11**, 298–314.

Katz, D. (1944) The measurement of intensity. In Cantril, H. (Ed.) *Gauging Public Opinion.* Princeton, N.J.: Princeton University Press.

Kaufman, E. L., M. W. Lord, T. W. Reese, and J. Volkmann (1949) The discrimination of visual number. *Amer. J. Psychol.*, **62**, 498–525.

Keats, A. S., H. K. Beecher, and F. Mosteller (1950) Measurement of pathological pain in distinction to experimental pain. *J. Appl. Physiol.*, **1**, 35–44.

Kelley, H. H., C. I. Hovland, M. Schwartz, and R. P. Abelson (mimeo.) The influence of judges' attitudes in three methods of attitude scaling.

Kellog, W. N. (1929) An experimental comparison of psychophysical methods. *Arch. Psychol.*, no. 106.

Kellog, W. N. (1930) An experimental evaluation of equality judgments in psychophysics. *Arch. Psychol.*, no. 112.

Kellogg, W. N. (1931) The time of judgment in psychometric measures. *Amer. J. Psychol.*, **43**, 65–86.

Kendall, M. G. (1948) *Rank Correlation Methods.* London: Charles Griffin.

Kendall, M. G., and B. B. Smith (1940) On the method of paired comparisons. *Biometrika*, **31**, 324–345.

Kingsbury, F. A. (1922) Analyzing ratings and training raters. *J. Pers. Res.*, **1**, 377–383.

Kirkpatrick, C. (1936) Assumptions and methods in attitude measurement. *Amer. Sociol. Rev.*, **1**, 75–88.

Klingberg, F. L. (1941) Studies in measurement of the relations between sovereign states. *Psychometrika*, **6**, 335–352.

Kluckhohn, C., and H. A. Murray. (Eds.) (1948) *Personality in Nature, Society, and Culture.* New York: Alfred Knopf.

Knauft, E. B. (1947) A classification and evaluation of personnel rating methods. *J. Appl. Psychol.*, **31**, 617–625.

Koester, T., and W. N. Schoenfeld (1947) Some comparative data on differential pitch sensitivity under quantal and non-quantal conditions. *J. Gen. Psychol.*, **36**, 107–112.

Kriedt, P. H., and K. E. Clark (1949) "Item analysis" versus "scale analysis." *J. Appl. Psychol.*, **33**, 114–121.

Laird, D. A., E. Taylor, and H. H. Wille (1932) The apparent reduction of loudness. *J. Acoust. Soc. Amer.*, **3**, 393–401.

Lawshe, C. H., N. C. Kephart, and E. J. McCormick (1949) The paired comparison technique for rating performance of industrial employees. *J. Appl. Psychol.*, **33**, 69–77.

Lazarsfeld, P. F. (1950) Chapters 10 and 11 in Stouffer et al. *Measurement and Prediction.* Princeton, N.J.: Princeton University Press.

Lazarsfeld, P. F. (1954a) A conceptual introduction to latent structure analysis. In P. F. Lazarsfeld (Ed.), *Mathematical Thinking in the Social Sciences.* Glencoe, Ill.: The Free Press.

Lazarsfeld, P. F. (Ed.) (1954b) *Mathematical Thinking in the Social Sciences.* Glencoe, Ill.: The Free Press.

Lazarsfeld, P. F. (ditto) The computation of latent distance scales.

Lazarsfeld, P. F., et al. (1951) The use of mathematical models in the measurement of attitudes. RAND research memorandum 455, unpublished.

Lazarsfeld, P. F., and J. Dudman (1951) Part II, paper 5 in Lazarsfeld, et al. (1951), The use of mathematical models in the measurement of attitudes. RAND Research Memorandum no. 455. Santa Monica: The RAND Corporation.

Lazarsfeld, P. F., and F. N. Stanton (1949) *Communications Research*, New York: Harper.

Lewis, D. R. (1948) Psychological scales of taste. *J. Psychol.*, **26**, 437–446.

Lienau, C. C. (1941) Discrete bivariate distribution in certain problems of statistical order. *Amer. J. Hygiene*, **33**, 65–85.

Likert, R. (1932) A technique for the measurement of attitudes. *Arch. Psychol.*, no. 140, 1–55.

Likert, R., S. Roslow, and G. Murphy (1934) A simple and reliable method of scoring the Thurstone attitude scales. *J. Soc. Psychol.*, **5**, 228–238.

Linder, R. E. (1933) A statistical comparison of psychophysical methods. *Psychol. Monog.*, **44**, no. 199, 1–20.

Lindquist, E. F. (Ed.) (1951) *Educational Measurement.* Washington, D.C.: Amer. Council on Education.

Loevinger, J. (1947) A systematic approach to the construction and evaluation of tests of ability. *Psychol. Monog.*, **61**, no. 4.

Loevinger, J. (1948) The technic of homogeneous tests compared with some aspects of "scale analysis" and factor analysis. *Psychol. Bull.*, **45**, 507–530.

Long, L. (1937) The effect of preceding stimuli upon the judgment of auditory intensities. *Arch. Psychol.*, no. 209.

Lord, F. M. (1953) An application of confidence intervals and of maximum likelihood to the estimation of an examinee's ability. *Psychometrika*, **18**, 57–77.

Lord, F. M. (1954) Scaling. *Rev. Educ. Research*, **24**, 375–393.

Lorge, I. (1951) The fundamental nature of measurement. In E. F. Lindquist (Ed.) *Educational Measurement.* Washington, D.C.: Amer. Council on Education.

Lorr, M. (1944) Interrelationships of number-correct and limen scores for an amount-limit test. *Psychometrika*, **9**, 17–30.

Lynch, J. A. (1938) A quantitative description of the stimulus. *Psychometrika*, **3**, 95–105.

Macdonald, P. A., and Robertson, D. M. (1930) The psychophysical law. *Phil. Mag.*, **10**, 1063–1073.

MacLeod, S. (1952) A construction and attempted validation of sensory sweetness scales. *J. Exp. Psychol.*, **44**, 316–323.

Madow, W. G. (1951) The measurement and prediction of attitudes. *J. Amer. Stat. Assn.*, **46**, 508–514.

Marder, E. (1952) Linear segments: a technique for scalogram analysis. *Pub. Opin. Quart.*, **16**, 417–431.

Margenau, H. (1935) Methodology of modern physics. *Phil. Sci.*, **2**, 48–72, 164–187.

Margenau, H. (1945) On the frequency theory of probability. *Phil. and Phenom. Res.*, **6**, 11–25.

Margenau, H. (1950) *The Nature of Physical Reality.* New York: McGraw-Hill.

Marill, T. (1956) Detection theory and psychophysics. Ph.D. Thesis, Massachusetts Institute of Technology.

May, Kenneth (1954) Transitivity, utility and aggregation in the preference pattern. *Econometrica*, **22**, 1–13.

McCarthy, P. J. (1951) A special review of *The American Soldier*, Vol. IV. *Psychometrika*, **16**, 247–269.

McCormick, L. C. (1948) A rationale for scaling unordered attributes. *Amer. J. Sociol.*, **54**, 31–35.

McGarvey, H. R. (1943) Anchoring effects in the absolute judgment of verbal materials. *Arch. Psychol.*, no. 281.

McGregor, D. (1935) Scientific measurement and psychology. *Psychol. Rev.*, **42**, 246–266.

McHugh, R. B. (1956) Efficient estimation and local identification in latent class analysis. *Psychometrika*, **21**, 331–348.

McNemar, Q. (1946) Opinion-attitude methodology. *Psychol. Bull.*, **43**, 289–374.

Merton, R. K., and P. F. Lazarsfeld (1950) *Continuities in Social Research.* Glencoe, Ill.: The Free Press.

Messick, S. J. (1954) The perception of attitude relationships: A multidimensional scaling approach to the structuring of social attitudes. Ph.D. Thesis, Princeton University.

Messick, S. J. (1956) An empirical evaluation of multidimensional successive intervals. *Psychometrika,* **21,** 367–376.

Messick, S. J., and R. P. Abelson (1956) The additative constant problem in multidimensional scaling. *Psychometrika,* **21,** 1–17.

Messick, S. J., L. R. Tucker, and H. W. Garrison (1955) A punched card procedure for the method of successive intervals. *Res. Bull.,* 55–25. Princeton: Educational Testing Service.

Metfessel, Milton (1947) A proposal for quantitative reporting of comparative judgments. *J. Psychol.,* **24,** 229–235.

Michels, W. C., and H. Helson (1949) A reformulation of the Fechner Law in terms of adaptation level applied to rating scale data. *Amer. J. Psychol.,* **62,** 355–368.

Milholland, J. E. (1953) Dimensionality of response patterns for the method of single stimuli. Ph.D. Thesis, University of Michigan.

Miller, G. A., and W. R. Garner (1944) Effect of random presentation on the psychometric function: implications for a quantal theory of discrimination. *Amer. J. Psychol.,* **57,** 451–467.

Minturn, A. L., and T. W. Reese (1951) The effect of differential reinforcement on the discrimination of visual number. *J. Psychol.,* **31,** 201–231.

Morgan, C. T., W. R. Garner, and R. Galambos (1951) Pitch and intensity. *J. Acoust. Soc. Amer.,* **23,** 658–663.

Mosier, C. I. (1940*a*) A modification of the method of successive intervals. *Psychometrika,* **5,** 101–107.

Mosier, C. I. (1940*b*) Psychophysics and mental test theory. Fundamental postulates and elementary theorems. *Psychol. Rev.,* **47,** 355–366.

Mosier, C. I. (1941*a*) Psychophysics and mental test theory. II. The constant process. *Psychol. Rev.,* **48,** 235–249.

Mosier, C. I. (1941*b*) A psychometric study of meaning. *J. Soc. Psychol.,* **13,** 123–140.

Mosteller, F. (1949) A theory of scalogram analysis, using noncumulative types of items: a new approach to Thurstone's method of scaling attitudes. Rep. no. 9, Lab. of Soc. Relations, Harvard University.

Mosteller, F. (1951*a*) Remarks on the method of paired comparisons. I. The least squares solution assuming equal standard deviations and equal correlations. *Psychometrika,* **16,** 3–11.

Mosteller, F. (1951*b*) Remarks on the method of paired comparisons: II. The effect of an abberant standard deviation when equal standard deviations and equal correlations are assumed. *Psychometrika,* **16,** 203–206.

Mosteller, F. (1951*c*) Remarks on the method of paired comparisons: III. A test of significance for paired comparisons when equal standard deviations and equal correlations are assumed. *Psychometrika,* **16,** 207–218.

Mosteller, F., and P. Nogee (1951) An experimental measurement of utility. *J. Pol. Econ.,* **5,** 371–404.

Munsell, A. H. (1909) On the relation of the intensity of chromatic stimulus (physical saturation) to chromatic sensation. *Psychol. Bull.,* **6,** 238–239.

Munson, W. A.   (1947)   The growth of auditory sensation.   *J. Acoust. Soc. Amer.*, **19**, 584–591.

Munson, W. A., and M. B. Gardner   (1950)   Loudness patterns, a new approach. *J. Acoust. Soc. Amer.*, **22**, 177–190.

Munson, W. A., and F. M. Wiener   (1950)   Sound measurements for psychophysical tests.   *J. Acoust. Soc. Amer.*, **22**, 382–386.

Nagel, E.   (1931)   Measurement.   *Erkenntnis*, **2**, 313–333.

National Industrial Conference Board   (1938)   Studies in personnel policy, no. 8.

National Industrial Conference Board   (1942)   Studies in personnel policy, no. 39.

Nelson, Erland   (1939)   Attitudes: III. Their measurement.   *J. Gen. Psychol.*, **21**, 417–436.

Nevin, J. R.   (1953)   A comparison of two attitude scaling techniques.   *Educ. Psychol. Msmt.*, **13**, 65–76.

Newhall, S. M.   (1939)   The ratio method in the review of the Munsell colors.   *Amer. J. Psychol.*, **52**, 394–405.

Newhall, S. M.   (1950)   A method for evaluating the spacing of visual scales.   *Amer. J. Psychol.*, **63**, 221–228.

Newman, E. B.   (1933)   The validity of the just noticable difference as a unit of psychological magnitude.   *Trans, Kans. Acad. Sci.*, **36**, 172–175.

Newman, E. B., J. Volkman, and S. S. Stevens   (1937)   On the method of bisection and its relation to a loudness scale.   *Amer. J. Psychol.*, **49**, 134–137.

Noland, E. W.   (1945)   Worker attitude and industrial absenteeism: a statistical appraisal.   *Amer. Soc. Rev.*, **10**, 503–510.

Nutting, P. G.   (1909–10)   A method for constructing the natural scale of pure color. *Bur. Stds. Bull.*, **6**, 89–93.

Osgood, C. E., and G. J. Suci   (1952)   A measure of relation determined by both mean difference and profile information.   *Psychol. Bull.*, **49**, 251–262.

Parducci, A.   (1954)   Learning variables in the judgment of single stimuli.   *J. Exp. Psychol.*, **48**, 24–30.

Parducci, A.   (1956)   Incidental learning of stimulus frequencies in the establishment of judgment scales.   *J. Exp. Psychol.*, **52**, 112–118.

Peters, H. N.   (1942)   The experimental study of aesthetic judgments.   *Psychol. Bull.*, **39**, 273–305.

Peterson, W. W., and T. G. Birdsall   (1953)   The theory of signal detectability. Electronic Defense Group, University of Michigan, Tech. Rep. no. 13.

Pfautz, H. W., and O. D. Duncan   (1950)   A critical evaluation of Warner's work in community stratification.   *Amer. Sociol. Rev.*, **15**, 205–215.

Pollack, I.   (1949)   Loudness as a discriminable aspect of noise.   *Amer. J. Psychol.*, **62**, 285–289.

Postman, C., and G. A. Miller   (1945)   Anchoring of temporal judgments.   *Amer. J. Psychol.*, **58**, 43–53.

Pratt, C. C.   (1923)   Bisection of tonal intervals smaller than an octave.   *J. Exp. Psychol.*, **6**, 211–222.

Pratt, C. C.   (1928*a*)   Bisection of tonal intervals larger than the octave.   *J. Exp. Psychol.*, **11**, 17–26.

Pratt, C. C.   (1928*b*)   Comparison of tonal distance.   *J. Exp. Psychol.*, **11**, 77–84.

Pratt, C. C.   (1939)   *The Logic of Modern Psychology.*   New York: Macmillan.

Preston, M. G.   (1938)   Psychophysical measurement methods.   *Psychol. Bull.*, **35**, 63–83.

Reese, T. W.   (1943)   Application of the theory of physical measurement to the measurement of psychological magnitudes with three experimental examples. *Psychol. Monog.*, **55**, no. 3, 251.

Reese, T. W., J. Volkmann, S. Rogers, and E. L. Kaufman (1948) Special problems in the estimation of bearing. Memorandum Report. 131–I–MHC 8, Special Devices Center, Office of Naval Research.

Remmers, H. H. (1934) Reliability and halo effect of high school and college students' judgments of their teachers. *J. Appl. Psychol.*, **18**, 619–630.

Remmers, H. H. (1936) Measuring attitude toward the job. *Occupations*, **14**, 945–948.

Remmers, H. H. (1954) *Introduction to Opinion and Attitude Measurement*. New York: Harper.

Remmers, H. H., and E. B. Silance (1934) Generalized attitude scales. *J. Soc. Psychol.*, **5**, 298–312.

Remmers, H. H., and L. Whisler (1937) The effect of the Presidents' speech on pupils' attitudes toward the proposed Supreme Court changes. *Sch. and Soc.*, **46**, 64.

Richardson, L. F., and J. S. Ross (1930) Loudness and telephone current. *J. Gen. Psychol.*, **3**, 288–306.

Richardson, M. W. (1938) Multidimensional psychophysics. *Psychol. Bull.*, **35**, 659–660.

Riesz, R. R. (1933) Loudness and the minimum perceptible increment in intensity. *J. Acoust. Soc. Amer.*, **4**, 211–216.

Riker, B. L. (1944) A comparison of methods used in attitude research. *J. Abn. Soc. Psychol.*, **39**, 24–42.

Riley, M., et al. (1954) *Sociological Studies in Scale Analysis*. New Brunswick, N.J.: Rutgers University Press.

Rimoldi, H. J. A., and M. Hormaeche (1955) The law of comparative judgment in the successive intervals and graphic rating scale methods. *Psychometrika*, **20**, 307–318.

Robinson, D. W. (1953) Recent work on loudness. *Acoustica*, **3**, 344–358.

Rogers, R. S. (1941) The anchoring of absolute judgments. *Arch. Psychol.*, no. 261.

Rosner, B. S. (1956) A new scaling technique for absolute judgments. *Psychometrika*, **21**, 377–382.

Ross, C. C., and J. C. Stanley (1954) *Measurement in Today's Schools*. New York: Prentice-Hall.

Ross, R. T. (1934) Optimum orders for the presentation of pairs in the method of paired comparisons. *J. Educ. Psychol.*, **25**, 375–382.

Ross, S., and L. Katchmar (1951) The construction of a magnitude function for short time-intervals. *Amer. J. Psychol.*, **64**, 397–401.

Rowan, T. C. (1954) Some developments in multidimensional scaling applied to semantic relationships. Ph.D. Thesis, University of Illinois.

Russell, B. (1938) *Principles of Mathematics*, Second Edition. New York: Norton.

Russell, J. T., and Q. Wright (1933) National attitudes on the far Eastern controversy. *Amer. Pol. Sci. Rev.*, **27**, 555–576.

Saffir, M. (1937) A comparative study of scales constructed by three psychophysical methods. *Psychometrika*, **2**, 179–198.

Satter, G. A. (1949) Method of paired comparisons and a specification scoring key in the evaluation of jobs. *J. Appl. Psychol.*, **33**, 212–221.

Scates, D. E. (1937) The essential conditions of measurement. *Psychometrika*, **2**, 27–34.

Scheffé, H. (1952) An analysis of variance for paired comparisons. *J. Amer. Stat. Assn.*, **47**, 381–400.

Schlosberg, H. (1941) A scale for the judgment of facial expressions. *J. Exp. Psychol.*, **29**, 497–510.

Schuessler, K. R. (1952) Item selection in scale analysis. *Amer. Sociol. Rev.*, **17**, 183–192.

Scott, W. D. (1918) The rating scale. *Psychol. Bull.*, **15**, 203–206.

Seashore, R. H., and K. A. Hevner (1933) A time-saving device for the construction of attitude scales. *J. Soc. Psychol.*, **4**, 366–372.

Senders, V. L. (1953) A comment on Burke's Additive scales and statistics. *Psychol. Rev.*, **60**, 423–424.

Shapiro, G. (1948) Myrdal's definitions of the "South": A methodological note. *Amer. Sociol. Rev.*, **13**, 619–621.

Shepard, R. N. (1955) Stimulus and response generalization during paired associates learning. Ph.D. Thesis, Yale University.

Sherif, M., and H. Cantril (1945) Toward the psychology of "attitudes". Part I. *Psychol. Rev.*, **52**, 295–319.

Sherif, M., and H. Cantril (1946) The psychology of "attitudes." Part II. *Psychol. Rev.*, **53**, 1–25.

Siegel, S. (1956) A method for obtaining an ordered metric scale. *Psychometrika*, **21**, 207–216.

Silance, E. B., and H. H. Remmers (1934) An experimental generalized master scale —a scale to measure attitude toward any school subject. *Bull. Purdue Univ.*, **25**, 84–87.

Simpson, R. M. (1933) Attitudes towards the ten commandments. *J. Soc. Psychol.*, **4**, 223–230.

Simpson, R. M. (1934) Attitudes of teachers and prisoners toward seriousness of criminal acts. *J. Crim. Law. Criminol.*, **25**, 76–83.

Smith, B. O. (1938) *Logical Aspects of Educational Measurement.* New York: Columbia University Press.

Smith, R. G. Jr. (1950*a*) Reproducible scales and the assumption of normality. *Educ. Psychol. Msmt.*, **10**, 395–399.

Smith, R. G. Jr. (1950*b*) A factorial study of attitude toward the negro. Ph.D. Thesis, University of Illinois.

Smith, R. G. Jr. (1951) 'Randomness of error' in reproducible scales. *Educ. Psychol. Msmt.*, **11**, 587–596.

Snedecor, G. W. (1946) *Statistical Methods.* Ames: Iowa State College Press.

Spearman, C. (1908) The method of 'right and wrong cases' without Causs' formulae. *Brit. J. Psychol.*, **2**, 227–242.

Spearman, C. (1927) *The Abilities of Man.* New York: Macmillan.

Spiegelman, S., and J. M. Reiner (1945) A note on steady states and the Weber–Fechner law. *Psychometrika*, **10**, 27–35.

Stagner, R. (1948) *Psychology of Personality*, Second Edition. New York: McGraw-Hill.

Stevens, S. S. (1934) The attributes of tones. *Proc. Nat. Acad. Sci.*, **20**, 457–459.

Stevens, S. S. (1935) The operational definition of psychological concepts. *Psychol. Rev.*, **42**, 517–527.

Stevens, S. S. (1936) A scale for the measurement of a psychological magnitude: loudness. *Psychol. Rev.*, **43**, 405–416.

Stevens, S. S. (1939) On the problem of scales for the measurement of psychological magnitudes. *J. Unif. Sci.*, **9**, 94–99.

Stevens, S. S. (1946) On the theory of scales of measurement. *Science*, **103**, 677–680.

Stevens, S. S. (Ed.) (1951*a*) *Handbook of Experimental Psychology.* New York: Wiley.

Stevens, S. S. (1951*b*) Mathematics, measurement, and psychophysics. In S. S. Stevens (Ed.) *Handbook of Experimental Psychology.* New York: Wiley.

Stevens, S. S. (1955) The measurement of loudness. *J. Acoust. Soc. Amer.,* **27,** 815–829.

Stevens, S. S. (1956*a*) On the psychophysical law. Harvard University, Psycho-Acoustic Lab. Rep. PNR–188.

Stevens, S. S. (1956*b*) Problems and methods of psychophysics. Harvard University, Psycho-Acoustic Lab. Rep. PNR-190.

Stevens, S. S. (1956*c*) The direct estimation of sensory magnitudes—loudness. *Amer. J. Psychol.,* **69,** 1–25.

Stevens, S. S., and H. Davis (1936) Psychophysiological acoustics: pitch and loudness. *J. Acoust. Soc. Amer.,* **8,** 1–13.

Stevens, S. S., and E. H. Galanter (1956) Ratio scales and category scales for a dozen perceptual continua. Harvard University Psycho-Acoustic Lab. Rep. PNR-186.

Stevens, S. S., and E. C. Poulton (1956) The estimation of loudness by unpracticed observers. *J. Exp. Psychol.,* **51,** 71–78.

Stevens, S. S., C. T. Morgan, and J. Volkmann (1941) Theory of the neural quantum in the discrimination of loudness and pitch. *Amer. J. Psychol.,* **54,** 315–335.

Stevens, S. S., and J. Volkmann (1940*a*) The relation of pitch to frequency: a revised scale. *Amer. J. Psychol.,* **53,** 329–353.

Stevens, S. S., and J. Volkmann (1940*b*) The quantum of sensory discrimination. *Science,* **92,** 583–585.

Stevens, S. S., J. Volkmann, and E. B. Newman (1937) A scale for the measurement of the psychological magnitude pitch. *J. Acoust. Soc. Amer.,* **8,** 185–190.

Stouffer, S. A. (1931) Experimental comparison of the statistical and case history method in attitude research. *Amer. Sociol. Soc. Publ.,* **25,** 154–156.

Stouffer, S. A. (1950) An overview of the contributions to scaling and scale theory. In S. A. Stouffer et al. *Measurement and Prediction.* Princeton, N.J.: Princeton University Press.

Stouffer, S. A., et al. (1950) *Measurement and Prediction.* Princeton: Princeton University Press.

Stouffer, S. A., E. F. Borgatta, D. G. Hays, and A. F. Henry (1952) A technique for improving cumulative scales. *Pub. Opin. Quart.,* **16,** 273–291.

Stratton, G. M. (1902) The method of serial groups. *Psychol. Rev.,* **9,** 444–447.

Strong, E. K. (1911) Application of the "order of merit method" to advertising, *J. Phi. and Sci. Method,* **8,** 600–606.

Strong, E. K. (1913) Psychological methods as applied to advertising. *J. Educ. Psychol.,* **4,** 393–404.

Suchman, E. A. (1950*a*) The logic of scale construction. *Educ. Psychol. Msmt.,* **10,** 79–93.

Suchman, E. A. (1950*b*) Chapters 4, 5, and 7 in S. A. Stouffer et al. *Measurement and Prediction.* Princeton, N.J.: Princeton University Press.

Suchman, E. A., and L. Guttman (1947) A solution to the problem of question bias. *Pub. Opin. Quart.,* **11,** 445–455.

Swartz, P. (1953) A new method for scaling pain. *J. Exp. Psychol.* **45,** 288–293.

Symonds, P. M. (1924) On the loss of reliability in ratings due to coarseness of the scale. *J. Exp. Psychol.,* **7,** 456–461.

Symonds, P. M. (1925) Notes on rating, rating versus ranking. *J. Appl. Psychol.*, **9**, 188–195.

Tanner, W. P. Jr., and J. A. Swets (1954) A decision-making theory of visual detection. *Psychol. Rev.*, **61**, 401–409.

Taves, E. H. (1941) Two mechanisms for the perception of visual numerousness. *Arch. Psychol.*, no. 265.

Terry, M. E., R. A. Bradley, and L. L. Davis (1952) New designs and techniques for organoleptic testing. *Food Tech.*, **6**, 250–254.

Thomas, G. J. (1949) Equal volume judgments of tones. *Amer. J. Psychol.*, **62**, 182–201.

Thomas, L. G. (1942) Mental tests as instruments of science. *Psychol. Monog.*, **54**, no. 3.

Thomson, G. H. (1912) A comparison of the psychophysical methods. *Brit. J. Psychol.*, **5**, 203–241.

Thomson, G. H. (1913) An inquiry into the best form of the method of serial groups. *Brit. J. Psychol.*, **5**, 398–416.

Thomson, G. H. (1926) A note on scaling tests. *J. Educ. Psychol.*, **17**, 551–553.

Thorndike, E. L. (1910) Handwriting. *Teach. Coll. Rec.*, **11**, no. 2.

Thorndike, E. L. (1920) A constant error in psychological ratings. *J. Appl. Psychol.*, **4**, 25–29.

Thorndike, E. L., et. al. (1927) *The Measurement of Intelligence*. New York: Columbia University Teachers College Bureau of Publications.

Thurstone, L. L. (1925) A method of scaling psychological and educational tests. *J. Educ. Psychol.*, **16**, 433–451.

Thurstone, L. L. (1926a) The scoring of individual performance. *J. Educ. Psychol.*, **17**, 446–457.

Thurstone, L. L. (1926b) The mental age concept. *Psychol. Rev.*, **33**, 268–278.

Thurstone, L. L. (1927a) A law of comparative judgment. *Psychol. Rev.*, **34**, 273–286.

Thurstone, L. L. (1927b) A mental unit of measurement. *Psychol. Rev.*, **34**, 415–423.

Thurstone, L. L. (1927c) Three psychophysical laws. *Psychol. Rev.*, **34**, 424–432.

Thurstone, L. L. (1927d) Psychophysical analysis. *Amer. J. Psychol.*, **38**, 368–389.

Thurstone, L. L. (1927e) Equally often noticed differences. *J. Educ. Psychol.*, **18**, 289–293.

Thurstone, L. L. (1927f) A unit of measurement in educational scales. *J. Educ. Psychol.*, **18**, 505–524.

Thurstone, L. L. (1927g) Method of paired comparisons for social values. *J. Abn. Soc. Psychol.*, **21**, 384–400.

Thurstone, L. L. (1928a) The absolute zero in intelligence measurement. *Psychol. Rev.*, **35**, 175–197.

Thurstone, L. L. (1928b) The phi-gamma hypothesis. *J. Exp. Psychol.*, **11**, 293–305.

Thurstone, L. L. (1928c) An experimental study of nationality preferences. *J. Gen. Psychol.*, **1**, 405–425.

Thurstone, L. L. (1928d) Attitudes can be measured. *Amer. J. Sociol.*, **33**, 529–554.

Thurstone, L. L. (1928e) The measurement of opinion. *J. Abn. Soc. Psychol.*, **22**, 415–430.

Thurstone, L. L. (1928f) Scale construction with weighted observations. *J. Educ. Psychol.*, **19**, 441–453.

Thurstone, L. L. (1929a) Fechner's law and the method of equal appearing intervals. *J. Exp. Psychol.*, **12**, 214–224.

Thurstone, L. L. (1929*b*) Theory of attitude measurement. *Psychol. Rev.*, **36**, 222–241.

Thurstone, L. L. (1930) A scale for measuring attitude toward the movies. *J. Educ. Res.*, **22**, 89–95.

Thurstone, L. L. (1931*a*) Rank order as a psychophysical method. *J. Exp. Psychol.*, **14**, 187–201.

Thurstone, L. L. (1931*b*) The measurement of social attitudes. *J. Abn. Soc. Psychol.*, **26**, 249–269.

Thurstone, L. L. (1931*c*) The measurement of change in social attitude. *J. Soc. Psychol.*, **2**, 230–235.

Thurstone, L. L. (1931*d*) The influence of motion pictures on Children's attitudes. *J. Soc. Psychol.*, **2**, 291–305.

Thurstone, L. L. (1932) Stimulus dispersions in the method of constant stimuli. *J. Exp. Psychol.*, **15**, 284–297.

Thurstone, L. L. (1945) The prediction of choice. *Psychometrika*, **10**, 237–253.

Thurstone, L. L. (1947) *Multiple Factor Analysis*. Chicago: University of Chicago Press.

Thurstone, L. L. (1948) Psychophysical methods. In T. G. Andrews (Ed.) *Methods of Psychology*. New York: Wiley.

Thurstone, L. L. (1951) Experimental methods in food tasting. *J. Appl. Psychol.*, **35**, 141–145.

Thurstone, L. L. (1954) The measurement of values. *Psychol. Rev.*, **61**, 47–58.

Thurstone, L. L., and Ackerson, L. (1939) The mental growth curve for the Binet tests. *J. Educ. Psychol.*, **20**, 569–583.

Thurstone, L. L., and E. J. Chave (1929) *The Measurement of Attitude*. Chicago: University of Chicago Press.

Thurstone, L. L., and Ruth C. Peterson (1932) The effect of motion picture films on children's attitudes toward the Germans. *J. Educ. Psychol.*, **23**, 241–246.

Tiffin, J. (1947) *Industrial Psychology*. New York: Prentice-Hall.

Tiffin, J., and G. F. Rabideau (1953) Harrison and Harrison's modification of the Muller–Urban weights. *Psychol. Bull.*, **50**, 474–476.

Titchener, E. B. (1905) *Experimental Psychology*, Vol. II. New York: Macmillan.

Torgerson, W. S. (1951) A theoretical and empirical investigation of multidimensional scaling. Ph.D. Thesis, Princeton University.

Torgerson, W. S. (1952) Multidimensional scaling: I. theory and method. *Psychometrika*, **17**, 401–419.

Torgerson, W. S. (1954) A law of categorical judgment. In L. H. Clark, *Consumer Behavior*. Washington Square: New York University Press, 92–93. Also *Amer. Psychologist*, **9**, 483 (abs.).

Tucker, L. R. (1948) A method for scaling ability test items in difficulty taking item unreliability into account. *Amer. Psychologist*, **3**, 309–310 (abs.).

Tucker, L. R. (1952) A level of proficiency scale for a unidimensional skill. *Amer. Psychologist*, **7**, 408 (abs.).

Uhrbrock, R. S., and M. W. Richardson (1933) Item analysis. *Person. J.*, **12**, 141–154.

Urban, F. M. (1907) On the method of just perceptible differences. *Psychol. Rev.*, **14**, 244–253.

Urban, F. M. (1910) The method of constant stimuli and its generalizations. *Psychol. Rev.*, **17**, 229–259.

Urban, F. M. (1933) The Weber–Fechner law and mental measurement. *J. Exp. Psychol.*, **18**, 221–238.

Urban, F. M.   (1939)   The method of equal appearing intervals.   *Psychometrika*, **4,** 117–131.

Urban, F. M.   (1950)   The equality judgments.   *Amer. J. Psychol.*, **63,** 282–284.

Valentine, C. W.   (1914)   The method of comparison in experiments with musical intervals.   *Brit. J. Psychol.*, **7,** 118–135.

Volkmann, J.   (1932)   The method of single stimuli.   *Amer. J. Psychol.*, **44,** 808.

Volkmann, J.   (1936)   The anchoring of absolute scales.   *Psychol. Bull.*, **33,** 742.

Volkmann, J.   (1937)   The natural number of categories in absolute judgments. *Psychol. Bull.*, **34,** 543.

Volkmann, J.   (1938)   The compression of an absolute scale.   *Psychol. Bull.*, **35,** 676.

Volkmann, J.   (1941)   Quantum theory in psychology.   *Trans. New York Acad. of Sci.*, Series II, **3,** 213–217.

Volkmann, J.   (1951)   Scales of judgment and their implications for social psychology. In J. H. Rohrer and M. Sherif (Eds.) *Social Psychology at the Crossroads.*   New York: Harper.

Volkmann, J., W. A. Hunt, and M. McGourty   (1940)   Variability of judgment as a function of stimulus density.   *Amer. J. Psychol.*, **53,** 277–284.

Warner, W. L., M. Meeker, and K. Eells   (1949)   *Social Class in America.*   Chicago: Science Research Associates.

Weiss, L. A.   (1933)   Rating scales.   *Psychol. Bull.*, **30,** 185–209.

Weitzenhoffer, A. M.   (1951)   Mathematical structures and psychological measurements.   *Psychometrika*, **16,** 387–406.

Wever, E. G., and K. E. Zener   (1928)   The method of absolute judgment in psychophysics.   *Psychol. Rev.*, **35,** 466–493.

Wherry, R. J.   (1938)   Orders for the presentation of pairs in the method of paired comparisons.   *J. Exp. Psychol.*, **23,** 651–660.

Wherry, R. J., and R. H. Gaylord   (1944)   Factor pattern of test items and tests as a function of the correlation coefficient, content, difficulty and constant error factors. *Psychometrika*, **9,** 237–244.

Whisler, L., and H. H. Remmers   (1937*a*)   A scale for measuring individual and group morale.   *J. Psychol.*, **4,** 161–165.

Whisler, L., and H. H. Remmers   (1937*b*)   The effect of the election on high school pupils' attitudes toward the two major parties.   *Sch. and Soc.*, **45,** 558–560.

Wilks, S. S.   (1938)   Weighting systems for linear functions of correlated variables when there is no dependent variable.   *Psychometrika*, **3,** 23–40.

Willis, R.   (1954)   Estimating the scalability of a series of items: an application of information theory.   *Psychol. Bull.*, **51,** 511–516.

Wilson, K.   (ditto)   Multidimensional scaling of data obtained by method of triads.

Winch, W. H.   (1909)   Colour preferences of school children.   *Brit. J. Psychol.*, **3,** 42–65.

Witryol, S. L.   (1954)   Scaling procedures based on the method of paired comparisons.   *J. Appl. Psychol.*, **38,** 31–37.

Woodrow, H.   (1936)   The measurement of difficulty.   *Psychol. Rev.*, **43,** 341–365.

Woodrow, H.   (1937*a*)   The interrelationship of conditions of difficulty.   I. The effect of change on number of various spatial separations on simultaneous letter span. *J. Gen. Psychol.*, **16,** 83–102.

Woodrow, H.   (1937*b*)   The interrelationship of conditions of difficulty.   II. Number, spatial separation, and illumination as conditions of simultaneous letter span.   *J. Gen. Psychol.*, **16,** 103–130.

Woodrow, H.   (1937*c*)   The scaling of practice data.   *Psychometrika*, **2,** 237–247.

Woodrow, H. (1946) The ability to learn, *Psychol. Rev.*, **53,** 147–158.

Woodworth, R. S. (1914) Prof. Cattell's psychophysical contributions. *Arch. Psychol.*, no. 30, 60–74.

Woodworth, R. S. (1938) *Experimental Psychology.* New York: Henry Holt.

Woodworth, R. S., and E. L. Thorndike (1900) Judgments of magnitude by comparison with a mental standard. *Psychol. Rev.*, **7,** 344–355.

Wright, Q., and C. J. Nelson (1939) American attitudes toward Japan and China, 1937–1938. *Pub. Opin. Quart.*, **3,** 46–62.

Young, G., and A. S. Householder (1938) Discussion of a set of points in terms of their mutual distances. *Psychometrika*, **3,** 19–22.

Young, G., and A. S. Householder (1941) A note on multi-dimensional psychophysical analysis. *Psychometrika*, **6,** 331–333.

Zerga, J. E. (1943) Developing an industrial merit rating scale. *J. Appl. Psychol.*, **27,** 190–195.

► *Index*